TOURISM IN INDIA

TOURISM IN INDIA

An Overview

(In Two Volumes)

Volume I

Rabindra Seth
Om Gupta (General Editor)

Publications

KALPAZ PUBLICATIONS

Delhi-110052

Tourism in India – An Overview

Rs. 1800 (set)

ISBN: 81-7835-328-8 (Set)
ISBN: 81-7835-329-6 (Vol. 1)

Published in 2005 in India by
Kalpaz Publications,
C-30, Satyawati Nagar, Delhi-110052
E-mail : Kalpaz@hotmail.com

Laser Typesetting at : Shiva Infosystem, Delhi
Printed at : Salasar Imaging System, Delhi

Contents

Preface

Ten years down memory lane, a meeting with the publisher, Santosh Goenka, ushered in the circumstances which brought me into association with the *Express Hotelier & Caterer* (EH&C) from its inception till today. I asked if the range of the journal's coverage should be limited to hotelier-ing and catering or extended to cover the entire reach of the tourism sector. Goenka, full of ideas, assured me that he had another journal in mind to cover the rest of the hospitality services but would begin with the EH&C. Looking back, the concept proved right because it filled a vacuum in hospitality services' journalism. A journal that could focus on a particular segment of the industry could set-off awareness for the entire sector.

These were the years when tourism peaked, dipped and has since plateaued on a lower level. The causes and effects of this oscillation have provided me all to sustain a column, week after week, during this period. Usually it is very difficult even for a full-timer to chase subjects relating to activities, particularly when at times it tends to get static to pick a topic and say something new about it in a column that is meant to be read by knowledgeable persons in a particular industry.

The publisher also deserves to be complimented on hiring and motivating the requisite staff to fill its columns every week with news about the central theme of the magazine. The boys and girls who have performed this job deserve a pat on the back, particularly when in the past years they had to be exclusive in coverage being in competition with a sister publication from the same stable.

There are trade publications, glossy ones with quality production; yet in the matter of news coverage, there has been no weekly journal – which has given EH&C an advantage. This weekly has a wider network of staffers and is clicked by the distribution system of one of India's foremost newspaper houses.

Fortunately, the first two years constituted a boom period for Indian tourism with double digit increases from 1994 to 1996. It dipped to 6.4 per cent in 1997 and the country will be lucky this year to touch a one per cent growth, thanks to both domestic and external conditions.

The factors which shaped tourism trends inevitably dominated the contents of the journal and my own commentary. The positive events on the domestic sector were an awareness programme, the entry of major businesses like ASSOCHAM, FICCI, CII and Ph.D. and the involvement of some political parties. At the same time, these trends did not have a uniform momentum.

The government of the day has a definite say in a situation where promotion and infrastructure build-up are the main concerns of the authorities. While P V Narasimha Rao did the honour of attending IATO's annual meeting, from the same platform he claimed that tourism was not a national priority for him. Even at an investors' meeting in Paris, he made it clear that tourism was not his cup of tea. This disinterest notwithstanding, the tourism minister, Ghulam Nabi Azad, was very vocal in support of the sector but little concrete action was evident in respect of strengthening the infrastructure. His sole claim of contribution to Indian tourism rested on his visits to 40-odd countries along a routine of officials at the tax-payer's expense. In a more accountable context, some should have queried what impact the ministerial jaunts produced on tourist arrivals. His successor in the United Front government, Srikant Jena, has had the dubious distinction of totally neglecting the ministry in his charge. The only pronouncement that he made and that too within hours of assuming office was that left to himself – he would introduce prohibition all over the country.

Jena was lucky in having a team of civil servants at the top who were committed to tourism's growth. They hammered out a draft national policy for the sector. Before it could get past the cabinet, the government changed. It must be said to the credit of the industry that it mounted a big campaign during the run-up to the last elections to personally contact and arrange round-table discussions on the relevance of tourism to the national agenda. They succeeded in getting acceptance by the BJP which by a turn of events assumed power. The rest is contemporary history – a tourism-friendly budget and initiatives for new incentives. And for the first time in 50 years, a ministerial group to coordinate tourism.

Lessons from the experience of other countries have also been recounted following visits to USA, South Africa, Israel, China, Indonesia, Thailand, Nepal, Sri Lanka, Turkey and Switzerland. One great lesson from the foreign experiences is that each country is a distinctive product that calls for special marketing and promotion. Yet, they have some common features too inasfar as the historical legacies and natural heritage and popular skills constituting tourism assets are concerned. Political will and professionalism are key to success everywhere.

This has been the constant refrain of this column for the last ten years. The industry is waiting for good days to come and hopefully, there may be a turnaround at least by the turn of the century.

Rabindra Seth

Introduction

Travel has been an integral part of human activity since antiquity. The reasons for travel have changed over the centuries. In the more ancient times the main motivations were pilgrimage, trade and conquest. It is surprising to find that several thousand years ago there were contacts among people separated by vast distances, seas and mountains. India and West Asia, for instance, interchanged ideas and knowledge. The Hindu temples at Borobodur in Central Java and the Gandhara School of Arts which developed following Alexander's invasion are classic examples. Emperor Ashok sent emissaries to Sri Lanka, Myanmar and other parts of Southeast Asia to spread Buddhism. In fact much of the knowledge about our social history in earlier periods is based on records left by visitors like Fa Hien and Hsuan Tsang, Ibn Batuta, Al Beruni and Marco Polo. Within India religion was the dominant motivation for travel. The concept of shrines in the four corners of India – Badrinath, Puri, Dwarka and Rameshwaram known as *Char Dam* seems like a well-planned effort to ensure travel throughout the country. And, to this day, pilgrimage continues to be the most important reasons for travel, although the country has entered the era of modern tourism.

In the West, particularly in Europe, tourism is the product of the industrial revolution. Holidays and surplus incomes created the urge to travel, mainly for change and relaxation in places with different or better climate, in the mountains or on the beaches or in search of the sun. These movements were initially confined to travel within a country but they played an important role in building a base for the future revolution in organised tourism. In other words, it was domestic tourism which became the foundation for international tourism. This is the first major difference between tourism development in India and the West. In India we have first build a base for international tourism and are using that as a foundation for domestic tourism! The reasons are clear: pilgrimage still accounts for much of travel and *dharamshala* and *dhabas* seem to be adequate to meet the needs of this category of travellers. The affluent and the professionals and workers with surplus incomes are the ones who are utilising hotels and other services built primarily for overseas visitors.

Organised or mass tourism as we know it today is a post-World War II phenomenon. In the past three decades or so tourism has become the world's second largest industry after oil, and, also the fastest growing. In 1951, 25 million tourists crossed international borders. The figure for 1983 is 287 million. These 287 million travellers spent the equivalent of 99 billion US dollars, excluding the cost of international air fares.

Tourism has come to play an important role in the socio-economic development of a country. There are more than two score countries round the world which virtualize off tourism. Spain is one of them and she welcomes every year more visitor than its own population of 24 million. What tourism means to India is aptly brought out in the Sixth Five-Year Plan's chapter on the subject: "Tourism both domestic and international, has rapidly won considerable recognition as activity generating a number of social and economic benefits like promotion of national integration and international understanding, creation of employment opportunities removal of regional imbalances, augmentation of foreign exchange earnings, thus redressing the balance of payments situation, etc. It is significant that many of these beneficial aspects of domestic and international tourism have special relevance to the socio-economic scene in India as emerging in the sixth plan period. Tourism also tends to give support to local handicrafts and cultural activities, both in urban and rural areas. Expenditure by tourists has a multiplier effect and also generates considerable tax revenue for Government, both in the central and state sectors. It is also relevant that the various multifaceted socio-economic benefits of tourism are achieved with a relatively low level of investment."

United we Stand

Tourism well-wishers have always emphasised that unity in the industry is a pre-requisite for the sector to have any influence on government decision-making. Trade associations and their leaders have been long on promises for unity but short on delivery. Last year, when the apex bodies presented a common pre-budget memorandum, hopes had arisen that alter all, the move towards unity was gaining strength. But, this year even the two hotel organisations, the older FHRAI (Federation of Hotel and Restaurant Associations), and the younger HAI (Hotel

Association of India), have submitted separate memoranda signifying that we are back to square one.

As is to be expected, both FHRAI and HAI have in the main concentrated on the need for reduction of taxes, particularly Hotel Expenditure Tax (HET) levied by the Centre and Luxury Tax (LT) charged by the states. Says the FHRAI memorandum: "One of the biggest factors responsible for the poor growth of tourism in India is the incidence of high taxes on the hotel sector." "Considering both central and state taxes," it goes on, "the burden in some states comes to as much as 50 per cent on the room rate paid by the guest....This is the highest incidence of taxes anywhere in the world and is far higher than the tax levied in all our neighbouring countries with whom we are competing." Adding to the burden is the luxury tax imposed by the states varying between 10 and 15 per cent. "Six states, it points out, are: levying this tax on the published rate and the actual incidence could be as high as 10 per cent of the discounted tariff which hotels offer for commercial or seasonal reasons, FHRAI, therefore, calls for abolishing the HET and asked the Centre to persuade the state governments to lower the luxury tax to 10 per cent."

HAI, too, would like to see the HET being 'abolished totally' but should this not be considered 'feasible', it would like foreigners and heritage hotels to be exempted; the threshold limit be raised to Rs. 3,000 from the existing Rs. 2,000, and, that it be limited only to the room rent and not other services. HAI's recommendation on luxury tax is that it should be levied on the actual bill and not on the published tariff. Also, some states which are charging this tax on telephone, health club and laundry should not do so. On service tax, both associations have suggested that hotels be exempted as it amounts to double taxation. HAI has dwelt at length with 80 HHD of the Income Tax Act under which. 50 per cent of profits earned in foreign exchange are deductible straight away and the remaining 50 per cent also if ploughed back into tourism within a given period. The memorandum lists the projects in which the remaining 50 per cent can be invested to ensure tax deduction. These include new hotels, purchase of cars/coaches (by travel agents); sports equipment, building of convention centres and subscription to certain equities. HAI feels hotels "should be allowed flexibility in the utilisation of the remaining 50 per cent of profits for which reserve is made as per the statutory requirements in any manner as deemed necessary and essential for hotels for normal hotel operations to provide world-class standard facilities to the tourists staying in the hotels." Under the existing section, the tax benefits are calculated on the basis of the foreign exchange earned through the settlement of bills only.

The association would like the benefit to be extended to money changed at hotel promises but utilised for services availed of in the hotel and other places as through money changers, in other words amount utilised through Money Changer Licence should also be considered as earnings in foreign exchange eligible for tax benefits.

Both associations have a common approach to the changes needed in Section 80-1A and 80-16 which are aimed at encouraging new investments in the accommodation sector in hilly areas, pilgrim places, rural areas and other locations specified by the department of tourism. The change suggested is that the tax reliefs be extended to Mumbai, Delhi, Kolkata and Chennai to "bring about accelerated infrastructure development in the tourism sector." Similarly, it is recommended that the income tax exemption available to those hotels to attract new investments also be extended up to 2005. FHRAI, however, says that the hotel industry should be recognised as an infrastructure industry just like power, ports, airports and communications. And, that the hotel sector should get concessions under Sections 80-IA and 23C (e) and not under Section 80-IR of the IT Act. In a separate memorandum, FHRAI has also submitted recommendations for the Exim Policy, 2001. It complains that the hotel sector is being recognised only as a service provider while it deserves to be treated as a service exporter. It hopes the new Exim policy will accord it that status. A list of 33 items has been appended as "additional capital goods for import under five per cent EPOC scheme."

This volume contains different installments of several columns and other writings. At this, the reader may find some of them unconnected but the underlying connecting thread is Indian Tourism, in its entirely and all dimensions touched, if not fully covered.

Om Gupta
General Editor

1

Tourism Industry: Past Developments and the Present Scenario

Introduction

Tourism has been a major source of invisible earnings on the current account of balance of payments. Growth of tourist arrivals and earnings had received a sharp setback in 1996-97 and 1997-98. There have been serious efforts at the Centre and State levels to accelerate the growth of tourism in India. These efforts are to be sustained and intensified. (Economic Survey of India, 1997-98). This observation reflects not only the aspirations of the government in regard to tourism but also a commitment to pursue its growth as an economic generating force. The new tourism policy which the government has promised is expected to be finalised soon by the cabinet (the draft has since been released). The tourism ministry has worked out the nitty gritty of the policy framework which hopefully will take care of the pitfalls the sector encountered in the past. These particularly relate to infrastructure and marketing.

Organised tourism in this country is fairly old. Kashmir had taken big strides in attracting visitors to the valley in fairly large numbers much before the independence, laying the foundations of such innovative activities as houseboats in the Dal Lake and tented accommodation at Pahalgam. But, in the rest of India foreign travellers started choosing this country as a destination as a post-World War phenomenon. Ninety-five per cent of the tourists travelled by ship taking as long as two weeks to reach Mumbai if they came from the UK and three weeks from the USA, which as then remain today also this country's largest source markets.

Almost the same percentage, if not higher, arrive by air. The years since independence have also been the period during which private and public facilitation for the traveller, in respect of accommodation, transport, leisure time pursuits or services expanded considerably. It cannot, however, be claimed that this expansion is comparable with other favourite destinations in our own neighbourhood, be it China, Malaysia, Thailand or Indonesia. At the same time the quality of the Indian tourism product has been enchanced significantly and its variety is now wide-ranging.

In the early years tourism was largely limited to the golden triangle of Delhi, Agra and Jaipur. Cultural attractions such as the Taj or the holy city of Varanasi is what overseas visitors came to see or experience. Thomas Cook was the only better known travel agency of the times. There was no registration of such agencies and even the department of tourism came into being towards the end of the 1950s.

Beginning of Change

The beginning of change in the toúrism sector could be traced to the time when Jawaharlal Nehru embarked on his programme of national planning and development. Tourism's potential was not visible then (the first reference to this sector came only in the Second Five Year Plan). But, as the architect of modem India, Nehru had vision that was attainable. An internationalist in outlook, he had a special reason to promote tourism. Such a movement of people, be thought, contributed to peace and mutual understanding besides giving India an international exposure. It was at his initiative and under his personal care that the Ashoka, India's first hotel built to international standards, and Vigyan Bhawan, the first modern convention facility came up in the capital. Indira Gandhi created the first separate Ministry for Tourism and Civil Aviation in 1967 under a Cabinet Minister with Dr. Karan Singh at the helm.

There was a steady increase in tourist arrivals. From less than 17,000 visitors in 1951, the figure rose to 2.3 million in 1997. Aviation had become the principal means of travel. Air India's Maharaja attained glory in the skies holding that lolly position for a decade and a half. Domestic air services took tourists to destinations far beyond the Taj and more foreign carriers chose India for their services to the Far East. Soon hotels too became profitable ventures with the deluxe segment attracting entrepreneurs. A new crop of five stars appeared on the horizon. Again, it was an Ashok in Bangalore, south India's first five star hotel. The 60s saw a movement of "flower children", hippy backpackers pouring into India and neighbouring countries. After growing up and changing their life-styles, they visited India again but this time stayed at classy hotels instead of the cheap joints they used to patronise.

Apart from hotels there was major growth in the travel agency sector. Joining the list headed by Thomas Cook, Cox and Kings and American

Express way, Sita. Orient Express, TCI. Ind Travels, Mercury, SOTC, Ambassador Tours, to mention only a few. The emergence of trade bodies was not far behind. FHRAI, Federation of Hotels and Restaurants Association and TAAI, Travel Agents Association of India are among the oldest while IATO, India Association of Tour Operators and Hotel Association of India are among the later entrants. Adventure tour operators, domestic tour operators and tourist transport operators have their own bodies.

Major Development

Another major development of the mid-60s was the setting up of ITDC, India Tourism Development Corporation to act as a catalyst in the development of tourism, a role it played ably at least in the first decade and a half. That was the time when the private sector was either unable or unwilling to invest in the sector. The opening of the country's first beach resort in Kovalam, a wild life facility in Kaziranga, an airport hotel in Kolkata, duty free shops at airports, authentic Indian Entertainment at the Ashok Theatre in the capital and promotion of Indian cuisine and ethnic decorate in hotels and quality tourism literature are among the many contributions made by this public undertaking. In the changed circumstances it is awaiting disinvestment.

Since the 1980s, tourism has been a major contributor to foreign exchange earnings. Receipts in 1997 are estimated at over $3 bn (some Rs. 13,000 crore), the second highest in net terms after garments with perhaps the lowest outgo in the world—seven per cent—spent on promotions overseas. With its multi-dimensional growth, the basic strengths, the variety and benefits of tourism came to be recognised as was evident in the Plan documents. Still, it is doubtful even to this day notwithstanding the tangible gains from tourism there is a requisite level of awareness among opinion makers on the crucial role of this sector. In fact, the hospitality industry leaders have been complaining loudly and for long that without the necessary political will tourism will not come on the national agenda.

To be fair, the role of tourism is being appreciated more and more, so much so that the Economic Survey too refers to its contribution to the balance of payments. But tourism is yet to be included as part of the core infrastructure.

The awareness programme launched by the ASSOCHAM tourism committee headed by the Managing Director, ITC Hotels, Mr..Habib Rehman, three years ago is now being followed up by a similar effort by the Pacific Asia Travel Association's India chapter which is presided over by the director general tourism, Ashok Pradhan.

National Action Plan

A national action plan presented to Parliament in 1992 by the then Tourism Minister, Madhavrao Scindia, had set two important targets: doubling accommodation to 88,000 rooms in three years and also doubling India's share of the world market from 0.4 per cent in five years. Six years later, the number of rooms has grown to just over 64,000 and there is no perceptible change in the country's share of the world market. Since then a strategy paper prepared by department of tourism envisaged an investment of some Rs. 33,000 crore to create infrastructure for hosting five million tourists. As was to be expected the resource crunch pushed the paper to cold storage.

Budget 1998 certainly offers new hope for tourism. A revival of the economy, its main thrust, should see the travel industry out of the sluggish growth of the last two years and the tourism-specific incentives in response to industry demands offer a positive opportunity for growth. Tourism's main constraint has been, apart from lack of political will, inadequate infrastructure—poor roads and road transport, unreliable power and telecommunication and lack of land for hotels. Economic reforms set in motion at the beginning of this decade gave hope that at least in the matter of roads and road transport, telecommunication and power, things would be looking up. In face, they are looking up certainly in telecommunications and road transport. STD and ISD booths even in villages are a common sight. Deluxe coaches are not far behind. Power projects too are coming up perhaps not at that fast pace as automobiles. The emphasis in the budget on the roads sector is encouraging. There is progress on proposals for privately-funded airports. Finally, land, there is good news here too. The Urban Land Ceilings Regulation Act is being repealed. Although this is being done primarily to release land for housing, the hotel industry is upbeat that it too will get some share particularly in metro and other major cities.

Sops

The target of doubling foreign investments over the next two years will have its own impact on tourism for it generates travel, business travel to be precise, which really means more dollars per visitor. The basket of sops for NRIs has its own significance for the travel industry. The PIO (person of Indian origin) with a visa-free regime will also spur travel to

India. And, the commitment to reduce government stake in Indian Airlines down to 49 per cent in three years will give the public sector airline a level playing field with privately owned carriers and provide the traveller with more services and greater satisfaction. Retaining the income tax incentives to the hotels earning profits in foreign exchange will lure investments into this capital intensive and long gestation industry.

This is not to suggest that all is well with tourism. It still has miles to go. A national tourism board is not yet in place, professional's need to man overseas tourist offices and "*Atithi Devo Bhav*" needs to be imbibed by taxi drivers and shopkeepers. The industry too is a divided house and is lacking in a common platform. But, the signals from the government as reflected in the budget are encouraging for tourism.

Global Advisor on ITDC's Future

The very first statement Madhavrao Scindia made after being sworn in as minister in the Rajiv Gandhi cabinet in 1991 was that government had no business running hotels. Since then a number of proposals have been considered to restructure the Rs. 310 crore India Tourism Development Corporation (ITDC) set up in the 60s to act as a catalyst in infrastructure growth for the hospitality industry at a time when the private sector was either unable or unwilling to invest in the sector.

One idea which was taken up in earnest was to go in for joint ventures with foreign chains offering two clusters of four hotels each covering the Delhi-Agra-Khajuraho-Varanasi and Delhi-Jaipur-Udaipur-Aurangabad circuits.

The proposal was given up because of a controversy over the valuation of the properties and concern over the fate of workers. Finally, the government managed to disinvest ten per cent of the corporation's equity which was picked up by Taj Group companies. That is where matters rested for some time.

More recently, the Disinvestment Commission recommended that government should part with upto 74 per cent of its Stock in ITDC. And, with the new government's emphasis on speedy action for reforms in public undertakings, particularly those not in the core sector, things have started moving again. SBI Capital Markets Ltd. (SBI Caps) a subsidiary of the State Bank has been entrusted with the task of advising the government on the future of ITDC. SBI Caps in turn is now looking for a global advisor for "restructuring of/disinvestment in/privatisation of ITDC".

According to a newspaper advertisement, the government expects the global advisor to examine "various alternatives/options of disinvestment". His responsibilities are spread over two phases. In phase one he will examine the various options and alternatives. And, in the second phase, based on the mode of "restructuring/disinvestment/ privatisation approved by government of India" he will "advise and assist in executing the transaction".

Initially the advertisement invites expression of interest from internationally reputed merchant investment banks, consulting firms and financial institutions who could apply singly or as a consortium.

The travel industry will be keenly watching the progress. Hopefully, the latest exercise will be fruitfully completed and within a reasonable period.

National Tourism Policy Gets States' Nod

Ministers and other senior representatives from 32 states and union territories meeting in New Delhi between August 6-7 unanimously approved the national tourism policy. One lieutenant governor, one chief minister and 17 tourism ministers after two days of deliberations at the Vigyan Bhawan unanimously endorsed the policy which union minister Madan Lal Khurana described as a milestone in giving this sector a push. The policy now awaits the cabinet's green signal after which it will be presented to Parliament, most likely in the winter session.

Prime minister Atal Behari Vajpayee was to address the state ministers but was pre-occupied with the Kaveri water settlement. His speech was read out by the minister of state, Omak Apang. The prime minister conveyed: "My government is aware of the problems that beset the tourism ministry. We have taken a number of steps to translate our commitment to tourism into action. We have set up a group of ministers so that policy issues regarding areas like civil aviation, surface transport, railways, culture etc. that effect tourism are dealt with quickly." Being a global industry, the speech expressed, tourism must remain at the forefront of application of modern science and technology. It referred to the Task Force on Information Technology set up by the government and added, "the ministry of tourism, state governments as well as the travel and hospitality industries need to apply information technology in a way that facilitates the smoother flow of tourists. The potential of the Internet, for example, has not been fully exploited by our state governments." Vajpayee's speech concluded: "With concerted efforts of the government and the private sector, tourism must emerge as a major economic activity of the 21st century in our country, for the benefit of all."

The state ministers' approval of the national policy came in the form of a resolution. They particularly agreed to extend their support and assistance to the action plan included in the policy document. The action plan lists April 1999-March 2000 as Visit India Year, a world Buddhist meet in October-November this year, the Khajuraho Millennium, a millennium package for tourists, the India Tourism Expo and the proposed Bharat Paryatan Bhawan in the capital.

In all, nearly 30 resolutions were adopted, many of them incorporating the various suggestions made by the states on their specific infrastructural needs or streamlining procedures. The civil aviation ministry, for instance, has been asked to "support and assist the formation of a regional airline and helicopter service covering Himachal Pradesh and other northern states like J&K, Punjab and UP, and the eastern and northeastern region,...Bagdogra and Guwahati airports should be upgraded and linked to SAARC countries." And, "inter-country travel to Bhutan, Myanmar and Bangladesh by air and road from Arunachal and Tripura needs to be made possible." There were two resolutions on the subject of environment. One said the environment ministry will be "asked to take into consideration the positive elements of tourism in improving and developing beach areas" while the other said "environment, coastal zone and forest regulations have to be enforced in a pragmatic manner for tourism projects and powers for approval need to be delegated to the states."

On the pattern of the group of ministers set up at the centre, the states would like similar arrangements on a regional basis to create a standing machinery to sort out issues among neighbouring states. They also want annual conferences of state tourism ministers covering regions. The vexed question of taxation is addressed thus: intelligent and fair taxation policies need to be adopted both by the union government and state governments in the tourism sector so that tourism promotion is not adversely affected.

The prime minister's address had also spoken of the state of upkeep of our monuments. He had said, "tourists come to places that they find beautiful or enriching. They will certainly not come to any place that is crowded, dirty or polluted." Keeping this issue at the forefront, the state ministers adopted a special resolution: "Beautification and refurbishment of pilgrim cities of touristic importance should be taken up as a campaign. About 40 such places will be identified every year for this programme."

Recognising the need for hassle-free holidays for travellers, the ministers resolved to improve facilitation and said the "states will consider measures to implement suitable regulatory measures in the form of tourism trade act. The states will also consider setting up special assistance police to ensure safety and security of tourists."

The ministers conference was also attended by leaders of the travel industry and before it concluded minister Khurana had some good news for them too. He has taken up with his cabinet colleagues the proposal for export status for tourism and he expected the formal decision to be announced soon.

India's Current Tourism Scene

For a land of milk and honey, critics complain that India does not milk off enough of the international tourist trade to match its potential. And going by figures alone, they would be right. Of the 40 billion US dollar world tourist trade, India accounts for just a meagre 1/3 of 1 per cent!

The question is often asked: Why this poor performance by India in spite of its splendid history, culture, size and the wide variety of its tourist attractions like mountains, beaches, valleys, forests, monuments, wild life and above all, a hospitable people. We do not stand in comparison even with other developing countries of the region like Malaysia, Singapore and Thailand which get twice as many tourists as we do. The answer to this cannot be a simple one.

First of all, the numbers game can be somewhat misleading. The half a million tourists who visited India last year spent an average of 28 days in this country (the second highest average in the world after Australia where the stay is almost a month). The average stay in Singapore is 1-1/2 days, in Thailand 3-1/2 and in Malayasia only a wee bit more. On this bases, India does five to six times better than her Asian neighbours.

Secondly, it ought to be remembered that more than 93 per cent of the world's tourist movements are within the developed world, i.e., within Europe on the one hand and North America on the other. Also much of the international figure is accounted for by regional movement among neighbouring countries in Europe and between the United States and Canada. In other words, less than 7 per cent of the world's tourist market is shared by the third world in Africa and Asia, where too, advanced countries like Japan and Australia siphon off a big slice.

Thirdly, political and military tensions in the area immediately surrounding India have robbed this country of a vast number of travellers who would be heading for this country in the normal growth of cultural and trade ties. Imagine, how much tourist traffic there would be within the sub-continent if there was free travel between India and Pakistan, India and Bangladesh, Myanmar and even China, not to speak of Sri Lanka,

Afghanistan and Iran. A larger part of the tourist traffic to Singapore, Thailand and Hong Kong after all is from the neighbouring lands of Japan, Indonesia and Australia.

Fourthly, India is a 'distant' land for the potential traveller in North America and Western Europe, which in the absence of the regional markets, remain this country's principal markets. Air fares to India, in spite of excursion and other concessional tariffs, remain an inhibiting factor.

Fifthly, and last, and most important reason for the limited growth of international tourism to India is our national aims and policies. Do we want mass international tourism and if so is it capable of achievement (Spain, for instance, gets 32 million visitors a year, a figure more than its own population, and, tourism is the mainstay of the country's economy)? Clearly, we do not wish to follow Spain's example, for tourism for us, is only a supplemental economic activity, the base of our economy being agriculture and industry. No wonder then that our planners have not given tourism the status even of a priority industry in spite of the fact that it is the sixth largest earner of foreign exchange. The demands of fertilizer, steel, technology and education have to take precedence over investments in tourism.

India's tourism performance must therefore be seen in this perspective. When tourism was taken into the ambit of planning, only a 14 per cent annual growth in tourist arrivals was envisaged in the light of the resources expected to be available for investment in this field. And it is this average 14 per cent growth that the industry has maintained in spite of several challenges like inflation and the oil crisis which affected tourist movements adversely in many parts of the world. Despite all these challenges, tourism in India has come a long way since we hosted 20,000 overseas visitors a year in the early 1950s. More than half a million foreigners travelled through this country in 1976. In just six years, to compare the figures for 1970, the number of foreign tourists has doubled from just over 2,80,000 to 5,34,000. Foreign exchange earnings in the same period rose from Rs. 406 million to Rs. 2,250 million, taking tourism from the 10th to 6th largest earner of foreign exchange.

Modest though our effort may be, it has shown resilience. For instance, when inflation and the oil crisis brought the global rate of growth to minus, India managed to keep its head above water with a modest 3½ per cent increase in that period. Even the average 14 per cent growth maintained by India is much above the world average growth rate.

While 1976 will be remembered for the half-millionth tourist landing on our soil, 1977 promises to lay the foundation for the millionth visitor to enter India in 1980, bang on the target date. Arrivals in the first nine months of the year show an average increase of 20 per cent over the same period last year. And if the trend continues—there is no reason to believe it will not—the cumulative effect of this growth will give us a million tourists before the year 1980 comes to a close. We will achieve what we are planning!

Has the Indian tourism scene changed over the years? The answer is a big yes and a small no. No, because 70 per cent of our tourists still come from the conventional markets of North America and Western Europe, although notable changes have taken place in movement from West Asia, Japan and Australia.

Yes, because the number of tourists coming to this country is steadily going up. Instead of a stopover point for most tourists on their way to some other part of the world, India is now a destination in itself. India to the foreign tourist no longer means Delhi-Agra-Jaipur. The country in its vastness has been opened to travellers. From Assam in the east (Darjeeling, Kaziranga) to Gujarat in the west (Gir lion sanctuary) to Kashmir in the north of Kovalam in the south. There is not just temple tourism or visits to historical monuments; there is also leisure tourism, beach holidays and resorts in Goa, Kovalam and Mahabalipuram. The Buddhist trail through Patna, Varanasi and Bodhgaya. Adventure tourism—trekking, golfing, skiing, fishing, you name it, we have it. And, the biggest of them all, convention tourism.

It was Jawaharlal Nahru who perhaps laid the foundations for convention tourism in this country. It was he who invited UNESCO to hold its first ever conference away from its Paris headquarters in India in 1956. The result was the Ashoka Hotel and Vigyan Bhawan. UNCTAD II held 12 years later gave the Ashoka its famed Convention Hall (which seats 2,400) and with which the Vigyan Bhawan offers one of the finest conference complexes in Asia.

The south, now has its own golden triangle which Air India, Indian Airlines and India Tourism Development Corporation are trying hard to sell. The triangle consists of Chennai (with Mahabalipuram), Bangalore (with Mysore and Hassan) and Trivandrum (with Kovalam Beach).

Two events will have a far reaching effect on the promotion of the South. In September 1977 the Department of Tourism invited some sixty travel writers from around the world to visit South India for a fortnight. And early next year (January 1978) PATA is holding its 27th annual conference in India and Sri Lanka. This two-part meeting (the main conference in New Delhi and workshop in Colombo) will enable (and even lure) many of the 2,000 delegates—the cream of the world's travel trade—to visit some part of the south as they travel between the two countries.

The eastern region too has not been neglected. The Airport Hotel at Dum Dum offers a new gateway facility to tourists visiting not only the great city of Kolkata but the whole region. Linked to Patna and Varanasi it becomes the base for Buddhist travellers as well as those transiting to Bhutan and Nepal.

Another area in which the tourism scene has changed is the rapid strides made by the hotel industry. In 1970, there were just about 8,000 rooms in about 150 hotels on the Department of Tourism's approved list. Most of these were concentrated in metropolitan cities and big tourist centres. Today, the number of rooms has doubled and that of hotels has passed the figure of 250. There are now class hotels even in remote tourist centres like Khajuraho, Hassan, Bharatpur, Kaziranga to mention only a few. Not only that, thanks to the trend set by India Tourism Development Corporation, now the country's largest hotel and transport chain, our hotels pride themselves on their Indian decor and Indian cuisine. The foreigner is discovering to his pleasant surprise that Indian food is not all curry nor even all tandoori. He can now sample the hundreds of vegetarian delicacies, *dosa-idli* included.

India now has 18 tourist promotion offices in various parts of the world, the latest addition being Kuwait. More such offices are planned in Teheran, Osaka (which will be the second in Japan after Tokyo) Bangkok and two additional offices in Australia—Melbourne and Sydney. These tourist offices work in close co-operation wth Air India in promoting tourism.

There is encouraging news in domestic tourism also: The new Union Minister of Tourism and Civil Aviation, Mr. Purushottam Kaushik, said recently. "While international tourism should grow, I strongly feel that the domestic tourist should also get a fair deal and should be provided with facilities and opportunities for an inexpensive holiday. This aspect of tourism has to be brought into focus—both in Governmental policy and in our approach to develop tourism through the private sector."

What we need is a chain of Janata (Peoples') hotels in different parts of the country to provide inexpensive accommodation and catering facilities to low budget tourists. We are already moving in this direction. We propose to build a Janata Hotel in Delhi as a pilot project. Work on this is to begin soon. The tariff of the Janata Hotel will be Rs. 15/- for single occupancy and Rs. 25/- for double.

2

India: Land of Different Seasons

India for the Summer Holiday Traveller

India is a tourist's paradise as it offers such a rich variety in everything one can long for. With its summer hill resorts like Shimla, Mussoorie, Nainital and the captivating beauty on the Kashmir, it is the ideal place for those tourists who insist on having cool weather even during the summer. Given the travel facilities provided by the international and domestic carriers, few should resist the temptation to visit the country, says the author.

India is so large, so varied, so full of contrasts that any time is the right time to visit this vast sub-continent. Each season has its own appeal. The Indian year has more than the four usual seasons. They are different from north to the south, from the great ranges to the warm sea coast, from the dry desert stretches to the tropical jungles and the sprawling flat central plain. There is more to a season in India than a mere change of weather. It is a subtle change of mood, a reason for celebration, for festivals and painting and song as well as for travel and adventure.

This is springtime! Soon it will be over. And, within a few weeks summer will be upon us. An Indian summer may be hot. But it is spectacular with a succession of magnificently flowering trees. Bazars flaunt the rich gold fruit, the mango. Alphonso is the king of mangoes and there are hundreds of other varieties. There are also the succulent lichis and juicy, fragrant musk melons—pure summer delights, missed in any other season.

While the summer may be hot, life is made comfortable by the air-conditioned hotels, restaurants, coaches and even railways in most parts of the country, particularly the large cities and tourist centres. But if you insist on cool weather even in the summer, India offers that too. Just head for the hill stations in the Himalayas to the north or the pretty mountains in the south. These charming mountain resorts fan out from most large cities. There is Shimla, once the imperial summer capital; Mussoorie,

Nainital and Ranikhet are within reach of Delhi. Kolkata's own magnificent resort, Darjeeling offers a glimpse of the lofty Everest and a breathtaking view of the whole Kanchenjunga range. Ooty and Kodaikanal nestle in the blue mountains of the south and western ghats of Mumbai have many little weekened hideaways. And a lotus-eating idyll in the Kashmir valley in summer is pure enchantment.

Now Kashmir is a complete holiday destination in itself. Jehangir, the 17th century Mughal emperor said when he first set eyes on the valley of Kashmir, "If there be a paradise on earth, it is this. . .it is this. . .it is this." In Srinagar, the principal city, are the famed Mughal gardens of Shalimar, Nishat, Chashma Shahi set around the Dal Lake. The smaller Nagin Lake is the hideaway for house boats. Thirty kilometres away is Gulmarg or meadow of flowers. At 2,370 metres above sea level it has the highest golf course in the world set on a rolling hillside and circled by pine forests.

India has for so long been a sightseer's paradise that the magnificent opportunity it offers the young, the sporty and the energetic often tend to be overlooked. Yet, there is a playground in the sun caters to a wide variety of sporting interests, Aristocratic polo, skiing, trekking and mountaineering in the spectacular setting of the Himalayas, sailing and swimming off sensuous, palm-fringed beaches are just some of the outdoor activities. I have already referred to the leisurely pleasures of golf, fishing, sunbathing as well as watching some exciting sports events like cricket, hockey, football, or best of all, joining in the celebration of India's colourful festivals and fairs that liven the countryside throughout the year. India has a special appeal to the young and the adventurous. This is especially so because it offers some of the most inexpensive travel and living facilities in the world.

Good starting points for trekking in the Himalayas are Pahalgam, Gulmarg and Sonmarg in Kashmir; and Shimla, Manali and Dalhousie in Himachal Pradesh. In the central region, Mussoorie, Nainital and Ranikhet, Almora in Uttar Pradesh make a good base. In the east, Darjeeling is a fine point. There are some flying clubs including one in Delhi and a dozen gliding clubs. For fishing there is one million square kilometres of marine waters throughout the country and a coastline of 4,700 kilometres with several hundred species of fish including shark, sardine, mackerel and trout.

Air India and several other international airlines operate a number of concessional youth and excursion fares to India all the year round. By road, the Asian highway provides a through route from Europe to Asia passing through Western Europe. Once in India, you can either travel by road or by air. Travel by rail is also exciting and inexpensive.

For accommodation, there are plenty of options, from luxurious deluxe hotels to budget hotels. There are several youth hostels where the charge per person varies from less than 10 cents to 50 cents a day.

The Indian summer invites you.

Monsoon in India

The word 'Monsoon' owes its origin to an Arabic word meaning 'season'. Believed to have been used by seamen some seven centuries ago, it describes a system of alternating winds in the Arabia sea. These winds appear to blow from the northeast for about six months and from the southwest for another six months. By far the most pronounced monsoon winds are those that flow over the Indian sub-continent between June and September.

The monsoon plays a vital role in our nation's life: it brings welcome relief to a dry and parched land in the form of rain and affects agriculture like a life-line. So great is the contribution of monsoon to the Indian economy that a Finance Minister once said his budget was 'largely a gamble on rain'.

But then this is not the only significance of the monsoon to us in India that makes it longed for. Monsoon is our most romantic season, even our real spring. Life virtually begins afresh with the monsoon. It is the time of dark thunder clouds, gorgeous sunsets, dancing peacocks and clear rain-washed air—enough to inspire the poet, the painter and the singer. It is also the season for love. In the ancient times, the monsoon inspired poet Kalidas to write:

> Tearing down the trees on the banks
> with swirling torrents of turbid water
> Rivers go surging to join the sea,
> So, too wanton women bespatter
> The men of their clean with mire
> By the vehemence of their wild desire
> And hasten to meet their wooer.

And what does the monsoon do to animals? Kalidas again:

> Wild elephants delirious with pride
> Fiercely trumpeting, ever and anon
> Challenge the thunder of the clouds.

To most Indian the monsoon is a little less than a mystic experience. It is a brisk walk along the main thoroughfares being splattered and slowly drenched by sea, river or stream gone wild. In most towns it is the crackle of pop of 'bhutta'—corn roasted over charcoal—smeared with lime and salt to be munched and savoured while raindrops keep falling on your head. It is little boys and girls, often joined by adults, jumping and shrieking with joy in water logged streets.

After heavy rainfall, the nights is thick with the voices of the frogs, profoundly deep base croaks and tremulous tenor quaverings singing the praise of rain together. Some may insist that it is a cacaphony and not a concert but to many it has a strangely soothing and sleep inducing quality.

I said earlier that life begins afresh with the monsoon. The trees and shrubs, bare of foliage in the heat, are now covered with fresh green leaves. And, this is the time for insects to assert themselves when lamplight attracts crowds of all sorts of fantastic varieties of beetles, moths tree hoppers and dragonflies. The tanks and lakes fill up. The water birds begin to breed and the air is humid and the earth soft and green underfoot. Umbrellas and mackintoshes in the towns and cities and an oblong cover of reed-matting in the villages are common sights.

The monsoon is also the season for festivals. The most colourful of these is in Rajasthan, in the pink city of Jaipur—the swing festival of *Teej*, when young girls put up swings in groves and hold swinging competitions. The climax to the festival is the traditional procession that is taken out from the City Palace. The procession consists of well-dressed images of the goddess Gauri, caparisoned elephants, beautiful palanquins and men dressed in traditional clothes.

An unusual and popular festival is *Nag Panchami* honouring snake deities. It is celebrated all ove the country, especially Maharashtra, Orissa and West Bengal. It is believed that on this day, Lord Vishnu rested on Shesh Naga or the many-headed cobra between the dissolution of one universe and the creation of another. In eastern India the goddess of snakes, Manasa, daughter of Lord Shiva, is worshipped. Stone images of snakes and snake trees are bathed in milk, and cobra and other snakes are offered milk. It is the proverbial Indian snake-charmers' day.

There is then *Raksha Bandhan*, the day when sisters tie a sacred thread or rakhi on their wrists of their brothers two promise to protect them from danger or evil.

The birth anniversary of Lord Krishna falls during the monsoon and is celebrated throughout the length and breadth of the country with great splendour. The festivals of Id and *Ganesh Chaturthi* are also celebrated by people across the country.

The foreign visitor who avoided India during the monsoon, is now discovering what he has missed. The South is particularly attractive at this time of the year.

Holiday Resorts for Autumn

For the visitor, India is a land for all seasons. But autumn has its own charm. Washed by the monsoons, the entire country wears a new green look. Dussehra is the most popular festival celebrated at this time. It recounts the story of Lord Ram and the abduction of his wife Sita by Ravana, demon king. Rama sought to wage war on him and was helped by the monkey god Hanuman and his followers. Hanuman could fly and was eventually instrumental in defeating Ravana and rescuing Sita.

Dussehra is celebrated all over the country but in different ways. The message is the same: the victory of good over evil. In the north, there is the dramatic representation of the events in the Ramayana. In the east, it is the worship of the goddess Durga—symbol of infinite power and strength, the avenging deity. In southern India, there is a resplendent pageant in the princely city of Mysore, while in western India there are nine nights of dancing and music in honour of Jagdamba, the great mother goddess.

This year Dussehra will be celebrated from October 2, the finale being on October 11.

For the Himalayan hill resorts stretching from Kashmir in the west to Darjeeling in the east, autumn is in fact the year's second season for holiday makers. In Kashmir the deep mellow richness of red gold autumn turns the trees to fire. Srinagar, the capital city, offers the quairt charm of a house boat moored in the famous Dal Lake or the Nagin Lake and journeys on a *shikara* past floating gardens. There is golf too at Gulmarg, the meadow of flowers, perhaps the world's highest golf course. And, then there is fishing, camping, trekking and riding in vistas of unimaginable splendour.

A little to the east is Kulu, the valley of gods. Kuku has one of the most magnificent celebrations of Dussehra. Each village has its own deity and they all assemble during Dussehra to pay homage to the presiding god, Raghunathji. There is a distinct bite in the cold air in October; the trees are aflame in autumnal beauty, Kulu is famous for its apple orchards, handsome people, folk music and dances and is the most accessible of the valleys that lie creadled in the inner ranges of the Himalayas.

Manali, at the head of the Kulu Valley is a picturesque little town where the tourist may enjoy all the comforts of civilization while exploring the mountains around. The valley floor on which it is situated, is at an altitude of 2,200 metres and the wooded slopes around it rise easily to 4,000 metres and more. There are innumberable walks through terraced paddy fields which take the visitor up above the tree line, into a world of snow and ice. The most famous is the trek up to the Rohtang Pass, 4,000 metres high, about 20 km. away. Manali also boats a 600 year old wooden temple set in the heart of a dense grove of ancient cedars. Close to the temple are hot sulphur springs.

Further east and you are in Shimla, once the imperial summer capital. It is much the same as Kipling knew it, sprawled across the crescent-shaped ridge which characterises the town. Tiny red-roof chalets, castle-like offices and a tin-topped bazaar are set among giant pines which add fragrance to the crisp Himalayan air.

Down into the plains and you are in Delhi, capital of India for 800 years, where sultan after sultan abode his destined hour and went his way. The court of the glorious Mughals and the citadel of the British Raj, it is today the seat of the world's largest democracy.

Autumn takes over Delhi lush and green after the monsoon rains. The summer has spent its fury and the more than five million citizens of the capital get ready for a season of festivals which lasts well into the winter. Dussehra, for the visitor, is an opportunity to see genuine theatre—not necessarily professional but perhaps more entertaining for being so. It is a tremendous spectacle. Neighbourhood groups set up make shift stages. The play begins in the evening and goes on through the night. The actors wear costumes and crowns, carry bows and arrows. Men dressed as women cause much amusement. After nine nights of drama people gather in parks to see the end of Ravana. Huge efficies of Ravana and his two brothers are filled with crackers. In a grand finale Rama and his brothers fire their invincible arrows to set the effigies aflame. Exactly twenty days later is the festival of lights or Deepawali.

A ninety minute flight and you are in Kolkata where Dussehra is celebrated as Durga Puja. In many senses in Bengal it is more than a festival. It is a cultural event. There are drama and music performances which give young artistes an opportunity to display their talents. Festive shopping is in full swing. There are cooking competitons, games of skill. On the last day, the statues accompanied by thousands of devotees are taken out in procession to the Ganga for immersion to the sound of bells and conchshells.

And now lets go south. Especially significant in the state of Karnataka, Dussehra is called by another name—and is a series of different celebrations. The city of Mysore has a princely history and the culmination of the festival is most spectacular here. Dedicated to the goddess Chamundi, another name for Durga, the festival is celebrated with great interest. Every home brings out a host of dolls stowed away from the previous occasion. The dolls are arranged in ascending rows with those of the gods and goddesses at the top. The display is known as *Bombegala Utsav*. Dolls made of blackwood depicting a man and a woman are inevitable in the display for their religious significance. One day is set apart for *Saraswati Puja* or worship of the goddess of learning. Another day is devoted to worship of weapons and instruments.

In Mysore city the final day of the festival is the occasion for a great pageant. Public buildings, some of them old palaces, are illuminated in the evening. A splendid procession goes through Mysore's principle streets with richly caparisoned elephants, camels, horses, palanquins and standard bearers.

Dussehra is just one reasons to come to India during Autumn. There are many others. Come, discover them.

Winter in India

It is with justification that India is called a land of all seasons. Sub-continental in size, it is so vast, varid and full of contrasts that any time is the right time to visit it. There are more than the four usual seasons and they vary from north to south, from the great snow ranges to the warm sea coast, from the dry dessert stretches to the tropical jungels and the sprawling central plain.

There is more to a season in India than a change of weather. It is a subtle change of mood, a reason for celebration, for festival, for music and painting and song.

Our winter is particularly welcome. It brings such a lovely blend of blue, sunlit days and crisp, cold nights in the north and mellow balmy days in the south. You can ski in the silent snowbound heights of Gulmarg and Kufri in the Himalayas or swim in the Arabian Sea at Kovalam. The big cities enjoy a splash of concerts and plays, parties and exhibitions. Travel and sightseeing is a delight everywhere.

Delhi is the royal gateway to the north and a good starting point for a discovery of India. Many ages meet in Delhi, all blended into one stimulating personality. Wide treelined avenues and gardens, vistas that open out to splendid stone and marble monuments that are Delhi's heritage from a rich past. One step and you are in New Delhi, the imperial complex that Lutyens built in glory of the British Raj. This is now the heart of modern India, the seat of Government and the nucleus of the city that New Delhi is today.

The winter flowers turn the parks and gardens into a riot of colour and the citizens eagerly await the Republic Day festivities which include the spectacular march past by the armed forces and the cultural pageant that follows it, folk dances and performances by massed hands and illumination of public buildings. Incidentally, New Delhi would be celebrating its golden jubilee next year when it will be fifty years old.

Agra, the city of the Taj, is only a few hours by road from Delhi and a few minutes by air. From Mughal Agra to romantic and chivalrous Rajasthan is a transition of infinite delight. This is the legendary land of pink palaces and sun baked forts and colourful people. Jaipur the rose-red city is the capital of this formerly princely region. A few miles journey by road and you are in Bharatpur, the famous bird sanctuary, which in winter is the home of migratory birds from as far away as Siberia. It is not at all difficult to spot the Siberian crane among the five hundred or so species in this bird watchers' paradise. The Sariska sanctuary is not far away and if you are lucky you might see the elusive tiger.

For those who love sport, Kashmir is ideal. An hour's flight from Delhi takes you to Srinagar, capital of the beautiful vale and a two hour ride by car to Gulmarg or the meadow of flowers, more than ten thousand feet above the sea level. Coated with thick soft snow, Gulmarg's gentle slopes are turned into some of the finest ski gradients anywhere. Circled by pinnacles of white, the air seems to sparkle against the ice as skiiers flash past. There is an intimate contact with nature among the grandeur of coniferous mountains. Gulmarg in winter is an experience of the Himalayas. The resort has a rope two, three T-bar lifts and a double chair-lift. The beginner's slope makes learning easy, with perfect snow conditions and a gentle gradient. Trained instructors are available and the most modern equipment can be hired. There is more to Gulmarg than just skiing. Skating, curling, ski-bobbing, tobogganing are some of the other sports activities offered. All this is wrapped up in a blanket of white that can turn pink or blue, depending on the angle of the sun.

If you are looking for a beach holiday, then again winter is one of the best times for it. Go to Kovalam, a few miles away from the point where three oceans meet and here you can feel the five thousand years of history and soak in eternal sun. Kovalam, endowed with one of the world's finest beaches, has mile upon mile of wheat coloured sand contrasting with the ice blue sea and a backdrop of gently swaying cocount trees. Added to the natural scenic beauty in India's first beach resort planned to international standards.

Then there is Goa which has beaches galore. Its one hundred mile long coastline is dotted with some of the loveliest beaches in the world. Calangute beach extending along the Arabian Sea in an inward arch of about 7 km may well be called the Queen of Goa beaches.

A former Portuguese colony, Goa is a blending of two cultures, Portuguese and Indian. There are magnificent 400 year old cathedrals; The Basilica of Bom Jesus where the relics of St. Francis Xavier lie and, the Convent of St. Gajetan and the Se Cathedral with its fourteen splendid altars. This particular cathedral took 75 years to build. Goa is also famous for its festivals, many of them religious. In a few weeks, Goans will be celebrating a carnival in the true Latin fashion for three days with much music, dancing and masquerading in the streets. On January 6 is celebrated Reis Magos to commemorate the visit of the Three Wise Men to the infant Christ.

There is an equally tempting beach on the east coast, just south of Chennai. Mamallapuram or Mahabalipuram, is also known for the famous shore temple and has been developed into a beautiful beach resort with cottages on stilts rubbing shoulders with a tiny fishing villages. The Shore Temple, a delicately carved survivor of seven, was erected on the sea shore more than twelve centuries ago. Here, history and relaxation get rolled into one. You may also taste the winter monsoon that makes the atmosphere pleasanter.

A wee bit further south and you are in Pondicherry. The French were here for nearly 3 centuries and have left their unmistake imprint. The look and ambience is that of a French provincial town complete with statue of Joan of Arc and some good French cuisine. But Pondicherry's atmosphere is pure Indian. Life here centres around the Aurobindo Ashram named after the zealous fighter for Indian independence who later became a philosopher and sage. This ashram is also the origin of an important project; the creation of an international city—Auroville—on the hills overlooking Pondicherry. Auroville will be a heaven of peace to all those seeking universal friendship and brotherhood.

There is much else to do in India in the winter. You can visit Kolkata, which is a dozen different cities all in one. It is a startling melange of mood and style and a strange mix of intellectual ferment and commercial pre-occupation. Get to the northeast and get a breathtaking view of the Kanchenjunga from Darjeeling or ride an elephant in Kaziranga to see the one-horned rhinocero. Or fly to Mumbai, vibrant vital city on the west coast and a base for the discovery of western India.

And so if you are planning travel in winter, India offers you irresistible of holidays.

Spring Time in India

India is so vast, varied and so full of contrasts that for a visitor any time is the right time to come. Each season has something different and distinctive to offer. A season has more to it than a mere change of weather. There is a subtle change of mood and a reason for celebration. Festivals and seasons go together.

When the supremacy of the winter begins to wane, it is spring, or Basant as we call it, that takes over. It comes with a quick blossoming and is soon over. Along the length of the Himalayas, mountain valleys, particularly of Kulu and Kashmir, Kangra and Chamba are a blaze of colour. The hill sides are covered with wild flowers and the valleys are covered with blossoms of pink and white.

In the plains gardens and parks are in full bloom presenting a riot of colour. Spring in India begins in February with Basant Panchmi, one of the country's gayest festive days. This is the fifth day of the bright fortnight of the moon in the Indian calendar month of Magh. Basant Panchmi is also a festival in honour of Saraswati, goddess of knowledge and wisdom. In eastern India, notably in West Bengal and Orissa, celebrations take on a sensitive form and images of Saraswati are carried in processions through the streets and immersed in holy rivers.

Books, pens and musical instruments are kept in Saraswati shrines for the period of the festival. Children are taken to the shrines for their ritual initiation to learning.

In northern India Basant Panchmi heralds the coming of spring. On this day people wear new yellow dresses and gather in open spaces for festivities. Yellow kites dot the skyline in a kind of competition with the blossoms on the ground. Delhi, the capital city wears a festive look. Most of its six million citizens spend the day out by the river side or picknicking in the numerous parks and gardens. The terraced Moghul Garden at Rashtrapati Bhavan – the President's palace – is open to the public.

Down south Tamil Nadu has its own spring celebrations, the floating festival of Teeppam. At the two famous temples of Chennai, the Mylapur Kapaleeswar and the Parthasarthy Swamy, the deities clothed in silk, bedecked with jewels and flowers are led in a grand procession to the temple tank, to the accompaniment of music and the chanting of hymns by priests. The deities are placed on lavishly decorated floats, illuminated by hundreds of earthern lamps. Floated around the tank seven times, in a touching ceremony, each deity is then taken back to its seat in the inner sanctums of the temples.

In the south-west of India, at the same time, as the rigours and fasting of Lent approach, the people of Goa, specially at Panaji, give vent to their exuberance and zest for life in a carnival that lasts a week. People celebrate and make merry. And with it comes the thing Goans love as well, music. Its rhythms are woven into the nights and days of the carnival as hundreds of guitars are strummed. Wearing bright colourful costumes and masks, revellers are on the move. Processions follow processions. Ingeniously made floats ply down the picturesque roads. And for an unforgettable week gaiety and joy have found a home amidst the sandy beaches and the beauty of Goa.

Up in the Kashmir Valley, where the winter has a longer innings, the first almond blossoms in March herald Sonth the spring festival which is even more widely celebrated in April and May with the approach of summer. The almond orchards near the picturesque Dal Lake become the centre of the city's social life. People collect there with their traditional Kashmiri tea pots not unlike the samovar. Sonth brings about a spectacular open-concert of folk singing and more and more forms of entertainment have since been incorporated.

The highlight of spring is yet to come. It is Holi – the spring saturnalia, the festival of colours. You can join the fun whereever you are but it would be nice to be in Mathura – the legendary town where Lord Krishna sported with the milk maidens in a battle of colour.

Or, at Shantiniketan near Kolkata where under the mango grove Tagore taught his students. You can join yellow *sari-clad* dancers. It is now that the jubilant spirit of spring sets in during Holi. An irrepressible splash of festivity colour the days before harvesting begins. It also marks the end of winter and the death of the demoness Holika. A spirit of abandon fills the people. They throng the streets in front of their houses rubbing powder colours on each other or tease and squirt colours through '*pichkaris*', the long syringes. Holi begins with a bonfire on its eve, the symbolic incineration of Holika. The next morning is a cloudburst the colour. Having destroyed evil in the night, revellers felicitate each other and make a festival out of mutual goodwill.

In western India, the villagers of Chhota Udaipur, near Baroda, celebrate Holi by re-enacting the story of Prahlad, whose aunt, Holika wanted to kill him by fire. Tribals walks across burning coal beds before the multitudes that congregate for the event. The most interesting Holi celebration is at the village of Barsana, near Mathura, where lived Radha, Lord Krishna's consort. This is called *Lathmar Holi.* The day offers Barsana women a chance to beat up the men without fear of male chauvinist retaliation!

The Gangaur festival is held in Rajasthan about a fortnight after Holi in honour of Parvati, the consort of Lord Shiva. Gaily attired young girls, gracefully balancing brass pitchers on their heads, went their way to the temple of Gauri, another name for Parvati, for the ceremonial bath of the deity who is then bedecked with flowers. In their invocation to Gauri, they ask for husbands 'such as the one you have been blessed with.' The festival ends in rejoicing, with the arrival of Shiva to escort his bride Gauri home, accompanied by caparisoned elephants and horses.

But with Baisakhi during April the Indian spring and its festivals are over. Baisakhi is the Hindu solar new year observed virtually all over the country. It is a socio-religious festival when people take a holy dip in the sacred rivers and visit temples. The river Ganga is believed to have descended to earth on this day. For the Sikhs, Baisakhi is of special significance. On this day about 300 years ago Guru Gobind Singh organised them into Khalsa, band of the Pure. In Punjab, Haryana, Uttar Pradesh, Bihar, Bengal, Orissa, Tamil Nadu and many other places farmers start harvesting with great jubilation giving an enthusiastic start to the new year.

There is much more then just spring in India. For the traveller major cities and tourist spots are linked by jet air services, sleak and comfortable air-conditioned buses and coaches and the famous Indian Railway network. And what is more the pound and the dollar go much farther in India then in most other countries.

3
Discovering North India

New Delhi – A Date with History

It is hard to describe New Delhi celebrating its 50th anniversary from December 1979 it is young and vivacious compared to other cities in the world. Yet it contains within its confines relics of many royal cities, the oldest of which dates back to the legendary times of Indraprastha, capital of the Pandava kings of the epic *Mahabharata* in 1000 B.C.

The heart of modern India, the seat of the government and the nucleus of the city, New Delhi boasts new skyscrapers flashing glittering smiles of glass and concrete, of wide tree-lined avenues and gardens, and vistas that open out to centuries old but splendid stone and marble monuments. The wide boulevards echoing the unending screeches of automobiles stretch as straight and true as an engineer's sliderule only to suddenly swerve aside precipitously as they encounter the implacable barrier of some ancient temples or mosques standing in the middle unmindful of the discomfort it causes to drivers and street planners.

Perhaps these temples or mosques contemplating the nation's progress are the best symbols of New Delhi. Theoretically, they could be pulled down and replaced with something more functional. In reality the thought is impossible. New Delhi is a city that reverse the old, though itself so new, always conscious of the silent monuments that testify so lustily that this too is only the latest incarnation of a series of cities whose history stretches to the very pit of time where legend and history are inextricably intertwined.

The older section of Delhi, (known rather obviously as Purani or Old Delhi) is still redolent of the past. Its maze of lanes, alleys and bazaars are dominated by the magnificent sandstone ramparts of the Red Fort, and the massive marble domes of the Jama Masjid. The ancient houses are still teemingly over-populated, each edifice a history page of its own, whispering of the days it has witnessed. New Delhi is by comparison a city unburdened by any overwhelming past. Its gaiet is that of open youthfulness and the planning of the city authenticates this.

National capitals tend to be dull and stolid cities, overful of pompous government offices and an inflated sense of their own importance. But New Delhi carries its vast power lightly. It is a city as much of bougainvillaeas as bureaucrats, as much of peaceful lawns as politicians. It is a city that delights in its fountains, its tree-shaded avenues, its gardens laden with vivid flowers, its tranquil parks offering secluded spots for the harried and the weary. New Delhi was practically foredoomed to lightness, humour and joy from the vary moment of its rather ludicrous conception.

The city was conceived of decidedly reluctant parents. Virtually everyone opposed the site for the new capital, from Mahatma Gandhi and Lord Curzon to the business houses of Kolkata. Also there was a hint of superstition that Delhi was 'a graveyard of dynasties' for at least seven royal cities had perished at the same site. However, Lord Hardinge the viceroy, over-ruling all objections, asked to choose a site immediately and a foundation stone was laid with great pomp and ceremony by King George and Queen Mary. Thereafter, a committee headed by Captain Swinton of the London County Council was appointed to survey the site.

In its report the committee criticised heavily the site chosen and recommended another further south. So one night the foundation stones that had been blessed by their august Highnesses were steathily dug out and conveyed by creaking bullock carts to the new spot. All those who might have been perplexed by a city having migrated several miles southwards maintained a discrest silence and construction was hastily started.

Edwin Lutyens and Herbert Baker, the two architects chosen for the job, proceeded with enthusiasm, imagination and a lofty disdain for financial constraints. Thereafter the Viceroy's enthusiasm for the city flickered as estimates mounted. And when freedom-fighters tried to assassinate him, his enthusiasm for India itself vanished. The solitary parent having disowned the increasingly expensive offspring, Lutyens charmed the Viceroy's wife into extending a motherly patronage over the project. Such was Lutyens' tact that when the Vicerine chided him once for some little matter, he swore to make amends by washing her feet with his tears and drying them with his hair. "It is true I have very little hair," he said, "but then you have such very little feet." Since part of this statement was true, the Vicereine was pleased to accept it in entirety.

The First World War halted work, but thereafter all the plans were ready. The architecture was a blend of European classicism embellished with Indian refinements and additions, particularly when most utilitarian, for instance in the use of sun breakers and latticed windows. The Viceregal Palace (now Rashtrapati Bhavan) and the administration building were started, both situated on a promontary, though both were kept at the same height, thereby denoting their equality according to prevailing democratic notions. This idea was Baker's who had been bitterly opposed by Lutyens who wanted the Viceregal palace to tower over the offices as a sign of domination. After this disagreement the two architectures ceased speaking to each other for several years.

Work progressed however. Raw material was quarried from different places and a special railroad – the Imperial Delhi Railway – was established with 15 miles of track and five miles of siding. Slowly the city rose. Over 3,500 stone masons worked on it, brick kilns were set up, 700 million bricks were used, trees imported from Africa and Australia were planted by the roads and slowly, in sixteen years instead of the predicted four, at a cost of £10 million, New Delhi was completed. India Gate, a memorial arch set in rolling stratches of lawn, bearing the names of 13,516 of the 70,000 Indians killed in the war, was among the last to be finished. New Delhi was finally inaugurated in January 1931.

As part of New Delhi's golden jubilee celebrations, the India Tourism Development Corporation has dedicated its annual diary for 1980 to the glorious history of the capital city. In this India Diary, a few of Delhi's many legends have been recreated through old etchings and photographs in sepia tones and colour. The fine sepia tones become all colour as the old Delhi nostalgia slowly lead onto the colourful presence of the new one. This diary is an excellent souvenir for those who wish to preserve the bygone moods and inflexions of this ever-changing city, and for those who've ever had any association or been charmed with its magic.

Delhi, The Gourmets Paradise – Dilli Daawat

Any discussion about Indian cuisine must begin with Delhi as the central point. There is a special reason for this. Delhi has no more than a thousand years been the capital of the various dynasties that ruled much of India. Each dynasty built a new capital, pushing the earlier one into suburbs or into history. The British-built New Delhi is said to be the eight identifiable capital. But whatever the fate of the various cities, nothing altered one legacy left behind by the various rulers—the excellence of its cuisine.

Every dynasty influenced, and enhanced, the city's food. Some of the delicacies became immediately popular; others took time to be accepted. The bland pilaff of the Steppes, for instance became an aromatic *pulao* spiced with cardamom, cummin, black peppercorns, ginger and garlic. Similarly, the ancient Persian pastry filled with kheema or minced Iamb, dry fruits and nuts, spawned the present day *samosa*, stuffed with *ajwain* spiced pea and potatoes. The English lamb chops are still grilled, but in the tandoor, after they have been made tender in a marinade of ginger, garlic and hot chillies.

The Tughlaki art said to be the fint to put Delhi on the culinary map. The kitchens of Mohammed-bin-Tughlak served two meals a day in gold and silver plates spread over a carpet. A recently published account of the kingly feasts of those days makes the mouth water. The first course, it says, was roasted lamb served with, *chapati* (unleavened – whole wheat-bread baked on a griddle). This was followed by exotic *parathas*—unleavened whole-wheat bread soaked in clarified butter and shallow fried spread with a combination of almonds, honey and sesame oil. *Samosas* were eaten before the third course of *pulao* garnished with a whole roasted chicken and served with a spicy curry. Dessert was usually sweets of Arab origin. Barley water and *paan* completed the meal.

When the Mughals decided to make Hindustan their home, they at once became patrons and connoisseurs of the then Indian culinary arts. The Mughal's own food had already been influenced. They favoured the Indian long-grained basmati rice and it was in their reign that a number of *biryani* and *pulao* dishes were introduced in Delhi. The Mughals also perfected the dam pukht delicacies—Samp and chicken gently steamed with yoghurt and combination of spices, in pods tightly sealed with dough. *Mutton Do piasa* is another of their favourites-meat cooked with onions, cummins, coriander, cardamom and cloves. Most Mughal delicacies have survived to this day almost unchanged.

According to an Indian food writer the British brought about a kind of polarisation of Delhi's food. The dominant Hindu Communities like Khatris and Kayasthas and the Muslims came to contribute their culinary styles to the Delhi cuisine. However, there being no tradition of eating out, mur's of the good food was cooked in the homes, the bazaars being left to specialise in breads, and snacks that were difficult to make at home. And snacks brought from the market accompanied the main meals prepared at home.

The same writer claim, and rightly so, that restaurant is at ion of the capital of free India began almost instantaneously when hundreds of thousands of Punjabis poured into Delhi at the time of partition. Thus the Punjabis introduced the joys of tandoori cooking to the city, their influence on the other foods grew rapidly, much, too rapidly bemoans. A string of restaurants and *dhabas*—the inexpensive truck-drivers rest place-cum-eatery—dotted the whole night. Unfortunately, says the writer and not without cause, what this new breed of entrepreneurs, not restauranteurs, were dishing out was not even authentic Punjabi food.

The endangered culinary reputation of Delhi found an *avatar* or saviour in tourism. The new deluxe hotels gave the city an exciting array of restaurants, restoring to the India, cuisine the authenicity it had managed to preserve over long periods of peace as well as upheavals. To quote the food writer friend again, Delhi today offers varied eating. It has become a jumble of restaurants dabbling in culinary delights from anywhere and everywhere. There are some very expensive restaurants and some providing erotic fare and other with more humble yet delicious dishes. The city has restaurants which provide occidental food including fast-food joints, speak easics, coffee shops and pizza parlours, and others that satisfy the craving of oriental delicacies. Above all is the fascinating varieties of Indian fast foods served from a plethora of eateries—*tandoori, kababi, moglai*, vegetarian Udipi, *chaat* shops and the ubiquitous *dhabas*.

Dhabas is where you get simple but delicious food served at a brisk pace and nominal price. Old Delhi is still the home of the most authentic Indian food. Be it the *Parathawali Gali* in Chandni Chowk, famous for its *parathas*, stuffed or plain, or the Jama Masjid area known for its pay a lamb rot fen slow rooked in a thin spicy gravy—and Bakarkhani, a rate leavened bread are memorable gourmet experiences, just inside the walled city near Delhi Gate is the renowned eatery that introduced the *tandoori* chicken not only to Delhi but internationally also. No tourist visit to Delhi is complete without a meal at this place. In another part of the walled city, Kashmiri Gate, is a restaurant which introduced authentic food from the North-West Frontier Province, also known as the frontier or *peshawari* cuisine. Two of the delicacies served here are worth mentioning. One is *Barra*, large chunks of tender lamb, marianated in spiced yoghurt and roasted in the *tandoor*. The other is – raan, whole leg of lamb marianated overnight and then roasted in *tandoor*. The same fare is now offered in posh five star hotels in the capital in see-through kitchens.

In one of the new areas of New Delhi is a *Dhaaba*, popular the city over for its fish delicacies, particularly Fish Amritsari, in which fish is marianated in lemon juice and dipped in ajwain-laced orange coloured gram-flour batter and then deep fried. Dishes like this adorn the menus of five star restaurants, too.

Indian cuisine comprises hundreds of dishes and innumerable variations, if would be impossible to explore all of it in one go. Let this be a brief introduction to the gourmet's paradise that Delhi is.

CHANDIGARH

Chandigarh Calling

Travel Guides find Haryana and Punjab have much in common; the most important being Chandigarh. It is a common capital and both states would like it to be their exclusive principal seat. And, until the claims are finally resolved the central government is administering it as a union territory. As a result there are two governors and a union territory administrator residing in the same city. The two state governments operate from the same impressive show piece secretariat but from different floors. But to a visitor it is Chandigarh that matters, not its future as a capital.

Independent India's first fully planned futuristic city evokes mixed reactions. Iconoclasts describe it as "the ivory tower school of architecture". For the fans it is the prototype of all Indian cities to come. Jan Aaron, author of India on $ 40 a day suggests, "looking around is the best way to understand these widely disparate views". "Chances are," she adds, "if you are an architect you will like the city better than other travellers do".

Named after goddess Chandi Devi (a temple dedicated to her is just 15 km away) Chandigarh has a rectilinear alignment of streets, a neat geometrical design of residential quarters, reinforced concrete structures (with an unfinished look) and self-contained area layouts. Central to the design are sectors—some fifty of them—each with its shopping plaza, academic and health care buildings, places of worship, open spaces, a green belt, and, of course residential complexes. To quote another guide, "the essential ingredient in each sector's planning has been the principal day to day functions of living, working, care of body and spirit".

Chandigarh and Le Corbusier are virtually synonymous but it is not widely known that the initial plans were drawn in New York by Albert Mayer and Mathew Novicki. The latter died in an aircrash in 1950 and it was then that the French master architect and planner was entrusted the job. And he was assisted by his cousin Peirre Jeanncret, England's E Maxwell Fry and Jane Drew, and a number of Indians.

Like Brasilia in South America, Chandigarh was solely planned as a capital. The four main segments of the city are: the capital complex comprising the Secretariat, Legislative Assembly and High Court in the north, with the hills as the backdrop; Sector 17, which is the city and district centre, with administrative and state government offices; in the west, a zone for under-graduate and post-graduate education (including the university) and institutions of engineering, architecture, Asian studies and medicine, and, an industrial area in the east.

The Secretariat is an elongated structure whose nicest part is its roof garden with a panoramic view. Nearby is the multipillared High Court, the most photographed of the city's buildings, with its strange stucco sun screen with a beautiful reflection in the pool. Atop the hugh chamber room in the Assembly there is a dome that can be removed to let in light. Adorning the building is an interesting Le Corbusier mural symbolising evolution. It was donated by the French government.

After satisfying the architectural appetite there is much for the culture fan. The city museum and the art gallery are worth a visit. Exhibits include modern works; others go back five thousand years or more to the Indus Valley civilisation. And, for relaxation there are "fantasies and flowers" in the form of now world famous Nekchand Garden and the Zakir Rose Garden, named after the late President. There is Sukhna Lake for a stroll or water sports. And scores of eateries offering the best of Punjabi and north Indian cuisines, roadside delicacies and air-conditioned restaurants, not to speak of decent hotels.

Aaron's description of Nekchand's contribution is worth repeating here: "Almost in the shadows of Le Corbusier's geometric buildings is the extraordinary 12 acre (and still growing) Garden of Nekchand, the highly talented, self-taught artist who has created an epic out of found objects. One of the most remarkable aspects of Chand's park is that he got hold of so many cast-offs." Nekchand's works have been exhibited around the globe and world TV networks have shown documentaries on his garden. The Zakir Garden boasts of 2400 varieties of roses. Barely fifteen km from Chandigarh is the Pinjore Garden, a gift of the Mughals. A popular picnic spot it also has accommodation.

Chandigarh airport serves as a hub for connections to Leh, Kulu Manali and much else of the western Himalayas.

And if you are a golfer, another treat awaits you.

HIMACHAL PRADESH

Visit the Gods

Next time you really feel bored with your surroundings, try something new. Visit the Gods. The area I have in mind is where almost anything can happen. What is more, it all happens at a price you can afford. If you have not guessed it yet, here are some more clues. The people are some of the prettiest women and handsomest men, and the gentlest. Where the sage Vyasa compiled the Mahabharata and Manu wrote his laws and Charaka gathered medical herbs and roots for his pharmacopoeia... not to speak of apples!

Yes, you have got it. Himachal Pradesh.

Where do I begin to talk of its many moods, its changing landscapes, its arts, its culture, history and its tourist spots. The thing that will strike you about Himachal, even as you set-off on your journey, is its diversity. Even your train or bus journey may not prepare you adequately for the people and activities you can come across. In a bus you may be sitting between a recluse and an aspiring pop singer.

There is so much to Himachal. The British, of course, could not just leave it alone and have bequeathed us a legacy of their summer capital. If it swung those day to *auld lang syne,* it now swings to the latest filmi hits. Himachal is a year round destination. In summer it offers refuge from the hot plains; it is refreshing and soothing with its perfumed alpine flowers and melting snows. Monsoons are a spectacle of lush greeney, cascading streams, impromptu water falls, gushing rivulets and willowy clouds, building a dreamland Autuman is pleasant sunshine spiced with moderate chill, glorious sunsets, a wonderful time to raise your spirits. And winter means snow and more snows that provide funfilled and exciting days at high altitudes and pleasant invigorating times in the valleys.

The seasons apart, there is so much in Himachal waiting to be explored. Many of its peaks are still unconquered, even some of the lower ranges are still inaccessible. The social whirl of Shimla contrasts with the Buddhist monasteries turked away in the far reaches of Lahaul and Spiti. Dussehra in Kulu vies with the spectacle in Mysore for worldwide recognition.

Let's begin our discovery of Himachal with Kulu. In the summer you can fly straight to this land, tailor-made for fairs and festivals, from Delhi or Chandigarh or by a more leisurely road journey.

A large open meadow stretches to the slopes above the river. This is the *maidan* where festivals are held in spring and autumn. Dussehra here is a particularly vivid celebration, a gathering of the Gods, all of whom leave their individual homes in the villages and journey down to Kulu for a week of music and merriment. Everywhere else in the country. Vijay Dashmi marks the end of Dussehra; in Kulu it is the beginning. There is another difference too. In Kulu no effigies of Ravana are burnt; only Rama's triumphant return is commemorated in the ceremonial installation of the image of Raghunath which is brought from Sultanpur and seated in a chariot. The other Gods of the valley assemble to pay homage to him. The pageant attracts people from all over the valley dressed in their colourful traditional costumes. They celebrate the occasion with singing and dancing, with drums throbbing all night through the week of festivities. Dussehra in Kulu mirrors the culture of Himachal in its entirely. You get a glimpse of the region's history, religion, social customs, way of life and the people's love of dance and music. The folk dance troupe from Himachal is a much looked for sight in the Republic Day parade in Delhi.

An hour's hop by road and you are in Manali, Kulu's twin and among India's top tourist attractions known the world over. This road journey is dramatic. The valley floor rises in a series of steps, the mountain walls close in and great rents appear in them though which the rocky snowcapped peaks of the central Himalayan range come into view. Even the river changes character, its gentle whisper turning into a deep throated roar. And, it is here one begins to see the dark cedars, two metres across at their base and more than 33 metres high. It is time to forget wordly wurries.

Manali is at the head of the Kulu valley. A picturesque little down where you can enjoy the comforts of civilization and at the same time explore the wild mountains around. The valley floor on which the town is perched is at an altitude of 2,000 meters and the wooded slopes around it rise easily to 4,000 metres and more. There are innumerable walks through terraced paddy fields which take the visitor up above the tree line into a world of snow and ice. The most famous and perhaps the most exciting in the trek up to the Rohtang Pass, 4,000 metres high, which begins at Kothi, a tiny village about ten km from Manali. From Kothi, Rohtang is only eight km but one has to make a vertical climb of 1,200 metres. The view from the top is well-worth the ascent: from the pass one looks at two different worlds, one to the south—lush green and inviting the other, to the north—cold and bleak, a mauve and ochre world of boulders and shale, rising to a series of ice peaks marching away as far as the eye can see. In a sense, one is looking at Central Asia. For, this is what its bleak windswept mountain ranges, the Karakoram, Kun Lun and the Altyn Tagh must look like.

Close to Manali, is a shrine well-worth a visit. It is a 600 year old wooden temple set in the heart of a dense grove of ancient cedars. Clinging precariously to the bill-side above the town is the pretty village Vashist, famous for its hot sulphur springs and an old temple with exquisitely carved panels depicting gods and goddesses. Most of the old houses of the villages have carved wooden panels. Mountaineering equipment and sherpas can be hired from the Himalayan Mountaineering Institute, and Hanuman Tibba, nearly 6,000 metres high is a two-day climb from Manali. And, if adventure is not your cup of tea, look for apples, first planted here a hundred years ago by an Irishman from Kolkata, Captain Benon. There are reasonably priced guest houses in Manali set amid apple orchards and you can pluck a fruit off the tree for breakfast, if the time is ripe.

One can go on and on about Kulu and Manali. But there is much more to Himachal than these two enchanting attractions. An angler's paradise it has some of the finest trout streams and of Mahseer. Pabbar river, upper reaches of Beas and its tributaries in the Kulu region, abound in trout. Mahseer is aplenty in the Satluj, Yamuna and lower reaches of Beas.

Himachal also boasts of a wide variety of wild life and birds. Bharal or blue sheep is reported in good numbers in Kinnaur; the Himalayan Ibex in Pangi and Bharmour, Musk deer, spotted deer, sambhar, barking deer and Himalayan black and brown bears, snow leopard and panther. The Tibetan Nian, a huge sheep as high as one metre often crosses into Himachal in search of food in the Spiti area.

Among the lesser known but equally fascinating tourist spots of Himachal is Kangra valley and like Kulu, dominated by the gigantic Himalayan peaks. Located on the banks of the tributary of the Beas, Kangra once a citadel of Rajput chieftains was at the zenith of its glory in the 18th century, when it emerged as the fountainhead of one of India's unique traditions—the miniature paintings that celebrated love, and the charisma of India's six seasons.

If you are interested in a deeper look into Himachal's cultural heritage, go to Chamba, sheltered by the snowy mountains from invaders. Well preserved are a richly carved and tastefully engraved group of six temples, three dedicated to Shiva and three to Vishnu, reflecting Chamba's glorious past. The Bhuri Singh Museum in the town, houses an extraordinary collection of paintings of Kangra and Basohli schools.

Starting from the south-eastern corner of Himachal you can discover something different—Paonta Sahib, Renuka and Nahan. Renuka is a stretch of water, shaped like a sleeping woman, where every year in November a fair is held to celebrate the immortality of Renuka and herson, Parsuram. Paonta Sahib, a city sacred to the memory of Guru Gobind Singh is also a bustling town. Greatly revered are the Guru's weapons and the majestic gurudwara Nahan, known for its pleasant climate round the year is the capital of the former Sirmur State and is famous for its temples, parks and ponds.

The gateway to Chamba is the quiet hill station Dalhousie, sprawling on five little hills. And Dharamsala stands on the spur of the Dhauladhar range, and is now a major attraction for the Buddhists. From here you can visit the famous temples of Chamunda Devi, Jwalamukhi and Baijnath and the tea plantation area of Palampur.

Bhakra, perhaps the youngest toursist attraction of Himachal, with its highest straight gravity dam in the world and its huge Gobindsagar reservoir, an interesting place for a night's halt or for the start of a motor launch trip to Bilaspur.

Another tiny hill resort in Chail, just off the Shimla-Kalka route. A royal resort of the erstwhile Patiala rulers, Chail is one of the best value for money tourist spots in the country. Here you can relax in royal comfort in the Maharaja suite for just Rs. 250 a day or in the ordinary rooms for as little as Rs. 60

And last but not the least, Shimla. This former imperial summer capital is now the capital of Himachal Pradesh and one of the most popular summer hill resorts in the country. Spread over a very long ridge at a height of 2,100 metres, Shimla is said to be the biggest hill town in the world. Our tourist brochure claims that Shimla is much the same as Kipling saw it. It is dotted with tiny red-roofed chalets, castle-like offices and a tin-topped *bazaar* and set among giant pines which add fragrance to the crisp Himalayan air.

There is much to see and enjoy around Simla. Wildflower Hall, which offers a panoramic view of the Himalayan snow and excellent accommodation. Naldera is another. This has perhaps India's oldest golf course. For winter sports, Kufri is the place.

Accessibility is one of the plus points of Himachal tourism. Good roads and comfortable and reliable bus and taxi services are available all round the year. While the more popular resorts of Shimla, Kulu and Manali have modern hotels, the state tourism corporation has done much by way of tourist bungalows and tourist huts tariffs are reasonable.

The rail journey into Shimla itself is tourist attraction. The metre-guage section from Kalka to the Himachal capital is a sheer delight apart from the engineering feat that it is. And, the railways are now planning a special train which will be as much popular with the foreigner as with the domestic traveller. Himalayan Queen, the name of the new train, will have a glass copula for a view of the mountains. Steamhauled, it will carry 75 passengers and will take eight to ten hours to complete the journey as a kind of a one-day rail package.

Himachal lives up to its promise a land for all seasons; with famous hill resorts in summer, orchards full of apples, plunes, cherries in autumn, winter sports, snow and warming sun in the winter; you pick the package for Himachal is gives you a holiday to remember.

THE ROYAL SPLENDOUR OF RAJASTHAN

Mount Abu

Rajasthan has aptly been described as the desert State of India. More than half of Rajasthan is desert or semi-arid, a continuation of the sand belt that girdles the world. And yet a visitor can expect to see the most unexpected—shimmering palaces on idyllic lakes or temples and forts or stunning artistry carved from stone that is honey or rose, marble white or sandstone red. In Rajasthan's painted streets pageantry and colour walk out of life-size frescoes. Brightly turbaned men with proud moustaches and equally brightly dressed women make Rajasthan the most colourful of the Indian States.

Of the many tourist attractions of Rajasthan is Mount Abu, a blossom in the desert. Surrounded by scorching, burnished sand all around. Mount Abu exudes a freshness. Balmy breezes waft in from the lush landscaped hills to create an enticing charm, Mount Abu is perched up about 1,200 metres above sea level on the highest point or the Aravallis, geologically the oldest mountains in India. It is considered a delightful summer and winter resort, decidedly one of the prettiest hill stations of India.

Mount Abu's beauty is enhanced by the verdant surroundings which are lush and charming interspersed as they are with huge granite rocks. The varied flora found here is a special feature of this hill resort. Some of it is so incredible that it has to be seen to be belived. There is a legend about Mount Abu's name. Abu, according to this legend stands for the son of the Himalayas-deriving its name from Arbuda, the powerful serpent who came to the rescue of the sacred bull of Shiva, Nandi, who fell into a chasm. Nakki Lake, one of the highlights of Mount Abu also has a legend. According to it, the Lake was excavated by the finger nails of the gods. Mount Abu was the seat of the great sage Vasishta. It was from the sacrificial fire of this sage, that Brahmin priests performed Yajana and created a race of warriors—the four Rajput clans. Besides being a hill resort, Mount Abu is also a celebrated place of Jain pilgrimage.

A special archeological interest in Mount Abu is in its five famed Dilwara Jain temples. A number of other monuments also add to its attraction. The main Dilwara Jain temples were built during the 11th and 13th centuries and are famous for their rich intricate carvings in marble. So exquisite is the work here, that the sculptors seem to have lent their soul to every tiny frieze. The architecture is a masterpiece.

Vimal Vasahi and Tejpal are the more important of the five temples. Vimal Vasahi was built about 950 years ago in the village of Diiwara. Made of white marble from Makrana mines it is plain from outside but the interior is richly ornamental with sculpture. The Tejpal temple was built two hundred years later. It is said the labourers were paid in silver and gold equivalent to the weight of the marble covered. The most striking feature of this temple is the marble pendant in the dome of the porch. It drops from the ceiling like an enchanting cluster of half-open lotuses whose cups are so finely carved that they appear to be transparent, Adhar Devi is another temple of great interest. Beautifully chiselled out of a huge rock, it is forced by a nature cleft. Also known as Arbuda Devi temple it is reached by a climb of 200 steps to the top of the hill.

Close to the Dilwara temples is the Nakki Lake. Lovely and placid the lake is an artificial sheet of cool green, water, studded with little islets. Overhanging this is the famous Toad. Rock, so called because it looks like a gigantic toad just about to leap into the water. A number of small temples and cave-dwellings of ascetics as well as bungalows built by the former Maharajas skirt the lake. There are boating facilities on the lake.

March to June and September to November are ideal seasons to visit. Mount Abu which has tourist accommodation. There is a tourist bungalow with cottages and Youth Hostel with dormitory accommodation. Conducted sightseeing tours are offered by Rajasthan Tourism which apart from covering the temples also take visitors to the sunset point for a tentalizing view of crimson colours of dusk splashed over the horizon.

The nearest airport for Mount Abu is Udaipur which is 185 km away The nearest railway station is Abu Road which is less than 30 km away. Mount Abu also has road connections with major Indian cities including Agra, Delhi and Jaipur.

A holiday in Mount Abu can begin at Udaipur especially if you are flying in.

Jaipur: India's New International Convention Destination

Convention facilities are as much critical to tourism promotion and marketing as natural assets or historic monuments. These call for integrated infrastructure and perhaps yield per participant a higher revenue; than leisure or even business traffic. Conventions draw larger groups for an exposure of the tourism product and the country's attainments. Both developed and developing countries for that matter with an eye to tourism promotion emphasize in their infrastructure plans construction of convention facilities. Even hotels find it a better source of steady revenue than food and beverages. Integrated infrastructure comprises not only conference halls, committee rooms equipped with the latest communications aids but, also in the vicinity include good accommodations, shopping malls, entertainment centres, sightseeing and relaxation. Everywhere tourism master plans provide for these facilitation.

Going by this criteria, Jaipur – the international destination for holiday makers today offers scope for developing the most modern and lucrative segment of tourism. With the commissioning two years ago of the Birla auditorium, part of the Birla Institute of Scientific Research, the Pink City can claim to have arrived on the convention map of India. It has a plenary hall that can seat 1,350 delegates, with a dozen or so committee rooms and exhibition area, the Birla auditorium is a state-of-the-art facility for conferences, concerts and other cultural activities.

Its choice as the venue for the 10th Adventure Travel and Eco-tourism Conference and Mart sponsored by the San Francisco-based Pacific Asia Travel Association (PATA) bestows international recognition to Jaipur's status as a convention city. The event is being hosted by the PATA India chapter, the Central and Rajasthan tourism departments as well as the travel industry. Some 300 delegates including 125 from abroad attended the mart. Among them were 60 buyers and 50 sellers from 30 countries and a dozen or so travel journalists from abroad.

A significant highlight of the PATA adventure travel mart was the interest shown by the Rajasthan Government. The chief minister Bhairon Singh Shekhawat not only inaugurated the three day meet but sat through the entire morning's session. In his welcome address he pointed to Rajasthan's great potential for the development of adventure and eco-tourism with its vast natural resources and diversity like deserts, hills, forests, lakes, national parks and sanctuaries. He took the opportunity to invite entrepreneurs to come forward and use these opportunities in Rajasthan. The chief minister reiterated the state government's policy of private investment in tourism. On behalf of the Government of India the delegates were welcomed by tourism secretary, MP Bezbaruah and director general, Ashok Pradhan who is also chairman of PATA's India chapter. Both emphasized their concern for sustainable tourism growth and protection of ecology. An interesting presentation on new eco-tourism products was made by John Edwards of Tiger Tops who chose Arunachal Pradesh as his theme. The keynote address was by Kevin Carton, chairman, Western Australian Tourism Commission on 'gearing up for competition', which is also the theme of the mart.

Rajasthan tourism officials and industry representatives are quite upbeat about Jaipur's emergence as a convention destination. They have reasons to be. The city has adequate accommodation to host conferences of even 500 delegates, with more than two thousand rooms in approved hotels, a thousand of them in the deluxe category and a modern convention hall. Plus there is Jaipur's own attraction as the third joint of the golden triangle with Delhi and Agra. And Jaipur has an enlarged new airport too. Sita Travels, one of India's leading travel agencies with a thrust on conferences, has bid for several international meetings. Soon after the PATA mart is an international conference of anesthetists, with some 350 doctors from overseas. Arjun Sharma, joint MD of Sita says Jaipur's easy accessibility from Delhi, availability of rooms, competitive tariffs (half of Delhi's rates), abundance of cultural entertainment and an ideal setting for theme parties makes Jaipur an attractive destination.

Taj group's Rambagh Palace and Welcomgroup's Rajputana Palace Sheraton as well as Clarks' Amer, Jaipur's leading five-star hotels now have two properties from the Oberoi Group also, the Trident and the Raj Vilas. As chief minister Shekhawat pointed out, the state government is making heavy investments in upgrading the general infrastructure which showed go a long way in facilitating tourists and enriching their experience of India.

Jaipur – The Pink City

Jaipur is the third point in India's golden triangle – the other two being Delhi and Agra. Capital of the State of Rajasthan, Jaipur is known as the 'Pink City' – its beautiful palaces, domes and forts touched in a rose-like hue. A strong wall encircling the old city is a symbol of strength. Tall, rugged men with handle-bar whiskers sport bright turbans. Comely, statuesque damsels in their flowing pleated skirts, add colours to the scene. Built 250 years ago Jaipur – City of Victory – 270 kilometres by road from Delhi.

For centuries, Rajasthan has stood for all that is best in Indian chivalry and romance; the proud Rajput princes will their high ideals of honour, and the selflessness of their womenfolk, who chose tope rish in flames in the ceremony of 'Jauhar' rather than have honour tainted by surrendering to their conquerors, all come to mind and present a vista of courage with Jaipur as the centrepiece.

There is a feast in store for the tourist. Ancient monuments in which one can breathe the fragrance of history; comfortable hotels that were once the proud palaces of kings; numerous parks and gardens, and other excursions make Jaipur a tourist's paradise.

Built in 1727 by Sawai Jai Singh II, Jaipur was the first planned city of its time. Blueprinted by a Bengali architect, in accordance with the principles of town planning as laid down by the ancient Indian treatises on architecture, the city is divided into six sections, separated by roads. At the cross-roads of these are market squares. It is in these squares that the origin of Jaipur lies.

The Maharaja chose a site that was on the main trade route between the imperial cities of the Mughal north and the ports of western India. The city's growth and prosperity was controlled, the buildings were to be strictly according to the approved plans. Even the heights of the buildings were fixed by the state.

To ensure that no one encroached on the broad thoroughfares that bisected the city, the shops facing these were built by the state. Nothing much has charted over these two and a half centuries except for the addition of a few places of worships, the victory Tower built near the Tripolia Bazaar, and the Hawa Mahal.

And, of course, the blush of pink which was ordered by Maharaja Ram Singh in 1817.

The City Palace is a historic landmark. The carved arches are supported by grey-white marble columns studded with floral motifs in gold and coloured stones. Two elephants carved in marble guard the entrance, where retainers who have served two generations of rulers are at hand to act as guides.

The palace interior houses a select collection of various types of Rajasthani dresses. The museum contains a fascinating armoury of Rajput weapons.

Jantar Mantar is one of Jai Singh's five remarkable observations. It is a stone and marble structure and its setting and shapes are precisely and scientifically designed and are, without a doubt, one of the high-points of medieval Indian astronomy. The two Ram Yantras used for gauging altitudes are unique in their isolation and one can almost imagine the grand Raja seated amidst his instruments.

The Hawa Mahal or the Palace of Winds is one of the most beautiful buildings in India, also one of the strongest. It has no depth, being almost all façade and no palace. It was built during 1751-68 as a summer resort for the maidens of the Raniwal Court who watched processions through its lace-like screens. Make up of niches and balconies, the pyramid-like structure rises perpendicularly from the street. Owing to the filigree some tracery, wind can filter through almost all parts of this splendid buildings, which has give storeys, built up of finails.

The Rambagh Palace, formerly the royal residence is now a hotel. It offers beautifully decorated suites, and well-kept gardens. There is a number of other good hotels, like Jaipur Ashok of ITDC and a range of accommodation is offered by Rajasthan Tourism.

On the National Highway, 11 kms from Jaipur stands the massive fortress of Amber, pronounced Ameer, a symbol of wartimed fortitude, the old capital of the Jaipur State. Amber, a much older city than Jaipur, was built in honour of Shiva and was the home of the Minas, before it was captured and occupied by the Rajputs. It is the site of numerous fiercely fought campaigns. Decorated elephants take tourists on a guided tour of the Amber Fort.

Shopping in Jaipur is an experience for many reasons. So much of India's ancient and excellent craftsmanship is for sale here and shops glitter with treasures. Beautifully printed textiles, heavy brassware and beautiful jewellery in quaint shops are great buys. Johari Bazar is one of the main shoping centres. Also sold here are silver bracelets and necklaces. The traditional visitor's circuit down the main street an and side lanes will bring him to the various chowks selling everything from fresh flowers to tie-and-dye sarees.

The people in and around Jaipur maintain a distinctive originality in their dress – a curious blend of the ancient and the modern.

While men wear a long, flowing tunic, thin muslin loin cloth and a fine large turban, the women are more gaily dressed. A cap-sleeved blouse, more like a bodic, is rounded off with a wide-brimmed, heavily pleated skirt, showing-off a bare midriff.

A large pendant hangs loosely on the forehead, while another lies heavy on the chest. Heavy silver or gold ear-rings and bangles adorn the ears and wrists. It is not uncommon to see women covering their faces with their colourful head-spreads.

Jaipur the gateway to Rajasthan is easily accessible. It has direct air connections with Agra, Ahmedabad, Aurangabad, Mumbai, Delhi, Jodhpur and Udaipur. It is also connected with many tourist centres in India by rail and road. A special train, the Pink City Express leaves Delhi early morning for Jaipur to return the same evening. Accommodation is aplenty and from budget to luxury. ITDC and Rajasthan Tourism run luxury coaches between Delhi and Jaipur.

Kashmir – Paradise on Earth

Eulogised through history as a paradise on earth, Kashmir amply vindicates every glowing adjective used to describe its incredible beauty. Nothing can begin to prepare one for the majesty, the peace the sheer loveliness that is Kashmir. A loveliness that is neither cloying nor static but constantly changing. Infinately varied in moods from dawn to dusk, from season to season. A continuous unfolding of the glory of nature, Emerald lakes and felt green meadows, mountainsides cloaked in pine beneath glistening peaks etched against the deep blue sky, are an incredible backdrop for the subtle changes of Kashmir in bloom.

As the dazzling whiteness of the snow begins to recede, timorous snowdrops push through the frozen earth heralding spring. A delicate green mantles the earth and the first wildflowers begin to appear. Timid violets, purple and blue irises peek through the grass. Clusters of primulas provide splashes of colour. Sap once again starts to rise and tender green shoots appear on trees. The feathery willow, the spreading Chinar, the stately Poplars step out of their winter mourning robed in a tender green. Gay patches of yellow mustard fields are scattered through the valleys and the lush Alpine meadows are sprinkled with flowers. Buttercups, narcissi, daiseys and panseys. Almost overnight the valley explodes with colour as the fruit trees blossom. Cherry, almond, peach, plum, pear, apricot and apple trees are just everywhere – spreading a pink and white mist over the valley – each a promise of the rich bounty to come. To this land of beauty, the Mughal emperors paid their own rich tribute – laying out terraced gardens with formal beds, intricate waterways, sparkling fountains, lovely lawns and shady trees. Amongst the famous baghs or gardens are Shalimar, Nishat and Chashma Shahi. Each a riot of colour, with gladioli, tulips, daffodils, dahlias, roses and innumerable other varieties vieing with each other for pride of place.

Nor is this restricted – every building and homestead has its own colourful garden. Even the mud-thatched roofs of the old houses are canopied with flowers. Drifts of wild roses line roads, drape hillsides, cascade over streams. With the lotus in full bloom event the valley lakes are solid with colour.

Shades of pink and green overlaying the green water are a starling contrast to the vibrant turquoise of the Kingfisher. Wafting through the air is the fragrance of a thousand flowers, the heavy scent of pines, the trilling of innumerable birds, the buzz of honey gorged bees.

As the fruit ripens, the green of the leaves is interspersed with vivid reds, yellow and purples. Each bush, every hedgerow is heavy with luscious berries. Soon the edges of the leaves turn to gold. The fruit has all been harvested. Slowly tones of russet and gold invade the vallies. Nature's last glorious stand before the winder. Sweeping through the higher fields and on denuded plateaus are swathes of purple fire as the saffron flowers. On a moonlit night, yet another memorable sight, another glimpse into the myriad of magnificent spectacle that is Kashmir. A world out of our time, serene and exquisitely beautiful – where men have escaped through the ages to commune with the glories of Nature – to lose themselves in the cosmic silence.

Winter Sports in Gulmarg

Bustling in the Himalayas and overlooking the famed vale of Kashmir is Gulmarg. Literally the 'Meadow of flowers' and also known as the Queen of Hill Stations. Gulmarg was once called Gaurimarg in honour of a deity. Its present name was given by King Yusuf Shah. It is said that the Mughal Emperor Jahangir once collected 21 different species of flowers here.

Once a mere side trip for those visiting the vale of Kashmir, Gulmarg is rapidly becoming a year-round destination in its own right. A convenient base for treks, it offers a magnificent view of Nanga Parbat, one of the highest mountains in the world and is an excellent area for winter sports. It also has the highest natural golf course in the world.

Two thousand seven hundred and thirty metres above the Indian Ocean, Gulmarg itself is a valley cupped high in the Himalayan mountains protected by tall pines and snow-cad peaks. Only 491 cm from Srinagar, the Kashmir capital, Gulmarg is accessible by road. Or, one can abandon the car or coach at Tangmarg and walk the last few kilometres or ride a pony through pine forests into Gulmarg.

Soon after the first snowfall, Gulmarg puts on its glamorous winter face. The slopes are covered in thick layers of snow. The ponies start their slow trek down to Tangmarg and an exciting hush descends on the scene.

Gulmarg is spectacular in winter. The skies are clear blue and sunshine is brilliant. Winter time is also ski time in Gulmarg. There is a choice of other sports too—skating, tobogganning or just soak in the sun shine and enjoy alpine scenery. Gulmarg offers fine ski slopes with 35° gradients, rims up to 2 jems and there is a 10 km run for the more adventurous-beginners to are well taken care of. There are excellent nursery slopes and well qualified ski instructors impart training in both skiing and ice skating. Snow conditions are good from December through early March.

Facilities at Gulmarg include a 500 metre chair lift, a 200 metre T-Bar and 180 metre rope tow. The highest lift served point is nearly 3,000 metres. The ski shop in Gulmarg is well stocked with the most modern equipment. Fibre glass and metal skis with step in safety binding, metal ski sticks, clip on boots, toboggans, anti-glare glasses and gloves can all be hired for moderate fees. Gulmarg has one feature not to be found in any other ski resort, i.e., the porters can be hired to carry the equipment to and from the ski slopes.

On a typical day, eight in the morning, the first of the skiers and other seekers of excitement are out in the slopes. Till about 4 p.m., when it begins to get chilly, cold and dark, they make the most of the snow. For the best part of the winter season, Gulmarg is blessed by a reasonable sun, but there are days when it snows heavily.

In the evenings, the colour and activity shift from the slopes to huts warmed by *bukharis*, while towering fir and pine trees keep a vigil outside. Whether in the huts, at a hotel, or at a mess, good food and stories are plentiful. On snowbound days, any time is tea-time in Gulmarg. The samovar is always steaming with piping hot Kashmiri tea, salt being added in place of sugar. Green leaves are boiled hard and a pinch of soda bicarbonate added.

At meal times, the Gustaba-balk of finely minced meat cooked in milk and spiced in saffron and zira, is one of the many mouth-watering Kashmiri specialities available at Gulmarg. Outdoor games give place to cards and carrom. Somebody strums a guitar; somebody also discovers the warmth of a *kangri* for the first time. It is strictly forbidden to cut down a chinar tree anywhere in Kashmir and the Kishmiris gather the dead fallen leaves of the tree and use them as fuel for the little portable stoves or kangris they carry under their garment in the cold winter months.

When it stem snowing, trainees, holiday makers and honeymooners alike step onto the fresh snow. Hand in hand, they move backwards and forwards in an attempt to pack the soft snow hard and make it fit for skiing, sledding and tobboganing. Once again, the snowclad slopes of Gulmarg become the scene of intense-activity as enthusiasts resume their weather-interrupted activities with whoops of delight.

The first outing after a snowfall always whets the sport lovers' appetite, for the air is clean and invigorating with the sweet smell of pines. Inspired, they often come up with impromptu sports like a snow tug-of-war. Taking the fresh snow, they erect a snowwall, about four feet high. A rope is then run through a hole punched in this wall. Each team endeavours to pull the other team through the wall, or to make them set go of the rope. Sometimes, a new sled game is improvised. From a team of two, one partner seats himself on the sled and the other pushes from behind and then leaps abroad and stand on the speeding sled. If he falls off, the pair is disqualified.

For those who wish to frolic on the snow on a quieter note, there is ski bobbing. It is safe, extra safe, for the ones who wish to get the feel of being whisked over the snow without flirting with danger. Ski bobbing and sledding seem to be in great favour with honeymooners.

A first timer recalls his experience thus: I remember vividly my maiden attempt at skiing in Gulmarg. The first hour found me a bundle of mixed feelings-nervousness vying with high expectations. Would it be able to keep me balance on the skis or would I come a cropper. As it turned out, under the expert guidance of a ski instructor, the nervousness and high expectations were quickly blended into confidence.

The pride of taking off a first run is simply marvellous and more than compensates for the almost inevitable result of indecorously finishing on your posterior. With a first run to buoy one under the belt, there follows a succession of blissful days. Each day at Gulmarg brings a fresh challenge to conquer and relish.

After you have had your fun and adventure in Gulmarg, there is always Srinagar for an ad-on mileage of the trip. The houseboat in the Dal lake will be a rewarding finale. Each houseboat, there are hundreds of them dotting the Dal and the other lakes in the valley, is a comfortable, well furnished home with a specious living room, dining room, bedrooms with bath attached, modern sanitation, a canopied sun deck and well trained servants who produce excellent meals and serve impeccably. There is also your own private shikara, a little paddle boat that can take you in a leisurely fashion almost anywhere in Srinagar.

You can relax in the comfort of your houseboat, swim, sunbathe, water ski, enjoy the view and just wait for all of Srinagar to come to you. And it invariably does. Shikaras will call at your Boor, laden with fruits vegetables, flowers, carpets, shawls, silks, cut sontes, jewellery and saffron. The vendor spreads his wares before, you.

You could also drift down towards the Jhelum river through the lovely backwaters and see the lake and river bound life of Srinagar. Women and children tend tiny floating gardens. Pagoda-like mosques drift by. A Kashmiri family takes its produce to market. Kingfishers flash in the sun-light. And there is a flurry of ducks as you glide past in the cushioned and canopied comfort of your shikara while the memory of the Gulmarg holiday is fresh and Kashmir beckons you to come again.

4
Eastern and Western India

Bombay (Mumbai)

Urs Prima Indes (India's number one city) is the country's commercial capital, something what New York is to the USA. This one time fishing village which a British monarch received as a part of dowry from his Portuguese Queen. Teems with millions of people from every part of the country dreaming a future for themselves. This city of seemingly endless skyline of skyscrapers over which the sunrises and set and the busiest stock exchange, which measures the fortunes of corporate giants of the mega polis has also a vibrant cultural visage.

It has numerous theatres nurturing the best of talent. It produces the largest number of films every year in any part of the world which has earned for is celloid world the Bollywood. Dance music and every other component in performing arts in all of India's variegated style flourish in this city.

It is a city that never sleeps. Industrial units operate night shifts. Night Clubs and Discotheques draw fun seekers.

International air carriers bring to this busy airport business and leisure travellers from everywhere even as its crowded portship vie with one another for a berth. It has numerous hotels, deluxe, including the famous Taj Mahal down-town and mid-town, as well as budget accommodation. It has the country's most efficiently run rapid transit system of suburban electric trains always crowded with commuters working in commercial offices, science and research establishments and factories producing every consumer item of fairly use. The best of medicine available in any part of the world is also available here of course at a price.

For those who want to take off from the humdrum of urban life, Goa, the beach resort can be reached on a hours flight or go on a 30 hours boat trip to see the incredible feat of human creativity in Elephanta Caves.

There are much to see in the city itself, the Gateway of India, built to commemorate the pinnacle of power of the Raja and the steps from which the last British soldier left, the famed Malabar Hill and marine drive, the prince of Wales Museum, the Film City, Victorian buildings including the railway terminus, the beaches at Chowpatty (Mumbai version of Hyde Park) and Juhu.

For the gastronomically inclined every Indian ethnic and international cuisine is available. Of course, for shopping and last. It is certainly no exaggeration to say at the visitor could not hope for a better bargain in any other part of the world.

Ajanta and Ellora

About an hour's flight from Mumbai, Aurangabad, the walled city built by Aurangzeb, is a convenient base from where to visit the Ajanta and Ellora cave temples.

Almost a hundred and fifty years ago a British officer went out to hunt tigers in the jungles near Aurangabad. From a prospect point across the scarp of a crescent-shaped hill, he detected a strange glitter in the foliage and rubble. Gathering helpers from nearby villages, the officer set out to explore. What he discovered were caves apparently empty, covered with foliage, the lair of tigers. Some were buried in the earth, others with their entrance almost completely obscured.

From that chance encounter, 150 years ago, Ajanta's world of 2000 years ago burst once again into living glory.

Today the wall-paintings, sculpture and architecture of Ajanta and Ellora are world famous. Thousands of visitors come here to marvel at one of the true wonders of the ancient world.

Today, one would be hard put to match the sheer grandeur of spirit, the virile exuberance and the spiritual inspiration of the art that hangs like tapestry from these sacred rocks.

The thirty rock-hewn caves at Ajanta, cut into the scarp of a cliff, are either *chaityas* (chapels) or *viharas* (monasteries). Most of these are constructed so that a flood of natural light pour into them a given times of day. Both the facade and the inside of the chambers faithfully reproduce the structural patterns known to these ancient builders.

On the walls are paintings, many still glowing with their original colours. On the outer walls are brilliantly executed sculpture. Here, ancient Indian art attained the zenith of its development and revealed a dynamic rhythm of life.

The Buddhist theme of Ajanta paintings depicts the pulsating world of many centuries ago. It recounts the life of Lord Buddha and tales of his previous earthly experience. You see in them the elegant timber-built interiors of spacious palaces, halls peopled by be jewelled princes and princesses, retinues of attendants, mendicants and market places, calestial musicians and furcapped foreign emissaries on unknown missions. Warhorses in colourful trappings, monkeys, peacocks and elephants and a host of other images dominate the world of these unknown artists.

The antiquity of these caves and paintings range between the 2nd century B.C. and the 8th century A.D. The work was completed in two phases, the first lasting between the 2nd century B.C. and 2nd century A.D. and the second commenced in the 5th or 6th century A.D. Despite the long intervals in time with separate these paintings, there is a remarkable unity of conception and design. Although the dominant theme is religious, the paintings, in their range and treatment, are really an epic of life during a span of almost a thousand years. Mere, in vivid colour, a whole age comes alive.

About 30 kilometres from Aurangabad is another sickle shaped hill. Hewn into temples and monasteries, this is Ellora. Unlike Ajanta, Ellora's shrines are not exclusively Buddhist. Here are temples of the Hindu and Jain faiths as well, chiselled into perfection between the 4th and 9th centuries A.D.

There are 34 of them, all hewn out of the sloping side of a low hill. The Buddhist shrines are relatively simple and austere. The Hindu temples carved between the 7th and the 9th centuries are marvellously elaborate. We see in these an attempt to surpass earlier Buddhist achievements in architecture and sculpture.

The most remarkable of the carved shrines at Ellora is the Kailasa Temple. It is some 50 metres in length, 33 metres wide and 30 metres high. This fantastic edifies has been scooped out by hand from a single rock with gateway, pavilion, courtyard, assembly hall, vestibule, sanctum and tower–all these out of the same enormous rock. Kailasa Temple has to be seen to be believed.

The Kailasa is approximately twice the area of the Parthenon and one had a half times as much in height. Lavishly carved and sculptured with epic themes, no nobler monument exists of India's genius, daring and skill.

BIHAR

Bodh Gaya — The Centre of Buddhist Culture

India's earliest tourists were pilprims. A large number of the modern day visitors also continue the same spiritual quest. Of all the centres which have drawn men and women through the ages, the largest concentration has been these with which the life of the great Buddha was associated.

The ancient towns in northern India through which he passed in his search for enlightenment and later for propounding the noble middle path after he had become the great enlightened one are all in this region. Gaya, where under the Bodhi tree he obtained the revelation, Sarnath where he delivered his first sermon, Nalanda, Rajgir and other places where the faithful flocked to him and Kushinagar where he spent his last moments are all hallowed spots visited by pilgrims especially from the Far East.

The Government of India has pushed through development plans making these once remote places easily accessible through surface transport. One sees in these places, more so in Gaya, a large number of monks from Thailand, Japan and China practicing hoary rituals in an atmosphere of quietitude that would transport the pilgrims to the days when a great master spent time here.

Bodh Gaya is to Buddhists what Varanasi is to the Hindus or Jerusalem to Christians and Mecca to Muslims. The esteem in which this holy spot is held is reflected in the temples and monasteries that have been built in the town by Buddhist communities the world over retaining their native architectural styles.

Bodh Gaya is a dozen kilometres from Gaya town, a district headquarters in the State of Bihar or the land of Viharas or Buddhist monasteries. Gaya itself is a hundred kilometres from Patna the State capital which has good air, rail and road connection with the rest of India and particularly with major religious centres of Varanasi and Allahabad and Kolkata.

It is said that Emperor Ashoka who renounced war in the hour of victory and embraced Buddhism visited Bodh Gaya a number of times and eventually had a temple built there. He also erected a Vajrasana, a diamond throne on the exact spot where the Buddha sat with his back to the Bodhi tree. The present Bodhi tree is believed to be the fifth sapling of the original tree which provided shelter to the Lord. Besides the sacred tree stands the Mahabodhi temple, perhaps the finest example ef Buddhist architecture. It is surrounded by reliefs of the jataka tales immortalised in stone which narrate the story of the Blessed One's life and his previous incarnations.

The Mahabodhi temple soars majestically 170 feet into the air and has a base of fifty feet by fifty feet. The Chinese traveller Hiunn Tsang who visited India in the seventh century gave this vivid account of the temple at the time: "The building is of blue tiles covered with plaster; all the niches in the different storeys hold golden figures. The eastern face adjoins a single storey pavilion, its projecting caves, its pillars, beams, doors and windows are decorated with gold and silver ornamental work, with pearls and precious gems lit into fill up the interstices". Much of what the Chinese chronicler saw may not be there now but the soaring pyramidal tower surmounted by the stupa inspires the devout and the tourist alike.

For 49 days and nights after attaining enlightenment, the Buddha remained seated under the Bodhi tree, deep in meditation. On the 50th day he set forth on his way to the Deer park at Sarnath now in the outskirts of Varanasi. It was here that the Enlightened one delivered his first sermon to his first five disciples. The Dhamek stupa marks the spot of the first sermon. Varanasi, like Patna is well-connected by air, road and rail services and draws hundreds of thousands of pilgrims and visitors from all over the world. At the Sarnath museum there is a remarkable statue of the Buddha, setting the Wheel of Law in motion. The Tibetan Buddhist Vihara at Sarnath enshrines sacred relics and is decorated with frescoes by the Japanese artist, Kosetsu Nosu.

Nalanda, once a great centre of Buddhist learning is some 90 kilometres from Patna. It is the site of a monastic university that flourished from the 5th century until 1199 when it was ransacked by Afghar raiders. At one time, the university had a vast library, some 2,000 teachers and more than 10,000 students from as far as Japan, Sumatra, Java and Korea. According to legend the Nalanda library had millions of volumes and it burned for six months after it was sacked. Nalanda is also hallowed by several visits by the Buddha.

Excavations at Nalanda have shown nine levels of occupation, six temples and eleven monasteries all built in red brick. The most imposing of the temples is the Sariputra stupa, built by Emperor Ashoka in honour of Ananda, the Buddha's first disciple. It is a three level structure, partly covered with stucco figures of Lord Buddha teaching at Bodhgaya, Nalanda, Rajgir, Sarnath and Vaishali. A Chinese temple has been built in Nalanda to commemorate Hsuan Tsang the Chinese traveller who studied at Nalanda in the 7th century.

A few kilometres away is Rajgir or Rajgriha. Capital of the Magadha empire in the 6th century B.C. Rajgir is a holy spot both for Buddhists and Jains. The Buddha is said to have taugh here for five rainy seasons. Here you will see the site of Venuvana Vihar, the monastery the local king built as an offering to the Buddha, the Karanda Tank where the Master used to bathe and the Japanese Buddhist temple Nipponzan Myoboji. Hot sulphur springs are a contemporary attraction for visitors.

Not to be missed is Vaishali, some forty kilometres from Patna. Capital of the Vijian Confederacy (6th century B.C.) a village republic, it is the birth place of Lord Mahavira and a holy place for the Jains. It was here that the second Buddhist Council was held in 383 B.C. All that now remains is an Ashoka pillar and ruins of Buddhist stupas. And at Vaishali you are almost close to Nepal. For the road from here leads to Raxaul, the border town on the highway to Kathmandu. A seven hour drive from here to the east takes you to Madhubani, the village now known in many parts of the world for its style of folk painting.

It is best to make Patna the base for visits to Bodhgaya and other Buddhist attractions. The city has its treasures to offer the tourist especially its museum which houses a collection of Buddhist sculpture bronzes and terracota pieces. Among the exhibits is a forty-five feet long fossil tree said to be 2,000 million years old and the longest tree fossil in the world.

Patna has a range of good hotels and modest accommodation is available in the Buddhist centres in the region. Come and discover the cradle of Buddhism.

Orissa: India's New Tourist Destination

Within a period of two decades, Orissa, a magical and mysterious eastern State, has developed into a popular destination that has something to offer to everyone. Exploring Orissa is visiting a country of green, dense jungles, blue hills, golden beaches and magnificent 1,000 years old temples.

There was a time when Orissa formed part of ancient Kalingadesa which had outposts flung across the sea in distant Java, Sumatra and Philippines. But all that was centuries before Christ. And it was here that Emperor Ashoka in 273-232 B.C. won the mighty Kalinga war. It was a victory which turned this great ruler away from violence and cruelty of battle towards the compassionate teachings of the Buddha.

However, that is a story from the past. Today, Orissa presents a beautiful sight of its past splendours and contemporary expression.

The journey in Orissa starts from Bhubaneswar, the capital of Orissa which provides the best base. It has good hotels, the latest addition being the Kalinga Ashoka, providing all facilities from comfortable rooms to transport for sightseeing. Moreover, Bhubaneswar is conveniently approachable as a part from its direct air-connection with Kolkata, the Indian Airlines has introduced a new direct flight between Delhi and Bhubaneswar via Varanasi. The new superfast train, Nilachal Express to Puri leaves Delhi thrice a week and goes via Bhubaneswar.

Centuries ago, the sacred Bindu Sagar lake was gindled by as many as 7,000 temples which provided a glorious spectacle of kingdoms that emerged. Today, only 500 survive in any case these are enough to justify Bhubaneswar's reputation as India's cathedral city. The chief of these temples is the great Lingaraj towering over the spires and pinnacles of other temples. Considered as the quitesence of Kalinga architecture, the Lingaraj temple is elegantly proportioned and is rich in surface treatment with superbly finished and refined details. Dedicated to Lord Shiva, it is the site of the annual Shivratri festival in February/March, when on the night of the new moon, thousands of pilgrims light lamps in a night long ceremony of devotion.

Another remarkable temple in the 10th century Mukteshwar temple which has a profusion of dazzling and intricate wall carvings. In Mukteshwar temples as well as in the 12th century Raja Rani temple, it is the woman which is there in different postures unbelievably voluptuous figures springing into life from ever niche.

Just nine kilometres to the west of Bhubaneswar lie the fascinating rock-cut caves of Udaigiri and Khandagiri, which date back to the 2nd century B.C. About 8 kilometres on the road to Puri lies yet another landmark, the famous rock edicts of Ashoka on Dhauli Hill. About 30 kilometres away from Bhubaneswar is the lovely Nandan Kana Park, where an area of 400 hectares is devoted to wild life and fauna.

The Sun Temple

The crowning glory of Orissa and one of the wonders of ancient India is the stupendous temple dedicated to Surya, the Sun God at Konarak. This sun temple alone is season enough for a trip to India. It turns every other adjective into a tired cliche. Konarak, the legendary 'Black Pagoda' for the medieval travellers, was considered by Mark Twain as one of the wonders of the world.

The sun temple is lavish, all pervading. It is designed in the form of a sumptuously decorated chariot mounted on 24 gigantic wheels and drawn by seven powerful horses. The temple gives the impression of being poised on the sands, speeding along the sacred passage across the sky...Today only the porch of the original temple stands. But there is enough to convey the splendour that must have dazzled worshippers six centuries ago and which holds visitors spellbound to this day.

Here at this temple, every aspect of life is represented, every surface is touched by the vibration of the sun. The first rays of the sun bring to life the scuptured kings and courtiers, warriors and children, birds and animals, women of incredible beauty and the naked images of lovers impelled by Surya's energy into a hundred postures of sublime love, and prayer. On the southern coast of Orissa lies the magnificent beach resort of Puri, one of the four great pilgrim centres of India. Puri is famous for its annual Rath Yatra or Car Festival held in June/July. Jagannath or the lord of the universe, draws thousands of pilgrims from all over the country during this festival when the deities are carried on gigantic wooden chariots, hence the word 'juggernaut', pulled by his devotees to commemorate the journey of Lord Krishna from Gokul to Mathura.

In refreshing contrast to Puri's temple festivals are the golden sands at Puri's beach. The beach at Puri is one of India's loveliest and it has a fine equable climate throughout the year. The surf at Puri is a thrilling experience, with the local fisherfolk in their conical, caps guiding bathers by hand through the magnificent breakers which roll in from the Bay of Bengal.

Another beautiful beach resort of Gopalpur was once an ancient port but today it is a modern beach resort. A sandy, silken beach and the big blue sea, Gopalpur has all the ingredients to make it one of eastern India's most pleasant beach resorts.

The wild life in Orissa has its own specialities. Separated from the turbulent waters of the sea by a long sandy ridge and studded with a sprinkling of small islands, Chilka Lake is a perfect habitat for many species of migratory and indigenous birds. The waters of Chilka are teeming with fish.

One of the nine 'Project Tiger' reserves in the country, Simlipal's lush green forest is an ideal wild life sanctuary. The most popular among visitors here is Khairi, the young tigress who was found as a cub and who is now an affectionate pet. The dense green jungles of Ushakothi are the refuge of a large and exotic species of wild animals.

And, Orissa like many other regions of India is a shopper's paradise. Applique work and mythological paintings are part of its rich repertoire of artistic handicrafts.

Orissa, then is the latest destination to be opened in India to tourists in search of a new travel experience.

Chilika

Orissa, the east coast state of India has been a popular destination for travellers the world over. It is better known for its giant Sun Temple at Konark and the holy city of Puri. Not so well-known but really enchanting in its touristic appeal is Chilika, the country's biggest inland lake. Nestling in the heart of Orissa the lake spreads over 1,100 square kilometres, arching across the lengths of the Puri and Ganjam districts. It connects the Bay of Bengal in a narrow mouth, thus forming an enormous lagoon of brackish water. The lake is dotted with a large number of emrald green islands. Some of them have colourful names like Honeymoon Island and Breakfast Island. Chilika is the home of the richest variety of aquatic fauna, sanctuary and winter resort of migratory birds from as far as Siberia. In fact Chilika is a veritable wonder of nature.

With its bounteous gifts of fish, the lake provides succour to thousands of families of fishermen as simple as mother nature herself. Hundreds of boats sail in the blue expanse of the lake everyday, in search of mackerel, prawn and crab and provide a living pageant of rural India at its colourful best. Chilika is encircled by picturesque hills all along its arched shape. It's colour changes in kaleidoscopic glory with passing clouds and the moving sun as its body rolls in languid abandon excited by the gentle breeze wafted from the Bay of Bengal.

Access to Chilika lake is easy. For those travelling by air the nearest airport is Bhubaneswar which has direct flights from Delhi and Kolkata and is linked with Mumbai, Hyderabad and Bangalore. By rail there is the Kolkata Chennai route on the Southeastern Railway which touches Chilika at Balugaon. And, by road, travellers can take the Chennai bound National Highway No 5 linking Kolkata-Cuttack-Bhubaneswar-Balugaon upto Vizag which runs along the Lake. Buses and taxis are also available at Cuttack, Bhubaneswar, Puri and Behrampur to Chilika. You can cruise on the lake for pleasure and relaxation. The Orissa Tourism Development Corporation provides water transport facilities by motor launches at Barkul and Rambha as well as at Balugaon. Country boats can be hired from private operators at these places.

For sightseeing within the lake there is the Kalijai temple abode of the presiding deity of the lake, located on a tiny island. Nalabana is the island home of migratory birds. There is a choice of several excursions from Chilika lake. Nirmal Jhar is 11 km from Rambha. This place is hallowed by the shrine of Lord Vishnu. The perenial stream that flows at Nirmaljhar is channelised to different ponds. As a picnic spot and a spot for religious worship, Nirmaljhar has earned considerable reputation.

A further 14 km away is Narayani, a picnic spot of great scenic beauty. By the side of a natural spring, the temple of Goddess Narayani adorns the place and is ideal for relaxation or meditation. Banpur, which is 8 km from Balugaon, is a centre of religious activities, revolving round the time honoured shrine of Goddess Bhagbati and the existing temple of Dakshya Prajapati, Nearly a 100 km from Barkul is Gopalpur-on-sea. It is one of the ancient seaports of Orissa and is now famous as a seaside resort. Being a quiet place, Gopalpur has become a favourite resort for visitors for countering the foamy waves of the sea.

Then there is Tatapani also 100 km from Rambha. This place is a pleasant health resort with a hot sulphur spring which has medical properties to cure skin diseases. The water of the spring is also carried to the baths of the Panthanivas tourist bungalow where travellers can enjoy this at leisure.

And when you have had the fill of Chilika lake and the other attractions around it, there is Konarak to see and appreciate. It is here some thirty km from Puri that the great Sun temple stands facing the stiff test of time. You can see on the sea shore Surya, the Sun God, speeding across the sky in a gorgeous chariot, all captured in stone. With its 12 pairs of giant, marvellously sculpted wheels and seven richly caparisoned horses straining their necks to pull the massive weight, the Sun temple is often described as a perfect allegory in stone, the highest point of achievement in the Kalinga school of architecture.

Fine carvings cover almost every inch of the outer surface, portraying with uninhibited fidelity the vast panorama of life. The erotic and amorous in the sculptural art of Orissa can be traced from the temples in Bhubaneswar. But at Konarak chiselled love and dalliance reach a peak.

Centuries ago this soaring and lofty structure was an important landmark to mariners navigating the coast. They called it the black pagoda to distinguished it from the white-washed white pagoda temple at Puri. All that is gone. What remains is a mere fragment of Konarak's former glory. But it still stands in majestic dignity amongst desolate sand dunes and still commands respect as one of the finest temples in India.

5
India's Southern Delights

Destination South India

India is perhaps unique as a tourist destination. Vast and varied, it defies description. Spread over 3,000 kms from north to south and east to west, it has three well-defined regions: the great mountain zone, the Himalayas; the Gangetic plain and the southern peninsula. The Himalayas extend over a length of 2,400 kms with depths varying upto 320 kms. The Gangetic plain is one of the world's greatest stretches of flat alluvium and also one of the most densely populated areas on earth. The southern peninsula is marked off from the Gangetic plain by a mass of mountain and hill ranges and flanked by the eastern and western ghats until it tapers off to Kanniyakumari or Capecomorin, the meeting point of three seas—the Bay of Bengal, the Arabian Sea and the Indian Ocean.

Nature and man have been generous to this sub-continent and given it something that a visitor from any part of the world would want to see or experience. Lofty snow-peaks, breath-takingly beautiful mountain resorts, lush green plains, jungles rich in wild life, sunny beaches, five thousand years of history, a vibrant culture in which the past lives on alongside the present, not in an archaic manner but in a gentle continuity. The sculpted temples and the citadels and minarets of the Mughal era merge with the modern industrial India.

Diversity is the soul of India. Travel a few hundred kilometres and there is a change in the terrain, the climate, the food, the dress and even music, arts and handicrafts. India could dazzle a visitor with her beauty, captivate him with her hospitality or baffle him with her contradictions. No wonder, India's tourist brochures invite a tourist to discover his own India. For India is not just another world but many worlds rolled into one. One such world, South India, comprises four states – Tamil Nadu, Andhra Pradesh, Karnataka and Kerala, and the Union Territory of Pondicherry.

Tamil Nadu's capital, Chennai, has always been the gateway to South India. Fort St. George, where most of the history of Chennai was written, has within its walls what is believed to be the oldest Anglican Church in the East. Another church, the San Thome Cathedral, is believed to be the last resting place of St. Thomas, the Apostle, who brought Christianity to South India barely a few years after the crucifixion.

An hour's drive along, the coast from Chennai in Mahabalipuram with its famous seventh century shore temple. Mahabalipuram now is a beach resort. Not far away is Kanchipuram with its one thousand temples. Equally famous of Tamil Nadu temple towns is Madurai with a history dating back to the sixth century B.C. The Meenakshi temple in Madurai has no less than nine sculpted gopurams crowded with figures. Rameswaram, Tiruchirapalli or Trichi and Thanjavur is another temple trio of Tamil Nadu. Lord Ramas is believed to have prayed at Rameswaram. Tirichurapalli has a striking rock fort and was the scene of battles fought between the British and the French. Thanjavur is well-known for its traditional handicrafts—art plates, antique gold and silver jewellery, bell metal castings, silk and carpets. Nilgiri hills, or the blue mountains offer an unspoiled retreat. Ootacamund or Ooty is a popular hill resort, also known for its impression of a little bit of England. Not to be missed in Tamil Nadu is its rich cultural heritage particularly the Bharata Natyam dance and the region's distinctive cuisine.

The State of Andhra Pradesh spread along the east coast has its own share of diversities, undulating hills and wild jungles, and lush green paddy fields. It is a synthesis of cultures. Temple gopurams and mosque minarets stand by the side of Buddhist stupas and church spires. Hyderabad, capital of Andhra Pradesh, exudes an atmosphere of 400 years of Muslim splendour. Symbolic of Hyderabad is the Charminar, architectural jewel of a stately rectangular building with four tall, slender minartes. Within a few yards from the Charminar stands Mecca Masjid, the most impressive mosque in south India. Another milestone of history is the tomb of Monsieur Raymond, the 18th century French adventurer who served under the colours of the second Nizam and who was popularly known as Musa Ram. Up the Krishna river at Nagarjunasagar, lie the remnants of Buddhism. Here, in the shadows of the tallest masonry dam in the world, were excavated the ruins of a lost city dating back to the 3rd century. South of Hyderabad is the venerated shrine of Tirupati, one of the most ancient in the country and also the richest. The shrine on the seven hills is dedicated to Lord Venkateswara. The temple is a masterpiece of the Dravidian school of architecture with an exquisitely carved gopuram facing the east.

Let us move on to Karnataka with its capital, Bangalore, the city of gardens. The biggest of the gardens, Lal Bagh, is spread over 240 acres and contains one of the largest collections of rare, tropical and sub-tropical plants in India, and you may wander around century-old trees, fountains, terraces, lotus pools, a rose garden and a deer park. Mysore, once the official capital and, today, the second most important city of Karnataka, has the lingering aura of royalty. During the Dussehra festival, for ten days in the month of September/October, Mysore wears a new bright look. The residents celebrate it both as a royal and a religious festival. The torchlight and daylight parades, the pomp and grandeur, or the worship of deities on decorated floats, the infantry, elephant and cavalry processions are just stupendous. The most impressive of Mysore's numerous monuments, though, is the Maharaja's Palace, one of the biggest in India. It is a harmonious synthesis of the Hindu-Saracenic architecture. For tourists the Lalitha Mahal Palace Hotel provides royal comforts. About 16 km away in Srirangapatnam fortress in the middle of an island between two tributaries of a river. It was once the capital of the Muslim rulers, Hyder Ali and Tipu Sultan, who in alliance with the French waged war against the British. It was here that Tipu was defeated. His summer pleasure palace, Daria Daulat, and his mausoleum, the Gumbaz, are situated outside the fort. The seemingly unobstrusive village of Somnathpur, 35 km south of Mysore, contains the largest of the exquisite Hoysala temples.

Drive south for 80 km from Somnathpur and the land becomes greener; deep forests cloak the hills. Here you find the Bandipur wild life sanctuary, one of the nine sanctuaries of India dedicated to Project Tiger. Go north of Mysore to Sravanablelagola, presided over by the colossal statue of the Lord Gomateswara, a sacred shrine to the Jain community. Another 100 km away lies Belur, a flourishing city some 800 years ago. The Belur temple, called the Chennakesava temple has the typical Hoysala architectural features covered with a profusion of intricate carvings, enough to take one's breath away.

The green crescent at the farthest south-western point of India, Kerala, lives up to a romantic dream of a tropical paradise. The Arabian sea crests its shores, palm and toddy trees reach upto the sky, and a benevolent sun warms the earth the whole year round.

Kerala is full of pleasant surprises. Here a Dutch Palace was actually built by the Portuguese; and churches have Hindu columns; graceful Chinese fishing nets festoon the banks of the waterways. An outstandingly beautiful Indian town, Trivandrum, the capital of Kerala, is situated on seven green hills. Within half an hour's run from Trivandrum is Kovalam, one of the world's finest beaches, lying languorously on Kerala's coast. Mile upon mile of wheat-coloured sand, blue lagoons and swaying coconut trees make this a paradise for seaside holidays. Fishermen with their catamarans take you for a surf ride a little distance away. Hidden among groves of palms is the magnificent Kovalam Beach Resort with beautiful cottages and rooms. It is an ideal base for a unique experience that combines all the fun of a beach holiday with easy lessons in Yoga and transcendental meditation and a rejuvenating Ayurvedic oil massage. There is also an open-air theatre for the spectacular Kathakali dance.

Up along the coast is Cochin, the historic and commercial capital of Kerala. To this day the old harbour-front of Cochin looke like a woodcut from an ancient book. Inside the old city are bastions and streets built by the Portuguese almost 500 years ago. The historic St. Francis Church was built in 1510 and is the oldest European church in India, where lies buried Vasco da Gama, the Portuguese explorer. At the Mattancherry Jewish synagogue are preserved the Great Scrolls of the Old Testament and a land grant recorded on copper plate.

And then Pondicherry—a French town in an Indian countryside. And just 10 km from it is a foretaste of the future; Auroville. Conceived as a tribute to Sri Aurobindo, Auroville is an entirely new concept in education and urban living.

Chennai

Mention of Madras is evocative of the best of cultural and art forms in South India. This port city on the eastern seaboard is directly linked by air with both western and Southeast Asian cities and thus is ideally located on the international trail running from London to Sydney. History of the past two hundred years has assigned to it a position of a thriving business centre in this part of India. But its importance as a key trading and industrial post has not minimized a wee bit the many – splendoured charm of Chennai whose lengthy Marina beach could be the envy of many seaside vacation spots.

A couple of hours' drive from Chennai to the south, west and the north would enable the visitor to experience a multifaceted tourism product. One could witness the temple towers now included in the world heritage list, the marvelous has relief protraying episodes from Indian epics in the vicinity of the shore temple of Mammallapura, the pilgrim hill of Tirupathi that redraws millions of devout people through centuries, amusement parks and even a crocodile and snake farm.

It is the principal rail junction for journey from the south to any part of the country. It has excellent bus connections with every place of interest including a hill top temple where through centuries at an appointed hour two eagles (whom the local believe to be God's emissaries) peck food offered by the priest.

One of the earliest British settlements, Morry has many relics of the Raj. Fort St. George which the East Indian Company established is the location of the headquarters of the Tamil Nadu state administration. The church where Robert Clive married survives to this day with the registry. Also, in Chennai is another Christian shrine raised in memory of one of the apostles of Christ, St. Thomas at the spot where he is believed to have been martyred.

It is one of the country's making educational centres with many institutes over a century old. Buildings suggestive of every reputed style of architecture stand out amidst modern skyscrapers.

The increase in business travel to this southern metropolis is reflected in the increase in exclusive facilitation available in hotels for this category. In fact, the largest business hotel in the south, Park Sheraton, is located in Chennai. Industries in the core sector like fertilizers, refinery and petrochemicals, and their ancillaries inevitably draw a large number of businessmen and technologists.

Even the briefest reference to Chennai could not overlook the rustle of silk specially woven in nearby Kanchepuram which has a claim to distinction in history as the city of thousand temples. Besides the Kancheepuram, silk, Chennai is the best hopping centre for bronacions and hand woven textiles and leather goods.

Pichavaram—The Place of Unparalleled Scenic Beauty

India's coastline stretches over several thousand kilometres along the Arabian Sea, the Indian Ocean and the Bay of Bengal. It is dotted with gateway cities, temple towns, bustling ports, beach resorts, enchanting backwaters and bewitching sunsets.

As tourist destinations, Goa, Kovalam, Kanniyakumari and Mahabalipuram (now called Mammalapuram) are well-known. Lesser known but a more attractive resort with unparallelled beauty is Pitchavaram in east-coast of Tamil Nadu, some 250 kilometres south of Chennai, the state capital.

Pichavaram is less than twenty kilometres from the famous temple city of Chidambaram which is well connected by road and rail with Chennai which itself on the trunk routes of air and surface connections with the rest of India. If Chidambaram is the base to discover Pitchavaram, then the charms of Chidambaram will have to be explored first.

Chidambaram is famous for its massive temple where Lord Shiva is depicted as Nataraja, the Cosmic Dancer. The temple, spread over forty acres has a golden roof over the sanctum sanctorum. Built out of enormous block of granite, the gopurams show in detailed sculptures 108 postures of Bharat Natyam the classical Indian dance. In keeping with its tradition as a centre of Tamil scholarship, the Annamalai University in Chidambaram is a major residential institution.

After the man-made warders of Chidambaram, a trip to Pitchavaram is a delightful transition to sheer nature. This 3,000 acre area is criss-crossed with enchanting back-waters forming several islands. The phenomenon of the ebb and flow of the tidal waters intertwining the islands presents and an unusual attraction to visitors. The Pitchavaram forest is no ordinary backwaters forest. It combines another rare occurrence—the mangrove forest—trees permanently rooted in a few feet of water. Pitchavaram is separated from the sea by a sand bar which is yet another patch of extraordinary loveliness.

To a botanist, a rare species like Avicennia and. Rhizophora will present a special attraction to a zoologist, no doubt, the sight of numerous birds like watersnipes, cormorants, egrets, storks, herons, spoonbills amd pelicans will be of special interest.

The mangrove species have several unique qualities of their reflecting nature's response to their special needs. They have a number of structural adaptations to suit factors like waterlogging, salinity, strong winds and lack of soil aeration. Stilted roots provide firm anchorage to the trees and breathing roots grow above the level of water. There can be seen standing in radiating rows a 11 along the banks and functioning as organs of respiration. Their fruits are adopted to float for long periods without deterioration. Germination in these trees takes place while the fruits are still with the parent plant and the embryo grows out or the fruit and then the fruit falls off and takes immediate root in the wet soil. These trees have a few uses as tanning and dyeing materials, poles, staves and fuel.

Pitchavaram also offers good fishing grounds and fishermen at work make interesting sights.

Those who wish to see Pitchavaram as an extension of their stay in Chennai City can take a two day coach package which will take them across Thanjavur, Velankanni, Nagore, Tirunallar, Poompuhar, Vaitheeswaran Koil, Chidambaram, Pitchavaram and finally to Pondicherry. But with Chidambaram as the base one can not only enjoy Pitchavaram more leisurely but also discover many other smaller but beautiful places of tourist interest. Take Vaitheeswaran Koil, only 24 kilomeres from Chidambaram is famous for the Shiva temple dedicated to Vaidyanatheeswarar, the healer of all diseases and his consort, Thaiyanaiki. Legend has it that a bath in the holy tank in this temple will cure all diseases.

Close to Pondicherry is Thiruvakkarai. Near this village are a large number of petrified tree trunks known as fossil wood which are of great interest to botany students. A little away is Genji or Ginji with a 700 year old fort running over three hills of huge and steep boulders. According to legend, the original fort was built by Kone Chiefs. The fort was ruled by Vijayanagar Kayaks, Marathas, Mughals, Carnatic Nawabs, the French and finally the British.

About 75 kilometres from Chidambaram is Arikarnedu said to be the earliest Indo-Roman trading post on the east coast of India. Excavations here have revealed Roman coins, wine jars and also evidence that the area was a Buddhist stronghold during the Sangam period.

Come, Pitchavaram is awaiting.

KARNATAKA
Travel Review

Bangalore

The most modern of Indian cities, Bangalore, interestingly dates back its foundation to the 1614 century and has since successively gone through several transformations—summer resort, garden city, industrial boom administrative headquarters and a major cultural total point. Old monuments and shrines, medieval pleasure palaces, a vast botanical garden and several parks, the grandiose Vidhan Sabha (legislature house) and spacious gallery auditoria featuring of fine arts and performing arts stows and the numerous industrial establishments bespeak of the continuing presence of the each stage of the transformations.

Well connected by air, road and rail to all the main entry points into India, Bangalore with its equable climate the year round could boast of providing something that any one could look for. It is the pivot for several radial routes leading to India's best known temple architecture, historical ruins, engineering marvels, hills and wild life sanctuaries.

In Bangalore itself dull moment for the visitor who wants to make the best one's leisure time. Perhaps next only to Delhi, Bangalore has the largest number of deluxe hotels. Numerous restaurants offer a world variety of cuisine. A place called the Tiffin Room is part of the itinerary of most visitors to the city to watch the making of and to taste the South Indian vegetarian delicacies in clean environs. Here people queue up even before the business hours start for breakfast. Bangalore has also a profusion of budget and low price hotels with restaurant facilities. Pubs are the latest additions to make for fun time. In fact, pub crawling has become a fad with both the locals and the visitors. Horse racing is a passion with many in the city and the turf is a major draw to the tourists too.

There are other places to go to unwind for the rising. Bangalore has a splendid golf green and many a club to spend the evenings. Some cinema houses feature exclusively English films. Incidentally, Bangalore has the largest number of cine halls. For those who want to get away from it all there is a sprinkling of country clubs and more are coming up.

Situated at a height of 3,000 feet, it was once called a pensioners' town for the mood of relaxation. It has since changed into a humming industrial centre manufacturing a range of high tech items which include aircraft, electronic instruments and computer software. As a result, business travel to Bangalore has increased manifold. The visitor on business or would be well advised to cover in eight seeing the Wesson Lake, Bull Temple, Tipu's summer Palace, Lal Bagh, Cubbon Park, Government museum Vidhan Soudh in Washington style and of, course, is not to miss the shopping on Mahatma Gandhi Road which has its latest attraction the largest toy shop in Asia is located.

Jog Falls

One of the most picturesque of attractions in Karnataka is Jog Falls, also known as Gersoppa Falls, Bangalore, Karnataka's capital and India's garden city, is a convenient base for visiting Jog Falls. Deep in the densely wooded mountainous region west of Mysore city and some 375 kilometres from Bangalore flows the mighty Sharavathy river. The short swift river plunges suddenly into a chasm over 260 metres deep, splitting into four cascades known as Rani, Raja, the Rocket and the Roarer. The columns of foam and sprays create an unusual myriad of prisms. At the touch of the rays of the sun a rainbow sparkles across the falls lending it an ethereal atmosphere.

You can go down to the bottom of the chasm. Steps are cut into the rocks. Breaking on the rocks below, the white foaming water leaps and spreads into clouds of spray. The roaring, swirling waters rush on to the west coast to join the Arabian Sea.

The Jog Falls are now a symbol of nature and man working in harmony for the benefit of humanity. The Sharavathy, like India's many other rivers conceals tremendous power. It has been harnessed in the Sharavathy Hydroelectric project generating ten million kw of electricity and is Karnataka's biggest power project. The power project has two main parts, the Mahatma Gandhi Hydroelectric Works and the Linganamakki Reservoir. The reservoir or the dam has a storage capacity of 1,56,000 cubic feet. The Dam is 2,461 metres long with a maximum height of 61 metres above the river bed.

Before the Jog Falls became part of the hydroelectric project, the best time to visit them was just after the monsoons. In the dry months they could be very disappointing and in the wet months too much mist would hide their beauty. But now, man regulates the flow of water. On the Sunday following the second Saturday of every month the waters of the Sharavathy River are let out from the hydroelectric works and Jog Falls come alive. In fact every second Saturday of a month there is a conducted coach tour from Bangalore which leaves in the afternoon for Jog Falls and returns to Bangalore the following evening. For those travelling by train the nearest rail head is Talguppa from where buses take about half an hour to Jog Falls.

With Bangalore as the base a visitor can also see the palace city of Mysore barely two hours' drive from the Karnataka capital, Mysore, the former capital of Maharajas, retains the aura of grandeur and royalty. The lavish ways of the Maharajas find reflection everywhere. Every edifice appears palatial, from a railway station to a technical institute to a government office, each marked by ornate domes and vaulting archways.

During the Dussehra festival (September-October), Mysore wears a bright new look for ten long days. Bathed in light, joy and colour the city appears at its best then. The citizens celebrate it both as a royal and a religous festival.

The most impressive of Mysore's numerous monuments though, is the Maharaja's Palace built about 75 years ago. One of the biggest in the country, it is a harmonious synthesis of the Hindu and Sarcenic styles of architecture. Archways, domes, colonnades turrets, colonnades and sculptures are evident in magnificent profusion. In the Durbar Hall where the Maharaja received the nobility, there is a grandstand awning which overlooks the court. Here rests the solid gold *howdah* in which the Maharaja sat when, on ceremonial occasion he rode through the city on elephant back, an the Kalyana Mandapa (marriage hall) hang beautiful paintings of the Dussehra procession. The palace is illuminated by thousands of tiny lights for the duration of the festival.

For those interested in the finer things of life there is the Chamarajendra Art Gallery which houses an excellent collection of paintings by reputed Indian artists like Ravi Varma, and ceramics, sandalwood, ivory, stone, antique furniture and ancient musical instruments. Or, you could go to the Sandalwood Oil Factory with its warm, slightly pungent smell of the oil that pervades the air. At the Government Silk Factory visitors can see workers weaving silk with shimmering gold borders, exactly the way their forefathers did centuries ago.

A short drive from Mysore is the Krishnarajasagar Dam and the Brindavan Gardens. The dam 2.4 km long forming a 129.5 square km lake, ranks among the biggest dams in India. It is built in stone without any use of cement and comprises parapets and a grotto for the river goddess Kaveri. The Brindavan Gardens which stretch out in terraced form below the dam have a French ambience, their landscape is a symphony in bright flowers, sparkling fountains and pools of various shapes and sizes.

Nearby rise the Chamundi Hills where the Goddess Chamundi destroyed the demon Mahishasura, thus bringing peace to the local people. These hills were once the site of the summer palaces of kings. About two thirds on the way up, a 4, 8 metre high and 7.6 metre wide statue of Nandi Bull, the vehicle of Lord Siva, carved out of a single boulder, sits poised and resplendent. The road to the hills is motorable.

There is much more to be discovered around Mysore including Srirangapatnam, the island fortress of Tipu Sultan, who in alliance with the French, waged war against the British. Let Jog Falls be your destination for your next visit to India.

KERALA – GOD'S OWN COUNTRY

Haven for Mortals

The conferment of international status on Trivandrum airport, the unveiling of plans by major hotel chains to launch a network of resorts, hotels and motels, and the state's own thrust in improving the infrastructure, all point to Kerala having become a most favoured destination in the south.

Precise statistics are not available but tourism, both domestic and international, has been on the upswing in the state. One reason could be mat the north is slipping out because of unrest in areas around places of tourist interest. But more importantly it is Kerala's tourism product, with its multifaceted attractions, and effective marketing and promotion by the state authorities backed by tour operators, which has brought Kerala into sharper focus in overseas markets. The government has responded by allowing charters to Trivandrum and hopefully the New Year will bring in plane-loads of holiday-makers.

The state has its traditional draw like golden beaches, boating in backwaters, wild life, plantations, unique in forms and some of the most ancient places of worship for all religions. It has the oldest synagogue, the oldest church and the country's first mosque. Besides, the place is dotted with temples where rituals continue as diety were practised several centuries ago. But temples are only one of the fascinating segments of the Kerala product. It is possible to stay in an 18th century palace one night and at a resort designed by a world famous architect the next day. One can study traditional wall paintings of rare and exquisite beauty, watch the last of the Travancore maharajas drive from his palace to the temple for prayers and relax under the hands of an ayurvedic masseur.

For lovers of sun and sand, the beaches are warm and the sea is gentle. Much of the coastline from Kovalam to Kozhikode is covered by white sand. The wonders of the water front are not confined to the seashore. There are innumerable backwaters drifting past coconut groves. One can take a journey right from Trivandrum, the state capital to Cochin (both have been restored their original names, Thiruvananthapuram and Kochi). The land's end, Kanniyakumari, could be reached in less than two hours by car from Trivandrum. Kanniyakumari is the home of the virgin goddess of the Hindu pantheon, where the sun sets on three seas—Indian Ocean, Arabian Sea and the Bay of Bengal. In the peace and quiet of its neighbourhood, Swami Vivekanada could not resist climbing a rock cutting out the sea to meditate. A memorial temple has been raised on the rock and is a must in any itinerary of a visitor.

While the journey to the south could terminate at Kanniyakumari, travel to the north through Kerala's midlands is eminently rewarding because one sees not only the backwaters where there is always a fiesta or a snake boat race to witness, but small hills which have many special spots, tea and spice plantations and the most sweeping scenery in the Western Ghats. Any traveller would better stop at: least once in a small restaurant or tea house (they all call themselves hotels) for coffee, tea or *idiyappam* (fermented pancakes). Shoppers too can look forward to carrying with them, apart from pleasant memories, textiles, antiques and jewellery which have reinforced the state's claim to being a favoured destination.

Cochin

Just like all the other cities in India, Cochin has a legacy and story of its own. Vasco da Gama arrived here searching for the exotic spices of the city. Later, the city passed into the hands of British. The city is the commercial capital of Kerala and is home to the country's ship building industry.

Cochin is not just a town but a complex of islands grouped right off the mainland town of Ernakulam. Willingdon, a man-made island connects Cochin harbour with the mainland by a bridge. The airport and the rail terminus are located on the Willingdon island. Another island in the group is Vyeen where fisherman still use Chinese nets introduced there centuries ago. Cochin's famous coir-makers hold forth on Gundu island. Bolghatty Island is the most beautiful of the lot and its colonial mansion formerly used by the Dutch Governor and later by the British resident is now a tourist bungalow. This mansion is a blend of Kerala and the Dutch styles of architecture. A French traveller who stayed here more than a hundred years ago described it the enchanted home of the sleeping beauty.

Fort Cochin and Mattencherry are the richest samples of the Port City's chequered history. Fort Cochin is believed to be the oldest European settlement and also the site for the first European church. Built by the Portuguese as the St. Franchis church, it was converted into a Dutch reformed church and later to an Anglican church. It is now part of the church of south India. Tombstones of all three European faiths line the aisles, the most famous of which is that of Vasco da Gama was died in Cochin in 1534. He was burried in the church but his remains were later removed to Lisbon.

Locked up in the church office are Dutch baptism and marriage records dating as far back as 1730. St. Francis is a quiet old church reminiscent of the Spanish style.

Mattancheri evokes even deeper interest. For, this is the home of white jew of Cochin with its world famous synagogue. The first emigration of Jews to Kerala is said to have taken place in the sixth century B.C. Built in 1568 the synagogue was considerably embillished in the eighteen century with hand painted tiles brought all the way from China. A visitor to Mattancheri, with its single blind street leading to the synagogue, cannot help being caught up in the serene old world atmosphere of the settlement. Most of the old Jewish families have emigrated, but they still maintain their links with their past by retaining their houses. Within the synagogue at once end in a tabernacle are the scrolls of the law, the crowns given by a Maharaja and a British resident and the copperplate inscription of the ruler who gave the community many privileges. Also worth seeing is the carved screen high up at the back of the Synagogue behind which, unseen, the women of the community sit during services conducted by the elders.

A bit of the Christian history is provided by COONEN CROSS lying on its side outside a church they near the Synagogue. Here, in 1653, tired of the pressures of the Portuguese to convert them to Catholicism, 20,000 Syrian Christians swore an oath that they would secede from Rome. The crowd was so vast that ropes were attached to the leaning cross and the faithful held these as they took their vow.

A relic of Cochin's colourful past can be seen in the bustling narrow streets that lead from the Chinese fishing nets to the Dutch Palace. The Dutch Palace was neither built by the Dutch nor was it, strictly speaking, a palace: no Maharaja ever lived here permanently, though many were crowned in the Coronation Hall. It was, in fact, built by the favour-seeking Portuguese in the middle of the sixteenth century and gifted to the ruler of Cochin in 1551.

And when Pope Alexander Borgia decided to divided the world between Spain and Portugal, the west half to Spain and the east half to Portugal, the famous Papal Bull was read from this edifice.

Quite apart from its associations with the competing European powers of colonial times, the Dutch Palace (so-called because the Dutch renovated it) has a rich heritage of local lore within its ancient walls.

The patron deity of the erstwhile rulers is enshrined in the centre of the courtyard and near the shrine is a temple dedicated to Shiva. Another temple, copper-covered and circular, is dedicated to Vishnu and lies on your right before you get to the long flight of steps leading to the upper floors of the palace.

The steps lead the visitor to the Coronation Hall of the Cochin Maharajas and the room is still rich with the trappings of another age. Here you will see the palanquins that were used by the royal family on ceremonial occasions, as well as the clothes they wore then, heavy with gold thread and jewels.

But the most interesting parts of the palace lie in the rooms off the Coronation Hall.

To the west is the Pallyiara or Royal Chamber, with 43 murals from Ramayana, and five scenes from the Krishna legend. The Ramayana scenes were probably painted in the second half of the sixteenth century.

Cochin truly is one of those rare places where ancient civilisations and the 20th century get along pleasantly side by side to the monuments to the days gone by are rising and co-existing modern India's new temples which Jawaharlal Nehru had once described as shrines where man works for the benefit of man. One such temple in Cochin is the Hindustan Shipyard, the country's biggest building and repair dock. The shipyard offers repair facilities to vessels upto one hundred thousand tonnes. At present the shipyard is building panamex bulk carriers of seventy-five thousand tonnes under technical collaboration with a British firm. The yard has firm orders for four such vessels, three of which are at various stages of construction.

Often referred to as Venice of the East or Queen of the Arabian Sea, Cochin is virtually a tourist paradise. Endowed with sun, sand and surf in a setting of shaded lagoons, wooded islands and canals winding past houses on stilts and enchanting back waters, Cochin is at the same time a symbol of resurregent India. A major port in India's overseas trade, Cochin is also an important base in South India's tourist circuit. More than that it is the charming people of Cochin that make this one of my favourite cities.

ANDHRA PRADESH

Hyderabad: A Rich Blend of Old and New

There is more to India than the Taj Mahal. The impact of this tourism slogan can be seen in the growth of tourist arrivals in the country, from a mere 17,000 in the early 1950s to over 1.3 million in 1983. And, not all of them came only to see the Taj. Scores of new destinations—gifts both of nature and man—have now been opened to visitors.

One of the new and popular destinations is Hyderabad, once the seat of the fabled Nizams and now the sprawling capital of the coastal southern state of Andhra Pradesh. A medieval city which has imperceptibly moved into the modern era. Hyderabad is a fine blend of the industrial age and the elegance of the old world. Palaces, mosques, minarets, centuries old metal craftsmanship, mouth-watering cuisine, gypsies and even a pearl market co-exist with a bustling metropolis that Hyderabad and its twin, Secunderabad, are today.

Although a meeting point of many cultures, Hyderabad exudes an atmosphere of 400 years of Muslim splendour. Symbolic of the city is the Char Minar. This is an architectural jewel of a stately rectangular building with four slender minarets, each more than 50 metres high, and a tiny mosque on the second floor. From the top one gets a fascinating view of the city and its crowded bazaars, like looking out of a sentinel.

This majestic monument was built at the close of the 16th century just a few years after the founding of the city. According to one account, the

Char Minar was built as a sort of talisman to drive away the dreaded epidemic that was ravaging the newly-founded city.

A few yards away from the Char Minar stands Meca Masjid, the most impressive mosque in southern India.

There are many legends about this mosque. According to one, the foundation of the mosque was laid by a Qutab Shahi king, a uniquely pious man who had not missed a single prayer since the age of 12. Another legend links its name to a brick which was brought from Mecca and which, they say, still adorns the building. The mosque has lofty colonnades and door arches made out of single slabs of granite brought from a stone quarry 11 kilometres away and pulled by 1,400 bullocks. To the left of the mosque is an enclosure containing the tombs of the Nizams who ruled Hyderabad after the Qutab Shahi dynasty.

Other landmarks of this interesting city include the tomb of Monsieur Raymond, the 18th century French adventurer who served under the second Nizam and who was popularly known as Musa Ram. The Archaeological Museum displays implements, sculptures, paintings, coins and textiles.

There are two picturesque hillocks overlooking the city. On one is laid out a hanging garden and on the other a marble shrine. The Nehru Park, Pre-Historic Animals Park, Ancient Life Museum, Natural History Museum, Lion Safari Park, and a children's train are some of the other attractions of Hyderabad. Just went to the city is the historic Golconda Fort once famous for its diamond market and the capital of the Qutab Shahi ruler. It is now partly in ruins.

But, perhaps, nothing captures the lifestyle of Hyderabad's old Nawabs, as much as the Salar Jung Museum. It has on display the private collection of Nawab Salar Jung III and is said to be the finest one-man collection in the world. The museum's 36 halls are filled with an intriguing array of treasures—as assortment of statues that includes that Veiled Rebecca and Mephistopheles and Margareta, bejewelled weapons including the Nawab's one diamond-encrusted sword; Indian miniatures and other paintings including canvases by Landseer, Watts and Cooper; furniture like Marie Antoinette's dressing table, illuminated manuscripts, priceless collections of jade, porcelain and crystal, ivory and bronze and a delightful collection of quaint clocks.

The gypsies or Banjaras, as they are known, travelled to the region with the Mughal armies and settled in and around Hyderabad. Despite changes in their lifestyle and occupation they have retained their distinctively colourful way of dressing and many of their joyous and festive customs. A visit to the Peral Bazaar is a treat, for Hyderabad is the country's leading trade centre in pearls.

Hyderabad's cuisine also retains its links with the past and is utterly unique. Pathar Kebab, introduced by the Nizam's African bodyguard, are flat mutton steaks grilled on heated slabs of stone. There is Haleem made of wheat and mutton and Nahari a soup of trotters eaten with soft sheeshmal bread. The most popular Hyderabad delicacy is Biryani, made of meat and rice. You will not only ask for more but will feel impelled to come back to Hyderabad!

Hyderabad is on the trunk routes of Indian Railways and connected to the main cities of India by jet services. There are good international class hotels and plenty of road transport.

Hyderabad could be good starting point for a visitor in search of history, culture and leisure.

6
Coastal India – Islands and Beaches and Other Lesser Known Beauty Spots

Sun, Sands and Coasts of India

India has for so long been a sightseer's paradise, that the magnificent opportunities it offers for holiday by the sea often tend to be overlooked. To these holiday seekers, India offers three oceans, five thousand years of history and eternal sun. The Arabian Sea, the Indian Ocean, the Bay of Bengal skirt a multitude of magic names: the Malabar coast, the coast of Coromandel, Kerala, Goa, Mahabalipuram and Konarak. Cape Comorin or Kanniyakumari, is where all the seas join beneath the world's most incredible sunsets. The entire coastline, stretching to several thousand kilometres, is laced with the rich history of ancient culture, palaces, temples, villages and great cities. Here was legendary Ophir, port of call for the ships of King Solomon, where Phoenicians once came as did Greeks, Egyptians Romans and Chinese.

If you can imagine how natural and unspoiled the sea coasts of the Mediterranean once looked, before the era of mass tourism, then you have at least some idea of what a perfect holiday is waiting for you in India.

Mumbai could be a colourful start to your holiday. India's commercial centre, Mumbai is uniquely gifted with honeyed strands of sand, golden, crescent-shaped beaches such as Juju, Versova, Marve, Madh and Manori. An hour's boat ride off Mumbai's busy harbour is Elephanta Island famous for its 7th century huge rock carvings magnificently executed on the walls of the cave temples.

An hour's flight to the south along the coast is Goa with its 100 kilometre long coastline endowed with some of the loveliest beaches in the world. Calungute beach extending along the Arabian Sea in an inward arch of about 7 kilometres may well be called the Queen of Goa Beaches.

Colva Beach is a rival to Calangute. It has miles of sand girdled by verdant palm-trees swaying gently in the caressing westerly breeze blowing from the ocean. Song, dance, music, conducted tours, historical monuments, fine foods, feasts, festivals, charming and friendly people make Goa a tiny paradise for holiday-makers.

Another hour's flight and you are in Kovalam very clear to the southern tip of India. Lying langurously on Kerala's sun-drenched coast is the magnificent new beach resort of Kovalam with one of the world's finest beaches. To its natural scenic beauty has been added a modern complex of facilities for a beach holiday. This comprise a village of beach cottages, an impressive five tiered hotel built on the slopes of a gentle hill overlooking the Kovalam Bay and plenty of water sports. A unique feature of Kovalam is the invigorating massage and oil bath, a famous Kerala health treatment which has been practiced in India for five thousand years. You can take yoga lessons too at the resorts Health Centre. And, Cape Comorin is just 80 kilometres away where the sun sets over three oceans.

Up the east coast is Mahabalipuram with its world famous shore temple. The temple is particularly fascinating for it is the lone survivor of seven erected on the sea shore more than 12 centuries ago by the Pallava kings. Mahabalipuram too has been developed into a fascinating beach resort with modern facilities for travellers.

Further north is Puri, the sacred city by the sea. This is one of the four most holy places in India. Its cultural attractions are a big draw. One of the most striking buildings is the great temple of Jagannath—a compound nearly 200 metres square, surrounded by a wall 6 metres high and served by 6,000 priests. In summer, 2,00,000 pilgrims converge on Puri for the Rath Yatra or the Car Festival.

Less than a 100 kilometres away is Konarak which has one of the greatest monuments in all India. This is the 13th century temple dedicated to the sun god. The temple is in the shape of a gigantic chariot on 24 wheels.

There is also Gopalpur on sea, a lovely sea resort. A little away is Digha and finally Kolkata where after a quiet beach holiday one feels in contrast another world, a pulsating metropolis and India's largest city.

One thing India's beaches can always guarantee. And that is unfailing sunshine.

Beaches of India

Winter is here with its nip in the air. It is time to wear a little sun and warmth. For a leisure holiday, then, there is nothing better than a time by a sea. And what better sea coasts to spend the time on than those of the peninsular India. Calm, blue seas; clear skies; an abundance of nature and rich hinterlands. India offers a choice of three seas, and one of the longest cumulated beach-line in the world.....the Malabar Coast, the coast of Coromandel, Kerala, Goa, Mahabalipuram, Konarak, Puri and many more that conjure up a magic all their own. Through the ages, travellers and traders have touched upon these shores......Phonecians, Greeks, Egptians, Romans, Chinese.....and spread tales of their beauty and richness. Yet, even today, these beaches are uncrowded and unspoiled, offering a warm, yet private holiday.

The climate along India's coastline is generally mild and steady. Tropical clothing is ample enough during the day. In the evenings however, you would do well to carry something warm to wear.

If you wish to spend your next holiday by the lapping waters of the great blue seas, you can expect a perfect one on any of the many beaches in India.

Let's start from the west, and Mumbai.

Mumbai is the commerical centre of India. An international airport, all-budget hotel and the foods of the world. And innumerable beaches—Juhu, Versova, Marve, Madh and Manori. Juhu is 20 km by road from Bombay air terminal, and city buses are routed thereon Sundays and holidays. There are good hotels in Juhu and you can spend a good weekend by the sea. Marve is 44 km, Madh 38 km, and Manori 40 km from Mumbai.

In the heart of Mumbai is Chowpatty where you can spend fascinating hours and be among the Bombayites in a park-like atmosphere. Across the Mumbai harbour, and one hour by boat is the Elephanta island. Here on the walls of the cave temples are executed rock carvings dating back to as early as the 7th century. From Mumbai, too, less than an hour by flight is Aurangabad, which connects to Ajanta and Ellora caves.

Andaman and Nicobar Islands

It is only in the last decade or so that the traveller is discovering that India is too vast a country and many splendoured. Visitors are no longer content with the golden triangle of Delhi, Agra and Jaipur. The Taj Mahal or the pink princely city or the capital of many a kingdom no longer satisfy the quest for the discovery that tourists seek in modern times. And so India has responded by opening up its myriad worlds to those who seek it. From the roof of the world – Ladakh – to the meeting of three seas at Kanniyakumari or Cape Comorin. And, in between much more. The Verdant South with its multi-hued cultures, languages, cuisines, customs, festivals and temple cities, the Himalayas and the plains in the North. The exotic east. And, now the doors are opening to yet another Indian world, Andaman and Nicobar Islands.

An emerald in the deep blue sea. Deep in the South Eastern waters of the bay of Bengal lies the archipelago of Andaman and Nicobar Islands with its capital at Port Blair. This wild land with scenic beauty stands isolated from India, some 1,300 kms. from Calcutta and 1,200 kms from Chennai. The islanders does longingly talk of the mainland.

Originally known as Kalapani or black waters because the islands were used as a penal settlement by the British rulers. Today, they are known as islands of the marigold sun. It is one of the most unexplored parts of India and also the most unexploited. It offers a quiet holiday in a serene setting.

Here the air is pure and unpolluted, the pace of life unhurried, the people gentle and hospitable. Surrounded by coral reefs and shallow seas, these islands boast of numerous long narrow stretches of sandy beaches. Endless opportunities exist for those who are interested in water sports.

The Andaman group five large islands; North Andaman, Middle Andaman, Baratang, South Andaman and Rutland. Each island is separated by shallow seas. To the south is the island of Little Andaman. Further south is the Nicobar group. The important ones are: Car Nicobar, Nancowry, Chowra, Katchal and Great Nicobar.

The Andamans are populated by Indians, Myanmar and the Negrito-tribals, still untouched by civilisation. The Onghies in Little Andaman are among the world's rarest and fast-vanishing tribes. The 22nd Onghi was recently born amidst great rejoicings!

The Jarawas on the west coast of South Andaman are a closed community. They shun overtures from outside and resist attempts at modernisation.

Nicobar Islands have friendly tribals. All tribals speak native dialects and worship the deities of rocks, trees, snakes and eggs. The islands and the waters around them provide rare sights – gambolling dolphins, flying fish and sea-crocodiles seven to ten metres long. Herbs of deer and galaxies of rare birds fluttering in the sky will gladden the heart of many a convervationlist.

Exploring these islands for Japanese war relics and beachcombing for fancy driftwood and corals and shells of various shapes and colours can be absorbing pursuits.

There is much to see in the Andaman and Nicobar Islands – The Cellular Jail; the Bastille of India – a relic of bygone days – where India's freedom fighters were incarcerated. Every cell has a tale to tell. The Chatham Saw Mill: The largest saw mill in Asia. Chiriya Tapu: this southernmost tip of South Andaman – the Bird Island – is a beautiful spot for picnicing and fishing. An ornithologists paradise. Madhuban: where elephants are trained for lumbering of timber. Mount Harriet: See the setting sun. Rose Island: it has the ruins of what was once the British Administration's headquarters. Permits to visit this island are issued by the Naval Office, Port Blair. Corbyn's Cove Sea Beach: a place for long lazy afternoons and sea-bathing, yatching and fishing. Anthropological Museum: the 'habitat' of aboriginal tribes in miniature. Marine Museum: it preserves over 350 species of sea-life. Zoological Gardens: holds in captivity salt-water crocodile, robber crab and crab-eating macaque, green lizard hornbills and a variety of deer and fish.

It is easy to get to Andaman and Nicobar islands. Indian Airlines operates a bi-weekly Boeing 737 service between Kolkata and Port Blair. The Shipping Corporation of India operates regular shipping services from Kolkata and Chennai to Port Blair. Occasionally, ships also ply between Visakhapatnam and Port Blair. Also, the Shipping Corporation of India and the Marine Department of the Government of Andaman and Nicobar Islands operate several services for inter-island movement of visitors. Small motor-boats are also available on hire. And for accommodation there is a Beach Resort at Corbyn's Cove, Port Blair, a Tourist Home and Government resthouse and inns in several islands.

For those looking for an off-beat quiet holiday away from the din and noise of the modern world, Andaman and Nicobar islands will be a rewarding choice.

GOA

Song, dance, music, historical monuments, fine food, feasts and festivals, the inebriating feni, colourful customs and a charming people...all these make Goa, a tiny paradise. Goa has among the loveliest beaches, stretching 100 km by the Arabian Sea. Of these, Calangute, 15 km from Panaji, the capital of Goa, is the most lovely and called the 'Queen of Goa Beaches.' It is also the most popular seaside rendezvous.

Six km from Margao, Colva beach is next only to Calangute in popularity, with stretches of sand girdled by green palm trees. Dona Paula is another picturesque spot, 7 km from Panaji. Facing the Marmagao harbour, it is an idyllic beach, good for picnics and a swim in the cool waters of the tiny bay. If you are looking for a quiet place, Vagator is the place, situated on the bay beyond the northern end of Calangute. There is a historic fort at the entrance of the bay, which enhances the picturesequeness of Vagator.

Moving down south, we come to Kerala, among the smallest and most beautiful of Indian states. It is a lush green land blessed with bountiful nature and innumerable rivers, dense forests, plantations of rubber, tea, coffee and pepper. And backwaters making way through paddy fields and villages. Kerala is truly a tropical paradise...the legendary Malabar coast.

Lying on Kerala's sun drenched coast is the tiny village of Kovalam, which now has become one of the most magnificent beach resorts in the country, and perhaps in the world too. The endless stretches of wheat coloured sand, the gently swaying coconut trees and an ice blue sea, make Kovalam ideal for a seaside holiday. The tourist complex at Kovalam is India's first beach resort to international standards. The complex comprises a group of air conditioned beach cottages, an impressive five-tiered hotel which follows the gentle slopes of a hill overlooking the Kovalam bay, and on the spot beach facilities such as changing rooms, restaurant, bar and facilities for water sports. The visitors can also enjoy invigorating massages and oil baths, as well as take yoga lessons at the nearby health centre.

Kovalam also makes an excellent base for excursions to Trivandrum, the capital of Kerala, to Cochin, to the Wild Life sanctuary at Periyar, and many more places. A favourite excursion is to Kanniyakumari, the southernmost tip of India. Here the Arabian Sea, the Indian Ocean, and the Bay of Bengal come together, making up the most spectacular sunrises and sunsets.

Chennai is the fourth largest city in India, but is quite uncomplicated city. Some people say that Chennai known only three seasons—hot, hotter and hottest, but they are wrong. However, harsh the sun, a cool sea breeze lifts early in the afternoon to bring relief through the day. Chennai has a fine line. Catamarans sail out on the sea. There is an abundance of excursions from Madras, the most popular being to Mahabalipuram, now known as Mamallapuram 60 km away. This is yet another beach which has been developed into a resort. The Shore temple at Mamallapuram is particularly fascinated. This one is the lone survivor of the seven, erected more than 12 centuries ago by the Pallava kings. Here, is both ancient history and relaxed holiday rolled into one 170 km south of Chennai is Pondicherry, a town with a French air about it. Life here revolves around Aurobindo Ashram, named after the great sage and philosopher.

A popular excursion along this Coromandel coast is Chidambaram, where there is a 6th century temple dedicated to Nataraja, Lord Shiva in his form as cosmic dancer. All of his 108 postures are represented in a series of rich and elegant carving.

Visakhapatnam, 800 km north of Chennai is India's fourth largest sea port, which is sheltered by a promontory from where one can have a splendid view of the bay and the town. Visakhapatnam's beaches are studded with secluded coves and creeks that are sunny throughout the year.

The small town of Waltair is about 3 km north of Visakhapatnam. It is a seaside resort known for its attractive wooded, hilly landscape, splendid beach and pleasant climate.

Puri, in Orissa, is a sacred city by the sea, among the four most holy places in India. In summer, a million people converge on this city for the Ratha Yatra or the Car Festival. Here also, you can enjoy some very good swimming and surf. The Puri sand is silver during the day and gold as the sun sets over the ocean.

Intent fishermen, of course, will prefer to spend their time hauling their catch out of the sea.

Further east is Kolkata—another world. Pulsating metropolis, it is the largest city of India and one of the largest in the world. This is the hub of Indian industry and much of its creative and intellectual activity. Kolkata is hardly a restful city but it is a vital and fascinating one and in complete contrast with the calm and quiet of the beach resorts.

So spend your next seaside holiday in India. Where there are more than a thousand beaches strung like pearls along her coastline. Each one is unique. They are, unspoiled, uncrowded, waiting to be discovered.

Lesser Known Beauty Spots of India

There is more to India than the Taj Mahal. The Taj is just one facet of this vast and diverse country that has something to offer to everyone. A visit to the Taj or to the Khajuraho temples or yet to the pink city of Jaipur is not a visit to India. For India is much more. There are many, many interesting places off the beaten track which are easily accessible but are yet to be explored.

In the heartland of India, Madhya Pradesh is a large plateau streaked with meandering rivers and majestic monuments which are full of romantic and heroic legends. The exquisite carvings at Sanchi, the stupendous fort at Gwalior, the superb paintings at Bagh, the remains of an ancient civilization at Bhimbetka make one ponder over the mysterious past. The Afghan capital of Mandu, 'city of joy', is scarred by sun, wind and battle and still stands with its formidable fort and imposing mosque. And, Bhopal, the lakeside city is today the capital of Madhya Pradesh and is a convenient base for visiting various places in Madhya Pradesh.

In eastern India, there are some new exotic places now open to visitors. The charming north-easternmost state of Sikkim has all the magic and splendour of the Himalayas. Its exotic flora and fauna; its colourful lamas and ever smiling hill folk, its mystery-laden prayer flags fluttering over the monasteries – all combine to make Sikkim a truly fascinating place for visitors.

The easternmost state, Manipur, though small in area, is rich in its culture, traditions, festivals, dances, handlooms and handicrafts. Its capital, Imphal, popularly known as the 'land of jewels', splits up naturally into two tracts – the hills and the plains.

A land of wooded hills, waterfalls and green dales, the eastern state of Tripura is a tiny, fascinating world in itself. A princely state for 13 centuries, Tripura traces its origin back to the days of the great Hindu epic, Mahabharata.

Situated close to the north-eastern border of India at an altitude of 1,500 metres, Shillong, the capital of Meghalaya state, is one of the largest hill stations in the country. Unlike most hill stations, Shillong is neither snowbound in winter nor over crowded in summer and is as yet untouched by the hundrum of ultra modern civilization.

Kaziranga and Manas are two famous wildlife sanctuaries in the east. The Kaziranga sanctuary is famous as the stronghold of the great one-horned rhinoceros. Its harbours over 700 species. Down south is the land of sun and warmth, of temples and legends, of silver lined beaches and blue mountains. In this lush and colour-drenched, sun-burnt and romantic region lie some of the most beautiful hill resorts. The states of Tamil Nadu and Karnataka merge in a lovely cluster of hills, the Nilgiris or Blue Mountains. Crowning the Nilgiris is the delightful hill station of Ootacamund, popularly known as Ooty, with a wealth of eucalyptus trees that give the air a distinct freshness. Further south is Kodaikanal, carpeted with wild flowers and faintly scented with honeysuckels.

Coonoor is the second largest of three hills stations of the Nilgiris. Standing on a lower ridge of the main plateau at an altitude of 1,858 metres, its climate is milder than that of Ooty. Known as the 'Queen of the Nilgiris', Coonoor is an ideal health resort.

Kotagiri is the oldest hill station on the Nilgiris and is protected by the Doddabetta ranges from the violence of the south-west monsoons. Nandi Hill is a popular hill resort near Bangalore and the fairly extensive plateau on its top is an ideal summer resort.

Karnataka has some of the most celebrated temples in the country. The 12th century temples of Belur and Halebid display a wealth of intricate and exquisite sculpture, lovingly and patiently carved in stone. The road from Bangalore to Belur (222 km) skirts the hills of Sravanabelagola with its colossal 17 metres high statue of Lord Gomateswara, the Jain apostle. A leap across the centuries brings you to Hampi, a fascinating ruined city which was the capital of the Vijaynagar empire in the 15th and 16th centuries. In northern Karnataka, there are some of the earliest temples of south India, cut out of the hillsides of Aihole, Badami and Pattauakal.

An hour'a flight from Mumbai takes you to Aurangabad, base for the rock-cut temples of Ellora and the marvellous cave frescoes of Ajanta that date back 2,000 years. Hewn out of solid living rock by generations of Buddhist, Jain and Hindu monks they are embellished with stupendous sculpture and painting.

In the north of Mumbai lies Ahmedabad, a wonderful blend of Muslim medieval and Corbusier modern. About 40 km from Ahmedabad lie the excavations at the ancient site of Lothal, seaport of the Harappan era that goes back 4,000 years.

A legendary land of pink places and sun-baked forts, preening peacocks and a proud and colourful people, the state of Rajasthan offers some of the hidden treasures that are yet to be explored. Jaisalmer, remote and medieval has yellow sandstone mansions and temples intricately carved that rise like a fantastic mirage out of the desert sands. From here, the camel safari takes you to the other desert towns of Jodhpur and Bikaner-completing the journey of the famous 'desert triangle'. And the great, gaunt, deserted fort of Chittor still seems to brood on a heroic end. These then are soem of the lesser known beauty spots of India.

7

Hotels: The Pride of Our Nation

Some Famous Hotels

Hotels as we know came into being in the first decade of this century. Their beginnings growth and transformation are woven into the web of history. In fact the distinct historic phases in the century are pronounced in their characteristics and development of these hotels. The Maiden's, the Grand, the Taj, the Connemara, Maurya Sheraton, Bangalore Oberoi and Rajputana Palace—the list by no means exhaustive—have all been a response to the needs of the times and bear witness to the process of development in the period.

These stand out as superb bookmarks in any narrative of the annals of Indian tourism and travel. Passage of time has not dimmed the lustre with which they had shone when, they were founded as, for instance, the Taj in Mumbai. From the Maidens to Le Meridien, in Delhi, from The Connemara in Chennai to Centaur in Mumbai, from the Grand in Kolkata to Rajputana Palace in Jaipur, these edifices of Indian hospitality services in their successive paces of growth have been in tune with the progress of the country from being a colonial outpost to almost the threshold of emergence as an economic superpower.

It needs to be repeated that the hotels referred to here are not exhaustive of a lengthening list. These are only typical of the period during which they were launched. All these fall into what are called big hotels with global linkages. Sheraton, Intercontinental and Kempinski are among the chains to which some of these are affiliated. But recent developments show that there is an equal urgency for medium hotels. Since they need marketing and promotion expertise special companies with international connections like Quality Inns India have moved in to fill the gap. In a short period they too have established a name for excellence and standard of service. Thus with the widening of the range and spread of the product, the saga of the hotel industry stretches from the days of the Raj to the immediate years after freedom and then to the era of economic resurgence.

Early Establishments

One of the earliest surviving hotels. The Connemara in Chennai, owes its name not to any location or people associated with its establishment in the last decade of the last century. It came to be known after the wife of the then Governor of Madras, Lord Connemara, who had taken refuge in the building at the hotel site protesting against the peccadilloic adventures of her husband.

The site originally acquired by an English surgeon, John Binny, passed on from his heirs to a succession of owners until it was bought by a local firm Spencer & Co. A French patissier first opened a pastry shop and then expanded to become a hotelier. It was in 1912 that the Spencers bought the area around the original site and developed it into a major hotel of the times. Incidentally, it was the same year that Spencers started the West End in Bangalore. The Spencers had a chain of hotels, and tie-ups with the Associated Hotels of India apart from running a network of departmental stores.

Connemara was always a hotel of class. In the 1930's it was an upmarket hotel of the times in the sense only British officers went there and it was out of bounds for ordinary soldiers even whites, its high ceiling rooms and *pankahs*, personalised services of one waiter attending on a single guest, among visiting Englishmen. At the same time, it was not an expensive hotel. An astounding announcement during the war years had offered gala dinner dance in aid of the War Fund at only Rs. 5 per head.

After the old patrons had left and a new class of visitors started coming in, making different demands, the Connemara had to change. By 1963 the hotel had been so completely renovated modernised that its former patrons would not recognise it. Yet the Connemara with the new look took full note of old values and traditions including the retention of covered courtyards full of plants and flowing water, temple sculpture and ornate wood carvings. Even the new addition, the open air restaurant called The Raintree, takes the visitor to the days of the House of on the Choultry Plain by which name it was known in the last century. The hotel with many historical associations and viewed as a retreat for power and wealth during the Raj, is now part of the Taj group with evergreen elegance.

Living Reminder

Edward Lutyens who built New Delhi stayed at Maidens for supervising the construction of the grand city reflective of the might of the *raj* and India's hoary traditions. So there were many others who had visited after the capital had shifted from Kolkata. One notable figure was the then Duke of Windsor in 1921. In its past was glory and it remains a contemporary favourite as a living reminder of a bygone age.

Maidens was founded early in the century by a person named Maiden and records show that it changed hands in 1916 to Associated Hotels predecessor to East India Hotels with the Oberois as the managing agent. The *de facto* take over by the Oberois came in 1943.

The Maidens is the lone survivor of the classy hotels of the times which came up in that part of Delhi before independence. Swiss, Cecil and Grand in the neighbourhood have passed into history, but the Maidens still exudes old world charm as a hotel.

This is in line with its claim to distinctions. Earlier it was the first hotel in Delhi to have modern plumbing, the first that was air-conditioned, the first to have a unique swimming pool with a Japanese style bridge and the first to have a discotheque. Repeat visitors from England and France do not mind the long and distance from the airport to stay in the Maidens. Its spacious rooms are fully occupied during the tourist season.

In this grand old hotel of Old Delhi much of the colonial architecture is retained. The original building started with what is now a coffee shop. Subsequently, the verandah and the ballroom were added. There is a deliberate effort to retain its original identity. For that reason, the management gave up the idea of providing false ceilings which would have cut the air-conditioning costs. Nor the room size has been trimmed. Some of the bathrooms are as large as bedrooms.

Even as the skyline in the entire neighbourhood has changed, the Maidens remains a spacious symbol of a change in continuity—traditional care with contemporary comforts.

Nation's Pride

Few establishments in any city have endeared themselves to a majority of its residents who have not even entered its premises as the Taj in Mumbai. It may be partly due to its historic origin as the first ever hotel of its kind open to Indians when the Raj was supreme. It came as an expression of maternal pride.

The great hotel that came into being on the Mumbai seafront in 1903 after ninety years of growth and expansion still retains fascination for the lookers-on who come to the Gateway of India in large numbers. Through its portals have passed men and women who have influenced the lives of mankind in various fields through successive generations. Here, its suites and rooms have been the temporary home of people from every continent. Despite the long drive from the airport it is still the number one preferred hotel of the "cream layer' of visitors on business or leisure.

The great landmark is as much sought after as an object of sightseeing as any other place of visitor interest. Today its restaurants and social and cultural functions attract a much larger cross-section of Bombayites than ever before. In the early part of the century the appearance of the sandstone edifice from distance at sea was the cheering sight for the passengers of the P&O shipping lines.

The Taj was launched because its founder Jamshetji Tata, who proved at that time Indian industrial capability wanted to demonstrate that Indians were competent enough to run a hotel and eligible to stay there. Hotels of this class until then were open to Europeans only. At the very beginning Tata wanted to build a hotel with a touch of class. After seeing many such hotels he commissioned a French architect to design the hotel. Since then this grand hotel has been a meeting place of great peoples of the earth. Royalties, artists billionnaires, Nobel Laureates, presidents and prime ministers, there is hardly any person of distinction having visited Mumbai and not been at the Taj. Coauthor of Midnight's Children, Dominique Lapierre speaks of the concern for the guests by the management by citing a personal experience: "the management of the hotel having heard that I had recently been married decided when we visited Mumbai to decorate our exquisite suite... I suddenly felt like emperor Shah Jahan bringing my French Mumtaz Mahal into the majic of an oriental dream." Many before and after him vouchsafe the memorable experience the Mumbai Taj Mahal Hotel can give in the age of jumbo jets and mass tourism.

Duchess or Debutante

Built towards the close of the last century on the site of a mansion one Col. Grand had acquired, the Grand Hotel has had a succession of incarnations until the master hotelier M. S. Oberoi took it under his wings in 1938. It was always associated with grandiose splendour because of its size, room strength and "The grand dame of Chowringee" as it was known, drew from his high ingenuity in management and persistence. After going through the successful war years, the Grand got a face lift by the late forties. That was the time the British empire was liquidated and the Oberois set out on their vast hotel empire. It did not take long for the Grand to assert its primacy in Kolkata as the hotel quickly readjusted itself to a new sort of clientele.

The Oberoi masthead has been there for the Grand for more than half a century. The most massive renovation came in its fiftieth year under the Oberois which in the words of Bachi Karkaria 'who wrote the Grand Hotel story, made those "who have seen the Grand through all its old glories watch and wonder what if the Duchesss becomes a debutante!"

She writes: From the cocooning chrysalis emerging a resplendent butterfly—a lobby agleam with marble crystal and brass: a set of deluxe suites ready to take on the celebrities who thronged to Kolkata for the World Cup : La Rotisserie, the city's first French restaurant: here a new tea lounge; there a new renovated Chowringee Bar or a Ming Court to replace the cuisine of Polynesia."

One of the best internationally known hotels whose name is sustained through the memories of six generations the name Grand justifies its literal meaning as it has come to mean the total integration of traditional opulence with modern luxury.

Ashoka and After

Ashoka Hotel in New Delhi in every manner of detail conformed to the grand design of new India which its architect Jawaharlal Nehru had envisioned. It was his view that the first great hotel of free India should blend traditional hospitality with contemporary efficiency. It was also the first major hotel in the public sector which had compulsively a role of primacy to meet the demands of those days. Nehru took personal interest in the construction of the hotel which commemorated the name of a historic figure he admired most.

The site chosen on the spur of a hillock in Chanakyapuri, the Diplomatic Enclave, its first guests were scholars scientists and litterateurs the world over who had come to attend the UNESCO session.

It acquired an identity of being truly Indian reflected in its decor, cuisine and entertainment. The massive 571-room hotel has been witness to developments in international relations of post-Independence India. Heads of state and government from far and near on state visits stayed here and had much of their social and formal engagements.

Ashoka has also introduced to the world of Indian performing arts most of its present day celebrities. In music, vocal and instrumental, dance and other art forms anyone who is somebody today had his or her debut in Ashoka.

Its vast convention hall with the capacity to accommodate nearly 2,500 persons at a time has been the venue of many international conferences. The warmth of Ashoka extends to its restaurants in the rugged fortess of Frontier, the Mughal splendour at Durbar, the Canton and Szechwan delights at China Town, the city's only Japanese restaurant, Tokyo, the 24-hour Samovar, the quiet garden bar and the bar-e-kebab.

Its extensive shopping arcade where Indian crafts of the widest range are available and facilities for outdoor facilities games like tennis courts, swimming pool and the like made it the trend-setter for India's latter day hotels.

Ashoka became the flagship of the ITDC chain which pioneered deluxe hotel in Kovalam, Bangalore as well as medium hotels in several other places of tourist interest. As tourism developed private hotel chains were not far behind to meet the accommodation requirements of the international traveller in new areas.

Business Towers

Maurya Sheraton and Towers in Delhi that came into being in the late seventies was at once an innovation to create demand and a response to the new class of tourists. Not only Maurya evoked a great epoch in the history of this country by its name and splendour, it truly provided corporate leaders with spatial suites to ponder and plan, facilities for business discussions and secretarial services. The latest technological aids were on hand. The tower concept fashioned the creation of a hotel within a hotel to cater to the upmarket executive traveller.

As the flagship of the ITC Welcomgroup it set a pattern of catering to a particular clientele that could afford to rent a business suite for months on end. The interests of the traditional customer were not overlooked. It has remained a favourite venue for parties and medium conferences. With the construction of the towers the two classes of clientele, the upmarket business traveller and the conventional patron, could pursue their interests without either inconveniencing in the least the interests of the other. The result is that it has become a revenue leader with a (1991-92) turnover of Rs. 54 crore and more.

Innovations enabled select groups to experience not only the in-house facilities but also sponsored programmes. The lobby ceiling is a masterpiece in creativity. Round the year exhibitions make its gallery the most frequented by art lovers. Its annual music and dance festival is an event that one looks forward to Delhi's cultural calendar.

Not the least of its attractions are its restaurants at least two of which have become virtually patented. These are Bukhara and Dum Pukht which has revived interest in the Avdhi Nabobi style of cuisine.

Maurya, The Oberoi, Taj Mahal, Taj Palace, Hyatt Regency, Holiday Inn, Centaur and Le Meridien have been among the contenders along with the Ashok for the favour of the upmarket since the seventies.

Newest Phase

The greatest hotels belong to all periods including the latest. The eighties and after could for the purpose be considered the latest phase. Airport, midtown and resort hotels were examplied by the establishment of Centaur (Juhu), the Leela, Sea Rock, the Retreat and the Resort—all in Mumbai—The Leela Beach in Goa, the Mughal Sheraton in Agra.

The Centaur and The Leela are of five star deluxe primarily catering to international travellers on business and leisure and stopover passengers. The two are located near Mumbai's international airport. Both have distinctive arthitectural style and, in spatial terms, are insulated from the bustle of the metropolis. Restaurants, bars, business centres, conference rooms and fitness centres seek to offer all that the international traveller would want there hotels.

The Leela Beach in Goa and, the Mughal Sheraton in Agra, typify the resort concept. Leela Beach is a cluster of peach painted Portuguese type villas and amidst coconut palms beside lagoons on the southern tip of the Colva beach. The accommodation is categorised into pavilions, vilas and deluxe rooms each pavilions/vila has a large air conditioned bedroom, well appointed bathroom and a private balcony. A large swimming pool, a kiddies pool and outdoor Jacuzzi, a health spa, two outside terraces with extensive food and beverage facilities are the other special features.

Palace Hotels

Indian palaces—repositories of opulence—have been glorified in fiction and history in the west. Not only the chroniclers of the Raj but visitors since the day of Huan Tsang and Marco Polo have spoken of the immense wealth of the Indian rulers as well as of the fabulous mansions they lived in. This always had a tantalizing attraction for travellers to India. But, only a very few of them had access to these palaces until recently. Now, it is no longer so.

Following the tradition in Europe of opening the great castles to tourists, the Indian tourism authorities have also encouraged the former rulers and princes to let others partake of a great heritage. The credit for pioneering the concept of Palace hotels in this country must go to the state owned India Tourism Development Corporation or ITDC. It converted the Lalitha Mahal in Mysore, a city famous for palaces, into a luxury hotel in the early 70s. An architectural beauty, the palace was built by the former ruler of Mysore as a residence for the Viceroy of India who might make an occasional visit to the state. Today it is a major tourist attraction and its Viceroy and Vicerene suites are the ultimate in luxury living. Mysore was soon followed by two Palaces hotels in Rajasthan, a state comprising more than a score of former princely territories with hundreds of palaces and forts. Rambagh palace hotel, in the heart of the pink city of Jaipur that forms one of the corners of India's golden triangle, and the Lake Palace in the middle of Lake Pichola in Udaipur, along with Lalitha Mahal Palace are among the best known hotels around the world. Built in the 19th century both were private residences of the royal families of Jaipur and Udaipur. The princess suite at Rambagh has its own terrace garden. The Chinese room with red and gold tapestry and antiques radiates an aura of the exotic.

In the past few years the turning of former princely residence into centres of hospitality has become a veritable movement and forms a key segment in the accommodation sector. These fall in the category of heritage hotels which receive state encouragement.

A short flight from Jaipur is Jodhpur with its Umaid Bhawan Palace, a massive edifice which is celebrating its fiftieth anniversary this year. Once considered the world's largest private residence, it is now part hotel and part residence of the royal family. In sheer grandeur it has few parallels. The palace hotel is a destination in itself for all lovers of art and architecture. Its museum, library, luxury suites, paintings can make even a brief visit a memorable experience.

An hour and half's drive from Jodhpur is the Sardar Samand Palace built in 1933 as a hunting lodge and country residence for the then Maharaja. This well-preserved structure located on high ground overlooks the vast Sardar Samand lake. The original dam was built in 1918. A guest wing was added and the work was supervised by a resident British architect deputed by Lanchester who had designed the Umaid Bhawan Palace and other mansions for the Maharajas.

The former Bundi state has its Brij Raj Bhawan Palace as a hotel. It is apiece with the rest of the complex of lovely palaces radiant with exquisite murals; everything reflected in a deep, lapping lake in the centre, Bundi is about 200 km from Jaipur.

Back in Udaipure, there is Shiv Niwas credited with "best views of any hotel anywhere." A former royal guest house overlooking Lake Pichola it has carved pillars, mosaics, ponds, delicate wall paintings, carved balconies and lavish space. Similarly, Jodhpur too has a smaller palace hotel, Ajit Bhawan, formerly the residence of a member of the royal family. A number of stone cottages have been added designed like a traditional villager's home. A hundred km away is Khimsar, famous for its Royal Castle, once a fortified home of a local ruler. Another 150 km and you are in Bikaner to sample its Lallgarh Palace another 19th century creation. There is jali work, freizes cover every surface, archways are scalloped and romantic copulas break the skyline.

A more recent experiment in converting a fort into a hotel which has been making waves internationally is Neemrana, barely two hours drive from Delhi on the road to Jaipur. For a long time Neemrana remained buried under the sands of time. Then suddenly in the late 1980s all eyes turned to this 15th century fortress when a group of art lovers recreated it stone by stone. And today it is a heritage hotel with international recognition. It has set the tone for conserving and preserving hundreds of such forts, palaces and mansions which were in the process of decay. Neemrana today is a stunning edifice with the matic suits, all done up in a feat of architectural restoration, a process which is still on in this fifteenth century fort. More rooms are being added. Its easy accessibility from the capital has made it a prime attraction.

Among the many other royal residence which have opened their doors to tourists is the Samede Palace near Jaipur which was the locale for much of the shooting of the Film Fair Pavilions. Castle Mandawa is another heritage hotel situated in the midst of several havelis-traditional Rajasthan mansions of the nobles in the Shekhawati area, famous for its frescoes.

The national action plan on tourism pledges support to heritage hotels and the Tourism Finance Corporation has been directed to give financial assistance to owners of palaces and entrepreneurs to convert them into hotels.

Although the initial response to heritage hotels' concept has been in Rajasthan the tourism authorities are confident that the movement will catch on in the rest of the country also, dotted as it is with palace, havelis and mansions. There were more than five hundred princely states at the time of independence with perhaps five times the number of palaces. If on an average one palace in each of those states is converted into a hotel, the number of heritage hotels alone could be more than five hundred. Palace hotels will then be a major segment of the Indian tourism market.

Leela Palace Makes a Mark

One of the world's ten most luxurious beach resorts – this is how the former Leela Beach in Goa is now being billed in its new texture as The

Leela Palace, a Kempinski Resort, after a Rs. 100 crore investment on renovations. It has also become it member of the Leading Hotels of the World. Spread over 75 acres and flanked by the Arabian Sea and the estuary of the Sal river, the upgraded complex is a unique blend of ancient Vijavanagara architecture of splendour with contemporay, if not futuristic, functional utilities. In contrast to the Vijayanagara temple and palace architecture of the main building, the resort's 143 rooms and suites are found within the portals of spacious Portuguese-style villas. Here, the accent is on stylish living within a gracious setting. You can choose a room or a villa overlooking tranquil lagoons with beautifully landscaped islands, the scenic golf course, or the Arabian Sea.

Among the villas, 17 are one and two bedroom suites and 74 are lagoon suites averaging more than 685 sq ft each. There is central air-conditioning and designer ceiling fans too. Eight of the suites have their own private plunge pools. Leisure facilities include a spa and fitness centre (with a variety of Ayurvedic massages on offer), tennis courts which can be floodlit, a nine-hole golf course, gaming room, a 300 metre private stretch of white sandy beach and a variety of water sports. Electric buggies are a reminder of the resort's concern for ecology.

Leela Palace's gourmet delights include the Jamavar, the Indian restaurant which offers regional cuisines and a decor which displays Leela's fabulous collection of original antique Jamavar shawls. The Waterfall Cafe, overlooking the swimming pool, offers sealing at two different levels – either to see the green vistas of palms and floral shrubs stretching up to the sea shore or to sit in quietude to enjoy a sumptuous breakfast (Continental, south Indian or Punjabi *parathas* and Kerala *iaai).* Or, you can choose, as this writer did, an exclusive treat at the riverside restaurant which nestles almost on a terrace over hanging the smooth glowing waters of the Sal. The decor, the ambience and the skills of Chef Roberto Il-lario come together to give you a truly Italian culinary experience.

The forty-year-old Swiss-born American general manager, Reto Torriani, has the right credentials for his assignment in India. He has been associated with the launch of some of the world's best known resorts in many continents. "Give me two years", he told me, "and Leela Palace will have acquired global recognition".

A Resurrection from Ruins

It is not unlikely that any query, possibly nearby Delhi or Jaipur, about Neemrana may find people puzzling about its location. In fact, it has given rise to the comment that if you want accommodation at Neemrana Fort Palace, make your booking in London, New York or Singapore.

The story of this medieval fort, built on nine tiers on a plateau, is the harbingers of a new movement in the hospitality sector. It is the first of a continuing string of heritage hotels built of old forts, havelis and palaces. Neemrana has come to be a word in hospitality circles for architectural cultural Renaissance. Its 42 well-appointed rooms created in the renovated structure have been patronised mostly by those seeking the experience of a lifestyle of 500 years ago.

The heritage movement owes its revival to two pioneers, Aman Nath and Francis Wacziarg. Nath, a history graduate began his career in the ad world as a designer and copy writer and Wacziarg, a Frenchman in love with India and Indian art, came to this country to set up an export business. The two are now sought after as restorers of monuments.

Flagging Off

With six heritage properties under their belt basking in the Neemrana brand, Nath and Wacziarg are now working on their seventh venture with eyes on projects as far south as Kerala. Of the six operating units, three are in Rajasthan and three in Uttar Pradesh. The latest project in hand is in Pondicherry.

Neemrana Fort Palace, artiste businessman duo's first experiment was just a dream two decades ago. Recalls Nath, "I first had a glimpse of the fort in 1971 when I was working on a book on Shekhawati. It was in total ruins and posed a dunting restoration challenge. But, after the successful renovation of two havelis, we gathered enough confidence to take on Neemrana. The fort was acquired in 1986 and the first phase with just 12 rooms and an investment of Rs 50 lakh from our own resources was commissioned in 1991."

So far, he said, Rs 3 crore has gone into the hotel but he has reasons to be upbeat about his investment. Neemrana broke even in the third year and has been paying a dividend from 1995-96. Even in the not-so good last two years for Indian tourism, Neemrana had recorded a revenue growth of ten per cent. So, what is new at Neemrana?

Loyal Patronage

Apart from the hardcore clientele overseas, the Fort Palace has become popular with the Indian upmarket travellers, corporate and is fast becoming a venue for exotic events like French opera, east-west music fusion, Indian classical dance performance, and celebrity weddings. Among the big names that have stayed here are Bernard Lacoste and Dominique Laiperre. Nath has a point when he says, "We have recycled historically wasted buildings into mainstream tourism revenue earners."

More to Come

The latest offering from the Neemrana Hotels, as the company is christened, is the Mud Fort at Kuchesar, a mere 88 km from Delhi into UP which has been given a soft opening. It has ten rooms with scenic views. And, it is not just the Mud Fort – its mud rampart; have a history of withstanding canon shells – but the surroundings that will appeal to the travellers. "There are orchards, mango groves and sugarcane fields. And it is just twenty minutes' drive to the Ganga." Glass House on the Ganges Neemrana Hotels' second property in UP is a tribute to a beautifully located historical site – once a private garden retreat of the Tehri Garhwal rulers and the only point at which the holy river flows northward. A little over 20 km above Rishikesh on the route to Badrinath, its ten rooms and cottages are named after the various Indian rivers. The third unit in UP is the Ramgarh Bungalows comprising the Writers' Bungalow and the Old Bungalow in the picturesque Kumaon – hills, both charming getaways.

The Hill Fort at Kesroli and the Piramal Havli at Bagar are the other two choices in Rajasthan, other than Neemrana. The seven-turreted Hill Fort stands atop the rare, dark Hornstone Preccia rocks, is older even than Neemrana and commands splendid agrarian views right in the heart of the Golden Triangle of Delhi-Agra-Jaipur. The Piramal Haveli in Bagar in the Shekhawati area has its own charm with traditional courtyards enclosed by colonial pillared corridors. Frescoes of flying angels and gods in motor cars adorn the walls.

The Neemrana initiatives has set a trend. Hospitality major, ITC Hotels, has set up a joint venture, clubbing together a dozen heritage properties under the WelcomHeritage brand name, including the prestigious Umaid Bhawan Palace in Jodhpur. But, this is only a beginning. According to Aman Nath, there are nine thousand-odd old monuments waiting to be renovated.

Environment Friendly Hotels – Ecotels

Uppal Orchid's Motto – Reduce, Reuse and Recycle

Builders have an advantage when it comes to diversifying into hotels. They have a nose for locating 'suitable land at suitable prices' especially in metro and big cities where archaic laws of land use leave virtually nothing for the hospitality sector. And, their construction expertise keeps costs under control.

It is with this edge, the Rs. 40 crore Uppal Group – capital's leading real estate developer in the residential segment – ventured into hoteliering.

Acquiring a designated hotel plot close to the Indira Gandhi International Airport, the group was lucky to add more adjoining area to make a grand size of 10.5 acres.

The group's 29-year old managing director, Manish Uppal says they were upbeat about adding another five-star property and realising a dream. But, they had no idea that it would be a unique offering – an internationally certified Ecotel which is the capital's first and Indian's third Ecotel hotel (the other two are in Mumbai). And, it all happened during the search for a partner to manage the hotel.

The group had approached the leading chains and companies specialising in this sector but the choice fell on Concept Hospitality Ltd. even in the early stages of negotiations with its chief Param Kannampilly. This was because of the fact that the Uppal Group was fascinated by the thought of an Ecotel particularly after the runaway success of the first such project in the western metropolis – The Orchid–An Ecotel Hotel, owned by Kamat Hotels.

Manish Uppal says as builders they were aware of the concerns about environment but to translate that into action in the nation's capital was an irresistible urge.

Commissioned just four months ago Uppal's Orchid has begun to make a mark in the market according to Pushpinder Kumar, general manager of the property, and has been averaging 90 per cent occupancy, fuelled partly by the revival of corporate travel and general tourist movements. Explaining the USPs of the hotel, Kumar says, "From its construction to the room service it offers, Uppal's Orchid provides the luxury that its guests deserve while remaining dedicated to the environment."

He adds, "The hotel prides itself in serving its guests 'luxury with responsibility'. Every inch of the property, the service and the operations of the hotel conform to the Ecotel concept."

Ecotel is an international brand, part of the famous collection of environmentally sensitive hotels that belong to HVS (Hospitality Valuation Services International). The collection was born barely a decade ago when the New York Vista Hotel reopened as the world's first Ecotel (certified) after the first bombing of the World Trade Centre. Since then some 1,100 hotels have applied for certification but only 34 have been successful.

There is a stringent system of norms, called globes, to qualify as Ecotel. Five is the highest number of globes that can be awarded. These cover; energy efficiency, water conservation, solid waste management, employee environmental education, community involvement and environmental commitment.

8

Indian Shopping Destinations and its Cultural Metropolises

Shopping in India

India is a paradise for the souvenir hunter. Expensive and not so expensive objects made all over the country present an unending variety of skill, colour and imagination. Kashmiri shawls, Varanasi brocades, jewellery, ivory carvings, papier mache articles, sandals, scarves, stoles and silk and cotton textiles of all kinds, inlaid metals and wood, pottery and painting – a wealth of objects awaits the shopper. Handicraft are produced in all parts of India. Every state has its special craft to offer. The variety is enormous, ranging from intricate and delicate work to rough-hewn colourful folk art made in village homes.

The diversity and richness of hand-made objects has a special appeal. Handloom are excellent. Indian jewellers are famous for their skill in filigree silver and heavy gold jewel work. Intricate enamel work from Jaipur even delighted the Mughals.

In cities, government emporia stock the country's handicrafts where one can explore without going through bargaining.

India adopts all shoppers. For the rich, there is ivory and jewellery, for the not so rich, the inexpensive handicraft. Each region of India has its own feast of offerings for the tourists. Each has its own craftsmen.

Shopping in Delhi

In Delhi the tourist is fascinated by the brilliance and variety of metalwork, particularly brasswork from neighbouring Moradabad. Vases, trays and ornate boxes are other attractions.

For the leather hunter there are ladies' handbags, pouches, wallets and suitcases, made from the finest hides, available at princes which are amazingly low. Most of these goods, though made in Kanpur, are freely available in Delhi.

The 'Cottage'

The Central Cottage Industries Emporium, Delhi, is a treasure house of Indian handicrafts. Carpets and rugs, pottery and ceramics of the highest quality are available. Copper and bronze statuettes are for sale and are a great attraction for any shopper. You may buy paintings and wall hangling featuring the heroes of Indian myths and legends. Ivory goods with their intricate carvings are in profusion, some of them the products of months of hard work. Also available are batiks which are reasonably priced. The aroma of Joss-sticks sold in Delhi woofted pleasantly in home all over the world. Trinkets, costume-jewellery and silverware of the highest quality are available under one roof at the Emporium which is manned by well trained attendants. The emporium sells handicrafts from all over India. For the tourist who is pressed for time, it is the ideal shopping centre. The Emporium is on Janpath, is the heart of New Delhi, and is air-conditioned.

The Cloth Mart

Chandi Chowk is a market which is situated in the walled city, opposite the Red Fort, it has an old world charm. There are scores of shops which sell cloth. Indian saris, now considered fashionable the world over, are sold here. Silk and raw silk saris, brightly coloured and with lovely brocade borders, are a special attraction. You may buy a 'sari' purse, finely woven and yet inexpensive.

Silver jewellery intricate and inexpensive, is available in Delhi.

Delhi markets have on display a wide-range of wall hanging which come from various states.

A must for tourists are the furs from Kashmir, sold in Delhi at the numerous emporiums including the Cottage Industries Emporium.

Dariba Kalan and Chawri Bazar are old Delhi markets the former specialising in jewellery.

Buying in Mumbai

Mumbai is a paradise for shoppers. The city markets the work of craftsmen from Maharashtra, Gujarat and Madhya Pradesh. A shopper in Mumbai is immediately attracted by the delightful applique—work toys of Kutch. For women would be able to resist the impulse to buy and hoard the magnificent silver jewellery for sale all over the city.

The Colaba Market has a wide ranges of items for sale, and the prices of most items are reasonable. The artisans of 'Pen' in Colaba District are famous for their skill in fashioning traditional statuettes from soft black clay and plaster of Paris.

Paithani Saris

Once a must for every Maharashtrian bride, Paithani saris, their name derived from a village in Aurangabad district, are made of heavy silk, elaborately ornamented with gold designs. They have now become popular with women from all over the world and are eagerly sought after.

Lacquerware a craft from Sawantwadi that once enjoyed royal patronage, is fast gaining popularity as one of Mumbai's gifts to the low-budget shopper. The Bidriware available in Mumbai's markets especially Crafford market, is of the finest quality. Bidri is a form of damascing in silver, where the metal ground is copper, tin and leads blackened on the surface by a solution of ammoniac and salt petre. Intricate designing and skilled craftmanship make Bidriware a must for every shopper.

Two of the most important centres of Indian jewellery are Hupre, famous for its exquisite silver ornaments, and Mumbai, where devoted craftmen turn out enchanting designs; both old and new. 'Western India's wide range of leatherware, widely admired for its texture and quality cannot be ignored by any shopper. Besides ladies' handbags, the Kolhapuri sandals have acquired worldwide fame.

Cloth dolls of all colours and sizes, dressed in different regional costumes, are to be had at very reasonable prices. Mumbai, Nagpur and Pune are famed for these dolls, and they may be bought at Mumbai's numerous emporiums and boutique.

Shopping in Kolkata

The shopper is absolutely overwhelmed by the array of goods, he sees in the bazars of Kolkata.

Rich silk saris from Banaras their borders broidered in silver or gold, and light *tasar* silk saris, are on sale in the city's numerous shops and emporium.

The pottery and ceramics of Bengal are famous. The potters of Bengal have maintained their high quality. All over Eastern India the shopper can buy Darjeeling Tea of the finest quality, rich in flavour.

Kolkata is famous for its colourful batik fabrics. Records of famous Indian classical musicians are to be had here in plenty. Records of sitar music are a must for every shopper.

Leather Goods

Kolkata has become very well-known for its leather products. Shops ladies' handbags and suitcases of all sizes are available in the various state emporium in the city, and their prices are fixed.

Another great attraction for tourists in Kolkata are the various Dokra's and Mother pearl products, which make very good gifts in the West.

In Kolkata, the shopper does not have to cover much distance to acquire these products. The New Market, the Air-Conditioned Market and the West Bengal, Bihar, and Orissa State Emporium will supply him with everything.

The silk saries of south India, both pure and raw silk are beautiful. A wide range of cotton saris are also available. Women all over the world yearn to war Indian silk saris.

Cotton is Cool

In Chennai you may buy inexpensive cotton garments. Chennai Cotton is of finest quality. One may buy saris, shirts, *kurtas* and *lungis* at reasonable rates.

The Chennai State Emporium the Kerala State Emporium and the Andhra Pradesh State Emporium stock all these goods and the rates fixed are reasonable and inexpensive.

Cultural Metropolises

Three major Indian cities celebrate their anniversaries this year. Kolkata the home of Tagore, Vivekananda and Satyajit Ray, has been a city with a soul, notwithstanding what its detractors have been saying.

Hyderabad is the epitome of India's fusion of cultures and a preserver of the unique legacies of all that is best in a bygone age. And, Chennai the southern metropolis is the gateway to a treasure-house of artforms.

For the record the beginning of Kolkata are traced to Job Cherneck, an Englishman who set up a factory spread over three villages which he acquired on rent. Little would he have anticipated that the year 1690 when he started the factory also signaled the ascent of the Raj. The villages were obviously existing much before the British came and thereby hangs a controversy as to when the story of Kolkata begins. But the fact remains that the area came into historical focus after the Honourable East India Company established its base there and built a fort at Kalikata completed in 1709. It was the year Aurangzeb died leaving northern India to the twilight of the Mughal era. For the next 200 years Kolkata held the centre in the spread of British hegemony, and, interestingly of the great Indian renaissance. Both have enriched Kolkata in every field of human endeavour. Since the 70s of the last century, when Kolkata acquired the reputation of being the second largest city in the British Empire, its multi-dimensional growth had become pronounced. The most intellectual giants came as if it were in a parade and left their imprint on history in a short phase of time. Many educational institutions which were the product of the age survive to this day. The Great Asiatic Society was born here. So many colonial structures still stand hearing testimony to the lifestyles of both the British and the Indian aristocracy. In fact, imaginative tourism campaigns could arouse deep interest in the English speaking world to experience this heritage. For all talk of Kolkata as a dying city or as lost in garbage the city and its denizens have shown a remarkable resilience and urge for renewal as for instance, the Metro.

Kolkata is the last city beside which the Ganga flows before merging into the Bay of Bengal. The symbiotic relationship between the river and the Bengalee is manifest in every aspect of their daily life. It is best illustrated by the sit of millions of people taking a ritualistic bath in the river while at a distance is the giant Howrah Bridge, Kolkata's most known identification mark, over busy with traffic that symbolizes the throb of business and industrial activity. The spirit of the city is also evident below in the waterway with ships, trawlers, steamboats and fishing vessels constantly on the move. Fort William, another traditional landmark of 300 years houses the eastern region's military headquarters. In the neighbourhood is the maidan that serves as the lungs for the sprawling metropolis. The other rights which are a must for the visitor are the Victoria Memorial, the marble edifice the British built that houses memorable of the Raj, the Birla Planetorium, the Museum. For a city that has seen much history, it has necessarily many structures associated with supermen and their achievements. On top of it all, the teeming millions of Kolkata going about their chores, should itself be a fascinating subject for observation and study. Rabindra Sangeet in its mellow tunes merge in the abandon of festivities like Durga Puja and political slogans of a highly articulate people of a temperamental city. Still in the overall, it is a city that is not lost in the past but one that works.

Hyderabad found by Qutab Shah 400 years ago is where the north meets the south. In the 17th century, it had become famous as a city that gave the priceless diamond Kohinoor, now encrusted in the British crown. Monuments, mosques and mistresses had lent splendour even in those days. In the wake of the decline of the Mughal empire, a noble of the court, Asaf Jha declared himself independent and founded the dynasty of Nizams which ruled Hyderabad for seven generations. Now the capital of Andhra Pradesh, Hyderabad and its twin city, Secunderabad, retain the quintessence of all it had charmed visitors since establishment. Its architecture, art forms, the music in its language, the very location gliding from Banjara Hills holding in their bosom, the Husainsagar Lake, make its glory. The most striking and lasting links with the past include the Charminar and the Golconda Fort. The Charminar rises and its bustling bazaars in silent arches and delicate minarets. It was built in 1591 by Qutab Shah as a form of *talisman* to drive away an epidemic sweeping the newly founded city. From atop Charminar, the view is that of entire city spread out below. During the Nizam's times, the privileged, view was forbidden lest the visitor had a glimpse of the ladies of the Royal houseful! The Golconda Fort to the west preceded the Qutab Shahis. Its battlements were rebuilt in 1525 by Qutab Shah who designed a fantastic accoustic system by which a handclap sounded at the gates could be heard right at the heart of the citadel. The most contemporaneous attraction is the Salarjung Museum, a private collection by a Hyderabadi noble, of oriental and western art, jades, ceramics, porcelains, miniatures, ivories, clocks, carpets and antiques. The piece de resistance is Rebecca, the lady in veil in chiseled marble giving the illusion of a transparent cover over her head. A growing industrial neighbourhood and a rich agricultural hinterland and a rapidly expanding educational centre, Hyderabad is a destination both for the business traveller and leisure seekers.

The Quaint little bazaars around Charminar are full of bangle sellers and dealers in pearls. The place echoes the gentle tapping of the silver beaters mallets. The fragrance of jasmine and the aroma of hot spiced kebabs mingles in the heavy air and wafts into the mansions of the aristocracy where hangs the most ornate crystal chandeliers. This is not all. Hyderabad's rich legacy extends to the pleasures of the palate. Different types of *pulaos* and *biryani* constitute a unique cuisine of skills. These have gone into the menu of most homes in the city on also a star hotels elsewhere in the country and even abroad. Truly, Hyderabad's flavours and sights are evocative and of fascinating detail to the visitor be he an Indian or a foreigner.

Chennai. The third city to celebrate an anniversary in 350 years old. Anyone who knows anything about India will recognise this harbour city with the longest beach is a starting point for a journey of discovery of the south. For a long time Chennai was synonymous with the entire south. To many north Indians anyone south of the Vindhyas was a Chennai. The appellation was perhaps justified because Chennai contained everything of the south, its traditions, artforms, temples, silks and cuisine. This is turn give a college of images, the whiff of jasmine, the rustle of silk, the sculpture of temple walls and towers, carnatic music and Bharat Natyam, a city of colleges and also of *idli dosa.* Chennai is also a maritime city and the second largest producer of feature films after Mumbai. Still, this one time presidency town, is full of surprises. For instance, it has a deer park in the heart of the city and a snake and crocodile farm on the outskirts. Here you have the largest concentration of practising believers going past rallies of rationalists.

For all its attachment to tradition, Chennai is a living heritage and not a fossilised one. Towards the close of the 17th century it was just a fishing hamlet on the Coromandal coast but part of the great creative kingdoms of Cholas and Pallavas. The fine arts and crafts of the city proudly proclaim Chennai's ancient lineage with pride, poise and dignity. Its cultural excellence has not been tempered by its position as a commercial city. In fact its ancient traditions remain apiece the most urban facilities. And that makes for Chennai's claim to be unique among Indian cities.

Places of interest in the city are many. Fort St. George, one time symbol of British power, today houses the headquarters of the Tamil Nadu government. In its vicinity is India's oldest protestant church, St. Mary's. Robert Clive who laid the foundation of the British empire in the sub-continent began life here as a clerk in the Fort. Then there is the Marina Beach, the second longest in the world. The global headquarters of the Theosophical Society, the Cultural University of Kalakshetra, a host of memorials to Tamil savants, one of the oldest museums, Kapaleeswarar Temple, dedicated to Siva and a fine example of Dravidian architecture and several shopping centres add up to the long list of attractions in this southern metropolis.

9

China as the New Tourist Haven

China as the New Tourist Haven

One of the earliest lessons learn at school is that a straight line is the shortest means of reaching the destination. All others are circuitous and long. 1 am reminded of it as plan for a scheduled visit to Beijing. I find that I cannot directly fly on a straight route to the Chinese capital from Delhi have to either fly to Islamabad, Karachi or Mumbai or Bangkok. Any of these will involve an additional eight hours of journey depending on flight schedules. Hopefully when the king delayed bilateral air agreement comes into effect there will be a direct link between the two capitals.

Having opted to go via Bangkok I had to spend five hours at the airport transit lounge. Unable to sleep on a chair all the time I take a few winks and admire the ambience the orderliness and facilities and I cannot resist contrasting with the situation at the start of the journey, Delhi. Its a five hour flight from Bangkok to Beijing. If the airport at Beijing does not appear as swanky as Bangkok it has far too many other compensations. The immigration and customs clearance is pretty fast and certain forms like health which the airline had insisted on filling up are not even looked at. The exit is smooth and perfect.

Excellent System

The coach ride to the town reminds one of a drive by our Ambassador, sturdy, spacious but low on the comfort index. Surprises begin as you leave the airport behind. Wide avenues, turnpikes, orderly fast flowing traffic and spotlessly clean pavements are on view throughout. The size and the grandeur of the hotel of your choice—the Kun Lun in ray case—matches with the best with what I have seen anywhere else. The check-in is a momentary problem over language resolved immediately by an English speaking staff. By evening I discover I am not required to tip anyone in the hotel or outside, nor does anyone expect it from me. This is certainly a culture shock in the reverse for someone coming from Delhi. I find myself free to go anywhere if only I can find my way back. In the five days I move about on foot or on the luxury coach that transports me to the venue of the travel industry conference I am attending. I crane my neck to find only, a solitary beggar trying to accost me. Instantly he is shooed away by passersby.

I notice that there are three kinds of metered taxis in all of which there is a glass partition as a protective barrier between the driver and the passenger. Of the three categories. deluxe, medium and van type, the most commonly used is the last one. There is also an excellent public transport system that provides access to all points with hardly any standing passengers. Except on one occasion I never had the feeling of being overcharged in a taxi.

Boom in Tourism

While roaming in the neighbourhood of the hotel I discover a flea market much like the Janpath wayside shops and across the street is a multistoried supermarket strangely called Lufthansa Centre. The experience since arrival at the airport leaves me with little surprise when given the figures of the tourist traffic. There is a deliberate effort to make the tourist stay pleasant and hassle-free, of course with the visitor remaining a tourist.

The boom is underlined by Prime Minister Li Peng himself who terms tourism as a supporting column of the economy. He is not exaggerating as figures of the World Tourism Organisation (WTO) vouchsafe China has leapfrogged to the fifth position as a global destination, China claims it received 51 million tourists last year while the WTO puts the figure at 26 million. Even the WTO assessment is a whopping twelve-fold gain over the Indian official figure of 2.2 million. The significance of the Chinese achievement is stark when it is recalled thai 20 years ago both these countries were on par as far as international tourism is concerned. Li Peng says he is not content even with the 51 million visitors as "there are still not enough overseas tourists and tourism revenues and we can expect more of boom in the future!"

He could prove correct. His statement reflects a political will and commiiment to tourism and a determination to achieve the goals. It is not a spur of the moment decision. Advance planning Mid strict implementation has brought the room capacity in Beijing alone to more than 50,000 a figure claimed for London. What China's capital boasts of is the estimated availability of rooms in the whole of India. China has shown that tourism goals, however ambitious, are attainable provided there is readiness at the top that percolates down the line did not Mrs. Indira Gandhi say in 1980 "I want Delhi's accommodation to be doubled for Asiad"? Indians proved it could be done.

Unusual Singapore

The island republic is truly surprising as claimed by its tourism promotion agencies. Where else could one find a top.civil servant after his office going straight to the kitchen, don a chefs apron and start working on the menu? The principal of a reputed college takes position behind the cash counter and half a dozen women in their silken best wait on tables taking orders from an international clientele. The ambience is totally Indian and cultural artefacts from every part of that country are on view. It is not only the food that is priced and for sale but all the items whether for decor or functional for guests like tables and chairs can he bought or booked to be shipped.

The restaurant, Annalakshmi, incidentally caters to the upmarket, not necessarily for those in quest of ethnic food. Its cuisine is Indian vegetarian and in the last few years of its functioning has gathered a select number of devoted customers. Also, it is part of an international chain which has outlets as far away as Australia. It has plans to open a unit in south India.

Annalakshmi is operated by a multi-functional complex which has a retail store, a school of fine arts and a handicrafts emporium. It is staffed entirely by volunteers and all surplus earnings are ploughed back for growth. The rationale of this unique institution started at the inspiration of a spiritual leader, Swami Shantanand Saraswati, who has a large following.

Kala Mandhir, the arts wing of the complex not only provides teaching facilities in Indian music and dance but also blends Indian classical art forms with themes from other lands.

Santosa, the island set real within the island republic, encapsulates its two hundred years of history in a museum. The colonial building was once used as a magazine of the then British defence forces. The place interests Indian visitors not only for its chronicling of the history of Indian settlers but also for recent history in which one of India's famous soldiers played part. Perhaps, nowhere else not even in General Thimayya's native Coorg, there is a lifelike model of him. In the museum, young Brigadier Thimayya (who later rose to be Chief of Army Staff) sits abreast with the Supreme Commander of the Allied Forces in Southeast Asia, Admiral Mountabatten to receive the surrender of Ihe Imperial Japanese forces at the end of the Second World War. The wax models a la Tussaud are placed in the very same fashion around the same table-on which the victors and the vanquished sat.

The museum has many other objects of interest to Indians. While the wax models depict the Japanese triumph and their final surrender, developments that took place in the interval are portrayed in visuals and pictures. There are a couple of pictures of Netaji Subhas Bose addressing Indian residents and prisoners of war in Japanese hands. There is another enlarged photograph which shows him and Capt Lakshmi (mother of the newly-elected Marxist MP Suhasini Ali) inspecting a guard of honour provided by the Rani of Jhansi Regiment of the Indian National Army. As if an amusing footnote to the Indian role in true history of this part of the world is a reproduction of an advertisement in the *Straits Times* of an Indian merchant on the morrow of the Japanese take over "Celebrate victory by flags of the rising sun "from our shop."

The Indian python in the Singapore zoo has an adopted guardian. The zoo management has evolved a system under which a visitor could make an endowment in favour of any inmate, be it an animal, bird or reptile. Outside the enclosures in this well-organised gardens of southeast Asia one finds many signboards of such benefactors to the denizens of the zoo. The Singapore zoo offers many lessons on how tourism management can be integrated with the development of every spot of sightseeing or leisure ground. Privately managed, it provides facilities for family outings with programmes of animal acrobatic and other animal shows. The visitors are also educated on the role of fauna and wild life.

Surprises are everywhere. All the choicest cuisines from many parts of the world are available in plenty. Of course Chinese. Indonesian and Indian predominate. But there is also unusual synthesizing. One could seldom imagine anywhere else a Chinese restaurant doing a good day's business not on chop suey or noodles but on egg paratha. How this Punjabi delicacy entered the menu card of the Chinese restaurant in Singapore where tourists are taken as part of the itinerary is a culinary riddle. Equally enigmatic is the side dish served vith the egg *paratha* — gravy of mutton curry, the restaurant manager affirmed that this breakfast draws the largest customers in the mornings. The owner and almost all the employees were Chines except the two who make the *paratha* were strangely south Indian but fluent in Chinese.

Come to Malaysia

Barely twelve years ago, this writer, on a visit to Malaysia discovered that tourism was the country's best kept secret, endowed though it was with all that travellers love to see and experience, be it man-made or God-given. Even quality infrastructure in terms of airports, highways, transport and hotels was in place. Spurred perhaps by the headway made by Singapore and other neighbours like Thailand, Indonesia and Hong Kong, Malaysia too unveiled its attractions and soon stood with them shoulder-to-shoulder as a tourism-success story, with arrivals shooting up to the seven million mark. When the currency meltdown struck the region, Malaysia too shared the misfortune with its neighbours, arrival and earnings plummeted by as much as 30 per cent. And, now that some of the Asian destinations are showing signs of remarkable recovery, especially Hong Kong and Thailand, Malaysia has not lagged behind. In 1999, Malaysia hosted 7.9 million tourists, a hefty increase over the 1998 figure of 5.5 million.

While the Malaysians, both government and the travel trade, have much to be pleased with, they have found to their dismay that their tourist attractions are hidden from the burgeoning Indian outbound movements. A bare 32,000 Indians travelled to that country last year, only one-tenth of the total who visit Singapore or Thailand. A good enough reason for a high-powered delegation led by the tourism minister, Dato Abdul Kadir Bin Haji Sheikh Fadsir with a thirty-member entourage of officials and industry leaders to visit the Indian capital and other cities to promote tourism. One whole day was devoted to a seminar where the minister, the Malaysian high commissioner and industry representatives interacted with the Indian travel trade to identify and remove the barriers that come in the way of tourist movements in both directions.

Lack of awareness and totally inadequate air services between the two countries were straightaway pointed out as the main stumbling blocks. The cumbersome and time-consuming visa procedure at the Malaysian high commission was another concern.

As for awareness, the minister said that the high commission will soon have a tourism section and a promotional campaign will be launched in the media. "The $31 million promotion budget will keep India in focus," the minister said," under the general theme 'Malaysia truly Asia'. "If you visit Malaysia," he added, "you have seen most of Asia." Pointing to the age-old ties between India and Malaysia, the minister said that 12 per cent of the country's population consisted of people of Indian origin who had contributed so much to its economy. Abdul Kadir also listed Malaysia's tourism USPs. "We are a green, clean and efficient country apart from being the most inexpensive in Asia for a quality vacation. Where else can you get a five-star room for $ 40-50. The same goes for shopping," he said. "The whole country is virtually duty-free, as many as 90 per cent of the items a tourist would want to buy – cameras, electronic goods, designer clothes and other branded items – carry no tax and soon the remaining 90 per cent will also be tax-free. In Malaysia you do not have to wait in queues at airports reclaiming your VAT," the minister said taking a dig at some of the European destinations. He also claimed that Malaysia is the 'safest place in the world' whether in the cities, on the beaches or in the jungles.

About accessibility, particularly air seats, the minister said that he is all set for a more liberal bilateral regime. "Let Air India, and for that matter, Indian Airlines and private carriers like Jet and Sahara, fly any number of services to any city in Malaysia," he declared.

"If Indian carriers do not have aircrafts, we are willing to help them out", he added. The Malaysian minister had a formal meeting with the Indian civil aviation minister and pleaded with him to allow MAS to increase its frequencies and acquire landing rights in more Indian cities.

Abdul Kadir said that more air service will encourage greater number of Malaysians to travel to India. He suggested that tour operators in both countries should set up a consortium to promote packages that will increase traffic in both directions. He said that scheduled air-charters could contribute to keeping package costs low.

"There is no stopping of Indians from travelling abroad but we also need to strengthen our marketing and promotions abroad to get more foreigners to visit our country," he observed.

ISLAND NATIONS — CYPRUS AND SEYCHELLES

Cyprus Jumps on the Bandwagon

The latest country to seek a share of the Indian market is Cyprus, the Mediterranean island nation of 7,00,000 inhabitants, which hosts three times as many foreign visitors every year. Sandy beaches, a warm sea, and 'invariably reliable sunshine' are not the only assets which have made Cyprus a popular destination. Home to the goddess of love – Aphrodite – and thousands of years of civilisation have left a heritage of Greco-Roman archaeological sites, medieval castles and Byzenline churches, which add considerably to its pull.

Interestingly, Cyprus is no ordinary success story where tourism is concerned. The quest for tourism began in right earnest in 1960, soon after the island gained independence from the British. By 1973, the bustling port city of Famagusta and the scenic harbour town of Kyrenia had become household names in the source markets in Europe, and arrivals soared to 2,64,000.

Came the Turkish invasion in the following year and both Famagusta and Kyrenia and much of the tourist infrastructure 'fell into Turkish hands. Tourist arrivals in what was left of Cyprus fell to 47,000 in 1975. Today's visitor count of two million plus speaks volumes of the hard work put in by the tourism authorities and the industry in the face of adversity.

The same spirit seems to be guiding the Cyprus government's effort in targeting the Indian outbound or for that matter cooperating with India to enable it to secure a share of the Cyprus market. This strikes you within moments of a chat with that country's dynamic high commissioner, Rea Ykmlamlis, busy as she is with her routine duties as her country's representative in nine nations, stretching from India to Vietnam.

At this particular occasion, he was also in the midst of finalising arrangements for the Cyprus Week in New Delhi, beginning with the national day on October 1, a tourism seminar on October 3, and, a whole week of a Cypriot food festival at Maurya Sheraton's famed West View restaurant.

The lady high commissioner opens the conversation by reminding you of a common recent past – the same colonial power ruled us; the two countries have had friendly relations and both tirelessly worked together in the non-aligned movement and at the United Nations. Almost with a tinge of sadness she says, "unfortunately despite all of this seeming and obvious closeness, Cyprus is not much known in India. And, not too many of my country's people have really made an effort to know your country."

The celebration of the Cyprus Week is an attempt to build bridges between our "two countries, this is not just a one-off initiative; it will be a sustained and ongoing effort."

It is at this point you discover that the high commission is going ahead in spite of constraints. At the initiative of Cyprus, the two countries had signed almost two years ago an agreement for cooperation on a two-way tourism. The Cyprus government ratified it within a month but the Indian Tourism Ministry is yet to reciprocate. Not only that. A bilateral agreement is a must before the national carriers of the two countries can start direct flights between the two countries, a first step for easy tourist movement.

For some reason bilateral negotiations always get postponed (it was hinted during the tourism seminar that these might after all take place next January). Rea Yiordmali s moves on to the symbiotic relationship between trade and tourism. Cyprus has a vibrant economy (its pound is ten rupees costlier than the British currency) and she invites Indian investors to put their money there and entrepreneurs to develop joint ventures and adds Cyprus "ideal" as a tax haven.

In less than four years, Cyprus will be joining the European Union. "We will be your European voice; you will be our Asian voice" is her vision of a new role for India and Cyprus in 2002. A two-day seminar on Cyprus; issues and prospects, was also organised as part of the Cyprus Week. Held at the Jawaharlal Nehru University it also discussed ways of expanding trade between the two countries.

The prospects of strengthening trade relations will get a more focused attention when a business delegation visits this country in January which will meet government and industry leaders in the capital New Delhi, and other metro cities like Mumbai, Kolkata, Chennai and Bangalore, and possibly Hyderabad.

Christos Moustras, marketing chief of the Cyprus Tourism Organisation, who conducted the tourism seminar said a visit to Cyprus could be combined with a cruise to Egypt and Israel at reasonable package costs. Five-star hotels in Cyprus, he said, charged tariffs of US $50 upwards but there were special facilities for visitors to stay with families or in villages homes.

He said he would welcome Indian travel agents to come to Cyprus on fam tours, an offer which was straight away picked up by Deepak Hasija, Gulf Air's district sales manager. Hopefully, our Ministry of Tourism will seize the opportunity and seek a share of the Cyprus market for India.

Environment Shells from Seychelles

Protection of environment and eco-tourism will be the.buzz words of the hospitality industry in the next millennium. Many countries have already set in motion strategies that will preserve the priceless assets bestowed on mankind both, by nature and human creativity. In India, the draft tourism policy awaiting the parliament's endorsement also lays considerable stress on the subject.

According to the World Tourism Organisation (WTO), the tops of the highest mountains, the depths of the oceans and the 'ends of the world are predicted to be the trendiest destinations for holiday makers in the 21st century. The ministerial conference on oceans and new tourism destinations organised by WTO in June this year, identified travel trends and destinations that will benefit from a tourism industry that is predicted to grow from 612 million international arrivals in 1997 to more than one billion visitors by the year 2010 and 1.6 billion by 2020. WTO secretary general,

Francisco Frangialli, is confident that eco products which are emerging today will dominate the market tomorrow, such as nature and tourism products, cruises, water sports and tourism in the great tropical forests of the world.

The WTO findings make one thing clear: tomorrow's travellers will be "poor in time and rich in money" and seeking maximum thrills in minimum time. One country, and a small one at that, Seychelles feels it is well-positioned to capitalise fully on these new holiday trends. The island republic's energetic tourism minister, Simone de Comarmond, in Delhi to attend the Indian Ocean Tourism Organisation (IOTO) meeting, shared the strategies her government is adopting. She begins by pointing out that environmental concerns have influenced major decisions on tourism infrastructure and services right from the beginning. Emphasis has always been on quality and not numbers. The government, she says, has committed itself to "protect, conserve, present, rehabilitate and transmit" to future generations a pristine environment.

The country has not just kept aside part of its very scarce land resources for conservation. Over the years, even dearer financial resources have been extensively injected into the upkeep and enhancement of the country's environment. Millions of dollars have gone into the development of an ecologically and economically sustainable tourism and leisure industry to give a range of opportunities for visitors and citizens to enjoy and appreciate the country's rich natural attributes, she adds.

Comarmond is satisfied that this has ensured a secured future for its natural and cultural values – a strong mandate to protect its bio-diversity, fragile habitat and special species of plants and animals with almost fifty per cent of the land of its 115 islands devoted to strict conservation. So, with justified pride she says, "Seychelles is a pioneer in the realm of eco-tourism and not an eleventh-hour attempt at taking advantage of an emerging trend." Hence its claim to the last sanctuary is genuine. In fact, she claims, Seychelles can be a role model for conservation and ecology.

Seychelles has two unique sensitive ecological areas on the world heritage list: Aldabra (one of the world's largest atolls) and Vallee de Mai (a unique palm forest which is home to the heaviest seed in the world), both of which are UNESCO sites, managed by the Seychelles Islands Foundation.

Minister Comarmond also unveiled a major initiative to be launched in 1999 to reinforce Seychelles pull as an eco friendly destination, a Gold Card concept which she described as the "lynchpin in a millennium strategy" being introduced by the country. It will be the world's first mandatory environmental Gold Card for all visitors from November 1, next year. The rationale behind the Card, she said, is the growing demand to "protect and enhance" the global environment coupled with the government's strong commitment to keep the islands in a pristine state at the expense of random developments.

The Gold Card, she explained will provide the necessary funds to protect and enhance the pristine environment for all the Seychelles islands; act as a vehicle to sensitise all visitors about the merits of conserving nature for future generations: to be a role model to other nations concerned about preserving their unique natural features and finally, to attract up-market nature lovers to Seychelles by developing consumer brand loyalty through a circle of 'friends of Seychelles'.

Seychelles gets a bare 1,30,000 tourists a year and Comarmond is not at all worried about the growth rate which last year, declined to one per cent. She is instead concentrating on improvement of the infrastructure and laying considerable stress on HRD to better the quality of service. "High tariffs must be matched by high standards of hotels and service," she said.

There may be a few lessons for our own planners and promoters now that we too will be getting down to implementing our environment protection policies and working out strategies to attract the up-market traveller a segment that has shown a continuing decline.

The Swiss Success Story

Switzerland is one European country which has a focused, industry–co-ordinated and consistent promotional programme for India. For several successive years, large delegations representing almost every segment of the hospitality sector plus the famous chocolate and watch-makers conduct road shows in Delhi and other metros with a certain regularity. Switzerland has another advantage. Its ambassador, Dr. Walter Gyser has earned the reputation of being the most tourism-friendly diplomat in the Indian capital. He occupies centre-stage in the promotional blitz and often manages to give it even an Indian touch. In the latest exercise on January 13, the media were treated to slick presentations on the various Swiss attractions from mountains to resorts and world class cities like Geneva and Zurich along with live traditional mountain music. This was followed by a lavish dinner which was joined in by leaders of the Indian travel industry in celebration of Lohri, the north Indian festival marking the peak of the whiter season.

This year's presentation had an unusual addition to Swiss allurements–a new dimension to tourism aimed at 8- to 18-year-old school children to enable them to become self-reliant and independent. This is done through experimental learning techniques which combine adventure sports activities, recreational, educational and social interaction between internationsal students. The man who thought of this kind of student tourism, Phillipe Stettler, was part of this year's delegation. He says that way back in 1987 as a school teacher in Lausanne he thought of an "extended arm for educating children in a fun way" and made a beginning soon afterwards with the first group of international participants in a makeshift camp in the small town of Verbier less than two hours drive from Geneva. Verbier, because of its location has the advantage of being suitable both for summer and winter adventure sports. The programme was a runaway success and by 1993 he had built special chalets for students who started arriving in larger numbers.

A young Indian housewife with entrepreneurial urges, Bibirani Nangia heard of this programme which was then being marketed as Les Elfes international summer and winter camps at the Delhi golf course in 1996. Remembering her own mundane school trips, the thought that children could have a productive holiday experience exciled her. What spurred her into action was that this programme would also give Indian children the opportunity to interact with students from other parts of the world. In the very first effort she managed to gather ten students and off she went to Verbier and returned with a happy experience. In 2002, she handled more than 300 students both for the summer and winter tours. And, she is so upbeat about the potential of this student tourism that last year she extended her operation to Australia. Her first group was as large as 60 students and the places covered included Sydney, Cairns and Byron Bay. Nangia says that at Verbier language conversation courses are part of the activities. The average cost of the programme for a week is $900 and for 15 days $2,000. Airfares are extra. The adventure activities cover skiing, bridge-swinging, para-sailing, sea kayake and surfing. There are also team building activities. Those opting for the 15-day programme also make trips to France and Italy. Bibirani Nangia can be contacted on e-mail: leselfes@dish-netdsl.net.

To come back to Swiss tourism, a century of just over 7 million people, Switzerland hosts 17 million visitors. In spite of 9 /11, it has had a sizable increase from India. The number of tourist from this country is said to have crossed the 2,00,000 mark in 2002 representing an eight per cent increase over the previous year. Indians, although they constitute less than one per cent of the total arrivals, are among the highest spenders. Gujaratis form the largest chunk of the Indian segment. Ambassador Gyser denied that Switzerland had lost its sheen for Indian film-makers who reportedly were heading for other destinations in Europe. If anything, he said, more film-makers are preferring his country in spite of tough competition, largely because of the one window access to all their needs. The ambassador provided a lighter touch to the serious tourism business when he said that like chocolates and watches the Swiss cow is also a popular sight. He said, "Like the people of India, we are also proud of our cows. We also decorate them at festivals." There is much Indian promoters can learn from the Swiss on how to promote tourism.

Let's Go Dutch

One of the tourism myths nurtured over the years particularly by Indian visitors is that London or Paris is the gateway to Europe in their travel for business or pleasure. Disproving the myth are 1.5 million international tourist arrivals every year to Holland. Many of them may nod in approval of what one writer said: "You can see Europe without leaving Holland."

Cruise in glass-topped boats in tree-lined canals and savour history and the delights which reminds one of Venice. In the richness of its museums one shares the legacy of great masters since the days of renaissance one might miss in London, Paris or Rome. Tulips and roses and a thousand varieties of flowers bloom in fields that stretch beyond the horizon as nowhere else in Europe. Its windmills and dykes are a constant reminder of the urge of the survival of man in the buttle against sea. This is not all. The place is as famous for its diamonds as its dykes. For three centuries, Amsterdam has been the mercantile and banking centre of Europe.

Still, in this compact country a journey through the past and present could be completed in a short time. Witness the drive from the spacious Schipol international airport to the nearest city, Amsterdam. In 20 minutes your go past traditional windmills and farms, where men work as of old in their wooden shoes, high rise and futuristic buildings, canals and cathedrals right to the inner line of the 17th century. All the other cities in Holland, the Hague, Leiden and Rotterdam from where families set sail to the New World could be reached in a matter of a few hours by road. If you feel the need to travel anywhere else in Europe, Schipol offers the most frequent service. Or, the Amsterdam railway station on which Japan in the early stages of modernisation patterned its Tokyo station, is linked with the European rail network.

For those who will be tied to business with a long work day, Amsterdam extends shopping hours by three hours at least twice a week. But guard your belongings. A wave of bag snatching has of late caused some disquiet.

How favourable the prices are depends on your tastes and travels. One account ranks Amsterdam as number 32 in the current list of expensive capitals. To connoisseurs of diamonds the Amsterdam cut signifies excellence. Diamond-cut ling establishments are apart of organised sight-seeing tours.

Amsterdam is compact with its attractions conveniently close to one other. It has 6,800 architectural Treasures—houses and buildings dating from the 16th century. Alongside the sparkling crescent of canals wealthy merchants built elegant homes. The windows are not curtained off as the Dutch like to display their flower arrangements and furniture. The best introduction to the wonderous waterways from which you can gaze at these homes, is via a cruise on board a glass-topped boat. The waterborne tours operate the year round.

Other favourite attractions in Amsterdam include its 40 museums, most famous of which is the Rijksmtiseum which receives one million visitors a year. It boasts a celebrated collection of works by masters including Rembrandt's "Nightwatch."

Marvellous furniture, silver and porcelain are on display. The comparatively new Vincent Van Gogh Museum is the showcase for the world's largest collection of his works—200 paintings and 400 drawings.

Amsterdam's Stedelijk (Municipal) Museum has acquired international fame because of its trend-setting permanent collection and temporary exhibitions of modern art. A former orphanage that dates back to 1,524, houses the Amsterdam Historical Museum. It offers a special bonus to visitors—free entry to the Civic Guard's Gallery, a glassroofed "museum street" lined with massive paintings. This connects the building's 17th century inner courtyards with the adjoining Begijnhof, the charmed circle of 500-year-old houses that forms a quiet oasis in the city's heart.

The Anne Frank House has an entirely different character and nearby is the home Rembrandt bought and went broke.

Amsterdam is a musical city as well—street musicians, the brightly-painted barrel organs and the centuries-old carillons high in their towers play a happy tune every quarter of an hour. Music, with a capital M, can be heard during noon-time performances and in the evening at the celebrated Concertgebouw (concert building) noted for its superb acoustics. Dutch orchestras perform there, including the Concertgebouw Orchestra. Jazz and light classical concerts are also given in the building. Almost any summer evening it is possible to hear an organ recital in one of Amsterdam's magnificent old churches.

Taking time off the business, shopping or museum visits, it is pleasant to sit and relax on a terrace overlooking a canal or in one of the tree-shaded "pleineea" (squares) and relax over refreshments. During the colder months many of the roofed terraces are heated and visitors are welcomed in Amsterdam's "brown cafes" any time of the year. Every neighbourhood has one or more of these old pubs with smoke-stained walls and overhead beams. Some of them have been serving drinks to congenial guests for centuries. It is possible to 'dine' in any language in Amsterdam whether the hungry traveller wants a simple sandwich-lunch or an extensive five course dinner by candlelight.

There are restaurants that feature French, Italian, Spanish, Greek and Japanese cuisine. A tasty souvenir of Holland's ties with the Spice Islands of Indonesia is the delicious "rijst-tafel" (rice table), a colourful array of up to 20 taste treats which are served with rice and large glasses of Dutch beer. There are a dozen Indian restaurants in Amsterdam and Rotterdam themselves with names which could make one nostalgic like Sangam, Mughal, Maharani and Tagore. Interestingly, the youthful owner of Tagore said he chose the name because he wanted to add an intellectual flavour to the business of food.

In this variegated culinary fare the Dutch are feeling lost about their own menu and now effort is on for a typical Dutch cuisine. The Dutch have a saying, "What the farmer doesn't know, he won't eat." And, admittedly, there are a large number of Dutchmen who pack potatoes and canned vegetables along with their camping gear when they head-off on a vacation in another country. They want to assure themselves of good, hearty meals.

Such delights are available in every town in Holland. Less than an hour's drive for Amsterdam is the Hague, the town of many faces—the seat of governmental fishing port, yatch harbour with two seaside resorts attached. It has many pedestrian promenades and passages. It is the court capital again now that Queen Beatrix has taken up residence. Also here is the massive Peace Palace housing the International Court of Justice.

On your journey in the Hague do not miss the Panorama Mesdag—a unique painting in, a gigantic circular canvas—(circumference 394 feet, height 46 feet, surface 18,00 feet). Its the creation of H.W. Mesdag, assisted by his wife Sina Mesdag giving a fascinating view of the old fishing village of Scheven-Sngen—in 1881 with its sea, sand and sky.

It is so positioned that the painting presents an optical illusion of a village while remaining a great work of art.

Also, near the Hague is Delft which has given its name to its celebrated earthenware which is beautiful to give and more wonderful to receive (it is quite expensive). Deftware is based on Chinese porcelain which the Dutch East India Company had brought in the 17th century. Fine flower, leaf and tendril motifs alternated by birds are typical land and sea scape are still the subjects for hand-paintings. But if anyone seeks to sell you what is claimed to be a piece of Delfrware ask for a certificate of authenticity. For, there are many fake claimants.

Holland is thus, full of heritage of crafts and skills, but it is also futuristic as evident in many of its structures particularly in Rotterdam. Built over the ruins of World War II it has all the high-tech link ups'tor a medieval flourishing port to turn into the most modern harbour. It is a focal crossroads of important routes by sea, inland waterways, airways and pipelines. Schipol is just 50 km away. With much of western Europe as its hinterland it is the region's trade nerve centre. It handles 250 million tonnes of cargo with the aid of a chain of 26 radar stations and a network of computers. These modern packages do not rob the place of the beauty endowed by nature. It has a floating restaurant stated to be the only Chinese joint venture in western Europe.

In cities as well as the countryside cycling is popular. Every family has a car and at least two or three bicycles.

Holland's culture and cuisine are cosmopolitan. In fact, it is so cosmopolitan that the query as to how most people speak English or French is met by the reply: "There are far too few here to speak Dutch." Holland could be the destination if you have no time for the rest of Europe. For here, much of Europe is on view.

10
Foreign Travellers and Travel Guides

Executive Travellers

The Executive Traveller is a fussy and fussed-over lot. And for good reason. From the common denominator of 'passenger' for an airline and 'guest' for a hotel, this specie of men on the move has crystalised into the executive traveller. His promotion, in travelese they call it upgrading, is not all his own doing. The culprit is the airlines marketing smart alecs who introduced honourable looking cover names for what used to be simply discounted, largely against airlines' own regulations, tickets, like excursion fare, apex fare, group fare, and so on. This created an awkard situation especially in the economy class: a business traveller, the erstwhile title of the executive traveller, would find to his dismay that his companion had paid anything from one third to one-half less than him for the same destination and yet he was enjoying the same leg room, food service, courtesies, and so on. And, while the executive traveller was burdened with tne stresses and strains of business and work, the companion was either going on holiday or returning refreshed from one!

Appreciating the problem and keeping in mind the higher revenue earned from the business traveller the airlines' marketing boys put their heads together and agreed that the full fare paying passenger needed a special deal. KLM, said to be the first to recognise that the executive traveller must be treated a cut above those with rebated tickets, introduced in 1976 a new class of traveller as triple F (or FFF) which stood for the uncamouflaged title of Full Fare Facilities. At the time, recalls KLM spokesman, K. K. Sharma, only a special sticker on the ticket and the baggage and a few minor courtesies distinguished the executive traveller from others in the economy class. This writer's own experience of being recognized as a special category of traveller was in 1979 on an Air India flight from Delhi to Frankfurt. A seat just behind the first class and close to the exit plus free drinks was all the perks that went with a full fare.

In the decade since KLM's first move, the full fare paying passenger on an airline has been given a distinctive identity, respect, amenities, comforts and courtesies that are excelled only for those travelling first class. Aircraft configurations have been changed to create a separate niche for the executive traveller, wider and fewer seats, more leg room, choice of food, free drinks, gifts and courtesies in the air and separate check in counters, handsome baggage allowance and several other amenities such as special lounges on the ground. And, at the destination special assistance in checking through customs and immigration, quicker clearance of baggage, meeting services. You name it, they have it. There are brochures galore reminding you of the importance of being an executive traveller. The airlines are nothing if they are not competitive. And in attracting the coveted executive traveller, it is not always the 'fittest' or the most efficient airline that succeeds; it could well be the gimmickiest.

Our very own Air India does not lag behind. It has published a 100 page business travel guide, the best part of which is the invitation to travel the Maharaja's executive class. Calling it a rich and rare experience, it gives details of what this 'class' offers, which will make you feel a lesser mortal if you are not an experienced flier. Says the guide: "On its Boeing 747's Air India's executive class offers 40 Weber First class seats—18 on the upper deck and 22 on the main deck. These spacious seats are 18 inches wide between arm-rests, with a seat pitch of 40 inches on the upper deck and 38 inches on the main deck. Seating is in a 6 abreast configuration with a 2-2 pattern; the central seat is folded down to act as a table and the emphasis is an ample elbow and leg-space to provide maximum comfort on long flights." Presumbaly, those with bigger girths would be taken to the upper decks (and, pray why have a seat in the middle which is only turned down to become a table. The revised edition of the guide will perhaps throw some light on this).

The splendour of Indian heritage too is thrown in by Air India in the cabin decor as also the lure of Indian food from superbly rich mughali to north and south Indian vegetarian fare. On prior request it also gives special meals for those on doctor's diet, Muslim, Kosher and pure vegetarian. And all this with the warmth of Indian hospitality.

British Airways shows special concern for the executive traveller who works even during a flight. The most uncomfortable thing, the airlines' brochure says, is to have a complete stranger reading over your shoulder. Especially when it's your company secrets they're reading. So, it is not only for more elbow room that their seats are as wide and as apart but also to "guarantee that your business remains your business." British Airways calls its executive class as Super Club and from the extent of literature produced by the airlines the range of facilities would seem more comprehensive and imaginative than most other lines. For instance, the Indian Visitors Service for super club travellers arriving in London would certainly take many an anxiety away. From a welcome at the aircraft door it take care of all airport formalities and for those with urgent business needs it arranges transport, conference rooms, secretarial services and even hotel reservations. Marketing wizkids of airlines can be trusted to bring in more sophistication into the art of pampering the executive traveller.

What airlines can do, hotels can do better. In fact, it would seem the hotels discovered the executive potential much earlier and developed their own sophistry in taking care of the executive traveller's ego as well as his hassles. To the Taj Mahal Hotel in New Delhi could easily go the credit for a whole-hearted application of the concept of a businessman's hotel, where every floor, every facility is geared to meeting the special needs of the executive traveller, especially those who in hotels are known as top of the market. With 80 per cent business traveller clientele, says PR Manager, Kerman Coulter, the whole hotel and not just a part of it, is an executive club. Guests can be met and seen off at the airport and within the hotel they even get not only personalised stationery, special toiletries, fruitbaskets but also towels with embroidered names. There is a twenty-four hour business centre and STD facilities from the room for overseas calls. Taj Mahal's sister, the Taj Palace specialises in caring for a new variety of the executive traveller, the conferencewalla. To his quality he adds quantity and his needs are wider; interpretation in foreign languages, small and large conference halls, banqueting halls, entertainment, spouses programmes and computers, word processors. One unique service provided by both the hotels is media relations consultancy.

Like different airlines the other leading hotels in the capital offer a variety of facilities to the executive traveller—separate floors with exclusive facilities. The Ashoka, father of the convention tourism in India, boasts of a presidential service with a valet and Mercedes car and the hotel's over 100 deluxe and executive suites. The Maurya Sheraton has given two of its floors to executive service but you pay a little higher tariff. With an extra higher tariff you get entitled to the Hotel's exclusive Tower Club. At the Hyatt Regency, executive exclusiveness is created into one compact floor called the Regency Club. Paying a higher tariff Club guests need a special elevator key to the floor and amenities include free breakfast, all day tea-coffee service and a happy hours bar service.

The executive traveller seems to be the apple of the travel world's eye with no competition round the corner.

American Traveller

Americans are great travellers. Over 25 million US citizens visited the rest of the world during 1983, spending the equivalent of 25 billion dollars. This would mean almost every tenth citizen took a trip abroad and spent on an average a thousand dollars. It is interesting to note that of these vast numbers more than half (14 million) went to the two border countries—Canada (11 million) and Mexico (3.9 million). Of the remaining ten millions US tourists 3 million visited the Caribbean and Central America. Europe and the Mediterranean received 5 million tourists (UK 1.9 million); France W. Beenay 1.2 million each. "Other Areas" covering the whole of Africa, Asia got 1.4 million. Of these nearly 96,000 came to India (this figure has not appreciably changed during 1984 and 1985). Taking India's share as part of "Other Areas" the showing is not as bad as it would seem at first sight. The only consolation India can draw from figures of arrivals in Europe is Portugal which too received 98,000 Americans a steep drop from the figure of 1,95,000 just four years earlier.

However insignificant the percentage of Americans travelling to India compared to other countries, the United States remains this country's biggest tourist market. Until a decade the USA's share in the Indian market was the largest when UK too over the number one position. Like the target of one million tourists has been eluding India for over five years, the arrivals from the United States too have yet to cross the 1,00,000 mark. Indian tourism authorities are however confident that 1986 may see the 1,00,000 American land at the newly commissioned Indira Gandhi International Airport.

It was only right that India made a major tourism promotion effort in the United States alongwith Europe. The largest number of tourist offices opened was in the United States. Even with the recent pruning of the tourist offices overseas, the largest Indian presence is still in that country with a Regional Director at the helm. Between 1975 and last year the number of American tourists has nearly doubled. Pran Nath Seth who once headed the India tourist office in the US, recalls that just fifteen years ago, Americans visited India as part of a round the world trip. Now more than fifty per cent Americans coming to India treat the trip as a destination and may at best include Nepal as part of their itinerary. According to him the major motivation for American travel is exotic India or a cultural experience of India. This country has yet to become a pure holiday destination like the Caribbean, although young Americans have started coming here both in search of culture as well as holiday.

Only ten or eleven per cent of the Americans come to India as groups; the rest love to travel individually. Mumbai and Delhi are their main entry ports for Americans and a vast majority of them cover Udaipur and Jaipur princiaplly to live like Maharajas in the Lake Palace Hotel and the Rambagh Palace Hotel. Agra, Khajuraho and Varanasi and some of the southern attractions like Chennai, Bangalore, Cochin are popular with them. Americans are great shoppers too. They don't buy plane loads like the Oil Sheikhs but they do order cartloads of carpets, marble topped tables, brassware, jewellery, silks. They would pay anything for antioues, sometimes it is enough if an item guest looks antique! This writer was witness to an American attending the Young Presidents Organisation meeting in Delhi ordering everything in sight at a hotel shop running a bill for $ 90,000.

American tour operators borrow freely from Indian tourism literature Annoness an American package tour brochure: Wonders of Asia—India, Nepal and Sri Lanka. It goes on to say: In a world tending towards uniformity, India is the most profoundly different country you can visit. An unparalleled continuity of civilisation 5,000 years old brings home to the visitor, the experience of living simultaneously in almost all the alges that have preceded this, the 20th century. And nowhere else does the present and the past coexist in such colourful promiscuity. But travel guides written by Americans, and there are quite a few of them, are quite candid in preparing the intending traveller to many of the Indian realities. I particularly like Myraa Waldo's Orient and Asia Travel Guide. In it she attempts to juxtapose India on the United States: Denver would become a seaport called Kolkata....Colorado a flat estuary named West Bengal. . . San Francisco would feel quite at home as a port called Mumbai. .. ..Alaska would come out ahead for it would be Kashmir. Tall bearded Sikhs would roam Washington State addressing one another as Mr. Lion. Oregan alas would lose its forest and become a semi-desert called Rajasthan. Myra Waldo turns Delhi Belly (intestinal disturbance) as somewhat of an international phenomenon comparing it with Montezuma's Revenge in Mexico and Tokyo Trots in Japan.

The most scintillating part of Myra Waldo's guide is the conversation an American tourist might expect with the Indian sitting next on an Indian airlines flight. Assuming that the Indian companion was a businessman or a civil servant, she prepares the American thus: If the conversation turns to politics, the businessman will be right of, and the civil servant, left of the Congress party line! The author candidly admits that most Americans find India's "neutralism" (they refuse to call it non-alignment) frustrating. The frustration it seems arises from the American feeling that India is neutral against the United States and in favour of Russia.

The USSR is perhaps the only bone of contention an Indian interacting with the American tourists might come cross. I have had personal experience of this several times over. Very recently, at a dinner with a group of Yale University Alumni, after Punjab had been discussed threadbare came India's relations with the Soviet Union. One group member seemd upset because he had seen so many Russian tourists at Mahabalipuram. He found it difficult to believe that only 15,000 Soviet tourists came to this country annually. Fortunately the subject got changed to the population problem which numbed the groups interest in serious matters.

Barring the Soviet factor, Indians and Americans as tourists have a lot in common. England and America, a wit said once, are divided by their common language but English would seem to unite Indians and Americans rather famously since both speak in so many accents. Among other discoveries they make about each other is that both want to be loved by the rest of the world. And, both love to talk. The Indian finds the American more than match in running down institutions and governmental policies; if the American sings a song about *tandoori* chicken, the Indian relishes Kentucky fried chicken. Much of this is communicated through jokes which then find their way to the cocktail circuits of both countries. The most current one is about the *Gandhi* film. The story goes that it was more popular on West Coast. It seems Americans living in that part found Gandhi had all they had always wanted to be: slim, tan and honest.

Tail piece: An American who returned the New York from a visit to India was asked if he had seen the Taj Mahal. Yes, he answered but added with a sad look on his face: unfortunately, they have turned it into a hotel.

What the German Traveller Wants

The Federal Republic of Germany has been traditionally one of India's best sources of tourists. Outside the United Kingdom, West Germany sends the largest number of visitors to this country. Statistics point to a 15 per cent growth in the inflow – almost twice the national average.

West German interest in India is not new. In earlier times, long before tourism became an organised industry, there had been a constant movement of scholars to India from famed German universities in pursuit of oriental studies. Similarly, there has been a movement of people from India to educational institutions in Germany. While this academic interest continues more mid more Germans now come to India for business tie-ups, transfer of technology and industrial cooperation.

Still it is worthwhile to examine where the German tourist is going, and why. Studies suggest that the German traveller looks for sunny declinations; shorter and more frequent trips every year; prefers special groups instead of mass groups; wants unspoilt environments and would like to holiday in a dub like atmosphere. The German tourist wants the hotel at the destination to be a second home with standard facilities at all times. Being a seasoned traveller the average German tourist has experienced several destinations and opts for the one that gives value for the money.

As a tourism product, India fits the bill. It should be so. Whether it is sun 'n' sand as in Goa or snow and skiing in Gulmarg or the marvels in stone at Mahabalipuram or Halebid or the cultural experience of Ajanta and Ellora. The options are one too many on a single package. Added to this, the German traveller knows of the shopping opportunities in places like Mumbai, Chennai or Delhi.

Simultaneously, there is a particular reason to concentrate on the German market and our tourist office in Frankfurt is one of the busiest outlets in Europe. According to P. K. Dong, Director of the office, "in 1984 the German tourists spent $2 billion more (more than Rs. 2,000 crore on travel than their American counterparts". A FATA survey in 1981 estimated that 26.5 million Germans take a main vacation every year. Of these, 1.5 million go on long haul vacations. India, as of now gets barely five per cent of this. For one, the German has to be convinced that India is an all-season destination. Secondly. German tour operators expect reliability of promised services particularly in areas like tennis courts and swimming pools. The average German traveller repeals the destination depending on experience. So, for that reason if there is cause for any disappointment with promised services a second vim will not materialise.

Fortunately, cases of disillusionment are few and far between and the estimation for India has continued to grow so as to reinforce Indian hopes of getting as many as 100 from West Germany by year visitors from FRG just less than 80,000.

Already a recognition is evident in the market are Otto Scneider. President Man Travel Agents would like an out of country meeting of his association in India.

He rightly argues that while India is traditionally a cultural draw the growth potential in that segment is limited. But the growth rate can he accelerated in beach tourism. He cautions however that a healthy environment around beach resorts is a must for holiday makers.

India's presence at the International Tourism Exchange (ITE) in Berlin which is annually the biggest event in the global tourism industry, has helped to provide increased publicity to the Indian tourism product and facilities. It has also facilitated proper feedback on Germany requirements one of which is accommodation in three to four star hotels. As Mr. Dong says, "happily, India is addressing itself this need and these medium rung hotels are now coming up at more tourist destinations." Hopeful trends indeed, as the country prepares for the Visit India Year in 1991.

Aaron's India

In the last 15 years Jan Aaron has guided hundreds of thousands of foreigners on what to see, where to go and stay and how to shop in India. She has given them the names of budget hotels and directions which sometimes pass through sidelines to destinations. So much so, many sincerely believe that what Aaron does not mention is not worth seeing.

She closely follows the inflation rate and the consequential rise in every hotel tariff and in the cost of their travel-related services and puts them in print down to the last paise. Her cuisine counselling is equally perfect: it informs the visitor which restaurant is reputed for what kind of food at what prices. In fact, many Indians too, come to know more about such travel details from Jan Aaron's India. In the past decade-and-a-half she has recommended an Indian holiday from $10 to $25 a day.

Aaron is an American bitten by the India bug ever since, she says, when she was seven or eight. At school in Denver, Colorado, a local magazine asked pupils which country they would like to visit when they grew up. Aaron had replied instantly India. It was the tales and legends she had heard from her mother that fascinated her most about India. Her mother had also told her about that great monument to love built by the richest Mughal—richer than any American—the Taj Mahal. Aaron had, however, to wait for many years before she could see it for herself to write about.

Since her first visit in 1965, Aaron has been coming to India every alternate year to update her book running into around 500 pages. She was recently in the country documenting establishments difficult, to find on one's own. She take, six months to sift, collate and confirm the massive data she collects before setting out to write. She also takes time to contribute to reputed journals and devote to her other main interest: cooking. She is the co-author of the *Art of Mexican Cooking* and *Lave of Spanish and Mexican Cooking.*

But her first love is to contribute to the India series travel books brought out by the internationally famous Simon and Schuster. Said she: "I do have definite goals, namely to encourage people to go to India with an open mind and carefree. I want everyone of my readers, all would be travellers, to give India a chance and not form an opinion before going to that country." Her last edition (1988-89) – *India On $25 a day*—went out of print after 1,00,000 copies were sold.

Has she any preferences among Indian destinations? "I recommend every part of India; but if someone persists in asking for my choice I say go to Kolkata, Ahmedabad, Mount Abu, Chennai and Pondicherry, not necessarily in that order."

Aaron recalls that she was prompted to write on India after she had seen Arthur Frommer's Fitmpe on five Mirny a day. Her obvious choice was India. She is now working on her sixth edition. With her sun-tanned face and in her *salwar-kameez* at lunch table in a five-star restaurant, few can mark her out as a foreigner except by her accent. To top it all, she is quite at home on Indian geography and history.

She meticulously notes down the additions, deletions and changes on each page of the previous edition pasted in her bulky notebook. To make the record absolutely authentic she repeats the visits to every place she has gone earlier. If there is any error, it is all due to inflation, "I make every effort to obtain upto-the-minute prices, but even the most conscientious researcher cannot keep up with the current pace of inflation. These traveller will add 15 to 20 per cent to the points quoted throughout the pages," she adds.

This veteran of India hand is happy, after so many visits, that she has an effective counterpoint to her detractors. They had once sneered: 'Ugh, you'! hate it (India). It is full of snakes and beggars, and so poor, and besides it's filthy'. "So what," she counters, "India undeniably has beggars (so does New York, for that matter) they are there, but so are many other things." As for snakes, "I never saw one except for the sluggish specimens displayed in the baskets of professional snake charmers or the occasional exotic breed to be found in a zoo. The average Indian familiarity with snakes is equal to a suburbanite's encounters with foxes."

There is the positive point too. "Above all else despite independence as a modern nation, since 1947, and a century-and-a-half before that of colonial rule; despite foreign aid, five-year plans, increasing industrialisation, a nuclear test and space experimentation—India is still very close to nature." The greatest PR person India could boast of.

Her documented India does not leave out anything that concerns the past and present: population, pantheon, gourmet glossary, currency and all essential information that a traveller needs. Going through the book one feels that those in charge of overseas tourism promotion would certainly recommend Jan Aaron's India. It will be fair to the traveller because it explains how to get value for money. For instance, she lists 14 Indian style hotels in Chennai and goes into the smallest of details such as plastic walls dividing the rooms in an Udipi Home in Egmore. Or, for that matter, she identified the year-old Victoria Training Institute's special room. There antiques and unusual items are .sold at bargain prices. Likewise there is a plethora of detail almost every place worth seeing, 'she relates to you the numerous palaces which have been turned into hotels and as a shrewd observer points to the sublime as well as the weird tastes of its former occupants as reflected in the decor of their bedrooms.

Her comprehensive coverage does not leave out night life. Bars, music, dancing discotheques, movies and cabarets are all discussed. Here is a tip on a Delhi cabaret, "Should half nude dancing girls with considerable lack of talent appeal, then these shows and the expenses involved are for you. Frankly, none of the performers is anywhere near as revealing or one iota as graceful as the statues on sonic of the celebrated Indian temples."

It is a safe bet that the readers of Aaron's India come to this country better informed than those who merely look at the tourist folders. This is acknowledged by tourist officials and all those involved in promotion of the in-bound traffic. On her visits both Air India, the department of tourism and different hotel managements try to assist her. For, they all know there are hundreds of thousands of people worldwide who have accepted her as their guide.

An Odyssey to Fulfilment

Yusuf Husain is an achiever. He was once a competent numismatist with the State Museum in Lucknow. His performances on the stage have received encomiums. But, for some strange reason the highly-competitive world of travel business attracted him. Here, too, he attained the goals he had set for himself and is now looking for fresh pastures.

The most fascinating chapter in the Husain story came about in a surprisingly very casual way. One day, years ago, he was leisurely going at the Indian Airlines flight tariff when he noticed that the lowest fare anywhere was between Delhi and Agra at Rs. 55. He started planning his first air journey and overheard a conversation that students were eligible for a 50 per cent rebate. He recalls that the observation "immediately triggered off an explosion in my head". And he lost no time in translating his brainwave into action.

He resigned his job and set up his travel business with no telephone or typewriter, but only an Indian Airlines folder. He went to a school and sold the idea of taking the children by air to Agra to see the Taj for only Rs. 50. After deducting for other expenses, he was left with a small profit of Rs. 10 per student. He brought them back by road.

The excitement of the children was infectious and many schools approached him for similar trips. And Odyssey International, founded in 1972, got into student-concessional routes. Kathmandu, Singapore, European and American destinations figured in his list. In four years as many as 1,00,000 students had availed of his package. Even with small margins he made a tidy sum.

But the Yusuf was already working on new ideas. He finally landed at the Caribbean islands and other remote parts of the world to promote India to fourth-generation people of Indian origin. The odyssey that he promised the West Indians turned out to be a very successful enterprise both in terms of the numbers who availed his offer and his own earnings. He won many prizes for several years as a foreign exchange earner.

Husain acknowledges that his wife, Salma Ajmeri, has been a big source of encouragement to him. For her, too, it was a change from her vocation as a Persian scholar and broadcaster.

His quest for fulfilment did not end. He gave up his flourishing travel business which he says "he no longer finds creative". He now wants to discover the India that he had all along been selling and showing to others. He also wants to set up a campus in a forest or near a river to teach young people about "life, environment, music, theatre and how to set up a business enterprise without big money".

If Yusuf, in his fourties, does not speak of what he proposes to do after the campus has been set up, it only suggests that the restless achiever is confident of blazing yet another trail.

11
Declining Trends

Declining Trends

The euphoria over topping the million mark in tourist arrivals has vanished faster than the worst sceptics would have foretold. Deliberate official briefings have sought to explain away this phase in the industry by citing bottlenecks and going into long sessions on how to overcome them. The new president of the Travel Agents Association of India, Vinod Kothari, who ought to know the direction of the tourism wind, has lamented the fall in the growth rate. According to him the growth rate dropped from 30 per cent last year to an estimated six to seven per cent so far during the current year. There are no indications to reinforce hopes of any pleasant surprise.

Kothari complains of the continuing inadequacy in the tourism infrastructure like airlines capacity and hotel accommodation. In this connection, a letter to the editor published in the *Indian Express* on September 12 is worthy of note as not only illustrative of the casualness of the officials of our air carriers but also for the adverse implications for long-term tourism perspectives. The writer, a British citizen of Indian origin, narrates how he had to wait for 12 hours at the Air India airport office in Delhi only to be told that he was waitlisted. He was desperate to get back to London to attend his father-in-law's funeral. He managed to end his agonizing wait only at the intervention of the British High Commission which arranged a berth for him on British Airways. The man, who out of a sense of pride for the country of his origin was keen on flying Air India, writes "I will never fly Air India again". This may be an extreme case but certainly typical of the response of airlines' officials to requests even on compassionate grounds. And the airline is losing not just a lone passenger but the country is losing many more would be visitors by this word-of-mouth adverse publicity.

For this reason alone the move by the International Airports Authority of India to introduce orientation courses for agencies handling traffic at airports should be welcome. But more than the content of the course the success will lie in the attitudinal changes these could bring about. Perhaps some of the airlines staff could be required to undergo training in hospitality and customer service.

Besides the airlines there are other segments of the tourism infrastructure which need a strong build-up and spread. Even last year when our tourism statisticians managed to present the million figure there were many parts of the country which did not get even a small share of this magic number.

It is true that tourism is and should by and large be in the hands of the private sector for the simple reason that public investments on the required scale would deprive priority sectors of adequate allocations. But even in areas where the government does not cease to boast of achievements as on the promotional side, the scene is far from impressive. ITDC, which claims to have launched tie-ups with international outlets, has lent its name to take a share of the turnover and profit from a new hotel in Cochin. The brand new hotel has meeting facilities and is very well furnished and conveniently located for business visitors or for those who come for leisure or pleasure. The ITDC linkage to the hotel was formalised six years ago though the hotel itself was commissioned only six months ago. Still, with this long back-up and relationship, this hotel is yet to reach a medium occupancy rate.

And ITDC persistently claims it is different from other private sector chains in so far as it engages itself in promotional and development of destinations. Unless the wise men of ITDC not think Cochin with its stunning attractions for visitors both from the scenic and historical point of view as a destination to be promoted specially, there is no logical reason for the low occupancy rate in the Cochin affiliate.

The list of such instances from other states would lengthen on minute scrutiny. It is not that the authorities are totally oblivious of the imbalances, their causes and consequences. A measure of this response to set matters right was the meeting recently convened by the union tourism secretary to identify and overcome the problems. Much of the solution emerging from that meeting attended by the cabinet secretary and secretaries of other ministries concerned was told that, namely, a package of financial concessions. This is not to minimise the relevance of their suggestions for concessional finance, tax reliefs, and customs reductions on equipment. But one wishes that the government would undertake a review of the implementation of the recommendations proposed even at a ministerial level for tourism development. It is common knowledge that the record of several state governments in practising or putting into effect its professions and promises is poor. Even states which have declared tourism an industry have not spelt out what it amounts to. Still everyone would like to get a slice of the tourism cake and for that purpose is prepared to call it a national priority sector. Unless the state governments, the airlines as well as a very strong section of the industry are prepared to fulfil their commitment to get more visitors to this land and to persuade them to stay longer and to come back again and again, the million mark that has now lapsed into history may long remain in the past.

HOTEL INDUSTRY DEMANDS ATTENTION

Central Authority Essential

All that glitters is not gold and five-star glamour is often a luxury mask. The story of the Indian hotel industry which to all intents and appearances is a high profit sector of the economy has many untold components which it would not like to show up.

For one thing, contrary to general belief, it is not a high profitability economic activity particularly in the professionally organised chains. At the same time, there is a segment in this business which does no credit either to the industry, tourism or the economy. Thus, the industry as a whole is a pointer to many contradictions in the economy.

The professionally organised and privately owned sector of the hotel business is close to nine decades old. Its origin, as in so many other areas, stemmed from the national urge to build institutions owned and controlled by Indians when the country had alien masters. Today this sector accounts for 85 per cent of the 'approved' accommodation for the upscale tourist on business, leisure or pleasure.

The private sector has not lagged behind the public sector as pioneers taking risks (in Goa, Khajuraho, for example). The investments and infrastructure the private sector has raised have been of considerable value to the nation as was evident during NAM, CHOGM and more recently SAARC. It may take a long time to get adequate returns from the massive investments made in these areas.

The availability of 32,000 rooms in nearly 500 hotels may sound a high figure but in a country of continental size and varied attractions it is not something which one could drum about. Countries of much smaller sizes have much more to offer with greater earning capacity. For that reason, it is worthwhile to examine why, in spite of the potential of tourism both in terms of earnings and employment, the hotel industry which is a key element of this sector, has not expanded to the desirable level. The contradiction is stark in the context of a projected demand for 59,000 rooms just three years hence, when the country hopes to reach a very modest target of 2.5 million arrivals. Even this winter with a small spurt in traffic, hotels are full with advance bookings for another three months.

Private Sector

This situation underscores the priority claim of this industry which is yet to be accepted by our planners in the matter of investment. The Government and the Planning Commission have made it obvious, for valid reasons, that resources for the hotel industry must come largely from the private sector, with government run hotels concentrating on low priced accommodation for domestic travellers. Certainly one cannot quarrel with this approach which suggests that the available funds should be used for top priority areas like the anti-poverty programme. Thus, it devolves on the private sector the responsibility for building up the deluxe infrastructure for tourism in the coming years.

On a rough calculation an additional room with attendant facilities should cost around Rs. 6 lakh. This has to be multiplied twenty-seven thousand times (Rs. 1,020 crore) if we want to ensure that those who come to our country in the 90s stay longer instead of getting stranded. Also, it is to be noted in the context of the rapidly changing nature of our economy consequent on the liberalisation of policies initiated two years ago, there is a new welcome wave of tourists of a particular class with a larger purse but more exacting demands. Understandably, this is the target group of the leading chains and other successful hotels.

The business tourists who constitute this group are not affected by normal or seasonal factors which sway the inflow of those who travel for leisure and pleasure (In fact much of the additional arrivals so far this year belong to this category). They want, apart from deluxe ambience, good food and service, efficient communications, exclusive inhouse entertainment facilities, meeting rooms, and excellent local transport as well as easier and reliable transit facilities.

These will involve not only high standards within a hotel but also the upgrading of services like telephones, telex communications, better taxis with educated chauffeurs, and dependable air bookings. The business tourist, it must be remembered, is a frequent traveller and earnings from this class of traffic will certainly be commensurate with any investment or upgrading of facilities and services.

Even official estimates, which are on the lower side, place foreign exchange earnings from tourism in the current year at Rs. 1,800 crore, at least fourty per cent of which is earned by hotels. A factor that cannot be overlooked is that this amount is brought into the country with very little outflow of any scarce commodities or assets.

Export Oriented

Having thus assigned to itself a pivotal role as a source for scarce foreign exchange earnings, the industry is justified in its plea for assistance particularly as the accounts of some of the professionally managed hotel chains indicate a lower capital profit ratio than in other comparable industries engaged in exports.

No less a person than J.R.D. Tata stated: "If recognition of the importance to the country of a greater flow of foreign visitors is to be translated into action, the government,' both at the Centre and in the states, must surely recognise the equal importance of the hotel industry as an export or export-oriented industry and to extend to it all the fiscal and other incentives available to export and other priority industries."

True, there is now a greater awareness on the part of the government of the relevance of tourism to tne national economy and the need to encourage the various segments of the industry. The government itself has stated that tourism should be recognised as an industry. But being a state subject, a national policy on a matter like this has inherent limitations. Possibly, at the time of the writing of the constitution, the potential of tourism could not be foreseen. So much so the thread of a central tourism policy so necessary in the existing context has many missing links.

Even now many states have not responded to the suggestion for industry status to tourism. Nor is there any coordination among the various agencies to which an entrepreneur will have to approach for setting up and running a good hotel. Incredible as it may seem, in the Capital itself the hotel industry has to run separately to as many as 30 agencies, many of which are least conscious or concerned with earning foreign exchange! The position may be worse elsewhere. Even in states which have declared tourism as industry, the situation is compounded by the total absence of support infrastructure like communications, transport, even water.

All these point to the need for clear enunciation of a national tourism policy to be pursued by a national authority which would facilitate a single window clearance for hotels and other tourism projects. Perhaps, such an authority could be strengthened by statutory sanctions by placing tourism on the Concurrent List. Besides, this authority with defined powers and strong teeth could differentiate between the cliff and the chaff. It could identify and encourage the real entrepreneur and also spot out those whose motivations are different. In that event, the hotel industry even if it retains the mask of glamour, will have acquired a face-lift.

Aviation Sector Hit

Gloomy Skies

It will take a very long time for India's domestic air transport to recover from the series of costly decisions on Airbus A-320 which remained grounded for more than 150 days. The country has lost over Rs. 100 crore on account of the cost of maintenance, salaries, training and loss of business apart from the spin-off effect on the national economy. In addition, it has had an adverse response from overseas tourism markets where tour operators consider the disruption of air services as the biggest constraint in sending groups to India.

By now it is fairly certain political considerations arising from the belief among the highest government circles that kickbacks and not technology influenced the purchase of these modern aircraft have led to the stalemate. In the rest of the world, airlines operate A 320 without any hitch. In India which boasts of being among the leaders in scientific manpower doubts are raised about the state of preparedness to handle this fly-by-wire machine, the type of which has been in use by the Indian Air Force for nearly twenty years. Whoever is responsible for the decision to ground the aircraft has not done either the country or the airline justice.

Most Airlines in the world prepare for augmentation of their fleets and modernization at least five years in advance. Their programme for the mid-90s must have already been finalised but we in India are yet to start on our fleet expansion scheduled for the late 80s! There has been little planning ahead.

It is amusing that in the circumstances a controversy has been aroused over the transfer or sharing of routes or licensing of air taxis. The air traffic demands would absorb even at the present level services with double the existing passenger capacity. For this reason it is all the more necessary that instead of expediencies, plans for the mid-90s should be immediately taken up lest there be a breakdown.

Some Plane Truths

Plane truth about aviation: "grounded by apathy" – a headline in a business newspaper aptly sums up the sad state of affairs in a sector so central to the growth of travel and tourism. In a status report the newspaper suggests that thanks to indecision "the government has done nothing to improve infrastructure, infuse competition and trigger growth". Concerned industry observers are dismayed that five years have gone by since the first draft of a national aviation policy was circulated and it is still on the drawing board. Upgradation of metro airports to contemporary international standards promised by the prime minister and supported by the finance minister with special sizeable allocations in Budget, 2003 is mired in the quest for a suitable legal framework for the Airports Authority through which to implement modernisation. Disinvestment of Air India and Indian Airlines was not allowed to take-off thanks to the disincentives built into the bid norms, and the aftermath of 9/11 has since virtually killed the idea. But after consciously saying goodbye to privatisation what did we do to help the national carriers fend for themselves and compete with big league operators like Lufthansa and British Airways in the west and S1A and Malaysian Airlines in the east or with private operators at home? Both Air India and Indian Airlines continue to be run by bureaucrats from the aviation ministry. Fleet expansion for both has been messed up. There is media type about the two boards meeting to take a final decision on which aircraft and how many to 'buy, and all-one hears at the end of the meetings is one word: postponed. Open-skies continues to be a dirty word at Rajiv Gandhi Bhawan.

Or, take the demand of the private carriers that they be allowed to share some of the foreign routes, now the monopoly of Air India and Indian Airlines. Whatever the policy aspects of this issue, their demand certainly has merit when Air India is unable to use half of its bilateral rights just because it does not have enough aircraft. It would be recalled that the former civil aviation minister, Shahnawaz Husain had in fact announced that Sahara and Jet would be given permission to operate to SAARC countries. It turned out but the matter had not even been placed before the Cabinet! The new minister Rajeev Pratap Rudy has now said that the private carriers' demand will be considered only after the aviation policy has been given final shape. To be fair to the new minister he has been promising to get things task force under Naresh Chandra, former cabinet secretary, to speed up the choice of modalities which the Airport Authority can use for modernising metro airports. Chandra will also recommend an independent regulator for the aviation sector on the lines of TRAI which takes care of the telecom segment. About time the minister appointed a full time chairman for the Airport Authority.

There is some good news about rural tourism, a thrust area emphasised in the National Tourism Policy unveiled last year. The department of tourism (DoT) has signed a tie-up with UNDP under which the international body will help setting up a new type of travel experience described as "endogenous tourism" (The dictionary explains endogenous as 'increasing by internal growth; formed within; with no external cause'). The UNDP-aided project for which there will be a financial assistance of US $1.8 million aims at promoting eco tourism besides creating livelihood opportunities for the rural people. Tourism and culture minister Jagmohan who was present at the signing ceremony said the project will be launched immediately and will be complete by the end of 2007. The idea is to boost village tourism, based on local culture and crafts with a two-fold objective: promotion of eco-tourism and generation of sustainable livelihoods. Both domestic and foreign visitors will be targeted to tour rural tourism sites. Initially, the project will be launched in villages in some states such as the Valley of Flowers region in Uttaranchal, Vishnupur village in West Bengal and Raghuraj village in Orissa. Eventually it will be extended to at least one village in each state and Union Territory to be identified jointly with the local authorities. Jagmohan said that DoT will contribute Rs. 50 lakh (to augment the UNDP allocation) for each village chosen for the project. The money will be used to train local residents in hospitality-related areas and for upgrading the traditional skills of rural artisans. These were precisely the recommendations made at a recent workshop at Bandhavgarh presided over by the Madhya Pradesh chief minister Digvijay Singh as reported in this column, a couple of weeks ago.

And, in a private sector initiative, the Oberoi group which has experience of organising cruises on the Nile as part of its hotel operations in Egypt is bringing the concept to Kerala's backwaters. Beginning November 1 the cruiser M. V. Vrinda will take guests on a cruise from Oberoi's Trident hotel in Cochin.

INADEQUATE INFRASTRUCTURE

Asiad Drew only 200 Paying Alien Fans

The recently completed 9th Asian Games attracted thousands of athletes and officials from 33 countries but drew only 200 paying foreign fans, a govenment tourism official says.

It may have been just as well that not all of the 5,000 foreign tourists expected actually came to the Nov. 19-Dec. 4 games since fewer than 1,200 of the 4,000 promised new hotel rooms actually were ready in time.

Kabindru Selli, divisional publicity director tor the Indian Tourism and Development Corporation, said recently that there were two basic reasons for the poor turnout.

First, he cited "adverse publicity" originating in New Delhi prior to the fames. The stories mentioned lack of facilities in the capital and dealt harshly with the disastrous "test" games held in September.

Secondly, Seth conceded that there had been a lack of coordination between the promotion and the marketing of the Asian Games. Much of the publicity was targeted for the west – for prestige reasons – and that was where most of the tickets, were sent, but the potential fans actually were in the participating countries of Asia and the Middle East.

"People went to the Air India offices (the official marketer abroad) and there were no tickets," he said with a shrug.

Seth discounted the fact that the Indian government decided at the last minute to require – as a security matter – all non-Commonwealth visitors coining to India during the Game to have visas.

Previously, all visitors were allowed entry for 3D days without visas (Commonwealth countries do not require them of each other's citizens). Indian embassies were unprepared suddenly to begin processing visa applications and issuing them.

Few people actually have been denied entry to India since the visa policy went into effect in mid-November, Seth said. Most of those who arrived without visas have been issued landing permits at the airport after screening by police officials.

He failed to mention that the major airlines, having been advised of visa requirements, will not let passengers board their planes unless they have the proper stamp in their passports. This is because regulations make the carriers responsible for their passengers having the proper travelling papers.

As for the hotel rooms, Seth said the four public and nine private hotels being built provided a total of 1,185 rooms for the Games.

Only one of the projects, a major 125-room addition to an existing hotel, was completely finished. Six of the privately owned hotels under construction failed to provide a single room.

One of these, the Air France affiliated Meridien, even held a grand opening, but tour weeks later does not answer its telephone, and has its front entrance barred.

Seth, said the hotel management "wouldn't let people past the lobby. One enterprising reporter asked to see the guest list and they refused because they said it was a matter of security. The reporter asked how many guests were staying there and they said that was a matter of security too."

The government earlier made land and scarce building materials available to the hotels, helped with financing and cut red tape. In return it demanded the hotels have at least some rooms ready for the Games, and threatened to confiscate private facilities that did not open. So far the threat has not been carried out.

Meanwhile, Seth said he had no figures on how much money India might have made or lost on the Games.

"I heard the silver shops did pretty well but I can't say if that was from foreigners or from Indians from other parts of the country," he said.

Asiad officials earlier put the cost of the Games at 85-95 million US dollars. That was for strictly Asiad items such as stadiums and did not include the new hotels, seven major highway overpasses, other municipal improvements and security and service personnel costs. Critics have charged the actual cost was as much as one billion dollars.

By comparison, Soviet officials said they spent 400 million dollars on new facilities for the 1980 (Moscow Olympics). This figure also did not include outlays or related items such as nine new hotels, the Olympic village and costs for service and security personnel.

INDIA'S NEGATIVE IMAGE

'Delhi Belly'

Visiting India has never been recommended for the faint of heart or stomach. Tourists from the time of Alexander the Great have suffered through everything from the water to the weather. "Delhi belly" is as common as an overcharging taxi driver. Heat and dust assume an intensity never before imagined. It is rare to find a tourist who doesn't have at least one major horror story to tell the folks back home.

Yet, few countries can match India's scope for tourism. The Steinbergs' houseboat sits on a picture-perfect lake. The soapstone factory is adjacent to the actual Taj Mahal, one of the few monuments in the world that lives up to its monumental reputation. With the Himalayas and Goa, India has a mountains-and-beach combination that is second to none. There are enough ruins, wild life, 'jostling humanity and exotica to satisfy even the most jaded sightseer.

"Both God and man have given every part of the country some tourist attraction," says Rabindra Seth, an adviser to the Taj group of hotels, which is owned by Indian Hotels Co. "India is a total experience, an assault on all the senses, a place you'll never forget," concludes "India—a Travel Survival Kit." That book is published by Australia's Lonely Planet Publications and considered the bible on India by many travellers.

Unfortunately, India's tourism industry is high on promise, but low on results. Tourism has developed helter-skelter, with little regard and assistance from the government, whose own tourism-related agencies can be just as avaricious as the sidewalk souvenir vendor. Tourists tend to be ignored or taken for granted by the government and become fair game for just about everyone else.

Large Agency

"Our frustration is ... the neglect of the industry for 35 years," says Inder Sharma, chairman of New Delhi–based Sita World Travel (India) Pvt. Ltd., one of the country's largest travel agencies. "If our country had no potential, then it wouldn't matter."

While Singapore and Hong Kong each routinely register three million visitors yearly, India's tourist arrivals topped one million for the first time only last year. For the year ended March 31, tourism-related earnings totaled a government–estimated record 17.8 billion rupees ($1.4 billion), a 22 per cent increase over the previous year. Industry officials say arrivals this year are running almost 10 per cent ahead of 1986.

The jump in 1986 followed five years of stagnation, when arrivals lingered at the 8,00,000 mark. Tourism was hardest hit in 1984, when large-scale riots, political turmoil and uncertainty followed the assassination of Prime Minister Indira Gandhi.

India has long been a must for the down-market, backpacking traveller who can still flop on any sort of bed for less than a dollar a night and wander about in dirt-cheap buses and trains. The average stay of a tourist to India is almost one month and some of the most popular "inns" are religious ashrams.

But only recently has India also gained cachet as a destination for upscale tourists such as the Steinbergs. The reasons are many. The country has basked in the romantic glory of several India-related movies and television series released during the past two years. The yearlong Festival of India, held in France, the US and now the Soviet Union, has what cultural appetites.

There are signs that the government also may be waking up to this newfound interest and the industry's potential. The single biggest barrier to growth has been "government's attitude toward tourism," concedes

S.K. Mishra, the highest-ranking bureaucrat in the Tourism Ministry. "That is gradually changing."

The Tourism Ministry has begun, for the first time, a sophisticated international marketing effort, including the use of TV advertisements overseas. Prospective visitors can obtain a tourist visa much faster than before. It finally is possible to confirm domestic air travel before arrival.

Old Structure

In New Delhi, at least, an arrival in India isn't as excruciating as it once was. Georg Pfluger, a West German student on his second visit to India after five years, terms New Delhi's year-old Indira Gandhi International Airport "splendid" compared with the crowded and dilapidated old structure.

Part of the problem, says Sita's Mr. Sharma, is that the government treats tourism as an "elitist activity," without understanding or appreciating its economic value. True, it is hard to justify sleek luxury hotels when millions lack housing. But many officials also regard the hotels as places for corrupt Indians to spend untaxed money rather than as accommodation for well-heeled foreigners. The hotels "are branded is examples of corruption," says Mr. Sharma.

Not that the country is exactly swimming in luxury hotels. Mumbai, India's premier business centre, has two five-star hotels, twice as many as Kolkata. During the peak season of November to March, they are full. Only New Delhi hosts enough first-class hotels to accommodate its visitors. But even that is getting increasingly difficult.

There is also a question of definition. The government-run India Tourism Development Corporation has a string of hotels they charge first-class rates but often lack first class amenities.

Most tourism facilities are either over stretched or non-existent. At Mumbai's international airport, three immigration officials handle an entire plane of arrival; Hotel reservations are impossible on short notice during the tourist season for the more popular destinations of Agra and Jaipur. During the hottest months of the year, May and June, it is common to have more than 100 waitlisted passengers ousting, shoving, cajoling and pleading for; single seat on a plane to Kashmir.

State-run Indian Airlines has a well deserved reputation for delayed flights and dreadful service. Uwe and Kerstii Achterberg waited hours in Agra's small airport for a flight to Khajuraho also booked solid for weeks during the tourist season—before being told the flight had been cancelled. Airline personnel offered neither assistance in reaching Khajuraho, about

15 hours away by bus, nor accommodation in Agra, says Mr. Achterberg, who runs a travel-book publishing house near Kiel, West Germany.

'Negative Image'

Many bureaucrats refuse to admit to industry shortcomings. Indian Airlines' former managing director, K. Chadha, claimed last year that his airline's inflight service was on a par with any in Asia. "The negative image of India has been created by the foreign media," says the Tourism Ministry's Mr. Mishra, who claims, among other things, that disease in India "isn't a problem now."

Tell that to Mr. Pfluger, the German student, who had to endure bouts of diarrhoea. He also had to stomach a government – run bus to Agra that was canceled because not enough tourists signed up, and he didn't get as many pictures of the Taj Mahal as he wanted because the film sold in Agra was defective.

But like other visitors, after finishing his litany of complaints, he says: "I've enjoyed myself." As "India—a Travel Survival Kit" says: "More than a few visitors are only too happy to finally be getting on the plane and flying away. Yet a year later, they'll be hankering to get back."

Paradise Lost – Islands Need More Development

The statement by Commerce and Tourism Minister Arun Nehru that the government, has big plans for development of Andaman and Nicobar Islands as holiday resorts has ironically come at a time when access to these places has been curtailed by the crippling of air services and reduction in shipping operations. If these are not enough, almost every night Doordarshan shows a cloudy path over Port Blair in the weather map suggesting heavy rain the morning after. If security considerations have for a long time regulated to some of the islands in the archipelago today environmental concerns are held as a deterrent to visit and experience the priceless quiet which is the hallmark of a leisure time tourism product. Still, periodically one hears pronouncements from the high-ups of the tourism set up that the great charms of Andaman and Nicobar should not be missed.

True, the islands are fascinating with a total coastline of 1926 km; which is about one-fourth of the entire length of India's seafront. Of the 572 islands, islets, reefs and rocks only 38 are inhabited. For all the bogey raised about the weather, the temperature ranges between 13 degrees celsius and 31 degrees celsius. In fact, Port Blair and, for that matter, most of the islands are not flatland. One of the islands has a volcanic mound.

The sea around Port Blair is the last home of many species of marine life. Nowhere else in South Asia could we find dolphins. A cruise in a glass bottomed boat unfolds a myriad facets of life under water including the best grown live corals. Incidentally, it takes many years for a coral to be fully grown. Watching them glisten in bright sunshine in the emerald shallows around the islands is an experience possible only in a few parts of the world now. And, the Andaman sea is one of the few such waters.

Though Andaman as known to us has barely two hundred years of history, geographically and geologically, it dates back to several millenia. Our mythological enthusiasts have not been wanting in enterprise to suggest that Andamans was a corrupted term from Hanuman! It was some time in the middle of the 19th century that the British made it a settlement as a rescue station for their shipping lines. Quite a few of the early settlement were killed by tribals. This in turn provoked the British to pursue a policy of enlightened selfishness resulting in the ruin of the Andamanese race. Port Blair itself with its undulating terrain has many pleasant walks in the morning and much to see later in the day. The Cellular Jail, a historic paradox of a horror structure rising in an idyllic setting is in any event a must for the visitor. It is doubtful if any part of the world, not even St. Helena where Napolean was exiled, could claim to a place in history because of its Jail as Port Blair. Kala Pani has since lapsed into history and the jail is a national memorial that every night comes alive with the outcries of the anguished souls of its inmates as conveyd in a light and sound shown. Andamans has no favulous museum but it certainly deserve one that could house an enthropological, historical and natural exhibits under one roof. Even so the present anthropological museum in the ramshackled building provides an insight into the lives and customs of the tribals with whom the visitors are barred from any contact. The reason of course is to respect the sensitivity of the tribals some of whom are totally hostile to outsiders. The administration tries to help them develop in their own way but are not prevented from the mainstream facilities if they choose so. The museum through a series of charts, photographs and implements makes visitors acquianted with tribal lifestyles.

As one drives through the length of Port Blair (named after Archibald Blair who founded the first British settlement), the flora and other dense vegetations come into full view. Though not very much known, the Botanical Garden attached to the soil conservation station is an attraction in itself. Giant flowers at once fragrant and radiant, not seen in any part of the mainland are grown here. Visitor can buy exotic seedlings but one isn't sure how many of them survive in unfamiliar soil or climate. On the way to the garden is another monument raised for fifty odd innocent Indians whom the Japanese during their occupation executed on suspicion of collusion with the British. The names of the victims are a roll call of national integration as it includes people of every faith and almost every region of the mainland.

Leaving thoughts of brutality behind the drive further on for a few minutes lands one on a jetty where boats wait to take the visitors to the unspoilt islands like Jolly Buoy, Red Skin and Havelock.

The Union Territory administration sets much store by these assets and has formulated a perspective plan for promotion and development of tourism. It is estimated that Port Blair and other places of interest together would require accommodation of an additional 900 beds. The plan envisages hotel accommodation for domestic and foreign tourists, development of Port Blair airport to international standards, introduction of luxury liners for inter-island services, a floating restaurant, an orchidarium, a butterfly pen, Asian's first dolphinariam and provision of a cable car connecting the topmost point on Mount Herrict with Ross Island on the lines of Singapore-Santosa Island link. One is not sure whether in the context of national priorities funds would be forthcoming for all the enterprises at once. The central government it is learnt has agreed to provide facilities for aqua sports but more investment would be necessary. Here, the private sector could be enlisted as is already being done in the mainland. In fasiness to the private sector, it has done some pioneering effort particularly for the upmarket by setting up two hotels, one by the Welcomgroup and the other by TCI. Welcomgroup's Bay Island is a Charles Correa creation, a three-tier of building in modules all gliding from an elevated rock to the waterfront. The building itself is a architectural masterpiece that blends with environment. The management very thoughtfully keeps its facilities attuned to that of a retreat with a definite prompting to the guest to be in communion with nature. (If the guest does not get any metropolitan newspaper from Delhi, Kolkata or Chennai, he does not miss it.) Every balcony has a view of the sea. The sight is so absorbing that few waste time in caring to read the disheartening headlines of the day. Still, for addicts there is newspaper stand in the lobby. Nor, have the rooms any TV. There is a compulsive need for more people from the mainland to visit the island chain to foster a sense of belonging. One wonders how many of our people know that India's southernmost extremity is Indira Gandhi Point and not Kanniyakumari. These islands are as much part of India as any other territory in the country. As for foreign tourists (now the overseas visitors are only Russians because of the low priced package) there is considerable potential in the markets of western and northern Europe. But it is imperative that air services will have to be more frequent. From the 12 normal services a week, which were far from being adequate, Indian Airlines now operate only 7, four from Chennai and 3 from Kolkata. A single return fare from Delhi for any Indian to visit this part of this land will cost as much as Rs. 8,000 while it would cost much less for a week's holiday in Bangkok, fare included! As Khatri pointed out there is urgent need for subsidised fares as is done in the northeast.

Which leads on to the thought why not put Port Blair on the Indian Airlines Bangkok route? Port Blair is a mere 450 km from Bangkok and this could generate foreign traffic as well. The only additional investment is improvement of the airports customs and immigration facilities already exist in Port Blair. A few more islands nearer Port Blair could be opened and a few more faster boats could be provided to prompt the visitor to stay longer. If these are done, Andamans could reduce the burden of the central subsidy and there will be meaningful content to Arun Nehru's optimistic statement.

Will the Boom Days Return

It was the best of times, it was the worst of times. That is, perhaps, how 1983-84 will go down in the annals of Indian tourism. The period had begun on an extremely promising note. The Asiad held in the closing weeks of 1982 gave India tremendous exposure around the world.

More concretely, it meant 10 new hotels for the capital (thereby doubling New Delhi's room capacity) widened roads and flyovers.

Then came NAM and CHOGM both bringing even more exposure to India as well as declaring an assertion of the country's ability to be the venue for large international gatherings.

Around this time films like *Gandhi, Passage to India, The Far Pavillions* and *Jewel in the Crown* did much to foster interest in India as a rich and colourful tourist destination.

Back home, the tourist arrival target was set down to 2.5 million, only a little less ambitious than the original target set in 1967. The resistance to air charters decreased and the first ever tourism policy was enunciated. Publicity and promotion, both by the government and the industry, picked up and the year 1983 ended with a modest recovery, the growth rate in arrivals going up by *2.9* per cent.

Many of these promising gains were offset by disturbing events. Recession continued to take its toll whilst the increase in tourism-international peace is one of them—made their influence felt on tourist arrivals. Overland traffic which had been affected by events in Afghanistan and Iran was further affected by the Iran-Iraq war. Even the turmoil in Sri Lanka made its impact on Indian tourism because of India's close proximity to the island.

And finally there was the question of visa restrictions. Initially imposed for Asiad they were continued for NAM and CHOGM and were not lifted ever after the two events. The uproar in the tourist industry has abated, as later events have vindicated the pragmatic stand taken by the Home Ministry (they were the final arbiters in this matter and proved that issues like internal safety and defence had to be given priority over tourism requirements.

The impact of the recent tragic events that engulfed the country can be gauged by taking a look at the tourist arrival figures for 1984. Official data is available for only upto the end of October. The first ten months show an increase of two per cent (almost the same figure as that of the previous year. But November must have been one of the worst months. According to unofficial estimates the drop in the arrivals was as much as 25 per cent and even if December shows an improvement the final count for the year would for the first time show minus growth. At this point it is pertinent to briefly sketch India's achievements in the tourism sector.

A late-comer to the race for international tourism India took rapid strides. From a mere 17,000 tourist arrivals in 1951, the number of foreign visitors grew to nearly 1,60,000 in 1966. A more than nine-fold increase in a decade and a half. This has turned out to be a land mark in the country's tourism effort.

In the following year, i.e.,1967, a separate Ministry of Tourism under a cabinet-ranking minister was set up. So encouraged were the tourism planners by the performance of the previous fifteen years that for the first time the country was given a target of one million overseas visitors by the end of the 70s. Meanwhile, the three years before the target decade began—1967-68 and 69—turned in even more encouraging trends A growth rate of 29.6 per cent in 1969 is a record yet to be surpassed.

The target of one million tourists by 1980 was based on a growth rate of 15 per cent. Surprisingly the country did manage to achieve an average growth rate of 13 per cent and an arrival figure of 8,00,000.

Surprising, because this was the'period when the fuel crisis overtook the world which greatly affected travel costs, brought in recessionary conditions, not to apeak of the Bangladesh crisis. Incidentally India's tourism growth rate waft almost twice as high as the average world growth rate during the 70s which was around eight per cent.

And, although, an early warning of an impending crisis in tourist arrivals did come in 1979 when the growth rate look a nose-dive to 2.2 per cent from the previous year's 16.8 per cent, the then tourism minister felt emboldened to set a target of 3.5 million arrivals by 1990. Assuming thereby a growth rate of 15 per cent. It was hoped that by 1985, 1.7 million travellers would come into India. And, it was not just the high growth rate of the 70s that had led the government to fix an ambitious target. The tourism infrastructure too developed at a rapid pace.

From a total of merely 8,000 rooms in international class hotels in the country (Bangkok city alone had more rooms) at the beginning of the 70s, there were in 1980 nearly 20,000 rooms.

Indian Airlines, once a deterrent to foreign travellers because of a paucity of seats and low confirmations had now augmented its fleet and streamlined its reservations, it was also offering a competitive Discover India Fare. The Railways introduced the Indrail Pass (like the Eurait in Europe). Tourism publicity had received a shot in the arm from such events as the meeting in India in 1978 of the Pacific Area Travel Association (PATA) and of UNIDO in 1980.

In fact the growth rate picked up in 1980 to 4.6 per cent and to 6.6 per cent in 1981. But it was around the same time that other factors began influencing tourist traffic. Recession, especially among the tourist generating countries in the west, was at its worst. Events in Iran and then Afghanistan, not only choked the sizeable overland traffic into India but also turned many an intending visitor to this sub-continent to other 'safer' destinations. The result: 1982 was the first year in which the growth rate dropped to less than one per cent, zero to be precise.

It would be wrong, however, to take a pessimistic view of the situation. A concerted and co-ordinated effort on the part of both Government and the industry can not only retrieve lost ground but provide for a more rapid growth. This would require both long term and short-term measures. The first need is to restore confidence among the intending travellers to India.

A Public Relations blitz overseas, both by sending a number of delegations (consisting both of government and industry) as well as by inviting larger numbers of travel agents and travel writers to India, would go a long way in assuring the foreigner that in spite of the size and diversity of this country and the enormity of the passions aroused, peace was restored in less than three days.

Not only that, the country was able to gear itself for a general election, a stupendous exercise even for advanced countries. No tourist came to grief. India continues to share its hospitality and warmed with the honoured guests, as we call the visitors from overseas. A good beginning has already been made by the Director General of Tourism who has himself led a delegation to the Gulf countries.

As for the visa while considerations of security must reign supreme, a lot could be done by strengthening consular staff at our missions, streamlining of procedures and a liberal approach to those travelling as groups or those who travel with escorts.

In the long-term, there is need for a more realistic attitude to prohibition, improvement in infrastructure like airports, railway reservations and removing such deterrents as touts, beggars and lack of hygiene in public places. Not all of this costs money.

Now that tourism has become the number one earner of foreign exchange—some 1,300 crores—let the Planning Commission lift it from the bottom of its list of priorities to a more respectable place. The answer to this question and many others that have hampered the growth of tourism will have to wait until the new government has had time to settle down.

Tourism: 1990 – Expectations Belied

It was at once a year of expectations and that of disillusionment. 1990 in fact began on a euphoric note. The industry and the government had agreed to organise an 'India Tourism Year' in 1991. There was every indication of a positive response from international hotel chains to invest for the first time in hospitality services. The new government made it obvious that atleast in respect of tourism promotion and development the policy will be one of continuity of liberalisation and incentives. A major irritant until then namely inadequate capacity on the domestic services was to be removed with a bang through the augmentation of the IA fleet with 19 A-320s. It was thought that at the political level the new government would be able to take initiatives in resolving the problem of law and order in parts of Northern India. The mood of expectancy was on the swell, reinforced by announcements made by big hotel chains of plans to invest more and expand the accommodation sector.

Things took a different turn early enough to belie the expectations. The turmoil in Kashmir not only slowed the tourist inflow into the state but also snowballed into cancellations of group visits to other parts of northern India. The aircrash of an A-320 in Bangalore in February put paid the hopes of Indian Airlines to emerge out of rather troubled times. The domestic air-transport bottleneck was again seized upon in the principal tourist markets of the world as a major deterrent to tourism promotion. Delegations both official and non-official which went to scour the markets returned with little to enthuse about. No wonder then, the growth rate registered a decline for the first time since 1984.

Government did make some SOS efforts to strengthen the infrastructure in alternative destinations. New fiscal incentives were offered to entrepreneurs who build hotels in rural and hill areas. The South was billed as an all-season destination which could be covered by surface transport. The multifaceted tourism product in the South was offered to a variety of interests ranging from architecture to 'sun and sand'. Special meetings of the regional groups including state officials and representatives of all segments of tourist trade met on more than one occasion. Still, at the end of the year, it is found that much more needs to be done to familiarise the attractions of the peninsula to markets which are interested only in the golden triangle of Delhi, Agra and Jaipur with a few extensions. As months progressed Kashmir became virtually lost to tourism both domestic and foreign. An attempt to make Himachal Pradesh as an alternative to Kashmir did not catch on because of lack of facilities and absence of quick communications.

The only sunny streak in an otherwise dismal shadow cast was Goa and for this was more due to tradition than innovative promotion. In the last two years, Goa has been a major draw in the European market in winter months during which there is a great movement of people towards warms beaches anywhere. Goa's share is still low of this traffic. But the hopes have been sustained by charters from Germany and Austria. At the same time Goa-bound traffic which formerly used to stop over in the north underwent a change in the itinerary. The India stay was reduced to that extent.

Though tourism in Sri Lanka picked up a little with its fallout benefit to the southern destinations in India, the totality of the scene pointed to stagnation and slide down. The unrest in Nepal fora while disrupted the inflow for adventure tourism and pilgrim traffic in eastern India. There were signs of revival towards the middle of the year but these vanished as many parts of northern India were gripped by the anti-reservation agitations. As if these were not enough, the governments of the United States and France, both main markets, advised their citizens on the hazards of travelling in India. Also about the same time Saddam Hussein triggered the Gulf crisis raising apprehensions of a global recession which is certainly not propitious for tourism, particularly leisure travel to long-haul destinations like India. Business travel, not normally affected by problems of law and order in remote places also suffered a damper when word spread of political instability at the Centre. Businessmen looking for new collaboration contracts preferred to postpone or cancel their trips for the present as they were not sure whether commitments would be abiding.

Also the controversies about liberalisation enunciated as part of the revised industrial policy inhibited many from undertaking visits at the present juncture. The communal tensions over Ayodhya and the world-wide publicity it received proved a further deterrent to India-bound travellers. The cumulative effect of all these developments was the low occupancy in hotels, poor sales of handicrafts and the consequent drop in foreign exchange earnings on this account. In any event matters would not remain bleak for ever. The industry has admirably responded to the situation by demonstrating its faith in the future. It is going ahead with the plans for expansion of hotels and other services. This is perfectly justified as when conditions improve and international tourism revives, India could not fall short of the expectations. Twenty thousand additional rooms are in the pipelines, expected to be commissioned in the next 18 months.

The setbacks of 1990 have not deterred the industry and the department of tourism from going ahead with programmes for 'India Tourism Year' that will begin on new year's day. Indian Airlines too is getting back to its normal services after the painfully slow return to operations of A-320. The south is directly being linked to European tourism generating markets. Kolkata cannot be far behind if the enthusiasm shown by the state government in its new found interest in tourism is any indication. The situation at the year-end enables an optimistic though cautious outlook for 1991. Of course much would depend on the developments in the coming weeks. Once again expectations are aroused and one can hope disillusionment will not repeat.

How Serious are we – A Note of Caution

The travel trade has done well in cautioning the government that all the spendings on specially promoting "India Tourism Year" 1991 will be of no avail, if the infrastructure remains inadequate. The travel trade ought to know what it is talking about, because most of the tourism is developed by private enterprises. Many in the business had been worried in the last few months of group cancellations from overseas. At least one Australian tour operator engaged in Indian business has pulled back. The others Britain, major ones at that, (and mind you, UK is the number one generating market) have slowed their promotional efforts and conveyed to their Indian handlers that they might follow the Australian's action. The reasons are not necessarily the troubled situation in Kashmir. In fact, this was bluntly brought home to a high level Indian tourism delegation led by the Secretary of the Ministry himself during his European itinenary. In West Germany, tour operators told the delegation "our worry is not Kashmir or Punjab but the mercurial fluctuations of domestic air services". They were not far off the mark. Indian travel agents could vouchsafe for any number of instances in recent months of delayed, cancelled or aborted flights upsetting the schedule of entire groups.

In the circumstance, one could appreciate the sigh of relief from the trade on prospects of resumption of A-320 operations. Bur all the 14 grounded aircraft and the four yet to be taken delivery of, will take weeks before they are fully inducted. Indian Airlines itself has claimed that the resumption of operations would be phased. This would mean that the situation may not go through an absolute turn around for another couple of months. Low occupancies in hotels in all centres of tourist and business interests will continue. So much so, July and August might prove the leanest months for Indian tourism in years. Normally business travel should not be swayed by factors which influence tourist movements. But in the present situation the confusion caused by the contradictory postures in the ruling party on economic policies particularly in regard to investments is certainly not going to unleash India-bound business traffic.

Only five months are left for India Tourism Year to begin. Tourists plan their visits abroad eighteen to twenty four months in advance. The only step they take at short notice is cancellations. In the light of the setbacks of recent months, the trade is apprehensive of the trends in the overseas market. Doubtless, the easing of visa regulations in the United Kingdom for travel to this country, is a welcome step. But this has to be followed up elsewhere in the existing and emerging markets. If there is any bilateral move with other countries to relax the visa regulations including the lowering of the high visa fees, it seems to be a treasured secret. The trade is not aware of it and the spokespersons of generating markets have given no indication of it either.

The authorities cannot plead that there was little time for preparation for the year. As early as May 1989, in Chennai at the annual convention of the Travel Agents Association, the government spokespersons mooted the idea of tourism year which they preferred to term as Visit India year. Probably the sponsors were carried away by the success of similar exercises by other favoured destinations like Thailand. But in fairness to the trade, even at that time, fully aware of the constraints, its representatives wondered if the country was ready for meeting the challenges of a tourist influx. On consequential revised thinking the sponsors renamed it "India Tourism Year" whose main objective was scaled down to arousing awareness about

India as a destination and not so much as to receive a far larger number of travellers.

Even this limited objective has not been reinforced by an offer of substantial facilities to the visitors. On the other hand recent reports raising the possibility of closure of overseas tourist promotion offices would deprive the would be traveller of outlets for basic information. While it is stated that this work could be transferred to the Indian missions, such an exercise, needless to say, would be least productive without saving any expenditure. In fact, that would be the surest way of turning away visitors to destinations other than India. By now, the generating markets should have been flooded with information on what special things the country would offer during the year not only in terms of sight-seeing but also in package costs. For instance, there should be discount offers and incentives all along the line, more duty free entitlements, rebated hotel accommodation, concessional domestic air travel, and other indigenously made items in government emporia and shopping complexes during the India Tourism Year, 1991. An innovative medical cover would be an added attraction. There is hardly any sign of such initiatives here. A calendar of festivals on mangoes, kites and the like which has been drawn up is hardly a substitute for incentives to come to India. The president of Indian Association of Tour Operators (IATO), O.P. Ahuja was not wrong, when at a recent convention in Jaipur he chose the focal theme "Tourism; Are we serious?" There was no affirmative answer in the deliberations.

The situation was best illustrated in the scenario in Rajasthan where the IATO meeting took place. The State Minister for Tourism waxed eloquent on all the delights the state offered. A few days later she levied taxes that raised the cost of the tourist product in the state. In neighbouring Gujarat, where enforcement of prohibition keeps hotel revenues down, a thirty per cent luxury tax hits the industry and the customer alike. And this, in addition to the 20 per cent hotel expenditure tax levied by the centre. In fact, there is very little co-ordination on tourism taxation policies among the states. Nor are the benefit entitlements to entrepreneurs uniform. According to the National Committee on Tourism, the country needs 6,000 additional rooms a year.

There has been much talk of big foreign chains eager to invest their money and expertise on the Indian hotel industry. Big industrial houses have also spoken of plans to venture into the accommodation sector. The ITDC and similar public sector undertakings in the states have spoken of plans of going in or medium priced hotels. But all these have not gone beyond, at best, the drawing boards. The Planning Commission has made its point clear: development of tourism has to be in the private sector. But such is the tangled procedural web that bureaucracy has spun that these plans get stuck there. It is in this context that the note of caution struck by the trade has become relevant.

AS USUAL – UNFULFILLED PLANS

Of Mega Plans and Projects Fading into Oblivion

Dream projects of the mid-nineties have become faded memories in less than five years. Yet, these were the projects which the tourism sector set much store on strengthening the infrastructure in terms of accommodation, business needs and transportation. Every one of the seven projects was hailed as a reflection of a great vision and requisite mega thinking on tourism's needs.

At the time these projects were conceived, the expected deadlines for their completion was well before the turn of the century. Now, just six months before we enter the next century no one talks about it except that it never was. Interestingly, all these mega projects were contemplated immediately after tourism had reached its peak as far back as in 1995 and 1996, giving rise to speculation about shortages if that momentum had been sustained.

Of course, the momentum was lost for varying reasons, mostly beyond the control of the industry if not of the country itself. All the projects surfaced as if in a burst of investment interest in hospitality services. If there is one lesson to be inferred from their collective fiasco it is that such projects can materialise with considerable advance planning, involving the widest industry participation and coordination in public-private partnership and Centre-state cooperation.

The first project that comes to mind is the great hotel-cum-convention complex in the Bandra-Kurla area, masterminded by the Mumbai Metropolitan Regional Development Authority (MMRDA). First conceived in 1994, it envisaged an investment of over a thousand crore of rupees on a 750 room hotel along with a five thousand-seater modern convention centre, which would have been the biggest in South Asia.

Tenders were floated and the Mumbai-based Leela venture successfully bid for it only to withdraw within the year on grounds of technicalities. Another year passed before the Authority could float a fresh global tender, which this time was picked up by the Taj Group. The Taj Group abandoned the project because of a change in investment policies which favoured consolidation of the existing assets. After being bitten twice, MMRDA seems to be shying away from a third attempt. The impasse could have been avoided had there been adequate homework.

It is the same malaise of lack of advance planning which aborted a twin hotel project in south Delhi, which HUDCO wanted to contract out. It was to consist of a four-star hotel and a five-star deluxe. Here too, two bidders successively sunk crores of rupees only to be mired in legal disputes. And now there is the astounding revelation that the Capital's Master Plan did not even provide for a project of this type!

Another ambitious scheme was Delhi's Hotel City project, in which the former director general of tourism, Ashok Pahwa, in his previous tenure as DDA vice-chairman had initiated. A whole complex of hotels in various categories, shopping malls, entertainment centres and conference facilities were to have come up as a model to the rest of the metro cities. The scheme was unveiled with great fanfare.

It was to have a spin-off effect on neighbouring Gurgaon, where a second Hotel City was to spring up. The promoters, DDA had not taken into reckoning what a few environmentalists can do to delay if not foil the project. It is now on hold and no one in authority or outside, in DDA, Ministry of Tourism or the Environment Ministry or the would be bidders talks about it. The Airport Authority of India (AAI), which persuaded the tourism sector to dream of an international class golf course in the Delhi airport area as well as larger duty-free shopping facilities. Several bids later, both projects were throttled by red tape and inter-ministerial wrangles. One is not sure if they would ever be revived.

Much has been written and argued about Bangalore's possibilities as a Convention City. The state government itself was keen on a big convention centre and several possibilities were explored. The last one heard fit was that Leela venture, on its initiative, acquired land for this purpose but has had to put the project on hold for its own reasons. The Bangalore airport project, which is to lend great infrastructural support to tourism's focus in the south, presents an all too familiar 'now on, now off' dismal story.

Experience makes anyone skeptical of the hope recently aroused by an understanding between the state government and the Airport Authority. If the story of these projects of the past makes depressing reading, a very recent human tragedy points to the shortfall in the response of the industry and the ministry. To say the least, it is callous and uncaring, particularly when the industry is promoting cruise tourism through a media blitz.

The ill-fated Sun Vista cruise ship that left 120 Indian holiday makers stranded once again, heightens the need for safety and security of tourists.

Shockingly, not even the travel agency which booked the passengers has come out with any sympathy or details.

Budget 2001 Ignores Tourism

The hospitality industry had great expectations from Budget 2001. These expectations had been fuelled by the 'audience' granted by the finance minister on the eve of the budget to a delegation representing all segments of tourism – hoteliers, travel agents, tour operators, transporters and even the tourism committees of various chambers of commerce. Tourism minister Ananth Kumar led the delegation signifying that the industry and the ministry spoke with one voice, a rare occurrence. Their demands had been narrowed down to three areas: infrastructure status for tourism; abolition of Hotel Expenditure Tax (HET) and liberalisation of concessions available for deduction of profits earned in foreign exchange. The delegation was conscious that the havoc caused by the Gujarat earthquake may inhibit Yashwant Sinha from giving too many sops but it was confident that after years of lobbying, the government was now convinced of the role tourism could play in generating employment and creating wealth. But industry watchers heard with dismay as the finance minister announced sops for IT, gems and jewellery, even automobiles, while there was nothing for tourism, not even a mention of its contribution to the economy, in spite of the fact that without any priority status it is earning the third largest amount of foreign exchange. The finance minister has created a record of sorts by ignoring tourism for the third time in a row.

One must hasten to add that the budget has been hailed as one which is both reformist and growth oriented. The thrust on highways, power and telecom will ultimately help tourism. But there are a number of challenges before this sector, especially the burden of taxation, which needed to be addressed. Travel industry doyen Inder Sharma puts it succinctly. "As a tax payer, it (the budget) is welcome. But tourism continues to be one of the most heavily taxed industries. Almost 40 per cent of the land cost goes into various taxes' and government revenues." He adds that, "The treatment given to tourism is a clear indication that neither the industry nor the ministry has been able to carry any conviction with the finance minister.

Lalit Suri, President, Hotel Association of India (HAI) in his comment, laments that the budget 'has failed to lay a road map to unleash the vast untapped potential of tourism to boost the growth rate of the national economy'. Globally, he points out, the tourism sector accounts for 10.5 per cent of GDP while in India tourism accounts for only 1.5 per cent of GDP. Suri says, "Given the righ; incentives and environment for the growth of infrastructure, tourism could help raise the GDP growth from six to 6.5 per cent as envisaged in the budget." The HAI president is said that the tourism industry's long standing demand for grant of infrastructure status has been ignored; its plea for abolition of HET, which amounts to double taxation (as state governments also levy their own luxury tax on hotels) has also not been considered. He adds that the tourism industry depends for its success on the health of the economy which, of late, has witnessed a slow down. There are encouraging signs, Suri notes, that the budget will stimulate growth and lead to enhanced and improved connectivity with its emphasis on related infrastructure like roads and airports. But, he cautions, "The fine print will, however, need to be studied for a fuller assessment of the impact of the budget."

On behalf of the other hotel apex body, FHRAI, secretary-general Shyam Suri also expressed disappointment that tourism did not find even a mention in the budget despite being the highest employment generator and third largest foreign exchange earner. He said that on the finance minister's own admission, the services sector (of which tourism is a major part) contributes as much as 50 per cent to the GDP. Yet the only reference to it comes in the context of widening the tax net by extending service tax to more activities. For him, the only redeeming feature is that there is no increase in the existing levies on tourism.

The past president of the Indian Tourist Transporters Association (ITTA), Mukesh Goel, said the travel industry deserved a break as high taxes had made the Indian package uncompetitive in south-east Asia, which has been aggravated by the recent hefty increase in entry fees to national monuments. He is unhappy about the countervailing duty imposed on the import of second-hand cars and utility vehicles. While this may serve the interests of indigenous manufacturers, it will have an adverse impact on tourist transporters who desperately need utility vehicles for adventure tours, which are yet to be manufactured within the country. He is also afraid that the pace at which conversion to CMC is being insisted upon in parts of the country may drive tourist coaches off the road.

A deeper study of the budget would, however, show that there are a number of proposals which would bring in long-term benefits to tourism. Apart from the prospects of better roads, uninterrupted power and efficient telecommunication, the proposed changes in the labour laws will be a boon to companies employing less than 1,000 workers. For the rest, the travel industry must try, try again.

Fee Hike's Discrimination to Hit Tourism

Rationalisation of taxes has been a longstanding demand of the travel industry, voiced over the years at successive trade association conventions. The central Department of Tourism (DOT) has been supportive of this demand and even went to the extent of getting state tourism ministers at the last two conferences in the Capital to agree that they would address this issue seriously. More recently, at the FHRAI conference in Mumbai, minister Ananth Kumar offered to lead a delegation of industry representatives to the finance minister in this regard, saying that he himself was fully convinced that rationalised taxes on hotels, road transport and other tourist services, both at the central and state levels, would go a long way in giving a push to tourism.

The plethora of taxes, their high incidence and vast variations from one state to another, has not only made the Indian package costly but is also a factor in making it lose out to competition from neighbouring countries of Asia, besides being irksome for travellers coming on repeat visits. It is, therefore, surprising that the tourism and culture minister, far from persuading his own Cabinet colleague in charge of finance, and ministers, holding that portfolio in the states, has allowed the department of culture to increase the entry fee for foreigners visiting Indian monuments fourfold at one go and with less than a week's notice. And without any consultation with the trade on the practical aspects of the hike. It is not known whether the department of culture, which authorised the Archaeological Survey of India (ASI) to revise the entry fee for all the monuments in its care, ever took the DOT into confidence or sought its views. Probably not. For, DOT would have advised its sister department about the global practice of giving a changeover period of at least three months before revising the entry fee to enable the trade to adjust its contractual obligations to its clients. Take one instance related to this writer by Davinder Puri, chairman, Ezee Travel, who has just conducted a group of 23 visitors from Chile, South America, around Aurangabad, Delhi, Agra, Fatehpur Sikri, Khajuraho and Varanasi. It cost him an additional US$ 125 per tourist, which he had to pay from his own pocket, as the package was priced on the basis of the earlier entry fee.

The issue's not the losses that tour operators and travel agents handling inbound traffic will have to incur. In fact, the Indian Association of Tour Operators (IATO) made a tactical error in using this plea (of losses) in their writ petition, which the Delhi High Court declined to entertain and instead directed them to approach the department of culture for a redressal. Also, it is nobody's case that the fee should not be raised at all. Not only does ASI need a lot more money for the proper upkeep of the monuments, but it is conceded by everyone that the present rates charged in this country are ridiculously low as compared to the rest of the world. The real issue is the extent of the increase and the short notice of less than a week for its implementation, and, equally importantly, its impact on the cost of the Indian package which is under severe pressure from competing destinations.

Industry vetern Inder Sharma Chairman emeritus, Sita Travels, says the entry fee would now account for 25 per cent of the total cost of a package, compared to about six per cent earlier. He adds that increased air-fares and higher luxury taxes, plus a hefty 30-35 per cent hike in the visa fees, are 'bound to affect the flow of tourists to India'. Already, Indian promoters have been having a tough time dispelling the erroneous impression abroad that our hotels are over priced. They will now have a tougher time answering queries about the higher entry fees and the so-called discrimination against foreigners.

The department of culture has not bothered to explain why the fee could not be hiked in phases, 'nor why no' notice was given to the trade. But it has effectively defended itself against the charge of discrimination. Dr RV Vaidyantha Ayyar, secretary, has been quoted as having said that 'it was only a taxation measure linked to the paying capacity and a sound and accepted principle of public finance'. Differential tariff, he said, is prevalent in many parts of the world. In Nepal, for instance, the entry fee for Bhaktapur is NR 50 for SAARC nationals and NR 750 for others. Similarly, in Sri Lanka, a visit to Anuradhapuram is free for the locals but foreigners have to pay US$ 15. Entering only the pyramid complex in Egypt costs a local one Egyptian pound, while a foreigner pays 20, and to enter a pyramid itself, foreigners have to pay 40 pounds while Egyptians pay only five pounds. IATO, whose members will have to bear the brunt of ASI's hasty action, is naturally up in arms. Its president, Subhash Goyal, has, in an emotional outburst, threatened to 'gherao' the minister and have the matter raised in Parliament. Founder president Ram Kohli, in a letter to Ananth Kumar, expressed the trade's shock over the sudden increase in fee and said that the magnitude of the hike and the timing (when the tourist season has just begun) are 'unparalled anywhere'.

Spirit is Willing but the Action is Weak

At a post-budget interaction with IATO, tourism minister Anant Kumar seemed to agree with most of tour operators' demands but that left one wondering why he could not persuade the finance minister a little earlier to make at least a reference to tourism's contribution to growth. But, that did not prevent him from promising the IATO functionaries that he would now take up their cause with Yashwant Sinha. It is doubtful if any positive result could come from such an exercise in the context of the tone and tenor of the budget speech. The IATO president and his aides lost no moment in raising with the minister their obsessively familiar complaint about Service Tax. Only the previous day Sinha had categorically told parliament that a committee would go into the entire coverage of Service Tax in order to make it more widely applicable and until then the status quo will continue. The status quo in respect of tour operations means that the levy is in abeyance. Still, one is puzzled by the minister's promise that he would take up the matter with the finance minister the next day.

If the finance minister does not share the urgency of tour operators or his cabinet colleagues to treat tour operators apart from those covered by the levy, it is in line with his seeming reluctance to refer to tourism at all notwithstanding all talk of prioritisation.

Sinha did not deem it necessary to refer to the gains from tourism acknowledged by his own ministry in its Economic Survey. Instead of offering any incentives to the generation of benefits he announced a definite disincentive, namely, taking away from the bulk of industry incentives for export. True, all exporters are covered by the five-year phase out-of-tax exceptions but unlike in most cases the outgo in the case of the tourism sector is minimal. As much as 60 per cent of the profits of major hotel chains are in foreign exchange. It is common knowledge that even in this period of comparative stagnation these chains are continuing with their massive investment plans. The three largest – ITC, Taj and Oberois – account for a commitment of Rs. 4,000 crore. One reason for their readiness to invest is the incentive that has been available to them so far under the income tax law. Under this concession, while 50 per cent is exempt straight away, the entire balance is eligible for total tax relief if re-invested in tourism. So, all chains preferred to create new assets availing of this incentive, thereby lessening accommodation shortages which constitute the biggest infrastructural inadequacy in the tourism sector. Tourism, along with IT, is recognised worldwide as a sunrise industry with immense potential for the creation of wealth and generation of employment. Whether the finance minister at the end of the budget debate will make a concession in the respect of tourism on this score remains to be seen. It will be in the interests of the economy and the revival of tourism that he treat the travel industry as a special case particularly when it has not been given any other relief in the budget. Hopefully the tourism minister will have some success in this effort.

Without belittling the role of tour operators in fostering tourism growth it has to be mentioned that even when every segment has been ignored in the budget speech they try to claim one upmanship in intra-trade disputes. For instance, at the interactive session where the minister had been invited to hear the industry's demands which have been overlooked, IATO members raked up the controversial claim of being the first recipient of foreign exchange remittance. It was amusing that when the relief is zero here is a section clamouring for a share. Worse, they also used the occasion to articulate their feud with hoteliers on the so-called dual tariff question. The minister drew cheers from them when he proclaimed his support to a single tariff. But neither the minister nor the IATO officials sharing the dais with him cared to remember that the entire matter is subjudice.

There were other issues also on which the minister and others demonstrated they were yet to be updated. For instance, the minister showed over enthusiasm by claiming that he hoped to double the number of international arrivals to five million within the year. Obviously he had not given much thought to that unlikely event and its implications. How will an additional two million people travel to India when the available air capacity is less than 50 per cent? And, where will they stay? The country is short of 60,000 rooms. And the finance minister has not helped his cabinet colleagues in overcoming the shortages in five years.

Tourism Momentum Still Elusive

Going by the figures released by the department of tourism (DoT), a slight recovery in arrivals is noticeable. While the fall in October – the month immediately following the events of September was a hefty 28 per cent, the decline came down to 24 per cent in November, and 15 per cent in December. Of course, the year as a whole has ended with a minus six per cent growth wiping off the good showing in the months prior to September. The count for 2001, the first year of the new millennium is 2.48 million against 2.64 million in 2000. It is too early to say if there has been or will be a major impact on arrivals because of the tension on India's western borders. Any further escalation could only scare travellers away from the subcontinent.

There has been much talk of initiatives to meet the situation created by terrorism and slowing down of economies in a large part of the world. Minister Jagmohan and director general Vinod Duggal have been travelling overseas and also interacting with industry leaders at home. But, beyond a minor relaxation in the service tax on hotel banqueting, no major step has been announced either on behalf of the government or as a joint public and private sector initiative. Prime Minister Atal Bihari Vajpayee's announcement that dual citizenship for Non-Resident Indians (NRIs) is in the offing is to be welcomed but it would be many months before the scheme (to be approved by the cabinet) is ready for implementation. In any event, this and the much hyped PIO (People of Indian Origin) card with specific facilities can only bring in long-term benefits. Interestingly, though Jagmohan's predecessor, Ananth Kumar had assured the industry that within a year the elusive target of five million tourists would be made good by NRIs alone.

Some observers feel that lack of unity in the industry is largely responsible for various segments like airlines, hotels, travel agents, tour operators, transporters and even shops not coming together to offer attractive packages which countries like Sri Lanka, Malaysia and Thailand have done with good. Small wonder that the new tourism secretary, Rathi Vinay Jha, at her very first interface with the industry IATO's monthly lunch on December 5, 2001. Stressed the need for unity not only between the government and the industry but also within the industry itself. Pointing out that a similar united approach was necessary for Centre and the states in addressing the needs of tourism, she sought the industry's help in this task. The states need to be persuaded to rationalise taxes and industry should lobby with them providing data and an assurance that rationalisation could bring higher revenue while reducing the burden on tourists. She was hopeful that DoT's pleas with the finance minister for reliefs will reflect a positive response in the coming budget. The main item on IATO's lunch meeting was to welcome the new secretary and to bid farewell to M. P. Bezbaruah, who retired at the end of November, after a five-year stint in tourism and a life-long distinguished career in IAS. Maharaj Wahi, IATO president presented a momento to Bezbaruah.

Director general Duggal, who also spoke at the meeting, recalled the assurance given on behalf of the Planning Commission for a much larger allocation for tourism in the tenth plan now under preparation. With additional funds, he said, DoT would be in a position to finance direct cooperative marketing with international airlines (American carriers to begin with). He said he was also hopeful of reviving the market development fund under which the department contributes to promotional efforts abroad of travel agents and tour operators. He also shared with IATO members the good news that the government had restored the cut (of nearly, 50 per cent) in DoT's overseas budget which was imposed recently.

In a related development, the PHD Chamber of Commerce and Industry, which has been actively lobbying with state governments on behalf of the travel industry through its tourism and civil aviation committee headed by

V. N. Dalmia, has secured a measure of relief for tourist transporters in Madhya Pradesh. The state government has issued a notification exempting approved tourists vehicles from transport tax for two years. Of course, there are a number of 'conditions and restrictions' including one which requires such vehicles to be painted white with a blue ribbon. And, in order to avail of the exemption, the owner of the vehicle will have to deposit a security amount of Rs. 1,00,000 which can be forfeited if the conditions of the permit are violated. It is not known how tourist transporters in Madhya Pradesh will react to the conditions and the requirement of such a hefty amount of security. But it is a laudable move on the part of the state government. Hopefully other states will follow suit.

India Tourism – Many Miles to Go

Annual General Meetings (AGMs) of the corporate sector are often used by captains of industry not only to review their individual performance and future prospects but also to air their views on the state of the economy and government policies. Two such meetings held towards the end of July have considerable significance for the hospitality sector. The message from ITC Ltd., which is close to completing the implementation of its over Rs 1,500 crore plan for new hotels and expansion projects, is a reaffirmation of the company's faith in the future of the accommodation sector of the travel industry. Chairman Yogi Deveshwar, who also heads the subsidiary ITC Hotels Ltd. told share holders in Kolkata that "globalising markets and the expected higher rates of growth of the Indian economy will lead to growing demand for high quality accommodation. India is greatly under-roomed and it is estimated that hotel capacity will have to at least double over the next five years to keep pace with the expected growth in demand." He pointed out that "only companies like ITC, with a strong balance sheet that can contribute effectively to the creation and sustenance of such capital intensive and long gestation projects like hotels, which constitute an important part of infrastructure for the growth of trade, commerce and industry."

He also gave an update on the status of the various projects. He said that the 80 room super deluxe extension to Maurya Sheraton, which has been christened ITC–One, is now ready for guests. Another super deluxe project, ITC Grand-Maratha, at Sahar in Mumbai, is expected to be commissioned towards the end of the year. Work on a second hotel in the western metropolis in Upper Worli has also begun while there has been satisfactory progress on the ITC Sonar Bangla in Kolkata. The second hotel project in Delhi (to be named WelcomHotel) may be commissioned in the next few months. Deveshwar said given the high multiplier effect of investments in hotels, it is estimated that ITC's expansion programme will create 20,000 and more additional direct and indirect jobs.

Referring to the prospects of moving into the international arena, Deveshwar said, "ITC believes that with skills and expertise developed; over the years, it is possible to build a global hotel business by owning and managing hotel properties overseas." This objective is part of the company's strategic direction and added, "will be embarked – upon after establishing a dominant position for the ITC-Welcomgroup chain in India."

The other AGM, which earned media headlines is EIH Ltd. – the Oberoi Group, also in Kolkata. Vice chairman and managing director, Biki Oberoi echoed the disappointment of those who wish to see tourism play its part in the well being of the nation. After pointing out what tourism can do to generate employment and help preserve the arts, crafts and cultural heritage apart from earning valuable foreign exchange, he said, "One would have thought that this important industry would have been embraced by the central and state government as key instrument to promote employment and rapid economic growth." But, he added, "for the past 50 years, the story of tourism in India has been one of sheer neglect."

He pleaded for a 'bold and path breaking' initiative – a tourism vision for India 2020 aiming at achieving the twin target of 50 million employees in the sector and 40 million international visitors. Oberoi feels, these targets are realistic and offers supporting evidence from a recent study by the World Travel and Tourism Council (WTTC). The council had projected that subject to policy initiatives, India could by 2010 take its tourism employment to 25 million, Oberoi recommends a seven point agenda.

First, he would like to see priority attention for the sector. This, according to him, could be achieved by creating a joint public-private sector Tourism Mission which would move India towards Tourism vision 2020. Its progress should be monitored by a cabinet committee headed by the Prime Minister and comprising of ministers of finance, external affairs, commerce, aviation, railways, surface transport and, of course, tourism. And, declare tourism an infrastructure industry to give it access to low cost capital, technology and resources to keep it globally competitive. The remaining six suggestions are along familiar lines demanded by the industry at almost every forum. These are: Ensure easy access to India by increasing air seat capacity through a liberal bilateral policy. He believes with more frequencies foreign airlines will promote India in furtherance of their own interests. Abolish visas for major markets like US, European Union and Japan and provide visa on arrival for other countries. Improving the airports is his next point. He says, "We must float global tenders for private companies to design, build and operate airports." Professionalise overseas tourist offices and rationalise taxation, especially in the states.

And, lastly, the Oberoi chief would like to see a national trust put in charge of the country's heritage particularly the great monuments 'where the state owns the assets and the private sector manages them'.

The question that arises is : Do we have the political will to let tourism play its rightful role ?

What Ails Indian Tourism?

At an informal gathering of what could be described as a group of analysts engaged in various fields, the discussions turned towards-tourism. As is common on such occasions there were quick comparisons with our south-east Asian neighbours and several questions were raised why Thailand, Malaysia or Indonesia get three times the number of tourists than India meagre less than two and a half million foreign visitors. Finally, the questions were narrowed down to one: What ails Indian tourism?

The knowledgeable among the group then put their heads together to identify 10 major obstacles to this country's quest for a bigger share of the world market than the present less than half a per cent of the 600-odd millions who trot the globe every year. Here they are. The first is the absence of political will. Political parties and leaders who eventually form governments have, until very recently ignored tourism's potential as a generator of massive employment apart from being a major earner of foreign exchange. The result, the sector has not been on the national agenda nor given any priority in the general developmental plans. In China, they call tourism a 'pillar' of the economy.

Secondly, for decades, tourism has been perceived as an elitist activity especially by the socialism-inspired politicians and bureaucrats. Even where the awareness of tourism's potential is high, they shied away from supporting it in public for fear of being branded anti-poor. How can we have 'islands of affluence in the midst of poverty' was their refrain. And, so tourism was merely tolerated. The third obstacle was created strangely by the Planning Commission. Plan after plan it persisted in an erroneous distinction between international and domestic tourism: it reserved the international segment for the centre and the domestic for the states. This clearly prevented the evolution of a national approach to tourism as a whole.

Fourthly, the federal nature of our Constitution and activities constituting tourism spilling into both the central and state lists, has come in the way of a coordinated national effort. For instance, aviation and railways are a central subject while road transport comes within the purview of the states as do hotels. Monuments are a central responsibility while law and order in their environs, is in the states realm.

The fifth hurdle is the inadequacy of infrastructure both in sizes and quality whether it is accommodation, airports, roads and road transport, power, water or telecom. Just one example will suffice. A billion strong India has less than 70,000 hotel rooms. China, with a comparable size, and which 20 years ago was on the same level with India tourismwise, has 4,00,000 rooms. Archaic land and land use laws and an approvals regime have combined to permit only a painfully slow development of infrastructure especially hotels.

Civil aviation policies was identified as the sixth stumbling block. It would seem bilaterals have been so administered that they have contributed little to increasing seat capacity for travel to India although, they may have protected the interests of the national carrier. The next point is visas. Here too, a strict regime based on considerations of security and reciprocity has not helped create India's image as a hassle-free destination. Many countries now provide visa on arrival.

At the eighth place is taxation. There is a plethora of taxes, central as well as state. Vast variations in incidence has made Indian packages not only difficult to put together but uncompetitive with destinations in our neighbourhood, which have become less and less expensive by currency devaluation.

India's promotion overseas comes next. There is a vast network of tourist offices, a score of them, but they are handicapped due to jack of professional manpower. Also, they have yet to reorientate themselves to the 21st century technologies. The world over diplomatic missions give a helping hand in promoting travel to their countries. Indian missions abroad are yet to be initiated into this activity. The absence of a crisis management mechanism at the tourism ministry headquarters is another handicap faced by the tourist offices overseas.

Finally, there is no unity among the various segments of the travel industry itself. Hotels have two apex bodies, the older FHRAI and the younger HAL. So is the case with travel agents, they have TAAI and IATO. Domestic tour operators and adventure outfitters have their own associations and so do tourist, transporters. There is no common platform from where the entire industry could speak with one voice which alone could influence decision-makers.

This is not to suggest that there are no moves forward at all. Politicians are beginning to see some merit in tourism. Economic reforms will have their own impact on the growth of infrastructure. But one thing is clear: Indian tourism has many more miles to go.

12

Conventions, Conferences and Special Tourism Events – Promoting Tourism Vigorously

A Week of Tourism Overdose

World Tourism Day (September 27) around which the department of tourism (DoT) built a three-day International Travel and Tourism Mart, FHRAI's annual convention, an ASTA (American Society of Travel Agents) seminar and the Qutab Festival sponsored by Delhi Tourism made the last week of the month pretty hectic both for industry as well as media-persons. Surprisingly, except for the Qutab Festival which had on offer some interesting entertainment and cultural programmes, the media took little or no notice of the other events. And, it isn't that nothing worthwhile was said at the convention or participation in the Mart was not satisfactory. Either there is something missing in the media relations effort of the various organisations or signs of fatigue are showing in the media. It is time the industry did some introspection.

FHRAI can pat itself on the back for its ability to have on the dais at the inaugural function at the prestigious Vigyan Bhawan both ministers, Jagmohan and Vinod Khanna, after their absence from both the IATO and TAAI annual conference in Kolkata and Kochi held earlier in the month. Besides, the FHRAI convention also had some outstanding overseas speakers including the former president of ASTA, Michael Spinelli and the present chief of IH&RA (International Hotel and Restaurant Association), Eric Pfeffer. Both had some sound advice on how India could cope better with the fallout of 9/11 (in some places in the United States it is now being referred to as 11/S). From the government, secretary Rathi Jha unveiled yet another initiative after taking the industry by surprise at the TAAI meet when she offered to share space at overseas tourist offices with (unanimously) chosen representatives of the hospitality sector. What she offered to FHRAI is the government's desire to withdraw from the responsibility of classifying hotels in star categories and leave classification to the industry to set up its own mechanism as is the case in most other countries. Jha explained that the move is in line with the spirit of deregulations generated by economic reforms. She would be willing, however, she said in reply to questions, to agree to a one-time project approval at the initial stage to ensure a government cover for any requirements later. Another piece of good news she shared with the delegates was the revival of the marketing development fund from which DoT subsidises overseas promotion trips by industry. The limit of assistance, she said, has been raised from Rs. 60,000 to 75,000.

When Jagmohan started to show his now familiar audio-visual on cleaning up the environs of Ajanta and Ellora there were some in the audience who murmured "No, not again" but they soon discovered that the minister was conveying an important message. He pointed out that operation clean-up was not just beautifying the space around monuments but that a host of visitor facilities are being created like accommodataon, eateries, entertainment, communications and interpretation centres which opened up avenues of profitable investments apart from generating employment. More than that, he said, such improvements will help enhance visitor experience and also contribute to correcting the country's image about the way it looks after its heritage.

From the ASTA president Spinelli, the delegates heard a detailed account of the impact on the travel trade of the attacks on the World Trade Centre and the Pentagon. Most of the workers in travel agencies who have been laid off, their number goes into thousands, have now set themselves up as one person shops at home with their computers. Which means a burgeoning use of the internet, both for transactions as well as data dissemination. There are portals in the United States, he said, which are willing to share with agents such information as who travelled where and whether he bought a bargain package or a high end tour. With access to such data, Spinelli said Indian companies could reach out to Americans (and for that matter Europeans too) who travel long-haul to say China or Japan and lure them into taking a second destination like India in their future itineraries. Pfeffer, the IH&RA president, had as his theme "Who is responsible for improving your business" said governments can and do help (as they did in the case of airlines) but ultimately it is the industry itself and its individual components who have to adopt creative and proactive strategies. In a comment on India he thought the $10 million campaign proposed to be launched overseas would be a drop in the ocean to whcih Jagmohan's response was that developing countries could not match their resources with the rich nations.

It certainly was a week of tourism overdose.

IATO'S CONFERENCE IN RAJASTHAN

Tourism in the Spotlight

After the 'historic' announcement by Atal Behari Vajpayee in his Independence Day speech from the Red Fort promising a progressive tourism policy by the end of the year the question asked in the industry circles has been where do we go from here. Fortuitously, the Indian Association of Tour Operators (IATO), was holding its annual conference in Jodhpur from August 23-26, 2001, which offered the right forum to seek answers to the question.

Gathered in this Rajasthan city, fast emerging as a major tourist destination, were minister Ananth Kumar, secretary, M. P. Bezbaruah, director general, V. K. Duggal, additional DC, Mohan Khanna, joint secretary, Amitabh Kant, and, apart from IATO president Major Murli Dhar, such celebrities of the industry as Inder Sharma, S. K. Misra, Pradip Madhavji (president TAAI), Behram Dumasia and upcoming leaders like Pawan Khanna (Rainbow Travels) and Ajoy Mishra (Taj group). But, one participant who virtually stole the show was N. K. Singh, who recently moved from the PMO to the Planning Commission as its member-secretary. His intervention in the discussion. Drought cheer to the record attendance (there were 400 delegates not counting the spouses). His announcement, rather a commitment, that the Tenth-Five Year plan will have a much larger allocation for tourism was greeted with tremendous applause as were his suggestion on how to remove the various impediments to the growth of the sector.

Yogesh Chandra, former DG tourism and secretary aviation and now secretary general of the World Travel and Tourism Council's India Initiative, made a presentation on the latest study which urges this country to seize the opportunity to become a frontline tourist destination. But, let us return to the minister for some of his major announcements. The long-standing demand of the industry for visa on arrival, said, is about to be implemented. The home minister has agreed to try this out as a pilot project granting visa on arrival to citizens of 1 6 select countries (he did not name them) and a special team is already on the job of setting up visa counters at the five international airports. As for entry fees to monuments, a sore point with the trade has finally offered a sop. ASI, he said, has been asked to work out a package, which will cover visits from one day to a week and there will be special tariffs for students and scholars. "The package will be tourism and tour operator friendly," he added.

On major initiatives that he and his team at the DoT (department of tourism) are working on to give a push to tourism, he said, these include a series of meetings at various levels beginning September 10. The first of these would be, the work of overseas tourist offices (directors and their promotional agencies have been invited to New Delhi) which will be reviewed. Then, tourism secretaries from the states will be meeting to prepare an agenda for consideration of chief ministers and tourism ministers, the very next day when the draft tourism policy will also be considered. The CMs and state ministers meeting will be addressed by the prime minister.

Doing what he called loud thinking he said, the tourism policy apart from encouraging private sector-public sector partnership in tourism development will define government's role as a liberaliser, rationaliser, facilitator and motivator. In the various presentations made to the home minister, the finance minister and even the prime minister, DoT has sought to project the vast potential that tourism offers in earning foreign exchange, employment generation and general economic development. He disclosed that, the home minister has agreed in principle to make Port Blair an international airport (the runaway has already been extended to take Boeing 747s and develop more islands for tourism). A suggestion made by N. K. Singh that empowered group of ministers should take decisions on tourism to ensure that the initiative of one ministry was not scuttled by another. A similar arrangement could be done for the states. The suggestion triggered greater expectations and the consensus was that ideally, there should be a cabinet committee on tourism on the lines of the one on economic affairs.

It is proposed to increase India's share in the world's tourism market upto 0.75 per cent by 2010.

PLANNING THE RETREAT AT AGRA

A Retreat to Decide the Way Forward

The London-based influential World Travel and Tourism Council (WTTC), comprising chief executive the hospitality industry, which launched its 'India Initiative' in 2000, is organising an event of great significance for the sector in Agra later this month. Coming together for three days of deliberations at the Oberoi's Amarvilas, made famous by the Vajpayee-Musharraf summit, there will be internationally acclaimed experts, leaders of India's tourism industry representing both government and the private sector, MPs, ambassadors, opinion makers and editors of major newspapers and periodicals. The number of participants is being restricted to 50 to ensure that the "group will be small yet impactful". 'Retreat, as the meeting is christened, will, as WTTCs' India Initiative secretary general, Yogesh Chandra explains, "Aim to address for the first time, with purpose and depth, the twin areas of travel and tourism". This, he says will be in the background of the current crisis in the industry as well as the success stories in the neighbourhood such as Malaysia, Thailand and Dubai. The Retreat is being hosted by PRS Oberoi, chairman of EIH, a key player in getting WTTC to choose India to give the country a helping hand in creating "Awareness of the economic importance of tourism as a creator of wealth, economic prosperity, business opportunities and avenues of employment."

WTTC president, Jean-Claude Baumgarten will be guiding the deliberations at the Amarvilas which will open with a presentation of the Council's status report on tourism on the evening of August 23. The main discussion will be kicked off the next morning by minister Jagmohan who will speak on 'Can India Harness its Tourism Potential?' The role of government in travel and tourism will be addressed by a panel consisting of Rathi Vinay Jha, secretary tourism, K. Roy Paul, secretary, civil aviation and secretaries from the ministries of external affairs and finance, Shashank and Ajai Vikram Singh, Finance minister Jaswant Singh is expected to lead a discussion on the impact of image on investing in India. Eight subgroups will meet concurrently and come up with recommendations on creating a brand image for India; setting up pressure groups to highlight travel and tourism; impact of aviation on tourism; the visa regime; tourism and innovation and partnership between industry and government.

Three turnaround cases will be presented at another session. The speaker for the US study will be Bernard D. Freelat, president and CEO, Rail Europe Group. On Indonesia, the presentation will be by the country's Tourism Promotion Board chief, Feisol Hashim and minister of tourism and antiquities, Aron Jordan who will talk about the Middle East.

The immediate impact of 9/11 on American Express will be referred to by the agency's vice president for global alliances, Kevin Carey. How IT can help with crisis management will be explained by a specialist from the Rail Europe Group. A presentation on behalf of FATA will be made by Peter de Jong the company's president and CEO.

A session that promises some light and maybe some heat too is billed as 'Travel and Tourism: The Wrongs and the Rights', and it has nine industry stalwarts on the panel including heads of the three main hotel chains; PRS Oberoi (EIH), R. K. Krishna Kumar (Taj) and Habib Rehman

(ITC Hotels). The others are Adi Katgara (ICI), Ashwini Kakkar (Thomas Cook), Maharana Arvind Singh Mewar (Historic Resort Hotels), Maharaja Gaj Singh (Maharaja Heritage Resorts), Lalit Suri (Bharat Hotels), and Inder Sharma (Select Holiday Resorts). The moderator will be Suhel Seth, CEO Equus Advertising.

Speakers at the final session on August 25 are expected to include the civil aviation minister, Shahnawaz Hussain, Vinod Khanna, minister of state for tourism and culture, Arun Jaitley, former law minister, N. K. Singh, member, Planning Commission and Shekhar Gupta, CEO, *Indian Express Newspapers*. Other media personalities invited to the Retreat are M. J. Akbar, editor-in-chief, *Asian Age*, Satish Jacob, BBC, T. N. Ninan, editor, *Business Standard*, Sanjay Baru, chief editor, *Financial Express*, Karan Thappar, TV Anchor, Bachi Karkaria, editor-in-chief, *Mid-Day*, Vinod Mehta, editor, *Outlook*, Chandan Mitra, editor-in-chief, *The Pioneer* and Rajdeep Sardesai, *Star News*. Among the MPs who have agreed to attend are Pritish Nandy, Ashwani Kumar, Margaret Alva, Balbir Punj, Amar Singh, K. Yerranaidu, Jyotiraditya Scindia, Renuka Chowdhury, Mani Shankar Aiyar and Nitish Sengupta. Another union minister, Shatrugan Sinha and Kerala's tourism minister, Prof K. V. Thomas, have also confirmed their participation, as have director general of tourism, Vinod Duggal and joint secretary, Amitabh Kant. A 'Retreat Declaration' is planned to be adopted at the concluding session. The travel industry will be watching with great interest the outcome of the liberations.

WTTC: A Reason to Cheer

The World Travel and Tourism Council (WTTC), has every reason to feel encouraged that it's effort to bring together decision-makers, opinion builders and industry leaders for a frank and serious discussion on the possibilities of giving tourism a chance in this country was successful. The Retreat at Agra's prestigious Amarvilas Hotel attracted more than a hundred participants comprising influential members of Parliament, editors, tourism and aviation ministers and secretaries. The foreign secretary, Kanwal Sibal and Planning Commission member, N. K. Singh provided added lustre to the high-powered presence of Jagmohan, Vinod Khanna and Sripad Naik, minister of state for civil aviation.

Overseas participation was no less impressive. Apart from WTTC president Jean'Claude Baumgarten, there was the chief executive of PATA (Pacific Asia Travel Association) Peter de Jong, Jordan's tourism minister Dr. Taleb Rifai, chairman of Indonesia's tourism board Feisol Hashim and such industry stalwarts as Alwin Zecha executive chairman, Pacific Leisure and Bernard Freelat CEO, Rail Europe Group, USA's largest outbound tour company.

On the Indian side, apart from tourism director general Vinod Duggal, secretary Rathi Jha, joint secretary Amitabh Kant and aviation secretary K. Roy Paul, the hotel industry was represented by chief executives like R. K. Krishna Kumar, Biki Oberoi, Habib Rehman and Lalit Suri as well as Maharana Arvind Singh. Among the editors was Shekhar Gupta, M. J. Akbar, Chandan Mitra, T. N. Ninan, Vinod Mehta, Satish Jacob, Rohit Bansal, Bachi Karkaria and TV anchor Karan Thapar.

The discussions, as was programmed ranged over the rights and wrongs, the experience of other countries and the way forward for India. Six sub-groups went into the details and came back with specific recommendation on major issues like branding India, accessibility, facilitation and the tax burden. While these recommendations will be forwarded to the government, Baumgarten announced that the follow-up action will be assessed at the next Retreat slated for Kochi in January. Briefing newspapers on the Retreat in the Capital, Yogesh Chandra WTTC's secretary general of the India Initiative, said that the main thrust of the Council's approach to the government from the Retreat is in the area of the tourism set up, restructuring of which alone can provide the necessary push to tourism. Its one point conclusion in Chandra's words is, "The Agra Retreat recommends the need to set up a cabinet committee on travel and tourism under the chairmanship of the prime minister." It will be recalled that in an earlier report to the government, the WTTC had said the same thing but without mentioning the Prime Minister specifically and limiting it only to the highest office in the land.

Samajwadi Party MP, Amar Singh, who along with other MPs like Mani Shankar Aiyar and Dinesh Trivedi of the Congress and the Trinamool Congress took a leading part in the discussions and offered to lead a delegation of MPs, tourism ministers and industry leaders to the Prime Minister to ask him to set up a cabinet committee for the sector under his own charge.

Answering questions the secretary general said the consensus in Agra was that the decision, since kept in abeyance, about visa on arrival for a select 16 countries should be implemented without further delay.

Planning Commission member N. K. Singh, respected by the industry for his tourism friendly views made a few important observations at the Agra meet. He fully agreed with the need for an India brand, but pointed out that such branding should cover the entire gamut of the country's interface overseas, "Only then tourism will benefit from the image created by that brand." He came down heavily on the aviation policies pursued by the government. He described the reciprocal element in the bilateral regime as a dog-in-the-marger attitude. "Rethink this approach more fundamentally," he said. He was also unhappy about the inordinate delay in privatising major international airports. "Four years have passed and we still have not decided which route to take as we had been moving from privatisation to leasing and now to joint ventures. Civil aviation is an area where we need to demonstrate far greater credibility," he added. Singh shared the industry's concern about the heavy burden of taxation on the sector which in India was much higher than the international average. He also referred to the allocation of Rs. 2,900 crore to tourism in the Tenth Plan and expressed the hope that it would be spent, "Purposefully in partnership with the private sector."

The success of the Agra Retreat means that the WTTC has moved one step forward in creating greater awareness of the role and potential of tourism by ensuring greater support from decision-makers with the help of opinion makers.

Second Retreat of WTTC

The second Retreat organised by WTTC the World Travel and Tourism Council, at the Taj Exotica in Goa from February 14-16 was significantly different both in composition and content. At Agra, where the first Retreat was held in August last year a large number of foreign experts including ministers joined our own tourism and aviation ministers, civil servants, editors and industry leaders to share with them their success stories and strategies post 9/11. Almost the entire spectrum of tourism was discussed. But in Goa, as WTTC president Jean-Claude Baumgarten and secretary general Yogesh Chandra explained, the effort was to make the Retreat an interactive exercise. And, so there were no ministers, Indian or foreign, and no overseas experts barring a keynote speaker, Stefan Pichler, chairman and CEO Thomas Cook whose Indian arm is a major player in the hospitality sector.

Apart from WTTC members of the India Initiative, which incidentally is into its fourth year as an internationally-backed think tank for Indian tourism, there were like at Agra, senior editors, secretaries of tourism and aviation, Rathi Vinay Jha and K. Roy Paul and senior MPs including Margaret Alva, Prithviraj Chavan, Ashwini Kumar and B. J. Panda. A welcome addition was Ajay Piramal, OSD to deputy PM L. K. Advani. With no ministers around it was easy to do away with speeches and plenary sessions. Instead, the 50 odd participants divided themselves into five groups for an indepth study of key issues like the aviation policy, visa regime, infrastructure, branding India and crisis management. Each group then made its recommendations.

Before we take up the recommendations, it would be necessary to take note of the fact that the most important proposal made by the Agra Retreat that a sub-committee of the cabinet be set up under the prime minister is still lying in cold storage. This came out in the question-answer session in Goa. Reportedly, minister Jagmohan feels that the present arrangement of a group of ministers (GoM) presided over by himself is adequate and that there's no need for a cabinet committee. Sadly, there have hardly been any meeting of the group of ministers! The consensus in Goa was that a cabinet committee is a must for any progress in tourism and M.P. Prithviraj Chavan volunteered to carry the flag.

There was unanimous support for creating a crisis management group by the government with representatives from the ministries and media. The group should be a proactive body. On aviation a major step forward was secretary Roy Paul's assurance that the virtual open sky policy for International carriers during the peak season would be announced sufficiently in advance to allow airlines to take advantage of it. He also said that his ministry has recommended that ATF (aviation turbine fuel) be made part of "Declared Goods", and, if this is accepted by the finance minister in the next budget there will only be 4 per cent central sales tax on ATF.

On the visa regime, while participants shared the security concerns that have prevented any liberalisation, one suggestion that found favour was introducing electronic visas. This, it was pointed out, was one step ahead of visa on arrival and some countries including Australia are already practicing it. Branding India, the participants said, was a good beginning but greater resources would be required. It was recommended that industry should contribute to a marketing fund at least up to 25 per cent of the government spending.

Planning Commission member, N.K. Singh who is a popular figure at travel events and whose tourism-friendly approach has endeared him to the industry, felt that tourism promotion abroad should be an integral part of a coordinated effort encompassing exports and attracting FDIs. He suggested that there should be a Rs. 200 crore fund for India promotion. Singh, who feels strongly about the aviation sector, said he would like to see the day when air travel becomes affordable. This could be achieved by rationalising the taxes on ATF and by withdrawing subsidies to non-lucrative routes. He is all for industry to absorb the non-viable services.

But, he said, let us first have a civil aviation policy. He would also like to see urgent action on privatising international airports. Already much valuable time has been lost. Public resources, he said, should not be used for upgrading airports when private enterprise is willing to take on the task.

Baumgarten reminded participants that by giving priority to tourism and by expanding infrastructure and connectivity India can create 25 million additional jobs. After China, he said, India has the potential for the fastest growth in tourism in the coming decade. Goa is certainly a step forward in the tourism effort. Everyone, however, is keeping fingers crossed about developments over Iraq.

PATA'S NEW DELHI CONFERENCE

PATA's Quest for New directions

Pacific Asian Travel Association which set up a task force some time ago to look at the challenge of 2000 A.D. now has a report titled "Direction 2000." Sharing the report with member countries, Pierre Doley, who was elected president of PATA in April this year was in New Delhi towards the end of August accompanied by Kane Rufe who has recently replaced Ken Chamberlain as the Executive Vice President, a semi-permanent position. Talking to media persons at a lunch hosted by Inder Sharma, chairman, PATA India chapter (who was a member of the task force), Rufe explained that under Direction 2000 PATA's focus would be on strategies rather than tactics. In order to achieve this, he added, the PATA board has formed an advisory council for different areas like education and research. The council would act like a think tank on how to tackle strategic issues. The new executive vice president gave these as the basic aims of Direction 2000 to enhance PATA's own mission as promoter of travel to and within the region through beefed-up marketing programmes; with Europe 1992 already a reality, to open a PATA office in Europe to attract larger traffic to the PATA region; advocacy of greater travel to the Pacific Asia from global markets; streamline PATA's own decision making through the advisory council and by strengthening regional offices and by merging the executive and management committees into one single management committee; and finally, more result oriented work by the membership committee. Kane said at present there were 16,000 members from 42 countries but notable omissions were China, Cambodia, Laos, Myanmar and Mongolia Vietnam which had also stayed out of PATA has indicated its desire to join the association. A major step already taken, he said, was the setting up of an Intelligence Centre at headquarters in San Francisco. This would be a data-based centre with ability to analyse information to help the advisory council in its assessment of strategic issues. Answering questions, the new PATA president, a senior executive with an international airline (KLM) estimated that in the next decade the number of visitors to the Pacific basin was expected to rise from the present 38 million to 100 million on an 8 per cent annual compounded growth. He would not say what would be South Asia's share in this growth but volunteered advice to the region on how to maximise its share. First, he said, each country should prepare a master tourism plan with involvement of the entire industry and not just by governments or segments of the industry.

Secondly, liberal non-protectionist policies would help. This, he said, was particularly important for countries which hitherto had been mistakenly adopting closed-sky policies to protect their national carriers. Open skies policies, he said, were the best way of attracting tourists and gave the examples of Singapore and Holland where he said, not only had traffic increased, the national carriers had also benefited. In the case of this country, Air India was hardly helped by official policies, while it lost many more tourists who would have come to India had there been more frequent services by other airlines. In his view AI with its lower overheads could easily compete with international carriers. Foreign airlines, Doley said, would operate through India only if their operations were viable which for this country would mean more tourists. On infrastructure, Doley felt that India should have a fair mix of facilities for both upmarket and less affluent travellers as airlines offered airfares to both segments. He thought India was perceived as a country with a lot to offer and, if "merchandised properly," it could be a model for the rest of Asia. As an example he said Americans have a special interest in Hinduism, in Ashrams and the like but there was not much awareness of these attractions. "Have duty free shops in the town – airport duty free shops are no longer popular" he said.

THE PATA CONFERENCE

Tourism-N Technology: Hand in Hand

The 48th Annual Conference of PATA, held in Nagoya, Japan, on April 21 was dominated by the millennium concern, technology and the Asian crisis. Keynote speaker Yotaro Kobayashi, Fuji Xerox Chairman, in his address "Bridge to the New Future" warned against too rapid Anglo-Americanisation of the world and said that nations should not lose sight of their own values.

Twenty-first century managers, he said, will have to develop a new *esprit de corps* to keep in step with the rest of the world. Commenting on technology's impact on the industry, he felt Internet virtual travel was no substitute for genuine travel with physical contact and the real exchange of experience, emotions, insights, pleasures and challenges.

Only by physical movement from one area of culture to another would 'real globalisation', take place and real travel was about hearts and minds not just numbers.

Over a thousand hospitality industry leaders from all over the world had gathered in Japan's fourth largest city. India fielded the fifth largest delegation, including a large number of media persons. The inaugural function at the sprawling convention centre was a colourful affair with a concert by the Nagoya Philharmonic Orchestra and by the Nagoya Boys and Girls Choir. Prince and Princess Takamado represented the Royal family to lend charm to the event. There were many references to Japan's unique contribution to tourism.

This year's PATA chairman, Terry Francis, said, Japan is the only country in the world which at the governmental level encourages its citizens to travel abroad (in 1998 more than 17 million Japanese visited other countries, while only 4.2 million foreigners came to Japan). Japan's tourism minister told delegates that his country was giving financial and technical assistance to other countries in their tourism projects. For itself, Japan has set a target of seven million arrivals by 2005.

Francis said that technology will be the single biggest influence in tourism's future. The Internet is leveling the playing field among suppliers and has now made it a true 'global village'. The continued emphasis on the Net for information, and now sales, will force change faster than any of us anticipated a few years ago, he said.

Francis felt that while these changes were inevitable, the travel industry also needs greater recognition and respect. The value of tourism is a question asked everywhere, he said, and added, "it has been addressed in Canada through the establishment of Satellite Accounting System that measures the benefit to each sector of the economy."

DATA CEO, Joseph McInerney, in his annual report described the move of the Association's headquarters from San Francisco to Bangkok earlier this year as 'drastic'. He said, "relocating to Thailand put us much closer to the core of our members in the Pacific Asia region, and as a result, we now have a much better understanding of the problems and opportunities throughout the region, and have the ability to communicate more effectively with all our members."

McInerney announced that a task force had redefined to geographical boundaries of the PATA region, which has enabled the Association to admit Maldives as a new member. He said PATAnet, the organisation newly redesigned Website will meet the requirements of the next century. Created by a San Francisco company, it will provide a free hyperlink from PATAnet to a member's Website, free classified listings for job openings in member companies and a password-protected access to a special members–only area of PATAnet for Strategic Information Centre Data, conference proceedings and PATA publications. PATA CEO also referred to the 50th anniversary celebrations due in 2001. "A diverse committee has been assigned to lay the ground work for what will surely be a spectacular year of celebrations," he said.

A concurrent session, which drew a large number of delegates, was on 'sustainable tourism' where the panelists included speakers from India and Pakistan. Much appreciated was Mandip Soin's work on an environmental pledge in India and inclusion in tourism brochures the visitor's right to ensure that hotels and other facilities he is using are eco-friendly, From Pakistan, Shirin Walji, a leading travel agent and environmentalist made a presentation on a project where 'the cultural heritage as well as the historic and natural heritage sites have been preserved and managed.'

The project, under the aegis of Aga Khan Trust for Culture, has been carried out at the remote HUNZA valley in the northern part of the country. The valley's unique BALTIT Fort is now under conservation and will be reused as a museum. The other aspects of the project are town planning assistance, economic development and housing.

For the hotel industry, Bangalore-born Ravi Saligram, head of Holiday Inn International – Bass Hotels, had some interesting forecasts like the merging of airlines and hotel chains, which will leave the segment in the hands of four or five giants; though in Asia this may not happen just now. Tomorrow's guest he said, would prefer a hotel with a 'can do friendliness'.

At the socials, Indian participants – particularly media persons – were much in demand for briefing on the political developments at home. "So you will have an Italian as your Prime Minister?" was a common question.

PATA 2002 Showcase India's True Potential

Any assessment of the gains from an international event like the 51st annual conference of the Pacific Asia Travel Association (PATA) held in the Capital from April 14-18, 2002, will have to take into account three factors. The first is the quality, spread and size of participation. The second, the quality of debate and efficient arrangements for delegates' stay, meetings facilities, food, entertainment and relaxation. And, finally the host country's ability to showcase itself in order to increase its share of the world market.

On the first count, it has to be noted that this must have been the most challenging year for PATA to gather its flock after the havoc suffered by tourism in the wake of September 11, followed by the military operations in Afghanistan and the India-Pakistan stand off, not to talk of the concerns raised by Ayodhya and the riots in Gujarat. At one stage, it looked as if the number of delegates may not even cross 500. But it goes to the credit of both PATA and the Indian organising committee headed by director general Vinod Duggal that the final count was a respectable thousand plus. And, there was no dearth among them of CEOs of hotel groups, airlines, travel agencies and government leaders. They came from 41 countries.

As for conference arrangements, thanks to this country's track record in this field, there was never any doubt that the industry would put its best foot forward. Whether it was welcome at the airport, transfers to hotels or movement between venues everything went clockwork. Sessions began on time and the use of modern technologies in presentations was much in evidence. The welcome dinner hosted by tourism minister Jagmohan at the picturesque Nehru Park across the road from the great Ashoka Hotel, venue of the conference, where the Capital's leading hotels joined hands to present the kitchens of India was a culinary experience that was enriched with cultural performances. Delegates were heard making comparisons with similar offerings in other countries but the consensus was in favour of the evening at Nehru Park.

On the quality of debate there was unanimity. This was reflected in the packed halls both for plenary and breakaway (concurrent) sessions. Good attendance was also the result of the keenness with which delegates were looking forward to answers and leads to meet the challenges thrown up by global terrorism. The galaxy of speakers included the secretary general of the World Tourism Organisation, Francesco Prangialli, Jean-Claude Baumgarten, president, World Travel and Tourism Council (WTTC), Michael Elliott editor-at-large, *Time* magazine, Brock Friesen of Star Alliance, Nik Cowing from BBC World, Richard Gordon, secretary, Philippines department of tourism, and Clara Chang, head of the Hong Kong Tourism Board. India fielded apart from Jagmohan, M. P. Bezbaruah, former tourism secretary and chairman PATA international in 2001 and Dr. Karan Singh as a keynote speaker on the opening day. Under the general theme of "Tourism – Looking Ahead and Beyond" the subjects covered such issues as the changing world and its impact on tourism key trends for the future and main influencers and aviation.

On the central issue of concern, the set back to the industry, there were words of comfort from the PATA CEO, Peter de Jong, who quoted from a recent WTTC study which indicated that 2003 would be a year of recovery. Prime Minister Atal Behari Vajpayee, who inaugurated the conference told the delegates, "India is now all geared up to reach its true potential in tourism". Calling upon the tourism fraternity to intensify the campaign against terrorism he said, "All of us should know why terrorism has hit tourism the most...because it is an antidote to terrorism and extremism." Jagmohan said that, "Tourism needs a new face" and added that "we must think of how we can break new ground and use tourism as an instrument to reduce disparities and alleviate poverty."

One of the most absorbing sessions was the one addressed by futurologist Richard Neville. He regaled the audience with such remarks as, "Our accelerating pace of change has turned time into a scarce commodity. Harassed executives are driving a new trend: Power, leisure, short intense periods of ultra relaxation, orchestrated by a stop watch." As you ready for power tourism he asked and added, "Twenty minutes for the Taj Mahal, ten minutes for lunch and the rest of the day at the Internet cafe replying to e-mails."

That brings us to the third assessment factor. Did we showcase India effectively. Yes, if you go by the 30 minute spectacle put together by Amitabh Kant of the department of tourism with 300 folk dancers from all of India at the inaugural and the Ritu Kumar extravaganza of a fashion show "Free of Life" at the dosing ceremony, PATA CEO summed it up by saying, "The delegates got the feel of India." For more tourists we shall have to wait for the delegates to go back and start promoting India.

A Seminar that made an Impact

A Step in the Right Direction for Inbound Tourism

It was a tourism seminar with a difference, organised as it was by a national daily in the capital which has specialised in providing a forum for public debate on issues of national importance. The difference lay in the fact that it was not thought up by a travel industry apex body or one of the chambers of commerce. Besides, *HT City*, the daily's colour supplement, structured it thoughtfully. The theme, 'Strategic initiatives to drive inbound tourism', was well chosen, as was the panel with the eminent travel journalist. Hugh Gantzer as moderator. The panelists were tourism and culture minister Ananth Kumar; Oberoi group president Ravi Bhoothalingam; Veenu Kashyap, who was deputising for Indian Airlines' chairman; Francis Wacziarg of Neemrana fame; Ram Kohli, founder president of IATO; Matthew Spacie, CEO-Ezeego Travel; and Arun Pandeya, regional manager–Air France. The audience consisted of a few industry leaders, including Inder Sharma, and a large number of young executives. The venue was the capital's Taj Palace Hotel. Gantzer set the tone for the discussion limited to the two-and-a-half hour allotted for it by specifying 'what we do not want to hear and what we do want to hear'. In short, he advised the panelists to stick to the main issue of how to get more tourists to come to India. Since the minister wanted to have 'the last word', Bhoothalingam took the floor first. He focused on three main issues which needed to be addressed urgently: air seat capacity, visa hassles and what he called 'extortionist taxes on hotels'. Availability of air seats was only half of the 10 million demand. The whole world was moving towards no visa or visa on arrival; even countries with major security problems like Sri Lanka and Pakistan were offering visa on arrival. And, the plethora of central and state taxes were amounting to as much as 50 per cent of a hotel bill. Kashyap, however, felt that air seats were no longer problem and according to statistics available with him, there were 16 million seats against an actual demand of 11 million. The recent bilaterals, he said, had further eased the shortage. Pandeya's diagnosis was that it was not the shortage of seats but ineffective marketing which was not bringing in more visitors. "We need to learn from other countries who have made a success of their marketing," he said.

It was left to Kohli to make a frontal attack on the authorities.

"Everything is wrong with tourism," he said, "and instead of bureaucrats running the tourism department, it should be managed by a professional board." He was particularly harsh on the government for the abrupt increase in monument entry fees. "We are not against the increase," he clarified, "but against the manner in which it was done without any notice at all." He reminded the minister that in other countries, the travel industry is always consulted before any major changes in policies and practices, Wacziarg said the fee hike was not exorbitant but it was introduced inelegantly. Money for upkeep, he said, could also be raised by developing facilities like shopping and cafes around monuments. Stacie saw in the absence of data and research a great impediment to India's marketing effort.

The minister surprised the audience by appearing not to be in a hurry to attend another meeting, as is the practice with politicians on such occasions. He listened attentively and smiled through all the criticism, giving the impression that he had an answer for all the complaints. The only glad tidings he had for the industry was in respect of visas and permits for visiting the North-East. A decision on both the issues, he said, could be expected within the week as the home minister will be taking a final view. He expected that visa on arrival will be agreed to at least for 10 selected countries (among the source markets) and that permits will not be necessary for most of the North-East.

About taxes, he tried to disarm the critics by agreeing with them that they were on the high side but defended his inability to influence the finance ministry by suggesting that the government had compulsions like the burdens placed on the resources by tragedies like the Orissa cyclone and the Gujarat earthquake as well as the Kargil war. Where he seemed to be on a weak wicket was entry fees. He skirted the issue of notice to the industry and, as a sop, offered a package that is being worked out for clubbing monuments in the same city. Tour operators in the audience did not seem impressed.

To come back to the main issue. Did the discussion throw any light on how to get more tourists? Well, visa on arrival for visitors even from 10 countries will be a major step in that direction.

KERALA TRAVEL MART (KTM)

Capital View

With the successful conclusion of SATTE 2004, eleventh in the series, in the Capital in the last week of March, the industry is now looking towards the next major travel show—Kerala Travel Mart or KTM as it has come to be known. Held every two years in Cochin it will be in its third edition since its debut in 2000. The dates are September 30 to October 2. EM Najeeb, chief of south India's leading destination management company, Great India Tours, has been re-elected president of the KTM Society which makes the event happen. For KTM III he is also general convenor of the organising committee. Kerala's tourism secretary, T Balakrishnan is chairman.

Najeeb, who was recently in Delhi in a chat with this writer, reviewed the contribution made by KTM I & II to Indian tourism generally and to Kerala particularly and, how KTM III will be different. KTM I, he said, succeeded in establishing a communication link with tour operators and media largely in West Asia and Europe. "We could also showcase most of our major products at the mart as well as through pre and post-conference tours" he said, and added, "as a first attempt, it was well received.

A significant spin off was that smaller players could establish networking at a lower cost." Najeeb described KTM II as a "wondrous success" when around 1,000 buyers including media representatives from all over the world attended and went back impressed with Kerala's approach to marketing. This was possible, he said, because of combined teamwork of industry and the state department. The chief minister held a special function in Trivandrum to congratulate the organisers of the mart. The two KTMs he said have completely changed the profile of Kerala's tourism business and this was reflected in the 30 per cent growth achieved during 2003-04. The off-season in the state has further shrunk and April and May have joined the peak season.

Learning from the experience of the first two marts, Najeeb said, but for KTM III it has been decided to host only 500 travel professionals including media. The objective in reducing numbers is to bring in more quality and make the event more meaningful by better thrust and greater focus. Restricted numbers will ensure better interaction between buyers and sellers which will also help build closer relationships. This will also in some way he added, in the existing infrastructure being further developed and strengthened. He is happy that the accommodation sector (the state has less than 5,000 rooms in good hotels) is now growing with an eye on quality. "We expect at least 15 to 20 per cent increase in the room count in the next two years" he said. Like in earlier marts, Najeeb said this time too there will be pre and post-conference tours. All airlines operating to Kerala, hoteliers and tour operators are jointly hosting the invited buyers. Each of the previous KTMs had cost between five and six crore of rupees but the government's contribution was only Rs. 50 lakh, the rest all came from the private sector. It will not be any different in KTM III. Which means, he said that the initiative of KTM is largely with the private sector with only the necessary support from the government. India tourist offices overseas and the central department of tourism have extended full support before and will do so now in identifying the right buyers as well as in arranging passages. Sri Lanka Air he said, has promised to bring some of the best buyers from Europe. He said, "this is the only mart which has been initiated by the private sector for the industry without any profit motive". To come back to SATTE. As part of the buyer – seller meet four interesting and educative seminars were also organised dealing with heritage tourism; connectivity; facilities for the handicapped and the Incredible India campaign. Heritage tourism was chaired by Jayant Sanyal, member core group of the Planning Commission and panelists included Rakesh Mathur, MD, Welcomheritage, Ramesh Chandra, member-secretary, INTACH, Rajesh Aggarwal from UNESCO and Maureen Liebl of Mehrangarh Port Musuem. Mathur pointed out that setting up a heritage hotel needed a huge effort compared to standard hotels. A standard property, he said has only two processes, construction and making it functional. In the case of heritage there are four stages—repair, restoration, conversion and finally operational. The costs involved in the first three steps are far more prohibitive than in a standard property. In addition, most heritage properties being located in rural areas there is the extra requirement of connectivity and communication. The owners too need to be trained to manage their converted properties to international standards. His solution: the central government should draw up a separate heritage tourism policy in which financial Assistance and training facilities are built for future heritage hotels.

It was India's day at the fourth global summit organised by the World Travel and Tourism Council (WTTC) which brought together some 700 of the planet's most influential leaders which included chief executives of hotel chains, airlines, travel agencies, car rentals, media barons and investors, in Doha, capital of Qatar, in the first week of May. Resurgent India was the theme of a presentation made by N K Singh, member Planning Commission, to a special breakfast session chaired by Jean-Claude Baumgarten, president WTTC. Co-panelists with Singh were hotelier Lalit Suri, who recently took over as president of WTTC's India Initiative, Amitabh Kant, joint secretary, department of tourism, Raymond Bickson, the new managing director,Taj group. Ashwani Kakkar, head of Thomas Cook and Redha Bhatia, chief of Amadeus.

Pointing out that India's economic growth is the fastest among major countries, Singh said that with an estimated growth of 9 per cent this country hoped to become the third largest economy in the coming decades, a jump from the present 12th position. The GDP growth of 10.4 per cent in the quarter ended December last was the highest among all economies of the world. And, according to Goldman Sach's projections, Indians GDP will exceed Italy's in 2020, France's in the same year and Germans in 2025. What is of special significance for tourism is that the services sector of which it is a major part, has grown considerably from 40.6 per cent in 1990-91 to 51.0 per cent in 2003-04. It was to this India awakening and a world of opportunity that the Planning Commission member invited foreign investors. There are myriad openings for investment in hotels, travel related services and even aviation, particularly airports. He said tenders have already gone out for privatisation of major international airports, peak periods open skies policy is in place, private carriers have been permitted to fly overseas and the massive 7,000 km Golden Quadrilateral linking Delhi-Mumbai-Chennai-Kolkata is scheduled for completion next year. India would be needing between 1,00,000 and 2,00,000 additional hotel rooms in the coming years and one hundred per cent foreign investment is welcome in the accommodation sector.

Later speaking as a panelist in the plenary session on Flow of Money (investments) Singh summed up the positive factors that make India the preferred place to bring money into. It is the world's largest democracy with political stability; a safe place to do business; has a large reservoir of skilled/semi-skilled manpower and where economic reforms are changing the character of business. More importantly, it has liberal and transparent investment policies—policies that are backed by a degree of national consensus carrying an element of continuity. Sharing a thought with the audience he wondered if there could be a special fund created to protect international investors. On his opening remarks at the breakfast meeting, Baumgarten threw light on how WTTC decided to launch the India Initiative. It all started five years ago, he said, when Biki Oberoi, chairman EIH, at a council meeting in London pointed a finger at Baumgarten and said "you do nothing for India" (Biki was in Doha but could not participate in the summit because of his indisposition). Baumgarten said he made a quick decision to visit India, get together industry leaders with whose help chose Yogesh Chandra as secretary general and soon India Initiative was making waves.

N. K. Singh began his presentation with a tribute to the workdone by India Initiative. Addressing Baumgarten he said "your most important contribution has been to make India Initiative a real catalyst for change. Tourism in India, Singh said, was driven by religion, and "you have made tourism a religiom". Secondly, from merely being the concern of the government, tourism is moving into a partnership between the public and the private sector. There is growing synergy and symmetry of action, the three Retreats organised by Yogesh Chandra "who is familiar with the ways of government" brought together MPs, editors, ministers and industry leaders. The outcome, he said, has been dramatic PM's historic address from the Red Fort prorating high priority for tourism.

The presentation on India included a section on the Incredible India campaign which has won two PATA gold awards at last month's annual meet of the association in Jeju, South Korea for best marketing and best print campaign. The current size of the Indian market was given as 520 million domestic movements; 4.8 million outbound and 3 million in bound. The Incredible India campaign has enhanced the country's earning by $ 600 million (foreign exchange growth of 23 per cent) and an increase of 15 per cent in arrivals. The Lonely Planet lists India among favourite destinations and Condenast Traveler among top ten destinations.

Indian tourism was certainly shining in Doha.

Through centuries travellers dating back to Marco Polo, Ibn Batuta, Fa Hian and Al Baruni, have related their tales, all true, but not the whole truth. They saw the truth in part and laced it with their perception of men and matters of the time. So, if their present day descendants, travelling or; their own or on conducted tours run into "areas of darkness" or "islands in the sun" and return with the impression that all of India is what they have seen or experienced. They could not be blamed.

The Steinbergs have every right to be resentful of the attempt at extortion by the houseboat owner in Kashmir. It is a pity that they could not go to the proper authorities and get redress. Kashmir, as everyone knows, sets much store by the rise in tourist traffic, particularly from abroad. There is a Tourism Department which is specific in its task to ensure visitor satisfaction. The episode also exposes the lacuna in the Tourism Department's information systems. The avarice and greed of a single unscrupulous houseboat owner is not illustrative of the experience of many others savouring this "paradise on earth".

The frequent traveller is pretty familiar with the pattern of squeezing dollars be it in Rome, Athens, Hong Kong or for that matter in India. But a visitor planning a holiday will find it worth the while to study a little in advance the realities in tourist destinations. Everyone know's tourist bus drivers/conductors the world over halt at cafes, restaurants or shopping centres where they get sizable cuts. There is however no compulsion to be led into these places either. A little forethought on the part of the tour operator could obviate such irritants. This is not to justify the grabs. Again, if the tourism authorities make it part of the media effort to publicise what and where to bargain and reach the message the visitor would have no cause for complaint. In fact, he would go back fully satisfied having obtained full worth for the money spent. A major thrust of India's tourism publicity abroad should be on its attraction as a shop-over centre.

We should not be very sensitive if someone talks of India's poverty or its beggars. It is not that we encourage vagrancy as there is a law that forbids begging. But more to the point is that we would like the visitor to see what India is doing to lift itself from the morass of poverty. The achievement so far and what India could offer in a range of tourist interests. No one disputes that there has to be attitudinal change on the part of the bureaucracy and the various agencies with which the traveller comes into contact. But there is nothing wrong in subtly conveying the message that Indians are Indians like the Dutch are Dutch, New York cannot be New Delhi. There is no mugging in New Delhi which keeps visitors confined to rooms in the American metropolis.

For every case of fraud, shortchanging or overcharging or inefficient service, one could cite hundredfold instances of display of absolute integrity. Innovation and efficiency. For that reason there could be no generalisation. India experience is variegated. So are its images. In some there should be a conscious effort on the part of everyone concerned with tourism promotion to develop some commitment to minimise the complaints as well as to acquaint the visitor the uniqueness of Indian experience.

The Rajasthan Tourism Event – An Exercise in Reinvention

The dream of achieving the heights attained by the Edinburgh Festival in Great Britain may not be easy to realise but Rajasthan Tourism, in close association with the corporate sector, the hospitality industry and organisations actively involved in preserving India's cultural heritage, have made a good beginning. The two-week Jaipur Heritage International Festival got off to a good start on January. The newly elected state chief minister Vasundhara Raje flagged off a colourful carnival pageant. Reflecting shades of the grand Republic Day parade in Delhi, it was replete with richly caparisoned elephants, swaying ships of the desert, the camels, horses, bands and an unending array of folk dancers from almost every part of Rajasthan. A spectacular laser show brought the pageant to a close in a sort of a bridge between the past and contemporary times.

The principal players that joined hands to make the festival happen are the Jaipur Virasat Foundation and the state tourism department. The central department of tourism has given a hefty grant. Among the corporates who have extended support and participation are Reliance, Hindustan Lever, Ambuja Cement and HSBC. The travel trade was represented by hotels, tour operators and national carriers.

Like Edinburgh, the whole of the Pink City, as Jaipur is known the world over (it sounds even better in Hindi-Gulabi Nagri), provided a backdrop to the festival, India's first ever international city-wide festival for a packed fortnight of events and activities. On show were the region's rich cultural legacy with events hosted in the city's spectacular heritage buildings, temples, forts and parks, presenting the very best in music, dance, theatre, arts and crafts from local as well as international artistes. The festival programme also included such activities as heritage walks, talks and seminars, sports, culinary delights and shopping. Each day there was a special occasion as Children's Day, Women's Day, Crafts Day, Heritage Day and even Special Needs Day. The organisers believe that since the wide ranging programme holds an appeal to all interests and age groups and also encouraged participation, the exercise will help create greater awareness of the wealth of local heritage and even the common man will not only start discovering its value and potential but it will also encourage him to innovate ways of using heritage spaces for performance and exhibitions. In their briefings to the large number of mediapersons invited from Delhi and even abroad, Rajasthan's tourism secretary, Arvind Mayaram and Faith Singh, honorary director of the festival and founder trustee of the Jaipur Virasat Foundation, had this to say about their effort: it has been a "real labour of love, of passion and commitment to the extraordinary rich cultural heritage of the city of Jaipur, the state and the nation at large, which we need to celebrate and showcase so that it can continue to grow." Both conceded that international acceptance of the festival and significant participation by overseas visitors will depend on how extensive and concerted marketing efforts are made. Mayaram pointed out that a beginning has already been made at global trade marts and a major effort is planned for the coming LTD in Berlin. Overseas tour operators are being persuaded to include the festival in their brochure for 2004 onwards. And, Singh explained that even the Edinburgh Festival had taken a decade's effort to attain global recognition (it is into its sixth decade).

The Jaipur Heritage International Festival is indicative of the awakening in the states of the potential of tourism. Rajasthan's foray into mega thinking has also been spurred by the discovery that its earlier tourist lure is now being shared by destinations like Goa of 365 Days of Holiday fame and Kerala, God's Own Country. Interestingly, the new and young lady chief minister of Rajasthan has kept the tourism portfolio under her own care. According to Mayaram, Vasundhara Raje is committed to making tourism "the main engine of growth for the economy". On top of the state's agenda, he said, is infrastructure like roads, accommodation, civic services. As much as Rs. 1,600 crore has been set apart for upgrading six selected cities—Jaipur, Jodhpur, Udaipur, Bikaner, Kotah and Ajmer-Pushkar. Next on the priority list, he said, are a regulatory framework, promotion and marketing and refurbishing of existing products. And all this, he said, is to be implemented with the active participation of the private sector.

The hospitality industry can only wish good luck to the Jaipur Festival and see it grow as a major event in India's tourism calendar.

A Millennium 'Sunrise' for Indian Tourism

Recently, tourism has been in focus at quite a few conferences where international figures have made key contributions. Of course, from the media point of view it was hype for Richard Branson all the way but from the long term perspective, contributions made by some of the other celebrities also merit an equal amount of attention. These include the former and present presidents of the World Travel and Tourism Council (WTTC), the private sector counterpart of the UN affiliate of government representations -World Tourism Organisation (WTO).

While the WTO headquarters are in Madrid, WTTC is based in London. WTTC's present chief, Jean-Claude Baumgarten, a French national and expert in aviation succeeded Geoffrey Lipman only two months ago.

A year ago, the organisation presented the Indian government with a special study on the potential of travel and tourism to create jobs. Investing special relevance to this visit is the Asia initiative – whose key component is the Indian section – which WTTC proposes to launch in February. Baumgarten has had several rounds of discussion with the tourism minister, senior officials and industry representatives regarding this initiative.

The Delhi discussions centred around four issues: Why is India missing the boat where tourism is concerned; why are air connections to India so inadequate; is travel and tourism a government priority; and, what action is required for the Indian tourism industry to develop fully. The new initiative is expected to provide answers to these questions.

The India-centred initiative, he explained, emerges from the realisation that the potential of growth and the economic benefits of a coordinated travel and tourism policy will be most effective in India as opposed to other countries in Asia, P R S Qberoi, vice chairman of the Oberoi group and member of the WTTC executive council will be the chief coordinator of the India Initiative. He will be aided by a WTTC nominee chosen from the country.

The Council is also looking for an Indian entrepreneur who has had experience in the private sector and maintains a good rapport with the public sector as well. Baumgarten will come to Delhi for the launch of the programme.

WTTC is approaching leading travel companies for enlistment. Membership benefits include opportunities to network with leaders of the industry in other countries and to address regional issues such as taxation, employment and capital investment. While the WTTC focus is on finding practical solutions and on implementing programmes which will be of real value to the industry. Baumgarten's own prescription is that the private sector should first set its own house in order and unite to survive and succeed in influencing governmental decisions.

He says "the key to success is unity." Though he did not say so specifically, this is certainly central to the Indian industry which is divided and fragmented. Only recently, a unity exercise found itself shorn of meaningful content at the IATO convention in Jaipur.

The second point in his formula, equally important to the Indian situation, is the need for an open skies policy. Unless there are more aircraft landing in this country, more tourists will not be able to come. To facilitate more services, a radical change in the civil aviation policy is called for. The mindset of the present bureaucratic and political leadership, if one were to go by the experience of the last several years, has to be transformed.

Baumgarten is confident that his prescription cannot only cure the malaise that affects Indian tourism and reactivate it, but also generate spin-off effects in terms of employment. According to him, at the present growth rate, the figure of 18 million persons employed in the tourism sector will rise to 25 million by 2010. But, he believes an additional 26 million jobs could be created if India adopts policy shifts and "does the same thing that the average European Union countries are doing for travel and tourism".

To the WTTC president "in order to achieve the full growth potential of travel and tourism in Asia, the right conditions need to be developed. Tht include maintaining economic and political stability as well as a whole host of specific industry issues."

He did not mince words in saying that progress is being hampered by the lack of priority status, infrastructural inadequacies, bureaucratic restrictions and poor regional promotions.

Hopefully, the millennium sunrise will usher in the right forces to lift tourism.

13
Promoting Tourism

Development of Various Tourist Spots

Indian planners working on national development for the next five years have identified tourism as a major resource. They have been supported in this view by the experience in the last few years during which tourist arrivals end foreign exchange earnings on their account have made a quantum jump. Though India has still only a small share of the tourism market, the increase in arrivals has been steady and last year it topped 1.3 million. Foreign exchange earnings which a country needs to spend, on national priorities have soared to about 1.5 billion US dollars. Now as the country chalks out an elaborate programme for India Tourism Year 1991 to promote and strengthen global awareness of its attractions, new facilities are being built.

As part of the effort to diversify tourism and also to make full use of the spread of attractions across the country new extensions to traditional circuits are being developed. These circuits will enable the visitor to experience more of Indian culture and other delights. Most people who come to India want justifiably to see the Taj but the attractions are far too many beyond the Taj as well. Even according to the established circuits Agra is linked to an itinerary that includes Delhi of seven cities dating from epic times to its current phase of expansion as a modern bustling capital. The other points in the circuit are Varanasi, the city on banks of the Ganges sanctified by faith and hope through the millennia. And, Khajuraho which is a museum by itself of the finest specimen of Indian sculpture expressing art forms as well as erotica. To this itinerary is now added Orcha.

Orcha is an archaeological delight. It is a complex of battlements dating back to 14th and 15th centuries now sheltered by dense forests. Royalty of bygone years had made the place a retreat and a refuge in those uncertain times. The Mughal emperor Jehangir, father of the builder of the

Taj is believed to have taken shelter in Orchha while being chased by his father's troops after a rebellion. The guest house built for him is known to this day as Jehangir Mahal. Some finely carved temples abound in Orcha where during the time of later day chieftains called the Bundela rulers musicians painters sculptors and men of letters flourished. They have left their imprint on life in the area. Orcha is now made easily accessible by India's superfast train, Shatabdi Express that reaches Agra from Delhi in just over two hours and Jhansi an old time British cantonment to which Orcha is next door.

Likewise, there are other established circuits to which new destinations have been added. Travellers familiar with Mumbai-Aurangabad-Udaipur can now avail themselves of facilities to see more of the glory that was Rajasthan whose annals and antiquity have been a perennial source of excitement to scholars, art lovers and explorers. Jodhpur where the visitor could relive the life of Maharajas in the palace-turned hotel. Mount Abu a hill retreat uniquely fashioned by nature in the vicinity of the desert. Chittorgarh whose forts and towers proclaim the valour of a proud people who defied the might of medieval rulers. They are all linked by air and surface transport. In the south of India, the popular circuit is Chennai-Bangalore-Mysore. But to these have been added the great temple cities of Madurai, Thajavur and Tiruchi, Kancheepuram, Mahabalipuram famed the world over for the shore temple, and Pondicherry, the one time French settlement. Each of these tourist attractions treasure the best preserved scuplture in temples where the worship has continued uninterrupted for a thousand years. The Gopurams, which are essentially towers built over the entry points of these temples, have on them countless pieces of sculpted pieces in stone, bronze and wood unmatched in ornate details. Tiers and tiers of these towers were added in successive centuries by ruling dynasties, ground these temples have also grown trade like silkweaving, stone carving and metalware. So the most expensive silks which find their way in western boutiques originate from here. A particular texture is known by the place where it is woven, called Kancheepuram. In this circuit extension it is better to travel by road as there are far too many bonus sites, on the way which one should not miss.

In the east, Chilka lake, a dream place for the angler as well as for boating and sailing, is brought into the circuit that links Kolkata-Bhubaneswar-Konarak and Puri, all abounding/masterpieces of art, sculpture and seaside resorts. Chilka is one of the largest of the fresh water lakes in India. It is studded with islands which provide a perfect habitat for many species of migratory birds from Siberia. The lake, 72 km long and 16 km wide is idyllic for small game and fishing. Other additions to this circuit are Lalitagiri and Ratnagiri, which shelter the remains of Jain and Buddhist shrines built two to three centuries before Christ. They are located in the valley of the river Mahanadi and the nearest railhead is Rourkela, a steel city in the east.

Further up in the northeast, Kolkata-Guwahati circuit is the entry point to areas where travel permits have been liberalised for foreigners. An addition to this itinerary is the Kaziranga sanctuary famous for its one-horned Rhino, the wild buffalo, the swamp deer and the fishing eagle.

The list is long and still by no means exhaustive. The Indian Department of Tourism has identified established 18 circuits to which double the number of tourist centres have been added. New infrastructural facilities like accommodation, air-taxies, eating houses have been provided to make these places easily accessible. Beyond golden triangles and squares of tourism, Indian destinations have become multi-demensional net only in terms of location but also in the variety of attractions.

STATES PROMOTING TOURISM

For Promoting Regional Tourism

Witnessing the strides made by states like Rajasthan and Goa in attracting larger number of visitors, both domestic and foreign, and the more recent initiatives launched by Kerala, West Bengal too has started tapping the vast potential of tourism. Its effort is a little more innovative, as perhaps for the first time, a state has attempted to involve neighbouring states to take part in the initiative.

It was thus that the Teesta Tea and Tourism Festival covering Sikkim, Dooars and Darjeeling was organised from December 24, 2000 -January 17, 2001, bringing together the tourism authorities and the industry segments of West Bengal, Darjeeling Hill Council and Sikkim Tourism. People participation in the festival was not of a high order because of the inadequacy of lead time for promotion but the enthusiastic response of official agencies and hotels and travel trade had spurred the West Bengal government's tourism department to cover a much wider canvas and to make the event an annual show.

It will now be known as the 'Eastern Himalayan Tourism Festival' and in addition to the existing partners – West Bengal, Darjeeling Hill Council and Sikkim – Arunachal will also join in. In addition, cultural troupes will be taking part in the main celebrations from Bhutan and invitations are also going to Assam and Meghalaya to participate. West Bengal is also making an effort to see if cultural delegations could come from Nepal and Bangladesh also.

The Eastern Himalayan Tourism festival, this year will be kicked off in Gangtok, on December 11. Spread over three days, the activities, will include cultural shows, archery competitions, food courts, visits to monasteries and trips to Nathu La at 14,400 feet, where a thin wire separates Indian and Chinese troops on Tibet's border with India, as well as to the scenic Chhangu lake at 12,000 feet. And, of course spectacular views of the world's third highest snow peak, Kanchenjunga.

On December 15 the festivities move to Arunachal Pradesh, where also for three days this northeastern state will unveil its tourist attractions in the Taeju-Walong sector of Lohit district. The scene shifts to Darjeeling on December 22 until Christmas eve. Again, three days of festivities, which will include more spectacular viewing of Kanchenjunga especially, the sun rise from Tiger Hill. There will be rides on the Darjeeling Hill Railways (the toy train), which has recently been bestowed the status of a world heritage in celebration of which a quaint museum has been set up at the Ghoom station recording the history of this engineering marvel. This writer witnessed a Japanese TV team from Tokyo Broadcasting System (TBS) making a documentary on the train, which will be shown in its world heritage series. The team has also been assigned another documentary on Delhi's Qutb Minar and Humayun's Tomb. Unknown to many of us in the tourism industry, the channel has already telecasted documentaries on the Taj, Konark Sun Temple, Ellora, Nanda Devi, Khajuraho and Elephanta Caves'near Mumbai. Eisuke Kono, programme director of TBS, told Express Hotelier and Caterer that at least half the Japanese population watch the world heritage series, so popular is the programme, TBS teams' Indian itineraries have been handled by Indiana travels which opened the Japan market to India.

To return to the festival, Darjeeling has a new attraction, a snow-leopard breeding centre at the Padmaja Naidu Zoo. From Darjeeling the festival moves to Dooars for its last leg of four days of exciting activities beginning on Christmas day. Starting with a one day travel and tourism fair in Siliguri, the base for discovering the Eastern Himalayas, the packages will include Dooars on Wheels, train ride through wild life sanctuaries (don't miss Jaldapara and its one-horned Rhino and Phuntsoling the foothills town in Bhutan is only 30 km away) and, of course, visits to tea gardens where you will see miles and miles of acres manicured bushes looking like an unending green carpet. Watch the deft hands that pluck two leaves and a bud and how within 12-18 hours machines convert them into the wonder brew with which most of us start our day.

On the cards is also an all India conference on eco-tourism at the North Bengal University Campus near Bagdogra, the Siliguri airport. Plans are also being worked out for an East Himalayan Car Rally from Gangtok to Arunachal Pradesh.

The Automobile Association of East India (AAEI) will organise the rally and the event will be sponsored by Indian Oil. The postal department is expected to release a special stamp and first day covers for the Eastern Himalayan Festival.

Subrata Sen Gupta, operational manager (north), West Bengal Tourism Corporation, who briefed travel journalists on preparations for the festival said the state government is also preparing a 20 year perspective tourism plan with help from professional consultants with special emphasis on eco-tourism. employment generation and raising the state effort to the national level.

The industry will be keenly watching West Bengal's effort at promoting regional tourism whose success might become a model for other states.

There's Something About Alwar

If Kerala set the ball rolling in promoting an individual state as a destination, Rajasthan can take the credit for extending the idea further to a part of the state. The young collector of Alwar district, Tanmaye Kumar is unhappy that while Sariska, the tiger sanctuary, and the Neemrana Fort Palace, the heritage attraction, are pretty well known in India and abroad as coveted tourist spots, few know that both are part of Alwar district whose headquarters, town and the surroundings have as much to offer. Alwar, a former princely state before it became a district of Rajasthan, has its own share of palaces, forts, temples, a rich culture, music and dance as well as cuisine and handicrafts.

Alwar lost some of its importance when a new route was opened to Jaipur from Delhi avoiding this city and the few who do manage to visit it are people in transit to Sariska or the spillover from Sariska when the season is at its peak. Now, with a dose of infrastructure the state department of tourism and Alwar city authorities are determined to make Alwar a destination in its own rights.

The media fame tour organised in the run up to this year's Utsav, comprising travel journalists and reporters from national newspapers, was itself a welcome change from past practice in most parts of the country. The initiative came from the industry – hoteliers, service providers, caterers, Pepsi, even Alwar's swanky and brand new private engineering college. The city now has its first classified (two-star) hotel, the Aravali, whose managing director Achal Kakkar was the lead organiser and accompanied the journalists right from the starting point in Delhi's Bikaner House. Of course, Rajasthan's tourism department is supporting the effort with full assistance from the district authorities.

Alwar's city palace, built over 200 years ago, is a fine blend of Mughal and Rajput styles and has graceful marble pavilions. Much of the palace is now used as government offices but a part has been converted into an interesting museum whose armoury section has swords said to belong to Mohammed Ghori, Akbar and Aurangzeb. There is the Sala Qila, a fort built in 928 A.D. but which never saw any bloodshed. The cultural assets includes the Mewari *gharana* to which Pandit Jasraj belongs. Many communities such as Mirasis, Jogis and Meena have preserved their folk music traditions and the Meo Muslims of Alwar are famous for singing the *Pandu Ki Kada* – retelling the Mahabharata.

Vegetarian cuisine is popular in Alwar and the city boasts of its equivalent of Jaipur's LMB – the Prem Pavitra Bhojanalaya with plenty of pure ghee preparations but sans garlic and onion. Janaki Prasad Beniwal, who came penniless to Alwar some 50 years ago now has a turnover of half a crore of rupee and is waiting for his son to finish his hotel management course to open branches outside of the city. Rajasthan is famous for its footwear, especially the Jeoti and Alwar has its own distinctive variety.

Travelling to Alwar from Delhi you also have the opportunity to visit an important Jain temple at Tigara on the way, and, once in Alwar, Sariska and Neemrana and the nearby Silserh are also must.

Sariska Palace, once a royal hunting lodge, is now a heritage hotel in the tiger sanctuary and there are a number of ancient temples and forts including Kankwari. It is in this fort that Aurangzeb had kept his brother Dara Shikoh prisoner in the succession war. And, of course, you see a lot of wild life and with luck even a tiger.

The mystery of an engineering college being among the sponsors of the media fam tour was soon solved when we met the promoter of this first private sector enterprise in Rajasthan, Dr. Vishnu Agarwal. His foray into engineering education was inspired by his engineer father but his own spirit of entrepreneurship urged him to extend his experience as a medical practitioner into the hospitality sector. He has just launched a sprawling health resort a little off the Delhi-Jaipur highway some 30 kms short of the pink city. Christened Sunrise Chandra Health Resort, it has a 40-bed Ayurveda hospital and 60 cottages for stressed out corporates and families and those looking for relaxed holidays with a gym, yoga, meditation and Ayurveda oil massages thrown in and medical aid for those in need of it. The Alwar experience is worth replicating elsewhere.

14

Encouraging Trends Shown by the Industry

Tourism in India is looking up again after the sluggish growth in the early Eighties and the nose dive during the 1984-85 seasons following the tragic events of the last months of 1984. Final figures of tourist arrivals during the calendar year, 1985, is 836,908 – just about reversing the negative growth rate into a meager 0.2 per cent increase over 1984. But January 1986 has really brought good news. Arrivals during the month were 17.3 per cent higher than those in the same month in 1985, a record increase since tourism's halcyor days of the Sixties and Seventies. Gone are the long faces of hoteliers and travel agents. Whether in the capital, New Delhi, or in the metropolitan cities of Mumbai, Chennai, Bangalore, or resorts like Goa, hotel had near 100 per cent occupancies right through October till the end of April. Delhi, which just two years ago was groaning under the weight of "over-built" rooms, could have done with a few hundred more, considering the shortage of accommodation in the better known hotels.

Travels agents and hoteliers are agreed that the spurt in travel to India is not caused as much by 'pure' tourists as those moving around for business and conferences. And those travelling for business of conferences do spend more than tourists because their expenses are paid by companies or organizations sponsoring their visits. Which means that in the last few months, hotels and other services points in the tourist industry must have earned much more per traveller than in earlier years.

Take the case of an international conference (held in the capital this March) of the Young Presidents Organisations, an American-based body with worldwide membership of those who became chief executive of companies before attaining the age of 40. Five hundred spouses (or guests) attended this seven-day get-together with a 14 hour-day schedule packed with work session and relaxation. A whole five-star was 'taken over' by the organisers with strict security and well-rehearsed *bandobast.*

The special point of interest for the travel trade is the revenue fallout for the industry. One estimate is that the hotel which hosted the YPOs, earned the equivalent of Rs. 1 crore in room rent, food, drinks and other services. W Scott Supernaw, president of Olson-Travel world, a pioneer in promoting travel to India from the United States, who attended YPO meet, told a Delhi newspaper that the country must have earned an equal amount (Rs. 1 crore) from the shopping sprees of the YPO wives. According to him, one shopper had ordered goods worth Rs. 90,000 from the hotel's shopping arcade alone.

And for the promotional fallout let us turn to Supernaw again. According to him, five hundred chief executives, engaged in varying trades and industries, would certainly their own trading and industrial organizations to consider India as a venture for their future conference. Supernaw also pointed out that at a personal level, chief executives would be better able to remove misgivings and fears of visiting India (what with its poverty and lack of drinking water!) than lesser mortals. Supernaw's projection is that in the current year there should be a hundred per cent increase in travel from the United States to India. Incidentally, the USA is India's second biggest market for tourism. Some 85,000 Americans visit this country every year.

Business travel to India has been growing steadily. The country's emergence as a major industrial power and the recent steps to encourage investment from abroad, have been the real factors in the growth, have been the real factors in the tourist trade. Foreign collaborations, especially the more recent ones in the automotive sector, have meant dozens of technicians, consultants and specialists travelling frequently for signing agreements supervising installation of machines, training manpower and being present at the 'launch' of the products.

Then there are scores of delegations visiting this country at the inte-governmental level as well as at private levels. Women pilots from around the world came to Delhi to confer on safety and education. Women entrepreneurs from neighbouring Pakistan felt the urge to meet their counterparts in India. The Australians came here to share their expertise on water resources. Pierre Cardin, apart from interesting us in getting into his high fashion, also wants to develop Indian garment exports to the Soviet Union. Then there is the European Economic Forum which holds meetings with captains of Indian Industry. And scores of chambers of commerce regularly send delegations to meet leading lights of the Indian chambers.

While the sun shines again on international tourism, concern for domestic tourism has passed the lip service stage. After decades of neglect, signs of a serious effort to make travel for the 'native' comfortable and attractive also, are discernible. About this, some other time.

New Incentives for Tourism

Two major decisions announcement by the National Front government will have far reaching effects on the tourism scene. The first and this concerns aviation, will ensure an almost open skies policy on charters and air taxis. And, the second gives further incentives to the hotel industry to encourage investments in hills rural areas and those centres where there is shortage of accommodation. So far as air taxis are concerned, almost all restrictions on their operations, size of aircraft, flying schedules, airports to be used, have been removed.

Similarly, charters can now land anywhere and touch more than one point. And, to ensure that genuine tourists travel by charters a minimum ground expenditure of Rs. 350 per passenger is to be levied. It is obvious both these steps have been taken in the teeth of opposition by our national and domestic carriers but industry circles appreciate they are in the larger interests of tourism promotion. These circles also feel that early action will be necessary to provide back-ups to air taxi and charter, movements. For instance, if a chartar is to land at an airport other than an international one, immigration and customs facilities will have to be provided.

The new incentives to the hotel industry include exemption from expenditure tax for ten years and a 50 per cent rebate on income tax for a fixed period. Industry circles are however awaiting the notification of the areas where the inducements will be applicable. In any case, they point out that the real problem is lack of suitable land at suitable prices and unless this is solved first no large scale investments in new hotels are likely to flow. Also, there is need for a single window clearance for hotel projects; the present practice of knocking at 30 different agencies' doors is too time-consuming. Hopefully, the tourism ministry is applying its mind to this problem.

TOURISM GETS POLITICAL SUPPORT

Tourism Finally Gets Recognition at Red Fort

Tourism is a big source of employment generation and foreign exchange earning. Indeed it is the fastest growing industry in the world today." What, another plea repeated day in and day out by those in the hospitality industry who have been espousing the cause of tourism? No, this time you are wrong. It is the Prime Minister of India, Atal Bihari Vajpayee, speaking from the ramparts of the historic Red Fort in Delhi on Independence Day, August 15, 2001. Many in the audience and millions who watched him on television must have rubbed their ears when he added, "To achieve this end, we shall unveil a progressive national tourism policy before the end of the year."

It was indeed a great moment for tourism which has come after a long wait of 54 years. It does not mean that the sector has overnight been accorded the degree of priority it deserves; but, it does mean that WTTC's dream expressed less than a fortnight ago that tourism be driven by the highest authority in the land has started taking shape. At this point all he has signified is that he sees the potential of employment and foreign exchange in tourism. And, all he has promised is that a 'progressive national tourism policy' will be unveiled before the end of the year. One must hasten to congratulate minister Ananth Kumar and his team at DoT (department of tourism) for their quiet work which has culminated in the recognition to tourism in the Red Fort speech. It remains to be seen how progressive the tourism policy will be or whether there will be a time bound action plan also with an assured mechanism of implementation.

There are encouraging signals from other high places. After the stirrings in the Planning Commission in its mid-term appraisal of the ninth plan, which, after conceding that tourism had not received priority in national development, had merely identified the causes of the sector's poor performances and made some suggestions for remedial action.

In a follow-up development, the commission's task force on employment opportunities under Montek Singh Ahluwalia has recommended a few solid action points in a chapter on travel and tourism, it would be useful to quote from the task force document, 'India's potential for both domestic and international tourism is greatly underutilised. Expansion in international tourism could contribute a substantial expansion in high quality employment opportunities in the years ahead'. It goes on, 'the following policy initiatives are extremely important from the point of view of developing tourism:

(1) Hotel room capacity in major Indian tourism centres especially of the mid-price variety is not adequate to support an expanded flow of tourists. Local authorities must take steps to earmark available land for hotel construction and expedite grant of necessary permissions for setting up good quality hotels with reasonable prices.

(2) The existing policy on bilateral air agreements needs to be urgently reviewed to ensure sufficient expansion in airline seat capacity.

(3) The combined effect of luxury tax and expenditure tax makes Indian hotels unduly expensive. These taxes need to be moderated; and

(4) The visa regime needs to be liberalised to obtain a visa on arrival as practiced in many important tourist destinations'.

It is interesting to note that the Planning Commission's task force is looking at tourism as offering 'high quality employment opportunities' and supports the industry view that it is taxes which have made Indian hotels expensive. The task force has rightly emphasised the need for faster development of the mid-market segment in hotels especially at tourist centres. While the awakening at the centre's level is to be welcomed, the states, at least some of them, are also beginning to see in tourism an instrument of development. Courtesy PHD Chamber tourism committee, the Madhya Pradesh government shared with industry representatives the good news that it too wishes to get into a development mode after years of neglect.

The state's tourism minister, Ajay Singh, assured that the aberration of luxury tax on rack rates will soon be amended to be levied on the actual bill, and, roads connecting wild life sanctuaries – the state's main attraction for tourists – are being attended to on a priority basis.

The assurance came after the chamber's committee chairman, V. N. Dalmia had pointed out how the state had been left behind in attracting both foreign and domestic tourists, and, a leading tour operator, Vikram Madhok (Aber Crombie and Kent) who brings in high spending foreigners, warned that he was taking Bandavgarh sanctuary off his itinerary because of 'pot holed roads' leading to it. MP tourism secretary, Susham Nath, said a mechanism for single window clearance for tourism projects would soon be in place.

Political Support Lends Wings to Tourism

The hospitality industry's dream of a prime minister-led tourism effort is nowhere near realisation. But, there is a silver lining – the sector has found some space as an instrument of development in the thought processes at the highest level. Ever since Prime Minister Atal Behari Vajpayee referred to tourism's potential in his Independence Day address two years ago – the first time this honour was bestowed from the ramparts of the Red Fort – the industry has been looking forward to August 15 for more leads. This year the Prime Minister moved ahead from identifying potential to action-oriented initiatives. What is more heartening, the President too in his Independence Day telecast the previous evening, spoke of tourism's "Tremendous potential for wealth generation," the first time the head of state has broached the subject. More importantly, Dr. A. P. J. Abdul Kalam went on to suggest that "Tourism be made the fifth mission," in the quest for achieving a 'Developed India' by 2020. And, to achieve this mission, the President said improvement of infrastructure is essential; thrust is required to be given for inland water navigation, hotels, communications and tourism promotion, "If we promote sustainable tourism, it will become India's core competence," he added.

To come back to the Prime Minister. The hospitality industry is fully conscious now that tourism can prosper only in a "Dynamic globally competent economy," the acclaimed objective of economic reforms launched in the early nineties and being pushed through by the present government.

The larger picture that Vajpayee painted did point to the move forward towards that goal. His promise of a mission to the moon (Chandrayaan I) by 2008 or that (software exports have already leap frogged from Rs. 8,000 crore to Rs. 50,000 crore should come as fascinating tools for promoting Destination India, as the confluence of a modern nation and an ancient civilisation.

The industry should appreciate that faster and quality growth of infrastructure as part of the country's general development is crucial for a push to tourism as well. A road network is one such area. In the prime minister's own words: "In the first five decades of independence, only 550 km of four lane highways were built. In other words, only 11 km a year. Now, we will build 24,000 km of highways at the rate of 11 km a day. The Rs. 54,000 crore national highway development project is progressing rapidly. Three lakh people are working on it. Next year, this number will go up to six lakh a day."

The Economic Survey had recently said that the 5,846 km golden quadrilateral linking the four metros will be substantially complete this year) and 817 km of the 7,300 km north-south, east-west corridor has already been built. This massive venture will be completed by 2007.

Turning to tourism-specific issues, the Prime Minister made quite a few significant remarks especially about Pakistan and Kashmir. Asking our neighbour to "Walk together on the road peace," he said, "Let people travel to and fro. Let more and more elected representatives visit each other's country. Let us expand bilateral cultural relations." Vajpayee shared with millions of viewers the good news on domestic movements into Kashmir. "This year, more than one lakh tourists went to Kashmir. There was a large turn out of pilgrims going to the Amarnath Yatra. Nearly six thousand students from different parts of India are studying in Kashmir," he stated.

Without naming union minister for tourism, Jagmohan, the Prime Minister paid him a tribute for his good work in cleaning up monuments. Pointing out that "India has limitless potential in tourism," he said, "Take the case of the historic Red Fort itself. It has been taken up for comprehensive restoration for the very first time in 350 years. I can see that a beautiful garden is coming up in the ground in front of me. It can be befittingly called the August 15 Park."

And, he asked the people, "I would like you too to emulate this example by undertaking such beautiful projects for the conservation of heritage in your own village or town." Interesting, President Kalam also referred to the same subject in his speech.

According to official sources a Tourism Infrastructural Development Fund is being created to "Speedily improve, through a strategy of public-private partnership, roads, water, power, sanitation and overall ambience in all the high potential tourist destinations."

Independence Day 2003 has certainly made the industry feel good.

Together, we shall Face the Adversity and Convert it into a New Opportunity for Indian Tourism: PM

It was tourism's big day when the prime minister, chief ministers and state ministers alongwith industry representatives were to sit together to give the sector "a new direction" got postponed, because of the sad events of September 11, finally arrived on October 30. But at the end of the daylong deliberations in the main auditorium of the swanky Vigyan Bhawan in the capital, the mood was certainly not upbeat. There were no announcements that would have set the Yamuna on fire nor were there any sops offered to the travel industry to tide over the current crisis. Expectations that some such decisions were on the way had been raised by media hype but industry leaders were finally reconciled that these were unrealistic. This is not to suggest that the first ever conference of chief ministers, state ministers, and industry representatives did not achieve anything at all. The fact that such a meeting did take place as a follow-up to Atal Behari Vajpayee's 'historic' reference to the potential of tourism in his Red Fort speech is in itself a significant step forward. It is largely in the states that action to implement the national tourism policy will have to be taken. The New Delhi interface will certainly encourage those states, and there are many of them, who have not yet woken up to the benefits of tourism as an employment generator and a sure engine for poverty alleviation, to learn from the initiatives taken by Kerala and Rajasthan.

The second and equally important contribution of the conference is that along with the prime minister, it was also addressed by the deputy chairman of the Planning Commission, K. C. Pant, and finance minister, Yashwant Sinha. Home minister L. K. Advani too was billed to speak but he couldn't come. The presence of the finance minister and Pant signified that at long last, the government as a whole or at least the important segments of it are looking at tourism's merits as part of the country's general development. The Planning Commission is about to finalise the Tenth Plan and it has already been indicated on its behalf that there will be a much larger allocation for tourism.

On the question of taxation, there was categoric support from the prime minister himself. Said he, "Lack of uniformity in taxes, laws and regulation also creates problems (for tourism)." These are further compounded, he added, by the complexity and multiplicity of taxes, which have a cascading effect on the ultimate price that the tourist has to pay. This also leads to confusion and inefficiency, reducing India's global competitiveness in tourism." "Therefore," the prime minister urged, "There is an urgent need to rationalise both central and state taxes on the tourism and travel industry." The finance minister thought, a solution lay with the states which in the past had stepped in with their own levies whenever the Centre reduced or waived its imposts. He commended to the states the mechanism of the standing committee of finance ministers for coordinating and reviewing the impact of taxation on the tourism industry.

The prime minister said he was happy that he would be able to fulfil his promise of 15th August to have a tourism policy in place by the end of the year inspite of the unexpected road block. And, he added, "In order to promote continuous interaction among various contributors to the successful implementation of this policy, we have decided to constitute a Tourism Advisory Council at the national level. Besides, having representatives of the Centre and state governments, the council will also have members of Parliament, industry representatives, and eminent public figures." He would like similar councils to be set up in the states. Briefing newspersons at the end of the meeting tourism minister, Jagmohan, said the Advisory Council would be set up "soon" and gave the assurance that it would meet regularly every three months. Doubts about the effectiveness of such a large body were expressed during the discussions by industry veteran, Inder Sharma.

Two issues that dominated the deliberations were the blanket rule against any construction within 500 metres of the coastlines and the harsh enforcement of forest laws. Several chief ministers and ministers from coastal states said the CRZ was coming in the way of any tourism development project. Others complained that environmental clearance for projects in forest areas was being generally denied or delayed with the result that very few projects were getting off the ground. A third issue, the proposal to put tourism in the Concurrent List (it does not figure in either the central or state list) was looked upon more favourably by the state representatives, even by those who had earlier opposed the idea.

The prime minister sought to allay the fears of the industry about the aftermath of the terrorist attacks in the US. He said, "What are challenges for, if not to be faced with confidence, and to be overcome with determination? Together, we shall face the adversity and convert it into a new opportunity for Indian tourism."

Inspiring words for the travel trade. But only time will tell whether tourism has found a new direction.

Unity in Political Debate Furthers Tourism

The most significant gain of the first ever political debate on tourism's contribution to the national economy was that it could be arranged at all. At least spokesmen of two major contenders for power, the BJP and the Congress, shared a platform with two former civil servants, a former cabinet minister for tourism, and travel trade leaders. Also, it was the first joint effort of the four apex bodies, TAAI, IATO, FHRAI and HAI, to come together on an issue of common interest.

What the organisers hoped to achieve through the political debate was to assess tho approach of the principal political parties to tourism and to secure from them a commitment to fully back the sector. Journalist and TV presenter Siddharath Bhatia acted as the moderator. If as a senior leader of the trade, Inder Sharma, contended that tourism had suffered because of the lack of political will, the political parties were not willing to buy it.

Jairam Ramesh, speaking for the Congress, pointedly rebutted the complaint saying the fault was not a lack of political will but it lay in structural problems. According to him a party's support to any trade or industry could not be measured by the wordage in a manifesto devoted to it. There could be a special chapter but it would mean nothing. He tried to turn the tables on the trade by asserting that instead of saying, 'support the tourism sector' the trade should focus on the most vital related issue of land use, power, telecom and so on.

Even so, he would agree that his party would back tourism, and for that matter any activity, that would generate jobs and help develop backward areas. The tourism sector stood the test on both counts. He was not very much impressed by arguments that it is a great foreign exchange earner as long as the sector would help other priority demands of employment and development. Ramesh's stand on foreign exchange was certainly not acceptable to other participants like S. K. Misra, former secretary tourism and civil aviation and Dr. Nilish Sengupta, former DO tourism and one-time revenue secretary. They maintained that inflow of foreign exchange through FIIs and debt instruments need to be repaid and tourism was a painless source of earning foreign exchange. The Congress spokesman also questioned the propriety of the trade's demand that revenue earned by way of tourism taxation should all be ploughed back into the sector.

On the point of ploughing back, Ramesh received support from the most unlikely quarter, Vijay Kumar Malhotra of the BJP. Explaining his party's approach he wondered how if taxes raised from a particular trade are to be ploughed back in entirely, social demands like education and health could be met. He agreed there was need for rationalisation of taxes and insisted that his party would favour uniform standards in respect of levies like sales tax. Malhotra scored over his political opponent in winning applause from the audience consisting of representatives of the travel industry when he declared unequivocally that BJP supported tourism all the way.

Interestingly, while both political spokesmen supported repeal of the Urban Land Ceiling Act that would make available land for hospitality services neither of them could explain why the constitutional requirement of legislative support for revocation by just two states was not forthcoming. This requirement had to be fulfilled to endorse the central legislative action to which the UF government was committed.

Though Malhotra held tourism as a sector positioned in the national interest he had to face embarrassing moments when questions were raised from the floor on the delay in giving approval to two new hotels in Delhi. And, Ramesh was quick enough to blame the stand off in the case of at least one hotel on the intra-party quarrel in the BJP.

The discussion, however, pointed to a consensus among all participants in favour of encouragement and incentives to the tourism sector. In what form these should be done there could be further debate. And, Malhotra suggested that in view of the national consensus on tourism all parties should sit together as a follow-up.

The trade's people had their own reservations on the approach of the political parties. Neeraj Ghei, president of TAAI, lamented that in the commemorative golden jubilee session of Parliament not a word was uttered about tourism's role. The absence of recognition of tourism reflected, according to Inder Sharma, the lack of political will. Dr. Karan Singh, who was the first ever cabinet minister for tourism, regretted the lack of sustained interest in the sector after his initial tenure of seven years in the late 60s.

The first ever debate of this kind could be a beginning for the awareness campaign which tourism surely needs.

Keeping Fingers Crossed

Until the advent of the first BJP-led government if a tourism well-wisher had been asked to name the biggest obstacle in the way of a breakthrough for this sector he would have promptly replied "lack of political will." It was for the first time since independence that a political party had included a reference to tourism in its election manifesto. Not only that, when it came to power, it gave charge of the tourism portfolio to a heavy weight, Madanlal Khurana. The minister lost no time and set in motion a number of initiatives which swelled hopes in the hearts of the hospitality industry *wallas* that tourism was on the way to acquiring a place on the national agenda. Among the steps taken by Khurana was the constitution of a ministers' group to coordinate and expedite policy decision on tourism and a committee of secretaries to implement them speedily. He took out from cold storage the draft of the national tourism policy, had it spruced up and got it endorsed by ministers in the states in charge of the subject. Proposals which would provide greater institutional support to tourism development, promotion and marketing, long pushed to back burners were revived. These included the controversial issue of a national tourism board with private sector participation for which a World Tourism Organisation expert had also given her recommendations. The industry's long standing demand that the tourism ministry ought to have its own PR set and a crisis management mechanism was at Khurana's intervention processed again. However, before any of the great initiatives could come to fruition, Khurana resigned and tourism became an 'additional' charge for another minister. And, before he could address any of the issues, the government fell. In the long run up to the elections and several weeks of polling and government formation, tourism slid back into the shadows.

Hopes rose again when Uma Bharti became minister, although there was disappointment that the portfolio was not headed by a cabinet rank incumbent. The lady minister quickly got down to business and provided the lead the ministry was looking for: spiritualism, alternative medicine and culture were India's unique draw cards as a destination and these must be at the core of the promotional and marketing campaigns. In fact, she won tremendous applause from a largely international hospitality industry gathering at the World Travel Mart (WTM) in London when she projected her India in a down to earth manner. But before her ideas could be converted into an action plan, she too resigned.

So, the travel industry is now building its hopes around the new minister, Ananth Kumar, who had earlier held additional charge of tourism. This time around by a happy coincidence he is also in charge of culture which is only the other side of the tourism coin and one can expect synergies to flow out of this union. Already, the minister has in a major initiative ordered that the National Culture Fund (NCF) set up as a trust in November 1996 be put on a firmer footing. NCF's aim to "preserve and promote our precious tangible and intangible heritage in partnership with the community." He has asked government to raise the corpus of the fund from Rs. 4.5 crore to nearly Rs. 20 crore and donations have been exempted from income tax. The council that administers the Fund is being reconstituted with representatives from the corporate world as well as media persons and opinion leaders. Better maintained monuments with good visitor facilities alone can draw tourists.

But what the industry is watching with great interest is the outcome of the minister's request to the prime minister to constitute a cabinet committee on tourism under his own chairmanship. This is certainly improvement over the earlier arrangement of a ministers' group. That Atal Behari Vajpayee took time off to preside over the Sindhu Darshan festivities in Leh shows that he cares for tourism. Home minister Advani was also present in the Ladakh capital and one hopes that Ananth Kumar did take the opportunity to persuade both Vajpayee and Advani for an initiative on tourism not only for a cabinet committee but also on such pressing demands as visa on arrival.

The tourism ministry is reportedly working on an alternative plan should the idea of a cabinet committee not take-off. This was indicated by secretary, M. P. Bezbaruah at an IATO function where he was felicitated on being elected chairman of PATA international. A high powered National Tourism Advisory Council is in the making with the prime minister at its head. It will have 50 members, half of them tourism ministers from the states, MPs, industry leaders, a few captains of the corporate world and media persons. Bezbaruah also said that another national committee on the development of pilgrim centres and to raise resources for the purpose is also being constituted. The travel industry can only keep its fingers crossed.

GREATER RECOGNITION GIVEN TO HOTELS

Export House Status - A Privilege, also a Responsibility

Hotel Association of India (HAI) has made a distinct contribution to the entire service sector by prompting the ministries concerned, other than tourism, to recognise its role in economic development and exports.

Its efforts have not gone unrewarded. At a national seminar in the Capital – to which the Ministries of Commerce, Finance and Tourism sent their senior functionaries - it was agreed that the next EXIM policy could have a special chapter on tourism. This is no small achievement as, even after securing a position as a top foreign exchange earner by export of services, tourism has remained ignored both in the long term and short term EXIM policies.

The seminar was also well-timed insofar as the participants could project their views just before the next policy statement is to be finalised. In fact, a major announcement at the seminar was the constitution of a task force on the initiative of the Commerce Ministry to expedite its report.

The task force is to comprise a representative each of the five apex bodies – TAAI, HAI, FHRAI, IATO and ITTA – with officials of the director general of foreign trade, which will have a major say in the finalisation of the policy. Coinciding with the seminar was the announcement that Indian Hotels Company Ltd. (Taj Group) has been given the status of super trading house, the highest in the export house hierarchy in terms of performance and entitle ment.

The convening of the seminar itself had aroused much interest in the trade in view of the discontent among certain sections over the eligibility clause for Export House Status in the tourism sector. While the earlier Commerce Ministry announcement had spoken of a Rs. six crore earning of forex as the minimum required for export status as measured against Rs. 12 crore in the case of other sectors, the travel trade – particularly tour operators – felt that most of them will be left out because they will not reach the threshold limit.

There has been intense lobbying by IATO supported by the tourism ministry to persuade the finance ministry to lower the limit. Both, trade and Tourism Ministry sources claim this has been agreed to but it came out during the seminar discussion that a formal notification is yet to be gazetted. But, it was promised on behalf of the government that it would be forthcoming in the next few days.

The promise however carried a caveat. Nripendra Misra, additional secretary in Commerce the Ministry, was frank that the trade should guard itself against fly-by-night operators availing themselves of the newly acquired status.

He also reminded the participants that the export status was not all privilege and no responsibility. For instance, permission to import goods on zero duty and the waiver of bank guarantee carried with it the responsibility of fulfilling a specified level of export performance. Failure would invite payment of duty and interest at the rate of 24 per cent. In any event, the seminar served to secure clarity on many equivocal issues arising from the announcement by the Commerce Ministry and tourism officials as also trade representatives some time ago. On the part of the trade, it was also significant that they could come together on a common platform.

It was educative for quite a few participants as it was explained to them in detail about the procedures and modalities for export benefits, the EPCG scheme as also institutional framework for securing the benefits, namely the Export Promotion Council.

HAI, under Habib Rehman, was definitely the initiator of the exercise but the role of the Tourism Ministry could not be minimised. Both, secretary M. P. Bezbaruah and D.G. Ashok Pradhan pointed out that their efforts in furthering the campaign of awareness about tourism's gains at the government and political levels had yielded results. The benefits which the trade has received in the past two years are illustrative of the positive achievements of the awareness campaign.

They did some plain speaking too as incentives by themselves do not foster the growth of tourism. Ultimately it is the quality of the product and service that is the final determinant. The trade was pointedly asked what it had done specifically on its own for product improvement.

Notwithstanding the demonstration of unity by different segments of the trade, a few of the participants perhaps found that old habits die hard and had to introduce some jarring note. The seminar's focus was on Export House Status for tourism but one or two tour operators deemed it necessary to question the norms of sharing tax benefits on foreign exchange profits.

And, it was left to a government functionary to point out that they had chosen the wrong platform to settle the scores.

Hotels are Back in Business

Predictions by international agencies like the World Tourism Organisation (WTO) that 2003 will be a year of recovery for the hospitality industry seem to be coming true, perhaps even earlier, if one goes by the third quarter results of the hotel segment. Established chains like the Taj, ITC-Welcomgroup and emerging groups like The Grand Inter-Continental of Bharat Hotels, Hyatt Regency of Asian Hotels, have recorded good performances. Some have a returned to black from red.

Only the spokesperson of the Taj group is on record on what led to improved balance sheets. He attributed the performance to both increase in market share and overall improvement in market conditions. Withdrawal of travel advisories and "aggressive marketing, enhanced recovery in business traffic" is another reason offered by the Taj functionary. Industry watchers add that the revival of conference, both national and international, has also helped. All this is welcome news, says Rattan Keswani, general manager of The Oberoi in the capital, but "we still have to go a long way to improve ARRs." Asked if the recovery trend was definite or a temporary phase he said as of now it was a definite swing but there is no knowing what might happen if there is war over Iraq. Any invasion and prolonged conflict could possibly create another serious setback for the industry. "We have to keep our fingers crossed," he added.

Now let us take a look at how individual hotel companies have fared. Of course, all of them have shown higher revenues as well as better profits. Indian Hotels, Taj group's flagship company, returned an 86 per cent increase in its net profit in the third quarter from Rs. 6.01 crore to Rs. 11.17 crore while total income jumped from Rs. 134.19 crore to Rs. 170.10 crore. A group company, Benares Hotels, improved its revenue from Rs. 2.65 crore to Rs. 3.24 crore and the net profit from Rs. 44.21 lakh to Rs. 71.14 lakh. A footnote ascribes this to the "increased focus of the company on domestic markets."

ITC Hotels has shown a spectacular recovery. From a net loss in the second quarter of Rs. 3.65 crore, it has recorded a net profit of Rs. 2.94 crore in the third quarter; the total income has moved up from Rs. 27.27 crore to Rs. 33.65 crore. Interestingly, the balance sheet is signed, in addition to the managing director Habib Rehman, by the newly appointed chief operating officer, Nakul Anand, and anointed in the line of succession. The chain's flagship, Maurya Sheraton in Delhi and its Mumbai arm, the Grand Maratha Sheraton, whose performance is reflected in the balance sheet of the parent ITC Ltd. have also done well. The hotels' segment in ITC's third quarter results shows revenues increased from Rs. 39.80 crore to Rs. 54.05 crore and returns from a loss of Rs. 1.66 crore to a net of Rs. 5.65 crore.

The public sector India Tourism Development Corporation (ITDC) with many of its hotels privatised has also come up with a better performance. Its hotel division's revenue is up from Rs. 19.75 crore to Rs. 27.03 crore, and from a loss of Rs. 6.38 crore in the second quarter it has notched up a profit of Rs. 70.89 lakh in the third quarter. A matter of concern for ITDC must be the higher losses from the international trade division (duty free shops) which have increased from Rs. 77.66 lakh to Rs. 2.09 crore. In the past good profits from this segment used to shore up the corporation's overall bottomline.

Lalit Suri promoted Bharat Hotels, which with the acquisition of three ITDC disinvested properties and its own greenfield projects has emerged as a deluxe chain, has also emerged from a net loss in the second quarter (Rs. 2.84 lakh) to a net profit in the third quarter (Rs. 2.56 crore) with revenue moving up from Rs. 13.67 crore to Rs. 21.19 crore. Bharat Hotels, which is being marketed under a new brand name of "The Grand Inter-Continental Hotels' already has five" operational properties in Delhi, Srinagar (the former Lake Palace managed by the Oberois), Ashoka-Bangalore, Udaipur and Khajuraho. Two new properties will be added in April in Mumbai and Goa.

And, finally, Asian Hotels, which for almost two decades was a single property (Hyatt Regency in Delhi), a product to the hotel rush of Asiad 1982, now has deluxe presence in two other metros – Kolkata and Mumbai. It has almost doubled its profits in the 3rd quarter from Rs. 3.03 crore to Rs. 5.97 crore; revenues are up from Rs. 21.69 crore to Rs. 28.75 crore. Kolkata's Hyatt Regency opened its doors in January this year while the hotel in Mumbai is undergoing trial runs.

The hospitality industry looks forward to an uninterrupted chance to the recovery mode.

Hotel Chains Tie Up with Each Other

The buzzword is brand name. The compulsions are capital and marketing. As many as twenty-one collaborations are in-varying stages of implementation in the hotel industry. The tie-ups are all for marketing and training so far with the Indian parties obligated to pay lumpsum royalty, a percentage of the turnover or both.

The collaborators form a who's who of the world's best known hotel chains belonging to Hong Kong, USA, UK, Germany, Switzerland, France. Australia is about to join the list. The Japanese have a small investment in partnership with Air India at the Buddhist pilgrim centres in Bihar and have a stake in a restaurant, already functioning at Ashoka Hotel in New

Delhi. Surprisingly two years after the government had agreed to majority equity participation from abroad, the wait for the first investor in hotels'continues.

Though apparently the advantages are ambiguous, closer examination points to considerable benefits from marketing pacts with international chains. Unlike other industries, a hotel in India which is called upon to maintain. The best in global standards has to compete with its counterparts in the international market. One has to be familiar with the consumers' preferences which change rapidly and unless the hotel is constantly in touch with the source market, it will miss the custom. It is neither easy nor adequate to keep pace with the consumer requirements. But a link up with an international group gives direct access to the market through worldwide reservation systems and market information data. Obviously, this is what Indian hoteliers look for. They do not seem to be keen on investment partnership because in that case they will have to concede a share in management for which there is understandable reluctance.

On the other hand, the potential foreign investors want the property not only to conform to their standards but also under their exclusive management. This probably explains the absence of any foreign investor's entry in the hotel business which in any event had not been encouraged until two years ago. The only one known offer is that of the Hong Kong based Regent International. The chain is a bidder for a world class hotel in the capital claiming that it will be a six-star affair and with hundred per cent foreign exchange investment of the order of Rs 100 crore. The group is also said to have offered to reclaim land in Mumbai at its cost, surrender part of it to the government, and take the rest on lease for building a hotel in that metropolis. Both the Bombay offer and the Delhi project for which tenders were invited two years ago are in deep freeze. The group has however signed up with an Indian entrepreneur for a Regent hotel in Agra as a joint venture.

The foreign chains which have an Indian presence by way of marketing tie-up are Intercontinental, Sheraton, Quality Inn, Holiday Inn and Radisson (all US names), Ramada International (UK), Meridien and Accor (France). Kempinsky and Robinson (Germany), Sofitel (Switzerland) and Hyatt (Hong Kong). Of these Intercontinental has agreements with the Taj Hotel in Mumbai and Taj Palace in Delhi Sheraton is linked with six hotels of the Welcomegroup, Maurya in Delhi, Mughal in Agra, SeaRock in Mumbai, Park and Chbla in Chennai and Windsor Manor in Bangalore. Quality Inns name a joint venture with A.K. Dave Associates for franchise agreement. Hilton is said to have arrived at a memorandum of understanding with the

Chhabrias for an undetermined number of hotels which are yet to come. A few other chains like the Merriot and Oriental and the Mandarin are also said to be waiting in the wings.

The agreements cover marketing, reciprocal reservations, training manpower and technical services. For these services payment varies depending on the number of rooms (generally 3 per cent of net room revenue) plus a lumpsum for royalty. For instance, Asian Hotels (Hyatt — Regency, Delhi) paid Hyatt 1,50,000 dollars on account of "pre-opening technical fee". This is in addition to the 3 per cent royalty on room sales. Similarly, Leela Hotel in Mumbai paid Kempinsky 1,60,000 dollars as lumpsum.

Apart from marketing and reservation, the agreements provide for training, an area in which India is handicapped. Besides western hotels use a range of new equipment and techniques which would add to productivity and efficiency. Much of this training is provided free of cost and hence the collaboration fees do not hurt.

Interestingly, sharing of hoteliering expertise at least in the case of India, has not been a : one way traffic. Both Oberois and Taj have had an international presence for long.

Lately, the brand name has had an appeal in the reverse direction too. Welcomgroup's Bukhara has been franchised by Sheraton in Hong Kong and will soon be extended to Singapore.

Getting Connected for Good – Tourism and Technology

The infotech rage need not scare the travel trade, particularly the travel agent and the tour operator. Of course, hotels are confident that the portals are friendly and facilitating. The catch phrase is 'total solutions'. In just a week in the capital there have been enough seminars, road shows and presentations where the trade was shown assured prospects of easy business, access to a vast range of products, and at the same time, speedy communication with service provides and customers, even banks, anywhere in the world.

At the Infotech Hotels Expo 2000 new technology was presented as a one-stop hospitality industry showcase. It was a question of which is overtaking what, technology or tourism. As minister Mahajan put aptly, what future guests will be looking for may not necessarily be luxury hotels but intelligent hotels. A time may come soon when the wonder cyber cafes will become antique pieces. Another event signifying the new trends is the website launch of www.india.com. The promoters claim that the site would enable 'online reservations, bookings, confirmation credit payment and could carry out business-to-business and business-to-consumer contacts. Shopping, trading, marketing, even bookings for entertainment shows are all possible under the single shop facility. What should interest the travel agent particularly is the opportunity it provides to improve personalised service through its packages.

The third event was the first road show on the e-commerce platform and Internet portal which make possible total solutions for tourism requirements.

The road show was the promoters' introduction of omnis-online, a global e-commerce portal on the launch of regional operations in India through omnis-India.com in partnership with Electronic Software Solutions (ESS) a company owned by the Bird Group. Bird is a well-known travel outfit with varied interests in the aviation market and has had successful innings in popularising Amadeus, a leading central reservation system. ESS will market omnis-india.com in India, Sri Lanka, Nepal, Maldives, Bhutan and Bangladesh with its USP as the first-of-its-kind travel portal that brings together all tourism products and services providers on a common platform.

The onrush of technology may puzzle the trade but it certainly will reinforce resources in satisfying guests with speedy needs.

Connectivity is core of the travel demand and the application will enable the travel agent of today find friendly solutions. The pioneers will have a leeway.

About the omnis tie-up, Ankur Bhatia, CEO of omnis-india.com said: "We are pleased to bring to India the first truly online and global travel e-commerce site. Not only will travellers benefit, it will also create a niche market for providers to avail themselves of the much-talked of business-to-business trading on the Indian subcontinent." This is where the trade should look for opportunities and make full use of the portal. The facility is backed by its international connection, the Berlin-based omnis-online Tourismus Services. Incidentally, the German carrier group Lufthansa's IT Services have a fifty per cent share in the facility which is essentially a new Internet platform for the tourism and travel trade. Through its use, the Indian trade can offer direct bookings on any and every travel-related service, be in the air, on sea or on the ground, along with a host of other services like restaurants, entertainment, shopping, etc. The managing director of the German collaborator, Paul Byerley is optimistic on the Indian business prospects. Says he, "the Indian subcontinent has a vast travel market and we are delighted to present to Indian travel professionals an opportunity to market themselves through an international brand. Also, trading within travel organisations should lead to an exciting new manner of operations in the region.

Omnis-india is among the early birds in marketing this technology. There will definitely be more entrants in the future with new incentives to travel agencies, resellers and users alike. Whatever be the response, the new technology represented by the portal has come to stay and it will revolutionise marketing trading and reservations in the tourism sector.

GIVING BOOST TO ECOTOURISM

Make Money by Preserving Nature

The credit for focusing sustainable livelihoods for communities living in eco-tourism areas must go to the PHD Chamber of Commerce and Industry (P-HDCCI) and the Madhya Pradesh government which came together at a high powered workshop to address this important aspect of the hospitality industry. Chief minister Digvijay Singh, tourism minister Ajay Singh and secretary department of biodiversity and biotechnology, R. Parasuram, PHD secretary general, Dr. B. P. Dhaka, co-chairperson of the Chamber's tourism and aviation committee, Mukesh Goel, and Rakesh Mathur, president, WelcomHeritage as well as Dr. A. Jayathilak, MD Chhattisgarh Tourism, experts, naturalists, environmentalists and foresters were among those who participated. Interestingly, the two-day workshop was held at Bandhavgarh National Park, 40-plus temperatures notwithstanding. The venue, we were told, was chosen at the instance of the chief minister who was present in all the sessions. He also used the occasion to release the state biotechnology policy. Also released was "A Handbook of Environment and Forest Legislation. Guidelines and Procedures in India" compiled by Ravindra and Sangita Saxena.

The keynote address was by Dr. Erach Bharucha director, Bharatiya Vidyapeeth Institute of Environment Education, Pune. He spoke on opportunities for employment generation through eco-tourism. A. K. Bhattacharya in his presentation talked of the linkage between eco-tourism, livelihood and biodiversity conservation. He is Faculty, Indian Institute of Forest Management, Bhopal while E.M.S. Rathore, forest conservator, Beoni talked of eco-regional planning for sustainable livelihood generation. K. K. Singh's paper dealt with capacity building for sustainable livelihoods. Among case studies Dr. Jayathilak referred to what Kerala had done in this area (he was formerly managing director, Kerala Tourism) and Deepti Neelakanthan unveiled Delhi's first internationally branded Ecotel (Uppal's Orchid) and the country's second (the first is in Mumbai). Rakesh Mathur outlined the eco-concerns reflected in WelcomHeritage's resort in Bandhavgarh including the use of solar cookers, turning solid wastes into manure and a herbal garden.

Dr Bharucha pointed to the apparent conflict between the objectives of forest and tourism departments. The forest department has as its objective bio-diversity conservation and ensuring livelihoods of local people. The tourism department wants tourism growth and to convert general to speciality eco-tourism and support for local people. This involves synergy through the forest department; involving local stakeholders; conflict resolution through income generation, and, livelihood opportunities through community based eco-tourism; generating work opportunities in hotels and allied activities; training as guides; training in small scale industry – artifacts, garments, food; sale of ethnic food; local agricultural and horticulture products; demonstration of art and culture, and local artisan support – baskets, pottery, sculpture, painting, jewellery and soon.

Whatever the segment of tourism – monuments, adventure, wild life or eco-tourism – infrastructure, specially connectivity is crucial for success, a point rightly emphasised in the concept paper presented by PT-ro. "Improve air and rail connectivity and quality of access to national parks and sanctuaries," it says after pointing out that Madhya Pradesh has the country's largest share of these assets. The chief minister conceded that the state had only limited airlinks and roads too had been a matter of worry. But, things are moving now and by December the Satna-Bandhavgarh stretch would be a smooth affair which will also halve the driving time between Khajuraho and Bandhavgarh to four or five hours.

On decongesting national parks and sanctuaries, an issue raised by participants, Digvijay Singh had his own recipe: open additional entry points and instead of jeeps use larger vehicles which could carry more visitors. He said an interpretation centre is a must for each park and lamented the fact that no one had thought of developing decent souvenir shops in these places. "Why don't we offer safari clothes to visitors," he asked and suggested there could be a dress code and garments made available at parks at reasonable prices. Entertainment for visitors is another area that calls for some innovative thinking. If it is felt, he said, that tribal dances need to be supplemented with something different he invited tour operators and hoteliers to sit together and work out new ideas. He promised his support. The chief minister said the state which already has a large forest cover has in the last decade added more to it. And, it has been steadfast in maintaining the eco-balance in spite of the fact that it gets no compensation from the Centre. He estimated that the state is losing Rs. 100 crore annually on this account and expressed the hope that one day it would be reimbursed.

The participants experienced some exciting moments too when they drove through the national park in the morning. Although this writer was able to sight only one tiger, most others saw four of them.

PLANS TO PROMOTE TOURISM BY STATE GOVERNMENTS

Chhattisgarh's New Weapon – Tourism

Of the newly created states of the Indian Union, Chhattisgarh is first off the mark to unveil its tourist treasure, kept hidden for whatever reason by Madhya Pradesh of which it was a part until two years ago. And, the way it has gone about this business would serve as a lesson to those states which are still waiting to tap their tourism potential. Ajit Jogi will soon join the ranks of just a handful of chief ministers who look upon tourism as a powerful weapon of development. With political will backing the sector – a rare commodity in other parts of the country – he searched and found the right person to lead the tourism drive. He has borrowed Kerala's star performer, Dr. A. Jayathilak, a medico-turned IAS officer, who alongwith Amitabh Kant (now joint secretary at the central department of tourism) put Kerala ahead of other states as a tourist destination. Jayathilak is managing director, Chhattisgarh Tourism Board, virtually a one-man show who believes in outsourcing as much of his work to the experts in the private sector as possible.

In a focused approach the young state has rightly decided to concentrate its tourism effort on Bastar (known even abroad for its tribal lifestyles), and conscious of its cultural and environmental fragility, go only for quality and upmarket tourism. Long-haul, long road journeys and expensive tented camps demand that approach. The return airfares from Delhi to Raipur, the state capital and the nearest airport to Bastar is more than Rs. 13,000 and Jagdalpur, headquarters of Bastar district (the country's largest) and on to Chitrakote (not to be confused with Chitrakoot elsewhere in Madhya Pradesh) with its spectacular waterfall on Indravati river where holiday makers would stay in 'royal' tents is another 450 km each way. There are plans to provide helicopter services from Raipur although the road journey is a delight as much of it is through thick forests and there is much to see and experience on the way, the Kankar Palace being one of them, where the teenaged scion of the erstwhile royal family would be happy to host lunch for you. Surprisingly, the road to Bastar is incredibly good. The Toyota Qualis by which this writer was driven to Chitrakote, was doing 90 kmph much of the way. At Jagdalpur the young Bastar Maharaj Kamre Chandra Bhanjdeo is happy to spend time with you and share a cup of tea in his palace. After considerable thought and planning, Chhattisgarh Tourism chose the right moment to launch its promotional drive – Dussehra, Interestingly, the Bastar Dussehra. is not about Ram returning to Ayodhya. It celebrates Sri Danteshwari Mai, the tutelary deity of the Bastar royal house. After a road show in Delhi with a big response from the media, a half a dozen groups of journalists, opinion makers, travel agents, consultants, and theatre personalities were invited for a three-day discovery of the newest tourist destination. It was a treat staying in the 'royal' tents rented from Jodhpur Maharaja Gaj Singh and the camp managed by a team of professionals led by Lakshmi Singh Sinclair. More than a dozen youngmen welcomed the guests at the airport and acted as guides as they looked around through serene Bastar villages or savoured the natural beauty of the Kanger Valley National Park. You could spend hours at the great museum in Jagdalpur badly in need of a proper home which would give it the international stature it needs for its rare anthropological treasures. Apart from the Chitrakote falls, there is another enchanting phenomenon at Tirathgarh. With a good monsoon, Chitrakote is a mini Niagra.

Bastar's handicrafts deserve a special mention. The Harappan and Indus Valley flavour of Bastar's handicrafts heightens their appeal amongst the tourists. Narayanpur and Jagdalpur are famous for their terracota crafts such as the elephant with bells and a selection of decorative pots and table top items. Jagdalpur is also famous for kosa silk weaving. Bell metal and wrought iron work is the speciality of Kondagaon and Jagdalpur. Memorial stones are one of Bastar's oldest crafts.

Jayathilak lists five good reasons to visit Chhattisgarh: nature, adventure, culture, history and handicrafts. The camp organised at Chitrakote for the 15 days of the Dussehra festival is only a sample of what will be on offer on a regular basis for a six-month season beginning October 2003. He hastens to add that the camp will be run by the private sector with full infrastructural support from his Board.

Chief Minister Jogi who found time to visit the promotional camp told media persons that he had already spent Rs. 1,200 crore on road improvements in the last two years and bigger plans were in the pipeline for two north-south express ways and four linking east with the west. He is keen to follow a liberal tax policy to encourage the private sector to invest in Bastar's tourist development. Well begun, they say, is half done.

AP's March to Numero Uno

Kerala had better watch out. It may soon have to share its numero uno position in the quest for tourism with Andhra Pradesh. Chief Minister Chandrababu Naidu told a group of visiting tour operators and media persons on July 11 in Hyderabad that in two or three years his state will emerge as the leader in tourism just as it has taken the lead in information technology. His confidence comes from several factors, among them is his Vision 2020. In it, tourism has the highest priority after IT and is based on larger national goals of a 9.50 to 10 per cent GDP growth with a high rate of growth of the services sector. So far as tourism is concerned, the chief minister has used the best talent available in the country and abroad like McKenzie and PKF and lately even the World Tourism Organisation (WTO) to translate his vision into action plans which are now under implementation. In a foreword to the WTO document he says, "We have a vision of tourism for the development of the state. The vision converges on improved quality of life for the people, economic growth in a trajectory higher than known before and employment opportunity for the people." He would like to bring the world to Andhra Pradesh and take Andhra Pradesh to the world but emphasises strongly that, this does not mean that we do not know the promise which the huge domestic market holds for us. After all it, is on the back of domestic tourism that international tourism is built".

Naidu is equally dear about the need for speedy and quality implementation of plans. He says, "Vision without action is a mere dream, action without vision is a mere wastage of time, but vision with action is a powerful empowerment. Hence our vision is about creating a champion of tourism in Andhra Pradesh, our action relates to creating the environment for public-private partnership, augmenting infrastructure and putting our faith on a joint marketing effort with the industry."

Unlike other states, the Andhra CM has not allowed the resources crunch to slow down his tourism effort. He has been spending as much as Rs. 32 crore from the state kitty. But, much more than that, he has been able to persuade the rich temple trusts to spare funds for developing the environs of holy places. The Tirupati Devasthanam, he told the tour operators, has put at his disposal the Rs. 450 crore it receives in offerings, as has the trust that manages the Lakshmi Narasimha Swamy Temple in Vizag which annually receives Rs. 250 crore, thus making a total of Rs. 700 crore. The rate at which peoples' offerings were rising, he expected Rs. 2,000 crore to be available annually in another five years. This should be music to the ears of the central minister Jagmohan, whose judicious use of the temple funds has transformed Vaishnodevi into a truly spiritual experience for visitors.

A factor on which the chief minister is banking on heavily for a push for tourism, is the state-of-the-art international airport project in Hyderabad, which after several hiccups is now finally on the way to being implemented. He quipped that the struggle he had to bring to get the project approved through the corridors of power at the Centre will help neighbouring Karnataka to get the Bangalore airport project also off the drawing board. Hyderabad city in the last few years has changed considerably. Easily, the cleanest state capital, flyovers smoothening traffic, scores of new buildings with glass and chrome facades, swanky new hotels, the hi-tech city (now in its phase II), the Shilpakala Vedik (with its 2,500 seater modern auditorium) and the enchanting Ramoji Film City, not to speak of pearls and bidri work and mouth watering Hyderabadi biryani, make the Andhra capital an inviting destination not only for the domestic traveller but also for foreigners looking for a different experience of India. The city's beautiful lake – Husainsagar – with the tall Buddha statue placed majestically in the middle and extensive landscaping all around it and air-conditioned cruises provide evening's fun and entertainment missing in similar locations elsewhere in the country. It is the hotel scene which is the most promising. After ITC brought class to hotelering with its Grand Kakatiya, the Taj group has moved in a big way renovating the Krishna (formerly run by the Oberoi's) into a world class property. The group is busy converting the former Nizam palace – Faluknama – into a heritage hotel and is also investing in a golf course and resort, a missing link in Hyderabad's tourist infrastructure. The Viceroy, another new deluxe hotel also has the city's largest convention hall.

The visiting tour operators, headed by IATO president Maharaj Wahi, in their interface with the chief minister pleaded among the other things for a reduction of taxes on road transport which they said were the highest amongst the states. Chandrababu promised to review the matter. The FAM tour was organised by V. Subramaniam, a travel industry professional who is now working as events manager for Andhra Pradesh Tourism. The consensus among tour operators was that Naidu's dream of making Andhra a tourism leader is realisable.

Aviation is Flying High

Observers of the tourism scene would recall that some of the harshest criticism for inaction was reserved for the ministry of civil aviation. The inordinate delay in finalising an aviation policy or privatising international airports, the heavy burden of taxation on ATF and air travel were among the reasons for dissatisfaction. As late as last September, N. K. Singh, member, Planning Commission, had said at the WTTC Retreat in Srinagar that civil aviation had become a case where "vacillation has been invested with an aura of statesmanship". The new minister in charge of this portfolio, Rajiv Pratap Rudy may have taken his time to get down to business but he has within a few weeks done enough to convert criticism into applause. When Prime Minister Vajpayee announced open skies for airlines of ASEAN countries during his visit to Indonesia, it was the beginning of a series of initiatives which, when completed, will not only make aviation policies and practices tourism friendly but also make affordable air travel an achievable goal.

The ASEAN development was soon followed by the offer of open skies to SAARC countries along with a more momentous decision to permit private sector carriers to fly to SAARC capitals, beginning with Colombo. No mystery surrounds the fact that such steps forward which must have required the Cabinet's approval were initiated by the aviation minister. And, that is not the end of the story yet. Finance Minister Jaswant Singh took off where the prime ministerial announcements ended. He stunned the nation through his mini budget with his withdrawal of the 15 per cent 1ATT (Inland Air Travel Tax) and even the Rs. 500 airport tax charged from those travelling abroad. The real bonanza the finance minister has given is the halving of the central excise on ATF from 16 to 8 per cent which will on one hand reduce operational costs of domestic carriers and on the other bring down air ticket prices, something that has already happened. The rationalisation of import and other duties on other segments of the economy will have its own impact on both domestic and international travel.

By a sheer coincidence, it is in this feel good atmosphere that the Indian Association of Tour Operators (IATO) which had just recovered from its organisational set back when the entire executive committee was dissolved, had organised an interactive session with the aviation minister. This was on January 15. It so happened that the minister was to come to the IATO meeting straight from a Cabinet session where some more forward steps on aviation were to be approved. The gathering to which tourism secretary, Rathi Vinay Jha and other senior functionaries had also been invited included one of the largest attendance of IATO members. The air was thick with expectations that Rudy would bring back the government's approval for a total open skies policy for all international services. And, patiently they waited for the minister's arrival who was three hours behind schedule. Rudy's bag of announcements did not include a total open skies but a radical decision on charters. You can now operate outbound charters; Indian passport holders can travel on inbound charters whose frequency and size of aircraft will be unfettered as also the choice of the airport. He even promised immigration and customs facilities at short notice at airports which do not have them.

While waiting for the aviation minister, Subhash Goyal, who has returned as IATO president (with Major Murli Dhar as senior vice-president) utilised the time for interaction with the tourism secretary. Rathi Jha said she shared the feel-good factor with the industry but higher occupancies should not make us complacent. "What we have achieved," she said, "is laudable but it must be remembered that in the big picture it is only a drop in the ocean. Much hard work remains to be done." The states have to play their part. And, in evolving public-private sector partnership, she said, the department of tourism (DoT) would welcome from the industry both ideas and investments. She also said that it would help the cause of tourism if civil aviation were combined with it under one ministry.

A day earlier there were some interesting presentations made at a Reality Check organised by publisher Navin Berry. One of the speakers was Amitabh Kant, joint secretary, DoT and chairman ITDC. He asked the industry to be prepared to offer the experiences today's traveller was looking for. This is an imperative, he said, especially now that the Incredible India campaign has created greater awareness of destination India. The private sector, he said, should now move as fast as the government is moving with policy initiatives. The Planning Commission member must be among the happiest today as will be Naresh Chandra whose committee's report has obviously influenced many of the aviation initiatives.

Open Skies: To be or Not to be?

After the successful effort of the PHD Chamber of Commerce and industry to bring substance to the work of its tourism committee by bringing together the northern Indian states for synergies in integrated development, it was the turn of ASSOCHAM to attempt a similar exercise by getting the tourism and civil aviation ministers to share the same dais. It is another matter that the exigencies of ministerial responsibilities did not permit Jagmohan and Shahnawaz Hussain to listen to each other. But, it was quite apparent, and pretty welcome at that, that Jagmohan, who also holds charge of culture, and Hussain have already set in motion initiatives that would lead to a coordinated effort between tourism and aviation.

The occasion was the national convention on Aviation and Tourism: Opportunities and Challenges, masterminded by ASSOCHAM expert committee chairman Subhash Goyal who for many years now has been espousing the cause of open skies as the only way to give tourism a chance. That there is a clear divide on the issue between the tourism and aviation authorities was evident from the remarks of Vinod Duggal, director general tourism, who expressed the hope that in the future bilateral negotiations national interest would be uppermost rather than the interest of the national carriers. Hussain's response was understandably not categoric. He conceded that while open skies was a laudable aim, the aviation ministry has to protect the interests of the national carriers especially in the matter of reciprocity. He gave the specific example of Virgin Atlantic asking for more frequencies to Delhi while the British Aviation Authorities were refusing Air-India landing rights at Heathrow for its additional flights. In fact, he prompted. Prime Minister Atal Behari Vajpayee, had written to Tony Blair for his intervention in support of Air-India's needs. Hussain explained, however, that in the matter of seat augmentation his ministry was virtually following an open skies policy in the peak months permitting international carriers to increase frequencies and use bigger planes at will.

Participants, who asked searching questions, pointed out that this selective open skies offer did not really translate into more seats as the lead time given to foreign carriers to arrange flight schedules and procure bigger aircraft was not enough. The minister seemed to appreciate the suggestion that in future such offers should be announced at least six months ahead of the peak months for it to be availed of fully.

The aviation minister had a lot more to share with the participants. An aviation policy which has long been in the making is close to being finalised. Aviation Turbine Fuel (ATF) on which most states are charging hefty sales tax and which has made domestic fares costlier than foreign travel, is another area where the centre appears to be making some headway, Andhra Pradesh is the first to take the initiative it has reduced the levy to just four per cent from the original 22 per cent. Hussain said he is trying to persuade other states to follow suit.

The minister announced that Air-India will soon revive its flights to Frankfurt and Chicago to re-establish its presence in Europe and to increase its share of the Trans-Atlantic market. He gave the assurance that work on privatising international airports was on course and he expected that all five airports would be privately managed within the year. Work on the nev international airports in Hyderabad and Bangalore was also proceeding on a fast pace, he said. Another welcome development was the near completion of the runway expansion and new terminal at Bodhgaya, which will now be developed as a South Asian hub for Buddhist traffic. "You will be happy to know," he said, "that Sri Lanka Air will be the first foreign airline to operate to Bodhgaya."

Jagmohan reiterated that governance and work culture are imperative whether we talk of tourism or civil aviation. He explained that he keeps repeating this at every forum because he does not want his audience merely to make a note of it but to 'absorb' the idea and start practising it. He said he was fully committed to a coordinated tourism effort with the aviation ministry and he was trying to achieve that even on a personal level. He said he had asked the Prime Minister to reintroduce leave travel concession (LTC) which would go a long way in boosting domestic travel.

Subhash Goyal said he would seek expert help in using the deliberations of the convention to prepare a Vision 2020 document on aviation, which will be submitted to the government to assist it in drawing up a long-term development plan for the sector. For his own part, he said, he would like to see each of the 29 states having an international airport.

With a Liberal Charter Policy

Can charters boost tourist arrivals? The department of tourism (DoT), which has been consulting the travel trade on such prospects, has finally come to the conclusion that a more liberal charter policy could result in twin benefits. First, it could ease the air seat shortage which has been identified as the main cause for slower growth of arrivals. And, second, it could bring in larger numbers of visitors especially in the peak period, October-April.

In the note prepared for the ministry of civil aviation, DoT has pointed out that part of the success achieved by our competing neighbours like Maldives, Indonesia, Malaysia, China, Singapore and Thailand has come from liberal charter policies. On the other hand, even the limited numbers of charters allowed into the country have declined though the number of travellers has changed only marginally. Statistics for the last three years show that in 1998, 505 charter flights brought 103, 212 travellers; the flights increased to 575 in the following year but the number of tourists was down to 93,876. During 2000, however, there was a steep decline in the number of charter flights, down to 466, but the passengers carried numbered 1,05,395.

DoT concedes that charters produce high volume but low revenue business. But it points out that India is a multiproduct destination with attractions for travellers in various segments of the market. Upmarket visitors would prefer scheduled flights and personalised service whereas budget travellers would opt for low cost charter packages. "If India is to increase its market share," DoT says, "we have to open our doors to all types of tourists" and adds, "Given the lack of availability of seats on international flights, encouraging charters appears to be the most feasible step in the short-term."

Charters on a regular basis were first allowed into India barely a decade ago. The director-general, civil aviation, is the nodal authority for approving such flights. The last review of charter operations was done by the committee of secretaries in April last year. The committee made a number of recommendations to ease restrictions on charters. The more important ones among them, which are yet to be implemented, include lifting the ban on NRIs travelling by these flights, removing the restriction that only Air-India and Indian Airlines should do ground handling and that there should be no limit on air seat capacity for outbound charters.

Among the recommendations which are in the process of being carried out is the inclusion of Port Blair in the Andamans in the list of designated airports for charter flights. The civil aviation ministry has already signified its approval. The committee of secretaries had also suggested that in addition to the 12 international airports plus Agra, Varanasi, and Jaipur, which can accept charter flights, four more airports – Calicut, Srinagar, Lucknow and Patna – should be added to the list. The committee had also suggested that the department of tourism should, from its funds, set up redemption centres for tourists arriving by charters and also take measures to improve facilitation. DoT is providing funds for this purpose in its budget for the current financial year.

It is yet to be decided who will meet the cost of new equipment needed at designated airports to handle charters, which is estimated at Rs. 44 lakh per airport, as well as recurring costs (including staff) of Rs. 16 lakh per airport. Apart from funds, the biggest stumbling block in implementing a liberalised charter policy are airports controlled by defence services, especially Goa, the most popular charter destination which is operated by the Navy. For its own operational needs, the Navy permits landing of charters only on three specified days of the week, often leading to congestion and higher landing charges. Small wonder, the travel trade points out, that in a global survey reported by the World Travel and Tourism Council (WTTC), Goa has been rated as the worst airport in the world.

Charter operators, in their discussions with DoT, have been urging that the minimum expenditure limit of $ 350 per tourist is rather on the high side and should be reduced to $280. Besides, faster approvals for flights and improved handling facilities at airports could not only include those who have stopped flying to India to come back, but also encourage new operators to include this country in their growth plans. Visas make up another area which could promote more charters. Visa on arrival would be an ideal solution but Indian missions should be geared to grant visas at short notice and not insist on a week's notice since a large number of travellers decide to join a charter only at the last minute. One suggestion made by charter operators, which DoT is willing to consider subject to availability of funds, is to offer incentives by way of reimbursing landing fees and handling charges to promote non-traditional destinations.

According to a recent assessment by the consultant agency, A. T. Kearney, an additional charter flight a day can bring in foreign exchange worth Rs 100 crore annually and also 20,000 additional jobs. DoT's initiative is therefore a welcome development.

Air India Disinvestment: A Test Case of Govt's Commitment to Privatisation

It is not surprising that as the Air-India disinvestment process sets into the final stages, those opposed to privatisation are also becoming more active and have stepped up their campaign through the media. The latest to fire a salvo is Congress leader, Priya Ranjan Dasmunshi. In a series of allegations in a letter he says he has written to the prime minister, he alleges that the manner in which the disinvestment process was being done, would lead to a single bidder remaining in the fray (It has since been officially confirmed by disinvestment minister Arun Shourie that there are only two bidders, TATA-SIA and Hindujas).

Dasmunshi's fears seem to be based on earlier media reports that the Hindujas were planning to pull out because they wanted Air-India to lose its PSU status before the specified equity (40 per cent) is offloaded. One news report says that the Hindujas have shelved their plans for withdrawal, if they had any, after an assurance from disinvestment minister of a fair and transparent process.

Dasmunshi's is a two pronged attack. A single bidder, he claims, will lead to under-evaluation of Air-India. He has been told, he says, that the national carrier's worth was pegged at Rs. 9,000 crore. His second target is Morgan Stanley which has been advising the government on the bidding process. He wants Morgan Stanley's services to be dispensed with immediately because of the reported association of its chairman as a director with one of the TATA companies.

It is not clear whether Dasmunshi is acting on behalf of Congress. He is the party's chief whip in the Lok Sabha which gives his letter to the prime minister a certain statue and authority. But, Dr. Manmohan Singh, who initiated the country's economic reforms when Congress was in power and who is the party's leader in the Rajya Sabha, did hot appear to be aware of the letter. According to one newspaper.

When asked whether the party supported Dasmunshi's stand, Dr. Manmohan Singh said. "I can only say that we have been insisting on a white paper on disinvestment."

There have also been persistent reports of differences between the disinvestment minister and Sharad Yadav who heads the aviation ministry with Air-India under its charge. Reports have been suggesting that Yadav is not in favour of privatisation and that his ministry has been adopting an unhelpful attitude towards the disinvestment process. A joint statement by the two ministers has however discounted reports of differences among them.

The official confirmation by the disinvestment minister of the two bidders as the finalists in the race for Air-India's Maharaja is a rather unusual step because the government has so far followed a strict policy of not disclosing the names of bidders with the sole objective of securing the best offer. Shourie unveiled the identity of the bidders at a meeting he had with Air-India unions and officials when he explained the disinvestment process to them. He also revealed that he had himself approached a number of big business houses and leading foreign airlines to bid for Air-India. "I spoke to Anil Ambani on the disinvestment process," he told a newspaper, adding, "we wanted a cash-rich Indian party to take part in the process so that the valuation of the airline goes up." But, the Ambanis were not ready to enter aviation at this stage. He spoke to ITC chairman, Yogi Deveshwar but the cigaretter and hotel major too did not respond. He also contacted Lord Colin Marshal to interest British Airways but a technical hitch came in the way. Heavy losses suffered by the steel industry prevented NRI L. N. Mittal from proceeding with his bid. Emirates had pul in a bid but later withdrew perhaps because it had secured equity in Air Lanka, and was developing the carrier as a hub in Colombo.

Although two bidders still remain, the government seems well prepared to carry the disinvestment process through even if a single bidder is left. It has been officially stated on behalf of the disinvestment ministry that in that event the reserve price of Air-India's equity to be offloaded would be kept in a sealed cover to be opened after the final financial bid has been received. And, the financial bid will have, to be higher than the reserve price for its to be accepted.

Of immediate interest, however, is the meeting of the cabinet committee which will take a look at the shareholders' agreement. Disinvestment secretary, Pradeep Baijal is on record that awarding five director to the strategic partner was necessary in order to fetch a better price for Air-India. In all there will be twelve directors. Baijal explained that under the Company Law the share purchase agreement had to keep one-third of directors (four) as neutral. Of the rest, the division could have been half and half between the strategic partner and the government. This, he said, would have fetched a lesser price. Hence it was decided to allocate five directors to the investor.

Air-India is being looked upon as a test case of government's commitment to privatisation. The smoother the change over, the better for the second generation reforms. And, of course, better days for Air-India, too.

Put Heritage Conservation on National Agenda

It does not require research to foresee the massive and wide ranging development that will follow the second generation of economic reforms now under way especially when we are envisaging a 9-10 per cent growth in the coming years. And, unless a holistic and integrated approach is adopted, some of our cities will lose their distinctive character and end up as concrete jungles. Mussoorie and Manali are stark examples of what has already happened in our mountains. It is not only historic monuments but also streetscapes, vernacular settlements, collectively in their natural and man-made environment that must be protected from unplanned urbanisation. It is obvious that the best conservation efforts cannot succeed without planning, regulation and legislation, that is, without the backing of various authorities.

Moved by this imperative, INTACH, the Indian National Trust for Art and Cultural Heritage, which has been seeking to enlarge the concept of heritage conservation into sustainable development, organised a three-day seminar on strategic partnership between state governments and INTACH, in the third week of July. The venue chosen was Fort Cochin, Kerala's famous port city which houses the heritage bequeathed by three colonial powers, the Dutch, the Portuguese and the British, and which is sought to be preserved in a joint effort by the government, the INTACH chapter headed by former mayor K. Sohan, and, his co-convener, Jose Dominic, whose reputation for building unique eco-friendly hotels and resorts has already travelled abroad.

Taking part in the deliberations were, apart from INTACH vice-chairman, S. K. Misra and member-secretary, Dr. Chuden Tshering-Misra, a score of conveners from Mumbai, Lucknow, Nalanda, Kolkata, Hyderabad and Chennai, INTACH's own conservation experts Shobila Punja and Hindu Manchanda, well-known environmentalist Shyam Chainani and secretary level officials from Pondicherry and Kerala. Significantly the Planning Commission was represented by senior consultant, Jayant Sanyal, who is currently working on tourism prospects in UP and Uttaranchal as part of the special development reports for the two states.

Interestingly, most of the sessions were held in the Brunton Boatyard, a charming old world hotel (though only two years old), a Jose Dominic creation over what was during World War I a mine-sweeper building yard, its stately architecture blending harmoniously with the flavour of Fort Cochin. But, the keynote address by Kerala's tourism minister, Prof K. V. Thomas was delivered at the historic Dutch Fort, also known as the Mattancherry Palace.

Commending INTACH's lead in evolving strategic partnership with state government, he pointed out that "heritage buildings and precincts in the states are now highly vulnerable targets of economic pressure, qualifying themselves as 'endangered'. Their existence, particularly in the urban areas is under severe threat." He saw INTACH's role in this great challenge for heritage conservation as "facilitator, catalyst and the educator." And, in his own opening remarks, S. K. Misra recognised that all states face budgetary constrains and have many other compelling priorities. On the other hand, he said INTACH is in a position to assist in planning, exploring ways and means for re-usage of old buildings, and finding funds through national and international agencies.

Finally, what the three days hard work put in by the participants produced is what has been christened as the "Fort Cochin Initiative" – a firm resolve to initiate immediate action to save our natural and cultural heritage from destruction and deterioration. "Towards this end," says the document which was supported at a public meeting presided over by the Cochin mayor, C. M. Dinesh Mani, "INTACH shall strive to establish, strengthen and sustain strategic partnerships with central and state governments, local authorities and panchayats, educational institutions, NGOs, voluntary organisations, media and enterprises both public and private, and maintain constant interaction with the community and its elected representatives. INTACH through such partnerships, seeks to create an awareness starting at school level, that heritage enhances the quality of life for all. INTACH," the Initiative goes on, "calls for urgent action for the preparation of inventories and lists of heritage sites and areas by state governments, local bodies and NGOs."

The Fort Cochin Initiative takes special care to emphasise that the needs of the people are important in addressing conservation concerns, a point INTACH vice chairman repeated at the public meeting. Says the Initiative: "INTACH, while recognising the importance of balancing the real needs of the community, calls upon the government and local authorities to take immediate action to put in place regulations to prevent damage and destruction of heritage sites such as buildings, artifacts, structure, areas and precincts of historic and/or aesthetic and/or cultural significance and, natural features of environmental significance and/or scenic beauty including sacred groves, hillocks, water-bodies, open areas, wooded areas etc." It reassures the people by reiterating "the need for obtaining economic benefits for the community as a result of restoration and conservation activities."

The last line in the Fort Cochin Initiative – INTACH resolve to put heritage conservation on the national agenda – is deserving of full support from the hospitality industry for heritage is Indian tourism's main draw card.

A National Policy for Heritage Conservation

A move by the Indian National Trust for Art and Cultural Heritage (INTACH), may well lead to the emergence of a national policy for heritage conservation and management. The Archaeological Survey of India (AS1), has – since its inception in 1862 – been looking after the 'protected' monuments. But, it was not until the mid-80's of the last century that INTACH came into being, as its present vice chairman, S.K. Misra veteran administrator and tourism guru points out, "to act as a vanguard for the vast number of unprotected monuments sites, arts and cultural heritage of the country." Beset as the country has been by numerous urgent demands, conservation concerns have received relatively low priority. Over the last 16 years however, he adds, there has been a build up of a steady concern for heritage whether it be built, natural or cultural. This concern has been represented by efforts of individuals and organisations like INTACH.

These efforts have resulted in the documentation of built heritage in some cities and towns followed by necessary protection, awareness, presentation and in some cases conservation of threatened heritage components. These efforts, Misra concedes, have not been sustainable and have not been gurded by a larger national policy or an action plan which is imperative for effective management and sustainable development.

So, while INTACH and ASI have been seriously considering steps to have a national policy in place, the impetus has come from a happy coincidence of the Somnath Chib Memorial Lecture organised annually by a trust headed by another tourism veteran and heritage activist, Inder Sharma. Having decided on heritage as the theme for this year's lecture, Sharma sought the help of the Austrian ambassador, Herbert Traxl, to persuade one of the world's best known authorities on heritage conservation and management, Frohlich to deliver the lecture. Seize the opportunity, Misra sent out an invitation on behalf of INTACH to the Australian conservationist to participate in a workshop being organised in association with ASI around the same time to prepare the framework for a national policy on heritage conservation and management.

Frohlich's claim to fame comes from his concept of turning heritage sites – into productive assets, which won him the chairmanship of a trust set up by the Austrian government to manage heritage sites. His team mate, Dr. Wolfgang Kippes, who actually manages the sites given over to the trust, will also be taking part in the New Delhi workshop. The Austrian model is now being adopted by many countries after the spectacular success of the very first site taken over by the duo – the Schonbrunn Palace. It is not only paying for its own upkeep but also giving a dividend to the government! Gradually more and more sites are being transferred to the Frohlich trust, Dr. Kippes will also be making a presentation at the workshop. And, appropriately the tile of Frochlich' lecture at the Chib memorial is 'Schonbrunn Palace – a success story.'

The INTACH workshop which will be held on February 14 and 15, will apart from the inaugural session, have four technical sessions, jurist F. S. Nariman will be the chief guest at the inaugural where Frohlich, Kippes and the Australian ambassador will be joined by Bonnie Burnham of the World Monuments Fund. Secretary culture, N. Gopalaswamy will represent the government. At the first technical session, urban growth, planning and legislation in heritage conservation will be addressed. Management of cultural and natural heritage is the subject for the second session with presentations by Richard Engelhardt, Dr. O. P. Agrawal and Dr. M. K. Ranjitsinh. A paper on disaster management for heritage properties from the internationally renowned expert, Bernard Fielden will be circulated. The third session will be devoted to heritage action plan and panelists include George Michelle, Karan Grover, Cyrus Guzder and Ratish Manda. Rajasthan tourism minister, Bina Kak will preside over the last session which is on heritage tourism and site management. The speakers are the new tourism secretary, Rathi Jha, Eugenic Yunis, Ashok Thakur and ITDC chairman and MD, Ashwani Lohani.

INTACH vice-chairman expects a large number of architects, heritage consultants and managers, policy makers, government agencies, NGOs tourism consultants, urban planners and cultural institutions to take part in the workshop which is being supported by the World Tourism Organisation (WTO), ASSOCHAM, IFFI, and the Austrian embassy.

Heritage is Indian tourism's major draw card. The INTACH-ASI move for a national policy on conservation and management deserves the industry's fullest support.

BRIGHT FUTURE

Forecast of Fortune

There is encouraging news for Indian tourism, and from a foreign source. An elite international body specialising in the sector has, in a study based on the satellite accounting system, come to the conclusion that travel and tourism is already contributing 5.6 per cent to the GDP and 5.8 per cent to employment.

It forecasts that in the next 12 years, that is by 2010, the GDP share could increase to 6.6 per cent and that of employment to 6.8 per cent subject, of course, to right policies being pursued and infrastructural adequacies being achieved.

The group that has done the study is the World Travel and Tourism Council (WTTC). Based in London, it comprises chairpersons and chief executives of some 125 hospitality companies around the world. From India, the Taj and the Oberois are members – Biki Oberoi is on the council's executive committee. It is headed by Geoffrey Lipman who was in New Delhi at the beginning of December at the invitation of CFI (Confederation of Indian Industry) to participate in an "exclusive" session on tourism organised as part of the meetings of the World Economic Forum.

Lipman said the WTTC study, a copy of which has been submitted to Prime Minister Vajpayee, has looked at the "full" economic impact of travel and tourism in India. Specifically, he said, it "shows the overall impact of the travel and tourism economy as traveller spending flows through the total economy. This impact includes the creation of jobs in many industry sectors, including upstream suppliers and downstream services in agriculture, construction, telecommunications, textiles, retail and manufacturing." It "also identifies the direct impact of the travel and tourism industry."

Lipman pointed out that in the next twelve years an additional eight million jobs could be created in travel and tourism-related activities. He suggested a five-point agenda for the success of the Indian effort; an integrated strategy which actively involves the private sector; strong, sustained policy implementation driven from the top; progressive liberalisation particularly of aviation; elimination of red tape, high taxes and similar barriers; and investment in infrastructure and human resource development.

WTTC commends the draft National Tourism Policy (soon to be presented to Parliament) especially its emphasis on sustainable human development, poverty alleviation and advancement of women and other disadvantaged groups. The Council, however, suggests there should be greater focus on tourism at both, central and state levels with increased funds for key ministries and incentives for foreign investment and private sector involvement. Priority should also be given to the funding of major improvements in a broad range of basic infrastructure which tourism relies upon, particularly transport links, energy and water treatment plants.

In the employment field, the study recommends introduction of "flexible" working practices to increase industry responsiveness, productivity and innovation reducing regulatory rigidity and protectionism, and policy mechanisms that enhance employment opportunities in rural, regional and peripheral areas.

On air transport, the WTTC study notes that the draft Tourism Policy is not integrated with the draft Aviation Policy and commends its own six-point programme for liberalisation. Among them is the controversial area of freedom of establishment and ownership. The Council's view is that any commercial enterprises should be allowed to establish operations in another country and to acquire ownership and control of an airline in that country.

It also recommends that "effective market access must be encouraged and legislative and the trade barriers should be eliminated in order that air services can operate on any route without restriction excepting normal competition rules which apply to all businesses. There should be no regulation of entry, capacity or pricing."

The study recognises that India has world class products to offer to international visitors, many of which are unique. It is important, therefore, it says that promotional budgets are upgraded to ensure continuing competitiveness. It urges the government to seek support from the international financing community to expand travel-related infrastructure and welcomes the liberal Airports Policy. At the same time, it says, border formalities and red tape should be cut to a minimum. Visa requirements, which are time consuming and expensive, should be eliminated wherever possible.

"Tax intelligently" is another important recommendation. It says Indian destinations, including Bombay and Delhi, are ranked among the most highly taxed in the world. About taxes on air travel, airport departure and highways, WTTC feels strongly that the principle of "User Pays – User Benefits" should be applied and a bulk of the funds raised thus should be spent on infra-structural improvements.

As Ravi Bhoothalingam, head of CM's Tourism Committee pointed out, both government and the industry would find much in the WTTC study to commend itself.

15

Future Steps and Policies to Improve Tourism in the Country

Need to Create More Tourist Resorts

Shouts of excitement over the arrival of the millionth tourist continue to reverberate, though we still have to reach even one per cent of the global traffic. The more reflective in the industry ponder what would have happened if ten thousand more visitors had come to Delhi in the year of the million. It is widely acknowledged that one disappointed visitor means a loss of ten tourists for all time to come. If the tourist does not find a good place to stay, or get a seat on a train or a plane or in an air-conditioned coach on a hot summer day, his word will keep at least ten others away from venturing to India.

So, today the most central problem facing tourism authorities is to ensure that destinations are spread, otherwise if all of them were brought to the traditional triangle, Delhi-Agra-Jaipur, it is bound to be counterproductive in the long run.

The promotion campaign has necessarily to take this into account. The visitor will have to be persuaded to go places in all seasons where infrastructure, at least accommodation-wise is adequate. Why not promote a campaign in the east and in the south as a concomitant process of development of tourism? For one thing is certain: more people will come to India in the coming years and the infrastructure in the traditional triangle will not be able to cope with the increase in the inflow.

Even according to official calculations or forecasts 2.5 million tourists are expected to come by the end of the seventh plan period—just three years away. And last year we were equipped just to receive—the numbers that arrived. Even so, some hotels had to ask their executives to vacate their offices to make room for the guests. And, the Government had to make a general appeal for those with spare accommodation to offer it to the tourists.

So, the question that stems from this situation is: Are we prepared even to receive this modest figure in just three years? Certainly we cannot afford to lose even one among them in view of the potential of tourism as a foreign exchange earner. Official estimates anticipate Rs. 5,000 crore as exchange revenue on this account by 1990.

The availability of 32,000 rooms in nearly 500 hotels may sound a high figure but in a country of India's size and varied attractions it is not something which one could drum about. It is worthwhile to examine why, in spite of the potential of tourism both in terms of earnings and employment, the hotel industry, which is a key element of the tourism sector, has not expanded to the desirable level. The contradiction is stark in the context of a projected demand for 59,000 rooms just three years hence.

The situation underscores the priority claim of this industry which is yet to be accepted by our planners in the matter of investment. The Planning Commissions and the Government have made it obvious, for valid reasons, that resources for the hotel industry must come largely from the private sector, with government-run hotels concentrating on low priced accommodation for domestic travellers. On a rough calculation an additional room with attendant facilities should cost around Rs. six lakh (taking the average of three to five stars). This has to be multiplied twenty-seven thousand times (Rs. 1,020 crore) if we want to ensure that those who come to our country in the '90s stay longer instead of getting stranded.

Also it is to be noted in the context of the rapidly changing nature of our economy consequent on the liberalisation of policies initiated just over two years ago, there is a new welcome wave of tourists of a particular class with a larger purse but more exacting demands. The business tourists who constitute this group are not affected by normal or seasonal factors which sway the inflow of those who travel for leisure (In fact much of the additional arrivals in recent months belong to this category). They want, apart from deluxe ambience, good food and service, efficient communications, exclusive inhouse entertainment facilities, meeting rooms, and excellent local transport as well as easier and reliable transit facilities. These will involve not only high standards within a hotel but also the upgrading of services like telephones, telexes, better taxies with educated chauffeurs, and dependable air bookings. The business tourist, it must be remembered, is a frequent traveller and earnings from this class of traffic will certainly be commensurate with any investment or upgrading of facilities and services.

True, there is now a greater awareness on the part of the government of the relevance of tourism to the national economy and the need to encourage the various segments of the industry. The government itself has stated that tourism should be recognised as in industry. But being a state subject, a national policy on a matter like this has inherent limitations. Possibly at the time of the writing of the Constitution, the potential of tourism could not be foreseen. So much so the thread of a central tourism policy so necessary in the existing context has many missing links.

Even now many states have not responded to the suggestion for industry status to tourism. Nor is there any coordination among the various agencies to which an entrepreneur will have to approach for setting up and running a good hotel. Incredible as it may sound, in the Capital itself the hotel industry has to run separately to as many as 30 agencies, many of which are least conscious or concerned with earning foreign exchange!

All these point to the need for clear enunciation of a national tourism policy to be pursued by a national authority which would facilitate a single window clearance for hotels and other tourism projects. Perhaps such an authority could be strengthened by statutory sanctions by placing tourism on the Concurrent List.

SAFEGUARD THE COUNTRY'S NATURAL RESOURCES

Sustainable Tourism Holds the Key

If there is a singular development that has influenced tourism in the 90s it is the awareness of the relevance of environment to the future of the sector. Both, host communities and more importantly, the visitors themselves recognise that tourism could survive only if there are adequate environmental safeguards.

Concern for environment among institutions engaged in tourism promotion is also growing. Tourism officials and trade representatives joined in observing World Environment Day on June 5. Most hotels held special functions to commemorate the day and pledges were renewed.

They committed themselves to alternate sources of energy for fuel, water recycling schemes, construction of eco lodges and resorts, use of local ethnic material in construction, proper disposal of non-biodegradable garbage and plants to be left in their natural surroundings. At the same time, vigilance is the price for sustainable tourism which means strict enforcement of environmental safeguards.

In fairness, Indian tourism cannot be accused of having created threats of contamination of air and water. The Ganga and the Yamuna have become unusable as clean hygienic water not because of tourism but because of years of neglect and deliberate pollution by people on the riverside villages and towns. But this is no alibi for tourism to keep its hands off environmental protection. On the other hand, it has a special responsibility as a social obligation and also in its own interests.

No visitor would be tempted to journey to a destination where denudation of natural assets has changed its topography and welcome features. Mass tourism for that reason is discouraged in island destinations with fragile systems. Mauritius and Seychelles, or for that matter Bhutan in mountain fastness, have rightly been insistent on selective tourism. The carrying capacity of a destination should be the ultimate determinant in marketing.

This does not mean that tourists should be totally barred. Perhaps, the arrival of the right number of visitors helps sustainable development. Everyone knows what happened to the valley of flowers. There was a ban on tourist traffic and no one was allowed to visit. The result was that this wonderful place of scenic splendour turned into a jungle of the wild, bereft of any charm.

There have been similar instances in other parts of the country where visitors are barred and poachers or graziers takeover. At the other end of the spectrum, everyone is familiar with what has happened to Manali, one of the finest retreats until the 70s, it has now become a teeming jungle of steel and concrete.

For that reason, the secretary general of the World Wide Fund for nature (WWF), Samar Singh, is absolutely right when he points out that tourism is essentially dependent on natural and unpolluted environment and on environmental services. It follows that tourism is both a responsibility and the need to understand and invest in the protection and proper upkeep of natural environment.

If undertaken sustainably, tourism can be a positive force for conservation and environmental protection. Interestingly, both the Constitution and legislative measures lay accent not only on tourism's responsibility but of the citizenry as a whole towards environment. Beginning with the Directive Principles, there are many other provisions which have been reinforced by legislative measures seeking to protect and conserve the eco system.

While the legal and constitutional framework safeguards the problem, as with many other well-intentioned legislations, there is little monitoring or enforcement. Of course, the judiciary has played a laudatory role is now seeking such enforcement. For instance, polluting industries have been ordered to be moved out of their existing locations to minimise pollution.

"The soul of tourism lies in environmental protection," says noted artist Kanwal Chaudhri, who presented at a Delhi function a series of artworks captioned 'Ode to Peace' using the simple motif of a lotus through its journey in life.

There are other reasons for which tourism is made accountable for depletion of natural resources. An international expert cites the example of a single guest in a Bali hotel consuming as much water as a citizen does in a whole month, which lends credence to the pledges mentioned earlier.

It is also appropriate that tourism associations and environmental bodies have joined in instituting special awards for conservation to individuals and institutions.

A handbook on Eco Tourism and Environment for PATA brought out by Mandip Soin, himself a recipient of many awards, is a good follow-up to eco-tourism guidelines contained in the draft National Tourism Policy.

IMPROVEMENTS NEEDED IN AVIATION

Indian Tourism : The View from Outside

Open Skies will Boost Travel to India

Pacific Asia Travel Association (PATA) which set up a task-force sometime ago to look at the challenge of 2000 A.D. now has a report titled "Direction 2000." Sharing the report with member countries, Pierre Doley, who was elected president of PATA in April this year was in New Delhi towards the end of August accompanied by Kane Rufe who has recently replaced Ken Chamberlain as the Executive Vice-President, a semi-permanent position. Talking to media persons at a lunch hosted by Inder Sharma, chairman, PATA India chapter, (who was a member of the task force) Rufe explained that under Direction 2000 PATA's focus would be on strategies rather than tactics. In order to achieve this, he added, the PATA board has formed an advisory council for different areas like education and research. The council would act like a think tank on how to tackle strategic issues. The new executive vice president gave these as the basic aims of Direction 2000 to enhance PATA's own mission as promoter of travel to and within the region through beefed up marketing programmes; with Europe 1992 already a reality, to open a PATA office in Europe to attract larger traffic to the PATA region; advocacy of greater travel to the Pacific Asia from global markets; streamline PATA's own decision making through the advisory council and by strengthening regional offices and by merging the executive and management committees into one single management committee; and finally, more result-oriented work by the membership committee.

Kane said at present there were 16,000 members from 42 countries but notable omissions were China, Cambodia, Laos, Myanmar and Mongolia Vietnam which had also stayed out of PATA has indicated its desire to join the association.

A major step already taken, he said, was the setting up of an Intelligence Centre at headquarters in San Francisco. This would be a databased centre with ability to analyse information to help the advisory council in its assessment of strategic issues.

Answering questions, the new PATA president as executive with an international airline (KLM) estimated that in the next decade the number of visitors to the Pacific basin was expected to rise from the present 38 million to 100 million on an 8 per cent annual compounded growth. He would not say what would be South Asia's share in this growth but volunteered advice to the region on how to maximise its share. First, he said, each country should prepare a master tourism plan with involvement of the entire industry and not just by governments or segments of the industry.

Secondly, liberal non-protectionist policies would help. This, he said, was particularly important for countries which hitherto had been mistakenly adopting closed-sky policies to protect their national carriers. Open skies policies, he said, were the best way of attracting tourists and gave the examples of Singapore and Holland where he said, not only had traffic increased, the national carriers had also benefited. In the case of this country, Air India was hardly helped by official policies, while it lost many more tourists who would have come to India had there been more frequent services by other airlines. In his view AI with its lower overheads could easily compete with international carriers. Foreign airlines, Doley said, would operate through India only if their operations were viable which for this country would mean more tourists. On infrastructure, Doley felt that India should have a fair mix of facilities for both upmarket and less affluent travellers as airlines offered airfares to both segments. He thought India was perceived as a country with a lot to offer and, if "merchandised properly," it could be a model for the rest of Asia. As an example he said Americans have a special interest in Hinduism, in Ashrams and the like but there was not much awareness of these attractions. "Have duty free shops in the town—airport duty free shops are no longer popular" he said.

Collective Marketing will Get India More Conferences

Is India underselling itself as a convention centre? Yes, say two renowned international experts who were in the Capital recently to speak at a seminar organised by the India chapter of the International Conference and Conventions Association. Lars Christensen, past president of the Brussels-based international Association of Professional Conference Organisers, and Helmut Sehwagermann, director. Congress and Convention Division of the International Congress Centre in Berlin (vanuefor ITB) said in an interview that the Indian promoters "underestimated their own product and its potential and seemed to give in too easily to competition from markets like Singapore, Bangkok, Hong Kong and Manila. India's unique selling points, two feel strongly, far outweigh those claimed by competition. But these had not been put across effectively. Collective marketing by the country's travel industry was another area which needed strengthening. "India needs more collective marketing by the industry," said Christensen and Sehwagermann.

Listing India's advantages, the two convention experts pointed out that the country was closer to Europe, a large generating market, in terms of flying time and more non-stop flights could save even more time for delegates. India might not have the most modern equipment but what the two experts had seen was certainly adequate. What was important was not modernity but reliability of the equipment. Apart from India's heritage, the country's scientific and professional resources were unmatched when it came to meaningful interface at international meetings. True, Delhi lacked a convention complex like Singapore or Manila but the city's hotels have good facilities for medium-sized conferences. Christensen and Sehwagermann pointed out that a major attraction Indian promoters should emphasise is the good value for money the country offers across the board whether it is hotel tariffs, food, taxis or shopping. Perhaps, the two conference experts said, India's greatest asset was its ability to present at the drop of a hat hundreds of scientists, doctors, bankers, technocrats, engineers to sit as peers with the best that the rest of the world could offer at any international gathering.

EASIER VISA RULES NEED TO BE IMPLEMENTED

Need for a Liberalised Visa Regime

Many years ago, during the 80s, Air India in association with ITDC was marketing quite successfully a low priced stop-over tour of Delhi for travellers flying long haul between UK and Australia. If memory does not fail me, for $25 to $30 a visitor could spend a night in the Capital at a five-star hotel and also get a half day free sightseeing before proceeding on to his final destination. An Australian travel writer, on a fam tour, who had a fascinating round of the Cottage Industries Emporium and other state emporia was overawed by the array of handicrafts available at what he thought were throw away prices, compared to what such articles would cost in developed societies. His advice to the then Air India commercial manager, tourism, S. P. Dutt, who accompanied him was: Stop promoting stop-over tours and start promoting shopover tours.

Whether the Indian tour operators took the advice seriously is another matter. I was reminded of this incident earlier this month, when as part of a group of four Indians we had to spend five hours at the Singapore airport after a 13 hour flight from San Francisco. Instead of relaxing at the airport, we decided to go to town at the instance of the compulsive shoppers amongst us. What about the visa? No problem, said the experienced traveller. Sure enough, by merely filling up the embarkation card at the immigration counter, it was no more than thirty seconds for each of us to be welcomed into Singapore. We discovered, there were many more like us waiting for connecting flights who had also taken advantage of this facility (which was at no cost). No doubt, for a free transit visa without any hassle, Singapore gained a lot by the hundreds and thousands of dollars, that visitors unloaded in the Island's shopping malls. Tourism is nothing, if it does not earn valuable dollars. Small wonder that Singapore attracts more than 3,00,000 Indians every year, a figure much larger in comparison to any other destination in southeast Asia.

The Singapore experience has been recalled to emphasise the part a liberal visa regime plays in promoting travel. Not long ago, when Indonesia took a conscious decision to boost its arrivals, it waived visa requirements for citizens of as many as 43 countries. In Thailand, a visa is sanctioned within minutes on arrival. If you are in Hong Kong and wish to visit mainland China, visa is easily available, even the same day if you are willing to pay that extra buck. But, it is Malaysia which takes the cake when it comes to a liberalised visa regime. As it is, citizens of only 13 countries around the world need a visa to enter the country. And even for this limited part of the world, the Malaysian government is reported to have decided in favour of a system unheard of before and which would sound revolutionary to Indian politicians and bureaucrats, not to mention those concerned with security.

According to a report in the Singapore-based trade weekly, *TTC-Asia*, the Malaysian immigration authorities have agreed to a request from Tourism Malaysia, the country's tourism administration, to empower it as well as the national carrier and believe it or not, Indian and Chinese agents to 'issue tourist visas into Malaysia'. Director general immigration, Datuk Asch Che Mat was quoted as saying, "We have agreed to this request by the culture, arts and tourism ministry in principle. The system will be implemented within two to three months." This timeframe will enable the immigration department to initially obtain clearance from the ministry of foreign affairs and update its computer systems, the weekly added. Significantly, *TTC-Asia*, says, "priority has been given to passing application requirements of those arriving from China, India and Pakistan." Travel industry folks in the Capital would remember that during a road show here the Malaysian tourism minister, Datuk Abdul Kadir Sheikh Fadzi had promised quick action on complaints of visa hassles.

The Malaysian minister has only succeeded in tackling the visa issue, but has also kept words about posting tourist offices in Delhi, Mumbai and Chennai as well as in Shanghai, and Beijing, within this year. Malaysia's leading tour operators, Eric Sinnaya of Morahols Travel, who is organising a travel mart in India next year, to promote Malaysia has welcomed the decision to empower selected agencies to issue visas. "It is fantastic" the weekly quotes him as saying, "it will increase Indian arrivals by 500 per cent."

The Malaysian tour operator's optimism is by no means misplaced. His country is a clear winner, in the return to the pre-currency crisis days of the revisited. According to statistics, released by FATA, many south-east Asian countries have had spectacular successes in 1999, "The best example" says FATA, "is Malaysia which terms of percentage gain grew by 42.9 per cent to rank as the best performer within the region and with a volume gain of almost 2.4 million arrivals." Incidentally, Malaysia is host to FATA 2001 which in turn is expected to add to its volumes, even more in the coming years. Is our very own tourism ministry listening? Will it succeed in persuading the home ministry to agree to at least visa on arrival for citizens of selected countries?

Changing Times Call for Visa Waiver

For too long tourism minister Ananth Kumar and senior officials of his department have been giving us hope of 'visa on arrival', a step which could go a long way in giving the country even a slightly better visitor count than the current 2.48 million, which is less than half a per cent of the global traffic. Analysts will tell you that even 2.48 million is an inflated figure if you count out NRIs (with foreign passports) and double entries of those who include Nepal in their itinerary. According to industry veteran, Inder Sharma, the number of 'real' tourists would be around 8,00,000. Inadequacies of infrastructure and poor marketing apart, visa hassles have been a major constraint in attracting larger numbers of visitors.

For some reasons, the tourism ministers have not been able to persuade their home and external affairs colleague (who have the ultimate authority to relax the visa regime) to learn from the experience of most other countries who consider tourism an instrument for development and prosperity. Among the Asian tigers who have also chosen tourism as a priority area, Indonesia, took the lead when, almost a decade ago, it listed more than 40 countries whose citizens needed no visa. Thailand and Hong Kong (even after its return to China) issue visa on arrival. Malaysia, with a 40 per cent increase in arrivals in 1999, showing the best turn around after the Asian crisis, is about to implement what could well be a revolutionary initiative. It will empower Malaysian Airlines and selected tour operators in source markets to issue tourist visa. Mind you the country insists on visas from less than 20 nations (including, of course, India), who have been chosen for this purpose.

Now, knowing the mindsets of our government and the genuine concerns about security, nobody would expect any bold initiatives in respect of visas. But, may be two of the latest developments, one in our next door neighbour Pakistan and, the other in the United States, will spur the tourism minister to lobby strongly with his colleagues in the home and external affairs ministries to agree to visa on arrival at least on a selective basis. Trade bodies and even some of the chambers, who are actively supporting the cause of the hospitality industry, have been urging the government to relax visa restrictions for countries which produce the largest number of travellers to India, namely, USA, UK, Germany, France, Italy, Japan and Australia. The immigration authorities have the right to refuse entry to 'unwanted' persons even when they are in possession of a valid visa. Any such element seeking entry into the country through the visa on arrival route could be easily kept out.

This is the argument that must have influenced the authorities in Pakistan and the United States. According to a report in an Islamabad newspaper, the military regime 'has allowed tourists from all over the world to fly into Pakistan, except those from India and non-resident Indians, without prior clearance from the country's missions abroad'. We need not worry too much about Indians being excluded because nobody in our own country is clamouring for visa waiver for our brothers across the border in the present state of relations between the two neighbours. But, an across the board no-visa offer for the rest of the world is a major step in removing barriers to free travel and worth emulating. Incidentally, Pakistan receives less than 5,00,000 tourists annually and like in India a large number of them are ethnic visitors.

The United States, which hosts close to 50 million tourists a year has chosen the reciprocal route in matters of visa. An agency report published in the *Tribune* says president Bill Clinton has signed a legislation 'that would allow citizens of many countries, to enter the USA for business or tourism without first obtaining a visa'. The visa waiver, the report said, will apply to citizens of countries that grant similar privileges to American citizens. It is noteworthy that the President himself issued a statement signifying the importance attached to a measure aimed at facilitating travel. He said, "By facilitating travel to the USA in this manner, the visa waiver programme is helping to generate billions of dollars in tourist and business revenues for US companies." The agency says that United States has been running a pilot programme for 12 years to see if the visa waiver would work. The American President's statement also points to another aspect of the visa regime – burgeoning costs when millions of entry permits have to be stamped on passports and the manpower required to process applications. President Clinton said, "The programme would also allow the state department to reallocate resources as it would not need to issue routine visas in low-risk waiver countries."

Is the tourism ministry listening? Surely there is a case for undertaking a pilot project with 'low-risk' countries.

Promote Hassle-Free Tourism

Visas are a source of pleasure or pain in international destinations attract the largest number of visitors when either there is no insistence on a visa or it is easily available. Tourism planners and the travel trade in this country have been urging the authorities to make visas free of hassles so that tourism can be lifted out of its morass.

It is to be hoped that when the new government that will come into being later this month will if it is serious about tourism promotion pay attention to this demand of the industry. Travellers can recall umpteen instances where the ease with which visa obtained makes the journey so much more pleasurable. This writer's personal experience reinforces this view.

On returning from attending the FATA session in Beijing last year there had to be a stopover in Bangkok. Enquiries in Beijing dispelled any worry on this score on being told that the relevant papers will be available at the Bangkok airport itself. The only requirement was to furnish two copies of a passport size photograph of the applicant. To the pleasant surprise on arrival at Bangkok was a photo studio next door to the immigration ready to provide instant pictures any time of the day or night.

The entire process of photographing and obtaining of the visa took hardly ten minutes which justifiably made the Bangkok stopover an occasion to remember forever.

Such facilitation is available elsewhere in Asia too. Indonesia, a success story in tourism took a deliberate decision to abolish at one go the visa requirement for more than forty countries in the early 1990s. The result was arrivals went up hy 300 per cent in three years. In the 1970s, India had no visa arrangements with several countries but security reasons later forced a reversal of this position.

The government could take a more realistic stand in easing the visa formalities for genuine visitors. After all, even viewed from the security perception, it needs to be borne in mind that no extremist or saboteur will take the risk of obtaining a visa and passing through security checks! Which only goes to show the need for revamping the visa system.

In developed countries with equal concern for security there are mechanisms for checks visitors with little dependence on visa. The American tourist influx into Britain is the largest thanks to visa exemption for visitors from the US.

Even in respect of outbound travel from India, journey to Europe has increased since the introduction of the single visa for nine EU countries. Not only is there a saving on the visa fee which have gone up many fold, but much time is gained as the passport now needs a visa stamp at a single point instead of waiting at the countries in nine separate embassies.

For all the visa reforms, obtaining travel papers seems a complex affair even for the trade. Therefore a set of three publications brought out by Indira Varma of IV Associates, New Delhi, serves as the most intelligent guide to the trade on the subject. The publications are Source, a visa and travel information manual, which is most comprehensive covering a host of topics including visa tariff, diplomatic missions, country fact finder, reciprocal visa, international help address, maps, health, passport and annexures.

In fact, two of the volumes are in the form of annexures, one containing specimen visa forms of almost all countries in the world from Afghanistan to Zimbabwe. The forms vary for tourists, business travel, transit passenger, students, temporary residence and relations. Says Varma, "trying to obtain forms for valued clients or submitting outdated ones can be frustrating as they cause delays and rejections." It is no exaggeration to observe that these publications, the third of which is a list of world public holidays, are one of the best facilitating tools, for the travel trade.

Apart from these publications, Varma's International Visa Service, (IVS) can handle visas on behalf of outstation travel agents. A whole set of advisories, which the publications carry on each country should be of immense use particularly to travel agents promoting outbound traffic.

Source, the publishers claim, is the only one of its kind in the world. At least in India no such travel kit is available. Together the three publications are encyclopedic insofar as these provide information on the travel requirements of those journeying abroad whatever be the objective; employment, business, education or holiday.

These innovative volumes could also be made use of by the new set up in exploring possibilities of easing what is considered to be one of the worst hassles inhibiting international tourism.

TECHNOLOGY CAN BOOST TOURISM

Judicious IT Application could Pave the Way for Successful Tourism

If the presence of senior ministers and industry leaders is any indication of the success of an event, the Hotel Association of India's second Afro-Asian conference-cum-exposition on information technology in hotels, held in the capital in the third week of March, could be said to have got off to a good start. Apart from tourism and culture minister Ananth Kumar, there were two chief ministers, Farooq Abdullah of Jammu and Kashmir and Shiela Dikshit of Delhi. Industry leaders included HAI president Lalit Suri and Taj managing director R. K. Krishna Kumar. A galaxy of sponsors too were associated with the event, many of them with international credentials. There was the UN Economic and Social Commission for Asia and the Pacific (ESCAP), SAARC Tourism Council, SAARC Hotel Association, PATA and the International Hotel and Restaurant Association (IHRA), apart from representatives of the department of tourism and ministry of Information Technology. President K. R. Narayanan and vice-president Krishna Kant were among those who sent messages, as did Kim Hak-Su, under secretary-general of ESCAP.

The ESCAP functionary's message should be of interest because it speaks not only of the impact of technology on economies but also of the role of tourism in poverty alleviation. The Delhi conference, he said, 'will provide excellent opportunities to better understand the profound transformation in key segments of the tourism industry that has occurred and that can be expected in the future. This will include, amongst others, discussions on global distribution and reservation systems, the internet and electronic commerce, networking among travel agents, the automation of building and property management systems'. Kim Hak-Su says that for business to be successful, it is very important that the private sector associated with the tourism industry in Asia and the Pacific grasps the opportunities provided by the new information technologies that will transform the management and operation of facilities and services for tourists. It is equally important, he adds, for the government policy-makers and regional and international organisations to maintain and strengthen awareness of technological changes that will profoundly influence the contribution of tourism to national and regional socio-economic development.

The ESCAP under secretary-general says the future success of the tourism industry lies in its ability to grab the opportunities provided by the information technologies. Tourism, he adds, is making significant contributions to the socio-economic development of many countries in the Asian and Pacific region through its role in expanding their economic base, increasing foreign exchange earnings, providing employment and enhancing standards of living. "The role of tourism has become particularly significant in developing countries; where there may be few alternative development opportunities."

Kim Hak-Su believes tourism can help reduce disparities in income and employment within countries, since areas suitable for tourism development are often situated far from the locus of other economic activities. And, when tourism is developed in parts of the country outside the main commercial centres, it could contribute to poverty alleviation in rural areas. Talking of ESCAP's own work, he said this UN body recognises the important role of tourism in socio-economic development and has been undertaking a number of activities in this field. One important initiative is the establishment of a regional network to address issues of human resource development in the tourism sector. This initiative is linked to the need for qualified education and training institutes to meet the demand for capable, well-trained personnel.

Asked to comment on whether India should import technology or develop it indigenously, Taj's MD, Krishna Kumar, said, "There are pros and cons for both. However, before a decision is taken, technology must be very carefully evaluated and only that which suits the need best should be considered. At this point in time, the hotels rely more on imported technology as their requirements are not met in India or the quality does not match the expected standards." Are our IT whizkids listening?

Public-Private Partnership Essential for Tourism Enhancement

There has been no dearth of praise for the government and the industry over the success of the PATA conference held, in the capital last month.

Describing it as a 'landmark achievement on behalf of Indian travel and tourism; the president and CEO of the prestigious international body Peter de Jong has spoken of the 'exceptional professionalism and efficiency' of the team that put the conference together. "What most impressed the more than one thousand delegates was the warmth and generosity of Indian hospitality and the stellar beauty of the cultural performances. These have left an indelible impression in the minds of many hundreds of key decision-makers in our industry." India he added, had beautifully showcased her unique destination to those who make a difference: the world leaders – the multipliers – of our industry." That this is not a mere formal thank you note from an honoured guest is borne out by what a hard-boiled Asian journalist, J. P. Sho, editor of the widely read Korea Travel Press had openly said at a briefing attended by Indian media persons covering the mega event. "I am a veteran of 31 PATA conferences" he said with justified pride, "and this is certainly the best I have ever attended."

The department of tourism (DoT), minister downward, is indeed happy that things went well. But every one is keen to ward off complacency. Secretary Rathi Vinay Jha put it succinctly in an informal chat. "PATA was certainly a great show. But let us not be carried away by the hype" she told me and added, "the Party is over; let us start working." PATA, she said, will certainly go some way in bringing India back into focus as a preferred destination. But, we have a more challenging task ahead: improving the product and effectively marketing it in order to build on the goodwill released through the PATA conference. Fortunately, the recent tourism-friendly initiative taken by the government, especially the plan allocation for the sector, do change the environment in favour of a push to tourism. She confirmed that against a demand of Rs. 5,300 crore by DoT for the tenth plan, the amount allocated is Rs. 2,900 crore, five times the figure in the Ninth Plan. The outlay in the first year of the Tenth Plan – the current fiscal – is Rs. 225 crore, twice as much as last year. DoT has already started a dialogue with the states and is encouraging them to come up with major projects as part of the circuits strategy spreading over state boundaries. For instance, while Hampi in Karnataka is being developed as a full destination in itself others in the pipeline include Mahabalipuram-Pondicherry-Kanchipuram and Kulu-Manali-Lahoul Spiti-Leh. She explained that with larger funds now available the idea was to start work on six circuits in each year of the plan period.

The tourism secretary is keen to see a new relationship develop between DoT and the industry. She recognises the role of the department in forwarding the industry's demands to the finance and other ministries.

But, she said, tourism will flourish only when there is genuine partnership between the public and private sector. While the government has an important part to play in developing infrastructure like airports, roads and elements that ensure connectivity, safety and security as well as civic services, the private sector can play a major role in marketing India. Hotels and other segments, she said, are spending huge amounts overseas on their sectoral promotions while government underwrites the entire expenditure on the maintenance and promotional activities of the tourist offices abroad. "It is about time" she said, "we sat together and worked out how best we could use our limited resources jointly or in a coordinated manner." She intends taking the initiative towards this end.

Asked about the future of ITDC after disinvestment she said that now that it has been decided to keep the Ashoka as well as Samrat and Janpath in Delhi and Lalitha Mahal in Mysore out of privatisation, an in-depth review is in progress. She herself feels that the Ashok has good potential both as a heritage property as well as historic hotel, built as it was in free India's first five-star offering. But, it will need fresh investments to be on a level playing field with the private sector. The current chairman and managing director she said, had already initiated several steps to reposition the Ashoka. Feasibility study for conversion the Janpath into a one-stop tourist service centre is on. DoT has its work cut out.

16
Epilogue

Tourism in India

Travel has been an integral part of human activity since antiquity. The reasons for travel have changed over the centuries. In the more ancient times the main motivations were pilgrimage, trade and conquest. It is surprising to find that several thousand years ago there were contacts among people separated by vast distances, seas and mountains. India and West Asia, for instance, interchanged ideas and knowledge. The Hindu temples at Borobodur in Central Java and the Gandhara School of Arts which developed following Alexander's invasion are classic examples. Emperor Ashok sent emissaries to Sri Lanka, Burma and other parts of Southeast Asia to spread Buddhism. In fact much of the knowledge about our social history in earlier periods is based on records left by visitors like Fa Hien and Huen Tseng, Ibn Batuta, Al Beruni and Marco Polo. Within India religion was the dominant motivation for travel. The concept of shrines in the four corners of India – Badrinath, Puri, Dwarka and Rameshwaram known as *Char Dham* seems like a well-planned effort to ensure travel throughout the country. And, to this day, pilgrimge continues to be the most important reason for travel, although the country has entered the era of modern tourism.

In the west, particularly in Europe, tourism is the product of the industrial revolution. Holidays and surplus incomes created the urge to travel, mainly for change and relaxation in places with different or better climate, in the mountains or on the beaches or in search of the sun. These movements were initially confined to travel within a country but they played an important role in building a base for the future revolution in organised tourism. In other words, it was domestic tourism which became the foundation for international tourism. This is the first major difference between tourism development in India and the west. In India, we have first built a base for international tourism and are using that as a foundation for domestic tourism. The reasons are clear: pilgrimage still accounts for much of travel and *dharamshala* and *dhabas* seem to be adequate to meet the needs of this category of travellers. The affluent and the professionals and workers with surplus incomes are the ones who are utilize in hotels and other services built primarily for overseas visitors.

Organised or mass tourism as we know it today is a post-World War II phenomenon. In the past three decades or so tourism has become the world's second largest industry after oil, and, also the fastest growing. In 1951, 25 million tourists crossed International borders. The figure for 1983 is 287 million. These 287 million travellers spent the equivalent of 99 billion US dollars, excluding the cost of International air-fares.

Tourism has come to play an important role in the socio-economic development of a country. There are more than two score countries round the world which actually live off tourism. Spain is one of them and she welcomes every year more visitor than its own population of 24 million. What tourism meant to India is aptly brought out in the Sixth-Five Year Plan's chapter on the subject. "Tourism both domestic and international, has rapidly won considerable recognition an activity generating a number of social and economic benefits like promotion of national integration and international understanding, creation of employment opportunities removal of regional imbalances, augmentation of foreign exchange earnings, thus redressing the balance of payments situation, etc. It is significant that many of these beneficial aspects of domestic and international tourism have special relevance to the socio-economic scene in India as emerging in the sixth plan period. Tourism also tends to give support to local handicrafts and cultural activities, both in urban and rural areas. Expenditure by tourists has a multiplier effect and also generates considerable tax revenue for Government, both in the central and state sectors. It is also relevant that the various multifaceted socio-economic benefits of tourism are achieved with a relatively low level of investment".

Whether the Planning Commission's recognition of tourism as an instrument of economic development is reflected in the allocations to this activity is another matter. First let us see what India has achieved so far in tourism. That in 1951 this country received a mere 17,000 foreigners and that their number went up to over 1,030,000 thirty two years later is a creditable achievement. The 1983 arrivals include visitors from Bangladesh and Pakistan. The table below shows the growth pattern of India's tourist arrivals:

Year	*Arirvals*	*% Increase*
1951	17,000	
1961	1,34,804	
1962	1,34,630	
1963	1,140,821	
1964	1,56,673	
1965	1,47,900	
1966	1,59,603	
1967	1,79,565	
1968	1,88,820	
1969	2,44,724	29.6
1970	2,80,821	14.7
1971	3,00,995	7.2
1972	3,42,950	13.9
1973	4,09,895	19.5
1974	4,23,161	3.2
1975	4,65,275	10.0
1976	5,33,951	14.8
1977	6,40,422	20.8
1978	7,47,995	16.8
1979	7,64,781	2.2
1980	8,00,150	4.6
1981	8,53,148	6.6
1982	8,60,170	0.6
1983	8,84,731*	
		1,304,976

*Includlng visitors from Bangladesh and Pakistan, the total comes up to 1,304,976.

While world tourist movements have more than doubled between 1968 and 1983 (from 139.7 million tourists to 287 million), arrivals into India went up about four times. Or, in other words, India's growth rate has been almost twice as much as the world's. India's share of the world tourist market a meagre 0.14 per cent in 1968 was still a meagre 0.28% in 1983.

Now let us see what tourist arrivals are like in some of our Asian neighbours and competitors:

Country	*1978*	*1979*	*1980*
Thailand	1,453,758	1,591,455	1,856,801
Malaysia	724,279	771,662	895,104
Phillipines	843,005	966,873	1,008,159
Singapore	2,047,224	2,247,091	2,562,085
Japan	1,039,055	1,112,066	1,316,632
Korea	1,079,455	1,126,102	976,415

(Contd.)

(Contd.)

Hong Kong	2,054,739	2,213,209	2,301,473
Taiwan	1,270,977	1,340,462	1,393,254

It will be seen that tiny islands of Singapore and Hong Kong get nearly three times more tourists than India. Even Thailand gets more than twice as much.

As a tourist destination, India is unmatched. Its vastness and its diversity of terrain, people, languages, culture, history, a continuity of its five thousand years old civilisation, a country richly endowed both by man and nature, is a virtual tourist paradise backed by international standard facilities like Jet Air services, starred hotels, air-conditioned coaches, rail services guides etc. Why then India's poor showing?

It is poor showing only at first sight. A mere one-third of one per cent of the world tourist arrivals, less tourists than Thailand, Hong Kong and Singapore. For an appraisal of India's performance we must see what is it that this country get out to achieve, what is the share of the world market available to India, what is India competing with and what are the inputs that country is making available to the tourism growth.

It would be good to begin with the year 1967 when Tourism became a separate Ministry under a Cabinet Minister. It was then that the target of one million tourists by 1980 was set with an average growth of 14 per cent in tourist arrival annually. If we take visitors from Bangladesh and Pakistan into account, then the target could be said to have been achieved. Again, in the case of India arrival numbers do not tell the whole story. The average stay of a tourist in this country is estimated at 28 days (the second longest in the world after Australia where it is 30 days). A million (or even 8,60,000) tourists spending an average of 28 days in India is much higher in volume than 2 million tourists spending barely two or three days on an average in Singapore or Hong Kong. Besides, much of the traffic to these islands is for shopping and a majority of visitors come from neighbouring countries like Japan.

Similarly, take the pattern of world tourist movements. Eighty-two per cent of the tourist traffic is generated by 17 countries, twelve in Europe, two in North America and Mexico, Japan and Australia. More tkan 90 per cent of tourist movement is within Europe and between Europe and North America. Countries like India can aspire to get only a portion of the small share left for them outside of Europe/North America. In other word, India is one among a hundred or so other countries vying for the traveller from the main generating countries.

And, finally the inputs. As the table below shows, allocations to tourism since the second five year plan (the first plan did not even refer to tourism as an activity) have not been more than one-fifth of one per cent.

(Rs. in crore)

	Total Outlay	*Outlay on Tourism*	*% of Total Outlay*
2nd Plan 1959-64	4,500	3.36	0.07
3rd Plan 1964-69	7,500	8.00	0.11
4th Plan 1969-74	15,902	46.48	0.29
5th Plan 1974-79	39,322	65.50	0.17
Annual Plan 1979-80	12,600	28.02	0.22
Sixth Plan	97,000	187.46	0.19

Allocations to tourism do look meagre in comparison with the total Plan outlay. But we must not forget that the tourism infrastructure consists of a number of elements under other heads as well. For instance part of the money spent on improving or expanding airports or building new ones, on purchase of new aircraft for Air India or Indian Airlines, on the improvement of rail and road transport, on roads and public utility services, indirectly helps tourism. The Sixth Plan, to take an example, allocated nearly Rs.188 crore to the central and state sectors for tourism. Of this Rs. 30 crore is for the Department of Tourism, Rs. 42 crore for India Tourism Development Corporation and Rs. 116 crore for the States. In addition there is a sizeable allocation of Rs. 850 crore for the civil aviation sector which will both directly and indirectly help tourism development.

The reasons for such low direct investment in tourism in spite of the Planning Commission's recognition of the role of tourism in the country's development are not far to seek. For India, tourism is only one of the many instruments of developments. The demands of more urgent and critical areas like industry, chemicals, fertilisers, energy, social welfare, to name just a few, must take precedence over tourism.

Thus taking all the factors into account India could be said to have done reasonably well in her tourism effort at least during the 70s in spite of the fuel crisis, worldwide inflation and disturbed conditions in India's immediate neighbourhood.

No wonder the country entered the 60s with a certain amount of optimism. It set for itself a target of 3.5 million arrivals by 1990 and 1.7 million by 1985. These were ambitious, targets and have since been scaled down to 2.5 million. It's difficult to say at this stage even if the revised target is realistic.

Now let us examine India's tourist markets. An analysis of the 1981 tourist arrivals by the country of residence shows that Western Europe accounted for a bulk of the traffic to India – 37.0% – followed by Southeast Asia (7.7%). Countrywise the United Kingdom is traditionally the major tourist generating market followed by the United States, Sri Lanka, France, West Germany, Saudi Arabia, Japan, Italy, Malaysia and Canada:

Following are the top 15 suppliers of tourists to India:

Country	*Arrivals 1981*	*Arrivals in 1980*
UK	102,266	89,392
USA	77,438	73,399
Sri Lanka	75,030	66,737
France	57,186	58,426
W. Germany	53,918	54,332
Saudi Arabia	29,842	27,604
Japan	29,025	30,679
Italy	28,591	29,108
Malaysia	25,677	23,489
Canada	23,079	21,547
Singapore	18,749	16,608
Switzerland	14,917	14,012
Afghanistan	12,841	10,813
Iran	10,618	19,612

Barring the emergence of the Arab and the Buddhist markets, India's tourism generating region have virtually regained static. In the ten years 1971-80 West Asia showed a more than eight-fold increase, with Saudi Arabia jumping to the tenth position in 1980 and sixth in 1981 among the top countries sending tourists to India. Most other regions showed a three-fold increase.

According to one tourist expert, India has depended too much on cultural tourist and 70 per cent of the visitors to this country do seem to be attracted by our ancient civilization, rich in monuments and temples, area and culture. According to him we have ignored the holiday market, make no special effort to promote short-haul regional tourism, and done nothing to encourage ethnic populations. The holiday tourist is usually looking for water climates, sunshine and warm water beaches beyond the

Mediterranean and Caribbean. It is not surprising that ninety per cent of the traffic to the neighbouring Sri Lanka is of these seeking a holiday by the sea. Of course, India has made a beginning with developing, beach resorts in Goa, Kovalam, and Mahabalipuram. and Orrisa is next on the list. But a more concerted effort in exploiting our vast coastline could secure for us a much larger share of the beach holiday tourists.

Ethnic visitors, i.e. visitors of Indian.origin is another huge market waiting to be tapped. A few years ago the number of Indians settled overseas was estimated at about 12 million. About a third of them are said to be descendents of those who migrated two or three generations ago and most of them have not seen India. It can however be assumed that they have preserved their religious and cultural traditions and may be longing to visit the land of their origin. Another one-third have become citizens of the country of their domicile and the rest still hold Indian passports. We could follow the example of countries like Italy and Ireland and even East European nations like Poland and Hungary, to run regular campaigns inviting the old citizens to visit their home country. There are large Indian communities in the UK, USA, Canada, Trinidad, Guyana, Surinam, Mauritius, Fiji, East Africa who could be interested in visiting India.

Then there is short-haul tourism. A large part of the world tourist pattern is based on this. The fuel crisis and rising airfares have only strengthened this pattern. Of the 287 million tourists of 1983, 200 million visited Europe, but eighty per cent of them travelled within Western and Eastern Europe. Similarly, the USA and Canada exchanged nearly 22 million and the USA and Mexico another 7 million visitors. There is great potential in our part of the world too, within Southeast Asia and East Asia. The countries of this region supply to one another nearly 50 per cent of their visitors. A new middle class has emerged and is eager to travel. But India gets too small a share of this. In 1980 we had only 60,676 visitors from the five countries of Southeast Asia and probably half of them were of Indian origin domiciled in Malaysia , Singapore and Thailand. East Asia supplied only 37,152 of which 30,679 were Japanese. The 67,000 visitors from Sri Lanka must have included a large number of Ceylon Tamils who came by sea. One can imagine how many millions will be travelling between Bangladesh and India and between India and Pakistan if there were no travel restrictions. Hopefully this will be possible in the net too distant future.

We have not touched on the foreign exchange India earns from tourist. The table below shows these earnings have grown:

(Rs. in Crore)

Year	Foreign Exchange Earned
1966	22.60
1967	25.18
1968	26.42
1969	33.11
1970	39.03
1971	40.38
1972	48.32
1973	67.50
1974	69.70
1975	104.20
1976	225.00
1977	270.00
1978	330.00
1979	338.00
1980	482.00
1981	560.00
1982	750.00
1983	878.00

Foreign exchange earned from tourism represents the third largest amount earned by the country from her exports. India does not spend more than 6 per cent of the foreign exchange earned from tourism on its promotion oversees. India is perhaps among the few developing countries which not only retains most of the foreign exchange earned from tourism but also earns additional amounts from overseas consultancy services, a field in which India's private hotel chains, notably the Taj Group have been pioneers.

The 876 crore earned in 1983 is an estimate of the Department of Tourism. Unofficial estimates put the figure at 1,000 crore. The counting fuel import bill, said to be Rs. 5,000 crore in the current year could greatly effect the balance of payments position. The immense potential of earning foreign exchange from tourism therefore assumes greater importance in the context of balance of payments. Achievement of the target of 2.5 million tourist arrivals by 1990 would earn foreign exchange of nearly 2,000 crores on current prices even according to official estimates.

As stated earlier, while the country ended the decade of 70s with a reasonably good performance and entered the 80s with a fair account of optimism, certain trends, mostly beyond India's control, have been causing concern. The growth rate in tourist arrivals which took a nose-dive in 1979 coming down to a low 2.2 per cent, picked up a little in 1980 with 4.6 and in 1981 with 6.6 and dipped again to 0.8 ner cent in 1982. Unless we restore the growth rate to about 10 per cent we have no hope of achieving the target of 2.5 million in 1990. However, the first two months of 1983 i.e., January and February have shown a 15 per cent growth and it is to be hoped that the situation will improve in the coming months with the renewed interest in India thanks to the Gandhi Kiln and the India Festivals.

While recession was the main reason for sluggish growth of tourism to India introduction of the visa system has had its tolls. At the moment there seems little hope that visa requirements will be withdrawn but there have been some other encouraging developments like charter traffic to country. On the infrastructure Big Asiad was good news for tourism planners and the travel trade. Ten new hotels in the capital have doubled the accommodation from the existing 3,000 to 6,000 rooms will enable New Delhi to stake its claim as one of the world's major conference and convention capitals.

Asiad is only the first seed to the Olympics. Already there is talk that India might make a bid for the 1992 event. Both Air India and Indian Airlines have augmented their fligts. The Airport at Mumbai has been expanded. Palam is getting ready to open the new terminal. Facilities at airports have vastly improved though still behind the developed countries. The green channel at the customs is a major advance, available only in India this side of the Suez. But the porters and tail drivers still need to be trained in the handling of a sensitive commodity called the tourist.

Turism has vast potential for India, we have only scratched the surface.

India-Destination of the 90s?

This year's convention of the Travel Agents Association of India (TAAI) has greater significance as it has been christened "Indian Travel Congress" reflecting a wider platform for the industry. Participating in this annual convention are not only travel agents and tour operators but also hoteliers, airlines, central and state tourism agencies and manufacturers of the industry's product requirements. The theme chosen for the meet, to be held in Kolkata from September 8-11 is 'India: Destination of the 90s?" The question mark lends importance to the deliberations as the travel industry is not enthusiastic about the observance of 1991 as tourism year nor is it confident that with the present pace of development, the country can become the destination of the decade. On the tourism year, representatives of TAAI are in fact reported to have cautioned the department of Tourism against wasting money unless the infrastructural inadequacies were first attended to. The industry as a whole is also concerned about the fallout of adverse publicity overseas, over Kashmir and the continuing disorganised state of affairs in domestic air services. The much publicised reinduction of A 320s (even though in a phased programme) is nowhere in sight. The recent ministerial pronouncement that there was no sanctity to the date for re-induction has only strengthened the widely-held belief that decisions on the controversial airbus are politically motivated.

Another development that has distressed industry circles is the decision, in the name of economy, to close down some of the tourist offices overseas. Sydney, Stockholm, Singapore are said to be among them. That this should be done on the eve of the tourism, year is surprising. One would have expected the Department of Tourism to strengthen, its overseas promotional effort, not reduce it.

But there are some hopeful signs, too. Our High Commissioner in UK, Kuldip Nayar, who persuaded the Foreign Office to liberalise visa rules for people of Indian origin in that country, has been able to get the relaxation applicable for their families. Not only that, no sooner had he announced the changes in the visa regulations he also announced a unilateral reduction of visa fees from £ 23 for a short term visa to £ 10, and from £ 69 for a long term permit to £ 15. Nayar has appealed to the British government to reciprocate the gesture.

The other encouraging news is that privatisation of aviation is about to take one more step forward. After the successful launch of the first air-taxi by UB air, which operates regularly from Bangalore to Mangalore and Chennai, a second airline, Air Asiatic is, set to commence services initially, with a Boeing 737 also in the Southern region. (UB Air has begun its service with a Kanpur-made Dornier).

Tourism: The Invisible Exchange Earner

India has mad big strides in tourism. From a mere 17,000 tourist arrivals in 1951, the figure for 1983 is 8,84,731. And if visitors from neighbouring Pakistan and Bangladesh were to be included, the number of arrivals in 1983 would be more than 1.3 million. And the foreign exchange earned from tourism in that year is estimated at close to 1.1 billion rupees, making it the largest single earner of this scarce resource. The seventies were a particularly good decade for tourism. The country maintained a steady growth rate of around 12 per cent, higher than the average world growth rate.

In spite of this good showing, our planners have not given tourism any priority. In fact in the Planning Commission's list of precedence tourism ranks only higher than light houses, which is the last item! This would be obvious from the allocations in the previous five year plans. The First

Five-Year Plan did not so much as mention tourism as an activity. The Second Plan provided 33.6 million rupees (utilisation 22.1 million rupees) together for the central and state sectors. In the Third Plan the allocation was 80 million rupees and utilisation 57 million. The Fourth Plan figure jumped to 458.8 million with an encouraging utilisation of 413 million rupees. The Fifth Plan showed a whopping increase to 781 million rupees with over 90 per cent utilisation. And, finally the Sixth Plan which originally provided for 1.8 billion rupees may also close the period with a similarly impressive utilisation. Taking the entire period of planned development from the Second Plan onwards till 1981-82, the total allocation to tourism comes to 2.3 billion rupees with a more than 100 per cent utilisation. Impressive indeed if one were to compare the second plan figure of 33.6 million with the 1.7 billion provision in the current Sixth Plan but it is depressing to note that the percentage of tourism allocations to the national effort have in no plan more than one-fifth of one per cent! (Incidentally, India's "impressive" 1.3 million tourist arrivals in 1983 also amount to less than one per cent of the world tourist traffic.)

It isn't that the Planning Commission does not recognise the important role of tourism. The Sixth Plan document spells it out in glowing terms: its contribution to balance of payments, employment, revival of handicrafts and village industries, regional development, international understanding and what is even more important to the country, national integration, not to talk of the multiplier effect of the tourist dollar, which in the case of this country, is estimated at three and a half times. Then, why such low investments in tourism? Part of the answer is the competing demands on resources. The other part is attitudes of decision-makers. For a politician benefits from tourism are not as possible (to the electorate) as an irrigation canal, a dispensary, a school or a factory or even a bank loan.

And those in the tourism industry who have been campaigning for a better deal to tourism have not been helped much by the tourism goods in the recent past. The eighties have been a period of sluggish growth what with world recession and disturbed conditions in the region and the recent sad events at home with the result that for the first time the growth rate in 1984 might well turn out to by zero, the lowest on record. And this at a time, when India should have been reaping a rich harvest from the tremendous interest created in this country tourismwise by events like the ASIAD, NAM, CHOGM and worldwide screening of films like Gandhi, Passage to India, Far Pavilions and so on.

Fortunately, recession seems to be receding and tourist movements are picking up. Two other major developments have given cause for hope.

First, we are on the eve of formulating the Seventh Plan, and, second, the country has a new government with promise of a 21st century approach and plenty of room for "change".

It is indeed the first time that the Approach paper to a five year plan has even referred to the subject of tourism. The approach to the Seventh Plan says: "There is a vast potential for development of tourism in the country. Tourism should be accorded the status of an industry. Private sector investment will have to be encouraged in developing tourism and public sector investments should be focused only on development of support infrastrcture". Significance is attached not only to the first ever reference to tourism but also to the need to give tourism the status of an industry. But more important is the clear enunciation of the roles of the private and the public sectors in the future development of tourism. One interpretation of this is that the public sector will only play the development role i.e., opening up new destinations and buildings that part of the infrastructure which the private sector is either unable or unwilling to undertake. One consequence of this may be no more five star hotels in the public sector. However one has to wait until the Seventh Plan is formualted to see the impact of the approach document.

Some indications are available of the projection of investments on tourism in the next five years. The revised target of tourist arrivals by the end of the Seventh Plan period (1990) is 2.5 million with an estimated annual foreign exchange earning of 3 billion rupees. The Central Department of Tourism would like an allocation of 3.6 billion rupees for the Seventh Plan of which 1.5 billion is for ITDC.

Diversifying the tourist product would be one of the major strategies of the Department of Tourism. Beach tourism, convention/conference tourism, trekking, wild life, incentive and holiday tourism and winter sports are some of the areas which are proposed to be rapidly developed. Among the beach areas to the further developed are Puri, the Andamans and Lakshadweep. There will be greater promotion of the southern and eastern regions as tourist circuits. A special effort is planned for ten new destinations as National Heritage Centres. Water sports too are proposed to be developed. There will be a bigger and wider effort to promote India overseas.

OPPORTUNITIES IN TOURISM SECTOR

Skills: from Cuisine to Computer

India's travel and tourism trade requires an estimated 28,000 persons every year only a fraction of which is met by the existing institutions. With the various catering colleges and craft institutes unable to produce enough managers for all levels, big hotel chains have developed their own in-house training programmes to fill critical gaps. Even so, the range of requirements is so wide—from a guide at a monument site (to a ground hostess at the airport, from the bell boy to the general manager in a hotel, from ticketing to translations—that no single institution can provide training in all the subjects. Still the trade offers immense employment opportunities particularly as tourism is the world's fastest growing industry. Our national target of tourist arrivals for the mid-nineties is 3.5 m. Though this is a miniscule percentage of the global movement, the large figure is indicative of the expansion potential of this service industry.

Career prospects in travel are obvious at the airport itself, the first point of contact for a tourist. Immigration is the first counter where the visitor is to be serviced. The government and industry are agreed that there should be a separate immigration cadre. A beginning has already been made for training the first batch. Curriculum in some universities provides for teaching of immigration procedures. Customs services have been in existence as a separate cadre but, here again as the volume of traffic increases, the number of counters will have to be 'increased manifold. If we have to match our facilities with what is available in competing destinations, the time taken at the counters has to be reduced to the minimum. If there is a bunching of flights, the customs check at the red channel counters results in long queues, frayed tempers and losses in repeat visits Transport is a related sector that provides employment. There is considerable scope for self-employment particularly for the educated where knowledge of a foreign language is an additional asset. Coaches and tourist cars with educated drivers are in increasing demand. Facility for bank loans for acquiring these vehicles is available. In fact this area offers scope for large-scale employment. A measure of the relevance of this section of employees to tourism promotion is the introduction of a special training course initiated by the Indian Institute of Travel and Tourism Management, (ITTTM) the apex body for tourism training. The average income could be upwards of Rs. 3,000 a month.

Perhaps the largest requirement of manpower is in hotels and the skills required are of a great variety, from cuisine to computer, There are at the moment 42,000 rooms in the approved category (with star ratings) in about 700 hotels and another 60,000 rooms in the other hotels. In the star hotels specialised training is required for food and beverage, housekeeping, accounting, marketing, recreation and other services, computer applications, financial management, engineering and maintenance, security, fire-fighting and public relations. Star hotels pay reasonably well. The more experienced get high salaries and perks at a young age. Diploma holders from institutes like the one at Pusa in Delhi are in good demand and they can hope to start at junior management levels. Promotion could be rapid not only because of growth of demand but also because of opportunities to improve skills including scholarships abroad and overseas training programmes of major chains.

The commonly held notion that in hotels people dress elegantly, work in plush air-conditioned buildings, meet celebrities and vine and dine is only a very small part of the truth. The jobs have become increasingly challenging and in recent times sophisticated technology is a key element in the hotel milieu. This is evident at the hotel reception counter itself where the computer is the principal tool. As time advances the need for elimination of any delay at the counters gets increasing emphasis. Automation will play a major role but the compulsions of personalised attention in a service industry will continue. This will mean that there will be a greater need for human resource: people would be needed to man the machines at every stage. At the same time, by the very nature of the industry, the human interface will continue to be a necessity.

The extent of human resource development required by the turn of the century is radicated by the projected absolute demand for 60,000 additions, rooms. A five star hotel creates three direct jobs and many more indirectly per room. To cite only to direct jobs, there will be 1,80,000 vacancies to run approved hotels in the next ten years. The global dimensions of tourism's job potential in this area are of a far greater magnitude. There are as many as 13,000 hotels and motels owned and managed by people of Indian origin in the US alone. The number of Indians working in hotels in the Gulf and in parts of Europe and in the UK is huge. Even at the highest level of management the annual requirement within the country is of the order of 850 according to the report of the national committee on tourism. For that reason the national committee recommended full time management courses to be taken up in the universities.

Hotels apart, travel agencies, tour operators, visa services, foreign exchange facilities and other travel-related services, credit card companies and airlines, both Indian and foreign, are the other employers in the business. Some institutes conduct part-time courses in airline ticketing and reservations, inbound tour operations, basics of outbound tours and travel marketing. There are a few colleges of vocational studies offering courses in tourism. Creative writing for tourism promotion, travel writing, TV and video films on travel are some of the newer areas of employment.

Shops and guides provide two travel-related services where the young could seek gainful self-employment With an eye to the preferences of visitors from different parts of the world, special curio and gift shops, which have a spin-off effect in rural employment as well, could be opened in larger numbers as more tourists come to these places. Young graduates with a flair for history and languages could function as licensed guides. This in fact generates local employment in places of tourist importance. By combining the tasks of a chauffeur with those of a guide, one could raise one's income to a much higher level. While these jobs relate to cultural tourism the trade is getting diversified which in turn could absorb more people. For instance, a party seeking adventure tourism would like to enlist the participation of like minded youth in the host country on payment.

Yet another segment of tourism where work opportunities abound are conventions and conferences. Here translators, ushers and secretaries as well as organisers of social and cultural events, even florists are required. Permanent business centres in hotels also take in such young qualified men and women. Thus, there is bound to be a huge demand for professionals in this field well into the future. The IITTM as the apex body takes care of education in the universities. The catering institutes as also institutions run by the Welcomgroup and the Oberois are turning out professionals, but the country would need many more of them. If there is any activity where job opportunity exists with certitude, tourism is one such.

Index

J

K

L

M

TOURISM IN INDIA

TOURISM IN INDIA

– An Overview

(In Two Volumes)

Volume 2

Rabindra Seth
Om Gupta (General Editor)

Publications
KALPAZ PUBLICATIONS
Delhi-110052

Tourism in India – An Overview

Rs. 1800 (set)

ISBN: 81-7835-328-8 (Set)
ISBN: 978-81-7835-330-2 (Vol. 2)

Published in 2005 in India by
Kalpaz Publications,
C-30, Satyawati Nagar, Delhi-110052
E-mail : Kalpaz@hotmail.com

Laser Typesetting at : Shiva Infosystem, Delhi
Printed at : Salasar Imaging System, Delhi

Contents

Preface

Ten years down memory lane, a meeting with the publisher, Santosh Goenka, ushered in the circumstances which brought me into association with the *Express Hotelier & Caterer* (EH&C) from its inception till today. I asked if the range of the journal's coverage should be limited to hoteliering and catering or extended to cover the entire reach of the tourism sector. Goenka, full of ideas, assured me that he had another journal in mind to cover the rest of the hospitality services but would begin with the EH&C. Looking back, the concept proved right because it filled a vacuum in hospitality services' journalism. A journal that could focus on a particular segment of the industry could set-off awareness for the entire sector.

These were the years when tourism peaked, dipped and has since plateaued on a lower level. The causes and effects of this oscillation have provided me all to sustain a column, week after week, during this period. Usually it is very difficult even for a full-timer to chase subjects relating to activities, particularly when at times it tends to get static to pick a topic and say something new about it in a column that is meant to be read by knowledgeable persons in a particular industry.

The publisher also deserves to be complimented on hiring and motivating the requisite staff to fill its columns every week with news about the central theme of the magazine. The boys and girls who have performed this job deserve a pat on the back, particularly when in the past years they had to be exclusive in coverage being in competition with a sister publication from the same stable.

There are trade publications, glossy ones with quality production; yet in the matter of news coverage, there has been no weekly journal – which has given EH&C an advantage. This weekly has a wider network of staffers and is clicked by the distribution system of one of India's foremost newspaper houses.

Fortunately, the first two years constituted a boom period for Indian tourism with double digit increases from 1994 to 1996. It dipped to 6.4 per cent in 1997 and the country will be lucky this year to touch a one per cent growth, thanks to both domestic and external conditions.

The factors which shaped tourism trends inevitably dominated the contents of the journal and my own commentary. The positive events on the domestic sector were an awareness programme, the entry of major businesses like ASSOCHAM, FICCI, CII and Ph.D. and the involvement of some political parties. At the same time, these trends did not have a uniform momentum.

The government of the day has a definite say in a situation where promotion and infrastructure build-up are the main concerns of the authorities. While P V Narasimha Rao did the honour of attending IATO's annual meeting, from the same platform he claimed that tourism was not a national priority for him. Even at an investors' meeting in Paris, he made it clear that tourism was not his cup of tea. This disinterest notwithstanding, the tourism minister, Ghulam Nabi Azad, was very vocal in support of the sector but little concrete action was evident in respect of strengthening the infrastructure. His sole claim of contribution to Indian tourism rested on his visits to 40-odd countries along a routine of officials at the tax-payer's expense. In a more accountable context, some should have queried what impact the ministerial jaunts produced on tourist arrivals. His successor in the United Front government, Srikant Jena, has had the dubious distinction of totally neglecting the ministry in his charge. The only pronouncement that he made and that too within hours of assuming office was that left to himself – he would introduce prohibition all over the country.

Jena was lucky in having a team of civil servants at the top who were committed to tourism's growth. They hammered out a draft national policy for the sector. Before it could get past the cabinet, the government changed. It must be said to the credit of the industry that it mounted a big campaign during the run-up to the last elections to personally contact and arrange round-table discussions on the relevance of tourism to the national agenda. They succeeded in getting acceptance by the BJP which by a turn of events assumed power. The rest is contemporary history – a tourism-friendly budget and initiatives for new incentives. And for the first time in 50 years, a ministerial group to coordinate tourism.

Lessons from the experience of other countries have also been recounted following visits to USA, South Africa, Israel, China, Indonesia, Thailand, Nepal, Sri Lanka, Turkey and Switzerland. One great lesson from the foreign experiences is that each country is a distinctive product that calls for special marketing and promotion. Yet, they have some common features too inasfar as the historical legacies and natural heritage and popular skills constituting tourism assets are concerned. Political will and professionalism are key to success everywhere.

This has been the constant refrain of this column for the last ten years. The industry is waiting for good days to come and hopefully, there may be a turnaround at least by the turn of the century.

Rabindra Seth

Introduction

Osama Bin Laden and his Al Qaeda monsters, it is now clear, knew exactly what they were doing to America, when the nineteen terrorists crashed three aircraft carrying innocent civilians into the Twin Towers and the Pentagon on 11 September 2001. But, one wonders if they had the ghost of an idea of what they were doing to the world of tourism globally. The biggest impact, of course, was in the United States itself where the fear of flying kept hundreds of thousands from leaving home. Larger numbers stopped travelling to Europe and other parts of the world and traffic into the United States too dwindled. The first impact was felt by the airlines and quite a few big league carriers went into bankruptcy not only in America but across the seas in Europe and down to Australia. Those that survived made drastic reductions in their workforce as did tour companies, hotels and other tourist services. Sure there has been some recovery and if one is to believe the statistics released by the World Tourism Organisation (WTO) tourist movements over the calendar year 2001 only marginally dropped by 0.6 per cent. Against 698 million in 2000, the figure for 2001 came to 693 million although individually some destinations had suffered a decline of as much as 50 per cent. WTO's deputy secretary general Dr Dawid de Villiers at a recent seminar in India had explained that the overall figure was not affected significantly because the loss of long-haul traffic was made up by an increase in intra-regional movement especially in those parts like northeast and southeast Asia which were not directly affected by the events in the United States or the military operations in Afghanistan. India, however, could not or did not take advantage of the intra-regional opportunities. We will come back to this later.

First, how did this country face 9/11. It has to be conceded that Indian tourism was already under pressure thanks to many of the world's major economies not being in the pink of health. Added to this was the slow-down of India's own economy followed by the Gujarat earthquake and the disturbances in the state. And, as if this was not enough, came the border tensions with Pakistan and the foreign media-hyped fear of nuclear war in south Asia and the travel advisories. An industry lacking in unity and a government unresponsive to the need for tax waivers or reduction left Indian tourism in a state of virtual inertia. A severe indictment of this country's inability to meet the challenge was delivered by a senior Indian functionary of WTO, Dr. Harsh Varma, who is in charge of the world body's Asia and Pacific region. Speaking at the same seminar in which Dr. de Villiers participated, he said Indian tourism failed to recognise the new patterns that emerged after 9/11; it failed to put its finger on the market place. It did not recognise, he went on to say, that the trend to shorter holidays would exclude long-haul and yet India kept on focusing on USA and Europe instead of concentrating on East Asia. The Indian industry refused to recognise that travellers have become cost-conscious and he asked, "how many new packages or new hotel tariffs were floated and himself answered, "none". Dr. Varma also felt that India had outpriced itself and had not adopted any new strategies adding that countries with dynamic strategies had targeted those countries which had not been affected by 9/11 like Japan, Korea, Taiwan; even China had redrawn its promotional plans. Statistics released by PATA just a few days ago show that China in fact received more visitors during 2001.

Dr Varma did not refer to it but it is obvious that the Indian industry did not learn anything from what Sri Lanka, Thailand and Malaysia did to lure the nervous Indian traffic away from the west to their own peaceful shores and so soon after 9/11. Sri Lanka's buy one package and get one free at prices just less than domestic airfares between Indian destinations was a runaway success. Thailand and Malaysia did not lag behind and managed to attract significant numbers of Indians who would otherwise have gone to Europe or the United States.

To return to the reference made to the issue earlier, these countries were able to secure an edge over India because of unity in the industry and commitment to public sector-private sector partnership. Sadly, the various segments of the industry in our country did not get together even once (although they kept meeting the department of tourism functionaries) to work out a Sri Lanka type package. To be fair to them, it seems they have after a year's labour worked out some 60 packages which will soon be offered in the Gulf countries. Meanwhile, hotels and travel outfits have learnt to live with shrinking balance sheets and recovery nowhere in sight. Marketing guru, Larry Malarkar of TLC Marketing, however, can spot some good that 9/11 had done. India, he says, has finally recognised the truth that domestic tourism is the only sustainable base for the sector and both government and the industry are happily concentrating on it. Besides, hotels and tour operators are learning the value of efficiency in competition. These, he says, are good signs for tourism future.

This volume contains different instalments of several columns and other writings. At this, the reader may find some of them unconnected but the underlying connecting thread is Indian Tourism, in its entirely and all dimensions touched, if not fully covered.

Om Gupta
General Editor

1
Challenges and Solutions

Showcase India: Challenges and Solutions

The Confederation of Indian Industry's (CII) fourth International Conference-cum-Showcase India: Tourism and Heritage – Challenge 21, was held in Hyderabad.

China was the partner country and the Peoples' Republic sent its second-most important functionary, Cu Zhaoxi, vice-chairman of the National Tourism Administration. As partner state, Andhra Pradesh was represented by its dynamic chief minister, N Chandrababu Naidu. From the centre came Rathi Vinay Jha, tourism secretary and Amitabh Kant, joint secretary, who is also chairman and managing director of ITDC. CII's own top brass included the deputy director general, M Roy and Andhra chairman, K Satish Reddy. Maharaja Gaj Singh of Jodhpur who is chairman of CII's national committee on tourism and heritage, was guiding the two day proceedings, as well as Ravi Bhoothalingam, former committee chairperson. Among experts were Nepal's director general of tourism, B D Rana, China's deputy director general, marketing, Liu Shijun, John King, former chairman of Australian Tourism Commission and now head of Tourism Tasmania and Tim Hunter, vice-president, New Zealand Tourism Board. Industry leaders who participated included Ranjit Malkani, head of Sita-Kuoni, Ravi Santhanam, CEO, Mahindra Holiday Resorts, Radha Bhatia of Amadeus, Madhur Bajaj and Ajoy Misra, senior vice-president, Taj group, and Vivek Nair of the Leela group who has recently been elected president of FHRAI. The subjects discussed ranged from integrating regional tourism to investments and returns and the heritage thread.

But, as has been the case with CII conferences on tourism, the highlight of the event has always been the CEO's Conclave from which emerged recommendations on major issues facing tourism. N K Singh, member, Planning Commission, admired by the industry for his interest in the sector, is sought after by CII (and indeed other bodies like the World Travel and Tourism Council) for the practical solutions he comes up with for difficult issues such as a tourism set up that would ensure intervention at the highest level at the Centre with a mechanism that would also achieve coordination with the states. And, this time around, it was precisely this subject on which he had done some homework. He examined the two proposals on the table-putting tourism in the Concurrent List and a cabinet committee on tourism under the Prime Minister himself. Amending the Concurrent List, he said, would take a long time. A cabinet committee would at best smooth matters at the Centre while most of the action on tourism lies in the states. A workable solution he thought would lie through the National Development Council (NDC) of which the chief ministers are members. The next meeting of the NDC is due in a few months time. CII and other chambers and trade associations, he said, should persuade chief ministers like Chandrababu Naidu who have taken commendable initiatives for the sector to suggest to the Prime Minister to constitute a committee of chief ministers to give a push to tourism and make India a world class destination.

He also addressed Vivek Nair's point about the requirement of Rs. 20,000 crore for new hotels only to meet the demand of five million overseas tourists. The answer to this, Singh said, lay in the industry striving for debt restructuring on the lines of the steel and textile industries as a special purpose vehicle being set up by government with external borrowing for financing hotel projects. The Planning Commission member also had something to say about the Incredible India campaign. It is a good beginning, he said, and a "definite facelift over previous marketing efforts," but added, market research is necessary for focus and clarity on consumer needs and not on what states can offer. The India Development Fund with the commerce ministry can be innovatively used for building the tourism brand.

In his address, the vice-chairman of China's tourism authority spoke of the importance his government gives to tourism. Last year, he said, China hosted 98 million overseas visitors (13.6 million of them non-Chinese). He referred to the recent development in the strengthening of tourism relations with India and said, "Let us work hand-in-hand for a more promising future of the Sino-Indian Cooperation."

Rathi Vinay Jha told the delegates that if tourism is to be a positive influence on people's lives, it must be fundamentally ethical in its treatment of people as consumers and employees, to host communities and the environment.

CII's effort in Hyderabad also brought forward several positive ideas on promoting regional tourism which 9/11 has pushed to centrestage.

Tunisia: An African Success Story

Tunisia's effort to make a foray into the Indian tourism market which was halted by the aftermath of 9/11, was relaunched in the last week of September when the country participated in a big way at the Indian Travel and Tourism Fair organised in the Capital by the department of tourism (DoT). A high powered delegation led by the chief executive of the Tunisia Tourism Board, Saifullah Lasram and vice-president of the national carrier, Air Tuni Mohamed Mzah and joined by the ambassador in Delhi, Elyes Kasri, had meetings with senior functionaries of the department of tourism and the aviation ministry as well as representatives of trade, office bearers of TAAI (Travel Agents Association of India), as well as IATO (Indian Association of Tour Operators). The ASSOCHAM tourism and aviation committee chairperson, Subhas Goyal, whose Stic Travels has already been named Air Tunis GSA in India, also organsied a seminar for the Tunisian delegation where it had an interface with leaders of the hospitality industry.

Tunisia, with an advantageous location in the Mediterranean and much to offer to visitors by way of history, archaeological sites, monuments, sunny beaches and leisure spots, is already Africa (and the Gulf region's) number one destination with five million arrivals. Ambassador Kasri told *Express Hotelier and Caterer* that in spite of this success his country is keen to establish a two-way tourist traffic with new destinations like India and China. He and his two colleagues from the tourism board and Air Tunis agreed that ideally a direct service between India and Tunisia would be the best way of promoting travel. But, until that happens – negotiations are on for bilateral arrangements – it has been decided to use the Dubai air hub for building traffic. Both Air India and Indian Airlines, they pointed out, have scores of flights a week from Tunis to the UAE and Air Tunis will this December start two flights a week to Dubai with quick onward connections to Europe and the UK. Air Tunis vice-president Mzah explained that the airline is working out an arrangement with the Indian national carriers under which a ticket from India to Europe would offer two stopovers in Dubai and Tunis at no extra cost. In other words, Indian travellers could add on two more destinations to their holidays or business trips to the west. Similarly, Europeans (who make up the bulk of traffic to Tunisia) could be lured to fly on to Dubai and to India. Most destinations in Europe, he said, are within the two-hour flying range and Air Tunis flies to some 40 cities. According to Mzah, there are large India communities living in Spain and other western European countries who could also benefit from Air Tunis-Air India/Indian Airlines Dubai connection.

Ambassador Kasri said that once Air Tunis's Dubai link was established late in December there will be an exchange of fam tours both of trade and media persons. Tunisia's minister for tourism Mondher Zenaidi, he said would be visiting India in January for talks with his counterpart Jagmohan to give a fillip to tourist movements.

In a related development, the tiny former Portuguese colony of Macau, now a Special Administrative Region of China, which already hosts 10 million visitors is also keen to increase its share of the Indian market. In spite of 9/11, the territory has witnessed a substantial increase in arrivals from India which in the first seven months of 2002 recorded a growth of over 25 per cent, although Indians account for a very small percentage of the ten million that flock to Macau. Conscious of the Indian potential, Macau has set up a representative office in the capital, its 16th overseas outfit. Formally launching the representative offices in Delhi, the director of the Macua Government Tourist Office, Joao Manuel Costa Antunes described India as "the fastest emerging outbound market in the world". Antunes said in reply to questions that although Macau's main attraction was its casinos but in the Indian market they would be emphasising leisure activities like family activities, golf, museums and relaxation. In addition, Macau would also be promoted as a base for discovery of Hong Kong and mainland China. Visas for the mainland are easy to obtain in Macau, he said, and added that no visa was required for Macau.

Talking of former colonies, our very own Pondicherry is all set to offer domestic and overseas tourists its special blend of spiritual aura, French colonial heritage, Tamil culture and the cosmopolitan flair of many nationalities in the seaside resort. The state's tourism minister, K Lakshminarayanan kicked off the promotional effort with a road show at Delhi's Ashoka Hotel before a large gathering of the travel industry and the media. Pondicherry already has a strong appeal in the domestic market thanks to the Sri Aurobindo Ashram and the easy access from Chennai which is a factor in its favour.

Crossover Tourism

Nepal has experienced a thirty per cent increase in arrivals from India in the last few months, but the industry is still not upbeat about its future prospect. At best, it is only 'cautiously optimistic'. The reason is that it is conscious that the larger inflow from India is the result more of diversions caused by the fear of SARS in some of the popular destinations in southeast Asia than any increase in the pull of the Himalayan kingdom.

This reality check emerged at the two-day joint conclave in Kathmandu, organised at the initiative of TAAI Northern Region with segments of the hospitality sector in Nepal including the government. The TAAI northern region chairperson, Rajji Rai, who led a delegation of more than 50 travel agents as well as media persons, said the exercise was part of the effort to promote regional tourism. Those taking part from the Nepal said included the Nepal Tourism Board (NTB), Nepal Association of Travel Agents (NATA), the Hotel Association of Nepal (HAN) and the Nepal PATA Chapter.

NTB's chief executive officer, Tek Bahadur Dangi, welcomed the Indian initiative as timely as Nepal is in the midst of drawing up strategies to meet the challenges of not only 9/11 and the more recent developments like the Iraq war and SARS, but also the damage to the country's image from Maoist activities. Fortunately, he said, the ceasefire with the Maoists has somewhat retrieved Nepal's reputation as a safe destination, although he wished the international media had taken note of the Maoists' solemn declaration not to target tourists. Dangi spoke of the importance of the Indian market for Nepal-India accounts for more than a third of arrivals – and said that throughout the period of set backs the Indian share remained constant. However, he said the liberal forex allowed to Indians travelling abroad plus the abundance of imported goods available in India was robbing Nepal of some of its tourism, USPs.

Dangi as well as chiefs of NATA, Jai Dewan, HAN, Narendra Bhattacharya and PATA chapter past president, Ashok Pokharel, seemed keen in their separate meetings with the Indian delegation to learn what more could be done to lure larger numbers from this country. The Indians did not disappoint them and came up with quite a few constructive suggestions and did not hesitate to list some of the trade practice which came in the way of greater inflows. As Rajji Rai summed up in the last session, "Nepal needs to grow out of selling just Kathmandu and casinos" and aggressively offer other attractions like Pokhara and Chitwan and its beautiful mountains. Climate, said Rai, is a major consideration for Indians looking for a holiday. It was also pointed out to the Nepal industry leaders that they were not encashing Lumbini, the birth place of the Buddha. With the infrastructural improvement in India's Buddhist circuit – Bodhgaya becoming an international airport – Nepal could promote this great asset jointly with India.

Pokharel, had mentioned the possibility of Indians driving their own cars to Nepal. Yes, everyone on the Indian side agreed it was a good idea. But, it would work only if there we're hassle-free entry of cars at the border. And, prompt came the assurance that this would be done and a guidebook on formalities would be circulated soon.

A sore point with the TAAI members which came up several times was about the way the Royal Nepal Airways (RNAC) functioned in India. Far from doing business with IATA agents (TAAI members), the carrier was exclusively dealing with non-IATA operators. It transpired that RNAC was unable to go through IATA agents because it is not a member of the BSP. RNAC managing director M P Khanal assured the Indian participants that the airlines will soon be joining BSP which will facilitate working with IATA agents.

Dangi was candid in admitting that the tourism board has not been active in India in the recent past and said he is keen to perk up promotions. He did not give any reasons why promotions had slackened but a board member confided to this writer by suggesting that the financial resources had gone down by almost fifty per cent in line with the decline in arrivals (The NTB funds come entirely from a two per cent cess levied on hotels and other tourist services). The Indian delegation was impressed by the fact that Nepal had stolen a march over this country in putting in place a national tourism board, while in India it is still a slogan the industry raises at every travel event.

Hyatt Regency where the Indian delegation stayed is Kathmandu's latest address, a five-star deluxe hotel with 290 mega size rooms (a few more than the good old Soaltee), set in a distinctive Newari style architecture. It has as its general manager a familiar Delhi face, Harinder Singh who has been a Hyatt loyalist ever since she preferred hoteliering to IPS two decades ago.

A Minister in Love

Regulars at the TAAI and IATO conventions would easily recall a familiar figure who would regale the audiences with his witty remarks about the 'way politicians function in this country.' The reference is to Vijay Mankotia, himself a soldier-turned politician, who was tourism minister in Himachal Pradesh when the state was ruled by the Congress(I). He would not spare even the prime minister when it came to pointing out his failings. His main thrust, of course, was on the poor performance of the tourism sector especially in relation to what many of our Asian neighbours had achieved. It was, I think, at one of conventions held in Hyderabad that he made the most interesting suggestion. India, he said, could do well only if we had at the helm a minister who is passionately in love with tourism.

Well, while this country is still waiting for someone with that qualification to take charge of the tourism department at the Centre, one of our Asian neighbours – Malaysia – seems to have found one. A look at the phenomenal rise in tourist arrivals shows that he is not only fully committed to tourism but that his strategies have achieved the desired results. He is the 60-year old Dato Abdul Kadir Bin Haji Sheikh Fadzir. He began his career in the foreign service but gave it up after five years to study law in the UK and returned to Kuala Lumpur with a Bar at Law and straightaway entered politics. Beginning as a parliamentary secretary in 1962 he soon became a deputy minister moving from foreign affairs to domestic trade, HR and home affairs. It was only in May last year that he became minister of culture, arts and tourism and also took up chairmanship of the Malaysia Tourist Promotion Board.

This was the time the South-East Asian region was struggling to emerge from the havoc left behind by the currency melt down in the region. Look, what he and his 'dedicated team' as he describes his colleagues in the ministry, the board and the travel trade, have achieved. In 1998 tourist arrivals had touched a low of 5.5 million. Relying on conventional wisdom that regional, tourism is the safest bet in any effort at faster and more sustainable growth, he launched a vigorous advertising, publicity and PR campaign in the South Asian source markets where Malaysia was already a popular destination and in the emerging markets of China and India. He personally led-trade delegations to the region's capitals and other big cities carrying with him senior officials and leaders of the industry and the national carriers plus a large sized troupe to cash in on the Malaysia Truly Asia theme chosen for promotion.

At the PATA conference in Hong Kong earlier this year, the Malaysian evening was one of the most enduring memories the world's tourism leaders had carried back. Minister Fadzir was in his elements. His message was simple and delivered in a down to earth manner; Malaysia is the melting pot of Asia; it is a shopping heaven where virtually everything sold in the marketplace is duty free; the fixed Ringett exchange rate gives tourists a forty per cent currency advantage; exotic cuisine, expressways and a new international airport and so on.

India has been on top of Dato Fadzir's agenda and he has made two trips to this country, first in March and the second earlier this month. Backed by his now familiar delegation which included Tunku Isaknder, president, Malaysia Association of Travel Agents, there was a whole day travel mart in the Capital's Maurya Sheraton hotel followed by an interface with the media and trade representatives. He had come prepared to face criticism by tour operators about visa hassles and delays. In fact, he had brought along the Malaysian High Commissioner to assure the audience that he meant business. When a travel agent suggested that visas should be made available at least on the following day of submission of applications, Dato Fadzir promptly said and with a nod from the High Commissioner, "Why the next day, why not on the spot or at least the same day?"

The minister had not yet played his trump card. He confirmed reports that his ministry was close to 'signing and sealing' an arrangement under which the Malaysian Airline and selected travel agents in source markets (including India) would be authorised to issue tourist visas. He emphasised that liberal visa and bilateral regime is the key to the rapid growth of tourism.

To come back to the recent successes of Malaysian tourism. The arrivals in 1999 crossed the eight billion mark, an increase of 60 per cent and this year are likely to touch the figure of nine million. The number of Indian visitors has jumped from 30,000 to nearly 1,00,000 in the first nine months of this year and the total may rise to 1,20,000 by December end. Surely Malaysia has done well. We in India must continue to pray for a minister who is in love with tourism.

Future Beckons

It was a rare gathering of industry captains, ministers, officials and executives from all segments of tourism. They had assembled in the banquet hall of the Ashoka Hotel in the capital at the invitation of the Department of Tourism for a presentation on 'Travel and Tourism – Present Scenario and Future Prospects', by the deputy secretary general of the World Tourism Organisation (WTO), Dr David J De Villiers, assisted by Dr Harsh Verma, WTO's senior functionary in charge of the Asian region. Sharing the dias were union minister for tourism, Jagmohan, minister of state for tourism and culture, Vinod Khanna, secretary, Rathi Vinay Jha, director general for tourism, Vinod Duggal and joint secretaries Amitabh Kant and Rashmi Verma. An interactive question and answer session was also on the cards.

With the help of slides, Dr De Villiers took the audience through the growth of tourism globally especially from 1995 onwards and the impact of 9/11, much of which WTO's secretary general, Francesco Frangialli had already shared with Indian trade representatives during PATA and SATTE just three months ago in April. The only bit of new information was that there was only a 0.6 per cent decline in tourist movements worldwide, down from 698 million in 2000 to 693 million in 2001 (PATA had been told that the fall had been as high as 50 per cent in some parts of the world).

Unlike Frangialli who had promised 2003 would be a year of 'recovery', De Villiers confined himself to encouraging words like fear is fading away and that there is continued improvement in economies. But, he was certain that in the long term, WTO's projection of 1.5 billion tourist arrivals in 2020 would be achieved. He also said that poverty alleviation was at the heart of tourism among the developing world and WTO is now actively working with the UNDP (United Nations Development Programme) in a special campaign christend 'STEP'– Sustained Tourism to Eliminate Poverty.

It was now Dr Harsh Verma's turn to turn the spotlight on Asia, particularly south Asia. In his case too, it was much of the same date he has shared with those taking part in SATTE. Except that when he came to India's response to the challenge of 9/11, many in the banquet hall, especially the industry leaders along with ministers and officials on the dias, must have been jolted. After pointing out that India's performance in tourism in the last fifty years has been unsteady, erratic and alarming in respect of tourist expenditures, he came straight to the point to suggest that the country was refusing to see where it's real competition lay. India, he said, was feeling buoyant by comparing itself with Maldives, Sri Lanka, Pakistan or Bangladesh. Whereas if it wanted to be considered in the 'A' league, it should compete with China which now receives 65 million visitors and Malaysia, which gets 12.8 million visitors. In any tourism strategy, the key factors should be cost, duration, booking habits, motivation, product promotion, safety and security. He fell that except for security over which India has little control, not enough had been done in all other key areas. In a candid assessment, Dr Verma said Indian tourism failed to recognise the new patterns that emerged after 9/11; it failed to put its finger on the market pulse. In a more direct indictment he said the Indian industry refused to recognise that travellers have become cost conscious and asked, "How many new packages or new hotel tariffs were floated and answered? None at all." The Indian industry, he went on to say, outpriced itself and allowed itself to be pushed out of the market. Also, it did not recognise that the trend to shorten holidays would exclude long haul and yet India kept focusing on the USA and Europe instead of concentrating on East Asia. "It is the beaten track that the Indian industry has been following with little or no attempt at product diversification. Please offer something new," he pleaded. He said countries with dynamic strategies had targeted those markets which had not been affected by 9/11, like Japan, Korea, Taiwan. Even China had redrawn its promotional plans.

Dr Verma's forthright remarks brought a riposte from minister Jagmohan who said, "As far as the government was concerned, it had given maximum concessions to industry. But, it is the politics of terrorism which some sections of the international community are practising that is hurting Indian tourism." He wondered whether WTO could not have intervened on the issue of travel advisories. Meanwhile, De Villiers explained that WTO could at best convey the feelings of the countries affected by the advisories to those issuing them. On behalf of the hotel sector, Shyam Suri, secretary general, FHRAI, said that tariffs had indeed gone down, adding that it was the cost of air travel which made the India package costlier. The interactive question and answer session that petered out to demands of restoring ITC and pertaining more foreign airlines access to India.

The question that industry captains must ask themselves in whether it is possible for them to sit out to work out new packages with new tariffs even at this stage. Also, what next after the withdrawal of the advisories?

Incredible India

With the Incredible India campaign well underway it was quite appropriate for the PATA India chapter to organise a seminar on 'Brand Building of Destinations' in the capital in the last week of September. Teaming up for presentations were two foreign experts – Creenagh Lodge, chairperson. Corporate Edge, UK and Lea Banwell, chief services director, TBWA, Malaysia. Joining them were Piyush Pandey, chairman, O&M and Amitabh Kant, joint secretary at the department of tourism (DoT) who has masterminded the Indian brand building effort. Secretary tourism, Rathi Vinay Jha who also heads the PATA chapter, was in the chair and PKF chief, Uttam Dave played the moderator. The large audience at the Le Meridien hotel benefited greatly from the case studies presented by the UK expert on Britain and New Zealand and by Lea Banwell on the success of 'Malaysia Truly Asia'. Piyush Pandey whose agency has been associated with the evolution of 'Incredible India' gave an insight into how this brand name was chosen. "Incredibility," he said, "is difficult to compete with."

Building a brand for New Zealand, Creenagh Lodge said, was a very difficult challenge. The island suffered from an image of "70 million sheep and three million people." Geographically and destinationwise, it was trapped between a vibrant Australia and the icy Antarctic. The earlier image building efforts were apologetic and lacking in confidence. In the latest moves, determination was the driving force for creating an effective brand for New build a brand. "Clear thinking backed by talent can build brand equity of great appeal," she said. Simplicity, she added, formed the starting point of the guest, which ended in "100 per cent pure New Zealand" whose runaway success can be measured from these developments: New Zealand is now recognised as the world's number one outdoor destination; the country is viewed as a different entity from both Australia and the Antarctic; it is confident and not at all apologetic; and, more importantly, the government and the people are united in delivering the promise of 100 per cent pure New Zealand. Not just tourism, Lodge said, the country's exports too have benefited from the branding exercise. The logo that goes with the brand name is a guarantee for quality and alongwith is punishment for non-delivery. She concluded with a quote from an IT marketeer: A successful brand is a promise that is kept among the travel industry fraternity but the millions who travel abroad or are planning to do so. This shows the strength of the brand as well as its dissemination in the media and through roadshows in a sustained manner. And Lea Banwell was candid in conceding that "since Asia has already been sold as a preferred destination (Singapore used to call itself' 'Instant Asia') we took the opportunity to use this to our advantage." Malaysia's brand vision, she said, is that it is the only country in Asia which is truly multi-radical and multi-cultural. In building the brand, four components were used in developing a memorable identity. These are a 'Malaysia Truly Asia' jingle; 'Malaysian Lego Typa' (with specific positioning recommended for consumer and trade creation); five-girls icon (representing the five main races – Malay, Chinese, Indian, Kadazan and Bayak) and signature greeting (hand on heart – the Malaysian gesture of warmth and sincerity).

The media strategy is aimed at reaching primarily international travellers in Europe and Asia Pacific with particular focus on Germany, Japan and Australia, the main thrust was via satellite and terrestrial TV, business and travel magazines in selected time-frames. And, what has been the result? Spectacular, by any standard. In 1999 Malaysia hosted 7.9 million foreign visitors. In 2000, the figure rose to 10.2 million (25 per cent). Last year, it touched 13.3 million showing an increase of five per cent.

An interesting point made by Banwell was that crisis management is a crucial part of protecting brands. A reassurance campaign was developed to counter the negative sentiments that Malaysia is a Muslim country; Malaysia Truly Asia was amplified as a country of peace, tolerance and harmony.

In her opening remarks Rathi Jha said while Incredible India has made a good start "we should not jump to conclusions as we have miles to go." A lot of infrastructure is yet to be built.

Tourism with a Conscience

The disabled account for ten per cent of the population which, in the Indian context, would be close to a hundred million. Ritualistically every year a World Disabled Day is observed when a few VVIPs deliver homilies, leaving this vast number hapless and uncertain about their future. The saving grace is that in the middle class families they are taken care of in some measure by the rest.

At the same time this dependence makes them less self-reliant than the handicapped in the advanced countries where with grit and determination they find their way up in life. Some of them, basing on their experience, make it a mission to raise public awareness about the problems of the handicapped in travel and other day to day life.

Such a man with a mission is 29 year old Scott Chesney, an American paralysed from a rare stroke in the spinal cord for the last fourteen years. Scott and his "angel" wife, India-born Prateeksha, a physiotherapist have been touring Indian cities in what they call their "Devotion to Motion", meeting public figures and bringing home to them the problems some millions face with little or no help.

Much of these relate to motion which inevitably turns to travel. The Indian transport system and the hospitality services are yet to wake up to the full dimensions of the problem. In these times when the elderly and the infirm have, for family and other reasons, to travel there is hardly any facility in the related services. In the entire country, only a couple of railway stations have even ramps for wheelchairs to move up or wide enoughh doors to guest rooms or toilets.

Toilets for the handicapped are non-existent except for the classy ones in the metros or major tourist centres. Otherwie, even hospitals do not have this facility. Therefore, the Scott-Prateeksha visit will serve as an eye opener at least in those sections with which they establish contact.

Incidentally, as the country seeks a larger share of the tourist traffic it should be noted that a larger section of travellers from advanced countries are infirm, handicapped or aged. So, it is all the more necessary that tourism planners and the trade should focus urgent attention to enriching the travel experience of this particular class. Scott, who is a US national, attributes the great advance made in his country in meeting the needs of the disabled to some of the greats of that nation who themselves were handicapped like Franklin Delano Roosevelt, four term American head of state, and Helen Keller, the great educationtists who lived in a world of darkness and silence. Thanks to the policy changes they shaped, every new building in the US has to have special parking for the disabled, easy access (through ramps or escalators) and special toilets.

As for the old buildings, they have been given a time frame of two years to make the requisite changes. All this is part of the law. The industry too has responded with innovative tools to help the disabled to be independent. Interestingly, as Scott points out, many of the tools – particularly wheel chairs – have been designed by the handicapped themselves. There are separate wheelchairs for every kind of motion – moving within the house, going to the market or the park, travelling by car or by air. There are as many as thirty-five to forty different kinds of wheel chairs of various brands in America, Among the promoters of such devices are airlines.

The tourism sector is primarily concerned with movement of people and has a special responsibility towards the disabled. Not only in giving suitable placement in their own establishments, but the industry also has a social obligation to raise public awareness about the needs of this section of society,

It is a welcome move that the ITDC has devised a very special offer for disabled persons which provides for fifty per cent discount on room rent, free stay for the attendant and thirty per cent discount of food. The Central Public Works Department (CPWD) has issued guidelines to hotels for providing special facilities for the handicapped.

All new hotels under development in the ITC-Welcomgroup are introducing state-of-the-art conveniences in toilets and bathrooms which ensure both comfort and safety. The Taj Mansingh in Delhi has created a special room where Scott and Prateeksha stayed during their Delhi visit. In fact, there is a move to ensure one out of fifty rooms in any hotel will be specially designed for the disabled.

Hopefully, the newly aroused awareness will catch on and influence politicians who could not be sure how the disabled would have voted in the current elections. Their number, close to a hundred million, should make them eligible to be treated as a vote bank, which politicians for their reasons have missed.

Investors' and entrepreneurs' interest in the tourism sector remains undiminished despite three consecutive years of virtual stagnation in this area. Opinion leaders do seem to have recognised the contribution of the sector to national economic development. Captains of the industry and top professionals see a great future in the growth of the sector. All of which goes to show that the tourism awareness programme initiated by various sources has caught on. The Associated Chamber of Commerce

(ASSOCHAM), in its electoral agenda presented for reference by national political parties, emphasises that along with IT industry, tourism holds the key to the future of economic regeneration.

ASSOCHAM has followed it up with a seminar attended by most political parties to discuss the agenda. By and large, at least insofar tourism is concerned, there is a broad consensus. Hopefully, it will be reflected on the party platforms. The ASSOCHAM document identifies tourism as the industry of the next century to ensure sustainable development and generate employment. But, the right policies have to be in place. Globally, in the last fifty years tourist movement has gone up from 25 million to 625 million while their spending has risen from 2.1 billion dollars to 445 billion dollars. This particular growth has taken in its stride wars and war-like situations, oil crisis, recession and currency upheavals. As far as India is concerend it has the potential for considerable growth in international business and leisure arrivals over the next 12 years, supplemented by a significant growth in domestic tourism. Needless to say, as a catalyst for wealth and job creation, the growth has enormous potential benefits to offer India.

According to Habib Rehman, MD, ITC Hotels and president, Hotel Association of India, if India were to attract double the number of present arrivals (2.30 million), a highly achievable target (4.78 million) it will ensure foreign exchange earnings of the order of 7.5 billion dollars, Rehman anticipates that these earnings will meet the oil import bill fully and the consequential growth of tourism will generate ten million jobs directly and 20 million indirectly. Rehman has proposed a nine-point programme to achieve this objective:

1. Position India Inc., build tourism brand equity
2. Concentrate on infrastructure
3. Adopt an open-sky policy ensuring optimal usage of existing airports
4. Enforce a national and consistant taxation policy in the tourism sector
5. Get a commitment from the individuals states to support the new tourism thrust
6. An intensive awareness programme of the Indian product through international media
7. Incentives to private sector to contribute to the tourism mission
8. Easing of visa restrictions,
9. Creating a tourism authority

The ASSOCHAM document is in line with Rehman's prescriptions in addressing key issues. These are: difficulties in getting new hotels off the ground; lack of adequate infrastructure; need for fiscal incentives; cumbersome border formalities and poor marketing.

Admittedly, despite the quality of the product India has been unable to attract as much attention of foreign visitors as competing Asian destinations. Obviously, India has not been marketed very well as a tourist destination.

Thanks to the awareness programme, many in the industry and in the ministry have agreed to prioritise marketing in which the private sector will have a better say. Besides, marketing will be professionalised. It will all be done under the aegis of the newly registered society—Destination India—with contributions from industry majors. Marketing will not be for any segment or establishment but will follow a holistic approach. Mere registration will not solve all the teething problems. There has to be maximum cooperation from all segments of the trade and coordination among all the agencies concerned, the centre, the states and the industry itself.

The ASSOCHAM document mentions certain steps to be taken which will be worthy of consideration by Destination India society. These are: Tourism promotion budgets should be augmented to enable the sector to meet promotional expenses like advertising. The sector should have the same incentives and infrastructure as exports. Private marketing councils should be established as a mechanism to boost international image and awareness. The focus should be on marketing India in convenient clusters which would result in creating islands of excellence, and thus help build brand equity.

While tourism's contribution is acknowledged, it devolved on the new government to reinforce its three pillars: awareness, infrastructure and marketing.

India Facinates All, Attracts Few

Breast beating over public apathy and media hostility overseas is a familiar pasttime with many in the trade. Numerous instances could be listed over a period of time. Yet there is another side to what is happening. This is the positive side of growing interest in India and its achievements. This was obvious to this writer on a short visit to Europe.

Shortly after taking off from Delhi on an SAS Service to Copenhagen, I picked up the airline's inflight magazine Scanorama (June 1999 issue) to find a seven-page illustrated feature – Magical Mystery Cure – on Kerala's Ayurvedic health resorts written by Miki Dedijer, a Stockholm-based writer. Says the blurb: More and more westerners swear by it in India it's been around for 3,000 years. Delving into the philosophy of Ayurveda, Dedijer quotes practitioners as saying, "We don't cure the disease. We encourage health." About the system's popularity, he points out that out of India's one million practicing physicians almost half hold government-recognized qualifications in Ayurveda and other ancient systems of medicine. The feature ends with a half page of travel information on Kerala.

On the next leg of the journey, from Copenhagen to London, it was hard to find an English language newspaper among the scores of European language publications. The air hostess finally dug out a copy of the *Financial Times*. There it was. A half page article by Keving Pilley on Varanasi – 'Once in a lifetime is not enough'. Describing it as India's most sacred city, a place of pilgrimage where a millions Hindus a year go to purify themselves, Pilley ends by saying: "But Varanasi is the Ganges and one day and one dawn boat ride is not enough. Varanasi should be visited more than once in every life. It is India compressed into 12 square kilometres.

London's India connection is too obvious to be detailed here. But Indian cuisine served at hundreds of restaurants in the city and cultural events, exhibitions and talks keep the connection alive all the time. A chance meeting with veteran broadcaster and former AIR colleague Mahendra Kaul, now a successful restaurateurs who with Delhi's Rohit Khattar of Old World Hospitality fame has replicated Chor Bizarre in the British capital, enabled me to be part of the celebrations of a theatre festival. Chor Bizarre was flowing with celebrities from India as well as London's Indian glitterati and journalists. There was Shabana Azmi, Shobha De, M F Hussain, Shakira Caine, Lilette Dubey, Siddharth Basu and the new director, India Tourist Office, Alka Kohli.

'What's happening with the Explore India in the Millennium Year?' I asked Kohli. Come to a lecture by Mark Tully at the V&A (Victoria and Albert Museum), she said. It was part of an exhibition, 300 years of the Khalsa, at the museum. 'From the Heart of India, was the title of the talk and Tully did speak from his heart to a predominantly British audience. He emphasized India'a age old tradition of tolerance and spirit of accommodation pointing out that this ancient land is not only the birth place of great religions like Hinduism, Jainism, Buddhism and Sikhism but also home to Christianity and Islam. He received a standing ovation. I had just missed a major event. This was the launch of Trevor Fishlock's book 'Cobra Road—An Indian Journey' which has received rave reviews both in Britain and in this country. The function was held at the Nehru Centre where Fishlock read excerpts to an appreciative audience..

Incidentally, Mark Tully in his review of Cobra Road has described it as a beautifully written tribute to a part of the world that never ceases to fascinate readers.

Catching up with Fishlock and his wife Penny, also a well-known journalist, was the launch of an unusual tour brochure on India by yet another old India-hand Bruce Palling, who was The Independent's first correspondent in Delhi and decided to become a tour operator on return.

His company is called Western and Oriental (W&O) and the brochure (The sub-continent 1999-2000) is a collector's item both for its design and innovative content. This is best illustrated in the introduction. The most exciting thing about the sub-continent, it says, is that you can organize anything to anywhere and at any time. Should you have a special interest in cookery, painting, botany, bird-watching, sport, architecture or Ayurveda, we can advise you on how to tie these in with a relaxing holiday. W&O also offers guest-lectured tours with well-known historians. But what is more heartening for the travel trade is that the agency is targeting up-market travellers.

A second visit to Chor Bazaar was also on the cards. This time to partake in a wine tasting festival... which wine goes best with which Indian dish. It was a quite a treat to rub shoulders with London's top food and wine writers, and ITV's wine expert Charles Metcalf while chefs Depinder Sondhi and Manpreet Ahuja took us through a 13-course feast of the flavours of Jammu and Kashmir, Punjab, Kerala and Tamil Nadu.

All these are not to detail my personal diary engagements but only to confirm what was emphasized at the outset – a growing interest abroad in India. Which left me puzzling about why with so much interest so few are coming to India.

Two Ms for India

Any observer of the Indian economic scene would be realistic enough not to look for too many sops at a time when the industrial growth is down, inflation is high and exports are stagnant. It should be particularly so with tourism, which in its global dimensions is in turmoil because of worldwide recessionary trends in general and the East Asian crisis in particular.

According to the World Travel and Tourism Council (WTTC), internationally the industry was down by $117 billion in lost revenues. Destinations everywhere are examining how to reverse the downturn. Rarely one comes across any higher budgetary support than before for tourism. It is another matter that the Indian allocations have already been poor measured against others.

Still, in the context the tourism trade in India could draw comfort from an earnest effort to revive the economy through the budget. After all, tourism is bound to be a beneficiary when there is general economic recovery even though the finance minister may not have provided any special concessions or reliefs for the sector.

The most rational response to the budget from the industry has come from the HAI president, Habib Rehman. He said, "the tourism industry depends for its success on the health of the economy. And, there are indications that the budget will hopefully stimulate the growth of the economy." With the same emphasis, but conveyed a little differently, what the WTTC president Geoffrey Lipman remark applies aptly to the current situation. "Ninety per cent of what happens to tourism depends on big economies," he said.

If a majority in the trade are disillusioned that Yashwant Sinha had little new to offer, it could be because last year they got most of what they had wanted and were hopeful that the yet unfulfilled demands would be met this time.

They voiced far too many expectations like total tax exemptions on services to foreigners, scrapping of HET (hotel expenditure tax), inclusions of hotels in core infrastructure, exemption from excise-duty for tourist vehicles, a five to 10 year tax holiday for travel agents in backward areas and extension of interest subsidy to travel agents and tour operators as well. Of course, the finance minister did not deem it necessary to oblige.

At the same time, he did agree to one of the long standing demands about the income tax concession under 80 HHD. Under the existing provision, profits earned in foreign exchange are deductible straightaway to the extent of 50 per cent. The other 50 per cent is also deductible if ploughed back into a tourism project. It will now be possible to invest the remaining 50 per cent into buying equity of any new hospitality facility.

Though the finance minister has not increased the budget for tourism promotion, he has at least kept it at last year's level of Rs 160 crore.

Of course, there is a strong case for a higher grant for overseas marketing and publicity especially when the country is set to launch a Visit India Year next month. Can it be a casualty of Madan Lal Khurana's exit?

In any event, the answer to India's current problem of shrinking tourist arrivals is marketing and aggressive marketing. Marketing certainly has a price tag and one should be careful that the right persons are entrusted with the right job.

Mere spending of money does not ensure results. PR and publicity have to be professionalised. Competing destinations in the rest of Asia spend three to four times of what India allocates. And, they do the job so thoroughly that the results are obvious to see.

Illustrative of such results is the Thai performance. In the crisis-ridden region as many as seven million tourists visited the Kingdom last year, a whopping increase of 16 per cent. A Thai minister who was in India recently is confident that this year, there will be a further improvement.

In the Indian context, it is time that all the agencies in the private sector and the government, which have anything to do with tourism, come together and pursue a policy under the aegis of an autonomous Central Tourism Authority. The proposal for such an authority has been long kept on hold. It is time the government decides to establish such a body with enough teeth.

The need is best summed up by Ashoke Chatterjee of the National Institute of Design and one of the best known experts on tourism promotion and marketing. Laying accent on meeting customers' needs, he says, "what's imperative is genuine business professionalism, resting on marketing management."

An Eye-opener

The spate of seminars organised as part of India Tourism Week occasioned some serious thinking on what still needs to be done if this sector has to make strides. Trade veteran, Inder Sharma minced no words in pointing to certain imperatives. Few in the concourse of industrialists, officials and media persons, could disagree with him when he suggested that what ailed Indian tourism was not lack of a new policy statement but implementation of what has been committed earlier.

Recalling what the hotel tycoon, Hilton had cited as a prime need for industry – location, Sharma's prescription was implement. Sharma was a panelist at a seminar organised by FICCI on National Tourism Policy. He also reminded the travel media that it would do well in monitoring how ministers kept their word, promises were made all around but whether they were kept or not was no one's business.

The seminar threw up quite a few suggestions which on behalf of the government, minister Madanlal Khurana and secretary, M P Bezbaruah welcomed. Safety, security, and comfort of the visitor needed top priority. Incidentally, quite a few participants referred to the widely publicised reports that coincided with the launch of the week but were not complimentary to the tourism security administration.

In one case, a Japanese visitor was found murdered and his body dumped in a drain in New Delhi. Obviously, the Japanese media would have extensively featured the ghastly story slurring India's image as a safe destination. Another report, also appearing on the same day, spoke of the nexus between unauthorised guides, owners of shady restaurants and unscrupulous doctors in Agra to rob the tourists.

Their modus operandi is to persuade a guest to choose a particular restaurant where adulterated food would be served and then taken to a particular nursing home where the unsuspecting visitor would cough up his dollars.

One solution suggested by L P Gupta who pioneered the first deluxe hotel in Agra, The Clarks, was to warn guests not to patronise restaurants outside the hotel of their stay. This is too simplistic a suggestion but the problem is grave and calls for a strict vigil and strong action against those indulging in malpractice.

Apart from the emphasis on implementation of past commitments, and guarantee of safety and security to visitors, the discussion served to expound the efficacy of tourism's social ethos and role as an instrument of change. Bezbaruah remarked that measure of tourism's achievements should go beyond the number of visitors and forex earned, and, instead focus on the improvement of the living conditions of the people, and cited the Mexican example.

TFCI chairman, P V Narasimhan was in line with him when he asked for concentration on backward areas with tourism potential like Himachal. This would also ensure removal of imbalances in growth.

Balanced growth in a different context was mentioned as an imperative for tourism's development as infrastructure. Sharma contrasted the availability of fine hotels in Delhi and the pathetic condition of taxis at the airport.

Minister Khurana was all with the trade on its requirements of incentives but did not fail to impress on them their responsibility in building up the infrastructure and also to conform to standards of ethics and fair practices.

The minister also used the occasion to disclose that fifty destinations would be taken up every year for beautification and improvement of civic services for which the cost will be equally shared by the centre and the states. For each destination the centre will offer a matching grant of Rs one crore to begin with. Khurana earned compliments from almost all participants for infusing dynamism into the tourism sector in a short span.

IATO president, Subhash Goyal went to the extent of saying that Khurana had achieved in nine months surpassing the record of all his predecessors in the last fifty years.

Goyal also wanted the minister to ensure integration of civil aviation policies with tourism development. According to both, the minister and the secretary talks are in progress with all tourism-related ministers, which explains the delay in the finalisation of the National Tourism Policy.

There was broad consensus that tourism should be of national concern. The government's own commitments as also the interest shown by chambers of commerce and industry bear testimony to its place on the national agenda.

Another valid point forcefully argued by participants was to extend the visa free concession available to people of Indian origin to visitors from the top generating markets, a practice which had prevailed before 1984.

Overall the Indian Tourism Week carried a meaningful note insofar as issues pertinent to tourism growth but seldom focused came in for serious debate.

For the Good Times...

Organisers of the India Tourism Week could congratulate themselves on the response to the invitation for participation in the Expo which began on 19th January. It is particularly so in the context of the global tourism scene marked by general concern over a fall in traffic resulting from global recession. Further, the time for preparatory work was limited to just four months. Still, there has been a forty per cent increase in the number of booths and participants as compared to last year when it was launched as an experiment. Besides, ten other countries have contracted to take up stalls.

It is a moot point whether a tourism event organised on a national scale to focus global attention on the Indian tourism product should have arrangements for promotion of outbound tourism.

The problem in such a case is that the main event will lack its focus, for after all, expo as other events scheduled for the week long programme which in a way is a rehearsal for the Visit India Year due to commence on April, is a promotional exercise. While the organisers could justifiably take credit for mobilising response, it cannot be overlooked that a large number of participants are state tourism corporations as also those sections of the trade who have a close liaison with the government. In other words, the success of the event should have as its parameter not the percentage in the increase in participation but the quality of participation that will be competent to deliver.

It may take quite some time how and when the queries registered at the expo are turned into actual business. In any event, the Indian expo is still in its infancy and hopefully with experience gained, in the coming years a decision will be taken on whether it should be a consumer travels show or an occasion for Indian sellers to meet their overseas buyers.

Alongside the expo, several other events will feature in the Tourism Week. The scheduling is quite relevant as in the face of a negative growth, due to extraneous factors the country cannot sit back waiting for better times. Constant promotion is the price for successful marketing through good and bad times.

These promotional shows should go on. It is quite possible, not all of them, for varying reasons yield results. For instance, the Buddha Mahotsova as also the Parikarma train have not been able to evoke much response from the target groups. At the same time, if the expo is an indication, prospects of a turn around cannot be ruled out.

The additional director general tourism, M K Khanna reaffirmed the objectives of the Week and the expo as generating awareness among decision-makers to secure their policy support and among consumers both, nationally and internationally. And, in addition to use this platform for evolving a consensus in the industry on ways of meeting challenges in such fields as human resource development.

In fact, a heartening development in the Indian tourism scene in recent months has been the coming together of different sections of the trade not only in pursuit of their individual and common demands but also for promotion marketing and sale of the tourism product. Individual organisations have sent to the ministry their own action plans for the Visit India Year coupled with a commitment that they will settle for only a marginal profit for the sake of the success of the event.

Apart from cooperation from among themselves in organising the programmes, they have addressed separate proposals to each ministry concerned with tourism. Even in respect of the Tourism Week, an elaborate programme has been prepared by not only the trade organisations but also chambers of commerce and industry. Seldom before have so many associations provided inputs for a collective effort. While FICCI has organised a seminar on tourism policy and investment in the sector, ASSOCHAM is focusing on awareness.

The Indian Convention Promotion Bureau, ICPB, has invited the EIBTM chairman, Ray Bloom, to deliver a keynote address on meetings, incentives, conferences and exhibitions. Several PATA functionaries from the newly set up headquarters in Bangkok are among speakers at the various seminars.

As part of the Week, India Tourism Day will commemorate the day with the creation of a separate department. The day's engagements will be also feature the honouring of those in the industry who have performed well with a pat on the back by the Prime Minister. Surely a week of much serious talk and some attempt at providing relief to the sombre scene.

The Same Coin

It is no secret that the department of tourism at the Centre (it lost its ministry status following its clubbing together with culture) has been fighting the sector's battles all by itself. Hardly any other segment of the government, be it finance, external affairs, home or even commerce, has ever treated tourism as part of the national agenda. There has been some mention of tourism in manifestos of political parties, but its importance has yet to translate itself into government policies. Let alone a change in policies (or mindsets about tourism being 'elitist'), no effort seems to have been made to create synergies among the various official agencies which could help tourism. So, when culture was taken away from human resource and put together with tourism under one minister, the hospitality industry, started dreaming of great days ahead. Culture and tourism have a symbiotic relationship and are two sides of the same coin. Seventy per cent of the leisure seekers who come to India, surveys have told us, come for a cultural experience. But, sadly, there are no signs of that dream being realised, at least not yet.

This is evident from the run up to and the final inauguration of the six-month long German Festival. True, the ministry of tourism and culture is involved in its organisation, but it is only the officials of the department of culture, secretary downwards, who are running the show, of course with the active participation of ICCR (Indian Council for Cultural Relations), an external affairs, ministry outfit. Queries at various levels of the department of tourism brought only discreet answers that the festival, thanks to the media coverage, will have a positive impact on travel to this country irrespective of whether the department was associated with it or not, Industry-watchers are surprised that if two departments under the same minister and ministry cannot create synergies, how could the department expect help and coordination from other ministries of the government or, for that matter, the state governments? The festival has a special significance for tourism because Germany is a major source market for

India. Arrivals from that country have been inching towards the 100,000 mark (they were 5,000 short of the figure in 1998) although, for unexplained reasons, there has been a six per cent decline in 1999. Sore tour operators have blamed the set-back to lack of air seats, The industry, however, looks on Germany as a market with great potential for India and cites the festival, on which the federal government and private sector are spending millions of Deutsche Marks as evidence of interest in this country as a destination both for business and leisure.

Had the department of tourism been associated with the planning of the festival, it could have drawn up promotions and advertising campaigns in Germany from its own resources of expertise to coincide with the event in India. A few tours for travel agents, opinion makers and journalists, including those from the electronic media, could have been invited. The tourist office in Frankfurt could have been instrumental in getting coverage in the German media for the various happenings during the festival. Before the festival ends on March 31-next year, as many as 160 events would have take place spread over 26 Indian cities. The international press in Delhi (and it is in a sizeable strength including global TV channels like CNN and BBC) could be persuaded for 'extra' coverage. But then, the department of tourism is still awaiting procedural clearances before it can appoint a PR agency equipped to handle such specialised tasks. Unless some headway can be made even at this late stage, the German Festival in India would be another missed opportunity for tourism.

The department of tourism, apart from lobbying with the government for priority for the sector, is also earnestly getting down to organising PATA 2001 which India is hosting. This international body which brings together leaders of all segments of the travel industry – the number of participants can go upto 1,800 – for an annual conference in a different country every year, helps promote the host country's tourist attractions. As the venue for the 2001 meet, India gets an opportunity to host an evening at the PATA 2000 which is being held in Kuala Lumpur next April. The department of tourism sent a high-powered team of industry leaders to the Malaysian capital for a 'recce' of the city for a suitable place for the Indian evening. The team, which included Ram Kohli, Ashok Anantram, Ragini Chopra and Amitabh Kant (tourism secretary, Kerala) has recommended the Mandarin Oriental Hotel. It has also suggested that in projecting India at the evening, a new concept of showcasing India's cultural heritage and modernity should be adopted, moving away from merely presenting classical dances, as has been done in the past, Secretary M P Bezbaruah and DG Atul Sinha, who carry the responsibility of organising the PATA conference with the support of the industry, will take a final decision. They have hinted that they would be associating with experts to take a decision on the them for the evening.

Hopefully, the department will leave no stone unturned in an area where its own writ runs.

Time to Play it Right

Looking back over the last five decades, it is an interesting discovery to find that huge doses of hospitality sector infrastructure were driven by the decision to host international events, be they conferences or sports oriented. It was in 1955 that Jawaharlal Nehru's impromptu invitation to UNESCO, while addressing its annual conference in Paris, to meet in the Indian capital in the following year, resulted in the building on a crash basis of the Ashok (India's first hotel built to international standards) and Vigyan Bhawan, among the first convention centres in Asia at the time. A dozen years later came UNCTAD II (United Nations Conference on Trade and Development) and the Ashok got its 2,400-seat convention hall and more rooms. The public sector's flagship got still more rooms in preparation for UNIDO in 1980 making the Ashok the capital's largest property, an honour later shared by Hyatt Regency.

But the biggest infusion of infrastructure, not only in terms of hotels but also sports facilities like the Nehru Stadium, Indira Gandhi Indoor Stadium, Games Villages, flyovers and upgrading of civic amenities – all on war footing – came in the run up to the Asian Games of 1982. Nine new hotels, among them Hyatt Bharat, Kanishka, Le Meridien, Centaur, Surya were built and two were expanded. And, although in the 20 years since the Asiad, a couple of new hotels like Park Royal, Radisson and Uppal's Orchid have come up, many more may be added in the six years that remains for making preparations for the Commonwealth Games due in 2010.

This time around however, it is not just the hospitality sector and selected civic amenities that will benefit; Delhi may finally be in a position to claim the status of a world class city after all. What is equally important is that Delhi will also emerge as the country's sports capital and both the department of tourism (DoT) and the travel industry can make a beginning with marketing India as a sports destination. The city already had a number of international class golf courses and with the additional sports infrastructure planned for the Commonwealth Games, it would have much more to offer.

The budget for the Commonwealth Games is said to be around Rs 2 billion. Much of the money will of course go into infrastructure like stadia and accommodation for athletes, but quite a lot is proposed to be spent on sprucing up the city, improving public transport, and the airport. Fortuitously, a string of flyovers has already smoothed traffic in many parts of the city and plans to privatise and modernise the Indira Gandhi International Airport (IGIA) are already in hand. Aviation secretary, K Roy Paul is reported as saying that by the time the Games are held, IGIA will be a mini city in itself with convention facilities, golf courses, shopping and entertainment centres. The metro would by then be fully functional with links not only to the airport but also to the Games Village which will come up in East Delhi (or Yamuna Paar as it is popularly known) bringing it on par with the other maintained parts of the capital. According to official sources a fleet of at least 2,000 modern energy efficient buses will be added which, after the Games, will be available for commuters.

Hopefully, DoT will soon be associated with preparations for the Games so that unlike the 1982 Asiad when we could not attract even 200 visitors, this time we should be able to do a much better job now that we have a Jagmohan-Rathi team at the helm. There is enough time to draw up strategies and to extend the Incredible India campaign to cover sports. A role model for DoT could well be Australia. Although infrastructure and organising tine Sydney Olympics was left to those who know-how to handle it better, all overseas publicity for attracting visitors was in the hands of the Australian Tourist Commission. This writer has it on the authority of a senior functionary of the Commission, Maggie White that it had in fact set a target of 100,000 fans need to look afresh at the future needs of accommodation. A good reference point would be the situation during 1995 and 1996, tourism's best years in the last decade, when the shortage of rooms in Delhi was estimated at 10,000. Even without the Commonwealth Games the recent turnaround of the economy and the growth rates being predicted during the rest of the tenth plan period point to significant increase in demand.

Globally, sports tourism is a major and growing segment of the sector. In India, for some reason we have only been promoting World Cups and Sharjah events. About time we made a beginning with inbound sports tourism.

About PR and Promotions

The PATA India chapter organised an industry meeting in the Andhra capital, and apart from Rathi Vinay Jha, those participating were, vice-chairperson, Ragini Chopra, secretary Pawan Khanna, executive director, Ashok Bhatnagar and members Ashish Kumar Singh (MD, Maharashtra Tourism Development Corporation), Uttam Dave (PKF), Rohit Kohli (Creative Travels), Mandip Soin (Ibex), Dileep Kapoor (Air India), G S Manchanda (ITDC) and Vikram Madhok (Abercrombie and Kent). Also present were L H Thangi Mannon, secretary, tourism, Nagaland and Andhra tourism secretary, Chandana Khan, who played host for the meeting.

After detailed discussion on what the chapter should do in the coming year, it was decided to give priority to reviving the tourism awareness programme (TAP) kept on the back burner because of pre-occupation and preparations for the PATA International Conference. The chairperson felt there is urgent need for creating a crisis management mechanism and she would be seeking assistance from the World Tourism Organisation for a seminar at which we could learn how other countries are addressing the issue. It was also agreed that workshops on different aspects of tourism would also be revived along with the training the trainer programme. There was consensus on the need for a PR agency both at the national and international level. One suggestion was that a professional be hired who could be the anchor for PR activities. A sub-committee will go into the subject more thoroughly and come up with final recommendations. About overseas promotions, Jha said she has taken up the question of reviving mandatory passages on Air-India for familiarisation tours and a beginning will be made on case to case basis. She expressed unhappiness that the industry has still not responded to her offer of sharing space and promotion expenditure at India tourist offices overseas.

The Industry meet, as Ashok Bhatnagar explained, aimed at strategising inter-state tourism promotion. The large number of travel professionals who participated had the rare opportunity of learning what other states are doing for the sector. Ashish Kumar Singh briefed the quorum about Maharashtra's initiatives and future plans while Thangi Mennon talked of how Nagaland is striving to carve a niche on the tourist map of the country. Chandana Khan's was of course the story of rapid strides made by Andhra. The special good news from her was that the Charminar is all set to be lit up, and more importantly she said that her department has acquired a piece of a 100 acre land where a 'mini India' will be built representing the whole country and its cultural heritage.

Uttam Dave's presentation covered a wide field of the post-9/11 scenario around the world. His in-depth study of the domestic tourism potential and the role of the industry was revealing. While the scale of domestic tourism is massive, in terms of revenue, it is small. His research shows that while domestic travel is 67 times that of international in numbers. The revenue it produces is only three and a half times. In other words domestic tourism is not yet lucrative enough for the travel industry, particularly the travel agent community. This is largely so because the consumer prefers to go directly to the supplier. And, so packaging is the main challenge before the industry.

Answering questions, Jha said that henceforth central assistance to the state will be given only for integrated projects. She said the first ever promotion campaign on the electronic media overseas aimed directly at the consumer is about to be launched under the newly acquired 'Incredible India' brand. The campaign, it will be recalled was masterminded by the Experience India outfit set up jointly by DoT and the industry three years ago and was originally woven around the slogan 'India: One Country Many Worlds' Rs 10 crore is being spent on the incredible India version of the campaign now being released.

The Hyderabad hoteliers raised with Jha the anomaly in the hotel expenditure tax (HeT), and about the revised three fold hike on a per person basis instead of a per room basis. She explained that the DoT had taken up the industry's complaint with the finance ministry.

GOITOs: Impactful or Unproductive?

The department of tourism (DoT) which has the responsibility of promoting India as a destination overseas has been doing so through a network of offices established since the 60s in what was perceived as source markets, largely in north America, UK, Europe and selected points in West Asia and Asia. In the beginning and until the mid-80s the staff manning these offices, which came to be known as Government of India Tourist Offices (GOITOs) came from a specially recruited cadre of tourism professionals and many of these have left an imprint of their pioneering and dedicated work in addressing the challenge of correcting India's image. But, with little or no replenishment of the specialised cadre, the department started looking for personnel from outside its own domain but still confined to government servants. This brought in a mix of good and mediocre state tourism department employees. The IAS put its foot into the door and started claiming a share of what was now reduced to mere foreign postings. This is not to suggest that they did not include bright minds. The industry's worries (and one is sure those of the senior functionaries of the departments) only grew when attempts were made to post ministers' personal staff to these offices. Fortunately, this did not happen but it had the effect of highlighting the urgent need for a relook at the structure of GOITOs and their performance especially in the age of Internet and technology.

At various trade meetings successive ministers made promises that GOITOs would be made accountable for their performance but indecision and frequent changes of governments and ministers did not lead even to a formal review of the role of tourist offices. The issue however came to the forefront when the Planning Commission released its mid-term appraisal of the 9th Plan with the first ever chapter on tourism. Industry observers and even the understandably media concentrated on what this august body had to say about the larger picture that tourism had not been given its due – and there was little or no comment on the sharp criticism of the overseas tourist offices. After pointing out that DoT was spending half its budget on overseas offices the Commission said, "In order to make effective use of the resource for overseas publicity, the application of information technology needs to be promoted in the sector, it may be advantageous to close the GOITOs and promote publicity through the Internet and television." The Commission did not stop at that. Reportedly, it slashed the department's overseas budget by half for the current year which apparently was restored on assurances that restructuring was on the cards.

The new team at the helm of tourism led by minister Jagmohan whose reputation as a doer travels ahead of him has finally acted. Both industry observers and travel media must have been surprised by reports in a number of national dailies about the decision to close down five of the eighteen tourist offices abroad. The offices chosen to be axed are: Madrid, Stockholm, Moscow, Tel Aviv and Buenos Aires. The announcement of the decision came in a chat Jagmohan had with media persons on the sidelines of a seminar in the capital. One newspaper quotes him as saying, "We are reviewing whether their utility as tourism promotion offices is commensurate with the expenditure on them." He gave the reason for closure as "non-performance". The estimated saying on the do-sure is Rs 6 crore. It is not clear if Jagmohan's announcement is a first step towards a major restructuring which would need some more time. He did indicate that, "Wherever offices are closed, embassies and industry would be requested to showcase India."

This approach has to be welcomed. Only a few weeks ago this column reported how diplomats from advanced and developing countries have been playing an active role in promoting tourist movements to their own countries in close co-operation with the travel industry. It will not be an easy task for Jagmohan to persuade our ambassadors and high commissioners to done the mantle of tourism promoters but he must try.

The first thing that needs to be ensured is that tourism is one of the subjects taught at the academy where our future diplomats are trained. There can also be refresher courses for middle-level foreign service personnel. Interestingly, using embassies for promoting tourism is exactly what the British Tourist Authority is doing after it decided a few years ago to reduce the number of its overseas tourist offices.

Ideally, it would be best to set up a national tourism board as suggested by the Yunus committee fourteen years ago, which could put together the best professional expertise from both the public and private sector for promoting India.

Gearing up for the Future

Governments generally tend to play down the adverse impact of setbacks to the hospitality industry. Perhaps the intention is not to create a sense of despondency. And, so it was that the new minister of state (MoS) Vinod Khanna told newspersons with hardly twenty-four hours in office that the 17 per cent drop in tourist arrivals since 9/11 was "not very sizable" and, by way of encouragement to the industry, he added, "This is not a big setback and with a focused approach the damage could be controlled." Apparently he was speaking to a brief provided by the Department of Tourism (DoT).

Whatever be the official appraisal of the tourism scene, balance sheets of hotels – the only segment that share its performance with the public – tell a different story. Published results for the fiscal 2001-02 of the big chains and major stand-alone hotels show steep falls in revenue and alarming declines in profits, and net losses in a few cases. Indian Hotels (IHC), the country's largest chain in the fourth quarter suffered a drop of nearly 84 per cent in its net profit. For the full year total income came down from Rs 716.34 crore to Rs 604.88 crore. It posted a net profit of Rs 80.7 crore compared with Rs 116.79 crore for the previous year registering a fall of 30.9 per cent, but as an analyst pointed out, boosted largely by extraordinary income arising out of sale of its stake in the air catering business, EIH, the Oberoi group's performance is on similar lines. Its net for the year saw a dip of 62 per cent from Rs 94.82 crore to Rs 41.89 crore. Total income went down from Rs 518.31 crore to Rs 427.33 crore. The third biggest private sector chain, ITC Hotels slipped into a net loss of Rs 3.12 crore against a profit of Rs 12.69 crore in the earlier year. The total income dropped from Rs 134.57 crore to Rs 113.41 crore. As for dividend to the shareholders, Indian hotels says it will stick to the interim 80 per cent recommended in May, Oberoi's will give 60 per cent while ITC hotels has decided to skip it this year.

The worst sufferer of the terrorism fallout on travel has been the public sector India Tourism Development Corporation (ITDC). This multifaceted hospitality giant posted a net loss of Rs 59.47 crore against a net loss of Rs 27.59 crore. The loss suffered by the corporation's hotels division came to Rs 53.57 crore compared with the previous year's loss of Rs 44.23 crore. Among the single units, Asian Hotels' Hyatt Regency in the Capital recorded a total income of Rs 93.26 crore, down from Rs 118.05 crore. Net profit was almost fifty per cent lower at Rs 12.97 crore against Rs 23.85 crore. Dividend too is lower at 40 per cent compared to the previous year's 70 per cent given in two instalments. In spite of the gloomy picture with only faint hopes of early recovery, it is remarkable that the hotel industry, the most capital intensive and long gestation period segment of tourism, is carrying on virtually full steam with its expansion programmes, ITC Hotel's 225-room super deluxe Sonar Bangla in Kolkata, which it is said will be redefining luxury, is due for soft opening during Durga Puja while the company's second new property in Mumbai, in upper Worli, which is being christened Grand Wekom Hotel is also nearing completion. Two more prestigious properties from the Hyatt and Meridien stables will soon open in Sahar in Mumbai, while another Hyatt is getting ready in the eastern metropolis. Surely, the hotel industry has faith in its future.

In another development, PRS Oberoi has taken over as chairman of EIH, Putting on the mantle of his legendary father, the late Rai Bahadur Mohan Singh Oberoi. He was earlier vice-chairman and managing director. S S Mukherji, who has been the company's deputy managing director has been appointed managing director.

Industry, watchers are surprised that while hotels and air carriers have stirred themselves to offer special tariffs' for domestic travellers, the industry, the government and Air-India have not sat together to work out packages for overseas visitors on the lines of what Sri Lanka, Malaysia and Thailand have been doing for months. Nor has the finance ministry responded to pleas for lowering taxes even on a temporary basis. It is a pity that the initiative taken by Andhra Pradesh in reducing the state sales tax on aviation turbine fuel (ATF) from 25 per cent to 4 per cent has not been emulated by any other state. According to reports in some newspapers, tourism and culture minister Jagmohan has written to the finance ministry demanding that the Inland Air Travel Tax (IATT) which adds 15 per cent to the cost of an air ticket be waived as also the central excise on ATF be reduced. The industry has for quite some time been demanding that the ban on LTC (leave travel concession) be lifted. All these measures could considerably help increased domestic travel. Perhaps the new finance minister Jaswant Singh will take a fresh look at these demands.

Yesterday Once More

In assessing the impact of disinvestment of public sector hotels both from the stables of ITDC and HCI, this column had on aft earlier occasion commented that it was leading to strengthening of existing chains and emergency of new ones of even providing a flagship to a group that needed it. A brief recap will be in order. Ajit Kerkar's Tulip Star, the successful bidder for HCI's Juhu Centaur in Mumbai, is poised to reposition this former Air-India run deluxe property as a flagship of the growing chain. The little known Lotus Nikko Hotels which has won ITDC's Bodhgaya Ashok is now the only chain in the Buddhist circuit. Lalit Suri's Bharat Hotels, which started with a single unit in the Capital and which now has presence in Srinagar and is "about to open" new properties in Mumbai and Goa, has spread down South with the prize catch of Ashok Bangalore, the peninsula's first five-star hotel built by ITDC Bharat Hotels is also the highest bidder for Khajuraho Ashok. Similarly, another prestigious hotel of ITDC, Kovalam Beach Resort near Thiruvananthapuram, has gone to M Far Hotels, an NRI-promoted company which already owns the Meridian in Kochi providing it with an established circuit in Kerala with the additional USP of convention facilities.

The trend has continued in the latest phase of disinvestment. ITDC's Kanishka in the heart of New Delhi has received a bid of Rs 96 crore, the highest so far for any hotel in this group (the Lodi has gone for Rs 72 crore) and the winner is the Eros group which already has a five-star deluxe hotel in the city, Park Royal Inter-Continental. Although the bid is yet to finally accepted by the cabinet committee on disinvestment the promoter Satish Sood, has already spoken to the media on his plans for Kanishka, currently a four-star property. He is quoted as saying that he plans to spend Rs 35 crore in renovations to upgrade it to five-stars and is also looking for foreign affiliation possible away from his own tie up with Six Continents chain which has in its fold apart from Inter-Continental such brands as Holiday Inn Crowns Plaza. Reportedly Sood is negotiating with Hilton, Radisson and Marriott because the Capital already has two Inter-Continentals and one Crowne Plaza.

Kanishka has an interesting history to it. The plot on which is stands (along with Ashok Yatri Niwas since renamed as Indraprashta and a shopping plaza linking the two) had a couple of Lutyen's bungalows which housed the Communist Party's MPs and their offices right though into the 70s. It was then that the plot was earmarked for a hotel. At that time DCM which had tied up with Hilton for a hotel project make a bid for it but was not successful. The government then toyed with the idea of a complex that would house all travel and tourism related agencies including airlines. There was even talk of a helipad on top of the building. However, this too did not convert into a firm decision. The next development was that ITDC should build a three star hotel. Came the emergency. Sanjay Gandhi, as the story goes, was appalled that a prime place of land was being wasted on a three-star hotel. So, the plans were changed in favour of a five-star unit. End of the emergency and the Janata government's heart bled for the common man. No five-stars was the new order. It was at this point that ITDC played its cards adroitly and got the government to agree to a Yatri Niwas for the common man (the initial tariff, believe it or not, was Rs 15) and a three-star hotel for the 'foreign' tourists. The impetus for carrying through the compromise formula was provided by the Asian Games and both properties were commissioned well to time for the 1982 deadline. Eventually, the Kanishka was upgraded to four stars.

Kovalam, India's first beach resort of international standards, has its own interesting story to tell. A UNIP team sent to India in the late 60s to advice the department of tourism on beach tourism identified three areas for development – Goa, Kovalam and Mahabalipuram (now called Mamalalpuram) and in that order. It suggested priority for Goa because of easy accessibility from Mumbai. Assigning the task to ITDC, the government, however, decided to spare resources for Kovalam and Mahabalipuram, leaving Goa to the private sector. ITDC hired Charles Correa as the architect for Kovalam and sent him on a tour abroad to study beach resorts. Phase one of Kovalam, forty beach cottages called the Village was commissioned in December 72, several years before Taj group built its resort in Goa. Phase two of Kovalam, the main hotel built on the promontory was opened to guests in 1974.

While the commissioning of Kovalam Beach Resort was a landmark in the tourism development of the country and a feather in ITDC's cap, it is also a sad example of lack of coordination. The Airport Authority took years, perhaps more than a decade, to lengthen the Thiruvananthapuram runway to enable the airport to take wide bodies aircraft. The resort had to make do with whatever tourists a Boeing 737 could bring.

Disinvestment: A Good Entry Point for Many

When the hotel sector was opened to FDI (foreign direct investment) first up to 74 per cent and later to 100 per cent those unfamiliar with investment patterns especially in Europe and the Americas had expected a rush on India. It slowly dawned on us that many a foreign chain although keen on establishing a presence in the emerging Indian market was largely interested in management tie-ups and if this were not possible then franchise arrangement. Most of the big league chains stick to management as their core competency and leave investments to banks and consortia. It is not surprising that in the decade since economic reforms little or no investments have come into tourism and certainly not in the hotel segment although one or two chains like Hilton and Inter-Continental did say they had investment designs on this country. Even in their case they were deterred from going in for greenfield projects because of the absence of suitable land and the formidable 'approvals' regime in metro cities where they would naturally like to make a beginning.

It is in this background that the Asia-based Silverlinks Holdings famous for their super deluxe Sukothai and the exclusive boutique Aman Resorts grabbed the opportunity offered by disinvestment in ITDC hotels and made a successful bid for the ideally located Lodi walking distance from the Oberoi in the Capital. Silverlinks has paid nearly Rs 72 crore cash down for the property and reportedly spent another Rs 11 crore in VRS payments to the staff, which as one newspaper said, was availed by the entire staff from general manager to the doorman (Both the department of disinvestment and ITDC deserve credit for making VRS an integral part of the sale/lease process).

There has been little official news from the new owners of Lodi about their plans. But one thing is clear. The present edifice is beyond upgradation and with a hundred per cent successful VRS the owners plan to build afresh. There has been some speculation in the media about the shape of things to come. One report would have us believe that Silverlinks may use the five acre space for two hotels and introduce both their brands on the same plot of land – a Sukothai with 200-250 rooms and an Aman Resort with 30-35 rooms. And, according to one estimate Silverlinks will be investing around Rs 150 crore on the new complex. If this money also comes from abroad, you have an FDI in the hotel sector of over Rs 230 crore, a significant amount considering that virtually nothing has come since globalisation. Industry observers agree that unless there is a drastic change in our policies on land, land use and building bye-laws, foreign investments in this sector will come only through acquisitions or may be joint ventures. Meanwhile the slow and steady progress with disinvestment of public sector hotels has crossed yet another stage.

In the category of all's well that ends well is the Juhu Centaur of Air-India subsidiary Hotel Corporation of India (HCI) which has finally changed hands after reports that the deal with Ajit Kerkar's Tulip Star Hotels might fall through. In a judicious handling of the situation and six months of patient negotiations, the hotel had finally been handed over to the new owner. Even after Kerkar had paid the bid money of Rs 153 crore a new hitch arose over the stamp duty. Good sense prevailed on both sides and this hurdle too was crossed and Juhu Centaur was handed over to Kerkar. Given his track record at the helm of the Taj group, it should not be long before Juhu Centaur under whatever new name it is launched as part of the Tulip Star chain, will stand tall among Mumbai's great hotels.

That is so far as HCI goes. ITDC has managed to give up four more of its properties in the latest disinvestment exercise. A fifth hotel which was also on the block – Khajuraho Ashok – did not get any bid and so will stay on hold until the next lot is up for sale. The four that have received successful bids include the prestigious properties like Ashok airport at Kolkata airport and Ashok Aurangabad and the resort hotel in Manali. The new owners of Kovalam Beach, India's first seaside resort commissioned by ITDC in December 1972, are M Far Hotels, an NRI promoted outfit which also owns the Meridien in Kochi. The company will pay Rs 43.68 crore against the reserve price of Rs 41.70. The Meridien has an adjacent convention complex and Kovalam has its own 500 seat conference facility, a marketing advantage for M Far Hotels, the Airport Ashok will fetch the government Rs 20.01 crore; the reserve price was Rs 14.83 crore. Aurangabad Ashok will fetch the government Rs 20.01 crore; the reserve price was Rs 14.83 crore. Aurangabad Ashok is being sold for Rs 17.40 crore to Loksangam Hotels while Manali will go to auto Impex, possibly newcomers to hoteliering, as seems to be the case with the bidders of the Airport Hotel – Bright Enterprises.

Hotel Industry Down the Ges

It all started with the currency melt down in southeast Asia followed by pressures on the economies of some of the leading source markets for tourism in Europe. At home the mid-term elections and the ensuring political uncertainties dimmed the enthusiasm of the overseas investors who in earlier years were coming in large numbers to explore possibilities. They adopted a wait and watch policy and seem to be sticking to it.

The slowdown of India's own economy affected domestic business travel. Adding to the industry's woes has been the steady decline over the years (unconnected with the economic ups and downs) in the quality of visitors in search of holidays. Small wonder that while the ministry of tourism has been reporting growth in arrivals, the yield per tourist has been going down. It is currently estimated at just over $43 compared to more $350 for Singapore.

Even when there was a boom, caused largely by the influx of business visitors, tourist locations were selling rooms at depressed tariffs. A look at India's neighbourhood will show that this country is not alone in the tourism set backs. China which stunned the world with its spectacular achievements in recent years had a minus growth of 2.4 per cent in the first half of this year. Hong Kong recorded a minus growth of 21.0 per cent and Singapore, the shining star of tourism was minus 17.2 per cent.

Only Thailand had a positive growth of 4.0 per cent. In Europe, most destinations saw a decline in arrivals, this year partly because of economic reasons and partly believe it or not, because of the World Cup played in France! It is explained that people either went to France or stayed home to watch the game on television.

In spite of all this less than enthusiastic scenario nobody has pressed the panic button. For, it is generally believed that tourism and its major component, hotels, is a resilient industry. It has survived wars and warlike situations, ethnic violence economic pressures and even natural calamities, tourism has come a long way from that sunny afternoon in 1841 when Thomas Cook, an Englishman took, a trainload of people from Leicester to Loughborough for a penny a head giving birth to the organised sector in travel.

Last year, according to the latest report of the World Tourism Organisation (WTO) 613 million tourists crossed international borders. Every tenth human being is part of the tourism workforce. WTO forecasts that by the turn of the century, the number of international travellers will go up to 700 million and rise to one billion in 2010. For South Asia, where India accounts for half the arrivals, the figure projected is 10.4 million. Which means that if the World Organisation's assessment is correct, India will achieve the coveted five million arrivals in just over eleven years from now – a dream which the then tourism minister, Madhavrao Scindia, had hoped would be realised in 1997.

It is quite possible however that we may achieve the target much earlier thanks to the ongoing economic reforms, the present government's declared commitment to tourism and the push to infrastructure like roads, power, telecom and airports.

The tourism-friendly budget that the finance minister presented to Parliament and the Government's response to the trade's demands about the Hotel Expenditure Tax (HET), the service tax and the latest conferment of the Export House Status has strengthened the industry's faith in its future. That is why in spite of two successive bad years with no silver lining for the current period, none of the hotel chains or individual entrepreneurs have pulled back from their proposed or committed investments.

ITC Welcomgroup plans a massive investment of Rs 2,000 crore; Taj and Oberoi have set apart Rs 1,000 crore each and a number of emerging chains like Leela, Asian and Bharat Hotels have announced projects running into hundreds of crore of rupees. The Tourism Finance Corporation of India (TFCI) is assisting a large number of entrepreneurs and some 30,000 rooms are said to be in the pipeline, involving an outlay of upwards of Rs 10,000 crore.

But even the addition of the 30,000 rooms will leave a huge gap of more than 40,000 rooms if we have to accommodate five million tourists. Land, or the lack of it all suitable locations and prices, has been the main hindrance in the faster growth of the accommodation sector. From an average of 1,800 new rooms per year in the 80s, we have reached on average of 4,000 rooms per year in the 90s.

The pace of growth has to be doubled or trebled even to meet the modest target of five million arrivals. Apart from land availability which may somewhat ease at least in the metro and other big cities from the expected repeal of the ceilings legislation, a sea change has to take place in land laws and building by laws and the plethora of approvals required for hotel projects.

While the industry must await reforms in these institutional areas, hotels have done a commendable job in meeting global challenges and responding to emerging customer preferences. The deluxe segment of the industry is second to none in the world and many Indian hotels have international reputation. There has been a smooth transition to segmentation. From catering to all categories of travellers, they first specialised into leisure and business hotels.

ITC Welcomgroup gave the lead in adopting the Sheraton and Towers concept of 'a hotel with in a hotel' for the business traveller. Other chains and single unit properties followed with executive floors and state of the art business centres. In the next round resort hotels are being offered as a distinct category. Heritage hotels, mostly palaces are another innovation. And, in industry has quietly corrected the imbalance in the deluxe and mid-market share.

The 60:40 ratio of rooms in the deluxe and mid-market has in the last decade been reversed. Even the major chains are consciously developing the mid-market as part of their growth strategy. The Taj group came up with Gateway and Regency brands and the Oberois have adopted the Trident as their mid-market route. ITC Welcomgroup has set up a subsidiary, Fortune Park, to develop (his segment, credit must go to A K Dave Associates for bringing in Quality Inns to India which showed the way to new entrepreneurs non-five-stars too have a future.

Talking of the future, two trends are clear. Hotels will be more and more technology driven, more modular, more functional. There will be less and less human touch to many activities. Self-help will replace personalised service.

Demands of specialisation will force owners to rent out space for restaurants to professionals. The other trend will be in infrastructure growth.

If the economy revives in the coming months as promised by the finance minister and the pace of reforms is sustained, the country may after all have 1,30,000 rooms in the next ten years and a quantum jump to 3,00,000 in the following decade.

Tourism Policy – Fulfiling Promises

It is because Prime Minister, Atal Behari Vajpayee had kindled hopes of a better future for tourism by his reference to the potential the sector offered that the hospitality industry also raised its expectations of new government initiatives. He had also said in his now famous Red Fort last year that in order to tap this potential a 'progressive' national tourism policy would be unveiled before the end of the year. For whatever reason that deadline could not be kept and the policy was finally placed before Parliament after its approval by the cabinet this year. Spread over 30 pages, the document has a preface, an introduction and two long chapters detailing the current situation and prospects, and, goals, objectives and strategies. There are also a few annexures and a model that illustrates what it will cost to build additional rooms to service one million extra tourists or invest in more aircraft and what this investment will lead to in terms of employment and earnings from tourism and aviation, an excellent innovation for a policy document.

There is general agreement among industry leaders that the policy is indeed not only progressive but also comprehensive although there is virtually unanimous criticism that there is no mention of the creation of a National Tourism Board, a long-standing demand which was strongly endorsed by the Yunus Committee as far back as 1988, CII president, Ashok Boota has welcomed the policy as 'forward looking' and 'timely' which 'encapsulates a comprehensive and holistic strategy for the development of tourism.' FHRAI chief, B K Gupta hails the policy because it "covers almost all the segments of tourism and has made an attempt to put forward tourism as a national priority and clearly defined the vision and objectives" but add that only through a National Tourism Board would we be able to "implement the marketing plan in a professional way in the competitive market." On behalf of TAAI, secretary general Subhda Joshi would have preferred a more categorical commitment to open skies and said, "It would have been better if a civil aviation policy had also been announced along with the tourism policy."

In the months before the policy was announced an impression had gone round that an action would be part of it. Obviously, that was not the department of tourism's intention. In the brief 'summary' at the end of the document it is clearly stated that "India's tourism industry through the capacity of its tourism resource, facilities and services and as yet relatively untapped market potential has considerable scope for expansion and development. The tourism policy elucidated above aims at setting up a framework that will allow the various stakeholders to fully develop the potential of tourism and to harness this to the national development priorities." According to one analyst this framework will have to evolve its own dynamism to enthuse all stakeholders to play their part effectively. Of course, any commitments made in the policy will have to be carried through. In other words implementation now assumes greater importance. For instance, the directions indicated for positioning tourism as a national priority are clearly in the area of action by the government, particularly the inclusion of tourism in concurrent list, setting up of the Tourism Advisory-Council which will act as a think-tank and the adoption of the satellite accounting system or even visa on arrival. The policy document claims that in one area at least – effective linkages and close coordination between departments -- action has already been taken and a 'group of ministers on tourism has already been constituted'. It would be a good idea if the department of tourism would let the industry know if this Group has met and what decisions have been taken.

There is progress on the proposal to include tourism in the Concurrent List. According to the document a majority of the states has already supported the proposal. Surprisingly, some industry leaders have reservations about the Concurrent List. S K Misra, former tourism and aviation secretary and now CEO of INTACH, feels the centre must tread carefully as the states are possessive of their constitutional rights. A better way would be to seek their cooperation or assist them with modal legislation, he says. On its part the policy document clearly spells out its considered view; "it will provide a constitutional recognition to the tourism sector...and enable the central government to legislates for tourism development."

In sum, the tourism effort will have to "evolve to be government-led, private sector driven annd community-welfare oriented." The industry would look forward to that happening soon.

Who will take the Lead?

For years the various chambers of commerce have been nursing committees on tourism and aviation as some kind of a mandatory activity holding a seminar here and a workshop there, some even with international participation, but mostly ending up as talk shows. Recently however, thanks to the pressure by industry leaders as well as a somewhat more responsive government, these committees have become more focused and purposeful and are doing useful homework in collecting data to buttress their case vis-a-vis official policies and practices. Reflecting this change is the conference organised in the capital by the PHD Chamber of Commerce and Industry. Recognising that where tourism is concerned it is the state where the action lies and it is they who need to be motivated to step out and do something for the neglected sector, which has tremendous potential for socio-economic development, the chamber thought of this exercise. Inspired by the initiative taken by the southern states earlier this year, the PHD tourism and aviation committee headed by V N Dalmia, organised the New Delhi meeting on 'Integrated Tourism Development: Synergising Northern Region States', which brought together ministers or tourism secretaries from 10 States comprising the region J&K, Himachal, Punjab, Haryana, Delhi, Uttaranchal, Rajasthan, MP and Chhattisgarh. And, sharing the dais were minister Jagmohan and secretary, Rathi Vinay Jha. Participating in the conference were leading representatives of the various segments of the hospitality industry. It was a welcome surprise for the participants to find among the papers circulated useful data on each state about its tourism budget, arrivals both domestic and foreign (the irrational) taxes imposed by them on road transport, hotels and other services. Some of the data was indeed an eye opener not only to the audience, but also perhaps to some of the states themselves. On tourism budgets, consider this: Kerala spends Rs 55 crore, while UP from which it: separated recently can spare only Rs 16.36 crore. Punjab takes the cake with a provision of Rs 1.15 crore!

When it comes to taxes, particularly the levels on tourist transport, the scene is entirely different. MP, Rajasthan and Chhattisgarh charge whopping rates on coaches plying with all-India permits in the range of Rs 28,000; Rs 28,500 and Rs 21,000 per month respectively, and, if you have wondered why it is cheaper to fly to Bangkok from Delhi than to Chennai or Bangalore, you have only to look at the sales tax charged by the state on aviation turbine fue! (ATF). The same three states are in the lead, MP takes 25 per cent; Rajasthan 23 per cent plus 15 per cent surcharge and Chhattisgarh 25 per cent. The same is the case with Luxury Tax on hotels in the three states, all charging 10 per cent.

The PHD committee chairperson enlivened the proceedings. As ministers and secretaries made presentations, the screens highlighted what the states were spending on tourism development and the high rate of taxes in each case. A major recommendation on which there was consensus was the constitution of a committee of northern region tourism secretaries for coordinating and integrating regional efforts for tourism development. It was announced that the first meeting of this committee would be held within three months and that the Delhi administration has offered to play host.

There were other recommendations too which the participating ministers and secretaries endorsed, but also said they would have a hard disk getting their finance departments to fall in line. One recommended an immediate relief to the hotel sector by waiving Luxury Tax till the end of March 2003, and after that, in line with the proposal of the Central Tax Rationalisation Committee peg taxes on hotels at 10 per cent. On transport tax a ceiling of Rs 12,000 was suggested per quarter and a single point collection system. A similar 10 per cent cap was also suggested for the levy on ATF.

Minister Jagmohan's advice to the states was to make the best use of available resources and made it clear that the centre "will help only those states which help themselves". It is not always money that can bring about change. It is also important to change attitudes to such issues as governance, hygiene and orderliness, he said. Rathi Jha was equally forthright on the issue of funding state project. Instead of depending solely on central assistance, she said, the states should create a conducive environment for joint ventures or direct investment in tourism infrastructure.

"Stick to your USPs," she told the states, and "do not spread your resources thin in doing what others can do better."

The PHD Chamber has given the lead. How the states respond only time will tell.

Give the Deserving Their Due

After the government has agreed to the withdrawal of service tax on tour operators, one demand that has been pending for long has acquired strident support – for export industry status to be granted to tourism.

The demand is not without justification as inbound tourism has minimal outgo and proportionately maximum inflow of foreign exchange receipts for any export product. Happily, this demand is not of any particular segment but binds the entire travel industry, including hoteliers, travel agents, tour operators and related services.

In fact, the Travel Agents Association of India (TAAI) deputed a team that called on the commerce minister, Ramkrishna Hegde, to press its case for an Export Promotion Council. The team pleaded with the minister to recognise tour operators and travel agents as export houses. Tourism, it was pointed out, ranked as foreign exchange earner only after gems and jewellery and readymade garments.

The tour operators too, at a special function organised by IATO, drove home the same point drawing a commitment from the tourism minister, Madan Lal Khurana, to represent their case. Incidentally, Khurana's credibility with the trade is quite high as he has been able to keep his promises and deliver the goods.

The Hotel Association of India (HAI), in a separate meeting with Hegde, suggested the establishment of an apex Tourism Export Promotion Council with a view to developing a country-specific strategy. All three organisations had most pleasant meeting with the ministers who promptly agreed on the justifiability of their demands.

Even so, it is not certain in whether the commerce ministry could overcome certain procedural snags and accept the request for a promotion council. If it was easy, such a body would have been sat up by now. For, Hegde had declared his support in principle to the Council concept long before the travel agents and the hoteliers called on him with their memoranda. Be it as it may, persistence by the trade with the demand might yield results of some form in their favour.

The broad framework and the nitty-gritty of an export promotion body for tourism has been clearly spelt out in the HAI memorandum, which proposes a marketing corpus of Rs 330 crore. This amount is equal to three per cent of the foreign exchange earned from tourism in 1997-98. As with similar promotion councils for other export products, the trade will share equally the requisite funds.

In a welcome development, the Federation of Indian Export Organisations (FIEO) has lent full support to the proposal for a Tourism Promotion Council. The delegations which met Hegde returned satisfied with his response. Hegde informed them that he would call a meeting of ministers and senior officials of the Ministries of Tourism, Railway, Civil Aviation and Finance as a follow up.

An Export Promotion Council can assist tourism establishments in market development assistance, export incentives, export house recognition, special import licences, institutional alliances, travel trade missions and similar promotion activities. Being industry-specific, such a Council can obtain relief under various incentive schemes for the import of essential items required by tourism establishments. Besides, the Council could recommend grading the establishments on the basis of their revenues.

For instance, an export house can be on an FOB value of exports of Rs 20 crore; a trading house for receipts of Rs 100 crore; a star trading house for a turnover of Rs 500 crore and a super star trading house on an FOB value of Rs 1,500 crore.

As already mentioned, the travel trade has a claim to be considered on par with other export industries. Though they take pride in the fact that all segments of the trade have forged links to fight for revocation of service tax, lowering of luxury tax and reduction of other levies, is it not time for them to come forth with at least a code of conduct for themselves?

It is strange that in the free market atmosphere, they want everything to be handed by the government. On their own part, they have done little to add to their credibility by organising meaningful research and creating a data base.

A beginning has apparently been made by IATO in formulating an alternative tourism plan and also by HAI in making a special study of the hotel tariff issue.

Certainly, much more needs to be done as the future can emerge only from a full-fledged public-private partnership.

Cooking up Tourism Conveniences

According to the latest report of the World Tourism Organisation (WTO) 613 million tourists crossed international frontiers during 1997. This does not include domestic movements which must account for several billion. Travel and tourism has become the world's largest industry, generating over $3.7 trillion in output which is 10.7 per cent of the global GDP.

Employment figures are no less impressive. Two hundred and sixty-two million people work for the sector or 10.5 per cent of the world's workforce. In the next ten years it is estimated that the number of employed will rise to 380 million and output will go upto $7.1 trillion. Visitor count at the turn of the century will touch 700 million and one billion, in 2010. Tourist expenditures which in 1997 were $444 billion (excluding airfares) are likely to increase to $600 billion in 2000 and jump to $1500 billion by 2010.

The tourism forecast for South Asia, where India accounts for half the arrivals is a six per cent growth upto 2010. In numbers it will be 5.76 million by 2000 and 10.4 million by 2010. Which means that if this country's one share of the South Asian region remains constant we will achieve the magic target of five million tourists only in 2010!

Perhaps, the economic reforms and the growing awareness of the potential of tourism at the highest political level will take India much beyond the WTO forecasts. But, there is little doubt about WTO's forecasts on tourism's growth globally coming true.

Even the present dimensions are pretty incredible seen in the context of how organised tourism began some 160 years ago.

The birth of tourism was recounted in New Delhi, when a new travel product was launched. You have guessed it right. It was a Thomas Cook offering – a plastic card version of the traveller's cheque. But, first about the story of tourism.

"The Story is a dramatic one, an eminently Victorian epic of achievement, which saw the construction of a new industry out of nothing more than a brilliant idea," says a company brochure. "On a sunny afternoon in 1841; an Englishman named Thomas Cook took a trainload of people from Leicester to Loughborough, for a penny a head. The train journey marked the beginning of the tourism movement, and the genesis of a remarkable organisation," it adds.

From this humble journey was born Thomas Cook the company, that was soon ministering to royalty, arranging the travel of Maharajas and pilgrims, and transporting a British army up the Nile. Among the company's prized possession is a 'certificate' from Mark Twain: Cook is your banker everywhere and his establishment your shelter when you get caught out in the rain.

Thomas Cook not only pioneered the travel industry, it has in its 158 years of existence, contributed significantly to its growth and refine of the various service including many firsts corporate travel, foreign exchange, traveller's cheque and now Visa Travel Money Card. Even the launch, ceremony in the capital had a special touch to it. Two directors of the parent company Thomas Cook Group Ltd., Ulrich Zierke, chief executive and John McEwan, deputy MD, flanked Pradip Madhavji, Chairman Thomas Cook India Ltd., after attending a board meeting earlier in the day.

The parent company has a forty per cent holding in the Indian set up. Thomas Cook India's top brass was there too – Ashwini Kakkar, CEO and managing director, Jayram Kelkar, executive director, forex and Sameer Govil, director business development, South Asia – to explain the merits of the Visa Travel Money Card (VTM).

As reported in the media VTM available at 33 Thomas Cook foreign exchange offices in 14 cities in India, is a prepaid card that the traveller can buy before leaving on foreign travel. The customer can choose the amount in US dollars to be stored on the card depending of course on his or her entitlement. And while he or she is abroad, money can be withdrawn in local currency from more than 4,40,000 Visa ATMs (cash dispensers) in 117 countries.

Access to cash is available 24 hours a day, 365 days a year and is extremely safe, quick and convenient to withdraw. Madhavji gave the assurance that card holders will get the most favourable exchange rates and that the card is protected by a personal identification number (PIN) and backed by a 24-hour helpline service in case of loss or theft.

John McEwan had some more good news for Indians travelling abroad – extension of the Thomas Cook Global Services to this country from the new year. One phone call will bring you immediate help in any travel emergency, legal, medical, money, itinerary, baggage, even flowers (bribe spouse back home on his or her birthday. Thomas Cook, and McEwan will continue to be leader and innovator. Looking at the company's track record since it set foot in India in 1881, few would question the claim.

But, the thoughts uppermost in the minds of those who wish Indian tourism well are whether the government and the industry will come together to raise this country's share of the world market from the present 0.4 per cent to at least one per cent.

A Matter of Ethics

Sensible people in the industry will by and large agree that it is high time that it should be subject to certain discipline by consensus or by law.

This is necessary for the betterment of infra-trade relations and protection of the consumer. For, good business ethics is the sheet anchor on which an industry could grow by enhancing its credibility.

There have been attempts in the past to realise this objective through a voluntary code of conduct or comprehensive legislation, including provisions for the protection of the consumer. If will be in the fitness of things that with a friendly tourism administration in place this need is fulfilled. This is imperative for the growth of the industry which is not passing through the best of times.

One could cite several illustrations reinforcing the need for safeguarding the interests of the consumer and maintaining ethical relations between the provider and the supplier in this totally service-oriented industry.

This writer recently had an experience of how the consumer's interests are brazenly ignored. Membership of the time-share exchange entitles the owner to a week's holiday as specified in the agreement. The particular week is also specified. But the management of the company did not deem it necessary to explain or compensate why the week would not be availed of. All that the writer received was a curt notice that for some unstated reason the holiday week would not be available.

The member has made an investment and the company is obligated to honour its commitment or to compensate. The company's approach may not necessarily be the same in all the time-share properties. But even in a single case when a contract is breached for no consideration the entire concept could be called into question. In fact, it is such experience with different customers which has stymied the time-share movement which has a vast potential in India.

It is possible that the aggrieved person could go to court but a person intent on a short holiday would not settle for a long litigation is here that a consumer protection oriented to tourism should help.

In other segments too there have been cases of breach of faith and trust, like last minute cancellation, off-loading confirmed ticket holders and non-provision of agreed facilities Added to these is the issue of safety and security of the holiday maker, where the government comes in.

Much of these problems also arise from want of proper intra-trade understanding. The industry had for spoken of a self-imposed code but they could not agree to its provisions. Both TAAI and FHRAI have a different annual conventions repeatedly stressed the urgency for a self-discipline system. After all, such a voluntary effort will find greater acceptability than a government enforced norm, which in the special circumstances of the industry can have only limited scope.

Now that the different organisations have agreed to operate from a common forum on matters of common interest, the proposal for a code should receive priority attention. Not only will such discipline smoothen relations between the different segments, particularly tour operators, it will also benefit the consumer.

Incidentally, the laws safeguarding the interests of the travellers are very stringent in several countries of Europe and other source markets. These laws have implications for the industry here too as the overseas counterparts expect adherence to their commitments to the clients wherever they go.

It is not infrequently that tour operators charge hotel managements with bouncing confirmed groups at the last minute, causing embarrassment and loss both to the operators and the consumer. A few years ago, when business travel had peaked tour operators lamented that hotels were turning away leisure travellers.

The hotels have their own tale of woes. They blame the operators for making dummy bookings in more than one hotel for the same group and making the final choice at the last minute for the best bargain. In the process hotels are left in the cold, unable sometimes even to recover retention charges.

Another cause of friction is related to payments. While travel agents and tour operators collect their money in advance, they seldom pay the hotels and other suppliers on time. Old timers in the industry will recall that a code modelled on the IATA-UFTAA accord was in force until the late 1970s. Since then, it got waylaid somewhere. Domestic air services also figure in disputes of breach of contract.

For all these reasons a comprehensive code backed by legislation, at least in part, is called for to sanction business ethics in this industry.

Hope for Tourism Revival

No segment of the travel and tourism sector has lowered its sights or modified its plans. Its problems are now essentially external to its functioning like the economic slowdown at home and recession abroad. But, it cannot throw up its hands in despair. Expectations that changes in the world economic situation will have its necessary fallout on the tourism scene have spurred the different segments to pursue their plans.

The years schedule is a demonstration of this optimistic approach. In the very first month, January, the Indian Expo which is at once consumer-oriented and also a marketing exercise for the industry, has received a good response in terms of world be participants.

In its first year, that is 1997, the Indian Expo organised in the capital was a consumer show. But, both the ministry of tourism and the event manager have this time enlarged it to cover a buyer seller meet and to develop it as an international event.

According to Navin Berry, who has been designated event manager for the 1999. Five hundred stalls, more than twice the number sold last year, have been provided making it the largest travel fair in Asia. Doubtless, this will be a major step forward in the joint efforts of the industry and the government towards tourism's revival.

The functioning of the newly-constituted Tourism Export Promotion Council (TEPC), headed by Habib Rehman, managing director, of ITC hotels, is another cause for hope. It has provided a promotional forum, bringing into it representatives of every section of the industry, related agencies and departments concerned. This is the first forum of its type constituted after long years of pleading. Earlier initiatives by one segment or the other, and on occasions by the government itself, to form a joint body could not fructify.

Of course, the circumstances in which the Council was constituted after the industry had been conferred the 'export house status' are different from the past when consultations were called to settle only intra-trade differences and not organise any collective promotional or marketing campaigns.

Hopefully, the new body will not get bogged down in any controversy. Also, participation in the Export Council should encourage fostering a sense of commonality of approach to issues facing the industry.

Such a joint approach has been made possible by the decisions of different apex organisations to appear together before the finance minister in the pre-budget discussions to present the case of the tourism sector, in the past, each organisation has been handing in a separate memorandum of sectoral demands which even sometimes clashed as between tour operators and hoteliers.

The Action Plan in pursuance of the draft Tourism Policy will acquire a more meaningful content once each of the task forces assigned to report on the requirements of infrastructure, marketing and human resource development completes its recommendations. Implementation of their recommendations should facilitate a clearer perception of investment areas and outlays so that Indian and foreign entrepreneurs can have a closer look at the possibilities. Needless to say these possibilities will become reality only in conditions of political and economic stability.

Yet another prospective factor that will bring about a change on tourism fortunes is the launch of Visit India Year. While the industry feels that the preparatory period is too short, with some innovative moves it should be possible to get some mileage. This reality is reflected in the decision to have a limited number of events but with a wider impact through higher visibility.

It is proposed to have strategic alliances with non-tourism partners and go in for co-branding.

For instance, there could be collaboration with the credit cards for shopping. The industry keenly awaits a decision to ease visa norms so that a visitor on arrival could be given a landing permit for a fixed duration.

The Visit India Year also coincides with the Millennium celebrations of Khajuraho temples, one of the greatest cultural assets of the country. On the infrastructure side too the industry looks forward to new developments, which will benefit the sector.

The massive investment in roads, introduction of greater competition in air service through disinvestment and repeal of the Ceilings Law, which will make available land for hospitality services units, all contribute to make the last year of the century, THE YEAR OF HOPE.

Indian Tourism: Chance to Make its Mark

The elevation of M P Bezbaruah as chairman elect of PATA is at once a personal honour and recognition of India's proactive role in furthering tourism in the face of adverse conditions. The high honour sits lightly on the civil servant of over three and a half decades in top positions in various fields. In an exclusive interview to EH&C, he expressed the view that his prime concern would be to carry India alongwith the rest of the PATA membership in making full use of the tools of technology.

He considers it an advantage that there is a national consensus in favour of prioritisation of tourism and he is hopeful for that reason there will be little problem in ensuring continuity of the several initiatives taken in the last two or three years. The transitory status of the present government should not be a handicap. Nearly a year after the draft National Tourism Policy was formulated and endorsed by the State Ministers Conference, it is yet to receive the official stamp of approval by the Cabinet. With all states having endorsed the policy document coupled with the acceptance by all agencies, concerned that tourism benefits percolate to the grassroots, there is no reason why the final sanction needs to be delayed.

Bezbaruah and his colleague – director general, Ashok Pradhan – are virtually the authors of the document, which covers all aspects of tourism and have proposed an Action Plan as a follow up. In fact, the Action Plan has already been underway with the launch of he Explore India Year, now midway through its first quarter. As with other national policies on which there is little dispute, tourism should not be a casualty of political changes. At the same time, it cannot be overlooked that tourism is bound to be hit during election time.

By a happy coincidence, this period has stretched to the usual leaner months of the tourist season. But, preparations like advance publicity and promotional campaigns should not be delayed. Happily, the industry and the Tourism Ministry have agreed to go ahead with their projected road shows in the United States and other source markets.

In this connection, it will be very appropriate if the Ministry secures clearance for appointing a well-equipped agency for promotion and crisis management through public relations. This proposal has been pending before the government for a long time. Equally, if not more important, is the establishment of an autonomous National Tourism Board to oversee and coordinate raising of resources, funding, promoting, marketing and infrastructural growth.

This proposal has been formally with the government for eleven years since the National Committee on Tourism submitted its report to the then government of Rajiv Gandhi, which for its own reasons failed to give effect to. In subsequent years all the apex trade organisations, without exception, have been asking for it. At one stage, a WTO consultant services were enlisted to work out the nitty-gritty of the Board. Again, being a non-controversial subject, government should not have any problem in approving it.

In any event, there cannot be any let up in aggressive promotion of the sector and strengthening of the infrastructure as desired by the Chairmen elect of PATA, that India should sustain its momentum.

Wearing his additional hat as PATA chairman, it will be Bezbaruah's endeavour to get as much international support to the Indian effort. The board of directors of PATA will meet in New Delhi in September, when about fifty or so leaders of the industry worldwide will be here, not only to carry out their agenda but personally apprise themselves of the wondrous improvement in the Indian tourism product.

Bezbaruah will also have a busy schedule of meetings with the participants of the World Tourism Summit, proposed to be held as part of the Explore India Year. The Summit dates will have to be finalised by the new government. Incidentally, Hong Kong – which hosts PATA 2000 – is planning an Asian Summit on Tourism along with the conference. Bezbaruah, with his gentle persuasive skills, should be able to persuade the organisers to synergise the programmes of the two summits to the advantage of countries in the region.

In his interview, Bezbaruah emphasised that the technological revolution is sweeping through every aspect of tourism like consumer choice at the macro and micro levels, ticketless travel and air safety. India will have to play a key role, particularly to ensure inter-linkages with all agencies globally so that Indian tourism does not slip when global tourism recovers.

While the soft spoken secretary, with his unconcealed strong commitment to tourism, is reckoned by the industry as a reliable prop, all who care for the sector share one wish: In the name of normal bureaucratic procedures and practices, Bezbaruah should not be shifted from the Tourism Ministry.

In that event, it will be an irony to find a person honoured by the most influential international body on tourism to be handling a subject far removed from the sector.

IATO's Commendable Initiative

Full compliments to IATO leadership for consistently encouraging participatory action. Its members are regularly briefed on trends and issues facing tourism. These are discussed threadbare at a working luncheon organised on the first Saturday of every month.

The members feel a total sense of involvement through its deliberations and are aware of what to expect as solutions to problems facing the trade within a time-frame. This helps not only in their dealings with the authorities but also in facilitating business operations.

At such a meeting held a month ago, it was brought to the notice of tour operators that some travel agencies in Ladakh have decided to totally boycott those engaged in the trade at the national level or in remote centres. The moment the problem was raised, the leadership took up the matter with the J&K authorities and established contact with the Ladakhi operators.

Some sort of a solution has since been found, in which the interests of the local trade will be safeguarded in what is essentially seasonal business. This is only illustrative of the issues that come up from time to time at the luncheon meet. The members are also informed about the court proceedings in cases taken upon behalf of the trade by IATO.

It must be said to the credit of IATO that at its last annual convention it brought together representatives of different apex organisations to sign a common memorandum to be presented to the Finance Minister on the eve of the Budget. Still earlier, IATO held a seminar to which it invited the spokesmen of political parties to secure from them a commitment of support to the tourism sector. The effort did yield results as at least one party, which formally led the ruling coalition – BJP – incorporated in its manifesto its support to the growth of the tourism sector, IATO did not stop at that. After a Minister for Tourism had been appointed, the organisation did intense lobbying and established rapport with the incumbent Madan Lal Khurana. Few, who had any concern for tourism or studied developments in the sector, would fail to acknowledge the contribution by Khurana to prioritise tourism on the national agenda and secure for the trade a host of reliefs, the most important of which was the Export House Status.

It is in this context that IATO's announcement of a similar election-eve seminar has aroused interest in the trade. According to Major Murli Dhar, IATO's secretary, this time the effort will be directed to persuade all major political parties, particularly BJP and the Congress, to be forthright in the support to the tourism sector as a source of employment and creator of wealth. IATO would like this commitment to be made not only a part of the manifesto but a component of a common programme of any coalition or alliance that takes over after the elections.

Another event which interests the travel trade, in which IATO has got itself involved, is the expansion of business activities particularly in the new markets. Though for some years, there has been travel to East and South Africa from Mumbai, there is an urge for a new emphasis to promote outbound travel to this part of the world, about which not much is known either to the trade or to the Indian holiday-maker.

It was thoughtful of IATO to have brought together the High Commissioners of Uganda, Kenya and Tanzania whose governments will shortly create a common community through a Treaty of Cooperation.

The splendour of the tourism product, as presented on behalf of the three countries by the Uganda High Commissioner, Joseph Tomusange, were revealing.

The questions triggered by the presentation showed considerable interest in the trade in the destinations. A query about visas secured an undertaking that while the objective was to arrange a common visa for all three countries fcr the present, the three High Commissioners gave an assurance that there will be no hassles. If any of the three countries issues a visa, the other two will automatically endorse the passports.

Meanwhile, one of the issues worrying the travel trade is the occasional violence that shakes hospitality services. In the recent past it had involved a couple of visitors who were taken for a ride by unscrupulous elements. The latest incident of a celebrity murder in a high society restaurant near a national monument in the Capital only heightens the need for a greater enforcement of protection for tourists. In this particular case, the unfortunate celebrity was a local model, but that it happened in a restaurant – part of a complex with a tourist appeal – will have its implications.

And United We Shall Be!

The significance of the joint memorandum submitted to the finance minister in a pre-budget exercise by the travel trade is that it was jointly formulated and signed by the representatives of all apex organisations. The demands may not be new but the fact that after several decades they could sit together and present a single list is a notable achievement.

The initiative it should be acknowledged, came from IATO which brought to its annual convention representatives of the other organisations like TAAI, FHRAI, HAI and TAFI and made them commit to collective action. It was followed up by the FHRAI convention in Jaipur and the TAAI convention in Hyderabad where formal announcements were made that it will be a joint effort this time. And, the newest of the associations, HAI also lent its full support.

The absence of any display of unity at joint fora has been the bane of the travel industry. It is ironic that on occasions the government itself unsuccessfully tried to bring them together on a common platform. A Travel Council as originally conceived by the then director general of tourism, Ashok Pahwa, did not materialise because, hoteliers and tour operators squabbled over arbitration in their disputes. And, truly enough there have been any number of causes for dispute.

For a long time the dual tariff kept the hoteliers and tour operators at loggerheads. The issue is still before the courts. Instead of settling the matter across the table the issue was handed over to the government for arbitration. Since there are periodic changes in the tourism ministry one cannot be sure whether the officials concerned handling the case at a particular time are fully familiar with the implications. While the court will decide as to whether the government is competent to scrap or sustain dual tariff in mediating the dispute, fortunately the stand off has not come in the way of the unity efforts.

The need for unity in the industry is at no time greater than now when the tourism sector is in the throes of a crisis primarily because of extraneous factors for which reason there is considerable unpredictability on the future of the sector, at least in the short-term. Collective action is called for in taking corrective measures in marketing, promotion, sales and product improvement.

Adding to the challenge is the technological transformation that has been brought about in the industry in recent years. Personalised service by every segment has to be necessarily coordinated if technology is to be taken full advantage of. There is growing recognition in the different segments of the industry on the need for coordination, particularly in marketing.

It will not be out of place to mention here the first eleven months of the year has seen a fall in tourist arrivals measured against last year's nearly four per cent growth. The task forces set up at the Prime Minister's level for service industries and at the tourism ministry level have focused on the urgency of corrective action.

Against this background, the joint memorandum offers the right response to the current situation. As already mentioned, it is not so much the demand as the united stand taken by the industry that will make a difference. As for the demands, the memorandum asks for:

(1) Exemption from hotel expenditure tax, luxury tax and service tax for payments made in foreign exchange now that tourism has been given the Export House Status. Incidentally, HET when it was first levied did exempt foreigners from its purview.

(2) Indirect taxes charged from the industry like sales tax, passenger tax and vehicle tax be reimbursed on the lines of incentives given to other export industries.

(3) The threshold limit of Rs six crore for eligibility to export house status should be lowered or scrapped altogether to enable larger numbers of travel undertakings to benefit from this status. As at present only chains and fifty odd travel agencies can avail of the benefits.

(4) The capital goods import facility limit of Rs one crore should also be waived.

(5) MAT (minimum alternative tax) should be removed from tourism units. The hotel segment wants further concessions in depreciation allowances especially for equipment purchased for environmental protection. The reinvestment condition under Section 80HHD for profits earned in foreign exchange should also be waived. And, hotels should be

declared infrastructure for tax benefits. In the context of the national economy, one is not sure whether and how the finance minister will reconcile his requirement of reducing the fiscal deficit and the industry's demands. But he has one advantage: he does not have to go through separate demands of five associations, often mutually contradictory.

Still Awaiting a Breakthrough

Agra was witness to two high profile tourism events in the latter. The first, organised by CII, held on the 13th and 14th was billed as 'India: Tourism and Heritage Challenge 21'. The second, which followed immediately after that was the 'Indian Travel Congress', a title which TAAI has assumed for its annual conventions for some years now. In terms of participation, the CII show was on a smaller scale with two hundred odd delegates whereas TAAI which seems to lay great store by records, had almost 1,800 representatives of the entire hospitality industry, spouses and children included. As was to be expected, some of the foreign speakers, celebrities in their own rights, appeared at both the meetings. These included Jean-Claude, Baumgarten, president World Travel and Tourism Council (WTTC), and Ian Angell, professor of informations systems, London School of Economics. Simon Bell of A T Kearney consultancy, was a star performer for CII. His 'Visitors to India' survey made headlines in the national media. Minister Ananth Kumar's address to the CII delegates also received wide coverage, largely because the chamber had taken the trouble of hosting media persons from the Capital. In comparison, TAAI did not receive much notice in the national media because it neither invited journalists from the mainline newspapers on its own nor did it coordinate with CII to benefit from its efforts.

Among the highlights of the CII gathering, apart from the Kearney survey, was an 'Agra Manifesto' presented by Ravi Bhoothalingam, chairperson of the chamber's tourism committee and president, Oberoi Hotels, which based on detailed studies recommends measures to upgrade Agra to a world class tourist experience and at the same time to preserve the city's heritage. Ananth Kumar's speech, largely a repeat of his inaugural address at the IATO convention, drew comment from delegates who keep a tab on ministerial pronouncements. They noted that he had promised at the IATO session that the long delayed tourism policy would be ready within a month but in Agra he extended the deadline to a 100 days. Tourism secretary, M P Bezbaruah who at various trade conventions has been pleading for cooperation between the public and the private sector said there could be no breakthrough for the sector unless there was a common agenda before the government and the industry.

Coming as it did just two days after his address to CII, the minister's speech at the TAAI inaugural could hardly be expected to have any fresh points except one more promise: A national tourism agenda task force which would be in place within ten days. The task force, he said, will meet once every two months and the 'agenda' would be suggested by the trade associations, themselves.

TAAI's theme 'emerging trends in the travel' pervaded most of the discussions. Technology's threat to the future of the travel agent of course popped up at almost every business session with little or no consensus on the extent of the threat in the Indian situation. But there were any number of useful suggestions on how to prepare yourself to meet the threat when it becomes real. Overseas experts pointed out that even in an advanced nation like the United States, where the Internet users numbered millions, barely 18 per cent of the bookings were being done online. There was agreement, however, that the travel agent, especially the medium and small-sized agency, must reposition itself in tune with technology and develop niche areas of business which the big operator or even the Internet cannot service.

Delegates showed considerable interest in the session devoted to mergers and acquisitions. Two of the panelists, Ranjit Malkani, whose own SOTC and Sita Travels, now form part of Kuoni Travels India Ltd., and Ashwini Kakkar, whose Thomas Cook is in the process of merging with TCI, made interesting presentations on the pre-requisites for successful mergers or alliances. A mismatch of work culture or lack of focus on objectives could be ruinous, it was emphasised. Synergies were also important. Malkani pointed out how SOTC's hold on the outbound traffic and Sita's on inbound business had been what he called a perfect fit to Kuoni, to emerge as the country's largest travel company.

Among the prominent overseas participants at the TAAI convention were the lady tourism minister from Seychelles, Simone de Comarmond, Udaya Nanayakkara, president, Sri Lanka Travel Agents' Association, Abdullah Jonid, Malaysia, DG tourism and Tunku Iskander, president, IOTO (Indian Ocean Tourism Organisation). Taking part in a discussion on Bonds Across Borders, they looked at various possibilities of regional cooperation. The consensus, however, was that going by the experience of SAARC, the political conditions were not ripe for governments to bring about such cooperation. It was, therefore, better that the private sector in the region took the lead. At the suggestion of Subhash Goyal, the IATO chief, Nanayakkara was persuaded to become convener for an initiative in this direction.

TAAI was meeting in Agra after 22 years. Conventional wisdom would have required the association to spare some thoughts to the City of the Taj which everyone agrees 'lacks in all basic needs of a tourist destination' but that was not to be.

Breakthrough, What Breakthrough?

Indian Association of Tour Operators (IATO), the more active of the trade bodies, chose for its annual get together a theme which prompted minister Ananth Kumar to assert that he is after all keen to remove some of the despondency in the tourism industry. The theme was 'Still Awaiting a Breakthrough' and Major Murli Dhar, the Association secretary and convention chairman in his inaugural address said that even after 50 years of independence the country was still without a tourism policy; the sector enjoyed the lowest priority and that even on such elementary things as coordination between the various ministries at the centre or between the centre and the states was not in place.

The minister asked for a month's time for the policy to be placed before the nation. "It is now before the cabinet for final approval," he told the delegates assembled at the Capital's Ashok Hotel on August 25, 2000. As for coordination he had a major initiative up his sleeve and hinted that he would soon launch a series of 'backdoor summits' with the states at the level of ministers and where necessary even chief ministers to sort matters out.

An immediate response to the idea came from Bina Kak, Rajasthan's tourism minister, who said she would welcome the first summit to be held in Jaipur. And, Kumar happily made a commitment for that first summit and equipped much to the amusement of the house, "I say the breakthrough has begun now."

Arun Jaitley, who has made a mark as disinvestment minister and is currently in charge of information and broadcasting, delivered the keynote address. He conceded straightaway tourism's role as a big provider of jobs as well as foreign exchange and it had therefore to be part of the overall economic development. But, the problem lay with 'mindsets' both at the central and state levels.

His panacea for the sector, however, lay in the higher growth rate of the economy. The future of five per cent growth of GDP in the past, he said, had perhaps made no difference to tourism. But, the expected growth of eight to 10 per cent in the coming years would certainly lift the sector to much higher levels.

Jaitley's thesis generated considerable debate among the delegates during the coffee and lunch breaks. Those who agreed with him pointed to how some of the insoluble problem in the way of tourism, growth has finally been got out of the away by economic reforms – the telecom revolution and the phenomenal growth of the automobile industry. The power sector is poised for a big push and so are national highways.

"Don't we finally have an expressway to Agra?" pitched in one of the delegates. "But who will change the mindsets and when?" was a question for which there were no answers. The pessimists, and there were quite a few among the delegates, were not impressed by the promised summits or higher GDP growth making any difference to the future of tourism. "I bet we will be saying the same thing at the next year's convention," said one of them.

One of the most interesting business sessions was under this topic 'New Millennium: Era of Partnerships and Alliances'. While there was an agreement on alliances being a natural outcome of globalisation, the panelists who included Ashok Anantram, vice-president, ITC Hotels, Rakesh Mathur, Asian regional chief of Bass Hotels and Prof Kapil Kumar of IGNOU, warned about the pitfalls of mergers.

Mohan Khanna, additional DC, who moderated the discussion took the opportunity to draw attention to the impact of WTO (World Trade Organisation) framework for the service industries which would have to be enforced in this country. He said that the broad implications of acceptance of the framework and discipline under it would entail that there would be no tariff barriers and non-tariff barriers too would have to be dismantled. The implications of the replacement of MRTP by a new Competition Law which will be drafted by the Competition Law Board were brought to the notice of the delegates by Anjana Gosain who advises IATO on legal matters.

Former union minister and currently president of the UP Congress Committee, Salman Khursheed, a popular speaker at tourism conventions and admired for his wit, bemoaned the fact that with the creation of Uttaranchal, his state would lose almost all of its mountain and forest cover and with it quite a bit of its tourism potential, although prime attractions like Agra, Allahabad and Varanasi would still be there. He wondered why our promoters had not thought of building tourism around renowned educational institutions like Aligarh or Mangoland like Malihabad on the lines of itineraries for Oxford and vineyards and orchards in Europe. There was also great scope for developing Varanasi and

Allahabad in the same way as the Vatican which attracted millions of tourists of all faiths.

IATO's Hall of Fame admitted two more stalwarts – M P Bezbaruah, tourism secretary who is this year's PATA international chairman and Ashok Pahwa, former DG.

In a few weeks, TAAI will be holding its annual convention in Agra, and a little later is the FHRAI in Mumbai. Will the discussions be more of the same the delegates must have wondered?

Tourism Gets Incorporated into Corporate Interaction

It was a welcome surprise to see tourism include in an exercise where the country's top CEOs sit together to share their visions. The occasion was the second edition of *The Managing Tomorrow Series* of corporate interaction jointly organised by *Business Today* and *Amity Business School* with Hyatt Regency playing official host, on March 25. The theme was "Vision 2010: The Growth Imperative" and the keynote speaker, N K Singh, member Planning Commission whose tourism-friendly initiatives have brought great encouragement to the hospitality industry. The four panelists who shared the dais with him were PRS Oberoi, EIH vice-chairman and M D, Jagdish Khattar, Siddharth Verma and Rajiv Kaul, managing directors of Maruti, Reebok and Microsoft India, respectively.

Briefly, Singh's vision of what he would like to see at the end of the decade is a GDP growth of 8-9 per cent; the number of people below the poverty line down to 10 per cent; drinking water for every village; forest cover to increase to 33 per cent; and every Indian to have gainful employment. He was candid enough to point to the imperatives necessary in making this vision realisable: a national consensus on and bi-partisan support to economic reforms fiscal management of revenues; more affordable cost of finance; reducing infrastructural inadequacies and regional disparities (some states growing at 8 per cent and some only at 2 per cent). And, finally, the pattern and quality of growth. The power sector, he said was still deficient with electricity boards losses totalling Rs 25,000 crore and transmission losses as high as 45 per cent. Progress on roads was commendable and speedy action initiated on privatisation of ports. Deregulation of telecoms was well under way. He also raised some questions relevant to tourism. Why is it, he asked, so many foreign airlines overfly India. And, why is our own civil aviation sector not doing well?

Oberoi was the first speaker after the Planning Commission member's keynote address. Coming straight to the point he drew attention to the country's dismal performance in travel and tourism. Compare India's 2.6

million arrivals with China's 27 million, he said. Even the 2.6 million figure is not reflective of the genuine tourists. If you take away people of Indian origin and business travellers, he said, that according to his analysis, the number of real tourists coming to India could not be more than half a million. In the rest of the world tourism has emerged as the largest industry and if its potential is tapped in India with the right policies and initiatives it could provide in the next ten years an additional 30 million jobs.

Oberoi was frank enough to say that it was not fair to put all the blame on the government; the industry itself has failed to create a body that could speak to the government with one voice. Also, we have done little to get the support of the media, be if the newspapers or television, and, for that matter even the people. It is only when the industry gets its act together will it be in a position to influence government policies. He shared Singh's concern about airlines overflying India and travellers preferring other destinations in southeast Asia like Thailand and Malaysia. On one hand, he said, we are pricing ourselves out and on the other the quality of our infrastructure, especially our airports and facilitation hassles like visa difficulties, were driving tourists away from this country. "I feel ashamed" he said, "When I compare our international airports with those in our neighbouring nations."

If foreigners complain our hotels are expensive, it is the taxes that make them so, he said. In Mumbai you pay 32.5 per cent tax on your meal and in Rajasthan the sales tax on imported liquor is 57 per cent, giving just two examples. The hefty Aviation Fuel Tax on Air Turbine Fuel (ATF) discourages foreign airlines from using Indian airports. And, look at our aviation policies, he said. "We encourage private enterprise to build an international airport in Kochi. And after it has been built and commissioned we do not permit foreign airlines to land there."

The EIH chief agreed that things were looking up where roads are concerned but wondered why the railways were not thinking of liberalising their operations. Why can't they let the private sector run tourist trains to places like Agra, he asked. On Visas he said that until the early 80s a thirty day visa on arrival was given to all visitors and it was time that practice was revived.

Once media shy, Oberoi has been actively espousing the cause of tourism by his association with the World Travel and Tourism Council's India initiative.

Get Focused on Pertinent Issues of the Industry

Meeting as it was barely ten days after the terrible happenings in New York and Washington, one would have thought the over 2,000 participants at the golden jubilee convention of the Travel Agents Association of India (TAAI) would devote a considerable part of their three-day meet to discuss the likely impact on tourism and how the industry should prepare itself for this unprecedented challenge thrown up by global terrorism.

It was pretty clear to everyone that this country would be the worst hit because of its proximity to the action point (Afghanistan) identified by the Americans with wide global support. Barring a brief reference in Pradip Madhavji's presidential address in which he declared 'tourism is under attack' and a minute's silence observed in the memory of those killed, there was no change in the agenda of the 'historic' convention. It is another matter that the tourism minister, Jagmohan took it upon himself to prop up the industry's morale on how to cope with the new situation and Dr Karan Singh, who became the first tourism and civil aviation minister in 1967, in his valedictory address continued, where the present minister left.

Said Jagmohan, "it is true that terrorism has put the world into a spin. But, it is for us to rise to the occasion, cut new channels and seek new directions." He pointed to the unlimited potential of domestic tourism and promised his own and his ministry's full support in tapping it. He emphasised, as he has been doing at various meetings since he took over, that only clean, orderly and landscaped cities, tourist places, monuments and pilgrimage centres attract visitors. He conceded that this is a gigantic task and urged the hospitality industry to give a helping hand.

All said and done, he went to say, tourism is much beyond the job assigned to a ministry; it is a question of governance, public behaviour and attitudes. He gave the example of Vaishno Devi, which now has a clean environment and quality civic services catering to five million visitors against 3,00,000 only a few years ago. The minister said that travel agents should concentrate more on domestic tourism especially now when there is possibility of a sharp drop in foreign arrivals. World over, he said, domestic tourism has been the true base for international tourism. The four highways that will connect Kashmir with Kanniyakumari and Mumbai with Kolkata will be the great race setters for tourism and travel agents and hoteliers should start planning ahead for that boom.

Dr Karan Singh, fully endorsed Jagmohan's recipe for Indian tourism and said, while the world battles with terrorism, we should also adopt a 'Look-East' policy to increase our foreign visitor count. Citizens among our neighbours like China, Japan, Korea, Thailand, Malaysia, Indonesia and even Australia and New Zealand could be wooed in larger numbers to experience India. The Asian Tigers he said had vast numbers of citizens with disposable incomes. But in order to achieve success in this policy, we need to reorient our marketing strategies. The former minister made an interesting suggestion on how to prevent hijackings. He said aircraft manufacturers should redesign the cockpit in such a way that once a plane is in the air, it should be sealed from inside by the crew. As designed now, only a swing door separates the pilots and the hijackers. Space should be created within the cockpit for a washroom and pantry for their needs of coffee and snacks (According to a newspaper report Air-India has decided to ask its pilots to bolt the cockpit door as a precaution).

It is customary at any TAAI convention for destinations, both domestic and overseas to make 'presentations. Malaysia, which in recent years has come to look on India as one of its biggest source markets, has been a regular participant. This year was no exception. The country's dynamic minister, Sheikh Fadzir was there as always. He invited TAAI to hold its 2002 convention in Kuala Lumpur. But if one was looking for a surprise exhibitor, there was China! In fact credit goes to TCI for launching its first China 2002 Tour series in cooperation with the China International Travel Agency, whose representatives along with the Chinese Consul General in Mumbai showed a film on China's tourist attractions (including of course the Great Wall and cruises on the Yangtze). Not to be left behind, the Russians had a kiosk promoting river cruises.

The Renaissance, on the edge of Powai Lake, with its nearly 2,000 capacity convention hall, the venue for the TAAI meet made its presence felt as the western metropolis new address for conferences, the city path-breaking ITC Grand Maratha introduced itself through a spectacular multimedia show at the inaugural function.

A touching moment during the awards ceremony came when the later S Dharmarajan was honoured posthumously. "In recognition of his exemplary ethics in travel writing."

Big Day Yet to Come

Wednesday, September 12, 2001 was to have been a great day for tourism. It was the final day of the three day conclave that has raised high hopes for the hospitality industry. The first two days were spent rather usefully.

First, those responsible for promoting tourism overseas, and who had flown in into the capital to share with the new team at the department of tourism (DoT) and the new minister, Jagmohan, what they intended to do was to get more visitors to come to India.

Joining in were leaders of the industry. There was general agreement that more aggressive promotion was necessary but first the infrastructural inadequacies need to be addressed, and of course, removal of irritants to tourism like visa hassles and lack of civic amenities. On the second day, it was the states' turn. The tourism secretaries made presentations to the same audience on what their thoughts were and what they expected from the centre and the industry. The minister set the tone. He reminded them that there was fresh thinking at the leadership level about the potential of tourism and no less than the Prime Minister had given a clear signal in his Independence Day speech.

It was necessary, he said, that everyone, government at the centre and in the states as well as all allied agencies and the industry should seek solutions to the country's poor performance in the tourism sector. He invited their comments on the draft national tourism policy as well as suggestions for action that will produce quick results.

Everyone agreed that the primary need was to give priority to tourism and supported the view that only a Prime Minister-driven effort will uplift the sector from where it has been stagnating for decades. There was consensus that a cabinet committee on tourism on the lines of similar committees on economic affairs and other core sectors should be set up for coordinated decisions and for securing implementation. A national tourism board should also be in place to advise government and to promote and market India abroad.

Third important suggestion was to create a mechanism for coordination between the centre and the states and among the states themselves so that uniformity of the Indian offer could be achieved. And, finally, creation of an environment through administrative, institutions, and fiscal measures for partnership between the public and the private sector which alone quicken the pace of infrastructural development ensuring at the same time the quality of service.

The visa issue did not figure much because the government had already announced its decision in principle to grant visa on arrival for a select number of countries and preparatory work is in hand. The heavy dose of taxation both central and state did come up in the course of discussions and the industry leaders, especially the apex bodies made a strong plea for rationalisation with the objective of reducing the number of levies and adjusting the incidence to levels which while ensuring revenues could lessen the burden on travellers.

And, so the last day, rather the 'big day' was kept for the chief minister and tourism minister from the state to sit with the Prime Minister, the home minister, and Jagmohan and his team and industry leaders for an interface which could result in spot decisions or promises of decisions.

There was a fair amount of speculation toward the end of the second day's deliberations on what the 'big day' had in store for tourism lovers. Many industry leaders and even tourism secretaries were confident that some major decisions would be announced. As one industry leader told this writer that even if the Prime Minister is unable to set up a cabinet committee on tourism he would certainly set up a group of ministers (GoMs), This would be a good beginning, he added.

There has been little or no support within the government over the demand for a national tourism board which was first recommended by the Mohammed Yunus committee on tourism as far back as 1988. Industry leaders feel that the idea may be more acceptable now in the changed atmosphere. But, taxation is one area where the industry expects little change. If at all, the centre may agree to rationalisation but, the state finances being what they are, no immediate relief is expected although there would be any number of promises.

Little did the participants in this latest tourism exercise knew that the 'big day' is not to be, thanks to the activities of global terrorism. The meeting had to be called off because of security concerns, a totally understandable action. Secretary M P Bezbaruah explains that it is only a postponement and that the 'big day' may yet come in a month or so.

The terrible happenings in New York and Washington will have a deep impact on world tourism which will need time for a fuller assessment.

Job Security Dominates Every Other Consideration

In the second generation reforms launched through Budget 2001, one aims at addressing what the finance minister described as 'rigidity in the labour laws', enshrined in the statutes during the Nehru era, when the nation was committed to building a socialistic pattern of society, it is now generally agreed, that these laws led to an over-emphasis on job security, but at a tremendous cost to productivity and lack of flexibility in reorganising businesses and industrial units. More importantly, it did not create more jobs. The specific law governing managements' right to hire and fire, is called the Industrial Disputes Act, which inter alia prohibits companies from employing more than 100 workers and from laying them off without permission from the government. An editorial in a leading daily sums up, rather succinctly, the impact of this legislation. "Lay-offs are a dirty word in India," it says, "where 'job security' dominates every other consideration. However, the drive to secure jobs by making lay-offs tough, has led to perverse outcomes. The labour market has become rigid. In good times, when the industry needs to expand, few businesses decide to hire people with new skills and talent, because older employees are impossible to dislodge. In bad times, it is impossible to downsize. The urning of new skills is slower, companies lose cost cutting flexibility and the ability to bounce out of recession quickly, both slow down growth and job creation."

The Industrial Disputes Act, with its threshold of 100 workers, now covers 87 per cent of all companies. The percentage may be much higher in the hotel sector where, on an average, there are three workers to a room. What Yashwant Sinha now proposes to do, will have far reaching consequences. He said in his budget speech, that the government will introduce an amendment to the Industrial Disputes Act, which will take almost 99 per cent of enterprises, out of the purview of the legislation and they will be free to hire and fire their staff. In the case of the hotel industry, the number of units employing more than a thousand workers, would be less than half a dozen, which include large properties such as, the Ashok Maurya Sheraton and Hyatt Regency in Delhi, and, The Taj Mahal and The Oberoi in Mumbai,

It is surprising, that the leaders of the travel industry, particularly hoteliers, have not commented on this aspect of the budget. True, that the proposed amendment, is yet to be placed before the Parliament, where vote bank and opposition politics, will make a determined bid to thwart its passage. It has to be noted, that the government too, is determined to complete the process of reforms. Of course, it will have to convince workers, that the change will benefit both workers and the industry. The finance minister has already indicated, that the amendment will also ensure higher lay-off compensation, as much as three times the present rates.

It has been pointed out by analysts, that even under the existing restrictive labour law, companies have been able to bypass regulations, by hiring people on various sorts of contracts. In this arrangement employees also lose out on the benefits that come with secure employment. These analysts feel, that if the amendment goes through, the labour market will become more flexible, more workers can be hired legitimately and can then ask for and get benefits, that come from legitimate, non-contractual hiring. They could also expect better work conditions, safety standards, welfare measures and health benefits. It is of course, upto the trade unions to choose between, concentrating on the positive aspects of the amendment and blocking the legislation.

A telling example of how the Industrial Disputes Act, has come in the way of reviving the Great Eastern Hotel in Kolkata, is there for all to see.

For several years, the State government has been trying to privatise the hotel, but each time, the unions have succeeded in blocking any progress towards that end. Even after Jyoti Basu gave his blessings to the tie-up with the French Accor and personally assured the workers of a fair deal, the unions have placed impediments in the way of the transfer of the management. Under an agreement with the workers, the hotel was to be handed over on March 31 and no bookings were to be accepted after that date. According to reports in the media, the workers have made fresh demands and the government has been forced to delay the handover to the end of June. Accor, it is reported, has set apart Rs 15 crore for the separation package for those who are not retained, but workers want employment in other government departments, instead of being laid-off. The state government now has to give the hotel Rs 1.63 crore to it tide over till the end of June (the new handover date), an unnecessary burden on the taxpayer.

Only time will tell, whether forces in favour of the economic reforms will continue to have an upper hand.

Preserving The Taj; Who will be the Final Arbiter?

There has been wide coverage in the media of the MoU signed by the Indian Hotels Company (IHCL) better known as the Taj group, the National Culture Fund (established by the department of culture), and the Archaeological Survey of India (ASI) for the 'preservation and upgradation of facilities at the Taj Mahal' in Agra. This is not surprising as the signing ceremony was a big show held as it was in the chandeliered Durbar Hall of the capital's Taj Palace hotel with a huge backdrop of the great monument and the presence of the chief of the house of Tatas, Ratan Tata, tourism and culture minister, Ananth Kumar and Uttar Pradesh chief minister, Rajnath Singh. So great was the electronic media response that photographers and TV cameras completely blocked the view of the dais from the audience.

That private sector's involvement in the daunting task of preservation and conservation of the nation's heritage is imperative has been recognised by the government for quite some time now. Minister Ananth Kumar underlined this by pointing out that the Rs 1-15 crore budget of ASI amounts to a bare Rs 7,600 per monument per month! Anticipating possible criticism – in fact a headline in one of the morning newspapers had suggested that the 'Taj was being handed over to the Indian Hotels Company for maintenance' – he hastened to clarify that the Tatas will "only fund and assist in conservation" and whatever they do will be under the aegis of ASI. He went to the extent of saying that Tatas "will not collect entry fees nor appoint the staff; government will continue to do that." For his part, Ratan Tata chipped in to say that it was a privilege to assist in the preservation of the Taj Mahal; this was not an activity "as part of the company's business."

Under the MoU, the Taj group will make available Rs 1.87 crore in the first phase. Says the MoU: "IHCL will be responsible for commissioning a professional agency to prepare a feasibility report on the conservation, beautification, restoration, upgradation of the monument and its surrounding areas." The feasibility report will be the basis on which work will be carried out "at and around" the monument. The MoU also lists 16 specific areas of work ranging from river water treatment to conservation of damaged stones and inlay pieces, to provision of "clean and hygienic rest room facilities." Plus, also planned are state-of-the-art communication facilities and a "one stop solution for all tourist queries."

The press note issued by the Taj group explains that "the question of the development potential of the area will be dealt with in the second phase of the programme. During this phase top professionals will be deployed to study the various environmental issues facing the Taj Mahal such as soil erosion, sedimentation, the high level of hydrocarbon and carbon monoxide in the air around the monument, inconvenient access to the east bank of the Yamuna, convoluted traffic within the city, formation of ravines and the incursion of the Rajasthan desert." Pollution control, enhancement of the river front and water management would be the three top priorities.

The press note that the Taj group will source expertise and support from reputed Indian and International agencies, some of whom have already carried out extensive studies on the Taj Mahal and its environs. These include Indian National Trust for Art and Cultural Heritage (INTACH), the University of Illinois, US National Park Services, the Getty Foundation and the Smithsonian Institute.

The hospitality industry, for whom the Taj Mahal is its biggest draw card should indeed be happy that the private sector has finally been allowed into the task of preserving the national monuments. But, observers point out that the choice of one hotel chain to be given the sole privilege of upgrading the Taj Mahal, even though its contribution will be limited to assisting the ASI, is bound to invite criticism. No other hotel chain or for that mailer any segments of the industry like travel agents, tour operators, the airlines, has gone public or voiced any dissent. But in private many have said that the Taj Mahal being the numero uno of the country's attractions; its preservation and upgradation should be a national effort in which not only the tourism industry but all sections of the corporate world should come together. Perhaps, a way can be found later to associate all those who are keen to help in the preservation of the Taj Mahal.

The only newspaper that has commented on the development is the *Indian Express*. In an editorial entitled Tata Taj, it says, "the big danger in arrangements where responsibilities are shared between principals and agents is that some areas are not clearly assigned and become no one's responsibility." Who, the paper asks, will be the final arbiter on conservation issue in each monument, experts employed by a company or the ASI? Another question raised in the editorial is: What kind of commercial spin-offs will be judged overly obtrusive and exploitative? These are pertinent questions that deserve satisfying answers.

Challenges Loom Large

It was at the 46th annual conference of Pacific Asia Travel Association (PATA) at Beijing in 1997 that global leaders of the hospitality industry heard with awe of China's breakthrough in tourism. Premier Li Peng told the delegates that in 1996, his country had received 53 million foreign visitors, and added with a flourish, "This is not enough; we want more." Four years later, it was Malaysia's turn to surprise the world. At the just concluded 50th anniversary session of PATA in Kuala Lumpur, the prime minister, Dr Mahathir, took credit for the Malaysian miracle. His country, he said, had not only doubled the arrivals from 5.55 million in 1998 to 10.22 million in 2000, but also made Malaysia Asia's second biggest destination after China and Hong Kong. Malaysia's performance is all the more creditable as the country was recovering from the staggering effects of the currency meltdown.

Malaysia's dynamic tourism minister, Sheikh Fadzir, in a chat with EH&C, readily shared the strategy he had adopted to recover the lost ground as well as to increase arrivals substantially. The first thing he addressed was the over-emphasis on promotional activities in the western markets which were producing marginal growth. Instead, he made hefty increases in promotional expenditure in the neighbouring countries. India, he said, was an excellent example of the success of this new strategy. Indian arrivals were barely crawling up. From a low of 15,000 in 1991, the figure had reached only 45,000 in 1999. But the million dollars spent in India on promotion during 2000 brought 1,45,000 Indian visitors during the year. He is hopeful of doubling this figure in 2001. "I will stop being aggressive in the Indian market when their number crosses the million mark," he added. And with the phenomenal increase in Indian outbound, the Malaysian dream of luring a million Indians does not seem far-fetched.

The 60-strong Indian delegation at Kuala Lumpur must have taken note of Malaysia's effective strategy in increasing tourist inflows, but their more urgent worry is how to make PATA 2002 – to be held in New Delhi – as great a success. There is no lack of skills in organising a conference of 1,000 or 1,500 delegates. We have an abundance of resources in presenting colour and pageant. Our reservoir of dance, music, cuisine, even medicine, includes great assets. Our five-star hotels are as good as anywhere else. But our airports, roads, hygiene and the way taxi drivers try to fleece tourists can be really off-putting. The thoughts uppermost in the minds of the Indian delegation were on these challenges and whether something could be done in the 12 months we have for the PATA meet.

Tourism minister Ananth Kumar, who was able to make it to Kuala Lumpur for the delivery of the customary invitation to PATA to come to India, seemed quite confident. He assured the delegates of a 'sea change' in India by the time they come here. "I am here to invite you on behalf of a billion people of India," he told them. "Ours is a vibrant and contemporary destination, one country and a thousand worlds ... our economy is opening up ... we are even opening our skies and we welcome 100 per cent direct investment." He spoke of the country's successive wins in the Miss World and Miss Universe contests and also of stride in IT. "I am happy to tell you," he said, "that we are a superpower in beauty and IT," much to the delight of the audience.

The mandatory India Evening, a privilege given to hosts for the following year's PATA, was a grand success, Kitchens of India, put together by a dozen chefs from the four leading hotels chains, served the best of Indian delicacies from the country's four corners. Classy dance performances were presented by Kerala tourism, which had brought a team of 32 artistes to give the delegates a taste of what to expect in India.

Earlier, at the closing ceremony, director-general Atul Sinha signed the formal contract with PATA for the 2002 conference, while tourism secretary M P Bezbaruah, who presided over the Kuala Lumpur meet, handed the baton over to his successor, John Standard of New Zealand, who will chair the New Delhi conference.

India's Ram Kohli, who has been heading PATA's prestigious Industry Committee, has been elected secretary-treasurer for 2001-02. Another feather in India's cap was the PATA gold award for the best training programming given to Amadeus India, whose young managing director, Ankur Bhatia, received it at a glittering programme hosted by National Geographic.

2
World is Coming

Slovakia Eyeing India

There is little to cheer the travel industry about possibilities of a revival of the inbound market. It is generally felt that the adverse impact of the series of setbacks since 9/11, the advisories being the latest, will take quite a while to wear off. Hardly any recovery is expected in the coming winter season. Hoteliers and tour operators seem resigned to live with the current situation and are trying hard to find some compensation in domestic tourism which certainly has picked up. Any significant recovery they say may come with the 2003-04 season and that too if effective marketing strategies are adopted.

The outbound scene, however, presents a totally different picture. True, there has been a decline of up to 15 per cent in travel to north America, particularly the United States, thanks largely to the stricter visa regimes now in place. This has been compensated by larger inflows into Europe and Asia. According to Arjun Sharma former COO of the Kuoni-acquired Sita Travels, and now managing director Select Hotels, there has been no let up in the growth of Indian outbound in spite of 9/11 and traffic has been growing at a significantly high rate of 15-20 per cent. This growth, he says, has been fuelled by the high domestic airfares; it is cheaper to take a fully paid holiday abroad than just pay the airfare between Delhi and Goa or Delhi and Chennai. Small wonder that Dubai, Thailand, Malaysia, and Sri Lanka have capitalised this advantage. In Europe, where London and Geneva continue to be preferred destinations, an Indian can take (an affordable) tour of six to eight countries for Rs one lakh. In this scenario, it is not at all surprising that many more destinations, particularly in Europe – have started looking at India as a source market knowing full well that Indians are also reputed to be big spenders.

The latest to eye this country is the Slovak Republic in eastern Europe with history and culture as attractive as in any other part of that continent.

And, as is a common practice with countries looking for more tourists, the spade work for opening up the market is being done by diplomats.

The Slovak ambassador Ladislav Volko who has spent two and half years in the Indian capital, is apart from being a successful diplomat, a renowned poet and film historian as well as president of the Slovak-India Society in his country's capital, Bratislava. He has been quietly meeting travel industry representatives and travel journalists to spread the word about Slovakia's tourist attractions. He reminded this writer that Bratislava was for two hundred years capital of the Hungarian part of the Austro-Hungarian Empire. Slovakia was part of Czechoslovakia until 1993 when it broke away to become an independent republic.

Describing Slovakia as a "small country with a big heart," Volko says it is multi-faceted and enchanting, possessing a rich cultural and historical patrimony with several sites protected by UNESCO as part of the world heritage.

Among them is the picturesque mining town of Banska Stiavnica, the Spis Castle and other buildings in its neighbourhood and folk architecture in Vikolinec. It has scores of museums, theatre, palaces, churches and cathedrals, some made only of wood.

"We do not have the spa," he says, "but we have mini Himalayas and plenty of scenic beauty." There are two aspects of Slovakia which he says would be of special interest to Indian visitors. One is its food, dominated largely by the Hungarian culinary arts and pretty close to India tastes. Goulash and chicken papri ka (locally called paprikas) are a prayer answered for Indian taste-buds. And, Hungarian wines have their own of pride of place among European competitors. The other is spas for which Slovakia is particularly famous for. The ambassador says located in picturesque surroundings in small towns, the spas are a bargain at US $100-120 per day all inclusive, accommodation (in star hotels), food, medicine and even therapy.

He concedes that there are no direct air services between India and Slovakia but is quick with a graphic description; of how it takes him just ten hours from his home in the Diplomatic Enclave to Vienna and on to Bratislava (by road) courtesy Austrian Airlines which has four weekly services. In any case quick connections are available from all major airports in Europe.

Volko says he is interested in promoting travel from both sides and would be happy to assist the travel industry to promote India in Slovakia. Even though on a limited scale, young Slovaks have been taking long holidays in India. Apart from the lure of India's great monuments and temples, he says, there is a growning interest among his people in the country's spirituality.

Is the industry ready to pick up the lead offered by the Slovak ambassador?

Spanish Thought

The Spanish dignitary, Antoni Subira I Claus, a minister in the Catlonia region said his country's success in tourism – it is the second largest destination in the world after France – came from a conscious effort to develop tourism infrastructure as an integral part of general economic development. He recalled that Spain had shut itself up from the rest of the world for nearly 400 years. But, when it decided to open up its economy in the 50s, it adopted a policy of development across the board including tourism. Governments, he said, can certainly foster tourism but the private sector has to play its part. In order to foster tourism, development of tourism infrastructure should be as an integral part of general economic development The World Economic Forum and the Confederation of Indian Industries (CII) come together every year for an India economic Summit in the Capital, an event looked forward to by all segments of the economy. The summit reviews the country's performance in the last 12 months and throws light on what the future holds. The gathering is addressed by the prime minister and several of his cabinet colleagues. Summit 2000 ended on November 28, 2000, and one of the financial newspapers said that it concluded with the 'same old demands for improving infrastructure facilities, speeding up of the economic reforms process as also cutting down on bureaucratic hurdles'.

CII's national tourism committee, headed by Ravi Bhoothalingam, president, Oberoi Group, in a thoughtful move organised a 75-minute mini summit on this sector on the last day of the main India Summit. The panel consisted of the tourism minister of a Spanish province and leaders of the Indian industry – Pradip Madhavji, TAAI president, R K Krishna Kumar, MD, Taj Group, Yogesh Chandra, the newly appointed secretary general of WTTC's India chapter and Mohan Khanna, additional DC tourism. Although participants lauded the CII initiative in putting the focus on tourism while an international gathering was taking a look at the Indian economy, some lamented that at the main summit tourism was not even mentioned.

Presentations by the panelists were on famliar lines. Yogesh Chandra who kicked off the discussion said tourism is not making any headway for lack of priority and absence of coordination between the various official agencies. The marketing effort too was flawed, he said. The Taj Group chief spoke at length about the need for building a competitive advantage for India which could be achieved only through a 'collective, intelligent effort by the industry as a whole'. He saw a glimmer of hope in this direction in the recent formation of the Experience India Society in which both the government and the private sector are contributing mone and expertise for effective promotion of India overseas.

Pradip Madhavji picked on finance minister Yashwant Sinha's stress, in his address to the main summit, on employment linked growth and diversifying the export base. He pointed out that in both areas tourism offered an unlimited potential. With less than two and a half million foreign visitors, the tourism sector employs 17 million people. And, what better avenue of diversifying exports than tourism, he asked. He felt that tourism had as much claims as IT did to be the government's blue eyed boy. Madhavji would like the government to promote the slogan 'Think of India, think of Tourism'.

The Spanish dignitary, Antoni Subira I Claus, said his country's success in tourism - it is the second largest destination in the world after France - came from a conscious effort to develop tourism infrastructure as an integral part of general economic development. He recalled that Spain had shut itself up from the rest of the world for nearly 400 years. But, when it decided to open up its economy in the 50's, it adopted a policy of development across the board including tourism. Governments, he said, can certainly foster tourism but the private sector has to play its part.

Mohan Khanna readily conceded the government's limitation in giving a push to tourism but pointed out that liberalisation did offer enormous opportunities to other players, the reference was to the private sectors, to make their contribution. The government had, he said addressed some of the more urgent issues including the pressure on air seat capacity. In the last few months as many as 34 bilaterals had been signed and more were on the anvil. This was, however, quickly countered by Subhash Goyal, the IATO president, who was part of the audience. He said more signing of bilaterals did not make more seats available. These bilaterals had to be converted into commercial agreements with the national carrier. According to Goyal, Air India had not concluded a single such agreement so far.

A casual remark by the Spanish minister that differential rates for foreigners and citizens visiting monuments would be 'unthinkable' in his country as such a practice would be against the law of the land, led to a heated, discussion on ASI's recent hike in entry fees. IATO's general secretary, Major Murli Dhar was ready with a survey reflecting the resentment of foreign visitors over what he called the abrupt and arbitrary increase in fees. A young lady executive in corporate finance, Caninder Gill advised the government...not to 'buckle under' – protests; pointing out that Indians travelling abroad were also being charged hefty entry fees. Khanna did hint that the various departments of tourism and culture were working out some solution but this did not satisfy the IATO functionaries.

The issues of air seats and entry fees, it seems, will at the remain center stage for quite some time.

Look Towards Hong Kong

The PATA 2000, Pacific Asia Travel Association's first annual conference in the new millennium scheduled to be held in Hong Kong (April 30-May 3), has special significance for India as the country's tourism secretary, M P Bezbaruah will be inducted as this year's president of the association. PATA meets have on occasion drawn as many as 1,800 participants including leading lights of the hospitality industry representing both, government and private sectors, airlines, hotels, travel agents, tour operators, transporters, exhibition organisers and experts in such fields as technology, sustainable development, environmental protection as well as safety and security. Organisers of the Hong Kong gathering, Hong Kong Tourist Association (HKTA) are confident that at least 1,500 delegates will attend in spite of the fact that the city did not have the usual three-year lead time for preparations. Hong Kong was the chosen venue after a last-minute withdrawal by Indonesia following the Asian crisis. HKTA's executive director, Amy Chan told EH&C in an exclusive interview that Hong Kong's confidence to attract large numbers of participants flowed from the city's track record of organising major events as well as other challenges facing the industry.

She said PATA 2000 will be "addressing the revolutionary changes that are redefining our industry. The special emphasis is on the Pacific, the growing markets of China and India and tourism activity along the Pacific Rim".

Commending India's efforts in tourism development, Chan said that with Bezbaruah presiding over the conference she expected a larger-than-usual Indian delegation to come to Hong Kong. Obviously, India's tourism chief will avail of the opportunity to promote the country within the limits of his role as president of an international association. He and his colleagues in the tourism ministry as well as industry leaders will be closely studying the organising skills of their Hong Kong counterparts as India is going to be host to the PATA 2002 conference which is coming to New Delhi after almost a quarter of a century. The last time PATA met in this country was 1978, then considered a huge success. With so much competition in Southeast Asia both in terms of price and quality of service, India will face a major challenge in the coming years to increase its share of overseas arrivals.

Thus, it will have much at stake at the 2002 conference, preparations for which must begin in right earnest now. Amy Chan even hinted that India might organise a spectacular evening in Hong Kong for starters. Tourism-wise the last three years have been bad both for India and Hong Kong but for different reasons, though the impact of the Asian crisis was common to both. The handover of the city to China created fears and uncertainties among travellers and arrivals took a nose dive with hotel occupancies going down by as much as thirty per cent while in India the factors were political uncertainties and frequent elections in addition to the slowdown of the economy. Hong Kong is now on the sure road to recovery with occupancies touching 85-90 per cent and arrivals back to nearly 11 million, the pre-handover level. But yields from tourism are still low as hotels have not reverted to the earlier high tariffs. Besides, there has been a shift in tourist profiles. A lot more visitors from the mainland are adding to the numbers and tourist expenditures are not picking up.

A bright spot in Hong Kong's recovery, according to Amy Chan, has been the Indian market. A ten per cent increase witnessed in 1999 was the highest from any country.

HKTA considers India as an important emerging market and "efforts and resources will be concentrated on New Delhi and Mumbai as bulk of the traffic is from these cities". Overall, 11.4 million tourists are expected in 2000, but the focus would be on improving yield and longer stays.

Indian planners and promoters should be interested in looking at HKTA's future plans listed by Amy Chan in the interview: consolidate and enhance Hong Kong's position as the pre-eminent international and cosmopolitan city in Asia; the preferred aviation gateway to Asia Pacific and mainland China and as the entertainment, media and events capital of the region; greater utilisation of consumer research in the market place; greater individualisation to regional marketing and promotions to appreciate changing consumer needs; changing source markets and increasing regional cooperation, innovative multimedia marketing for consumers and trade. The destination's pull will be built around such key products as family-oriented attractions and activities like international cuisine, Chinese and western heritage performing arts, culture and events, green tourism outdoors and nature and cruise ship port.

Amy Chan's, and for that matter HKTA's, sights are clear – by 2005, Hong Kong will have its own Disneyland and by 2010, Hong Kong will be able to take its place as the events capital of Asia. Indian delegates to PATA 2000 will have many opportunities to see for themselves that Hong Kong's tourism industry is on the right track. There is much that India can learn from Hong Kong's focused planning and determined implementation of policies and from the spirit of unity among the various segments of the industry.

Not Just Strengthening Bilateral Relations

State visits by presidents and prime ministers have gone much beyond the mandatory 'strengthening of bilateral relations'. They have become instruments of developing trade, commerce and cultural ties on a fast track. But, the president of Brazil, Luiz Inacio Lula de Silva, who was chief guest at the Republic Day parade in the capital on January 26, went a step ahead in the process. Considering that both India and Brazil which are poised to emerge as strong economic powers, one in South America and the other in South Asia, it was not surprising to see president Lula's entourage include government and industry leaders from trade, IT and even space programmes.

What was surprising was that he also brought along his tourism minister, Walfrido Mares Guia, who in turn was accompanied by the chiefs of international relations of the newly created tourism ministry as well as films department of the ministry of culture, Pedro Wendler and Jom Tob Azulay. And FICCI, the oldest apex body of Indian industry moved into ensure a wide ranging interface for the Latin American guests with the hospitality sector through a joint meeting of its tourism and civil aviation committees.

Specially invited to this interactive session with the Brazilian tourism delegation were India's tourism secretary, Rathi Vinay Jha, TAAI president, Balbir Mayal, and IATO chief, Subhash Goyal who also happens to be co-chairperson of FICCI's aviation committee. Playing hosts were FICCI secretary general, Amit Mitra, and tourism committee chairman, Lalit Suri, hoteliers and MP, and a large country valued tourism not only for its employment potential but also because it is an industry of peace and an effective instrument of integrating cultures.

His introduction to the tourism scene in his country showed a lot of similarities with India. As developing nations both look to tourism as a mean of economic advancement and both have not so far done well in this sector. Brazil's international arrivals last year were less than five million (compared to India's 2.7 million) was behind big league players like France and Spain, or China and Malaysia.

Only a few thousand tourists visit Brazil from India and so is the case in the reverse direction. The minister and Rathi Vinay Jha agreed that there is little awareness of tourist attractions of each other. The high cost of travel and the absence of direct air links has not helped either. Both agreed that now is the right time to initiate steps to facilitate travel between the two countries. They decided that the first step will be exchange of tourism delegations backed by promotional campaigns. The second is airlinks.

At present travel to Brazil is via the United States or a wee bit shorter route through Portugal. Tour operators suggested that flights via South Africa would not only be less expensive but also take much less time. Perhaps a code sharing arrangement could be worked out.

In a chat with this writer, the Brazilian minister said that an India-Brazil-South Africa Dialogue Forum set up in June last year during the Cancun meet of the World Trade Organisation, would be entrusted with the task of putting together a code-sharing arrangement among the national carriers of the three countries – Air India, Varig and South African Airways.

The inclusion of a representative of the film industry in the Brazilian delegation was seen by participants in the FICCI discussions as the homework done by the Latin American team before coming to India. Jom Tob Azulay was aware of the Indian film industry's insatiable urge to shoot abroad. But, what he proposed to the FICCI audience was Brazil's desire for joint production of films in both countries. He planned to have detailed discussions with India's ministry of information and broadcasting and leaders of Bollywood.

Walfrido Guia's introduction to the tourism scene in his country must have been of great interest to our own hospitality industry representatives especially the department of tourism functionaries. He spoke of an ambitious five point programme for a push to tourism. The programme is to be completed in three years, that is, by 2007, and, he said he is confident it will be achieved.

The first objective is to create 1.2 million jobs in the tourism sector. Second, develop at least three new tourist destinations in each of the states (much like India Brazil has 37 states). Third, double tourist arrivals to nine million. Fourth, more than double foreign exchange earnings from tourism to US $8 billion. And, finally to increase domestic air travellers from the present 35 million (the Indian figure is 11 million) to 65 million.

Interestingly, India's 10th plan which ends around the same year also has a target of 5.6 million foreign tourists with the same aim of doubling the present figure. Hopefully, both Brazil and India will succeed in achieving them.

Malaysia Impression

In its media briefings, DoT, the department of tourism, has been talking of efforts to meet the challenges, thrown up by the events of September 11. One initiative, if it can be called so, was to adopt a 'Look East' policy by strengthening promotions in Asia, which offers a vast potential for India but which the established markets in the West managed its keep in the second place. A report in the *Indian Express*, however, brings out how the 'Look East' policy is handicapped by the absence of senior functionaries in the India tourist offices in the region. For instance, the newspaper points out, "The thrust in policy is rendered useless as the tourist offices in the crucial capitals of Sydney and Tokyo remain headless." Both cities, it adds, have had no regional directors for the past one year and there is no sign of an appointment as yet as the selection process is still on.

While procedural hassles make sad reading for those who wish to see tourism grow, it is interesting to know-how our neighbours in Asia are going full speed ahead in securing a share of the burgeoning outbound market of India. Many of the, notably Sri Lanka, Thailand, Singapore, even Australia, have been actively promoting their destinations with attractive packages in the last three months. Sri Lanka has been offering an unmatchable bargain: a three night/four days holiday for just Rs 10,500 per person with airfare and hotel room thrown in. And, the Island Republic's high commissioner personally meets the travel trade and media to create an awareness of the package. But, if there is a prize for an Asian nation for the best promotion in India, it would easily go to Malaysia. The country hosted 46,537 Indian visitors in 1999, a figure that jumped 1,32,127 in 2000 (an increase of 183.9 per cent). In the first nine months of the current year the growth has been of the order of 16.4 per cent. This is not at all surprising considering that Malaysia is the only country in Asia, other than China and Hong Kong, which receives more than ten million foreign tourists. This speaks volumes for the country's promotional strategies because the magic figure was crossed in 2000 with a 28.9 per cent increase over the previous year.

Marketing itself as 'Malaysia Truly Asia' it has successfully projected the country as a peaceful multiracial society with a fair reservoir of history, culture and infrastructure as good as any developed nation. Tourism Malaysia, a joint private-public sector board that is charged with promoting the destination, has judiciously spent its resources on a mix of advertising (with a significant use of the electronic media), fam tours and road shows in source markets. The road shows are generally headed by the tourism minister Sheikh Fadzir, a familiar figure in international trade events and popular with the Indian travel trade.

The latest Malaysian Tourism road show in India was led by Mirza Mohammed Taiyab, a director with the tourism board as the minister was busy travelling through Europe. The road show usually comprises tourism officials, tour operators and Malaysian Airline executives. But, the 30 strong delegation that Taiyab brought with him had an unusual fashion team of a choreographer, two designers and eight models including Tan Su Wei (Miss Malaysia 2000). The road show, "With a graceful fashion statement to present the latest trends and designs from Malaysia," as the Malaysian tourism director pointed out, "is a novel way to attract and entice the Indian market." This time around, the road show was taken to, apart from Delhi to Chennai, Hyderabad, Bangalore and Mumbai.

Conscious of the fact that in spite of attempts to streamline the visa regime there are still complaints of delays and arbitrary refusals, a senior official of the immigrant department accompanied the delegation.

The official, Abdul Wahab, who seemed to have done his home work, had a few sops to offer to the tour operators who listed their complaints before him. After assuring them that his department is "very India friendly" he said that several relaxations have been introduced exclusively for Indians. Only an Indian citizen can get a visa to visit a relation. Also, only for Indian business persons the minimum age requirement has been reduced from 30 to 25 years. And, this applies to all nations, the transit pass for stop over visitors, will now be available for five days instead of three at present.

An example of how industry segments work together was given by a senior Malaysian Airline executive, Moor Amiruddin. Buy an MAS ticket, he said, and stay free for three nights in a hotel from a wide choice in a dozen or so destinations in the country. Two persons have to travel together to be able to avail of the offer.

Isn't it surprising that our own hoteliers, tour operators and international and domestic carriers have not come up with any joint packages ?

'Malaysia Truly Asia' Dazzles Delegates at PATA's Golden Jubilee Meet

The strong Indian presence of more than 70 industry leaders and travel journalists at the golden jubilee conference of PATA, the Pacific Asia Travel Association, in the Malaysian capital Kuala Lumpur, signified the country's desire to put its best foot forward when the world's largest hospitality body returns to Delhi for its next annual meeting in 2002 after a lapse of nearly a quarter of a century. It is not just the quality and extent of tourism infrastructure that Malaysia has put together (its new international airport in the capital would match the best in Europe) but it is also the 'welcome' skills that the industry has equipped itself with that would certainly amaze the Indian delegates. That Malaysia is a tourism success story thanks to the priority the sector has enjoyed on the national agenda, and the excellent public-private sector cooperation, comes out loud and clear from a cursory glance at the tourism scene. It was not surprising that the Malaysian prime minister, Dr Mahathir Mohammad, was the chief guest at the inaugural ceremony marked by a spectacular show of colour and pageant certifying that Malaysia is truly Asia.

Addressing the 1,400-odd participants, industry leaders from around the world in the state-of-the-art international convention centre, Putra, in the heart of the capital, the prime minister shared with them yet another breakthrough. Malaysia has achieved after its leap frog in the early 90s in tourism arrivals. During 2000, he told delegates that Malaysia had crossed the 10 million mark, emerging as Asia's number two destination after China and Hong Kong. Not a small achievement considering that Malaysia, along with the rest of south-east Asia, had suffered terribly after the currency melt-down just four years ago. Dr Mohammad said, foreign exchange earnings from tourism, now the second largest earner, have come to almost $5 billion. Malaysia, he said, will now position itself as a value for money destination. His dynamic tourism minister, Shaikh Fadzir, no stranger to India where he has led several promotional shows, pointed out that the country now has the infrastructure to absorb even a much larger inflow of visitors.

Dr Mohammad lauded the role of tourism in strengthening the world's economy and opening up fresh opportunities to larger employment, but warned that both the government and the industry have a responsibility to ensure equitable and sustainable tourism. While the positives outweighed the negatives, care had to be taken to preserve the environment. He emphasised that quality interaction was a tourism credo and added that 'even in a knowledge-based economy, the human touch is a key factor'.

Both the prime minister and Sheikh Fadzir referred to distorted media coverage in the international press and referred specifically to an isolated local incident being blown up as a racial clash. Shaikh Fadzir said, "We are creating one Malaysian nation (out of Malays, Chinese and Indians) as a meeting of rivers and ripples were bound to occur from time to time during the course of this great experiment in social engineering." Delegates could witness throughout the three days of the conference, especially in the cultural events, the sincerity of the tourism minister's claims, as racial harmony was so patently projected in all that was showcased for the benefit of delegates.

India had its own moments of glory at this historic PATA meet. Tourism secretary Bezbaruah, the second Indian to be elected chairman of PATA, presided over the Kuala Lumpur session. In his address he recalled Aurobindo's dream 'for the resurgence and liberation of the peoples of Asia' and said he is happy that Malaysia is at the forefront of the Asian economic resurgence. He also said that Indian settlers in Malaysia had contributed generously to the country's growth. "Because India and Malaysia have always been together in the old as well as the new Asian dream, I hope by the time PATA meets next year in Delhi Malaysia would be a major contributor to our growth."

The India evening being hosted on the last day of the conference is a much looked forward to event as an invitation to PATA 2002, and tourism minister Ananth Kumar will personally extend the invitation. D G Atul Sinha and his PATA India chapter team, responsible for next year's PATA conference, has been making note of the minute details of the organisational aspect of a gathering of this dimension. They surely have a daunting task ahead of them, India's infrastructure being what it is.

Chinese Way

Tourism minister Jagmohan has, in his post-September Eleventh utterances, been urging the industry to concentrate on apart from the domestic market to the vast potential among our Asian neighbours. Countries like China, Taiwan, Japan, South Korea, Thailand, Indonesia and even Australia could be good source markets. Promoting India overseas being primarily the responsibility of the department of tourism (DoT) the minister has lost no time in visiting some of these markets. He went to Japan last month and as these lines are written he has just completed a visit to China. And, within a few hours of his return home he left for London to attend the World Travel Mart, among the largest hospitality industry events held annually in the British capital. It is here that he will gather expert opinions on the impact of the sad events in the United States and how the rest of the world is adjusting itself to the new challenges. Hopefully, he will be sharing the feedback with media persons when he returns to Delhi.

Jagmohan's interface in Beijing with the government and industry leaders is likely to have a profound effect on him because of the spectacular success of that country in tourism. It is worth repeating that when China decided in 1978 in favour of "reforms and opening up," India and its northern neighbour both were on par in terms of foreign arrivals – 75,000. In a little over two decades since then, China has leapfrogged to 27.04 million foreign visitors (in 1999) while India is struggling with just 2.50 million tourists from abroad. In this period Chinese arrivals have jumped 3,505 per cent and India's 230 per cent.

The Chinese breakthrough was facilitated by the leadership's decision to make tourism an integral part of the economic reforms with a sizable share of the (hassle-free) foreign direct investments (FDIs). Whether it was airport, highways, hotels restaurants, shopping malls, entertainment/ cultural centres, the needs of tourism were as important as any other sector. Planners have of course made the maximum use of history and culture as the main draw card for tourists but they have gone a step further and created tourist attractions of a world class where non-existed before. The window of the world at Shehnzen, show-piece of China's economic advancement, with its miniature replicas of planet earth's best known tourist attractions (including those gifted by nature like the Grand Canyon) backed by numerous fun and entertainment centres, is a striking example of innovation. China culture villages, where the fifty-odd national minorities project their way of life in every detail, considerably enhance visitor experience. An imperial palace garden in ruins in Beijing has been replicated to its full glory in another upcoming business city.

What would have impressed Jagmohan most is the fact that tourism is an important part of the national agenda and figures prominently in China's five year plans. And, the Tenth Plan (2001-05) launched this year has clear goals for tourism. In the last year of the plan, the number of foreign tourists will reach 34.5 million and foreign exchange earnings are estimated at US $2 billion. China has already moved up the global ladder as a tourist destination to the fifth position.

Our own tenth plan is being finalised for launch in 2002 and some encouraging signals have already emanated from Yojana Bhawan. N K Singh, a senior member of the Planing Commission has already promised that the allocation for tourism will be 'much larger' than before. The Commission's deputy chairman, K C Pant in his address to the chief ministers and state tourism ministers conference at the end of October has, however, pointed out that "the key (to success) is policy coordination and clarity of objectives. It is not only plan funds that will make it happen but also determined policy initiatives that encourage the growth of this sector and boost private investment". He did conform that the National Development Council has approved the growth strategy of the tenth plan in which "tourism has been explicitly identified as the activity which has the greatest potential for stimulating a number of labour intensive sectors."

Jagmohan's reputation as a doer, the friendly response from the Planning Commission and the promise of the national tourism policy (with an action plan attached to it) being in place before the end of the year by Prime Minister Vajpayee, do add up the hope for tourism even in the atmosphere of gloom caused by terrorism.

How Canada does it

Many years ago this writer, on a visit to Ottawa, asked a tourism department functionary if Canada had any plans to attract more visitors from India. "No" he said categorically, adding, "we are quite happy with the numbers that come here on their own to visit friends and relations." But things seem to have changed considerably in the two decades since that conversation.

Canada is the latest destination that is making a serious effort for a share of the fast growing Indian outbound traffic. And, the way the country is going about its job should be of great interest to India's tourism planners and promoters. Recognising that lack of direct flights and visa hassles are the biggest stumbling blocks in the way of attracting tourists, the Canadian government and industry have swung into action to address these challenges first (Both Air-India and Air Canada had quite some time ago stopped the services between the two countries).

Fortuitously not just one but two Canadian airlines – Canada 3000 and Air Canada – have decided to link the two countries not only with direct flights but also non-stop service using the Polar route. On its part, the Canadian High Commission has streamlined its visa procedures, daunting even at the best times. Gone is the limit of 70 tokens issues everyday for those queuing up through the night, and, anyone with a US visa on his/her passport can use the 'drop box' facility. Application forms too have been simplifies. The High Commission's dynamic commercial counsellor, Bill Johnston has in the run up to the inauguration of air services in October been addressing groups of travel industry representatives and media persons, creating awareness of Canada's attractions.

Using the new and easier accessibility peg he will tell you, "Now is the time for Canadians and Indians to reach out to each other; Toronto and Delhi are only 12 hours away." That is the time a Canada 3000 flight will take to reach Delhi cutting the net flying hours (not counting the stop over in London) by four hours. This airline will have three services a week, two from Toronto and one from Vancouver in Canada's west coast. The Vancouver operation will take two extra hours in the air.

Air Canada on the other hand will have four flights a week but all from Vancouver. Both will be using the most modern Airbus A340 which has 300 seats in a two-class configuration, business and economy. Johnston is confident that the two carriers will achieve reasonably good load factors in both directions especially where leisure seekers are concerned. He bases this on the view that Canada and India have complementary weathers. When it is bitterly cold in his country, India offers warmer climes and when it gets too hot in India, Canada has its summer. He hastens to add, however, that he would only be supplementing the main promotional efforts to be launched by the Canadian Tourism Commission which will coincide with the introduction of the air services. Apart from tour operators and media persons who will travel on the inaugural flights, road shows are planned for Delhi, Mumbai, Chennai and Bangalore. Indian TV celebrities will be taken on a tour of Canada and their experiences will be beamed on Indian channels. Festival Canada is slated towards the end of the year. The Tourism Commission is also hoping to get a slot in the golden celebrations of TAAI in Mumbai in September.

Johnston is not waiting for the Tourism Commission to give him data on the India potential. He has it all on this table. Less than 70,000 Indians visited Canada during 2000, most of the VFRs and a few who added Niagara Falls to their US tour or the handful who took the Alaska cruise. The target, he says, is to take the figure to 1,00,000 in the next 12 months and to double the current figure by 2003. Unlike most of his counterparts in Indian missions abroad he is quite knowledgeable about his country's tourist attractions and fairly enthusiastic about promoting them.

Says he, "Indians will find Canada a fascinating destination stretching 8,000 km across from east to west with as many as 40 language groups among its citizens." From scenic beauty to modern comforts, entertainment, shopping, international cuisines, a cultural experience in the French speaking Quebec province, the adventure in the Rocky Mountains, skiing, golf and cruises on the Alaska coast, Canada has virtually everything today's traveller wants. Vancouver, he tells you with a justified sense of pride, is on top of the world's four best livable cities followed by Venice, Zurich and Sydney. And, as a further sop he tells you, the Canadian dollar is less expensive (by about 16 per cent) than the US dollar and that makes his country cheaper than its big southern neighbour, so popular with Indians.

Although it is obvious that the two way traffic that the Canadians are talking about would largely be the NRIs who would be using the new air services, hopefully our department of tourism and tour operators would also seize the opportunity to lure more Canadian tourists to come to India. Johnston says the High Commission and for that matter the Tourism Commission would be happy to lend a helping hand. Last year only 83,000 Canadians visited India most of them ethnic.

Sri Lanka Looks Beyond

Sri Lanka's tourism effort has been firmly focused on projecting complete safety in the tourist areas. This endeavour has been bolstered by prospects of a ceasefire with the LTTE, being brokered by Norwegian emissaries. The country has thought out strategies to reposition its tourism operations and set itself new goals and targets. Besides, it is empowering the private sector to take on more responsibility in managing tourism activities and even planning a private sector-led tourism promotion board to undertake destination promotion. Observers of the international tourism scene have been watching with interest the quick recovery made by several Asian destinations which suffered major setbacks in the fallout of the currency meltdown. Hong Kong was the first to return to its boomtime arrivals of 11 million-plus in less than three years of the economic crisis, which, in its case, was aggravated by the 'handover' of the territory to China. Thailand, which too retrieved the lost ground pretty fast, has been surprised by its own performance. It had projected a visitor count of 8.8 million in 2000 but the actual arrivals exceeded 9.5 million. Malaysia's spectacular success, already reported in this column, has few precedents. In just two years, 1999 and 2000, the country not only wiped off the losses of the currency crisis but also forged ahead to cross the 10 million arrivals mark, emerging as Asia's second top destination after China and Hong Kong. A common thread linking the three success stories is too well-known but can bear repetition: political will, public-private sector partnership and effective marketing.

While South-East Asia had made rapid strides in tourism, the south Asian nations are still struggling to put their act together, though some of the smaller countries have major initiatives in place. Sri Lanka is one example. In spite of an image problem, thanks to the disturbed conditions in the northern part of the island, the country's tourism effort has been quite steadfastly focused on projecting complete safety in the tourist areas. And, with prospects of a ceasefire with the LTTE, being brokered by Norwegian emissaries, Sri Lanka Tourism has launched a well-thought out campaign with the theme 'Beyond the conflict'. Tourism minister Lakshman Kiriella told this writer, "We have now begun to look beyond our problems and are focusing on scenario planning for times of peace." He added, "We have undertaken strategies to reposition our tourism operations. We have set ourselves new goals and targets. We are empowering our private sector to take on more responsibility in managing tourism activities and are taking action to set up a private sector-led tourism promotion board to undertake our destination promotion functions."

The Sri Lanka Minister, making a strong plea for regional cooperation, said, "We believe that all other destinations around us are our allies and partners. For example, there are synergies we can work on to promote tourism that combines Maldives with Sri Lanka; India with Sri Lanka; Bangladesh with Sri Lanka and Nepal with Sri Lanka, besides several other combinations."

Within a week of this conversation in Colombo, the Sri Lankan minister was in India heading a delegation of tourism officials and industry representatives to, as he said, 'revive the tourist flows of the earlier years' in both directions. Marketing wizard Benton de Alwis, a familiar figure on the international travel scene, is the new chairman of Sri Lanka tourism, and like his minister, is upbeat about the future. "We are determined," he told EH&C, "to move into the win-win mode." And they will do everything to develop the potential of the northern and eastern parts of the island also, he added. The effort to change the image of the destinations, he said, will also address the need to attract upmarket and affluent visitors and move away from being known as an 'all inclusive' destination. The new marketing strategy will project Sri Lanka as not only a beach country but also a place where one can enjoy 'nature, culture and adventure'.

At the recent PATA mart in Singapore, the Sri Lanka tourism chairman said, "We were able to project our eco-tourism products also. Not only that, we are also going to promote Ayurveda, a legacy we share with India." The market for this segment, he said, is very large. He also spoke of the new role of the reconstituted tourism board. In the 60s, the board was expected to provide leadership to the industry which, he said, has since matured. Now, the board will be a catalyst and facilitator assisting the industry to take on more and more responsibilities.

De Alwis said India will figure largely in the new promotional campaign. The present figure of 40,000 arrivals was not only too low but could easily be tripled. He conceded that potential travellers in India were not aware of the shopping opportunities in Sri Lanka, nor of the entertainment facilities, including casinos. Conferences and the honeymoon market are the other segments that the campaign will target.

The Sri Lankan minister shared with *Express Hotelier and Caterer* the good news that Air Lanka, which was part privatised just three years ago – Emirates picked up 40 per cent of the equity – is now in good health. New aircraft and better in-flight services have given the airline (since rechristened Sri Lankan Air) a competitive edge in the region.

Hopefully, our own department of tourism and the travel industry will see some merit in the Sri Lankan initiatives.

Marketing Tourism in India

A crying need of Indian tourism along with promotion of awareness and build up of infrastructure is the right marketing set up and strategy. On earlier occasions too attempts had been made for a proper orientation of overseas marketing. The annual meeting of the director of tourist offices abroad is an exercise in pursuance of this policy. There have also been attempts to assess market potential through country-specific surveys.

Not long ago, five such country-specific surveys were directed. But, the results have not been shared with either the industry or with the public. So much so, one is not sure whether the promised surveys were in fact carried out. But, even at that time it was not made clear what kind of strategy was to he adopted, While this is history, the enlistment of a World Tourism Organisation (WTO) consultant for a revamp of the overseas structure and strategy has engendered hopes of worthwhile action.

The consultant, John Blamey, has been assigned to India as part of a technical assistance mission on tourism marketing with special emphasis on overseas offices. Blamey has handled similar assignments in China, Jamaica, Pakistan and Belize. Even in India, it is not his first assignment. Two years ago he came here to draw up the marketing part of a Master Plan for Andamans and Nicobar.

He is full-time associate of the London-based consulting firm, Pannell Kerr Forster Associates. According to Blamey, one key rule of the book is that there must be one common central theme in Indian promotion in all markets with variations to suit local requirements, and a concerted PR effort must back up marketing.

Blamey's visit coincided with the overseas marketing conference in the capital and the state tourism ministers meet which should give him a proper appraisal of what is needed at home and abroad. At home, the obvious critical requirement is adequacy of infrastructure and abroad effective promotion oriented to different markets and interests.

The overseas meet was also attended by representatives of different segments of the travel trade. But surprisingly there was little interaction. They came, heard for a while, and left. Only a very few tourism loyalists stayed on through the entire proceedings. A sidelight arising from their presence was a short exchange of views on the 'Visit India Year' slated for 1999-2000.

One mandate given by the conference to the participants was to make the year a great success. But, it was left to an industry veteran to point out that with barely six months left, the lead period was too short. In his view it would be better if the following year, i.e., 2000-01 was chosen for the event. An alternative suggestion was to have observance of both years as 'See India Year' and 'Visit India Year'. What difference the terminological distinction will make for the preparatory effort was not spelt out.

The overseas tourism directors finalised at the end of the conference, according to an official release, recommendations more of a general nature. For instance, they were told that they have to be result oriented, they should be cost effective, explore new markets, coordinate with trade and industry and airlines, all of which added up to saying 'be good'.

The pet proposition of tourism minister, Madan Lal Khurana, that there should be focus on NRIs found specific mention among the recommendations. It was also suggested that the impact of marketing should be continuously evaluated and that there should be an effective mechanism for supplementing the monthly exchange of letters between the DG Tourism and the regional directors.

Quite a few of the other suggestions were far beyond the purview of regional directors of tourism, if they are to end at the conference. While it is possible for tourist officers to promote more charter flights, they have little say in the proposal for permitting about 60 foreign carriers to start operations to India. Nor have they any say in Indian Airlines operating additional flights to Leh, Varanasi, Udaipur and Aurangabad. Also, liberalisation of the visa regime is not within their reach.

All these proposals, valid as they are, require intervention at a much higher level. In fact, the right forum would be the Minister's Group set up by the Prime Minister recently. It is fair for the regional directors to show concern and raise these issues but it is for the government at the highest level to take action. Hiring of a professional PR agency has again been raised but hopefully some action will be taken this time.

In the circumstances, the recommendations of the WTO consultant related to the deliberations could help revamp both, the structure and strategy of overseas marketing.

Two-way Passage

The presence of the ambassador of Lebanon, Jean G Daniel at the launch by minister Jagmohan of the website of the Indian Heritage Hotels Association of India, highlighted the growing involvement of diplomats in promoting tourism. Chatting with industry representatives and media persons, the Lebanese emissary recalled West Asia's great tourism days until the 60s when Beirut was by far the most popular stop over on flights connecting Europe and Asia. He is looking forward to the day when Beirut will once again be full of visitors and "many of them from India."

The travel industry has watched with considerable interest the personal interest taken by ambassadors of countries who look on India as a burgeoning market. The Sri Lankan high commissioner has been interacting with the trade and the media with the island Republic's unmatched offer of 'buy one package and take one free' at regular intervals. The Malaysian high commissioner has been leading his country's road shows with presentations and fashion shows. In the latest promotion he did the unusual thing of bringing along a senior functionary of the immigration department from Kuala Lumpur to sort out on the spot visa hassles Indian tour operators were facing. Switzerland which claims a significant measure of success in its Indian effort also has its ambassador at the forefront. He surprised media persons when he said his country had not suffered any decline in Indian arrivals in spite of September 11. Apart from the conventional road shows, Switzerland is now turning to more innovative promotions. A few weeks ago, ambassador Walter Gyger organised a prestigious sports event in the capital – Swiss Polo Cup – alongwith performance of Swiss folk music by the famous Appezeller Women's Band, playing violin, double bass and dulcimer. The French ambassador, apart from the interface with the travel industry, has been adopting a more subtle approach. He sponsors Indian music concerts and Indian fashion shows.

The latest to enter the Indian tourism scene is the Tunisian ambassador, Elyes Kasri, who recently took up his assignment in Delhi. He hastens to tell you that he is keen to see a two-way movement of visitors between India and Tunisia which at the moment is barely into four figures in each direction. Tunisia, with a population of ten million, hosts five million tourists annually earning US $2 billion in foreign exchange, a success story. Kasri explains that tourist traffic to his country is almost entirely from Europe and north America. And, Tunisia has for quite some time been keen on attracting visitors from Asia, what with emerging markets like China and

India as well as other countries in the Pacific. Absence of direct flights from the region has also come in the way of build up tourist traffic. Air Tunis, the national carrier, says the ambassador, is being expanded. Of course, there will be more flights to the west also but, there will be special emphasis on opening the Asia-Pacific routes. A direct flight between Delhi and Tunis is on the cards, but to begin with the Tunisian carrier might go in for code-sharing with Air-India and depend for the time being on connecting flights. Subhash Goyal's Stic Travels has already been appointed GSA for Air Tunis.

Ambassador Kasri has already met Jagmohan and started a dialogue on developing a framework for tourism exchange. The two countries already have a bilateral agreement on tourism and what he has suggested is participation by both countries in the trade events and organisation of FAM tours for travel agents and travel journalists. A delegation of the National Tourism Board is due to visit India in March when an action plan for joint promotion will be drawn up. In September, tourism minister Mondher Znaidi will be visiting this country to participate in ITTM where Tunisia will be showcased. He will also be holding talks with the Indian government including the tourism and aviation ministries. He would explore the possibilities of Indian investments in the tourism sector in Tunisia. On its part, Kasri says, India could benefit from the Tunisian expertise in attracting western tourists as well as work out joint packages as an extension to India. He points out that Tunisia has the biggest share of the tourist market on the Mediterranean rim. Visitors sunbathe, dive, sail and fish along the 1,300 km long coastline and popular beach resorts include Tabarka, Hammamet, Sousse and Jerba. Punic and Roman archaeological sites in Carthage are a big draw as are masterpieces of Arab-Islamic architecture like the Great Mosque of Kairouan. Besides, ambassador Kasri says with justified pride, Tunisia is the Muslim world's most liberal society with a pride of place for women.

Tourism is a virgin field for both India and Tunisia with a vast potential waiting to be tapped. Hopefully, our ambassadors abroad can also spare a thought for tourism.

Today Berlin, Tomorrow...

A confident India flush with a 15 per cent increase in arrivals in 2003, participated in a big way at ITB Berlin, the Mecca of the world tourism buyer-seller meet. A 150 strong delegation, led by tourism secretary Rathi Vinay Jha, representing travel agencies, tour operators, hoteliers, airlines, tourism departments from a dozen states, was among the over 10,000 exhibitors from 179 countries that made it to this year's greatest travel trade show on earth in the German capital.

What made the Indian effort look more earnest was the presence of tourism ministers from Uttaranchal and Kerala, senior officials of the central department of tourism (DoT) including Amitabh Kant, joint secretary Rashmi Verma and Giriraj Kushwaha, regional director tourist office in Europe. Among the senior industry leaders were Ram Kohli of Creative Travels who is president designate of PATA 2005, Radha Bhatia, Amadeus, Subhash Goyal, president IATO, Ashwini Kakkar, head of Thomas Cook, Vivek Nair, Leela group's vice-chairman and FHRAI chairman, Anil Goyal of Indian Airlines, Arjun Sharma of Select Hotels and T Balakrishnan, tourism secretary Kerala. Apart from the major chains like the Taj, Oberoi and ITC, the Casino group under its new brandname of cghearth, the Kairali Ayurveda Group and stand-alone hotels like Delhi's Imperial were also represented.

For the first time the Express Group's Business Publication Division made a representation on its Travel World – the India International Tourism Forum slated for February 2005. And, another first for India at ITB was the release by Rathi Vinay Jha of MICE India QI, a follow up to the launch of MICE India 2004 Guide at WTM in November last. The MICE guide published by Worldroom India Limited seeks to buttress the government's efforts to increase India's share of this segment especially in view of the finance minister's announcement in his mini budget of plans to build four convention centres of international standards at Mumbai, Delhi, Goa and Jaipur. QI puts the spotlight on the northern region with special emphasis on Kashmir as an upcoming MICE destination.

The various booths in the India pavilion and those outside it were busy with meetings and negotiations much of the time reflecting the revived interest in Destination India. It was not only tour operators who were visiting and negotiating with their Indian counterparts but also international travel journalists and TV crews looking for what was new from the Indian sub-continent. Live dances by Indian artistes and mehendi demos attracted large numbers of visitors and photographers. The press conference addressed by Rathi Vinay Jha attracted a record number of media persons. Among the questions asked were those on aviation policies and adequacy of medical assistance in remote areas. The India Evening at the newly commissioned Marriott was attended by over 250 leading travel industry celebrities and scribes. This column in the curtain raiser on ITB had expressed the hope that the Indian participants would come back with bags full of orders. Most of them confirmed that this indeed was the case.

ITB is not all buying and selling. The occasion is used to gather global experts on travel, tourism and aviation to exchange views on trends, issues and challenges. On hand this time were the secretary general and his deputy from the World Tourism Organisation (a UN affiliate) Francisco Frangialli and Edward de Villiers, president of the World Travel and Tourism Council (WTTC) Jean-Claude Baumgarten and the PATA chief executive Peter de Jong.

The conclave at ITB virtually coincided with the terrorist strike in Madrid, and at the premiere seminar, the WTO chief Frangialli had a hard time explaining why no advisory had been issued in the wake of the Madrid bombing. A journalist and travel analyst Imtiaz Muqbil asked if this was not double standards. All that Frangialli could say was that WTO has been pleading with nations that issue advisories to be specific about particular areas that are disturbed instead of banning a whole country and that the affected destination's views should also be taken into account. The same question was put to Rathi Vinay Jha at her press conference. "There are," he said, "enough instances of such double standards. But we can only take up the issue through diplomatic channels".

Interestingly one of the speakers invited from India to a discussion on new trends in tourism and civil aviation was M P Bezbaruah, former tourism secretary. He made two important points: the benefits of recovery are not, at least in the short run, evenly spread; those destinations which are alive and responsive to the trends and take steps for crises management reap benefits. He foresaw large changes in the migration and employment situation in developing countries – stagnation in population in some and emergence of ethnic travel as a major component.

Among the many research papers circulated at ITB's massive press centre (the number of media persons registered was nearly 7,000, a third of them from outside Germany) was one by Karl Wolfgang Menck on Medical Tourism – a new market for developing countries. After detailing the cost differential for treatment in India, Menck predicted that "India can expect to earn around US $1 billion in foreign exchange once the recently implemented programme to promote medical tourism takes effect in 2012".

Another paper by Murray Bailey on outbound markets in Asia says, "India's performance has been less good than its reputation...development is slowed by high airfares, itself linked to a restrictive aviation policy. This hold down capacity growth, which keep up prices."

And for Indian tour operators servicing the German market, the Indian ambassador TCA Rangachari (who was present at the India Press conference) had a good lead: he said that 2005 marks an historic event –

the five hundredth anniversary of the arrival of the first ship load of Germans to India. So, grab the opportunity.

An Incentive

Ray Bloom has the most impeccable credentials to advise Indian tourism officials and the travel trade on the promotion of incentive tourism. This segment, though a thrust area of the National Tourism Policy is still in its infancy with unbounded potential. Bloom is the chairman of EIBTM (The European Incentive and Business Travel and Meetings Exhibition) whose annual event in Geneva figures top in the global tourism calendar.

Every country which wants its tourism to grow successively enlarges its presence at EIBTM in May every year to meet buyers from all over the world. These buyers from the trade and also big corporations look for exotic, different and new destinations where they could hold conferences and provide an incentive holiday to achiever executives or dealers. It has been a phenomenal success in just a decade and as Bloom bows out at the last exhibition of the millennium in another three months, he will have left an organisation whose annual show is a Mecca of the travel trade, going in search of business.

Bloom was in Delhi recently to speak to Indian tour operators, travel agents and government officials on what India could achieve through this specific segment of tourism. His engagement was part of the India Tourism Week programmes. After the coming Geneva show he will return to his home town Brighton in the UK where he experienced the beginnings of his great international tourist movement.

Born into a family of auto dealers very early in life, he realised that organisation of meetings with clients could be enlarged into a world business show encompassing those who want to sell a venue and those who want to go there to meet. He opted to go to Geneva because he found Brighton was not the right place for a pan-European exercise. He proved absolutely right.

The first EIBTM in 1988 drew 450 exhibitors using a space of 3,000 metres. Last year, there were 2,224 exhibiting companies from more than 100 countries and they occupied a floor space of 13,500 sq metres. The break up of visitors who came to discuss business with them was incentive houses 29 per cent; corporate executives 28 per cent; association executives 12 per cent; professional conference organises 12 per cent; travel agents out-bound 10 per cent and PR and promotion agencies nine per cent.

A far larger organisation than his own. Reeds Exhibitions, has since bought over EIBTM but the new owners persuaded him to continue until the end of the century. Because of his astounding contribution to this specific area he has been a trustee of SITE (Society of Incentive Travel Executives) comprising leading associations in the world of incentive travels well as MPI (Meetings Professionals International), which has 17,000 members.

When such a person speaks, the trade and the other agencies concerned eagerly looking forward for a breakthrough in a despondent situation, will necessarily heed his words. He told them, "you may rest assured that in my international travels I am a permanent ambassador for your country. You must cooperate as partners to ensure that a large scale diplomatic initiative to promote India for incentives is carried out in all appropriate target markets."

What are his prescriptions for India to seek a bigger share of this market. At present, it has far too minuscule a share of world conventions, conferences and incentive travel. And that is where the money is. First, India should pursue persistent promotion among top decision-makers to dispel several misgivings about this country and invite them for on-site inspection.

EIBTM, he reminded the audience, had already sent one such FAM tour to India and a second one is now on the drawing board. Secondly, Indian conference organisers should have greater interface with SITE and MPI, they should go out of their way to understand and appreciate how conferences and incentive tours can be better handled. Thirdly, incentive travel can become a seriously large scale and valuable market only if the perceptions of those involved are positive and confident.

A problem according to him is that too few incentive travel specialists have visited India or got to know its facilities. At the same time, India's advantage is that as a destination this country has everything, particularly for the tourist who has seen everywhere else and may be jaded and cynical. As a host country, India must remember what specialist incentive agencies look for are creativity, quality and reliability.

Incidentally, Veena Sanyal, a former tourism official based in Geneva and long associated with EIBTM, imbibing its ideals and concepts, has represented the organisation in this country. She is confident of record Indian attendance at this year's event.

Mileage from Clinton

In the March 20 issue of *Express Hotelier and Caterer*, the weekly's lead story on the likely impact of President Bill Clinton's visit on tourism observed, "We can really cash in on the dignitary's visit and make our country attractive on the world map if the ministry of tourism takes adequate and timely measures." This column, in the same issue, had also referred to 'deep stirrings' in the hospitality industry and reported the fact that the ministry did wake up, even though a little late, to the relevance of the event and went into consultations with a cross-section of the travel trade. With no briefing from any quarter, one has to turn to *The Hindu*, the only national daily to think of tourism's expectations from Clinton. In a report titled 'Tourism ministry takes a holiday' the newspaper's tourism writer Gargi Paras, referring to the large number of print and TV journalists accompanying the American President, says, "it appears that the tourism department and the industry are not geared to take advantage of the situation. The minister for tourism, Anant Kumar, given additional charge recently, was away most of last week in Berlin, and senior officials of the ministry are also abroad attending tourism conferences."

And so, in their absence, adds the newspaper report, "it was left to the additional director general to convene a hurried meeting of tour operators and hoteliers to discuss what best could be done to convert this opportunity into tourist arrivals from the US. They decided to institute an award for the best photograph taken of Clinton against a tourist spot monument during his visit. That's it. That's about all the tourism department and the industry could think of." This calls for little comment.

While there is no denying that the tourism sector did not avail of the opportunity presented by 200 odd American and other journalists' presence to persuade at least some of them to look at India's tourism product, all is not lost yet. Promotion built around events like Clinton's visit can only aim at long-term results, provided there is a sustained follow up effort. The tourism ministry, leading hotel chains and travel agencies could strengthen their promotional efforts overseas, particularly in the United States which is already India's second largest source market both in leisure and business segments as well as the burgeoning number of NRI achievers.

It must be conceded that even though there was no specific input from the tourism industry, global media giants like CNN, BBC and other, international channels did bring India into homes in North America, Europe and even Asia. The focus on Delhi, Agra and Jaipur must have served as a good reminder of India's golden triangle, Mumbai as the country's commercial centre and the emerging Hyderabad as Cyberabad. Most economic writers agree that the visit will certainly lead to faster growth in trade and investments, which for tourism converts itself into business traffic, the upmarket traveller we (especially hotels) are keen to lure.

Hotels must be the happiest segment as they benefited most from the visit, both in terms of business (whole hotels were commandered for the American President and his huge entourage) as well as the media coverage they have received both at home and abroad. It is not surprising that the lion's share went to Welcomgroup whose flagship Maurya Sheraton in the Capital has repeatedly been the preferred hotel for presidents, prime ministers and celebrities like Bill Gates.

Sharing the honours was the Oberoi group which played host to President Clinton at its super-deluxe Raj Vilas resort in Jaipur and The Oberoi in Mumbai. Both properties received extensive coverage in the run-up to the visit.

Maurya Sheraton was Clinton's first public exposure. ITC chairman, Yogi Deveshwar and ITC Hotels managing director, Habib Rehman were the first to welcome him in the hotel lobby while Clinton, breaking the security cordon, shook hands with everyone from the bell boy to the executives present. A little later he walked into the famed Dum Pukht restaurant for a reception in his honour by Ambassador Celeste and for dinner he chose the internationally known Bukhara where, presumably on the recommendation of his daughter (who with Hillary had sampled the Bukhara food on an earlier visit), he savoured the Sikandri Raan and kulfi. ITDC's Ashoka, yesteryears' favourite with heads of State was the venue for Prime Minister Vajpayee's banquet, and lived up to its reputation for great food.

Carpet trader Manzoor Wangnoo managed to sell a few rare pieces to the American President, as also have him sip Kashmiri tea at his showroom in Maurya's shopping arcade. That should be some promotion for Indian carpets. A few members of the Clinton entourage even managed to slip away to the Kairali Ayurvedic Centre near Qutub Minar for its renowned Ayurvedic herbal massage.

The one question industry watchers are asking is: Will the travel industry pick up from where Clinton left?

Consolidating Brand India at ITB

The International Tourism Bourse, better known as ITB Berlin is the travel world's greatest show on earth. Every year in March this historic German city attracts several thousand industry leaders from more than a 100 countries eager to increase their share of the tourism boom. This year the dates are March 11-16, 2004. An upbeat India, with a 15 per cent increase in arrivals and a hefty 23 per cent rise in foreign exchange earnings in 2003, and keen to ensure that its growth momentum is kept up, will attempt to make its presence felt. More than a 100 destination management specialists, hoteliers, national carriers and tourism functionaries will be operating out of the Indian pavilion in the Asian section of ITB, while a score will have separate individual booths. But for the general elections, minister Jagmohan would have led the Indian contingent. In his absence, secretary Rathi Vinay Jha would be the head, assisted by joint secretary and chairman, ITDC, Amitabh Kant, and additional director general, Rashmi Verma. The regional director, India tourist office, Frankfurt and heads of other overseas offices will also be there to give a helping hand.

Rashmi Verma told *Express Hotelier and Caterer* that this year's theme for the India Pavilion is 'Faces of India' showcasing the country's unity in diversity. Significantly, she said, the stirrings among the states about the realisation that tourism is a powerful instrument of economic development, will be reflected in the fact that a dozen of them – virtually half of the country will be represented in Berlin. All four southern states – Kerala, Karnataka, Tamil Nadu and Andhra Pradesh which have cornered a bigger share of international flow into the country, will be promoting the new destinations that are becoming popular as well as the new infrastructure in terms of hotels and airports. Among the northern states, Rajasthan, UP and the newly created Uttaranchal and Chhattisgarh, along with Jammu and Kashmir will be presenting their attractions. Assam from the North-east and the union territory of Delhi will bring up the rear.

And, to bring into focus the vast potential that India offers in the MICE segment, ITB will witness the release of India 2004 MICE QI, a quarterly follow up to the successful launch of India 2004 Worldroom MICE Guide at WTM in November last year. It is a publication of Worldroom India, a subsidiary of the London-based company, which operates the international travel portal www.worldroom.com. QI promotes states in northern India, their immense potential as ideal destinations for incentive travel and pilgrim tourism in addition to being ideal venues for business meetings. There is a special section on Jammu and Kashmir with its endless natural beauty, being promoted as an upcoming MICE destination. This is the first time that such an invaluable data has been compiled to target industry professionals in specific countries that comprise the most important potential MICE source markets for each destination in India.

Another segment that the Indian promoters will project at ITB is rail travel by steam engines for which there is a fast growing demand in the west particularly in Europe. According to one estimate the UK earns as much as 60 million pounds from steam trains. Ashwani Lohani, former chairman and MD of ITDC, and founder member of the Indian Steam

Railway Society (ISRC) told this writer that 15 or 20 fixed steam services had the potential of attracting 1,00,000 visitors from abroad. For starters, he said, the first regular steam train between Delhi Cantt and Farrukh Nagar will be launched in April and possibly a little later, a second one from Udaipur to Chittorgarh. Among other proposals the ISRC is working on is to convert to steam the Palace On Wheels along its 75 km run from Delhi to Rewari. It is also planned to convert all the five hill railways to steam.

Hopefully, the Indian contingent will return with a bag full of orders.

Singapore Sings for India

It is not always that destination management companies, more popularly known as tour operators, live up to their names. But we have to grant this to Creative Travels for having thought of getting the prestigious Singapore Press Club to make an out of the country visit to India. That a senior economic writer on the Island's *The Straits Times*, Narendra Aggarwal, has been the Club's honorary secretary for 15 years may have helped. The significance of the development lies in its timing when India is emerging as a major power. And, at the head of the 35 strong delegation comprising hard core journalists from the print and electronic media (not travel writers as is the norm in promoting travel), was Cheong Yip Seng, editor in chief of *The Straits Times*, who has been at the helm of the internationally renowned newspaper since 1987 and has spent 41 years of his 60 years in the profession, So impressed and overwhelmed he was by the melange of colours and joyous revelry at the Holi celebrations at the home of Creative Travels' chief Ram Kohli that he told this writer, "This is incredible; we did not know one can have so much fun in India" (Kohli was away to Pakistan as part of an Indian travel industry delegation organised by TAAI and PATA, and son Rohit played host to the Singaporeans).

The Straits Times' editor in chief's spontaneous reaction has a story behind it. He has been to a great part of the world but this is his first visit to India. He said candidly, "India was never on the radar screen of Singaporeans, except for ethnic Indians. And, so the rest of the world was a preferred destination (for us) like east Asia (Hong Kong, Taiwan, China and Australia) and to a lesser extent Europe and the United States." But now, he added, things have changed, India has been in the news in recent years. Hardly a day goes by in Singapore without some report about the impact India is making globally. Be it information technology, business process outsourcing or the opening up of India to foreign investments, they have all attracted a lot of attention. Tourism, Cheong Yip Seng said, is an important economic factor and, "our tourism board has established its presence in India this year to generate greater traffic both ways. So, you will see more Singaporeans coming to India. Sadly, no more than 50,000 Singaporeans visit India against 3,00,000 Indians who travel to the Island. Asked what India should do to promote itself in destinations like Singapore, *The Straits Times* editor in chief said, "India is not just about IT and BPO; it has 5000-year-old rich cultural assets which are not known abroad. You should create greater awareness." He went on to say, "Participating in Holi, I am ashamed to admit that I'have come to know of it for the first time. And, it is such an important part of life in India. For a media person not to know about it is a reflection of how little India is known to potential visitors from abroad." A more liberal aviation policy, he said, will also help Indian tourism.

Narendra Aggarwal gave some interesting facts about the Singapore Press Club. Established in the '70s, its founding chairman, Wee Kim Wee rose to be Singapore's president for two terms. It could be the only Press Club, which permits full membership to non-citizens who can also hold office. He cities his own example of his long tenure as honorary secretary. The Club has a policy of one trip abroad every year and so far, the countries chosen have been Mauritius, South Africa, Turkey, Romania, Philippines, Sri Lanka, and New Zealand, "We treat each visit as a goodwill mission to create friendship and understanding," he said. In India, they spent nine days, four in the capital and the rest in Agra and Jaipur. Among their engagements in Delhi was a meeting with President Dr APJ Kalam at Rashtrapati Bhawan, a dinner hosted by CII and a reception by the Foreign Correspondents Club and sightseeing which Aggarwal emphasised included a peep into real India. The delegation also visited the 24-hour news channel *Aaj Tak* and *Press Trust of India*.

Aggarwal pointed out that there is neither any sponsorship nor any subsidy for members of the delegation who are all taking time from their jobs and spending their own money. They are under no obligation to go back and promote India through their writings or by word of mouth. But judging by their reactions to Holi celebrations alone as witnessed by this writer it is difficult to see them holding back their pens.

Tourism Industry Needs a Common Voice

Last year a joint pre-budget memorandum was submitted by apex organisations of all the three major segments of the tourism industry – namely hoteliers, tour operators and travel agents – in a show of unity and concern for their shared problems. In the following months there has been talk of concerted action and a collective appeal to the finance minister. It was to demonstrate a new approach for the good of tourism.

While the problems remain, as little was done by the government in response to last year's request, there has been no renewal of the joint exercise on part of the apex organisations. FHRAI struck its own course and submitted its own memorandum without waiting to consult others. It is not clear at the time of writing whether the others presented separately their case for relief. Even so, there are signs of the industry getting its act together pushing its differences behind and it is quite possible that the start of the millennium will usher in a new phase of collective action helping the growth of the sector.

Illustrative of this trend is the accord on all minus points in the dispute between hoteliers and tour operators. It is a happy augury that the voluble IATO president, Subhash Goyal, has written to HAI chief, Habib Rehman, pointing to the futility of a continuing confrontationist approach on either side. He has also accepted the hoteliers' demand on prompt payments within the 30 day limit as well as voucher status on materialised group.

The only lingering issue, which in fact triggered the latest crisis in their relations, TT rates on currency, payments, over which there has been an exchange of ultimatums and hot words, will now be settled across the table within a set time limit of March 31.

The significance of the accord is not so much on resolution of differences between two sides over a matter that is only marginally relevant to tourist arrivals and earnings, as on bringing together different sections of the industry. In fact, it is the absence of unity that prompts different organisations to rush to the government every time there is a dispute.

In this case also, secretary tourism, M P Bezbaruah was called upon to use his persuasive skills. Needless to say such dependence on government on even intra-trade disputes certainly will not contribute to the health of the industry or realisation of its objectives. After all, all these organisations have been wanting the decision-making powers in tourism management to be transferred to a national board with adequate autonomy.

The tendency to seek government intervention at the slightest provocation will only reinforce those forces within the ministry resisting the creation of an autonomous board.

Another instance of the industry coming together, though at the initiative of an international body, WTTC (World Travel and Tourism Council), is for support to a five-year plan of building up awareness on the urgency for meeting the various requirements of the tourism sector.

WTTC president Jean Baumgarten has been able to mobilise the backing of industry leaders like ITC Hotels, the Taj Group and Oberois and Thomas Cook, for what it describes as the 'India Initiative'. A membership drive is on and he is confident that many more will join to make it a representative effort.

Interestingly, the founding members of the India Initiative signed their document at the peak of the hotelier-tour operator acrimony. The WTTC chief was able to get both sides into his fold.

If unity is necessary to create awareness, development of infrastructure and creation of more supportive services, it is equally important for most segments of the industry to stay in business. A recent independent survey by PKF claims that unless hotel managements cut their costs and offer value additions there is little prospect of the occupancy rate going up alarmingly low at present. They can do so only with an integrated programme involving other segments of the trade like travel agents and tour operators.

Similarly, the travel agents and tour operators are equally beleaguered by the impact of technological advances. They also need as much support from hotels and other providers of services. Any value addition by one section is possible to market only with the cooperation of the others.

To return to the budget, pronouncements by the finance minister and other spokesperson of the government leave little room for any big sop for the hospitality industry. It is very unlikely that the demand for scrapping hotel expenditure tax or service tax will be accepted. Nor will the Exim policy provide any relief in respect of imports like liquor, certainly not for 2000.

The industry should share the burden with the other sector in the national interest and focus on priority areas like infrastructure and marketing. It should seek to take advantage of the economic recovery in principal markets and come out with innovative packages and product improvement for profitability in a competitive environment. Of course, unity will remain central to any progress in tourism.

Fun in White Sands

An NRI multinational, Unicorn Holdings, based in the UK and Kenya, is all set to commission a classy resort in India's beach country, Goa. Unicorn is pegging its future to charters at a time when the hospitality industry is yet to recover from the fall out of 9/11. Unicorn Holdings with interests in trading, finance, computers software and telecoms is making a foray into hotels with a resort in Goa and acquisition of an operational hotel in Mombasa now under negotiations.

For its debut in India, Unicorn Holdings has tied up with the fast growing Carlson Hotels with a franchise of its Radisson brand, christened as Radisson White Sands Resort, it will open its doors to guests in December with 110 rooms with 50 more to be added in phase two. The project has cost Rs 100 crore. Briefing news persons at the Capital's Radisson Hotel in the presence of president and MD of Carlson Asia Pacific, Paul Kirwin and chief of Carlson India operations, Bhushan Kachru, Unicorn's executive vice-president, Hari Ravindranath explained how White Sands hoped to get more out of charters as well as domestic travellers. He said Goa has so far been exposed to low spending charters a bulk of which came from the UK. Secondly, while hotels do provide plenty of relaxation, there is little or no fun to be had. White Sands, he claimed, will fill this gap.

On charters, Hari said White Sands will depend more on those from Russia, a fairly new market with a younger crowd of holiday-makers and deep pockets looking for value for money. A major campaign is being launched in Russia and tour operators were being persuaded to include Goa in their offerings. A similar campaign aims at the 30-40 year old executives in our own metro cities has also been released. Spanning 39 acres of beach front in Varca in south Goa, Radisson White Sands Resort was built in a record eleven months from Bhoomi Puja to project completion. For its general manager Unicorn has hired Detlef Meisalein, a German expert who has specialised in commissioning new hotels for over a quarter century including a stint in Goa a decade ago when he was associated with the opening of Ramada. Hari said that in south Goa, White Sands will be the third 'best' hotel after The Leela and Taj Exotica. It is being positioned as a 'fun place'. He added, "It will be the only hotel which is going to talk of fun and life." There will be no formal management infrastructure. The staff will wear jeans and t-shirts. The telephone operator will respond with a 'hi' rather than 'thank you' for calling White Sands. Limousines that transfers guests from and to the airport will play Konkani and Portuguese music. And, within the hotel there will be a choice of three or four channels of World Space Music, satellite based transmission with the clarity of CD level.

Among the activities for guests Hari said there is 4,000 square feet of games area – a bowling alley (Goa's first), computer games, a video game arcade and a separate children's games room, a mini theatre, pool tables and a library of films. Specially trained teams will provide in-house activity from morning till night, a clown or a Mexican amigo to entertain children along with interactive working sessions for those interested in enhancing their culinary skills. Entertainment by artists from Africa like the Masai dancers (thanks to Unicorn's Kenya connection) will be a regular feature. Added Hari, "We want the guest to be a participant and not a spectator. The key is to think like a guest and not a hotelier."

Among other distinguishing features of White Sands are the Beach Bar and the swimming pool. The bar is housed on top of a fishing trawler and the pool is long enough to look like a shore line. And, of course, there will be the health spa, yoga, meditation centre and ayurveda massage. Flavours of India is the speciality restaurant for dinner with many cuisines and Water Falls Cafe will be a 24-hcur dining affair.

Carlson Hotels, a big league player in the travel world, has some 770 hotels and resorts under its belt as well as six cruise-ships. There are more than a dozen Radisson hotels in India. Other brands introduced in this country from the Carlson stable are Country Inns and Suites, Park Plaza and Park Inns. Asia Pacific president and MD, Kirwin says, "The opportunities for growth of our brands in India is immense. Since globally Radisson is the leader in the Hotel industry, we are destined to become a vibrant, and exciting new travel industry powerhouse in the next decade."

White Sands has enough time to live up to its claim of Goa's first fun place.

Sustaining Tourism in a Fragile Environment

The hopes raised by the imminent end to military operations in Afghanistan for revival of tourism have again been dashed by the mounting tension in Indo-Pakistan relations. The recall of the Indian High Commissioner and stoppage of the Samjhauta Express and the Lahore Bus followed by the ban on overflights of each other's national carriers and troop build-up on both sides of the border can only scare travellers away from the sub-continent. No one is yet talking of war, but the fear of it is enough to compel holiday-makers to think of alternative destinations. The incident of the abortive attempt by a single terrorist on an American Airline trans-Atlantic flight has aggravated the fear of flying which has gripped the United States and some other parts of the world. With continuing set backs to any return to normalcy, India's hospitality industry has to brace itself up to more cancellations and low occupancies and concentrate on the domestic market for survival. It is encouraging, however, to learn that New Year destinations like Goa, Rajasthan and Kerala have had a good response to keep the cash registers ticking.

Hopefully, India-Pakistan tensions will reduce in the coming weeks once our neighbour takes strong action against militant groups operating against this country. With little hope for the rest of this tourist season, the tourism industry can and should concentrate on putting its best foot forward in the preparations for the mega travel promotion opportunity that is being offered to India in just 100 days or so – the 51st Pacific Asia Travel Association conference in Delhi.

The good news about the PATA meet is that Bill Clinton, former US president, who has millions of admirers around the world (and who has won the hearts of many Indians during his earlier two visits) will be delivering the keynote address at the valedictory session. For its 50th conference in Kuala Lumpur in April 2001, PATA was able to get Buzz Aldrin, who along with Neil Armstrong, were the first human beings to step on to the moon. But, Bill Clinton who presided over the destiny of the world's only superpower should be a bigger draw card for participation in a global travel gathering of this kind. Both PATA headquarters in Bangkok and the Indian organising committee headed by D G Vinod Duggal are planning for 1,500 registrations including a large domestic contingent.

Considering the international and regional situation even 1,200 delegates would be considered a good show. There is yet another reason for greater delegate turn out. After the events in the United States and the assault on the Indian Parliament, the hospitality industry, the world over has to deal with terrorism as one of its main concerns. It is not known if PATA has included the subject in its agenda specifically, but the challenge of terrorism to tourism is likely to pop up in every discussion around the table or at informal gatherings. Prime Minister Atal Behari Vajpayee, who is expected to inaugurate the conference is bound to share India's concerns with global travel industry leaders.

As mentioned earlier in this year's PATA conferene is 'Tourism – Looking Ahead and Beyond' but the name of the keynote speaker is yet to be announced. But the panel for the first plenary session on 'The changing world and its impact on tourism' is confirmed and will be led by *Time* magazine's editor-at-large, Michael Elliott Richard Neville will be the other speaker. Key trends for the future and main influences is the subject for the second plenary session and the panelists are Clare Chong, chief of the Hong Kong Tourism Board, Lisa Henriques Hughes of the Oxide Nast Traveller, Richard Hartman, Six Continents Hotels and Shapiro Travel Resources chief functionary, Sue Shapiro. Concurrent sessions will address such issue as 'aviation: where to from here?' and, 'global marketing: new world, new challenges'. Two other concurrent sessions will take up 'economic and demographic change in the new world order 1 and, sustainable tourism in a fragile environment'. The third plenary session is devoted to learning from the past to prepare for future success. CNN, BBC and Burson Marsteller have been invited to nominate speakers. The final plenary session is on future HR needs, an area of special interest to India as well. The discussion will be led by Peter Burwash, president Peter Burwash International. The National Geographic Traveller Magazine will be making a multi-media presentation 'South-Southeast' by Steve Me Curry, one of the many side-shows of PATA. At the dosing session where Bill Clinton will be the keynote speaker, the association's current chairman, John Standford will pass on the baton to the new incumbent, Bo W Long. The travel industry will keenly look forward to the war against terrorism and return of normalcy to the sub-continent.

WTO Prescribes 2003 as Year of Total Recovery

The hospitality industry, if one goes by the financial results of almost all chains, is still reeling under the downturn caused by 9/11, the Afghan and Iraq wars, SARS and pressures on the domestic economy. Except for the ITC Group (both ITC Hotels and properties included in the balance sheets of parent ITC Ltd.) which has shown recovery, the others have recorded sizeable decline in profits in the fiscal 2002-03, though there has been an increase in revenues.

The revenue spurt is significant in view of the drop in overseas arrivals; obviously the domestic traveller has made up some of the shortfall of international arrivals, even though with lower yields. All hotels have done well in the last quarter though. Interestingly, the four major chains, Taj, Oberoi, Asian Hotels and ITC have not stopped or slowed down their investments in expansion and the commissioned hotels are in the gestation period. These should in a few years add considerably to the revenue and hopefully to bottomlines, provided, the recovery trends seen in the last quarter are maintained.

The industry's faith in its future as reflected in the massive investments is aptly summed up in the annual report of ITC Ltd. by chairman, Yogi Deveshwar. After outlining tourism's contribution to global economies, he says that, "in the Indian context, growth in the tourism and hotel sector is a sure and fast means of employment generation across a spectrum of skills." "This sector," he adds, "can therefore contribute significantly to the larger national goal of inclusive economic growth." Pointing out that progress in India's immediate neighbourhood brings home this potential, the ITC chairman says, "China currently clocks 31 million arrivals a year, while Malaysia and Thailand have crossed the 10 million milestone. In sharp contrasts India notches barely 2.5 million visitors annually. Just two decades ago China was on par with India with tourist arrivals of 7,50,000 a year".

According to the World Tourism Organisation (WTO) China today has more than 9,50,000 hotel rooms. Beijing by itself has as many rooms as the whole of India – estimated at 80,000. Deveshwar sees, "a growing appreciation of the significance of the tourism and hotel industry in contributing to the important national goals of employment generation and foreign exchange earnings. The government's (read Planning Commission's) ambitious target of attaining 0.62 per cent of world tourism market share by 2007, are reflected in the enabling proposals contained in the Union Budget and the Exim Policy, and the substantial allocation of funds for upgradation of physical infrastructure."

He adds, "tourism is an industry of industries. It will prosper as all-round development take place in the quality and scale of infrastructure. In the context of this potential, India is grossly under-roomed even in comparison with its much smaller neighbouring East Asian countries. Even to service a modest GDP growth of 6 per cent the capacity of hotel rooms in India would need to double over five years."

To come back to the performance of hotel companies, income of ITC Ltd.'s hotel division increased from Rs 162.38 crore to Rs 193.41 crore and profit rose to Rs 10.09 crore from a loss of Rs 0.50 crore. ITC Hotels recorded an increase of Rs 137.78 crore against Rs 129.91 crore. EIH, The Oberoi Group turned in a revenue of Rs 429.38 crore, up from Rs 427.33 crore, but the net profit showed a major dip from Rs 35.56 crore to Rs 15.47 crore. Taj Group's. Indian Hotels Company Ltd. (IHCL) notched up income of Rs 590.84 crore against Rs 538.16 crore (last year's figure does not include revenue from Taj Air Catering) and the net profit came to Rs. 40.48 crore compared with Rs. 80.70, inclusive of air catering. This year's profit also includes a profit before tax of Rs 23.34 crore from the sale to PIEM Hotels of Taj's Pune and Lucknow units. Asian Hotels, which has emerged as a chain with the addition to its New Delhi property, Hyatt Regency hotels in Kolkata and Mumbai is however down from Rs 12.97 crore to Rs 9.63 crore.

The public sector company ITDC's hotel division sans may of its units, which have since been disinvested, earned a revenue of Rs 87.84 crore, up from Rs 74.23 crore and a decline in its losses from the previous year's, Rs 31.43 crore to Rs 11.89 crore. Losses in the corporation's duty free shops are up from Rs 2.66 crore to Rs 7.75 crore.

Thanks to the new format introduced from this year, it is now possible to see first hand, Group turnovers of chains inclusive of their subsidiaries and associate companies. ITC Hotels, for instance had a Group gross income of Rs 175.03 crore if you add the ITCs hotel division, the figure will be Rs 337.41 crore; EIH Rs 479.38 crore and IHCL Rs 894.56 crore. Only time will tell whether WTO's prediction of 2003 as year of recovery comes true.

A Race to Recovery

With SARS in full retreat, a race is now on among southeast Asian tourist destinations to be in the lead for recovery. And, who is best prepared for this role? Thailand, of course. It is this country, which thanks to its innovative strategies took big strides in tourism and became the first 'Asian Tiger' to cross the ten million arrivals mark.

The successful, 'Amazing Thailand' promotion campaign, infrastructural development, connectivity and government – industry partnerships, have been the main factors that has given Thailand an edge. Tourism, until recently has been Thailand's biggest foreign exchange earner, now pushed to second place by electronic goods exports. A fine example of contemporariness of the nation's economic vision.

Although Thailand was not affected by SARS (There were no cases reported within the country), the scare created by the epidemic in other parts of the region took a heavy toll on tourist flows. In the first 15 days of May alone, arrivals fell by as much as 53 per cent. Phuket, famous for its beaches suffered according to the local tourist association president, Tanan Tanphaibul, a loss of business worth US $100 million (An interesting piece of information for Indian planners is that Phuket has 38,000 hotel rooms).

So it is not surprising that Thailand organised a Mega Fam trip in which nearly 350 leading travel agents and media persons from around the world participated. India, though not among the first ten generating markets yet, is considered a fast growing source and this was reflected in the size of the Indian delegation, the second largest after Australia's 94 againt India's 33. But, the largest number of media persons – 14- representing the mainstream newspapers and travel publications from Delhi, Mumbai and Kolkata were from India. After visits to Phuket and Pattaya and other tourist spots, they all converged on Bangkok for a conclave at the capital's elegant Queen Sirikit National Convention Centre.

The dais was occupied by Juthamas Siriwan, the lady governor of the Tourism Authority of Thailand (TAT), Vichit Na Ranong, president, Thai Tourism Council (Apex body of the industry) and the president of Thai International Airways, Kanok Apiradee. Governor Siriwan's message was simple and effective. "The Thai tourism industry would like to convey to your clients that they can come to Thailand and have a perfectly safe and enriching holiday. This is good for your business as well as our tourism industry."

She outlined the various promotions in place, like the 'Thailand Smiles Plus' campaign with hotel package of buy one, get one free. The Thai Airways chief chipped in with his offer of 20,000 free return tickets given in lucky draws on our flight to the Thai capital. A lively question answer session followed. Asked if additional budget had been provided for the recover campaigns, the TAT governor said the government had spared only 500 million Baht as additional funds, but segments of the industry were investing huge amounts, especially Thai Airways. She said new products are being added, which include health and wellness programmes as well as yatching. Siriwan was so upbeat about the future that she said she expected normalcy to be restored by which time she promised tourism in Thailand would have reached new heights.

The Thai Airways president said that in spite of 9/11, the Iraq and Afghanistan wars and even SAES, the airline has stayed afloat and is among the few carriers to expand its fleet. He said Thai Airways had spent a lot of money and effort on devising measures to prevent the recurrence of SARS-like outbreaks. A safety manual based on expensive research carried out by experts for Thai Airways will soon be ready and he announced that his airline will be happy to share this with other airlines.

The most striking aspect of the Mega Fam trip was the spirit of unity in the Thai industry and the rewarding partnership this has brought about with TAT. The Thai Tourism Council is the industry's voice representing all major segments – hotels, travel agencies and airlines -- which has also set for itself the additional role of training and upgrading skills for which it gets some financial assistance from the government. The Indian industry leaders working for a confederation of various associations could benefit from the experience of the Thai Tourism council.

Interestingly, Air India will be completing 50 years of its operations to Bangkok in August 2004. The airline's dynamic country manager, Alka Jayakar, the first lady to occupy the position in this male-dominated sector including all foreign airlines, is busy working on plans for the golden jubilee celebration. The Mega Fam trip also had much to offer India, both industry and government, on how to strengthen out own tourism effort.

No Retreat for Tourism

The state of affairs in the aviation sector – absence of a national policy and the inordinate delay in privatisation of international airports – was top of the agenda of the Srinagar Retreat of WTTC, the World Travel and Tourism Council. Participants, numbering over 70, comprising industry leaders, members of Parliament, editors and experts were eager to hear from the new aviation minister, Rajiv Pratap Rudy what his plans were to get things moving. The minister however cancelled his visit at the last minute much to everyone's disappointment. Planning Commission member N K Singh in his valedictory address said civil aviation had become a case "where vacillation has been invested with an aura of statesmanship". He added that four ministers and five secretaries, each one promising a new policy, have come and gone; The latest minister has set up yet another committee to draft the policy. He also referred to the demand made during the discussions for an open skies policy and said it would be more appropriate to think in terms of an 'open-ended' policy. And, for starters, the unutilised bilaterals could be given to the private carriers like Jet and Sahara. If necessary, such slots could be auctioned, he added. Privatisation of airports, the Planning Commission member said, had been talked about for a decade; it is sad that a unanimous decision taken by the Cabinet five years ago is still to be implemented.

N K Singh also had a word of advice for the department of tourism (DoT) which he said should gear itself up to meet the challenge of utilising the remaining Rs 2,500 crore allocation for the tenth plan in the next four years. He commended the Incredible India campaign but suggested that a more concerted restructuring of DoT's promotional apparatus would be necessary to effectively reposition India in the overseas markets. To the industry leaders he pointed to the tax reliefs in the central budget as well as the concessions offered in some of the states. The industry should assess the impact of these sops on the competitiveness of the Indian package vis-a-vis our neighbours and other markets well in time for the next budget so that the finance ministry could consider if something more could be done for the sector. He showed special concern for the hotel industry's debt burden which had been aggravated by the series of setbacks suffered by tourism. He repeated a suggestion he had made at the earlier Retreats that hotels should come up with a debt-restructuring plan along the lines of what the textile industry had done. He is sure debt-restructuring would facilities greater investment in the hotels segment.

N K Singh also said that there is need for tourism to draw synergy from the various infrastructure projects launched by the government for general development, especially roads and ports. He said as much as Rs 1,00,000 crore is being invested on the Golden Quadrilateral, the North-South and East-West corridor and rural roads. The tourism industry should put its feet together to get the maximum benefits from these investments.

An interesting presentation on the impact of tourism on the economies of the states was made by Jairam Ramesh, AICC secretary. He put his weight behind the idea of bringing tourism into the Concurrent List. The states need to be convinced, he said, that tourism cuts across state boundaries and the Centre alone can ensure massive funding required for its growth. As a concurrent subject the Centre will not only be able to provide resources but also the coordination that is essential for balanced regional growth! Not foreign exchange, he said, but the employment potential will bring the states round to the need for concurrent status for tourism.

WTTC's decision to hold a Retreat in Srinagar, third in the series after Agra and Goa, earned praise from J&K chief minister, Mufti Mohammad Sayeed who said it would strengthen the signals emanating from the state of a return to normalcy. Affirming that tourism has a 'bright tomorrow' in Jammu and Kashmir, the chief minister said his government is keen to expand the infrastructure. Inviting investments he said, "We offer you a single window clearance," When he said he looked for guidance from WTTC, the council president Jean-Claude Baumgarten announced that J&K is now a partner state, an honour it will share with Kerala, Rajasthan and Madhya Pradesh.

The Retreat, held in the first week had as its venue Inter-Continental The Grand Palace overlooking the Dal Lake, once the abode of the Maharaja and recently renovated and expanded by Lalit Suri of Bharat Hotels who now owns and manages the property.

In his inaugural address, Dr Karan Singh supported Srinagar's claim to be an international airport which he said "should attract direct flights from overseas". The Srinagar Retreat will be remembered for WTTC's expression of solidarity with the cause of J&K tourism.

Hot Turkey

The Turkish Airline's resumption of its direct flight to Delhi after a gap of five years, and, the exchange of tourism delegations between Turkey and India has achieved what the initiatives were aimed at – reviving travel between two destinations with abundance of history, culture, cuisine, nature's bounty, unique experiences and a shared vibrant secular democracy. The return visit of the Indian delegation, led by additional director general Rashmi Verma, led to the discovery. Pramod Singla of Services International, who was among the eight tour operators comprising the delegation, and, who has had previous experience of business with Turkey, told this writer that before the restoration of the airlink in September, barely three or four tour operators in Turkey were selling India; their number has now risen to 60.

Another member, Naresh Trehan of Twenty-first Century pointed out that although TURSAB, the Turkish association of travel agencies (Turkiye Seyahat Acentalari Sirligi) which hosted the Indian visit, was concentrating on Indian outbound, he did notice growing interest among Turkish agents for promoting travel to India. He and Singla feel that Bollywood, the golden triangle, Sufi dargahs in Delhi and Ajmer as well as shopping could attract larger numbers of Turks. And, for Indians, both feel Istanbul being as modern as any European city, could be clubbed with new packages covering the neighbouring Greece and even Cyprus.

Rashmi Verma, at a de-briefing session with the TURSAB president Basaran Ulusoy and vice president, Hulya Aslanta (who was part of the Turkish delegation that visited India in April and who also attended the Skal International Conference in Chennai) said the tourism authorities in the two countries have opened the gates to travel. It is now, she said, up to the industry on both sides to takeover. The exchange of delegations was the first step forward and more continuing contacts will go a long way to help the people to discover Turkey and India. She also recalled the active support that the tourism initiatives received from the two countries' diplomatic missions.

The Indian delegation, which spent a week in Turkey, travelled by road extensively over 2,400 km of excellent highways from Istanbul to the capital Ankara, with its imposing memorial to the founder of the Republic, Kemal Ataturk, on to Cappadocia (it has a spectacular open air museum created by volcanic eruptions and human creativity). Also, on the itinerary was Konya haloed by the 13th century Sufi saint, Maulana Rumi, whose shrine is visited by hundreds of thousands of devotees much like the dargah of Hazrat Nizamuddin Aulia in Delhi and of Khwaja Moinuddin Chisti in Ajmer. Cognisant of the great reverence of Indians for Sufism, the tourism chief of Konya, Abdussettar Yarar personally took the Indians around the Rumi shrine explaining its finer points. He also suggested that the international Sufi meet being organised in Konya in 2004 be promoted in India.

The TURSAB presentation to the Indian visitors brought out the impressive gains made by tourism. With only 1.3 million international arrivals in 1980, Turkey last year welcomed 13.24 million foreigners. "Turkish tourism has made remarkable progress over the last two decades," the TURSAB president said, "and tourism is one of the largest and fastest growing sectors of the economy." The number of hotels beds increased in the same period from 55,000 to 3,65,000, making a grand total of 7,15,000 together with those licensed by the local authorities. Since the '90s the

Turkish government and the industry have taken strides in diversifying the tourism product. Apart from sun and sea based holidays, Turkey is promoting eco-tourism and nature based activities like winter sports, culture based activities including faith tourism and a multitude of special interest tours.

A study of the TURSAB set up revealed some interesting facts. It is established by law. Its main aims are 'the development of the travel agency profession in harmony with the country's economy and tourism sector, and protection of professional ethics and solidarity'. A new agency can be established only after approval from the ministry of tourism and it is obliged to become a member of TURSAB. The association came into being in 1972 with 120 members. It now has 4,472 members including branch offices and is the only association of travel agencies in the country.

Hopefully TAAI, IATO and TAFI are listening.

PATA 2002: Gearing up for Success

The tourism industry, especially the official agencies, must have like the rest of the country, heaved a sign of relief that developments over Ayodhya passed away peacefully. The Gujarat riots had already been causing worries about a possible impact on participation in PATA 2002, the mega travel event that this country is hosting in the capital. It is in this context that Ayodhya had assumed importance and with the clouds having drifted away the department of tourism (DoT), the PATA India chapter, co-hosts, with the full backing of all segments of the hospitality industry, are now engaged in last minute efforts to ensure the largest possible attendance. PATA, which is now more than half a century old (its Delhi session is the 51st) has on occasions had as many as 1,500 leaders of airlines, hotels, travel agencies, tour operators, national tourism organisations and experts from around the globe come together for an annual pow vow. Small wonder that nations in search of tourists vie with one another to host PATA because it offers a rare opportunity to showcase their destinations.

India had won the bid for PATA in 1999 and had three years run up period to catch up with infrastructural inadequacies and to remove facilitation hassles as well as to make efforts to attract larger number of delegates. But, four ministers and three DGs did hamper a sustained effort towards a successful PATA conference. One must hasten to add, however, that the current team at the helm of tourism, minister Jagmohan, secretary Rathi Vinay Jha and DG Vinod Duggal, additional DG Mohan Khanna and joint secretary Amitabh Kant ably assisted by Ashok Bhatnagar of PATA chapter have done an excellent job of making up for the lost time. Apart from their own dedicated work, they have been able to secure the willing and enthusiastic cooperation of the industry. In fact, the organising committee headed by DG consists almost entirely of industry veterans like Behram Dumasia, Ram Kohli, Ashok Anantram, Bagini Chopra, Anil Bandhari, Sarabjit Singh and Sanjeet, who have taken on specific responsibilities in areas like airport welcome and transfers, accommodation, protocol, facilitation, special events ground arrangements and so on. Others who have been giving a helping hand include Rajiv Talwar, managing director of Delhi Tourism Corporation, Subhash Goyal, Pawan Khanna, Mandip Soin and M S Manchanda. Delhi chief minister, Shiela Dikshit has been taking personal interest in ensuring that the civic authorities and other agencies ensure that the capital is at its best when the PATA delegates arrive.

As reported earlier in these columns, prime minister Atal Behari Vajpayee will be inaugurating the conference on April 15, and Dr Karan Singh will be delivering a keynote address. PATA's new CEO, Peter de Jong who visited Delhi in January to take a look at the arrangement and went back satisfied, will see his first international meet through. The theme for the fifty-first session is "Tourism – Looking Ahead and Beyond" wide enough to permit discussion on any aspect of the industry. But, it is possible much of the debate would centre around the post-9/11 scenario and how to meet the challenges of global terrorism. A galaxy of speakers is listed. The secretary general of the World Tourism Organisation (WTO) Francisco Frangialli will deliver the valedictory address and those initiating discussions at plenary sessions will indude the editor-at-large of *Time* magazine, Michael Elliott. Other celebrities are: Dr Surin Pitsuwan, former foreign minister of Thailand, Clara Chang, executive director of Hong Kong Tourism Board, Thomas Oliver, CEO Six Continents Hotels, Jeff Hamblin chief executive, British Tourist Authority and Renton de Alwis, chairman, Sri Lanka Tourism.

At the time of writing more than 650 registration had come but the organising committee is hopeful that the delegate count would certainly touch the thousand mark.

On the heels of the PATA conference, another international event is taking place in Delhi – South Asia Travel and Tourism Exchange, which has come to be known as SATTE. Into its 9th year, SATTE which meets, will have several new features. According to coordinator, Navin Berry, there will be a lot more concentration on domestic tourism. Regional movement and inbound will also be in focus. He expects about 500 buyers among whom150 will be from abroad.

And, if Subhash Goyal the new chairperson of ASSOCHAMs tourism and aviation committee, can complete the ground arrangements, he has planned a national convention on aviation and tourism on the eve of the PATA meet where he hopes to present a Vision Document on challenges before tourism and aviation.

Look Ahead Optimistically: Jong

While India joins other nations to celebrate World Tourism Day sponsored by the United Nations affiliate WTO, the World Tourism Organisation on September 25, it has its own National Tourism Day also which is observed on January 25, coinciding with the Republic Day festivities in the capital. Earlier attempts to mark the day with events, a travel trade fair and seminars were last year given up turning the occasion into a brief function at which the national tourism awards are given away along with a foundation day lecture to mark the establishment of the department of tourism way back in 1956.

The highlight of this year's event was the foundation day lecture by the new president and CEO of the Pacific Asia Travel Association (PATA), Peter de Jong, the world's largest body representing both the public and private sectors in the hospitality industry. His theme "PATA's View: Travel Trends for 2002 and Beyond" was most appropriate not only because of the aftermath of September 11 (and in this country's case December 13 also) but also because PATA is holding its 51st annual session in Delhi April 14-18, 2002, with the promise of helping the revival of tourist traffic to India.

Jong came straight to the point – prospects of recovery in the global context – with a message of hope and encouragement. He said, "I think 2002 will be a reasonably good year. Experts predict that the global economy, starting in North America, will start its positive rebound by the second or third quarter." But, he also added a word of caution. "If there are no further security incidents," he said, "pent-up demand in the marketplace will also express itself." He recalled that in 1992, the year after the Gulf War, international tourism grew by 8.3 per cent. And, immediately following the currency melt-down in Asia during 1997 and 1998, arrivals in the region grew by 10.8 per cent in 1999 and 14,7 per cent in 2000. "In both cases, the recovery took place faster than expected. However, he went on to say that the "speed and extent of tourism revival in our region this year will mostly be driven by the security concerns and economic conditions in source markets. The biggest boost we can hope for in 2002 is simply the absence of terrorists attacks. The current stabilisation in Afghanistan is very encouraging."

The PATA chief also shared with the huge gathering that had come to listen to him at the convention hall of Ashok Hotel, the changing trend that have emerged after the Terror Tuesday: growth in short-haul and domestic travel; preference for perceived 'safe heavens'; more late bookings; realignment in marketing spend towards intra regional markets; further corporate price cutting, and more consolidation across all hospitality sectors due to financial controllers looking for economies of scale. According to Jong, hotel trends taking place at the moment include: aggressive marketing campaigns to build brand awareness; heightened customer demand for value; more consumer demand for hassle-free environment; simplification of the billing process; better-in-room telecoms, and, a growing shift towards fashionable boutique hotels marketed as 'cool' to the affluent under 40. Hotels which suffered severe losses from large scale cancellations of the MICE segment 'are writing more rigorous cancellation clauses' to safeguard their interests.

Jong had interesting things to say about another segment of tourist which at least in India has remained largely untapped. "Clever people in tourism," he said, "are also looking more at the young travel sector. And, for good reason". Young travellers benefit the host destinations because, although they spend less per day than the business traveller, they stay longer and often spend their money at small family-run outlets and street vendors. Youth travellers' money generally reaches the pockets of people who really need it. Talking to media persons later Jong said that it was this lack of appreciation of the economic impact of youth tourism that had prevented Indian travel agents from marketing this segment. It should be remembered, he added, that youth travellers are assured repeat visitors.

In his foundations day address Jong also said that his optimism for 2002 came from the two emerging markets, India and China. Outbound from China, he said, has doubled to 10 million in the last five years. India, too, has an equally important role to play in the future of global tourism. Destinations like Australia, Malaysia and Thailand are "wisely investing larger percentage of their marketing budgets in India."

Minister Jagmohan who was chief guest at the tourism day said that in addition to awards for best hotels and forex earnings, there should also be awards for clean cities, a requistie for visitor experience.

Capital Gears up for PATA 2002

Preparation for PATA 2002, to be held in New Delhi and which is expected to bring together some 1,500 decision-makers and professionals in the hospitality industry from around the world, entered the final phase when on February 4, minister Jagmohan, chairman of the National Host Committee presided over a joint meeting with the organising committee, headed by director-general Vinod Duggal. The organising committee consists of a dozen conveners, drawn mostly from the industry, each in charge of responsibility for activities like protocol, airport welcome, transport, accommodation, event management, publicity, PR and pre- and post-conference tours. Their common goal is to ensure that the capital and other places the delegates are likely to visit put their best foot forward and destination India is showcased in the best manner possible, Jagmohan's penchant for a clean environment being central to civic agencies, police, railways and even Delhi's chief minister, Sheila Dikshit, were all there to pledge their cooperation. Dikshit went a step further and gave the assurance that the city, at least those parts of the foreign visitors will be going round and especially all the monuments, will only be spruced up but the Capital will also wear a green look.

There is good news about political support for the event, which the country is hosting after a gap of 24 years (the last PATA conference was held here in 1978). It is now confirmed that prime minister Atal Behari Vajpayee will be inaugurating the meet and Dr Karan Singh is the keynote speaker. There is some bad news though. Former US President, Bill Clinton who had earlier agreed to address the valedictory session, has now dropped out. His participation would have given the PATA conference an added luster and even increased the delegate count. The tourism industry will take this in its stride as it has by now learnt to live with the consequences of the sad events of the past six months. But the Clinton fans in India, and there are quite a large number of them, will certainly be disappointed that he will not be making what would have been his third visit to this country within a short span. The main conference, as planned earlier, will be held at the Ashoka Hotel (which was also the venue in 1978) but the site for the India welcome dinner on the opening day has been shifted from the Kamali Jamali area of the Qutab complex to the Nehru Park besides the Ashoka Hotel. The official reason given is that is will be easier to shift the event inside the hotel in case the weather suddenly packed up.

The Capital's Pragati Maidan which hosts most of the national and international expos will for the first time share limelight in a global tourism meet. Lunches on all three days of the conference will be arranged in Hall No. 11 which is being specially done up for the occasion. Two of these will be glittering affair. At one, PATA Gold Awards, Instituted for excellence in various fields of tourism, are given away. The host this year is the Macau Tourist Board. And, at another the National Geographic Traveller Magazine will make a multimedia presentation, which always draws a full houses.

Two PATA site inspection teams have visited India to take a look at the ground arrangements. The second one which came at the end of January was headed by no less a person than the new president and CEO, Peter de Jong, who according to D G Duggal has gone back happy and fully satisfied with the 'bandobast'. Duggal also announced that the posts and telegraphs department will be issuing a special commemorative stamp on PATA 2002 which will be of special interest to Philatelists.

As mentioned earlier in these columns, the theme for the conference is 'Tourism – Looking Ahead and Beyond' a wide enough subject to cover every aspect of the fallout. There will be considerable interest among all delegates in a panel discussion to be led by the *Time* magazine editor-at-large, Michael Elliot on 'The Changing World and its impact on Tourism'. Lisa Henriques Hughes of the world's best known travel publication, the Condenast Traveller, will team up with professionals like Clara Chong, head of the Hong Kong Tourism Board, Richard Hartman of the Six Continents Hotels and Sue Shapiro chief of Shapiro Travel Resources on 'Key Trends for the Future and Main influence'. Concurrent sessions will take up aviation, which has suffered the most in the wake of the terrorist attacks in the US and the discussion will be 'Where to from Here?'. Sustainable tourism in a fragile environment is the subject for another breakaway session. And, to Indonesia will go the privilege of playing host the last evening as Jakarta is the venue for PATA 2003.

PATA 2002 offers India not only the opportunity to showcase itself at this juncture but also a occasion to learn how the rest of the world is addressing the challenges to tourism.

Conventions and Solutions

Omang Apang is young and earnest about tourism and makes a conscious study of different aspects of the subject which explains why his observations based on supposed feedback from overseas tour operators merits attention. But, what is puzzling is that his remarks, although related to the Indian context, were contrary to the information available with leaders of the industry present at the FHRAI convention in Jaipur. They were startled when the minister of state said that the perception abroad is that India is overpriced.

He addressed a query to the delegates who included all segments of the travel trade: Is the tourist getting value for his money? More puzzling was that the suggestion contained in the query went unchallenged from the dais where the managing director of the country's successful leading otel and president FHRAI, Sushil Gupta was in the chair.

Politeness alone would have prompted Gupta not to contradict the minister. Otherwise, there is little explanation of his silence which he subsequently explained to media persons at the end of the convention. "We have our own way of conveying the ground realities to ministers," he said. Surprisingly, this is not the first time that the tourism ministry has taken this view. Obviously, the ministerial pronouncement is influenced by the views of its advisors among civil servants. Everyone knows some of them share the perception articulated by the minister.

One wonders whether the minister has been told by his advisors that even in these days of depression in southeast Asia, in Phuket the occupancy rate is 75 per cent on a tariff of US $175. In the capital, Delhi, five-star hotels are reportedly selling rooms at US $75-100 when the season is supposed to have begun. The scene in tourist destinations like Agra is dismal where rooms can be had for as little as US $25-30.

If this contradiction could be overlooked the Convention had some good news to convey too. Hopefully, it should signify a trend, for the past one year hoteliers in Delhi have been asking for a relaxation of the luxury tax. The impost has been collected not on the negotiated or rebated rate but on the published rate. At a time when occupancies are down and rates are discounted; the levy has been harsh raising the cost of the package.

The Delhi finance minister, Jagdish Mukhi, announced that the state assembly has adopted an amendment to limit the levy to the actual lull. Only two weeks ago the Andhra Pradesh chief minister, Chandrababu Naidu has promised the travel agents convention that he was ordering an immediate review of his luxury tax on published rates.

Incidentally, luxury tax on live published tariff is levied in states which are in the frontline for tourism development, These include Goa, Karnataka and Tamil Nadu. Hopefully they will follow the example of Delhi.

The FHRAI convention as also the conference of other apex bodies TAAI and IATO have now only one remaining point at issue between the travel trade and the government. And that is tax rationalisation. Some other major problems have been sorted out in the trade's favour by the tourism-friendly government. Appropriately, the Jaipur convention had in the keynote address focused on the tax structure. The point also came up in the interventions.

For the keynote address, the organisers had invited Bernd Chorengel, president, Hyatt International Corporation. His description of India's pull was a copywriters delight. Taking a cue from the economists definition of tourism as a "search for experiences", he said "India offers it all – a lusty gratification of the five senses. From a winter walk by a placid river....

backwater cruises in Kerala... eco-tourism in the north-east... the sublime beaches of Goa... Kashmir, the serene Himalayan 'playground of the gods'... to the verdant golf resorts. Small wonder Hyatt International has plans for developing seven major hotels in India with local and foreign investors.

To come back to taxation. Chorengel suggested, a four point programme: Create tax incentives for the investor, develop tax into incentives to attract key global tourism investors to work in India, provide financial assistance to companies to venture into tourism-related investments, and introduce more rational and less complicated tax structure for the consumer.

Clearly the most informative and absorbing of the business sessions was the one devoted to trends in restaurants when Lalit Nirula of the famed Nirula eateries and Keith Haslam, general manager of the New Delhi Intercontinental, teamed up to peep into the future. Haslam fell the buzz-word for restaurants would be fun and hoteliers would rent out space for restaurants to professionals, while Nirula thought there would be a return to the yesteryears entertainment like cabarets. He also predicted good times for 'dhabas' with hygiene.

As already mentioned, with quite a few problems out of the way in the trade-government talks, now it is for the industry to meet challenges.

IOTO brings good Tidings for Indian Tourism

The Indian Ocean Tourism Organisation (IOTO) has as its rationale both, the economic and political compulsions which have prompted the littoral countries stretching from east Africa to Polynesian islands to Australia to come together to tackle shared problems and strive for shared prosperity.

India obviously has a major role in IOTO's future. At least five of its board members, including Ashok Pradhan, Director General Tourism, Ram Kohli, Founder President, IATO, and S P Dutt, Chief of Inter-Media, are from this country. The IOTO Board met for the first time in India in the second week of February at the invitation of the Department of Tourism. It holds promise of a continued linkage for Indian tourism with expertise available in international bodies.

One of the topics to which IOTO has already addressed is a very much hot issue for Indian tourism. This concerns coastal management and tourism. IOTO, by virtue of its membership that covers the paradise islands of south Pacific and other island tourism centres, has a keen interest in coastal management, IOTO's vision for the region is that every destination will optimise its tourist potential in a sustainable manner for the benefit of all its people.

It has annunciated guidelines for the national planning process and tourism development. It wants integrated planning to manage land development, the shoreline and marine resources keeping in view tourism opportunities. Data evaluation, approval of the needs of individual coastal tourism development, protection of natural coastal resourses, public access to these resources, constructive community review of the benefits of development, definition of clear targets for the success of coastal zonal management, avoidance of conflict, continuous monitoring of environmental impact and introduction of educational programmes for communities and travel related personnel, constitute the agenda that IOTO has set for itself.

Needless to say, every aspect of this programme is pertinent to the Indian situation in the context of environmental challenges as the country has plans for development or more destinations as beach resorts both, on the eastern and western seaboard. Another area that India might profit from the IOTO programme is marketing. One of the very objectives of the organisation is to enhance regional cooperational and understanding in promotional efforts.

IOTO secretary general, Dr Graham Hornell, who for several years directed PATA's PR, envisions marketing the region as a distinct entity. The time may not be far off, he says, when an event like ITB in Berlin will feature an Indian Ocean Hall as an umbrella for presentation of the tourism product from the countries of the region.

IOTO is the brain child of Tunku and Hornell, both of whom had been helping to shape tourism policies at the international level. In setting up IOTO, they have had the support of the Western Australian Tourism Commission, based in Perth, which is also the headquarters of the new organisation. The organisation has had resounding initial success in that most official and non-official agencies of the littoral countries have obtained its membership. Two of the board members are ministers of tourism, one from Madagascar and the other from Seychelles.

Tunku, as head of such an organisation, needs listening when he speaks of the prospects and problems of tourism in India. While he was certain that this country would make a significant breakthrough in the not too distant future, he would like to add a caveat. India needs to improve its accessibility, which in effect means more international airlines should be encouraged to increase their services without too much insistence on reciprocity.

Secondly, the currency meltdown in the southeast Asia has lessons both, to Indian tourism and to the Asian tigers which according to him, should look into the Indian experience for stability. At the same time, India will have to review its cost structures to stay competitive. If this is done, he is certain that his prediction about the future of Indian tourism would certainly materialise.

Buck Upon the Tourist Front

It was in the 90s that travel and tourism emerged as the world's largest economic activity accounting for 11.4 per cent of the global GDP. At the same time, it generated over $3.6 trillion in output with a manpower count of 230 million or 9.4 per cent of worldwide employment. These figures are for the year 1998 and carry the authenticity of World Tourism Organisation (WTO). It estimates that in the next decade, that is by 2010, the industry will generate $8.1 trillion in output or 12.5 per cent of GDP. The share of tourism employment will rise to 10.9 per cent and the number of people working in the sector will go up to 328 million.

With a three-four per cent growth forecast in tourist movement, the number of international travellers is expected to jump from the 1998 figure of 625 million to 700 million in 2000 and close to a billion in 2010. Last year international travellers spent the equivalent of $444 billion, excluding air-fares. This will go up to $500 billion in 2000 and $1,500 in 2010. Capital invested in facilities during the year was of the order of $779 billion; 11.8 per cent of total indirect taxes came from tourism.

Environmental concerns will be a major consideration in future travel decisions and eco-tourism will emerge as a major segment. Safety, both in terms of law and order and in product use will be of equal concern. There will be growing demand for development of man-made attractions that combine tourism activities with entertainment, fun as well as relaxation and outdoor opportunities. Ageing populations in many of the generating markets will revive interest in cultural tourism. As for accommodation, environmentally sound resorts and hotels are going to be preferred as uncontrolled, authentic and natural surroundings vis-a-vis closely controlled, purpose-built and enclosed structures. Local cultures, heritage and customs will dominate hotel and resort design. Incidentally, last year there were almost 9 million hotel beds in the world. China has 7,00,000 rooms, Thailand nearly 2,50,000 and Indonesia 1,87,000 and Malaysia just under 1,00,000. India's latest count is 68,000, the same number as China is said to be adding every year.

That was a peep into the global scene. Now let us look at the forecasts for the area of our immediate interest; South Asia. According to WTO, the region should be hosting 5.7 million tourists in 2000, a figure that should double in 2010. India's current share of the South Asian market is estimated at 52 per cent (2.37 million in 1998). And, if the country can retain its share, then by 2010 India should be reaching the magic figure of 5 million plus arrivals (Something that we should have achieved in 1997 if the target set by Madhavrao Scindia in his action plan of 1992 had been realised). A recent task force assessment, in which the planning commission seems to have found merit for inclusion in the 9th plan targets puts the figure of expected arrivals by 2003 at 3.25 million.

The questions arises whether this country will be able to host even five million overseas visitors by 2010. Our Southeast Asian neighbours crossed this total several years ago and are poised for greater strides in the coming decade. Five million is indeed a modest target and once we move out of the present slow-growth period, it should not be difficult to achieve. Quite apart from the initiatives set in motion by the Vajpayee government to give tourism a push, what will ultimately help put the sector on the fast track is completion of the process of economic reforms. Some of the once-insoluble constraints in the way of tourism growth have started to melt away. Telecommunications and road transport are two shining examples. There is definite progress, even though at a slower pace, in the field of power generation. At least one privately-financed international airport (Kochi) is finally operational and while the national highways authority is getting a grip on the daunting task of building expressways, at least the Delhi-Agra bit has been completed. There has been significant growth in domestic aviation while international carriers are still struggling to come out of the bilateral regime, to make more air seats available for travel to India.

Land and land laws are and will continue to be the biggest hurdle in the growth of accommodation. With the necessary political will, this can be got over by introducing the concept of land banks in various states. Not auctions, but graded lease arrangements as recommended by the Yunus committee, would make hotels more viable. That leaves the issue of the government's role. As in other tourism success countries, this should be limited to regulation and facilitation; promotion and marketing should be handed over to an industry-dominated board. It is equally important that the industry segments themselves come together on a common platform.

Last, but not the least, hopefully the electorate will give the country a stable government committed to tourists as a gift for the new millennium.

Indian Contingent Heads for PATA '99

Over a thousand hospitality industry leaders, including a large contingent from India are headed for Nagoya, Japan to attend the 48th PATA annual conference, the last to be held in this century. Leading the Indian group is DC tourism, Ashok Pradhan. Other participants include Capt C P Krishnan Nair, chairman Leela Hotels, Ram Kohli, Chief of Creative Travel, C S Wclinkar of Everett Travels and Inder Sharma, former PATA international president. A number of Indian media persons are also taking part.

Not surprisingly, the focus of the four day deliberations beginning April 18 will be the challenges of the new millennium. The theme chosen is 'Bridge to the new future: Challenges and opportunities for managers in the 21st century'. Yotaro Kobayashi, chairman Fuji Zcrox, known for his dynamic and articulate presentations will deliver the keynote address.

Indian participants will be keen to learn how various countries are facing up to the pressures on tourism now felt around the globe. 'What is travel worth to Pacific Asia' is a question that will be raised by Ravi K Saligram, president, Holiday Inn brand, Bass Hotels. He will speak on the Value of Asia Pacific: Today vs Yesterday in the first plenary session. Another plenary will seek to find out ways in which destinations, travel agents and suppliers can develop products and generate traffic in conjunction with mega events; panelists will use the 2000 Olympics, World Cup 2002 and 2005 World Exposition as examples.

With the growing popularity of breakout (concurrent) sessions, PATA this year has organised five of them. Global Travel Management will provide a panel discussion on how corporate discipline will affect the inbound market share frcm North America and Europe. Tima Reid, publisher, *Business Travel News*, will be the main speaker. A breakout session on 'Environment and sustainable tourism in the PATA region will bring together a diverse group of panelists including representatives from the Maori Tourism Development Board, the World Wide Fund for nature as well as experts from India, Pakistan and Thailand. The other concurrent sessions will address technology related subjects.

Silver Lining

A person whom the thirty-odd Indian participants at the PATA meet in Nagoya were looking for in four days of this great International event could not be traced anywhere around. The person was no less than the Regional Director of India's tourist office in Tokyo. The incumbent is supposed to promote India in the region and she could not have had a better opportunity when tourism business leaders from all over the world had assembled at a location just a two-hour train journey away from her headquarters. It is amazing that not even a representative from her office deemed it necessary to turn up at the event.

Ironically, at this very session, an Indian was unanimously elected chairman for 2000-01. Tourism Secretary, Madan Prasad Bezbaruah, who was thus honoured, himself could not be present because of developments back home. He is the second Indian to be chosen for this high office, the first being Inder Sharma. His absence was all the more reason why the Regional Director should have attended.

Reports current among Indian sources were that the Regional Director preferred to stay away because the Director General of Tourism was not attending because of personal reasons.

It was as if her job was not to promote India but to be on attendance to a visiting dignitary. It is a monumental commentary on the way our overseas tourism offices operate.

It is particularly galling that the Regional Director stayed away when the country had launched an Explore India Year, on which attention should have been focused to that vast assemblage of the world travel trade, it also underlines the need for a thorough survey of the working of tourist offices overseas and to what extent their programmes have had any impact.

The episode recalls to mind the claim that used to be repeated by Ghulam Nabi Azad, when he was Tourism and Civil Aviation Minister, that he had made visits to more than forty countries promoting the Indian tourism product. It is good as well that nobody took count of the extra visitors that resulted from his expensive exercise. It only means that it is not just visits or presence that is important but professionalism and commitment to carry out the task entrusted with the person, involving expenditure of public money.

In any event, PATA '99 will be remembered in the Indian context not for the lapse of the Regional Director but for the deserving honour conferred on Bezbaruah. A sincere and seasoned administrator, and author of a book on Indian tourism, his elevation to the highest elective office of this world body representing governmental and non-governmental agencies is most timely.

The stagnation in Indian tourism has been compounded by recent political developments, including a schedule for elections. Certainly, it is not the time when tourists come. Even is the lean season. But Bezbaruah's personal standing with PATA leaders will have its impact on refurbishing India's image as also a new orientation to the traffic flow.

The PATA agenda for the year includes a meeting of its directors numbering over fifty, from as many countries, in New Delhi. This body could be persuaded to assist in whatever form possible in the promotion of the Indian tourism product. Twice before, South Asia Year plans by PATA and WTO (World Tourism Organisation) did not materialise.

At the same time Indian tourism authorities should have more innovative programmes for the turn of the millennium.

Most cities of the world are already on the job. It will only be appropriate that such celebrations in this country could feature what has been described as Explore India Year, which needs to be stretched by a year to 2001 to coincide with Bezbaruah's chairmanship of PATA.

In the following year, 2002, India will be hosting the annual PATA Convention. The intervening period will give him an opportunity to apprise the concerned authorities of the preparations necessary for the success of the world event from India's point of view.

It has been a strange but unfortunate coincidence that Indian tourism receives a setback when expectations are aroused for a take-off. The uncertainties of the past few months and the election programme certainly will have their impact in a downslide. But, hopefully a bad year will be followed by better times.

Countdown to PATA 2002

After three successive years of stagnant arrivals and declining amount that a tourist spends one would expect the hospitality industry to look upon Pacific Asia Travel Association's annual conference in 2002 to be held in this country as an opportunity for a turn around. For, it is well known that a PATA meet brings together hundreds of tourism industry leaders of all segments, hotels, travel agents and tour operators, airlines, transporters, national tourism organisations, cruise companies and event managers. The host country thus gets a captive audience from around the world to showcase its tourists attractions and updates on what's new on offer. It is also acknowledged that PATA brings in its wake a significant increase in visitor arrivals for the host country.

Small wonder that there is intense competition among nations looking for more tourists, and they number more than a hundred, to be the venue for the next occasion. Bids are made three years in advance. This period is utilised by PATA to piece together its organisational needs in a different country each year. But, for the host country this timeframe is'barely sufficient to put its best foot forward. Some are content with getting good attendance (larger numbers than the last one) and a reasonable increase in visitor inflows. There is, of course, the remarkable example of Indonesia, which used the three years before the 1992 PATA in Jakarta as the base from which it leapfrogged to a phenomenal three fold growth in tourist arrivals.'By the time PATA' delegates arrived the tourism set up under the dynamic Jup Ave had broken through the political and bureaucratic Maginot Line ringing around a strict visa regime and aviation bilaterals. PATA was inaugurated with the fanfare of open skies and no visa for more than forty countries. Not only that, dozens of new hotels were built and a global publicity blitz was launched. Every Indonesian travelling abroad was enthused to become a tourism ambassador. In no time, the country joined the ranks of the other Asian tigers with a five million plus visitor count.

The more recent success story of cashing in on PATA conference is Hong Kong, this year's venue just three months ago. All the more creditable because the City of Life as it loves to call itself did not even have the customary three years but only two because it stood in for a defaulting bidder. PATA 2000 attracted 1,400 participants, among the highest attendance ever. In the two previous meets, PATA lured 900 in Nagoya (1999) and 800 in Manila (1998). Hong Kong showcased to the global industry leaders its brand new airport with its sleek rail link to the city, a renovated state-of-the-art convention centre, theme parks, fine hotels, rows and rows of shopping plazas, entertainment centres and a mind-boggling choice of cuisines and branded goods. And, more importantly a promise that by 2005, it will have its own Disney land. Which is when the charming executive director of Hong Kong Tourist Association (HKTA), Amy Chan says it will have achieved the unrivalled status of Asia's number one events city. With 11 million tourists visiting Hong Kong every year, it is already Asia Pacific's number one destination.

So, what is India planning, and hoping, to achieve from PATA 2002? It was fortuitous that tourism secretary, M P Bezbaruah, who at the Hong Kong session was inducted this year's PATA president, and the new director general, Atul Sinha were able to see for themselves what a convention of that size and significance expects from a host country. Sadly, we too have only two years lead time because a year was lost thanks to elections and ministerial changes, Bezbaruah downwards the officials seem enthusiastic about making a success of the big conference. After all this country did a good job when PATA last visited us way back in 1978. But industry watchers are a bit concerned about a lack of enthusiasm among the industry segments particularly hotels, travel agencies and tour operators and other service providers. It is not clear whether this is due to complacency or apathy. Someone needs to give a wake up call. The key to success lies in a coordinated cooperative effort between the government and the industry.

Three daunting tasks face the organisers: ensuring good attendance, smooth management of the conference and, enhancing India's appeal as a destination. Neither money nor effort should be spared. It is good to know that the government is willing to spare Rs five crore for organising the conference and efforts are on to secure an additional Rs one crore for the India evening to be hosted at Kuala Lumpur at PATA 2001, which will go a long way in attracting greater participation for the event in India. Managing the conference should not be a problem as there is plenty of expertise available. But, showcasing India is what will require more concerted efforts and even investments within the next two years. A face lift for IGIA is a must. The railways could earn the tourist industry's gratitude by extending the rail link to the airport. Luckily, the score of new flyovers being built in the capital will be ready, as will be part of the MRTS. Delhi now has a large number of deluxe hotels and among the latest additions will be the Grand Hyatt, ITC's Welcom Hotel and the first Japanese managed Nikko Metropolitan. One thing is clear. We cannot afford to miss the opportunity that PATA brings us. Hopefully, visa on arrival will be in place even if open skies must remain a dream.

PATA 2002: Shot-in-the-Arm for Indian Tourism

Pacific Asia Travel Association (PATA), now into its 50th year of existence, is the largest global body representing both governments and the private sector in the hospitality industry. It has played a significant role in guiding countries to increase their share of the world travel market. Its annual gatherings are so coveted that nations vie with one another to play host spending huge sums on getting their bid approved three years in advance. For that is the time needed to organise a conference where you get an opportunity to showcase your destination before discovering travel industry eyes from around the world and also prepare to meet the "fallout" from such an event, a sizeable increase in tourist arrivals by as much as 15 per cent.

It was this challenge and opportunity situation that spurred our tourism ministry backed by the industry to successfully bid for the 2002 PATA. This country has played host twice before in 1964 and 1978. As one who was associated, with the 1978 conference I can recall with some pride that it was rated by global leaders as among the best and certainly there was a significant increase in arrivals in the following years. But, 2002 is almost a quarter of a century after India's direct brush with PATA. There has been a sea change in the tourism scenario. China, Hong Kong and Asian tigers like South Korea, Taiwan, Indonesia, Thailand, Malaysia and Singapore have all leap-frogged to five million and 11 million arrivals range while we are struggling to touch two and a half million. Clearly, we have been left far behind. And, this would call for a much bigger effort to move a few points forward, if still unable to catch up with our neighbours.

Sadly, the tourism ministry, thanks to the intervening elections, has already lost a whole year and will have to achieve in two years what it would have done in three. There are, however, some compensating factors. There are signs of awakening in the political leadership about the potential of tourism as a great employer apart from the valuable foreign exchange it earns. Some policy initiatives could be expected in the coming months. On the other hand, the industry has more professionals at the helm than ever before, though lack of unity is still a matter of great concern. The apex bodies like TAAI, FHRAI, IATO and HAI all have more focused agendas and they are receiving good support from the various chambers like FICCI, CII and ASSOCHAM. And, so far as organising the PATA conference which is expected to attract up to 1,500 delegates, should not pose any problem, for the country has successfully handled many a conference with much larger participation.

The problem that is worrying industry observers (and surely tourism secretary, M P Bezbaruah and director general, Atul Sinha who participated in the Hong Kong PATA earlier this month) is how to ensure that destination India is showcased effectively and at the same time improve the existing infrastructure and expand it to meet that expected demand. India is a world class destination, a foreign tourism expert had told an Indian audience some time ago. What it lacks is its ability to offer a world class experience. He had said obviously, there are several elements that make up a world class experience. Among them are facilitation visa free regime (friendly immigration/customs/taxis), quality services at competitive prices, hygiene, safety, entertainment and reliable shopping. Ecology is a new buzzword at travel trade forums. The 40-strong Indian delegation, that went to Hong Kong (interesting, half of it was represented by media persons), I am sure, would unhesitatingly testify that the City of Life, as its tourism promoters describe it, does qualify for a world-class experience. Incidentally, after becoming Asia's number one destination (with 11 million visitors) Hong Kong is now aiming for recognition as a 'world city' in the same class as London and New York.

There is no doubt that Bezbaruah and Sinha will be discussing with industry leaders on how to meet the challenge of PATA 2002. The way Indonesia used its PATA opportunity could provide some useful tips to us. That country won the PATA 1992 bid in 1989. In the three year run up, it pegged its entire promotional and marketing effort to the PATA meet. On facilitation, it abolished visas with more than 40 countries. As much as $100 million was invested in new hotel projects. Hopefully, the tourism ministry supported by the industry will be able to persuade the rest of the government particularly Home, External Affairs and Aviation Ministries to give tourism a chance through PATA 2002.

A Time of Crisis is a Time of Opportunity

The world tourism summit planned for the Delhi was postponed for want of time, preparations and response. It would have been a major event on the Asian calendar of tourism happenings. But that was not to be, reflecting once again the inability or failure of the tourism authorities as also of the industry to make it happen as a great opportunity. Whatever be the official explanation for the summit not materialising, the lessons of the postponement have to be remembered. This is not the first time that such an abrupt cancellation of a tourism-related development has been announced. Not only did it affect the credibility of organisers, it also renders difficult such future meetings. In contrast to the Delhi fiasco, Hong Kong tourism which hosts this year's PATA in three weeks' time has shown remarkable organisational ability in putting together an Asian tourism summit as well alongside.

If the Hong Kong tourist authority (HKTA) claims "it has an excellent track record for handling major events", it is not wrong in the least. In respect of PATA it needs to be pointed out Hong Kong did not have the customary three-year period of preparations. Two years ago it chipped in when Indonesia, the earlier bidder, had withdrawn in the wake of the Asian crisis. PATA will certainly lend greater mileage in respect of tourism to Hong Kong where total arrivals in 1999 reached 10.68 million prompting a forecast for 2000 of 11.4 million. It demonstrates enhancement of Hong Kong's position as the pre-eminent international tourist spot in Asia as also the preferred gateway to the region. The complementary Asia Pacific Economic Cooperation (APEC) tourism summit fixed one day before PATA opening, is also an event that has aroused great expectations. Special significance is attached to the April conclave in the context of preparations of a ministerial declaration on a charter for tourism for APEC to be endorsed three months hence in July 2000. Official support has also been forthcoming for the forum as a major occasion at the beginning of the millennium to contribute to the future direction on key travel issues. The Hong Kong programme also demonstrates how long-term tourism planning, when integrated with the overall development of a region, will provide better direction for the industry, without much hiccups when a new event has to be inserted into the calendar. Hong Kong has a consistent record of competent marketing and innovative approach in tourism development. This policy has stood the region in good stead when an international gathering like PATA had to be brought in. This is one point which Indian tourism planners and agencies should keep in mind lest their plans go away.

As referred to in this column not long ago, India's tourism secretary, M P Bezbaruah will be inducted as the elected president of PATA's next convention to be held in Kuala Lumpur in 2001.

Incidentally, India will host PATA 2002 and it is a welcome development that the industry and the ministry have put their heads together to make a success of. The Hong Kong PATA which will be the 49th annual conference will have as its theme "The Future is Now". The industry, beleaguered by advancing technology, can look up to its deliberations for clues to survival and success. E-Commerce, the thing of all forms of activity will be discussed in detail at the plenary. It is expected to present an overview of the IT scene and how it will impact the future of the travel business. Another related subject is travelling worldwide with the Web. Development of satellite television is yet another subject regarding the knowledge industry's influence on the course of tourism. The subjects are thus well chosen for their relevance to current developments.

If the subjects are interesting, the speakers chosen are also of a genre that has grown with the space era. A keynote speaker is Buzz Aldrin, the astronaut who with Niel Armstrong walked on the moon. Author, chairman of National Space Society of SA as also head of Sharespace Foundation, Dr Aldrin is to discuss the development of tourism in the remote frontiers of space. Other contemporary and long time tourism-related topics like timeshare building in Asia Pacific, implications of the airline industry's development on travel and tourism and outbound markets figure on the PATA agenda.

Hopefully, the Indian contingent to Hong Kong, which will be in sizeable strength, will assimilate some of the novel ideas articulated during the discussions and build on them a very meaningful event in 2000 on our own soil.

Hijacking Hurdles

The Indian Association of Tour Operators (IATO) has every reason to worry about the hijack horror that originated in Kathmandu. For, most of its members market Nepal along with Indian destinations and the packages involve flights into Indian territory and then to Nepal, as also in the reverse direction. It is often that the packages are combined into circuits. So, any decision to suspend flights to Nepal and cancellation of tours by groups to the Himalayan Kingdom hurts them. It is therefore justified that they call for most stringent measures to ensure airport and flight safety. Their suggestion to issue visa on arrival in Kathmandu for visitors, Indians included, needs examination for its involves key aspects of bilateral relations. In any event, the hijack of flight IC 814 has exposed many weak links in the security chain within India as also on the border with Nepal. The problem should concern Southeast Asian tourism as a whole, as between the two countries the traffic accounts for over 50 per cent of the tourist inflow in South Asia. In the circumstances, it is time this issue takes top priority not only in regional tourism-related councils but also in other international organisations like PATA and WTTC.

A sizeable section of the passengers on board the Indian Airlines plane were honeymooners, and others travelling for pleasure. It is ironic that a leisure trip climaxes in a traumatic experience. While air safety has been taken up in global aviation organisations, tourism establishments should be as much concerned because of the damage that such incidents cause to tourist traffic. Within a week of the flight IC 814 incident, Nepal has reported a dramatic decline in arrivals. Incidentally, one-third of Nepal's visitors come from India and are among the high spenders in the Kingdom. Likewise, quite a number of visitors to Nepal during winter particularly include the golden triangle of Delhi-Agra-Jaipur in their itinerary. Any fall in number of arrivals will equally hurt the trade in north India.

Security at airports and counter terrorism outfits are outside the ambit of tourism departments in most countries. As with other disasters, a single hijack incident can influence adversely originating markets. So, alongwith counter terrorism measures which are the charge of security establishments and are required to swing into swift action, damage control exercise has to be simultaneously undertaken by the appropriate public relations and communications set up. For instance, in the latest incident while tourism would be momentarily affected in the region, it is essential to project the other destinations far removed from the affected area. Even as the trade was worrying about the adverse impact on the traffic, Goa is the place sought after by most during the festive season with the additional pull of the millennium.

International opinion, especially of the trade, should be mobilised for minimising the fears created by incidents like the Kathmandu hijack. In fact, it is surprising that in spite of the several hijacking incidents in the Asia Pacific region, the PATA agenda for the next annual convention in Hong Kong makes little mention of it. Since our tourism secretary, M P Bezbaruah, will be installed in Hong Kong as the president for the Kuala Lumpur session in 2001, he should be able to persuade the participants to pay attention to the alarming incidents of hijacking and terrorism. A further review of the progress of measure initiated in Hong Kong could be discussed in the subsequent meetings in Kuala Lumpur in 2001 and New Delhi in 2002. India will be justified in taking the lead.

It is very thoughtful of IATO to convey first the industry's concern over the hijacking. Particularly relevant in the IATO statement is the suggestion on introduction of visas. The statement reads: "IATO has always held national interest above narrow personal interest. Even though the members of IATO are the largest promoters of Nepal as a tourist destination and will be adversely affected, we urge the Government of India to introduce passports and visas and completely seal borders with Nepal, Visas can be given on arrival so that tourism can be saved and Nepal can be free from becoming a hide-out for terrorists infiltrating into India." While the spirit behind the statement is laudable, introduction of passports and visas in reciprocal actions by India and Nepal will be reversing a historic relationship. The best way perhaps is to list identity papers acceptable to both sides and enforce them strictly apart from a coordinated security cover.

PATA on the Back

The feel good factor has started manifesting itself in the tourism sector also. Arrivals from overseas have not only touched the highest figure of 2.8 million, an increase of more than 15 per cent over the count of 2002, but also there has been a hefty jump in foreign exchange earnings of over 23 per cent, from Rs 14,195 crore to Rs 17,049 crore. The department of tourism (DoT) ascribes the upturn largely to the initiative for the first time to brand the country with the primary objective of establishing a unique and a single positive identity – Incredible India. The campaign, an integrated one, was launched last year covering international print and television media as well as the internet.

And, now recognition for the Incredible India campaign comes from the Pacific Asia Travel Association (PATA), the world's largest body on tourism which are represented both by governments and all segments of the tourism industry. DoT has won two Gold Awards for 2004, one for the Incredible India campaign and the other for the Incredible India Spiritual Campaign. DoT's e-mail newsletter was also recognised through a special mention. From the industry, Outlook Traveller's 75 Holidays in Hills' has also bagged a Gold Award.

PATA Gold Awards were instituted years ago to encourage exceptional achievement in a variety of endeavours bringing acclaim to the best the travel industry has to offer. The awards are given away at a glittering function usually hosted by the National Geographic during the PATA annual conference. India will receive its awards at PATA 2004 which is being held at Cheju Island in South Korea in April. PATA 2004 is scheduled for April 18-22 when the world is experiencing a sure recovery from the aftermath of 9/11, the Afghanistan and Iraq wars as well as the SARS epidemic. The theme chosen is 'Tourism is everybody's business'. PATA CEO Peter de Jong explains that "one realistic claim our industry can make after all it has been through is the fact that tourism is everybody's business". The Cheju conference will address the reasons why everybody has a stake in tourism, no matter what their goals are – economic, social, financial, environmental, cultural and political.

Cheju is Korea's world class tourist destination known as the Island of Peace and has played host to several summits for world peace. UNESCO has designated Cheju as a biosphere reserve. Cheju's month of blossoms and Mount Halla, tall at 1,950 metres, is a constant companion for visitors.

The keynote address is one 'The World of Aviation in its Second Century' and the impact it has made on tourism. Other subjects to be discussed include Tourism Investments – The Big Picture as well as the more topical ones like bio-diversity and poverty alleviation, and, challenges for sustainable tourism development.

PATA 2004 has yet another honour reserved for India. At the closing session Ram Kohli, chairman Creative Travels and founder president, IATO, will be inducted as the elected president of PATA for the year 2004-05. Kohli, who has received several national and international awards and was recently named as the world's number one tour operator, will preside over PATA 2005 which will meet in Macau.

PATA's India chapter, headed by tourism secretary Rathi Vinay Jha and comprising representatives of states and industry segments has after much hard work finally set up a crisis management mechanism whose need was highlighted by the series of setbacks suffered in the last decade. Christened as PATA Action Council on Tourism (PACT) it has Jha as chairperson and veteran Inder Sharma as co-chairman. Joint secretaries from the ministries of external affairs and home will represent other wings of the government while the industry representatives will be the presidents of TAAI and IATO and permanent heads of FHRAI and HAI. Senior print and TV journalists have also been named. They are Bachi Karkaria (*Times of India*), S Venkatnarayan (Foreign Correspondants Club), Dr Yogesh Gondal (New India Publications) and Vikram Chandra (NDTV). Dilip Cherian of Perfect Relations has been included as a public relations personality. The group will meet regularly. Standby committees would be formed with representatives from other travel industry bodies. State government and other ministries would be invited as per need. PATA chapter's executive director, Ashok Bhatnagar says PACT's primary objective is to change misconceptions to positive perceptions. And, he adds it will anticipate, react and respond to ever changing situations, take decisions and set in motion a machinery for damage control, repair and restoration of consumer confidence through appropriate communications, before during and after the crisis and especially while prempting any crisis. The chapter deserves the industry's appreciation.

Short-term Remedies

It is nearly three months since the sad events and the industry is yet to recover from the price it has paid. The worst sufferer has been the aviation sector. Many a prized airline has gone under the bankruptcy hammer including such blue chips as Swiss Air and Sabena. The latest victim is Canada 3000, which had launched its much hyped Toronto-Delhi flight early in October in what appeared at the time to be swimming against the current. In the process, a non-stop 13 hours service over the Polar route to India – the first ever – turned out to be a shortlived dream. Three other major players, United, SAS and Northwest have pulled out of India severely curtailing flying opportunities between India and north America. An estimated 1,50,000 airline staff have been given pink slips globally and many carriers have reduced their services by as much as twenty to thirty per cent. Travel agencies too have felt the heat, America's number two outfit, Airtours has just announced it is downsizing its operations by asking 1,600 employees to leave.

Here in India, one has not heard of major lay-offs either in aviation, hotels or travel agencies although severe cost cutting measures are in place. Air-India, in spite of the shadow of privatisation, has shown some resilience in filling at least some of the void created by the withdrawal of several foreign airlines from this country. It has revived its coveted terminator flight to London and is adding one more flight each to New

York and Chicago. With this Air-India will be offering a daily service to New York (as before) and thrice a week to Chicago, all with a stop in London where travellers can get quick connections to destinations in North America including Canada. Incidentally, in the reverse direction, Austrian Airline is perhaps the only carrier to increase flights to India. It has added a sixth service to its weekly schedule to this country and plans to have a daily service early next year. Austrian Airlines is also hoping to secure a second destination in India in the next bilateral dialogue. Its flights now come only to Delhi.

Like the Delhi-Toronto direct flight there was another: shortlived period of excitement (and expectation) among travellers when British Airways announced a rock bottom Rs 28,000 return fare from India to the US and just Rs 18,000 to Europe including UK. An orchestrated campaign by rival airlines backed reportedly by regulatory bodies (DGCA in India's case) branding the move as 'illegal' forced British Airways to withdraw the offer killing hopes of affordable holidays. But, a few airlines particularly in Asia in cooperation with other segments of the hospitality industry like hotels are offering attractive packages to woo tourists back.

Sri Lanka Tourism, under its dynamic chairman, Renton De Alwis has come up with perhaps the most attractive package for holiday seekers from India. The package worked out in cooperation with Sri Lanka Air and star hotels is "Buy One Get One Free." For a mere Rs 21,000 a couple in Delhi can have a four night/five days holiday in Sri Lanka, airfare, bed and breakfast and airport transfers included. Apart from advertising, the package was personally promoted in the capital by the Sri Lanka High Commissioner at a meting with the travel trade and iiedia persons. Many of those who attended the meeting came away with the nagging thought why the department of tourism and industry have not thought of similar packages in India. They recalled that in the 80s Air-India in association with ITDC had successfully marketed low priced stop-over tours to India. Perhaps, it is not too late even at this stage to put together special packages in which not only Air-India but domestic carriers and hotles could join in.

It must, however, be said to the credit of domestic carriers that they have not lagged behind in offering sops to ensure their load factors remain at reasonable levels. Indian Airlines has tied-up with hotels in several cities and tourist centres and is offering packages in standard and up-market prices. On offer are also free tickets to foreign destinations if your spend certain specified amounts on domestic sectors. Jet Airways and Sahara have introduced inflight shopping and along in Indian Airlines all three have launched co-branded credit cards in association with leading banks. Air Sahara has just announced, a new frequent flyer scheme which promises to get the traveller to the "goal of getting a free ticket faster than the river carriers."

Short-term remedies are fine. What about the future?

The travel industry worldwide is keeping its fingers crossed. The prospect of a prolonged war in Afghanistan appears to be receding with the Taliban holed up in Kandahar and possible return of peace in the region. Tourism, they say, has a habit lf bouncing back. Nothing will please the industry more should that happen, in the coming months.

PATA 2002: A Ray of Hope

As these lines are written, the military action against terrorism by the US and its allies is entering the fourth day. It is generally expected that the operations, confined so far to air and missile attacks on targets in Afghanistan may not last more than two weeks or so even if ground support becomes necessary. Once the Taliban regime is removed, the action will then shift to the field of diplomacy. Of course, the battle against terrorism will be a long drawn out affair as the Americans and everyone else is saying. But from tourism's point of view once military action stops, the urge to travel will reassert itself although fears created by hijacked planes being rammed into commercial towers may take a while. The hospitality industry around the globe is therefore hoping, and praying, for an early end to the military activity and a return to normalcy or near normalcy in tourist movements.

The aftermath of the tragic events has played havoc with the aviation segment on a global basis. Blue chip airlines like Swiss Air have had to be bailed out by governmental intervention. Major players have reduced services by as much as 20 per cent abandoning a number of destinations. United Airline, which was to introduce a prestigious Chicago-Delhi flight over the Polar route pulled out of India. Hotels around the world are facing low occupancies and countries with liberal labour laws are experiencing massive lay-offs. There are conflicting reports about the impact on India. Director general tourism, Vinod Duggal is reported as saying that only six to ten per cent cancellations have taken place while some industry leaders are talking of thirty to forty per cent. Among the domestic carriers, Indian Airlines has reported that it has lost only three per cent of its load, while Jet Airways says its business had declined by twenty per cent.

Be that as it may, the Department of Tourism (DoT) has advised its tourist offices overseas to spread the word to tour operators that India continues to be a safe destination. At a meeting with industry representatives, the director general has set up a task force to monitor the situation on a daily basis and suggest remedial action wherever possible. Duggal had some good news about tourism's long-term prospects to share with the industry. The aborted meeting of the prime minister with chief ministers and tourism ministers from the states is now proposed to be reconvened when major initiatives for the sector are expected to be announced. Also, preparations are going on apace for the New Delhi conference of PATA (Pacific Asia Travel Association). This coveted gathering of 1,200 or more travel industry leaders from worldover gives the host country an opportunity to showcase itself. The theme the international body has chosen for 2002 (its fifty-first annual meet) is "Tourism – Looking Ahead and Beyond". And, the message that India will give the delegates is "One Country, A Thousand Worlds". Prime Minister Vajpayee is expected to inaugurate the conference. The venue is the familiar Ashoka Hotel, which played host to the last PATA conference held in this country in 1978 (There was one before that in 1966). PATA India chapter is co-host with DoT and the industry is giving a big helping hand in organising the event. In fact, hoteliers, tour operators, travel agents and transporters are all heading various committee putting together the arrangements.

At its latest meeting, the organising committee decided that the India welcome dinner will be held at the historic Jamali Kamali part of the Qutub Minar complex, where delagates will be able to sample the kitchens of India and also experience some of the country diverse cultural heritage. The organising committee is particularly happy that it now has the services of Amitabh Kant, who has recently moved from Kerala to DoT as joint secretary and who is credited with presenting one of the most spectacular inaugural shows at the Kerala Tourism Mart in Kochi, last year. The cultural events at the welcome dinner, the inaugural and closing ceremonies will now be masterminded by him. In fact it was Kant, who in a last minute arrangement, made the India Evening at Kuala Lumpur (where the 2001 PATA conference was held), so much more memorable with a troupe flown in from Kerala. The hoteliers' team under Ashok Anantram of ITC, which presented the kitchens of India at Kuala Lumpur is in charge of the food part of the welcome dinner at Jamali Kamali. Ram Kohli of Creative Travels, who is now a senior functionary of the international PATA, has drawn up a programme of pre- and post-conference tours for delegates.

The success of PATA conference as indeed of the tourism initiative will depend on how the world community comes to grips with the daunting challenge of terrorism. India made its strong presence felt at the recently concluded Pacific Asia Travel Association's (PATA) golden jubilee conference in the Malaysian capital, Kuala Lumpur. A significant growth in participation, with the presence of over 70 Indian industry leaders, signified the country's desire to put its best foot forward when the world's largest hospitality body returns to Delhi for its next annual meeting in 2002 after a lapse of nearly a quarter century.

M P Bezbaruah, PATA chairman, stated in his address that he is happy that Malaysia is at the forefront of the Asian economic resurgence (having received over 10 million tourists during 2000 and recorded earnings in excess of US $5 billion), "Indians in Malaysia have contribute generously to the country's growth. Because India and Malaysia have always been together in the old as well as the new Asian dream, I hope that by the time PATA meets next year in Delhi, Malaysia would be a major contributor to our growth," he said.

The India evening, hosted on the last day by Atul Sinha, director-general of tourism, in conjunction with the team of PATA India chapter, was attended by Ananth Kumar, minister of tourism, who personally extended the invitation to the members for attending PATA in Delhi.

Spirit of Unity

The terrible tragedy that struck New York and Washington on September 11 has not only taken a heavy tool of human lives but also set in motion developments that bring alarming signals for the future of tourism worldwide. Already, the closure of all airspace over America, even though for a few days, lias meant a loss of billions of dollars to US airlines and other carriers who fly across the Atlantic and the Pacific.

One American airline, United, whose two aircraft the hijackers crashed into the twin towers of the World Trade Centre, has announced it is pulling out of India, United had returned to the Indian skies after a gap of two years with it's round the world service which on October 8 was to be converted into, a non-stop Chicago-Delhi service using the Polar route.

And, as the United States readies itself for action in Afghanistan, uneasiness is overtaking tour operators promoting India in north America and in Europe. No large scale cancellation have been reported so far but a fair amount of corporate travel has been put on hold. What is worrying the Indian industry, both hoteliers and travel agents, is that there is no knowing when the military, action will take place and where (whether only Afghanistan or any other country) and how long such an action will last. In any scenario India's proximity to Afghanistan is enough to cause apprehensions in the minds of travellers.

Even if our tourist offices overseas and industry segments that do their own promotion can persuade tour operators and would be travellers that this country's tourist spots are hundreds of miles away from any possible conflict area, the fear of being stranded by cancelled or grounded flights acts as a great deterrence. Indian promoters are therefore faced with a daunting challenge and one can only hope that they can rise to the occasion.

International tourism, it should now be clear to all, is vulnerable to warlike situation and now also to terrorism of the kind perpetrated on America. The only viable answer to meeting this challenge is to have a sustainable base of domestic tourism which can act as a cushion to any significant fall in foreign arrivals. As the World Travel and Tourism Council (WTTC) has pointed out, the domestic demand in India has far outstripped supply in infrastructure like affordable accommodation, transport and other services.

This becomes obvious when you look at the figure of domestic visits (where paid accommodation has been used). In the last decade, according to WTTC statistics, which it has borrowed from our government, the number of visits increased from 64 million to 174 million. And, the latest count for 2000 (quoted by none other than director general V K Duggal) is 210 million.

Now, that we are in the process of finalising the national tourism policy (this process itself has been put on the back burner, hopefully temporarily, thanks to the events in the United States) we might take a fresh look at the future role of domestic tourism and reorient our infrastructure development thrust accordingly. Obviously we need to encourage vaster development of budget and mid-market accommodation and affordable road, rail and air services.

Apart from great pilgrimage centres, historic cities, monuments, and haloed spots there are vast untapped travel possibilities. Rural tourism is perhaps the single biggest opportunity. Fortuitously, even the Planning Commission has shown keen interest in promoting rural tourism. Addressed carefully, this could play a vital role in creating employment in the rural areas and preventing urbanisation in search of work. The industry is looking forward to the department of tourism (DoT) to revive the tourism conclave which was to lead up to the announcement of some major initiatives by the Prime Ministier; chief ministers and state tourism ministers who were to deliberate on the future of the sector on the day the sad happenings in New York and Washington unfolded themselves.

It is a pity the industry's oldest apex body, the Travel Agents' Association of India (TAAI) is meeting in Mumbai for its golden jubilee session in the shadow of the terrorist tragedy and the yet-to-be-assessed fallout on global and Indian tourism. TAAI's annual sessions have rightly been described as gatherings of the Indian Travel Congress, for apart from its own members, it attracts participation from all other segments of the industry, hoteliers, tour operators, transporters and airline people. Hopefully, the spirit of unity which has been evading the hospitality industry, will take root at the 50th TAAI and enable it to meet the daunting challenge ahead as a united group.

Special Significance

The Pacific Asia Travel Association (PATA), the world's largest hospitality industry body, representing both the private sector and governments, is this year celebrating its 50th anniversary. Apart from the yeomen's service it has rendered the cause of tourism, it has assisted the region in marketing and research and promotional activities. And, with Asia Pacific identified as the largest growth area in the coming decades, PATA is looking forward to an enhanced role.

PATA's annual conferences are a coveted lot. Nations vie with one another in playing host as it gives them an opportunity to showcase their destinations to over 1,000 industry leaders from the world over, who gather every year to discuss the challenges facing tourism. This year the venue is Kuala Lumpur, the Malaysian capital, where the hosts are expecting more than 1,200 delegates.

The 50th conference has a special significance for India as the 51st session is in New Delhi in April 2002. And, as next year's host, this country will exercise its mandatory right to an India Evening. Besides, tourism secretary, M P Bezbaruah, will he presiding over the Kuala Lumpur conference and handover charge to the president elect for next year.

The department of tourism and PATA India chapter, who will be mainly responsible for organising the 2002 event, have been burning the midnight oil for several weeks in putting together the India Evening which, apart from ensuring good attendance for the New Delhi meet next year, will also strengthen India's claim as a unique destination. There will be two slots for this country on the last day of the Kuala Lumpur meet. At the closing ceremony in the afternoon, a 10-minute audio-visual 'Invitation to India' will be presented, after which tourism minister Ananth Kumar will address the delegates to convey a formal invitation from the government of India. In his absence, DC tourism, Atul Sinha, will perform this role. The AV has been prepared by AIM TV, famous for its Namaste India TV serials. There will also be an Odissi dance performance by a Malay-Indian, Ram Murali.

As the sun goes down, it will be time for the India Evening. There will be the usual cocktails, but with heavy Indian snacks like *tikkas* and *samosas* followed by a huge Indian feast. Titled 'Kitchens of India', it will be masterminded by a dozen leading chefs from leading hotel chains reflecting cuisines from the country's four corners. The chefs will be carrying as much as 700 kg of ingredients not available abroad. There will also be a two-part entertainment. A multi-screen audio-visual will project tourist fashion and handicrafts. This AV is being made by the National Institute of Fashion Technology (NIFT). And, for a live performance Kerala Tourism will present an India Spectacle with 30 artistes, on the lines of the brilliant inaugural function organised in Kochi at the Kerala Tourism Mart (KTM) in October 2000, but with an all-India flavour.

Because of the travel industry's interest in making the 2002 conference a success, a larger than usual Indian delegation is expected to be in Kuala Lumpur. According to information available with the PATA chapter, more than 50 registrations have already been made, and, in addition, as many as 25 Indian media-persons are also attending.

In its 50 years' existence, PATA (it was earlier known as Pacific Area Travel Association) has visited India only twice before. The first time was in 1964, when Jawaharlal Nehru gave the nation the slogan: 'welcome a visitor, send back a friend'. The second PATA conference in this country was in 1978. And, so PATA will return to India after a lapse of 24 years.

In keeping with the historic occasion of the fiftieth anniversary, the theme of the Kuala Lumpur session is apt: 'Proud Past – Promising Future'. And, equally befitting the occasion, the first keynote speaker is ambassador L W 'Bill' Lane, who attended the very first PATA conference half a century ago. An acclaimed editor, he is also recipient of the PATA gallery of legends honour.

A presentation of special interest to Indians attending the conference will be 'exploring Pacific Asia's promising future'. Of course, delegates from other countries would be asking Indians what they are doing to give a push to their own efforts to increase their share of the world market. Hopefully, the tourism minister, if at all he goes to Kuala Lumpur will be able to assure those who ask happening in the sector to catch up with the spectacular progress made by other nations in the region.

3
Regional Tourism

Close on the heels of the hugely successful international travel event – PATA 2002 – the Capital was treated to yet another mega gathering of buyers and sellers who met for SATTE, the South Asia Travel and Tourism Exchange's 9th annual mart. In spite of 9/11 and developments on India's borders, as many as 155 international buyers from 25 countries and 240 sellers from 25 cities made it to this major item on the country's international calendar.

SATTE 2002 got an upgrade internationally as it was inaugurated by Francisco Frangialli, secretary general of the World Tourism Organisation, an affiliate of the United Nations, an honour usually reserved for such global events as ITB, Berlin and WTM, London. Of course, there was also full support from the department of tourism, minister Jagmohan down to secretary, Rathi Vinay Jha and DG Vinod Duggal, as well as industry leaders like Gaj Singh, erstwhile maharajah of Jodhpur, ASSOCHAM tourism committee chairman, Subhash Goyal and national carriers and hotel chains. A whole day was devoted to a WTO–SATTE seminar on regional tourism where, apart from Frangialli and WTO senior functionary Dr Harsh Verma, government and industry leaders from China, Nepal, Sri Lanka, the Philippines and Indonesia made presentations.

Jagmohan affirmed India's full support to regional tourism and spoke of the new initiatives his department had set in motion in this regard. For media persons SATTE coordinator had thoughtfully arranged an interface with the WTO boss on the sidelines of the seminar. Frangially shared with journalists the preliminary data on the fall out of 9/11 and the military operations in Afghanistan. He said that in the six week period to the end, international arrivals fell sharply virtually everywhere. Declines of 25-30 per cent were commonplace. India and Nepal reported losses of 30 per cent and Iran up to 70 per cent of its small but previously growing inter-regional tourist flows. The US market was decimated while Japan was also sharply down. From Europe, however, performance varied country-by-country with best achievement (that is the lowest falls) being recorded by the UK, France, Italy and Spain (in essence the countries with the best performing economies) and the largest falls from Germany and the Netherlands (both with weak economies).

According to this preliminary data during the final four months of 2001 total arrivals in the South Asian countries declined by 24 per cent compared with figures for September to December 2002. Taken together, the 1.2 per cent growth for the period January-August and the 24 per cent fall in September-December produced a decline for the year of 6.4 per cent. South Asia was less badly hit than West Asia (down 30.2 per cent in September-December and 8.8 per cent for the whole year) and suffered similarly to the Americans (down 24 per cent September-December and 7 per cent for this year). Other regions were less badly hit.

Frangially and Verma pointed to an interesting phenomenon in the fall out of the global terrorism on South Asia and Central Asia, or more precisely, ASEAN countries. While South Asia (SAARC countries plus Iran) took a big knock in arrivals, ASEAN nations were compensated to an extent for the loss of US and European markets by more visitors like Japan and Australia whose nationals preferred to travel within the region rather than go to Europe and America. South Asian countries were denied this diversion because of proximity to Afghanistan where military operations were under way and because of the tensions in the Indian sub-continent following the attack on the Indian Parliament and deployment of troops on the India-Pakistan borders.

Among the presentations made at the seminar China's was the most spectacular. In the two decades since the opening up of the economy, said Zhang Guangyu of China National Tourism Administration, tourist arrivals had gone up fifty times to 89 million making the Peoples' Republic Asia's number one and the world's fifth largest destination. Tourism receipts moved up 68 times to US $17.8 billion. Domestic tourists numbered 784 million and 12 million Chinese travelled abroad. China's motto, he said, is to promote inbound tourism 'aggressively', domestic tourism 'actively' and outbound tourism-moderately'. Some food for thought for Indian tourism.

Durga the Crowd Puller

Durga Puja is to Calcutta (or Kolkata as it now called) as Diwali is to north India and Christmas to the Christian world – a time for festivities and family reunions. Pujo, as it is popularly referred to in short, is an event that has an unbroken run for three centuries and is completely spontaneous. There is no 'organisation' which runs it; it is really a people-run happening. The panorama unfolds itself regularly as clockwork every year. Myriad individual and local worship centres spring up; they are synergy of explosive emotional energy and creative enthusiasm accumulated through the entire year in the hearts and minds of Kolkatans. But it was only three years ago that members of Concern for Calcutta, a group of citizens in love with the city, thought of organising a Puja Parikrama of pandals with a history and tradition of their own. A team of 20 youngmen with a penchant for research went round the city documenting their origin, backgrounds, evolution, anecdotes and nuances of the presentation of Durga Puja. In the following two years, tours were organised for Kolkatans with the same 20 young men now acting as trained guides. Those joining the Parikrama learnt for the first time why the lion Durga rides has the face of a horse as well as a moustache in pandals with a zamindari tradition. Because this reflected the prerogative of kings who rode horses and the moustache was a symbol of power. Another fact the team brought out is that while Durga's image is immersed the weapons are not; these are used again and again every year. The team has also recorded the evolution of the pandal structure over the centuries, from a simple design to intricate replicas of great monuments and such creative use of materials as broken LPs and cowdung. Another finding was that Lord Clive, after his victory at Plassey, came to the Shobabazar Rajbari Pujo, and could well have been the first foreigner admitted to a pandal.

Around the same time Concern for Calcutta discovered that in a parallel effort the West Bengal department of tourism under Jayanta Sanyal (currently senior consultant with the Planning Commission) was also toying with the idea of extending Durga Puja to a wider audience. Hotels and travel agencies have been involved in the exercise. The Bengal Chamber of Commerce and Industries is giving a helping hand. Sita Travels has put together a five-day tour beginning October 2 and the package cost is US $425 per person on twin sharing in luxury hotels and US $325 at the Country Club. A CD – 'Durga beckons, Pujo happens, Calcutta welcomes', promises a unique experience to the visitor from the time he/she lands at the airport to a welcome of the Dhaki (the indigenous drummer of Bengal), the traditional flowers-and-lamp welcome by the ladies of Kolkata, to the subsequent unfurling of more, and increasingly more, exotic happenings. After the first introduction to Kolkata, and Bengali cuisine (there is also a choice of western food), there is the Calcutta by Night Pujo party. Exotic rituals in selected pandals will be the last activity of the first day. The next day begins with a boat trip on the Ganga to witness the worship of the Child Goddess – Kumari Puja at the Ramakrishna Mission premises and a visit to pandals famous for their innovativeness or antiquity, with an opportunity to mix with families which trace their ancestry to the city's origin and its noble lineage. The evening is reserved for the Raj experience and dinner at the Tollygunge Club. The third day has a leisurely tour of the city covering among other places, Victora Memorial and Fort William and in the evening a taste of the rustic beauty and rural artistry of India – village handicrafts and authentic entertainment accompanied by food and drink. On the final day, when Durga bids goodbye till the next year, the visitors will see the diversity of Kolkata – the festival being celebrated by other groups, of other communities in their own distinctive way underlining India's unity in diversity. Before the grand finale, there is the Sindur Khela where the goddess is bid farewell by the ladies. And, finally the emotional scene viewed from a specially arranged boat, when the goddess is immersed in the river. And for those who have the time there are add on trips to North Bengal and Sikkim as well as to Assam, India's tea country. Experiencing Pujo for overseas visitors is a path-breaking initiative on the part of citizens of Kolkata and food for thought for those who live in and love the other great cities of India.

All Roads to Himachal

PHD, the Punjab Haryana and Delhi Chamber of Commerce and Industry, whose tourism and aviation committee has been conducting some meaningful one-on-one interactive seminars with the states, chose Himachal in the first week of September for its latest effort.

The subject, as in an earlier exercise, was Sustainable Tourism Development: Issues and Perspectives. Shimla was the obvious choice for the venus and chief minister Virbhadra Singh downward played hosts. To its credit, PHD managed to persuade union minister Jagmohan to participate and the state government leaders and officials were lavish in their appreciation of the Chamber's contribution. Industry representatives from all over Himachal were there to hear outside experts like J P Gupta, chairman, Jagson Airways, Rakesh Mathur, president, WelcomHeritage, Prem Subramanian, till recently British Tourist Authority's man in India, Sudhir Sahi, eco-tourism specialist and mainstream journalists from Delhi.

It is a pity that the interactive part of the deliberations was sacrificed to enable the union minister to fly off to Kulu-Manali for some on the spot discussions with the chief minister and the state tourism minister, Vijay Singh Mankotia. Still, the participants benefited from Jagmohan's now familiar audio-visual presentation on the clean up of our national monuments as well as his view that more than master plans it is the quality of implementation which will decide the growth of the sector. He said the centre has chosen three tourists hubs to be developed in Himachal. For one circuit in these hubs, which will promote adventure tourism, he had sanctioned Rs 7.50 crore. "Implement this project speedily", he candidly told the state government, and you will immediately get money for two or even more circuits."

The chief minister took the opportunity to allay the fears of investors which he said might have been fuelled by developments over the Wild Flower Hall – a joint venture between Himachal and the Oberoi Group – and gave the assurance that the state has an investor friendly approach. He pleaded for better connectivity for his mountaneous state and early action to extend the runway at Bhunar airport at Kulu so that ATRs could land there. The extended runway, he said, could be achieved by spanning the river.

Supporting the chief minister on the Bhuntar Airport needs, the Jagson Airways chief said traffic to Shimla by air was suffering because of lack of navigational aids.

PHD tourism and aviation committee chairman, V N Dalmia pointed to the low budget support to tourism by the state government. Its allocation of less than Rs five crore was far below the young Uttaranchal state which has allocated Rs 19 crore for the current year. Himachal's principal tourism secretary, Ashok Thapar spoke of what he called "winds of change." A part of the luxury tax collected from hotels, he said, is being passed on to the board for developmental work. Himachal's PHD chief, Dhian Chand gave several suggestions for enabling visitors to extend their stay in Shimla. He said a ropeway from Puranoo to Shimla would not only be in additional attraction but could also sit down the travel time and reduce the pressure on the road.

The union department of tourism joint secretary and chairman ITDC, Amitabh Kant acquainted the participants with the Rs 15 crore Incredible India campaign launched a few months ago on the electronic media in the major markets abroad and how it had already helped increase the flow of tourists.

Prem Subramaniam, who seemed to have done a good bit of research on Himachal, drew attention to a little known fact. Apples, he said, were introduced into Himachal in 1904 and the state should have been busy preparing to celebrate the golden fruit's centenary. Even now it is not too late he added. He had found on the internet 28 recipes of apple delicacies from other producing countries and none from India. A Himachal industry functionary said an apple blossom festival was planned for next year in April, though he conceded it, it is not part of any centenary celebrations. If Shimla wants to keep visitors longer than they normally stay, Subramanian said, "You must create activities for them to be busy with. Revive traditional pastimes like tattooing, body piercing, painting, photography competitions and so on".

Rakesh Mathur gave the participant some interesting tips on marketing destinations. Referring to the suggestion that Shimla be made a World Heritage site he advised the authorities to first run a bulldoser over the ugly structures in the once most prestigious hill station of India.

Since Jagmohan could not interact with the experts as he had to leave he invited them to meet him in Delhi where he promised to spend time with them.

Tamil Nadu Raring

That Chennai drew more than 500 foreign participants to the 64th SKAL World Congress – the largest ever – endorses the city's claim to have arrived as a major MICE destination. Other signals that emanated from the successful conduct of an international event crucial to the country's tourism effort is that not only the southern metropolis now has the infrastructure for large conventions it can also put together the best of cultural presentations and culinary experiences that add spice to a conference deliberations. But, the more important message to tourism well wishers is that the Tamil Nadu chief minister has joined the select group of state chief executives who are committed to ensure that the sector plays its full part in the socio-economic development.

Selvi J Jayalalitha's inaugural address, a special honour to the delegates and reaffirmation of governmental support to tourism, was perfect showcasing of Tamil Nadu's attractions. The centre was not far behind in its backing of the SKAL Congress. In the absence of Minister Jagmohan and Secretary Rathi Vinay Jha who were away to Beijing attending the World Tourism Organisation's General Assembly, additional director general, Rashmi Verma and joint director general Shankar Dhar were there throughout reflecting the importance the department of tourism attached to the event. Verma hosted a gala dinner which observers said would be one of the highlights of the social happening the delegates would take back as a fond memory.

Jayalalitha spoke of an ambitious US $4 billion development plan for Chennai (of which US $2 billion will be invested in the first phase) which as a Tamil Nadu tourism advertisement proclaimed will put the city in the league of Paris, Rome and Singapore. More about this later.

SKAL International, which Rashmi Verma in her welcome address on behalf of the department of tourism hailed as "an organisation of tourism industry professionals from around the world promoting global travel and friendship, chose India for its annual Congress for the first time in its 70 year existence. Credit was given to the Tamil Nadu SKAL Club whose president Manoj Virmani and his Skalleagues (as the club members love to call themselves) made a successful bid three years ago. For its organisation it secured enthusiastic cooperation from all segments of the hospitality industry, the state government, civic authorities as well as the central department of tourism. Rathi Vinay Jha and other department officials were in close touch with Virmani's organising committee to monitor the progress of arrangements.

By coincidence, the president of SKAL International, Mary Bennett is the first woman to head this global body and welcoming her was the lady chief minister of Tamil Nadu. The theme for the Congress was Tourism Through Friendship and Peace. Bennett in her presidential address mentioned that India, China and Russia are tomorrow's top destinations. The Chennai meet she said would go a long way in attracting more visitors to India. She added that India should market its history, culture and crafts and that the skills of Indian craftsmen and their variety of creations are unmatched, besides the prices which are a fraction of what one pays in the West.

In her address, Jayalalitha spoke of her determination to make Tamil Nadu a world class holiday experience. She said, "We wish to transfer Tamil Nadu from a gateway to south India to a tourism hub of this part of the world. She unveiled a seven point action plan for her tourism strategy; unlocking the hidden treasures of Tamil Nadu; positioning Chennai and Coimbatore as destinations for international conventions and exhibitions, twinning of destinations; improving international accessibility; upgrading the transport network; filling infrastructure gaps; and, aggressive and focused marketing. The chief minister also has big plans for Chennai which will be repositioned as the City Premier in South India as the country's eastern gateway to the world.

Jagmohan's message to the Congress was read out by Rashmi Verma. The union minister said the SKAL meeting in India was held at an appropriate time when tourist trends are showing promise of recovery and growth. India in particular he said, has posted an excellent growth rate of 15 per cent overseas arrivals so far this year. In the arena of tourism and culture Jagmohan said, India for quite some time had been a sleeping giant. It is fully awake now and making strides in the right direction. And, he said, in the recent past some new initiatives have been taken which synthesis the elements of tourism, culture and clean civic life.

Uttaranchal's Broad Vision

In yet another instance of the industry taking the lead in bringing into focus the challenges facing tourism, the Uttaranchal Hotel and Restaurant Association took advantage of the Nainital Festival to get media-persons from the capital to take part in a seminar on creating awareness of the potential of the young state and its once premier hill destinations. Although the state tourism secretary, N N Prasad could not make it to the seminar, Nainital's district collector (they call him DM) Amit Ghosh was there for an interface with media-persons. The Uttaranchal Hotel and Restaurant Association president, Saeed Sherwani and members of the Nainital chapter including Praveen Sharma to whom goes the credit for restoring the heritage property of Chaveron, were upbeat about the future of the lake resort. The collector said that thanks to the Supreme Court intervention no new constructions are allowed. As part of the move to decongest Nainital, Ghosh said as many as 17 government offices are being shifted out to Bhimtal and residential accommodation is being provided to staff.

The project to protect the lake is in full swing. Ghosh said for the first time this year there has been no silting and under High Court orders no bathing or washing is allowed. Boats are being provided with bins to collect throwaways. To improve connectivity a new bypass to Nainital via Kaladoongi (in the Corbett Park) is proposed and work will be completed in three years. The collector said that while Nainital's permanent population is only around 40,000 in the peak season, the floating population could touch the 1,50,000 mark.

Nainital, discovered by a British explorer in 1840, was the summer capital of Uttar Pradesh and among its architectural assets is the Governor's House overlooking the lake which is now the abode of the Uttaranchal governor whenever he chooses to visit the hill station from the state headquarters in Dehradun. Close-by is Nainital's 18-hole golf course, fortuitously well preserved and popular with lovers of the game who come from distant parts of the country. Hoteliers feel this attraction of the hill station has not been fully exploited.

Apart from the pull of the lake (there are many more in Nainital's well-connected neighbourhood like Khurpatal, an anglers' paradise) there are many other attractions. Naina Peak (formerly called China Peak) at a height of 2,610 metres offers a panoramic view of the Garhwal Himalayas. The state observatory devoted to astronomical studies has a powerful telescope for a close look at the planets. The visiting media persons had the thrill of looking at the near full moon and the Red Planet (Mars) Magnified 80 times over. Nainital has a number of fine hotels including the good old Grand on the Mall, The Claridges, The Swiss, and the Uttaranchal Hotel and Restaurant Association president's own Sherwani Hilltop Inn, once a family residence to escape to from Delhi's heat.

Another private initiative in the young state, the Kumaon Tourism Forum, representing off-beat resorts is headed by Dileep Gupta who pioneered the resort concept at Mukteswar, the 8,000 feet plus picturesque part of Kumaon's highest inhabited zone with spectacular views of the Himalayan peaks. The forum has been active in promoting awareness of the little known attractions of Uttaranchal and focusing on the area's infrastructural needs. Gupta is happy that the state government is taking tourism seriously and has in fact provided significant funds for development. The decision to privatise the state-owned Kumaon Mandal guest houses, he says, is a step in the right direction. It is good to see, he adds, that the government is thinking of mega projects for the state, particularly the new township near Ramnagar. But, he says, the same attention needs to be paid to existing infrastructure like hotels and resorts and such small but crucial areas as road signs. Water and energy, he says, are major problems facing resorts and yet no concrete steps have been announced so far (For his part Gupta has gone in for water harvesting at his own Mountain Trail resort at Mukteswar). There is no clear policy, he says, for assisting resorts with such things as subsidy or better support infrastructure. Garbage disposal is another major problem for hoteliers; resorts do not have the resources to handle it themselves. Ideally, he says, the government should develop new destinations and invite private sector participation only after basic support infrastructure like accessibility, water, energy, sanitation is in place.

Hopefully, the tourism set up in Uttaranchal is listening.

SATTE – Platform for Interaction

It may sound strange to exclaim that the Union Minister for Tourism after all attended a tourism-related event. What made it strange was that over the last years the incumbents found little time or interest to participate in such functions. To Madan Lal Khurana goes the credit for ending the spell of no-shows. Even he could not find time to sit through the just two-hour inaugural of SATTE (South Asia Travel and Tourism Exchange) in New Delhi.

However, in fairness, it was not entirely his fault as it came to be known that his personal staff had made a faux pas at some stage. In any event, he did not listen to the presentations of others and left the hall after a brief speech and lighting the customary lamp. The tourism minister had other priorities to attend.

It is the fifth SATTE, probably the only one travel show focused on South Asia buyer-seller meet. Though the object is specific, SATTE '98 coming after two successive trade shows had to be comparatively low profile this year. The organisers preferred to shift the inaugural function to the relatively smaller Durbar Hall of Taj Palace from the spacious convention hall of Ashok Hotel where the previous events were traditionally held with considerable glitter.

The highlight of the inaugural was an audio-visual presentation by the noted lensman Avinash Pasricha, which brilliantly captured the theme 'coming together' with music, slides and commentary. All seven SAARC countries were represented in the synthesised production. It could convey the message of what the coming together of those countries could achieve.

A unique dance art form combining the three main streams of Bharat Natyam, Kathak and Odissi by three top artists to a Rig Veda hymn ably rendered by a vocal artist was a symphony in harmony. This impressive cultural start regaled the 150-odd buyers who had come from various parts of the world. And, surprisingly, quite a few had arrived from Southeast Asia.

The impact of the Southeast Asian currency melt-down on Indian tourism was referred to by more than one speaker. While they were all hopeful that the crisis in the region was only transitory, there is no reason why India should not take advantage of it. The plain fact is India has not. The 1992, National Action Plan had projected international arrivals of the order of six million by the year 1997. The actual figure was less than 2.5 million. Why should it happen so?

The question was raised and answered by the keynote speaker, Inder Sharma, who has been in the travel business almost since organised tourism began in this country. There was much to be desired in marketing the Indian quality of the product. Sharma likened Indian tourism to a pyramid of layers which at the base were not strong. He referred to the first three layers not resting on solid foundation.

Domestic tourism, did not receive the attention it ought to have. Anywhere else in the world, particularly in countries of Europe, where tourism has succeeded both in national and international dimensions, the base was strong in domestic tourism.

Barring the case of Nepal, where visitors from India can go without visa or foreign currency, on a reciprocal basis, crossborder movement has to encounter restrictions. Sharma justifiably wondered what all the seven countries could have achieved from tourism if the India-Nepal crossing is to be the pattern.

SATTE, as a marketing exercise, could help correct the distortions at least in international tourism through interaction between the buyers and the sellers. Such interface would determine the quality of arrivals, enabling the creation of the facilities for the right type of visitors. But there is one hitch. It relates to the role of several travel shows in different cities like Chennai, Kolkata, Mumbai and the capital, without a connected objective.

The result is lack of focused marketing on niche markets. The director general of tourism, Ashok Pradhan's solution is to combine all the trade shows into a mammoth mart like ITB.

But the SATTE coordinator, Navin Berry, feels differently. He said any mart which is not object-specific would serve little purpose because currently the different shows centre on consumer interests, inbound and outbound traffic or just a 'mela'.

A serious study Is called for. Hopefully the initiative can come from the minister.

Branding Kargil

Kargil operations may have cost Indian tourism in some measure in terms of international arrivals. But, it has emerged as a potential tourist destination with its name familiar to most Indians and quite a large number abroad. Its snow-clad hill tops, uneven terrain and unpredictable weather together challenge the spirit of adventure. The place, hallowed by the blood of martyred Jawans, has become a destination for veneration for Indian patriotism. Media reports for over two months have conjured up visions of a mystic country in the Himalayan heights. In other words, Kargil has surfaced as one of the most tourism-fertile spots in the country in general and in Kashmir in particular. Incidentally, though referred to as a sizable area, Kargil is the name of the second largest town in Ladakh after Leh. It marks the midpoint of the journey from Srinagar to Leh. It is also the take-off spot for excursions into the Suru Valley and the remote Zanzkar Valley with exciting opportunities for mountaineering, camping, river rafting and trekking trails into Himachal Pradesh, Jammu and the Indus Valley. Once at the crossroads of a network of trade routes which led to Kashmir,

Baltistan, Afghanistan, central Asia and Tibet, Kargil is invested with the lingering air of romance. The two tributaries of the river Suru, the Dras and the Wakha converge here. Pretty walks around the town of Kargil provide breathtaking views of the mountains. Representative of Shia Muslim culture, it has two fine mosques built in Turkish style. Thus, naturally endowed, its attractions have been reinforced by the culture of a refined friendly people. Even in the neighbourhood it has very pretty areas. The Suru valley is one such. It runs for 140 km beyond Kargil to the Penzi La, the point of entry to Zanskar valley. Its verdant hills are intensely cultivated. Enough snow and water during the year sustains two crops. It is ironic that such a picturesque region has been the scene of bloody battles with infiltrators. Nonetheless, Kargil's claim to fame and familiarity in the last two months has set tourism analysts thinking about making it a popular destination like Srinagar or Leh.

The tourism authorities, in concert with the defence administration, will have to map a strategy for turning open to tourism as much area of Kargil as possible. Hopefully, the military authorities will accept a proposal for developing a complex around Kargil town which has a permanent population. Besides, it is already a transit point on the highway to Leh. The complex could provide the gear and the guides for adventure sports. A more significant attraction would be a national memorial to the unknown soldier who gave up his life in defence of the country. The memorial could be made as distinctive as possible as a reminder of one of the major historical episodes in recent years.

It could be a grandiose project which, even if it is completed over years, would be eloquent to coming generations of the great moment when fighting here rallied the entire country as one whole. Its planning should be entrusted to a national body formed of eminent people from all walks of life. Finance should not be a problem going by the popular response to the Kargil fund. In the process, a new tourist destination will be created for which the industry should take the lead. Kashmir is a tourism-oriented state in which the project envisaged will provide new assets enhancing the total quality of the tourism product. It will be a good follow up to IATO's decision to hold its next annual session in Srinagar in October. Though the delegates may not be able to visit Kargil as it will be snow-bound at the time it will be worthwhile if the convention devotes a special business session on building Kargil for the future. It need not be IATO's exclusive responsibility. Other trade organisations which are scheduled to hold their annual conference elsewhere can spare time and thought on creating a tourism demand in the battle-scarred Kargil.

A tourism complex in Kargil will have other spin-off effects. Jawans familiar with the snowy, mountain terrain and quickly-changing weather in surrounding areas could be encouraged as part of their resettlement programme to open and manage tourism – related establishments. Besides, in better weather conditions the Army itself could conduct domestic visitors to hallowed points like Tiger Hill.

Development of Kargil as a tourist destination with a memorial at its core will more than compensate what the operation cost in terms of arrivals.

Marketing the Millennium Sun

Most millennium celebrations are featuring the 'Explore India' programme. Preparations are already on for opening of Katchal island in the Andaman Nicobar group for watching sunrise on the millennium morning. In fact, worldwide several countries will be celebrating the event at the dawn of January 1, 2000 AD. Inspiration, however, for the celebrations world-wide has come from Britain where a village called Greenwich just outside London marks an imaginary line dividing the two hemispheres. Time everywhere is counted ahead or behind the Greenwich Mean Time (GMT). The observatory on a hillock here is the world's most famous time keeper. So, even while the rest of the world destinations are offering sunrise–watch to usher in the millennium, Greenwich reminds one that the great day starts there at midnight GMT. This writer visited Greenwich a few days back and talked to astronomers and others on plans for millennium celebrations which are not without controversy. At the same time, Greenwich offers a reminder, to those in search of tourism marketing strategies, of how even a natural phenomenon could be put to practical use. The Greenwich observatory is one of the many attractions that annually draws millions of visitors. With ten kilometres of frontage on the Thames river and vast acres of parkland, it is a place of beauty. Greenwich is where time begins. It is also a heritage site of world importance. There are royal palaces, the marine museum, and other vestiges of architectural and scientific achievement. Of course, its fame is perpetuated in the observatory founded towards the close of the 17th century to help ships at sea to discover longitude of points for perfecting navigation and astronomy. Thus, though Greenwich is primarily a science centre, it has vitality, a diversity of treasures and pastimes to make an evening out a night to remember.

The British Tourist Authority estimates that the millennium experience can generate upto 500 million pounds sterling through additional overseas visitors. More than 2 million visitors are expected to visit Greenwich to watch the mammoth dome, the world's largest, being developed to commemorate the millennium dawn. The dome has stimulated new interest in the use of the Thames as a major transport artery and tourist attraction. The social legacy of the dome and the challenge in education, environment, arts and heritage of Greenwich will be felt for years to come as a reminder to future generations that the 6 millennium was timed to make a difference.

Estimated to cost 750 million pounds, the grandiose project of the dome is not without detractors. Many wonder why such a colossal amount should be spent on a dome with limited utility. This has been countered by the promoters who point out that no money from tax revenues will be used. The budget comes from sponsorships and income from ticket sales, licensed merchandise, media rights, on-site catering and national lottery grants. Such is the huge size of the dome that it could contains Trafalgar Square, 117 tennis courts or 12 football pitches. It covers one million square feet of space and the Eiffel Tower could lie on its side in the dome. It could also shelter 18,000 double-decker buses. Arguments between supporters of the dome and the protagonists continue in the media even as work is going apace on the dome site. The construction is being managed by a joint venture between two of Britain's leading firms.

The quest for the millennium experience has spurred action in countries as far apart as France and Fiji. Indian interest so far has been limited to holiday makers visiting the dome site.

With India's national priorities different, a dome-like project is necessarily out of reckoning. But a date with the sun on the morning of the millennium over the mountains, beyond the desert horizon and at the confluence of three seas at Kanniyakumari should be a worthwhile marketing proposition.

Trade Shows

All favoured destinations in the world look up to trade shows as a means of promotion, sales and marketing. Linked with this participation, is getting into the media to reinforce this publicity. Incidentally, in the tourism sector most trade shows are organised by publishing houses which underlines this connection. Still, the basic question that arises is how relevant the trade shows are to different categories of users and providers in the tourism sector. Does generic promotion help the buyer or the seller or both? Does it help neither? The Indian travel trade as well as the tourism authorities have been scrupulously taking part without fail in ITB, WTM and PATA mart. So much so, one industry major who could not cite any tangible gain from participation in one of these major events pleaded he would continue to attend "because otherwise we will be missed in the reckoning for our overseas contacts." The question that inevitably arises is what sort of fairs or trade shows should one go to and with what expectations. How does one evoke interest in the travel media, particularly overseas, in any establishment

Answers to these queries were sought at a seminar in New Delhi organised jointly by the Ministry of Tourism and PATA (India) chapter. A noteworthy feature of the event was the effort by the tourism authorities as well as the trade representatives to use available international resources for assessment of instruments for promotion.

The discussions emphasised that mere participation in trade shows would not get the host country visitors. Much planning, homework, identification of target groups, access to data base and a clear perception of the buyer's needs were essential. Equally important was taking the right approach to media and other tools of promotions like brochures. The role of public relations has become increasingly central to marketing. Media persons from overseas spoke of opportunities offered by the media which could only be exploited by the trade through a professional approach. Media interests in the industry will have to be necessarily sustained. If a media person wants to meet the "boss" and the sales people the request should not be negated. The PR person should be thoroughly knowledgeable on the industry in general and his own undertaking in particular. The PR concept in the Indian tourism sector is its weakest link. Even top companies do not have designated PR professionals either in direct employment or on contract. A long-felt need of the Ministry of Tourism to have a PR agency of its own for regular communication or for crisis management remains unfulfilled. Returning to the conference theme "Getting the most out of trade shows," Bill Baker of the Sydney-based think tank Destination Development Group and Pauline Tan of TTG-Asia pointed to the imperatives of simple niceties and eye-to-detail in getting the message to the media. Media interest may vary and it is the job of those handling media relations to assess the different requirements of individual publications and respond accordingly. Besides, these professionals should have to acquaint themselves with the functioning of the media they cater to. A senior travel executive from Japan, Norihiro Kobyashi and TAAI's northern India president, Rajji Rai, held that the rationale of participation in trade shows should be directly based on the preference of target groups and the nature of the available product.

Navin Berry, coordinator of SATTE which held its sixth annual show in Agra in April and also event manager of Indian Expo during Tourism

Week took the opportunity to drive home that it is more relevant for Indian sellers to go to country or region-specific shows instead of the bigger all-purpose events like TTB and WTM. He saw nothing wrong in extending hospitality and free or rebated tickets to buyers when the purpose was to sell your own destination. Also, he dismissed complaints that not enough quality buyers were coming to Indian shows.

At the same time he argued in favour of extending facilities to even repeat buyers as also to members of Indian establishments overseas marketing the shows. He agreed, however, on the need for guidelines not on participation but on the location of the shows.

The need for a database in order to get the maximum out of trade shows was accepted by the additional director general tourism, Mohan Khanna. He appealed for the industry's cooperation in this task.

The director general Ashok Pradhan, who is also chairman of the PATA India chapter set the tone for the seminar by defining the norms which will result in productive participation.

The event turned out to be a useful experience for tour operators who spend sizeable sums of money on participation in trade shows around the world and also on the imperatives of carrying the media with them.

4
Heritage Restoration Demands Priority

The three task forces sent by INTACH – Indian National Trust for Art and Cultural Heritage – to the quake-affected areas of Gujarat have reported extensive damage to heritage properties and the natural environment. The team were led by Divay Gupta, Janhwij Sharma (both heritage conservationists) and Himanshu Grover (nature conservationist). They were joined by experts from other NGOs and agencies, including construction engineers, in assessing the damage as well as suggesting short- and long-term measure for restoration. Their report is being discussed at workshops organised by INTACH in the capital on Earthquake Hazards for Heritage Properties, where an international authority, Sir Bernard Feildon, will be the main speaker. The workshop will then draw up guidelines for the immediate task of preventing any further damage, supervised clearance of the debris in order to salvage artefacts and structural pieces. For the long-term, the guidelines will cover the areas of restoration, the costs involved and plans for raising funds from the corporate sector as well as the people, and finally, strengthening the properties against future shocks.

Briefing EH&C, Divay Gupta said his team had visited Kutch while Himnashu Grover went to Jamnagar, Rajkot and Junagadh and Janhwij Sharma to the Mehsana and Surendranagar areas. Kutch has been the worst hit; out of 250 listed heritage properties, as much as 50 per cent may have suffered damage in varying degrees. Of the 128 properties in the Rajkot – Jamnagar area, nearly 20 per cent have been affected, while in the Mehsana—Surendranagar area, 10 per cent of the 110 listed buildings have been damaged. Much of the devastation affecting heritage properties took place, in Bhuj where the buildings most badly hit included the Aina Mahal, Prag Mahal, Chattris, Sharad Bagh, Museum, Jubilee Hospital, Hatim Shah and Vegetable Market. Craft villages of Dhamadka, Bhujadi and Chavda, historic settlements of Koldi Mahadevpur and Kudhreshwar are among those which suffered heavy damage. Noha Darbargarh (palace), Tera Darbargarh, Than Monastery, Mandivi Customs House and Light House are also damaged, as are the Limdi Darbargarh, Morvi Darbargarh, Mani Mandir, Uleshwar Wat Mahal, Jamnagar Darbargarh and Willingdon Crescent (Gandhi Chowk).

The task forces' report also recommends guidelines for immediate/ emergency rescue of historical and landmark buildings in the affected areas of Gujarat: "After assessing the conditions on the ground, we feel there is urgent need for salvaging important architectural fragments from the debris of the collapsed historic buildings for their reconstruction. Dismantling needs to be done for parts of buildings that may be unstable or are not heavily damaged and sections that have partially collapsed. Preservation in situ is to be done for buildings and sections of buildings that have some damage but can be restored using conservation techniques."

The report suggests dos and donts on debris management and salvage of historical architectural material. It says; "do not disturb or dispose debris of a historical building. If the debris of heritage buildings has fallen on the road or any public area, it should be put back inside the compound of the building. Maintain status quo until technical assistance is available. Cordon off the debris to prevent pilferage for further damage. Salvage architecturally significant members like carvings, jharokhas, carved doors and windows, "brackets, columns, railings, decorative features like hardware, key stones, sculpture, painted wall sections, decorative plaster work, iron work and so on. Keep the salvaged material in a safe place, preferably covered with tarpaulin, to prevent damage or theft." The report of the task forces also has something to say about the dismantling of structurally unstable heritage buildings. "While dismantling, be careful about the safety of the persons pulling down the historical buildings," it emphasises. Prop up all structurally unsafe members like arches, domes, roofs and parapets before starting work on dismantling.

INTACH vice-chairman, S K Misra, has written to the government for stricter enforcement of the existing laws for the protection of monuments on debris management.

Outside of Rajasthan, Gujarat has the largest number of heritage hotels, almost all of them former palaces. An estimated half a dozen of these palace hotels have also been damaged. These include the famous Ranjitwilas Palace in Wankaner and palace hotels in Limbdi, Mandvi, Surendranagar and Bhuj, The Indian Heritage Hotels Association is holding a meeting in Rajkot, with support from INTACH, to draw up plans for the restoration of the damaged properties and seek assistance from the hotel industry. FHRAI and HAI have also been invited to participate.

The hospitality industry, according to media reports, has responded generously with donations for relief and rehabilitation in Gujarat. It also needs to spare a thought for the restoration of heritage hotels and other heritage properties that have suffered in the earthquake.

•

The Spiritual Route to Tourism

The recent International Conclave on Buddhism and Spiritual Tourism held at Vigyan Bhawan in the Capital and the dedication ceremony of the Mahabodhi Temple in Bodh Gaya which was recently declared a world heritage site by UNESCO, will be remembered as yet another major initiative by the Jagmohan-Rathi Vinay Jha team. It is the first time that such an event has been organised on an international scale with the twin objective of spreading the Buddha's message of peace and non-violence and promoting spiritual tourism. It was indeed a grand show which attracted 600 scholars (including 200 from India) and ministers and religious leaders from as many as 25 countries. And, among those who addressed them were India's President, Dr APJ Kalam and the Dalai Lama. Jagmohan's welcoming partners were the minister of state Bhavnaben Chikalia', culture secretary, Dhanendra Kumar and tourism joint secretary, Amitabh Kant and additional director general, Rashmi Verma. To Rathi Jha went the honour of formally welcoming the president, the Dalai Lama, foreign dignitaries and the learned men and women.

In a moving inaugural speech, Dr Kalam suggested that a university of 'universal unity and understanding' on the lines of the ancient seat of learning be re-established at Nalanda, and dedicated to the preservation of the teaching of Gautama Buddha. He said, "At this critical juncture of universal turbulence and instability arising out of mutual distrust and hatred leading to violence, the world needs such a university of peace, enlightment and great thought." He called upon the Ministers of HRD and tourism to undertaken the task of setting up the university.

In his address Jagmohan said that his ministry has already moved a proposal to elevate the status of Nalanda University to that of a 'deemed university'. "Efforts are also on," he added, "to make Nalanda into a great hub of learning, tourism and culture." The Chinese pilgrim Hieun Tsang's travels in India over a period of 16 years has also been converted into a Buddhist route and work is in hand to recreate his journey. India, he said, is the world's hope for spirituality. For, it is here that three great spiritual movements evolved. "There are many physical and spiritual signposts of these movements in the form of monuments, paintings and manuscripts. The international conclave will help acquaint the world with this wealth of knowledge," he said.

The Dalai Lama, who delivered the keynote address, dwelt on the experience gained by the world in the last century. The closing years of the century saw a widespread growth of awareness that improving physical facilities and material progress alone were not adequate. There was much greater public recognition of the need to employ non-violence, to work for peace and the protection of the natural environment." "Now," he went on to say, "it is timely and appropriate for every religious tradition to promote the positive qualities of compassion, tolerance, contentment and self-discipline." Said His Holiness, "I believe that the Buddha dharma in particular, which has flourished for over 2,500 years and which shares with other religious traditions teachings concerning compassion, kindness, tolerance and self discipline, has a special role to play in our modern world." Pointing out that the Buddhist traditions are preserved in scriptures in Pali and in Sanskrit, he said, "I would like to suggest that our Indian Buddhist brothers and sisters should take special interests in and responsibility for upholding the Sanskrit traditions, which proposed for more than a thousand years in this country."

The Dalai Lama saw merit in spiritual tourism. He said, "An important aspect of the Indian Buddhist legacy that concerns us all and that I understand is the focus of this gathering, is the existence of Buddhist sacred places. Naturally, they have a special significance for Buddhists." He referred to his first visit to Bodh Gaya and said that since that moving experience, "I have travelled far more extensively in India and in many other parts of the world. Having the opportunity to visit the pilgrimage places of other religious traditions, has led me to realise that spiritual tourism has a significant role to play in fostering inter-religious harmony and understanding."

As was to the expected, poor connectivity and lack of infrastructure in the Buddhist circuit was commented upon by many a participant in the conclave. Jagmohan, in a special presentation, assured them that this is being addressed in a concerted and focused manner, and unveiled his ministry's plans for improving roads and encouraging entrepreneurs to build accommodation and other facilities.

In a media briefing on the eve of the conclave, Jagmohan had said that depending on the success of the conclave, he would decide whether it could be made an annual event. Observers would readily concede that a good beginning has been made in promoting a segment which has immense potential.

Niche Tourism

Focusing on a niche market is central to any promotional success. But the identification of the product and the market segment will need careful study before any venture is launched. With the gradual diversification of the Indian tourism product, the potential and possibilities of niche markets have increased. At the just concluded IATO Annual

Convention in Jaipur, one fruitful session was devoted to marketing, at which several valuable suggestions which were practicable were proffered. It is hoped that the impressive number of the participants who turned up for the session on the closing day would get back and work on some of these suggestions.

Deepak Vohra, the youthful joint secretary in the external affairs ministry and popular TV personality, made some distinctive observations based on his personal experiences. Vohra is on transfer to Madrid where he will be minister counsellor at the Indian embassy. He told the audience of the rejuvenation camp that he had attended in Haridwar recently along with his wife. The camp was a blend of practices of Yoga, meditation and Ayurvedic therapy. He described the experience as exhilarating and was confident that it would offer a niche market, particularly to the Mediterranean and Latin American countries. The industry could well make use of his services which he offered in projecting India as a destination with a difference.

Health tourism has become universally popular with people over 55-plus constituting the bulk of travellers, particularly from advanced countries. They seek relief from stress which is the health problem number one in those nations. For a long time, the Ayurvedic massage treatment has been a USP with some major hotel and resort establishments in Goa and Kerala. The Taj Group, in its promotional campaigns, has highlighted it as an incentive to visitors to its Kozhikode property. In fact, as in many other things, ITDC in Kovalam had pioneered the project but some undesirable elements who had strayed into the hospitality sector brought a bad name to this ancient treatment. So, it was only proper for the management and the tourism ministry not to use the word 'massage' to describe this value addition service. It is now called Ayurvedic therapy in its comprehesive detail as the massage has unsavoury connotation with some other destinations in Asia.

Also, related to it was another piece of information which the diplomat shared with the tour operators. There are as many as 1,200 Satya Sai Baba centres in Latin America, to persuade at least 10 each of these centres to travel to the home of this seer would add up to substantial number of long haul tourists. The Sai Baba cult is not confined to South America alone. Like the Bahai's they are spread all over and to persuade them to visit India would be a rewarding exercise. Also, packages for such visits could cover the country's other attractions and this will provide a breakthrough in the Latin American market which, because of distance and language and also lack of information has remained untapped.

Coincidentally, Ram Kohli, IATO's founder president, recently reactivated the India chapter of Confederacion de Turiste Organisacion of America Latin (COTAL) which is an influential body of the travel trade in that continent, Kohli has been canvassing for a meeting of the executive committee of COTAL in India in January next. Efforts are on to enlist the support of Air-India and Maurya Sheraton for the stay and travel of committee members. Some of Kohli's new colleagues in the COTAL chapter have been over-enthusiastic in getting the Latin Americans here and want a general assembly to be hosted by India. Kohli himself is wary of such moves and has advised them to focus on the executive committee meeting.

The move for the Latin American links and Deepak Vohra's suggestion for concentrating on the traditional but little promoted aspect of the Indian tourism product, should facilitate the creation of a niche market. The tourism ministry, the travel trade, whose representatives heard Vohra patiently and the new marketing society, Destination India, should have a look at the move. Incidentally, the marketing session, as one looks back was the liveliest exchange of IATO at Jaipur. Among the delegates who participated were new entrants, all young to the travel trade.

A concomitant highlight is the refutation by the larger turnout and a growing membership of IATO, as of the other trade organisations of the doomsday merchants who use any available platform and pronounce that the Indian tourism has no future. On the other hand, as long as there are optimists like Vohra, who with their tell-tale experiences point to the niche markets that need to be tapped, there is hope for tourism.

CII Emphasises on Heritage and its Symbolic Relationship with Tourism

The just concluded three-day international conference on "India: Tourism and Heritage – Challenge 21" indeed was, as organisers CII claimed, a star-studded affair. Held at the capital's Taj Palace hotel, it brought together a galaxy of travel industry leaders, central and state ministers and leading tourism lights from home and abroad. Mauritius Tourism was a partner country and Uttaranchal, partner state. Sponsors included the department of tourism and the ministry of external affairs. Tourism minister Jagmohan, Uttaranchal chief minister, Nityanand Swami and his tourism minister, Kedar Singh Fonia were there. Overseas participants included Nandcoomar Bodha, tourism minister from Mauritius, who was the guest of honour and the Italian ambassador, Benedetto Amari. Among the faculty were Ingval Maxwell, director, technical conservation, Historic Scotland, S K Misra, vice-chairman, INTACH, Jayanta Sanyal, senior consultant, Planning Commission. Taking part in the various panel discussions were tourism secretary, M P Bezbaruah and director general Vinod Duggal, the immediate past president of TAAI, Pradip Madhavji and the new FHRAI chief, B K Gupta.

As was to be expected, the focus of discussions remained on the aftermath of the tragic events. In his inaugural address, Jagmohan came straight to the point. Do not ring the alarm bells too sharp, he told the industry, and, instead got down to meeting the new challenges. Industry should join government's efforts to project India as a safe destination and break new ground in attracting visitors from Asia, Australia, Korea, Japan, Taiwan, Malaysia, Thailand, Indonesia, since they are huge markets. Equally, important, he said, is the industry's help in backing a strong movement for changing attitudes which have harmed India's image – lack of hygiene and sanitation, poor civic services, beggars and touts, cattle roaming the roads, taxis and shopkeepers fleecing tourists. Also, the minister said, there is need to preserve and enhance our heritage, not only in monuments but also in our culture. With greater order, discipline and cleanliness, old and new Delhi could be an experience which would turn visitors into India's ambassadors. Similarly, an upgraded Varanasi ('which was existed before Rome was born') could easily attract five million tourists.

Jagmohan's plea for building domestic tourism as a sound base for international tourism was supported by Yogesh Chandra, secretary general, World Travel and Tourism Council's India chapter, when he made a presentation on the council's findings about the burgeoning demand of domestic travel in India against a painfully slow development of infrastructure. In an aptly titled session 'home truths' Hugh Gantzer, travel writer offered a three-point solution to the present crisis. With no glimmer of light emanating from the Euro-American market he said, we should adopt a policy of "consolidate, look in, look east." His recipe included such ingredients as sizable lowering of the prohibitive ATF (Aviation Turbine Fuel) prices to make domestric air travel less expensive and restoration of LTC. Taking over from there, Pawan Khanna, head of Rainbow Travels supported the view that domestic tourism is our best bet. But, we must do a lot of introspection to change mindsets particularly among decision-makers. Tell them, he said, to stop using tourists as a milch cow. He pointed out that the world had not changed east of Suez. Seize that opportunity and market India's spirituality to people seeking inner peace and tranquillity.

The highlight of the CII venture was the CEO's conclave with the participation of nearly 70 industry captains. Divided into eight groups, they discussed in detail tourism's needs in crucial areas like taxation, destination management, training, heritage, marketing connectivity, role of the government and community involvement. It was good that CII was able to involve N K Singh, member, Planning Commission with the conclave. He has his own ideas for tourism which he has been sharing with the travel industry at various fora and the recommendations of CEOs should help him crystalise his strategy for this sector now that the 10th Plan is being finalised. On taxation, the industry captains feel that the current fiscal policy actually penalises entrepreneurial spirit and is working as value destroyers. The lack of 2/3 star hotels they feel is due to high taxation which leaves very little ploughing back of surplus.

Heritage and its symbolic relationship with tourism was emphasised in almost every session. The Italian ambassador offered his country's expertise in restoration work. Dr Shobita Punja of INTACH gave a timely warning that if the country does not make the right decisions about preserving our heritage, tourism, will collapse.

Harnessing Heritage

A flash back to the genesis of the restoration movement so important to the hospitality sector was provided by INTACH, which has launched a series of lectures on the subject. Wacziarg's was the second in the series held at the Trust's headquarters in the capital recently. In the audience were travel industry leaders including Inder Sharma, British Council head Edward Maredan, INTACH's Delhi chapter chief for heritage activities OP Jain and Nayana Goradia, author of *Lord Qurzon – The Last of the British Moghuls*, about the Viceroy credited with initiatives for saving the country's great monuments. INTACH vice-chairman SK Misra, who presided over the lecture, recalled that Wacziarg, who had come to the country as the French Commercial Counsellor, was so fascinated by India's heritage that he decided to make this country his home.

Wacziarg reminisced that in the initial stages the trio (Aman Nath, OP and Wacziarg) were only interested in the restoration, turning the ruins of Neemrana into a museum was the farthest they had thought. The idea of a heritage hotel came up only when viability was discussed in detail. Neemrana, Wacziarg said, was a huge challenge both in the technical aspects of the restoration and also the bureaucratic hassles of obtaining the approvals necessary to convert it into a hotel. The state government asked for large sums of money as 'conversion charges', while the promoter kept wondering whether they should be rewarded or charged for restoring ruins to their original glory. However, their determination kept them going. The runaway success of Neemrana was followed within the decade by Hill

Fort, Kasroli; The Muj Fort, Kuchesar; the Piramal Haveli, Bagar; the Ramgarh Bungalows and the Glass House near Rishikesh.

The latest jewels in the Neemrana Hotels' crown – Hotel De L'Orient in Pondicherry and 'The Verandah in the Forest' in Matheran near Mumbai was the subject of Wacziarg's lecture. The Pondicherry hotel is an 18th century colonial structure used by the French and later the Indians as the office of the territory's education department. Through slides Wacziarg took the audience into a year's hard labour and tender care that went into the restoration. Today, the property is their most profitable venture after Neemrana. "France in the 18th century has been brought alive in India," he says about the impact made by the property. Matheran is the last hill station the British built in India and is Asia's only pedestrian resort. There is joy in reaching 'The Verendah in the Forest', a house built by a Capt. Barr in 1857. Though reaching the property means a 45 minute walk from the road head – you can also ride a pony or be carried in a palanquin – he lists it as a plus point in the Matheran experience. Solar heating and rain-water harvesting are innovations by Neemrana Hotels and Wacziarg is confident that the monsoon experience would be an added attraction.

TERI Shows the Way

In the run upto the millennium a noted international expert on environment had warned of peoples' resentment against tourism if hotels and other infrastructure continued to eat away community resources such as energy, water and food. Addressing a global gathering of the hospitality industry leaders in Jakarta in 1997, he had given a telling example of how a guest in a hotel in Bali was consuming as much water in a day as an island citizen would in a month. His advice to the industry and particularly hoteliers was straight: a twenty-first century hotel should create its own resources of energy, water and food and leave to the community what belongs to it. In other words, there was need for top priority to sustainable tourism.

In a welcome initiative, India's home grown conservation outfit – Tata Energy Research Institute (TERI) – has created the country's (and may be South Asia's) first habitat which epitomises sustainability. Christened RETREAT (Resource Efficient TERI Retreat for Environmental Awareness and Training), it is located at Gual Pahari in Gurgaon just 30 km from New Delhi and is awaiting inauguration by prime minister, Atal Behari Vajpayee. Once a swampy, degraded wasteland, the TERI campus is today a lush green, living and throbbing habitat. Built as a model training complex, RETREAT demonstrates efficient utilisation of energy, sustainable and integrated use of both natural resources and clean and renewable energy technologies, and efficient waste management.

RETREAT, which took three years to complete has a built-up area of 3,000 sq meters. This 30 room training hostel boasts of conference facilities for 100, dining space and kitchen, recreational area, computer room and a library. What makes RETREAT unique is its total independence of the city's grid system and near complete freedom from city services and infrastructure. Interestingly, energy planning in the building has led to a reduced load of 96 kW (peak) from a conventional 280 kW (peak), a saving of 184 kW. Another distinctive feature of TERI's Gual Pahari effort is the dedicated team effort that has made it possible to combine technology and architecture in a manner 'that the beholder's understanding of the environment, energy and buildings deepens.' An integrated design element, the solar passive architecture, renewable sources of energy, conventional and non-conventional heating and cooling and energy saving features, all stand out in an astonishing blend of the traditional and the modern.

According to a TERI spokesperson, a sustainable habitat design is an economically viable solution with minimal environmental footprint that can drastically reduce energy demands in buildings by 50-60 per cent. And, it can be done through reduced demands on the fossil fuels, reduced emissions, reduced pressure on natural resources like water, reduced waste generation and through recycling resources. All this has been attempted at RETREAT. A hostel is only a couple of steps short of a hotel; hotels too can be largely sustainable propositions now.

Mili Mazumdar, a young architect at TERI, who showed this writer around RETREAT which was being dressed up to welcome the prime minister, threw additional light on the Gual Pahari experiment which is likely to be replicated across the country. She said, "To make a building like this the thought of energy efficiency has to be there in the design stage." According to her, three basic factors were considered: (1) functionality of the building (how energy is used in it during the day or at night); (2) design can minimise energy demands by architectural intervention through passive concepts like solar orientation, lattice work for shading, insulation and landscaping; and (3) space conditioning and lighting demands can be met through energy efficient systems while electric energy demands are met by renewable energy sources. And so, said Majumdar, the RETREAT complex is powered by photovoltaic-gasifier hybrid renewable energy system, which uses waste biomass and solar radiation as sources of energy. RETREAT also has the country's first solar roof. Space conditioning and air-cooling is provided by an earth air tunnel, which consumes a fraction of the energy. The ammonia chiller and the evaporative cooling system provide air-conditioning equivalent to a conventional 35 tonne capacity. Waste water is treated using plants. Solar heating is used for both space and water. Dr Ajay Mathur, dean, energy environment technology division, TERI, sums up the institute's achievement in these words: "There was a need to develop a model habitat design of high equilibrium, with high level of thermal and visual comfort and with minimal environmental footprint, which is replicable in part or whole."

TERI has shown the way. It is for our entrepreneurs to contribute in the growth of sustainable tourism in the cities, rural areas, in the mountains or even in arid zones.

Conservation and Restoration

The Casino Group of Hotels and Neemrana Fort Palace in India, Kandalama Hotel in Sri Lanka and Dwarika's Village Hotel in Nepal have won the award for excellence in conservation and restoration presented by the Indian National Trust For Art and Cultural Heritage (INTACH). The awards were instituted by INTACH recently, in association with South Asia Travel and Tourism Exchange (SATTE), to spread greater awareness about the region's rich heritage and encourage conservation and restoration efforts.

The award; were given away by S K Misra, vice-chairman, INTACH, at SATTE 2001's inaugural function in New Delhi. Well-known conservationist duo, Aman Nath and Francis Wacziarg, received the award for Neemrana Fort Palace, which, the citation said, 'is perhaps the first example in India of taking on the challenge of waking an utter ruin from its crumbling facades and foundations.

The Casino Group of Hotels, founded by Dominic Joseph in 1954, opened its first hotel on Willington Island in Kochi. Today it has eight 'very exclusive boutique hotels and resorts'. All of them in Kerala, and it has won several national and state awards. The group's strong commitment to environmental protection and sustainable tourism has also won it distinction from the Green organisations.

The Kandalama Hotel in Sri Lanka's Dambulla district, created by the Aitken Spence Group is, according to the citation, a stellar example of a 'green hotel' which has won acclaim for its contribution to the cause of ecologically sensitive tourism.

Two Birds with One Stone

The signing of a franchise agreement with the owners of three heritage properties in Himachal Pradesh by WelcomHeritage not only increases accommodation in this category of the group but is a pointer to their growing popularity to leisure travellers. There are in all forty-six identified and approved heritage hotels now operating in this country offering a unique experience in comparative quiet in rural environment, lesser expensive accommodation. It is unique in the sense that leisure travellers who prefer to live through the lifestyle of bygone days come to these properties as a destination and not as a part of a package.

The concept was developed about five years ago with a view to converting old palaces, havelis, forts and residences built prior to 1950 into accommodation units as these traditional structures reflect the ambience of an era that is long past. At the same time, it seeks to ensure that such properties, which are landmarks of Indian heritage, are not lost due to decay but become financially viable properties providing additional room capacity for tourists.

The largest number of properties so identified is in Rajasthan, where the movement was pioneered with the entry of Umaid Bhawan Palace as a hotel under the Welcomgroup banner. Since the concept has caught on in other states as well as is evident from the Himalayan experience.

In fact, the heritage properties are placed in three categories according to their age – those which existed prior to 1920; built between 1920 and 1935 and the final category, which came after 1935 but were already operative before 1950. The three categories cover the new entrants to the fold of the WelcomHeritage, which is a joint venture mooted by ITC Hotels Ltd. and the Marudhar Hotels of Jodhpur, headed by Maharaja Gaj Singh. The three in the Himachal circuit are the fort of Nalagarh in Solan district which dates back to the 15th century Taragarh Palace, a princely summer resort which came up in the 1930s and Judge's Court, a quiel retreat built by a former judge of the then Punjab High Court as his holiday residence in the early part of the century. Both Taragarh and Judge's Court are in Kangra district.

Nalagarh Fort surrounded by ten acres of greenery providing a breathtaking view of the Shivalik hills, is the largest of three with 20 rooms, eight of them deluxe. Taragarh, again a well appointed resort at an altitude of 100 metres, has 15 rooms all comfortably furnished. Judge's Court, which is truly a heritage country manor at Paragpur, a truly "modern" village that has been declarge a heritage village, has seven large rooms of the Anglo Saxon tradition.

The enlargement of the WelcomeHeritage family by the inclusion of these operating hotels is a major development in tourism's growth. For the quality of the tourism product is very much enriched by the facilitation, the ambience and the traditions of these properties which once hummed with activity. Now, these are the places where the leisure traveller seeks the quiet of the Indian countryside comfortable with modern facilities enabling the visitor to contemplate the life and times of those who once occupied these places. It is quite possible that more people will have assured access to these places when the time-share facilitation is introduced. But, as far as WelcomHeritage is concerned, according to Habib Rehman, managing director of ITC Hotels, the group's immediate concern is consolidation. The process is going in earnest as it has already over a dozen forts, palaces and mansions sporting the WelcomHeritage logo. This is the largest single number an hotel chain has of heritage properties.

ITC hotels has been prompted to promote this group not only as a business proposition but also out of a sense of corporate citizen responsibility to preserving the national assets. WelcomHeritage is headed by one of its seniormost executives, Om Munjal, who is designated president.

Heritage property management is not just upkeep and maintenance of old structures. Each of these properties is integral to the local cultural scene and a landmark in the region's history. These are monuments to creativity of Indian genius and constitute a definite link in the Indian civilisational continuum. For instance, Umaid Bhawan Palace, the flagship of WelcomHeritage, embodies in itself a fascinating blend of the Oriental and the Anglo Saxon architecture, decor, and for that matter, even landscaping.

The heritage movement had started with Neemrana off the Delhi-Jaipur highway. It also typifies the transformation of a derelict, forgotten fort taken over by wild growth into an exotic example of restoration. It marks a new phase in Indian Renaissance. To Indian tourism it gives a lustrous reinforcement to is infrastructure; it offers to the connoisseur an experience not available anywhere else, and it vindicates the sector's claim to be generator of employment and that too in remote areas.

India Misses Opportunity to Project 'Explore India...Year' at PATA '99

India failed to utilise the PATA platform, which draws over a 1,000 hospitality industry leaders from around the world to its annual convention here, to project the 'Explore India in the Millennium Year'. Director general – Tourism, Ashok Pradhan, who was scheduled to make a presentation to a specially invited international media group could not come to Nagoya and the event was cancelled.

Apart from this, India had a windfall of honors. The most important of which is the unanimous election of tourism secretary, Madan Prasad Bezbaruah as the President of the International Body, the world's largest representing governments and industry, for the year 2000-01.

He is the second Indian to be selected to the office, the first was Inder Sharma, industry doyen.

Ram Kohli, founder president of IATO and MD, Creative Travels who is on the PATA Board of Directors and also a member of its executive committee was given the chairman's Award, are honour reserved for one leader every year for outstanding contribution to PATA and Tourism.

Mandeep Soin, chairman of PATA India Chapter, environmental concerns committee, was honoured for designing the environment Fledge which as Soin told a seminar in Nagoya "empowers travellers to assert their rights to environmental protection".

A feature on Oberoi, Raj Vilas hotel in Jaipur by a foreign journalist, Carol Lutfy, received an honourable mention at the PATA Gold Awards ceremony. The thirty-five strong Indian delegation donning Rajasthani turbans stood out at the inaugural function which was also attended by members of the Japanese Royal Family, Prince and Princess Takamado.

5
Tourism Destination

Room with a View

Marriott International, a leading global hospitality company with over 2,600 properties and a room count of close to 5,00,000, has seen phenomenal growth, particularly in Asia Pacific in the last ten years. This is best reflected in its foray into China where in just six years the company has jumped from zero to 45 hotels. Even in India the global major already has five properties including the capital's new address, Marriott WelcomHotel, and Mumbai's JW Marriott. Paul Cerula, Marriott's senior vice-president who was in Delhi recently told media persons that India with "its vibrant economy" offered a huge potential and that the company is looking for "the right partners" to spread its wings. He could not put a date to it but he hoped Marriott's next targets are Bangalore and Chennai.

Marriott's interest in India is not only to franchise or operate more hotels in the country but also to lure the burgeoning Indian outbound traffic to use its hotels worldwide. Only recently Marriott International had upgraded its global sales office in India promoting the livewire Sheema Vohra as director and opening a second outlet in Mumbai.

The main reason for Cerula's visit was to promote the Marriott Rewards launched in 1997 which he claimed was the world's first and largest multi-brand frequent guest programme (the chain's brands include apart from Marriott, Ritz-Carlton, Renaissance, JW and Courtyard). Already, he said, 19 million members are benefiting from the programme. Points can be earned through frequent flyer miles, AIR properties.

A little known facet of Marriott international that came out at the media briefing is the pride of place it gives to Time Share. A separate division, Marriott Vacation Club International (MVCI), has under its belt 52 resorts in seven countries with 8,300 associates, and 2,30,000 owners. Starting in 1984, the division's annual sales touched the billion dollar mark in 2000. As Cerula put it, MVCI members have a choice of experiences that range from the magic of Orlando to the Snow capped Rocky Mountains, to the sugary beaches of tropical islands. We are expanding too, he said. Each of our resorts, he added, is architecturally designed to reflect the lifestyle and ambience of its setting. Unlike in India where Resort Condominium International (RCI) has virtual monopoly of time-share exchange programme, Marriott has a tie up with competitor Interval International which provides its mem-programme, Cerula said, ensures the exchange in the same category of five-star resorts as those of MVCI.

The Marriott senior vice-president gave five advantage its vacation spots had over those of other companies. These were, he said: brand awareness and credibility via Marriott name; consistency and quality of product hospitality; access to Marriott system via Marriott Rewards; responsiveness to consumer need for flexibility, and, variety and geographic broadening of its vacation experience which includes beaches, islands, mountains, lakes and deserts. Currently, a bulk of MVCI time share resorts are in the United States spread over Florida, Colorado, Hawaii and South Carolina. There are three in Spain and one each in France, Thailand and Britain.

Giving a global picture of the time share industry, Cerula said since its small beginning in the French Alps in mid-60s, this segment of the hospitality industry now has 3.8 million member households who own units in 5,300 resorts in 95 countries. The segment's turn over is estimated at US $59 billion.

Cerula sees a good future for time-share. For investors there is an approximate 20 per cent operating profit margin. In the USA, the product is becoming "more of a sought good than an impulse buy." And, as disposable incomes rise, people are more willing to purchase high quality holiday products.ing for 37 per cent and 29 per cent share respectively. Mexico alone has seven per cent and all of southeast Asia including Japan only four per cent.

Time-share came to India in the '90s and already there are more than 50 resorts and some 40,000 unit owners. Both RCI and the All India Resort Development Association (AIRDA) have been working hard for its growth but the recently released classification norms by the department of tourism (DoT) denying recognition to time-share has been a set back. Hopefully, DoT will review its decision.

Good Times Ahead

15 per cent increase in arrivals, northward moving hotel occupancies and the entry of three of the most prestigious chains – Aman resorts, Four

Seasons and Shangri-La has been a shot in the arm of the hospitality sector beleaguered as it has been by a series of crises which began with 9/11. Claims that overseas visitors' count may touch the three million mark this year may be over-optimistic but, even a return to the previous best of 2.6 million would be an encouraging development.

Significantly, Aman resorts, the world's most exclusive top end of the market chain promoted by journalist turned hotelier, Adrian Zecha, is making its foray into India with four properties, three of these to be in operation before 2003 ends. The tiny 12-room Manor Hotel in the capital's Friends Colony is already functioning as is the Aman-i-Khas, a luxury air-conditioned tent complex near the tiger sanctuary of Ranthambor. Final touches are being given to what would be the chain's flagship in India, the majestic Umaid Bhawan Palace in Jodhpur, managed until recently by ITC-Welcomgroup where the number of rooms is being reduced from the existing 100 to fit into Zecha's norm of 30-60 keys. The fourth Aman resort will be the former ITDC Lodi Hotel which is at a walking distance from the New Delhi, Oberoi. The schedule for the successor or successors to the Lodi which had 200 rooms (the structure is yet to be demolished) is not known but there were reports that it will be replaced by two properties, one a typical Aman resort with less than 50 rooms and the other, a larger unit with more rooms but a notch lower than the Amanresort standard.

To be functional in 2005 is the Four Seasons' hotel in Mumbai in the Worli area. The Canada-based luxury chain has entered into a management agreement with Magus Estates and Hotels Ltd. whose co-owner Shiv Jatia is associated with the Hyatt properties in Delhi and Kolkata. Four Seasons Hotel Mumbai, as it is going to be named, will have 175 rooms and service apartments. Interestingly, Four Seasons, which is largely engaged in management tie-ups, is planning to invest in the Mumbai hotel up to 20 per cent of its equity. Chairman and CEO of Four Seasons, Isadore Sharp told media-persons that in the coming years the group would like to extend its presence to other metros like Bangalore and Chennai. Asked about the status of the talks for a tie-up with the Oberois, Sharp is reported to have said, "We have ceased discussions with the Oberoi group on that project." About any exclusivity in the arrangements with the Jatia group, the Four Seasons CEO said it would apply only in the case of Mumbai; for projects in other locations the Canadian chain is free to join hands with other hotel groups.

The managing director and CEO of Shangri-La, Giovanni Angelini said the same thing in Delhi when at the end of a seven-year search for an Indian partner he formally exchanged the management agreement initiated earlier in Hong Kong with the owner of Eros Group, R Sood, for the Kanishka Hotel acquired in the ITDC disinvestment process. For any expansion, Shangri-La is keen to have at least half a dozen properties in India, Angelini said. Only in Delhi there will be need for Eros Group's approval but elsewhere it is free to enter into arrangements with other parties. In fact, he said, Shangri-La is already in conversations with other hoteliers.

Sood said Kanishka is being completely redesigned by a Hong Kong-based outfit, Chhada Siembieda and Associates. The former ITC Hotels president, Kanwal Malhotra and first general manager of the trend setting Akbar Hotel of ITDC's halcyon days, is also a consultant on the refurbishing of Akbar to Shangri-La standards. The Eros chief said that the redesigned Kanishka will wear a contemporary look. Its 354 rooms will be equipped with high-speed internet access and wireless LAN as well as three new meeting rooms and a 450 square metre ballroom divisible into three. There will be two restaurants and a coffee shop with a porch terrace overlooking the main outdoor pool as well as an Asian restaurant offering Chinese, Thai, Malay and Japanese cuisine.

Kanishka's is a fascinating story. Built over a piece of prize land in the heart of New Delhi – 200 metres from Connaught Place – known as Windsor Place, which earlier was dotted with Lutyen's bungalows, home to Communist Party members of Parliament, it was designated as a hotel plot in the '70s. The Janata government, which came to power after the Emergency, scaled down the five stars originally planned to two units, one of one-star and another three-stars, Kanishka finally made its debut in time for the Asian Games in 1982 as a four-star ITDC hotel. The cycle has run its full circule and Kanishka will make room from Shangri-La as a super deluxe five-star hotel.

Sharing Good Times

The ministry of tourism views time-share apartment hotels as a means of increasing budget or moderately priced accommodation which is one of the prime needs of the sector. It has formulated guidelines for their recognition as such. Though the time-share concept is some 30 years ol: and has been operating successfully in many parts of the world, in India has been of recent origin, less than a decade ago. There are a total of 'ɔ operating time-share resorts. The ministry predicts the concept will gain momentum in coming years and will attract a large number of middle class foreign tourists apart from catering to the requirements of domestic travellers. It also fulfills a need of the hotel industry to sustain occupanies by tying up with global time-share exchange programmes. Hence growth is of topical relevance.

Illustrative of the success of the time-share movement within the country is that there are already about 1,00,000 unit holders, who have bought at least one week in a resort of their choice. Resort Condominium International (RCI) the world's largest time-share affiliating organisation places the Indian market potential in the next few years at 27 million week holders. Of this according to Markus Deutsch, executive director of RCI, who was recently in Delhi, 2.7 million may actually buy into the units. No less than 55 of the existing time-share properties in India are affiliated to RCI enabling their members to a choice of exchanging their week with overseas properties in about 3,000 locations, In fact, RCI has become a prized affiliation receiving enquiries not only from chains and single unit hotels but also exotic time-share resorts and by new entrepreneurs. A case in point is the interest shown by Mountain Trail, the lone resort at Mukteshwar in Kumaon hills in seeking a linkage. But RCI norms, however, are strict understandably because of its vast international clientele and need for credibility.

One distressing development in the Indian time-share industry has been the erosion of this credibility because of a few fly by night operators who sold time-shares without infrastructural backup. So much so, even major companies with a countrywide spread of properties in various stages of construction were adversely affected and have had to face a severe financial crunch. Hopefully, this will be a transient phase that will be overcome by compulsions of both developers and unit owners seeking an assured holiday at a lesser cost.

RCI has undertaken a major effort to educate both developers and consumers on the programme that is beneficial to them alike. RCI has a stake in this programme insofar, as it will increase the number of its affiliates with a consequential expansion of the global network. For, once an individual purchases time-share, he can have the option to select from the affiliates worldwide, a corresponding resort, at a convenient time.

It works both ways contributing to inbound and outbound travel. Deutsch claims that time-share is now the fastest growing segment of tourism. He cites statistics to show that two per cent of global tourist movements are intime-share time-share accounting for nearly five million families.

RCI studies show that the slice of time-share may increase 0.4 per cent within the next five years. Countries which already have a larger share are Israel and Hungary where it has climbed to five per cent. In the United States it is four per cent.

RCI's India chief, Shukla Bose speaks of increased facilitation services to Indian consumers. The latest is the fully operational Call Centre at its headquarters in Bangalore where not only all information about various services but even exchange transactions can be done over the phone. The Call Centre will soon be linked with a toll free system.

With the accommodation sector still to catch up with perceived requirements of the turn of the century, the time-share movements should be able to contribute to bridge the gap. The stagnation in global traffic is not uniform. South Asia of which India is the biggest component grew its arrivals by five per cent last year which is twice the rate of the world as a whole. According to WTO, tourism receipts also grew better than the world rate (2.8 per cent for South Asia and two per cent for the world) to reach the global figure of 4.4 billion US dollars.

A country-specific factor in envisaging the growth of time-share in India is of course the whopping increase of over 12 per cent in domestic tourist traffic to reach 175 million visits. It is this figure which makes the RCI functionary upbeat.

Luxury Sells: Climb to the Top

Cannes, the French resort city is better known in India as the home of international film festivals and awards. For the hospitality industry, it has a new attraction, the first in Europe, – an annual International Luxury Travel Mart on the lines of a similar trade show in the United States. It made its appearance in December 2002 when this country was still battling with the after-effects of all that has happened since 9/11, Afghanistan and Iraq wars and SARS, and participation was not possible without spade work. For its second show, however, in December 2003, the India tourist office in Paris, a few hotel chains including the Taj and the Oberoi as well as the standalone Imperial in Delhi made a beeline to Cannes. And, so did the youngest and hugly successful destination management company, Le Passage to India. It was ready with a well brought out four colour brochure 'Luxury Holidays'. As its chairman, Ghulam Naqshband explains, "In these days of hard competition among Indian tour operators Le Passage has come up with an original idea of entering this niche market." He adds, "We are the only company in India that has created this product."

Besides luxury accommodation, mainly suites, Le Passage also offers travel by chartered executive aircraft and luxury cars like Mercedes (Le Passage, which came into existence just over a year ago, has already joined the ranks of top ten agencies. In the ten months of the current year it has touched a turnover of Rs 25 crore, an unprecedented achievement. It hopes to close the year with Rs 34 crore).

Naqshband says India's vibrant economy has opened up avenues for yet another segment of visitor – the high profile business traveller and the upmarket tourist who demands the very best any country has to offer. Le Passage's 'Luxury Holidays' he says is aimed at the corporate traveller who would like to combine business with pleasure, and "who would not like to compromise on any aspect" whether it is the hotel or mode of travel. It is precisely for this kind of a discerning and demanding guest, Naqshband adds, "We have painstakingly compiled a list of 22 of India's finest hotels located in important business and tourist centres. The selected hotels, he says, are comparable to the foremost in the world, and more often than not, have much more to offer in terms of sheer size, opulence, grandeur and heritage. Moreover, he goes on to say, within each hotel we have identified the best and most luxurious accommodation, in decor facilities and amenities. Many of the suites have been patronised by heads of state, chief executives of multinationals and celebrities. The 'Luxury Holidays' brochure details the kind of experience a listed hotel can provide. Information on express check-in, breakfast, cocktails, bottle of champagne, beverages, internet connectivity, TV and DVD players, 24 hour butler service, designer toiletries and so on have been taken for granted and not even mentioned.

In addition, Naqshband says, Le Passage also offers other standard, superior and deluxe rooms at the listed hotels for those who prefer them for a business trip or leisure travel or both.

These are the hotels included in Luxury Holidays: from the Oberoi group Rajvilas, Amarvilas, Udaivilas and the main properties in Mumbai, Delhi and Kolkata. From the Taj stable, the chain's main hotels in Mumbai, Kolkata, Delhi and Hyderabad, the palace hotels in Udaipur and Jaipur, Taj Exotica in Goa, Taj West End in Bangalore, Taj Coromandal in Chennai and Taj Malabar in Kochi. ITC-Welcomgroup's Grand Kakatiya in Hyderabad and the flagship Maurya Sheraton in Delhi have been chosen. The Leela group is represented by its resort in Goa and the Leela Palace in Bangalore. Among the standalone properties figure The Imperial in Delhi and the Travancore Heritage in Kovalam. Luxury aircraft on offer are Hawker 125-700B Executive Jet which can carry eight persons and the smaller King Air C 90A which can carry five. And, there is a choice of luxury cars ranging from Mercedes to Toyota, Mitsubishi and Ford.

Luxury Holidays suggests two sample itineraries for leisure seekers, one for north and the other for the south, both can be tailored to suit the requirements and convenience of the travellers.

The initiative taken by Le Passage has come at the right time when travel is on the upswing again in most parts of the world. And, it is the first time that a focused attempt is being made to tap the upper end of the market which is imperative for the right mix of traffic to justify the massive investments which are being made in improving roads, airports and other infrastructure like super deluxe hotels.

Time-Share: Product of the Future

Low occupancies in the wake of September 11 attacks and military operations in Afghanistan have spurred hoteliers to look for alternative clientele. Time-share is one segment of the holiday market in which the hospitality industry has started seeing a lot of potential. Globally, time-share has had rapid growth. Now a US $6 billion turnover sector, it has expanded between 18 and 20 per cent in the last few years, much more than segments like airlines. Time-share was introduced into India barely a decade ago, but it has made steady though slow progress. Raju Shahani, managing director, RCI (Resort Condominium International), 'the swap company' which enables time-share members to exchange their weeks the world over, is upbeat about the sector's growth in India. He says, "When occupancies are down, when there is excess real estate space available, it is at such times that the hoteliers and real estate developers look at alternate means of selling their space. It is at times like this that the club business and time-share flourishes."

Shahani readily concedes that time-share in India has had a credibility problem caused mainly by a few unscrupulous developers and marketing agencies, which use questionable means in executing sales. But, thanks to several initiatives taken by RCI and supported by genuine developers, customer confidence is returning to time-share. First, and foremost some quality brand names have been brought into the market. Holiday Inn, Radisson, Meridien and the Mahindras are now part of the time-share business affiliated to RCI. In a review carried out of standards in RCI-affiliated resorts in: the last few months, half of the 98 properties have been delisted for 'poor quality and bad management'. Trustee companies have been brought in to protect time-share members' interests. Two UK-based outfits, FNTC (First National Trust Co.) and Hutchisons Trust Co. will ensure that if a developer defaults in any way, the company will relocate the purchaser to an equivalent or similar quality resort within the RCI system.

On its own part, RCI has decided not to affiliate with any resort, unless it is 100 per cent complete and commissioned. Shahani says, "RCI encourages the sale of time-share membership on site so you can touch and feel the product like test driving a car before purchase." There is urgent need for legislation to protect consumers, he adds, and RCI has been lobbying with the Department of Tourism (DoT) in this regard; it has sent a draft law based on the western model for its consideration.

RCI's India chief sees good days ahead for time-share. "I see it clearly as the product of the future. It is inflation proof; at today's price for the next 30; years or so," he asserts. The product is so flexible, he adds, that you can will it, gift it, sell it or, of course, continue to use it. About changing trends in time-share holidays he says that in the past vacation ownership (another name for the concept) has been confined to resorts in holiday locations. In the last few years, urban time-share (or city time-share) is gaining popularity. It started in New York five years ago and then moved to Paris, Rome, London, Edinburgh and Glasgow. And, last month, he says with a flourish, it has moved to India. The pioneer is Le Royal Meridien in Mumbai, which has put 14 of its one bedroom suites in the care of RCI. The same owners are building an all-suites hotel in Juhu – The Meridien Residence – which will open its doors to guests within a month. Forty-one of its 180 suites will be in the RCI bank. Shahani expects more hotel chains to introduce time-share and his own efforts are now directed to cities like Delhi, Chennai and Bangalore.

The 'thin and lean' RCI family in India, according to Shahani, now has 48 resorts with 42,000 time-share members. During the current year so far 15,000 member families availed of time-share holidays. Sixty-five per cent of them travelled domestically and thirty-five per cent went to resorts overseas. The domestic choices included Goa, on top of the ladder, followed by Manali and Ooty. The international preferences were Orlando (Disneyland), Scotland, and destinations in Southeast Asia.

Worldwide there are 5,390 time-share resorts in 100 countries and the number of households owning membership is 4.75 million. During 2000, 12 million people took time-share holidays and RCI's share of this was seven million.

Shahani takes care to point out that RCI is only a swap company: it does not own any resort or hotel nor does it sell any. Its role is that of facilitation to enable time-share members to exchange their holiday weeks around the world ensuring quality controls at the same time. The hospitality industry will be watching with interest RCI's efforts to bring credibility back to time-share in this country.

Survival by Vision

The Republic of India may have banned the use of titles bestowed in the Raj era. But when it comes to hotel guru Mohan Singh Oberoi it was difficult to address him as anything other than as 'Rai Bahadur' in the most affectionate terms during his lifetime, and now after his death. This is only a small part, perhaps, of the nation's everlasting gratitude to a man who put the Indian hotel industry on the world map backed by the export of Indian expertise.

His rags-to-riches story is well-known. But few know that he was a social reformer too. Bringing women to work in hotels was nothing short of a revolutionary change in those times. But the contribution for which he will be remembered and respected most is the realisation of his vision that hotels, a major economic activity in themselves, were part of a larger picture called tourism which could do much to generate employment and alleviate poverty. In other words, he put hotels on a larger canvas of the socio-economic development of the nation.

In his three terms as member of Parliament, two in the Rajya Sabha and one in the Lok Sabha, he missed no opportunity to espouse the cause of tourism. As the founding president of the Federation of Hotel and Restaurants Association (FHRAI), he built a strong trade lobby to influence governmental policies and decisions. It is another matter that successive governments, obsessed as they were with socialism, continued to treat hotels and tourism as an elitist sector. But it is evident that Rai Bahadur's pleadings are being increasingly taken note of more seriously in the climate of economic reforms.

For all his celebrity status and the fact that hotels are a peopled business, Oberoi was a private mart. Not that he was not an outgoing entrepreneur where work was concerned, wherever innovations were in demand or when staying contemporary in a highly competitive global environment was required. He was at the right place at the right time. But he was certainly not media-savvy. Even one-on-one interviews were rare. This writer had his first chance of an informal chat during the ceremonies in Munich in 1978 when he was admitted to the Hall of Fame of the world's largest trade association, ASTA, the American Society of Travel Agents. What he told me then—privatisation of domestic aviation and of airports—did not have many backers even in the private sector 24 years ago. It is a tribute to the Rai Bahadur's vision that private airlines are a reality today and steps are underway to hand over to private management the country's international airports. His plea for a rational tax policy towards hotels and tourist services has however so far received only lip sympathy.

Partition has blurred the fact that in the first phase of his hotel empire-building in the 30's and 40's, his chain had properties in Lahore, Rawalpindi, Peshawar and Murree. Their loss spurred him to build a new chain with Oberoi as the brand name. The Oberoi in Delhi was the capital's first private sector five-star offering that gave a new nuance to luxury. Then came Mumbai and a foray into the south with Bangalore and Hyderabad. Inspired by the father's legacy, son Biki has redefined luxury and service standards with hotels like Raj Vilas in Jaipur which Bill Clinton described as the best resort he had ever stayed at. A great tribute to the Indian hotel industry's grand old man.

Major Hotels Improve Profitability; Await Major Government Initiative

This is the time when hotels begin to share with the public their financial performance during the fiscal that ends on March 31. While most of the standalone hotels and even smaller chains have yet to announce their results, mandatory under the Company Law for public-owned enterprise, the four big chains have all published their balance sheets. Of them, EIH, the Oberoi group, has turned in what a newspaper headline said 'a five-star performance', the government owned India Tourism Development Corporation (ITDC) has gone deeper into the red. In-between came the Indian Hotels Company Ltd. (IHCL) which manages the Taj group and ITC Hotels Ltd. (ITCHL) which is responsible for the Welcomgroup. Both have recorded marginal increase in net profits although their revenue have grown better.

Take EIH. Income jumped 13.33 per cent for Rs 421.09 crore to Rs 4,77,06 crore but the net profit soared 30.84 per cent from Rs 72.47 crore to Rs 94.82 crore. Analysts say this is a creditable achievement considering "sluggish trends in occupancies and the resultant pressure on room rates." Oberoi group's vice-chairman, Bikki Oberoi, however, gives the credit to what he calls "political stability and improvement in business conditions" which he says resulted in better occupancy levels and ARRs (average room rate) as compared to the earlier year. He adds, "Whenever possible, steps have been taken to eliminate waste and contain costs." The EIH board has recommended a dividend of Rs six per share against Rs five given in 1999-2000. EIH also earned the country a whopping Rs 279 crore in foreign exchange against the earlier year's figure of Rs 258 crore.

Lets go to ITDC, the multi-faced hospitality giant which since its inception in the 60s always made profits, has not been doing well in the last couple of years. It made a whopping net loss of Rs 24 crore in 1999-2000. Last year the loss increase further to Rs 27 crore although there was a small spurt in its turnover which is around Rs 300 crore (ITDC is in the process of disinvestment). Note attached to the balance sheet offered no explanation about the continued downslide of the hotel major.

ITC Hotels has maintained its profitability and last year's growth in its net at Rs 12.69 crore is just over six per cent. Total income was Rs 134.74 crore compared to Rs 131,11 crore in the previous year, ITCHL board has recommended a dividend of 10 per cent. The comparative low figure of turnover is due to the fact that many of its properties, being associate companies, have separate balance sheets; flagship Maurya Sheraton finds a place in the accounts of the parent ITC Ltd. Welcomgroup's turnover as a whole would be around Rs 400 crore.

One of ITCHL group companies, Srinivasa Resorts Ltd. which manages Kakatiya Sheraton in Hyderabad, has 'turned the corner within five years' of is commissioning. Its turnover in 2000-01, at Rs 35.57 crore, was up by 27 per cent and net profit at Rs 6.61 crore showed a growth of 234 per cent. The hotel recorded an enviable 75 per cent occupancy during the year, Srinivasa Resorts chairman, C Shivakumar Reddy sees in the performance of the hotel a reflection of the acceleration growth Andhra Pradesh is witnessing.

And, finally India Hotels Company, the Taj group, now the country's largest chain. It too has maintained its profitability and the net profit in the last fiscal at Rs 116.79 crore was a modest three per cent increase. The turnover at Rs 687.50 crore (Rs 603.47 crore in 1999-2000) was up by nearly 14 per cent. IHCL board has recommended a dividend of 100 per cent. Analysts point out the company has achieved reduction in operating costs especially in food and beverages as well as in staff costs mainly through VRS. According to one estimate about 1,200 workers opted for VRS during the year.

IHCL associates company, Indian Resort Hotels Ltd. has reported a fall both in its revenue and profits. Total income decreased from Rs 22.06 crore to Rs 20.45 crore while profit after tax came down to Rs 2.15 crore from Rs 3.32 crore in the previous year. The fall has been attributed to the reduction in other income which declined from Rs 4.02 crore to Rs 2.48 crore.

An Oberoi group company, EIH Associate Hotels Ltd., has returned higher income and reduced losses. Total revenue increase from Rs 31.50 crore to Rs 37.17 crore while the net loss which was Rs 5.61 crore in 1999-2000 was reduced to Rs 1.54 crore.

It is customary for chairpersons to issue statements to the media along with financial results. Only vice-chairman EIH, Bikki Oberoi's statement was available at the time of writing. In a comment on the tourism scene he says, "It is unfortunate that the central and state governments have not yet appreciated the potential of travel and tourism as a job creator and as an important economic activity." He adds, "Unless there is improved infrastructure, better airports and reduction in the burden of multiple taxes on visitors, the travel and tourism industry will not realise its full potential."

The Oberoi chief's comments are one more reminder that the hospitality industry is still waiting for a major initiative from the government to put tourism on the national agenda.

Hilton Returns with Promise

When Golden Palm Resort and Spa, promoted by actor Sanjay Khan, formally opened its doors to guests in the scenic neighbourhood of Bangalore last month, the event also marked the return – on a third attempt – by the global hospitality major, Hilton, to India. While the Hilton managed resort will add to the quality of accommodation and leisure facilities in the South, which has recently seen significant additions to infrastructure, it has also brought in the promise of major foreign investment in the hotel industry. For Hilton not only wants to establish and strengthen its presence in India, it is keen to put its money into greenfield projects in this country.

Koos Klein, president, Asia Pacific Hilton International, who was in the capital to launch the Bangalore resort, also announced a strategic partnership in sales and reservations with Inter-Globe Enterprises, leading air transport management and travel technology company based in Gurgaon near Delhi. He said Hilton saw a huge potential in India both in the growing need for more quality accommodation and also in outbound travel, The tie-up with Inter-Globe will offer a choice of some 2,000 hotels around the world to Indian travellers, management of the Golden Palm Resort will pave the way for a growing partnership for Hilton with the hotel industry. Klein said Hilton had learnt its lessons from earlier forays into India – a management agreement with Bharat Hotels in Delhi was terminated in just two years while a similar agreement did not take-off with a hotel in Chennai just two months before its commissioning. This time around, he said, the company is better prepared to secure a firm presence. He declined to be pinned down to any figure for investment but said it could be from $50 million to $500 million. He hastened to add that Hilton was open to any route for expansion; management, lease, joint venture or even a wholly owned project. One thing Klein was sure Hilton wants to have 10 hotels in its chain in India in the next 10 years; one hotel a year is the target. After Bangalore, he said, obviously the preference will be for other metros like Delhi, Mumbai and Chennai. He disclosed that negotiations for hotel projects, all greenfield, were in the final stages for all three metros. He was hopeful of announcing the first deal within two or three months. He indicated that to start work in any joint venture, Hilton would take 26 per cent equity, which in later projects could go up to a higher figure. He conceded that foreign chains by and large did not invest overseas or even in their homegrounds but pointed out that Hilton was among the few chains that owned a big chunk of their properties. According to him, Accor, the French major, was leader in ownership and Hilton came next with as many as a third of its hotels owned by the group. "We are sitting on $1.6 billion worth of real estate," he told EH&C. Klein has picked up as his country manager for India, a former leading light of the Taj group, Leonard Menezes, with headquarters in Mumbai.

On his tie-up with Inter-Globe, Klein said, "Hilton has identified India as a strategic market. Indian travellers today demand world-class facilities, which we can provide through our partnership with Inter-Globe". He added, "Travellers will now be able to make reservations in any of the 2,000 hotels in more than 50 countries – represented by the two companies – simply by dialling a domestic toll-free number."

Interestingly, the idea of the Hilton Golden Palms Resort and Spa was born during the period Sanjay Khan was recovering in hospital from the burn injuries he received when a fire broke out on the sets of 'The Sword of Tipu Sultan' in 1989. He had promised himself that if he survived he would 'set up a place where people could go to promote their health and well-being'. Five years later and with Rs 125 crore in the bank with the promoter company, Khan and his wife Zarine set about planning and designing the resort on 14 acres of palm-filled land just 25 kms away from Bangalore.

Thirty-six years old Peter J Simson, who has grown up with the Hilton family, was executive assistant manager when the chain was managing the Delhi property. He is the general manager of the Golden Palms, which has 150 rooms designed in Mediterranean style featuring a large balcony or terrace with garden views. One room has been specially equipped for the handicapped. Says Simson, "Specially created to serve the increasingly sophisticated business community in Bangalore and discerning travellers from the world over, the resort offers an excellent array of facilities for business meetings and conferences." He adds, "The resort promises unprecedented exclusivity and comfort amidst a secluded environment blessed with immense scenic beauty."

The travel industry will naturally be happy that the South too has its own classy spa to match the Ananda in the North (near Rishikesh), while observers are keeping their fingers crossed, hoping that Hilton will be third time lucky.

What cash Crunch?

If the hospitality segment in the services sector, which incidentally is growing at a fast rate, has received a low Foreign Direct Investment (FDI), it is only because the hotel industry is in no desperate need for cash. None of the major chains, including ITC Hotels, Taj, Oberois and the ITDC has any foreign equity participation.

Maybe, standalone properties require overseas credit or some NRIs have brought in funds. At the same time, there is a continuing demand for brand equity obtainable through management or franchise marketing agreements. Even here, ITDC does not have any marketing tie up, Taj has an odd membership of the Leading Hotels of The World and Oberois have gone for the Trident brand for their mid-market segment. The Sheraton connection is limited to seven of the ITC Hotels.

But, the growing hotel industry seeking to maintain international standards in all its services and also because of compulsions of overseas marketing require international linkages. They are not keen on investment partnerships.

Illustrative of this relationship is the approach of the Delhi-based Bharat Hotels response to the proposal of its international partner, Bass Hotels, owners of Inter-Continental and Holiday Inn brands. The foreign chain, according J T Kuhlman, company president, is to invest globally $750 million in the next five years.

Asked how much of it is set apart for India, he was frank that, "It depends on the requirements of Bharat Hotels, whose flagship in the Capital flaunts the Inter-Continental banner under a modified management agreement. Bharat Hotels chairman, Lalit Suri, intervened to say "I have enough cash surpluses for my expansion plans" and that his three new properties will need a total investment of Rs 280 crore, all of which he will find from his own resources.

The occasion for these interesting exchanges was a news conference in Delhi on April 9, called to announce that Bharat Hotels is signing its three new properties also with Inter-Continental. Two of these, Srinagar and Goa, are due for commissioning next year while the third, in Mumbai, in 2001. Together, they will add 822 deluxe rooms to the 400 in Delhi, upgrading Bharat Hotels as an emerging chain, Suri said that after his two not so successful partnerships with Holiday Inn and Hilton, he has been lucky the third time "The relationship with Inter-Continental has yielded more than we expected" and this is what has prompted him to go along with Inter-Continental for his current expansion plans.

Both, Kuhlman and Suri were asked if now was the right time to invest in the hotel industry when tourism is under pressure in large parts of the world. The Bass Hotels chief said it made business sense to acquire properties when the prices are down. Both, he and Suri agreed that the present slowdown is a passing phase and certainly in India the hotel industry has a bright future considering that the country has so few rooms. Kuhlman added, "India is an important market and I am delighted that we shall soon be able to offer four excellent Inter-Continental hotels and 16 Holiday Inns to international and domestic travellers." Suri said that far from being discouraged by the current scenario, he was in fact expediting work on his projects.

The Grand Palace in Srinagar, now under extensive renovation, is due to be commissioned early next year with 56 palace suites, 60 standard rooms and 10 cottages with an estimated investment of Rs 60 crore. A similar amount is being spent on the Goa resort, which is due to open in September 2000. Set in south Goa in Raj Baga, Cana Cona, it is spread over 86 acres – straddled between two rivers – with a thousand metre beach. Its 300 rooms will include suites, villas and Club Inter-Continental rooms.

The last of the projects is in Mumbai, in Andheri East, on an 8 acre site. This is slated for opening early in 2001. Suri said it will be a nine-storey structure with a magnificent architectural facade and a large atrium and indoor patio. It will offer 400 rooms.

Kuhlman was also asked if there was any exclusivity in his Group's arrangements with Bharat Hotels. He said Bass Hotels was free to tie up with others but he would prefer to do so in association with Bharat Hotels. He said that over the years Bass Hotels had developed considerable hotel management talent from around the world and had in its chain managers from forty countries. An Indian is general manager of an Inter-Continental in Venezuela!

Foreign Chains Eye Indian Market

Hilton International, the UK-based big league chain which has been eyeing India for almost three decades, has made its third attempt to establish its presence in this country. It has signed a management agreement with film actor Sanjay Khan who has promoted Golden Palms

Resorts and Spa in Bangalore. Built on a 14 acre plot some 25 km from the city, the luxury resort which has cost Rs 125 crore is due to be commissioned in two months time. The promoters claim it will be a 'holistic' holiday resort in tune with the expectations of the modern corporate and entertainment personalities, will also double up as a convention destination. It has been part-financed by FIs.

If the Financial Express, which carried an interview with Hilton president for Asia-Pacific, Koos Klein is to be believed this upmarket international chain with a 60,000 room global spread has this time round come to stay, For, it is not just looking for management contracts with existing or upcoming hotels, it wants to invest in our country in a big way. The newspaper quotes Klein as saying that the chain has already identified four locations including Delhi, Mumbai and Chennai for greenfield projects. In the first project, Hilton will have a 26 per cent equity and in the rest, the stake: may rise to 50 or even 100 per cent. The initial investment he had in mind is $75 million. More funds will be brought in after two or three years as Hilton considered India a 'thrust region'. He also said he is looking for a management partner in this country.

Hilton's investment plans are indeed a welcome news for the hotel industry. There are more than a score of foreign chains associated with Indian hotels, with more franchises than management tie-ups at the moment. But, there has so far been little or no foreign investment except from NRIs. It will be recalled that when Bharat Hotels in the capital was rechristened as Inter-Continental, the chain's chief had offered to invest in India but the Indian promoter had spurned the offer as he had enough funds of his own.

Old timers will recall that Hilton's first attempt to enter India was made as far back as the early 70s when in association with DCM it wanted to build a hotel on the plot in the capital where now stand Kanishka and Ashok Yatri Niwas owned by ITDC. Hilton's condition for entering India was that it wanted only this piece of land or nothing. In the event the plot was not released for a hotel at that time although years later it was, to meet the needs of the 1982 Asiad Games. In its second foray, Hilton took up the management of the Bharat Hotels' property but, the arrangement did not last more than two years. Only time will tell whether Hilton will be lucky a third time.

Another overseas chain which has been making strenuous efforts to consolidate its presence in this country is the French Accor. If made its presence felt through lending from its stable brands, like Sofitel and Novotel. For some time, the Oberois had a deal with Accor to launch a string of Novotels in the mid-market segment but, finally settled for Trident. Accor is now managing four properties in India, three of them in a joint venture with Mahindras Guestline hotels with a thrust on their Novotel and Mercure brands.

The property in Jodhpur, the latest in the Accor chain, is christened Novotel Coralia Ummed, a resort with nearly 90 rooms. There is a Mercure in Juhu with 90 rooms and Accor has even taken some equity, although the chain's strategy is to look for management tie-ups. Then, there are Guestline hotels in Tirupati with 140 rooms and Bangalore with 100 rooms.

Accor now has a separate COO for its Indian operations based in Mumbai, He is Arnauldt Kindt. At a lunch with media persons in Delhi recently, Kindt spelt out Accor's USPs. He said the chain had developed expertise to reduce both construction and operational costs, while ensuring the quality of the product. This strategy which he said had been tried out around the world had made it possible to achieve guest satisfaction on one hand and give a fair return to owners and investors on the other. Accor, he said, had picked up a marketing specialist, Siddharath Roy, with considerable experience in the hotel industry, to look after four marketing centres set up in the country to sell not only Accor properties in India but also in popular, destinations in Asia including Singapore, Thailand, Indonesia and Malaysia.

The real feather is Accor's India cap is, of course, the MoU it has signed with the West Bengal government to takeover the Great Eastern Hotel. Hopefully, the MoU will be converted into a final agreement and the hotel will be restored to its past glory.

Third Time Lucky

Hilton International, the UK-based hotel major with a UK £2.4 billion turnover and nearly 400 hotels in its chain worldwide is back in India after two earlier unsuccessful attempts in the last few years. Its management tie-ups, first with Bharat Hotels in Delhi and then with actor Sanjay Khan's resort near Bangalore, did not last very long. This time, however, Hilton has adopted a route that promises not only stability but also longevity – a joint venture. It has joined hands with an Indian pharmaceutical company, Morepen Laboratories, with sales exceeding Rs 500 crore and which has already diversified into hoteliering, a good enough reason to believe that Hilton has now come to stay here.

The joint venture which was signed in Delhi in the presence of the media is between Hilton International and Blue Coast Hotels and Resorts Ltd. (formerly known as Morepen Hotels Ltd.). The two have formed a JV company, Hospitality Holdings India Ltd., to develop first class and luxury hotels and resorts in India. Present at the signing ceremony were Anthony Harris, chief executive; Koos Klein, president, Middle East and Asia Pacific, Hilton International; Lene Menezes, Hilton's India manager and Arun Suri, C&MD, Blue Coast Hotels and Resorts.

Harris, without specifically referring to the chain's earlier experiences in this country, conceded that India is a difficult market to understand. But he pointed out that the new arrangement is the result of an indepth study lasting well over 18 months and quipped, "We have begun to understand a bit of India." Klein explained that in the joint venture Hilton will hold one-third stake while two-thirds will stay with the Indian partners. In the first phase three hotels are planned in Mumbai, Bangalore and Goa (Morepen is already in collaboration with Hyatt International for a hotel under construction in Goa which will be a separate project outside of the JV with Hilton). Of the Hilton-managed projects the one in Mumbai will be a 175-unit Hilton Residences (comprising serviced apartments and Country Club). Bangalore will get a 250-room Hilton Hotel and Goa a 160-room Hilton Resort. The total investment on the three properties is estimated at Rs 500 crore. Suri said in reply to questions that negotiations are in the final stages for land acquisition and there is the possibility of local partners coming in.

Both Klein and Suri made it clear that there is no exclusivity clause in the joint venture agreement; both parties are free to enter into joint ventures or management agreements with entrepreneurs or national or foreign chairs. Suri said Morepen's tie-up with Hyatt for the Goa hotel is doing so well that the overseas partner has agreed to upgrade the property to Hyatt Park when it is commissioned. It will be among 20 hotels of its kind in the world. "In fact," he said, "after (the) successful completion of our resort development in Goa, we are upbeat about our hotel development capabilities and are glad to be associated with Hilton International." Klein said Hilton has a "long-term commitment to a presence in India, utilising a two pronged strategy: anchoring our presence with a strong local partner, and participating in the equity of our hotels." He described Morepen Labs as a blue chip company.

Asked about the timing of Hilton's return when the hospitality industry is still suffering from the after effects of 9/11, Klein pointed to two favourable factors—the burgeoning domestic travel market which must shore up the hotel industry and the fast growing outbound traffic which could be beneficial for Hilton hotels overseas. He said the three projects listed in the joint venture are only a beginning. Hilton is keen to have a hotel in the

Capital and other metro cities and business and tourist centres. He added, "Hilton will be bringing to India several new concepts of guest comforts and facilities evolved over a period in its hotels around the world." A new programme "Equilibrium" provides guests with an opportunity of relax, rejuvenate and restore the balance. A relaxation room will be a retreat to escape into after a heavy day. Suri did not miss the opportunity of rightly claiming Morepen 'a achievement in bringing the first foreign equity participation in India's hotel industry.

Suri is hopeful that work on the three new hotels would start in two or three months and the first Hilton, whether it is Mumbai, Goa or Bangalore, is not expected to be commissioned before 2005, the minimum average time it will take to complete the project. In other words, while Hilton has technically re-entered India, its flag will not fly for at least three years. Hopefully, Hilton will be lucky in its third effort.

Back on Track

It is now the turn of FHRAI, the Federation of Hotel and Restaurants Association of India, to discuss the burning issue before the hospitality industry, as secretary general Shyam Suri puts it, "Where do we go from here?"

Reeling under the pre- and post-9/11 fallout, the continuing stand-off with Pakistan and the near-real danger of war over Iraq is causing fresh concerns about tourist arrivals. Under an umbrella theme of 'Tourism – Everybody's Business', the hotel and restaurants' federation is meeting in New Delhi at the Hyatt Regency for its 38th annual conference.

There are some interesting aspects of the conference. It is perhaps the first time FHRAI is meeting in the Capital since its inception. Even old hands at the federation cannot recall if it ever held a convention here and Suri is certain that the city has not played host since the '80s insofar he could refer to the records.

Also, the New Delhi meet is coinciding with the World Tourism Day which falls when a travel expo and seminars are organised by the department of tourism (DoT).

The inaugural function which is being held at the Vigyan Bhawan for reasons of space is in two parts. The first is a seminar organised jointly by DoT and FHRAI on the topic 'Tourism Grows in Partnerships'. The keynote speaker is Eric Pfeffer, president, International Hotels and Restaurant Association (IH&RA) while Union Tourism Minister Jagmohan and Minister of State for Tourism Vinod Khanna will be chief guest and guest of honour.

Finance Minister Jaswant Singh has also been invited but his acceptance is awaited. The IH&RA president will enlighten the delegates on the current global scenario for the hotel industry and how to cope with the downturn and prospects for the future.

For travel industry observers there will be great interest in the first professional session titled 'Global Scenario in Tourism and What India Should Do'. Here again, the task has been assigned to an international expert, Michael Spinelli, former president of ASTA, the American Society of Travel Agents, the world's largest industry association. Suri says Spinelli, himself a leading, travel agent, will particularly touch on how Indian hotels and tour operators could increase their market share from the leisure travel segment of the United States.

Trends in hotel designs will be addressed by yet another overseas speaker, Michael Bedner, CEO, Hirscn Bedner and Associates (HBA), among the largest and most reputed hotel design companies. He will share insights into aspects of design which may enhance the value and business of hotels.

With the growing realisation that more attention needs to be paid both to the quality and numbers of budget hotels, for the first time (and in response to members' request) FHRAI has slated a separate session 'Trends and Potential for Budget Hotel in India'. The discussion will be led by Ajay Bakaya, executive director, Sarovar Park Hotels (which has a score of mid-market properties in its chain, the latest being the Peerless Inn in Kolkata), Ravi Appaswami, MD, Chennai based Regency Group of Hotels, and Homi Aibara, a management consultant.

A special interactive session has also been arranged which will be chaired by the tourism secretary, Rathi Vinay Jha and participants will include D G Vinod Duggal and tourism secretaries from the states. Suri says the aviation ministry, ASI and other government agencies servicing various tourism activities have also been asked to send representatives for this session where delegates would have an opportunity to ask questions. Uttaranchal, among the youngest of Indian states, will have a slot to showcase its attractions at the valedictory session where FHRAI's own awards will also be given away by Delhi Chief Minister Sheila Dikshit.

A hoteliers' convention is never complete without wining and dining. Taking a cue from the organisers of PATA 2002 in April this year, FHRAI will give its delegates a treat at the Qutub Minar with a cultural evening to be contributed by the Delhi Tourism Corporation. This will be followed by the president's dinner. Outstation participants will be able to sample the Capital's new address, ITC's Marriott WelcomHotel in Saket, south Delhi which is hosting a dinner. Taj Palace and Hyatt Regency are venues for the two other dinners. ITDC is among the luncheon hosts.

To come back to Shyam Suri, according to him the consensus among hoteliers is that since 80 per cent of the leisure traffic is in groups, they should strengthen their own promotional efforts with overseas travel agents and tour operators and for the time being not divert scarce funds to reaching the consumer directly.

Hopefully the conference will provide a lead on whether they are right.

Giving Back to the Children

Nearly a hundred years ago, Jamshetji Tata was appalled when he was refused entry into a British-run hotel in Mumbai. He went on to build the Taj Mahal Hotel, also in Mumbai, right on the shores of the Arabian Sea which not only welcomed Indians but also took its place among the world's great hotels. It is now the flagship of the Taj group, the country's largest hotel chain. A few decades later Mohan Singh Oberoi, the revered Rai Bahadur, rose from the position of a clerk is a Shimla hotel to found India's second largest chain with the Oberoi brand. Then came independence and to the architect of modern India, Jawaharlal Nehru goes the credit of bestowing the capital with the country's first hotel built to international standards, the Ashoka, around which the India Tourism Development Corporation (ITDC) grew into a major hospitality business sprang from entirely different reasons – his love and concern for children. He also stands apart from other hoteliers in that he is determined to stay as a one-unit owner of Best Western Resort Country Club in Gurgaon, some sixty kilometres from Delhi on the Jaipur highway. He says categorically that while he would continue to expand and upgrade the facilities at the Resort, he has absolutely no, intention of building another one. This is how his story begins.

An engineer with a private firm in the capital, he always felt he ought to have been doing something else. He was a member of the Chelmsford Club in the Capital, but he was very upset when he discovered that children were not welcome. An hour or two at the pool was all they were allowed and most evening when he and his wife would be in the bar or the dining room, the kids would be sitting in the car in the parking lot. Now he knew what he had to do find fulfillment. He decided to build a club that would be children-friendly.

Not only that. He also felt strongly that a club should offer facilities like horses, ponies, golf, open spaces and outdoors. It was time for his retirement and he got down to realising this dream in great earnest. By 1988, he had bought fifty acres of land and in just two years his dream country club was operational. Starting with membership fee of Rs. 3.000, new entrants are now willing to pay as much as Rs. 75,000.

Today, the Resort Country Club is a much a fun, entertainment, food and relaxation place for children and grown ups as it is for corporate houses who prefer to engage in serious business of conferences and training courses with an add on the leisure. Children are of course are a pampered lot. The Club has a nine-hole golf course designed by well known Australian architect Ronnie Durand, set in lush green surroundings. Resort Country Club has a franchise tie-up with the global Best Western chain, the first international flag in Haryana and is also a member of RCI (Resort Condominium International), the time-share people.

A large bar overlooks the swimming pools and there is adequate banqueting space for parties indoor or in the open. There are fifty well appointed rooms and Goel has started work on adding fifty more which would be ready within the next two years.

Goel, who is now chairman and managing director, says he is the most diversified hospitality complex of its kind comprising a country club, a hotel, golf resort and time-share facilities. What is more, even environmental concerns are taken care of. Since its inception, he has been assisted by two dedicated lady executives, Roop Sodhi who looks after the operations and Anita Rajput who takes care of marketing. Daughter Usha, an MBE, is finance director. He says he has specially trained kitchen staff and hotel guest, as a result of which corporate houses conducting residential courses have been quite appreciative of the fare offered in the dining rooms or at the theme parties.

With an average of 70 per cent occupancy (corporates account for a third), the Resort current turnover is Rs 3 crore. He hopes to take it to Rs 20 crore by 2020. Time-share fills 15 per cent of the rooms and among the corporate houses that use the facilities are IBP, Electrolux, Pepsi, Britanni, Wipro and Ranbaxy. The Resort also has a travel desk and foreign exchange counter. There are arrangements for transfers from and to city and airport.

Does he have another dream? Yes he wants to build cottages in the complex on ownership basis for elderly couples who wish to avail the service of a hotel, a golf course, a club and live comfortably especially when their children are abroad or live separately. Ranjit Goel's experiment can be replicated in many other cities of India.

Christel House: 'Hospitality' with a Difference

What does a successful executive do when he/she has reached the top of the ladder in the corporate world when still in the 40s and the urge to do something 'different' has begun to assert itself ? An easy way is to 'retire', play golf and lead a life of leisure. A more difficult one is to take up a social cause, do something for the deprived sections of society. Shukla Bose, who after a steady career in the hospitality industry rose to be managing director of RCI (Resort Condominium International) the US-based global time-share exchange outfit for its India operations, did not have to look far and wide to respond to her urge for change. Christel de Haan, the Dutch-born lady who founded the RCI and developed it into a multi-million dollar economic activity spreading the concept of time-share around the world, sold off her company while at the pinnacle of success and has been spending her time and money setting up Christel Houses with the mission 'to help orphaned, abandoned and impoverished children around the world, break the cycle of poverty and become self-sufficient, contributing members of their societies'. De Haan had been talking to Shukla about setting up a Christel House in India and she grabbed the opportunity. She is happy to be managing director, Christel House in Bangalore, happy to give up corporate perks and five-star lunches. Within a few months her make-shift Christel House in Bangalore's suburbs near the new highway to Hyderabad, is playing mother to no less than 320 orphaned, abandoned and slum children of this southern metropolis. In another 18-20 months, a modern school complex with a capacity of 2,000 children will be completed which will perhaps be the biggest of its kind in our part of the world.

Christel House is a unique experiment in schooling. Children continue to stay in orphanages or with their parents or relatives but it is at the school where they spend eight to ten hours that they are helped to better their lives. Shukla's colleagues include doctors, psychologists, dietitians, teachers and volunteers who specialise in various fields. Shukla told this writer, who spent two delightful days at Christel House, that her "first few days in school were spent in toilet training the kinds from the slums. Right now if you ask my children what their best subject is they will say 'oota' or food but I know one day it will be arithmetic and history". She added, 'Instead of boardrooms I conduct assembly everyday and teach my kids how to share, care and made a difference in the world."

Even a casual visitor to the Christel House in Bangalore can see the change in the way the children are conducting themselves, at studies, at play in competitions, excelling even in painting. Though many children's ambition is to be a bus driver simply because south India's matinee hero rose to Stardom from bus driving there are many young minds aspiring for bigger dreams. Six year old Hoiuno, an orphan from Manipur, told me he wants to be prime minister. Asked what he would do in that capacity he was quick to say he would abolish plastic bags and, hold your breath, he would teach people not to fight with each other and destroy the world! And, this after a just a few months of schooling.

Explaining Christel House mission, Shukla said, "We work with children who live below the poverty line and therefore would not normally have the opportunity to go to school and our goal is to help them to move out of their current social strata into a higher level socio-economic group. After their schooling we place them in jobs or sponsor them for higher education so that they will be able to stand on their own two feet. We expect that they will return to their communities and provide the opportunities that they have had to other children in their area." She added, "At the end of the day, we aim to have students who are self-sufficient, whose right to their dignity has been respected and who are successful in life."

Land for the permanent Christel House school complex has already been acquired and the project will be completed in three phases, each costing Rs 2 crore plus. Half of the total expenditure of over Rs 7 crore will come from Christel de Haan and the other half is being raised in India. It will be recalled that de Haan had delivered the 2001 Somnath Chib Memorial Lecture in the capital and her theme was social responsibility of the corporate sector. The hospitality industry which has now rightly started emphasising what tourism can do for poverty alleviation must support initiatives like Christel House not only by way of financial assistance but by offering training facilities and job opportunities to these sections of society. Among VVIP's who have visited Christel House in Cheries Blair, wife of the British Prime Minister. Captain C K Krishana Nair of the Leela Group has donated a deluxe bus for the school.

Looking Upbeat Going Strong

It is strange that the government, even at this stage when many an ITDC hotel has been disinvested – has not come out with any plan for what it intends to do with the rest of this premier and multifaceted public sector hospitality undertaking. The disinvestment exercise is limited only to hotels and there has been no word even from the department of tourism (DoT) in whose domain the corporation has been functioning since its inception in the 60s. Apart from hotels, ITDC runs the country's duty free shops at international airports as a monopoly whose profits have often come handy in shoring up its over all performance. Then there is the Ashok Travels and Tours which has been offering a range of services including ticketing, transport and arrangements for conferences. A consultancy division has been assisting state governments and entrepreneurs with hotel and other tourism-related projects. And, finally the publicity set up whose imprint can still be seen in the excellent tourist literature produced for DoT as well as state governments. ITDC diaries were once a collector's choice internationally. Old timers would remember some of the thematic advertising campaigns organised by ITDC's P&P division as it was then called, like 'tourism is everybody's business' or 'Keep your city dean – it is a tourist attraction' or the promotional campaigns on behalf of Kashmir.

Whatever the government as a whole or DoT have in mind about the future of ITDC which has played a laudable catalytic role in tourism development at a time when private enterprise was either unwilling or unable to invest in the sector, its current helmsman, Ashwani Lohani, the youngest C&MD (he is in his early 40s) is determined to ensure that there is life for ITDC sans its hotels. Interestingly, when Lohani first talked of a new-look ITDC with its residuary (and new) functions competing with the private sector, industry observers admired his faith in the undertaking's future but wonder whether his dreams was realisable. He has, however, carried on regardless. He has been rechristening his divisions (Ashok Creatives is one example) and making them independent profit centres and enthusing the staff to breakout of the strain of disinvestment. The most noticeable of his rejuvenation measures is what is happening at the duty free shops. Just a week ago the duty free shop at Delhi's Indira Gandhi International airport has a new section offering travellers 'rare arts and crafts objects' sourced from the Central Cottage Industries Corporation. Soon there will be designer sections for perfumes and wines. The travels division is branching into picking up state tourism promotion accounts as well as representation for overseas destinations.

Call it luck or compulsion of ground realities, ITDC will not after all be without any hotels properties. After two abortive bids for the flagship Ashok in Delhi, whose architectural grandeur has remained unmatched, will continue to be run by ITDC. And, perhaps so will the neighbouring Samrat (for security reasons because its rooms overlook the prime minister's residential complex) and so will Janpath in the heart of the capital which the government has now agreed will be rebuilt as a one-stop travel service station. It is likely that the Lalitha Mahal, a unique palace hotel in Mysore will stay with ITDC. But, the Ashok and Samrat with a total room count of

900 will be good enough to sustain ITDC and with the immense commercial possibilities of a Janpath Paryatak Bhawan, the corporation's viability can be ensured provided it is allowed a level-playing field in competing with the private sector. Lohani is particularly upbeat on this. The present teams at the head of the tourism set up, his reference is to minister Jagmohan, secretary Rathi Jha and D G, Vinod Duggal, could be expected to fully support ITDC's revival after partial disinvestment. Incidentally, for Lohani ITDC is an additional charge to his responsibilities at DoT as director tourism.

Even before a final decision on the future of Ashok Hotel was known the C&MD had set in motion a number of initiative to, refurbish both the image and facilities at the hotel. For instance, he has reopened the Ashok Theatre which since the hotel's commissioning in 1956 has played a major role in presenting authentic Indian entertainment and launching many an eminent artist. Now that the ITDC has to make a success of the Ashok, Lohani has plans to increase its turn over from Rs 40 crore in 2001-02 to Rs 50 crore in the current year and to Rs 60 crore in the following year, which will be the break-even point. There will be many more speciality restaurants he told me, and added, "A disciplined workforce with service orientation and aggressive marketing will, I am sure, return the Ashok to its halcyon days." He has plans to celebrate Ashok's 50th anniversary due in 2006 as a tribute to Jawaharlal Nehru whose vision and initiative brought the nation the gift of this great hotel.

ITDC: Future Unknown

After a decade of indecision, hiccups and road blocks, disinvestment in public sector hotels under the central government now appears to be on a somewhat smoother pace. Air-India subsidiary, HCI (Hotel Corporation of India) has already sold one of its prime properties – Juhu Centaur for Rs 153 crore (reserve price Rs 101.6 crore). The lone successful bidder is Ajit Kerkar, who in the four years since he retired from the Taj Group, has turned Tulip Star into a major chain with around twenty hotels. There were no valid bids for the remaining HCI units and fresh offers are being invited. ITDC, India Tourism Development Corporation, the country's largest hotel chain until the Taj group wrested from it the first position, after a few half-hearted attempts at disinvestment in the mid-90s, made serious moves last year thanks to the drive of the department of disinvestment (DoD). The disinvestment process is already complete for the first tranche of half a dozen properties put on the block. Of these, five are smaller hotels in Agra, Madurai, Bodhgaya, Hasan and Mamallapuram and have been sold outrights. The sixth, Ashok Bangalore (south India's first five star hotel) has been given on lease again to a lone bidder, Lalit Suri's Bharat Hotels for Rs 39.41 crore as an upfront payment plus an annual rent of Rs 4.11 crore. For the flagship hotel in Delhi, the Ashok, which was also offered on lease there were no bids reportedly because of the requirements of a very high bank guarantee as well as an annual ground rent of Rs 14 crore. Fresh bids are to be invited with revised terms which the government hopes will ensure a response. Accordingly to sources in DoD, instead of the hefty ground rent, the lease rental will be shared between ITDC and the urban development ministry in a 25:75 ratio.

In the second tranche of ITDC properties, mainly those in the capital – Şamrat, Qutub, Janpath, Kanishka, Indrapastha (Ashok Yatri Niwas) Lodhi, Ranjit – as well as Ashok Varanasi and Lakshmi Vilas Palace in Udaipur, alongwith the Delhi Ashok are being processed for disinvestment. Expressions of interest have been received and financial bids will soon be called. ITDC has now invited expression of interest in respect of nine more hotels spread over the country. These are the beach resort at Kovalam, Airport Ashoka, Kolkata, and hotels in Jaipur, Patna, Bhubaneshwar, Jammu, Khajuraho, Aurangabad and Manali. The qualifying amount for bidders for the Kovalam beach resort is a minimum net worth of Rs 15 crore. for Ko!kata and Jaipur it is Rs 5 crore and for the rest Rs 3 crore. The last date for expression of interest.

It is not clear what will happen to ITDC after all the hotels have been disinvested or as in some cases given away on long-term lease. It has several other activities which have a potential of growth, particularly duty free shops, publicity, travel agency and consultancy work in which it has considerable experience. The present chairman and manageing director, Ashwani Lohani has been unveiling a number of ambitious schemes to keep the ITDC going without the hotel component. Industry observers, appreciative of this premier-public sector undertaking's contribution to tourism, would like to see it continue to play its original role of a catalyst. An area in which ITDC gained even in national recognition is the development of tourism communication. Tourist literature produced by ITDC over the years has won national and global awards. Its diaries have been a collectors item. ITDC has also been a source of inspiration to the states in designing and printing their tourist literature and even making films for them. ITDC often masterminded media publicity for tourist destinations in the states. Until the mid-80s the department of tourism depended heavily on ITDC for its PR needs at international travel events and in projecting India through visiting journalists and travel writers. In fact, it was the communications wing of the department. Now that the department has been toying with the idea of hiring a PR agency for its promotional activities, it might consider restoring to ITDC that role which it had handled creditably in the past.

Consultancy in hotel management is another potential that a future ITDC can exploit. The wide ranging mix of hotels from deluxe metro properties, to beach resorts, wild life sanctuaries, airport hotels and properties in tourist and pilgrim centres has given ITDC a unique across the board expertise in hoteliering which entrepreneurs entering this field a fresh could immensely benefit from. There is no escape from disinvestment in hotels but the rest of ITDC can play a useful role in the tourism industry.

No, Dr Karan Singh

It was not until 1967, two decades after independence, that tourism was accorded the status of cabinet rank in the council of ministers. And, Indira Gandhi's choice of Dr Karan Singh to head the ministry, which had both tourism and civil aviation in its fold, was the best thing that could happen to the hospitality industry at the time. Under his stewardship, the two flag carriers, Air-India and Indian Airlines, and the newly created India Tourism Development Corporation (ITDC), made a significant and substantial contribution to facilitation, infrastructure and promotion of tourism. ITDC particularly gained from his dynamism and encouragement to talent in the three public sector undertakings. He took a lot of interest in upgrading the tourist literature being produced by ITDC to compete in the international marketplace. It was in his time that The Ashok Hotel in the Capital, as also those in other cities, offered the visitor an authentic Indian experience, in decor, cuisine or entertainment. His friends and admirers in the hospitality industry acclaimed him the country's tourism ambassador. He has been a familiar figure at most travel trade events delivering key note speeches. Only in April last, he addressed an international gathering in Hong Kong at the PATA annual conference, where he was given a big ovation.

But, his friends, admirers and perhaps the entire travel industry must be puzzled by his widely reported 'appeal' to the prime minister not to privatise The Ashok Hotel. If Dr Karan Singh is against privatisation, one can understand his love for the public sector; he would be welcome to suggest ways in which government-run hotels could perform better without disinvestment. But the alternate he has suggested is surprising, to say the least. He wants The Ashok and the adjoining Samrat to be turned into the offices of the ministry of external affairs and renamed Ashok Bhawan. He also has pleaded that the Lalitha Mahal Palace Hotel in Mysore be turned into a museum – "a really top class museum for the south Indian art." Dr Singh's reasons for turning the Ashoka, with its magnificent structure, into the abode of the external affairs ministry is to "provide it with an impressive and dignified location with adequate meeting and conference rooms." Public memory is proverbially short, and, we may have forgotten that The Akbar – the country's trend setting hotel and a jewel in the ITDC's crown – was in fact converted into offices of the external affairs ministry in the early 80s. It would be an interesting revelation to inspect the Le Corbusier-inspired architecture and its trendy interiors, including its conference facilities, to see if they are being used the way Dr Singh has a dream for The Ashok.

Not many people may know the fascinating story of how The Ashok came to be built. In his anxiety to provide India with a global exposure Jawaharlal Nehru had invited UNESCO to hold its first out of Parie meeting in New Delhi. That was in 1955. There was only the Imperial and a few small hotels in the capital. That is how The Ashok and Vigyan Bhawan came into being within a year and that to after a consortium of princes (Dr Singh himself discloses that he was one of them) failed to raise Rs 1.5 crore to fund the project. And that is precisely how it became a government hotel! Nehru took personal interest in its construction and old timers would recall the hotel being called Nehru's baby.

All this is being mentioned to point out that The Ashok was conceived as a hotel and it has played a major role as a host to presidents, prime ministers, kings and queens, celebrities and major international gatherings. No other hotel in the capital, existing or in the future can hope to have 25 acres of space, a convention hall to seat 2,500 and an architectural design that gives credit to the Mughal traditions, not to speak of its 600 rooms and culinary experience. All it needs is a level playing field with private sector hotels. Which is exactly what is aimed at through disinvestment or privatisation.

Dr Singh's proposal could be faulted on two other counts also. Delhi, like the rest of the country is terribly short on accommodation (7,500 rooms vs 60,000 rooms in Beijing). The hotel industry is a big creator of employment. Three jobs per room directly and many more indirectly. Dr Singh himself has been stressing that at many tourism meetings and seminars, and has gone as far as to say that this sector could contribute substantially to poverty alleviations. Should we add more rooms and create more jobs or close down the Ashok's 600 rooms and sack the 1,800 employees?

In any event, it is too premature to assume that The Ashok Hotel will be 'sold'. The modalities of disinvestment have yet to be decided. There could be strategic sale, lease or part disinvestment. Any route that gives The Ashok a chance to return to its past glory will be welcomed, certainly by those have the good of tourism at heart.

Gaining International Character

Hotels everywhere like to sport international brands. For the linkage suggests high global standards in all aspects of operations of the industry which go well with international clientele. A growing number of such travellers, particularly on business, prefer special brands whose services and standards they are accustomed to. A traveller familiar with Sheraton services in New York, Bali or Tokyo will opt to go to the branded property when he comes to India. It is a sort of loyalty built by the quality of services provided, for which the brand is known and the franchisee is committed to provide.

Besides, in this highly competitive business, marketing abroad involves special skills and facilities which individual hotels and even chains do not have. Franchise or management agreements make it incumbent on the brand provider to look after marketing and operations. Nonetheless, hotels find themselves free to change their brands if the providers do not compensate them well enough for the royalty received by them. Of course, all brand owners make big claims but the proof is in the survival of hotel-brand associations. Without taking names it may be mentioned that a particular hotel in the capital has changed its brand affiliations thrice in as many years whereas another chain has retained the brand for nearly two decades and the association is going strong.

The steady arrival of new international brands in this country is a sure enough indicator of the faith global groups have in Indian hospitality services. At the same time, the franchise experience for varying reasons has not been uniform. The have to pass through several vicissitudes before firmly establishing relationships. The brand provider, who offers to manage as well, has to demonstrate how well it manages itself. It is only thus the confidence could be generated among entrepreneurs or chains. Survival and success depends in efficiently fulfilling its commitment.

One international brand that has passed through such experience in India is Holiday Inn. It shared with Inter-Continental the honour of being the first to make a debut in this country in the 60s with a tie-up in Agra (now under Taj management). In the early 90s, the chain attempted to reposition itself through a joint venture with a Bangkok-based NRI with an ambitious dream of 70 Holiday Inns in this country in five years or so. For a variety of reasons, the dream remained unrealised and in 1996 Holiday Inn Worldwide decided to take matters in its own hands and set up its own corporate presence but with a new name and many more brands in its stable. Bass Hotels and Resorts, a UK company, acquired Holiday Inn and later Inter-Continental making it one of the biggest hospitality industry players. Its presence in India is now backed by 2,700 hotels and 4,50,000 rooms in some 95 countries with a guest count of more than 150 million annually.

Bass executive director in India, Rakesh Mathur, who has more than a quarter century experience in the industry both at home and abroad, is responsible for the entire, Southwest Asia (including Pakistan, Nepal and Sri Lanka). He is pretty upbeat about the future with 18 Holiday Inns and Inter-Continental hotels already in operation in the region, twelve of them in India and ten more properties under development. Ten Indian cities have Holiday Inns on offer. They are: Ahmedabad, Khajurao, Manali, Surat, Goa, Ooty, Hyderabad, Jaipur, Pune and Mumbai. And there are two Inter-Continentals, in Delhi and Bangalore. Four more Inter-Continental hotels are under development in association with Bharat Hotels (in Bangalore, Mumbai, Goa and Srinagar) while six new Holiday Inns are coming up in Agra, Bangalore, Baroda, Kandla, Rajkot and Siliguri.

Even amongst existing hotels, Holiday Inn has emerged as the largest chain with an international linkage. Mathur is confident that many more of the Holiday Inn brands like Crowne Plaza, Holiday Inn Express (Limited Services Category), Staybridge Suites (extended stay market) would soon be available in India.

Mathur says that his main objective after setting up the regional corporate Bass office in Delhi has been to upgrade the existing Holiday Inns to the company's global standards, an area in which he can claim some success. And secondly, to establish a good management company to assist growth. The number of properties under development shows progress in this respect also. Bass Hotels, he says, is basically looking for management tie-ups. Franchises could be considered for properties managed by professional hoteliers. He recalls Bass CEO's announcement in the capital a few months ago that the chain had set apart $700 million for investment overseas and Indian entrepreneurs could look forward to a share the funds.

The Bass executive director is keen to point out that their Indian properties will not only be promoting each other, something that was never done in the earlier set up, but are an integral part of the central reservation system which is now available to travellers through toll free calls. Industry observers are hopeful that the success of Bass may spur other big league operators to enter India.

ITDC: Looking for Direction

Reports in a business newspaper suggest that the government has yet again invited fresh bids for a global advisor for the 'strategic sale' of its equity in the hospitality major, India Tourism Development Corporation (ITDC). The earlier choice of HSPC Investment Bank has reportedly been cancelled. The tourism ministry, under whose charge ITDC has been functioning since its inception in the 60s, is said to be keen on the new advisor to be in place by the end of December. It is nearly 10 years ago that the then prime minister had categorically announced that the government had no business to be in the hotel business. In the decade since then and after recommendations of several committees and finally the disinvestment commission, all that has happened is that the government has offloaded 10 per cent of its stake in ITDC to the Taj group which itself has been a subject of controversy. The slow pace in initiating steps towards divestment of a sector which admittedly has not been in the core area has naturally drawn critical comment from industry observers who would like to see ITDC professionally managed like its counterparts in the private sector.

Interestingly, ITDC was not set up as part of Jawaharlal Nehru's concept of gaining 'commanding heights of the economy' but due to shear unwillingness and/or the inability of private enterprises to invest in tourism. Old timers would recall that the government failed in its efforts to get a consortium of Princes to put together just Rs 1.5 crore to build the Ashok Hotel in the Capital in 1955 as the city was to host the UNESCO conference the following year. The government itself had to step in and fund the project leading eventually to the growth of the country's largest hotel chain and provider of other tourist services like transport, entertainment (sound and light shows) and duty-free shopping apart from producing tourism publicity literature. To give credit where it is due, it must be noted that the government was quite clear in its mind that ITDC's role was primarily to act as a catalyst in tourism development, particularly in the area of infrastructure. After the initial gift of the Ashok and with it Lodhi, Ranjit and Janpath hotels in the capital in 1969, when ITDC took its present form, this public sector undertaking played a pivotal role in opening up the country to tourism. Hotel Ashok in Bangalore was south India's first five-star hotel (commissioned in 1971). Akbar in Delhi, which opened in early 1972, set trends in decor which are today's norm all over the country. (Sadly it does not exist as a hotel any more). In the same year, the Kovalam Beach resort was thrown open to guests heralding beach tourism in India. It was ITDC's pioneering effort that has eventually resulted in the rapid growth of beach hotels and other services not only in Kerala but in Goa and around Mahabalipuram (since renamed Mammalapuram) near Chennai. Or, take ITDC's lead in opening wildlife sanctuaries to tourists in the far off Kaziranga and Gir forest, or the next door Bharatpur bird sanctuary. True, it was Taj group's initiative in popularising palace hotels (Rambagh in Jaipur and Lake Palace in Udaipur) but ITDC's Lalitha Mahal in Mysore is in a separate class. The Corporation's contribution to mid-market hotels in main tourist centres like Khajuraho, Varanasi, Patna, Jammu, Aurangabad, Hassan and Bhubaneswar, to name only a few, is quite significant. Today, all the major chains as well as the emerging chains have recognised the mid-market as a thrust area.

Promoting Indian cuisine is one more feather in ITDC's cap. Not only *Mughlai* or *tandoori* delicacies but also regional varieties were made palatable particularly to foreign visitors. No less important is the undertaking's role in presenting authentic Indian dance and music performances. To the Ashok Theatre in New Delhi goes the credit of launching many an artiste of repute. The Ashok hotel can also boast of laying the foundations of convention tourism in India.

An achievement that would stand out in ITDC's report card of its heyday is its contribution to raising the standard of tourism literature to global levels, be it a poster, a brochure, ads, picture post cards and the coveted annual diary which rose to be a collector's item. And, although it had a largely developmental role, the Corporation as a whole always made profits.

This was ITDC's dynamic decade of the 70s. It must be concluded that the Corporation was able to achieve all this, thanks to a supportive political leadership and professional management from chairman downwards. Besides, there was little competition from the private sector which was still finding its feet in tourism.

Soon, however, the scenario changed. Spurred by ITDC's success, private investments into tourism started flowing. The government, on its part, had no time to review ITDC's role as a catalyst. Instead, political interference, aggravated by bureaucratic hassles and unionism started impacting ITDC's performance. The ills of the public sector, inherent or otherwise, made their appearance in ITDC too. Burgeoning private sector competition has only added to its woes. The uncertainty that has dogged the Corporation since the start of the economic reforms has had its own adverse effect on the morale of the staff.

On top of it, ITDC has been without a permanent chairman/managing director for over two years. An early decision on disinvestment and its quick implementation alone will give ITDC an opportunity to relive its halcyon days.

Foreign Hands for Greener Goals

A growing number of Indian entrepreneurs in the hospitality industry, particularly the greenhorns in the business, seem to opt for foreign expertise in management and marketing. Until a couple of years ago, international linkages in the industry had been limited to franchises as that was all that was permissible. This trend has changed, making possible new entrants from the global hoteliering scene to make their presence in this country. Alongside, it is also noticeable that the linkages confined to European and American concepts of hoteliering are changing. These are underlined by the announcement of Nikko Hotels whose parent company, JAL – a subsidiary of Japan Airlines – has announced a marketing, licensing and operating services agreement with the Delhi-based Sunair Hotels. Nikko thus make its entry into the South Asian market, traditional preserve of western chains.

Sunair itself is new to hoteliering, having been a subsidiary of an international trading house owned by a family in the Capital. Sunair has built a 170-room property claiming five-star deluxe status in a prime location in the Capital. The project has been hanging fire for more than a decade and the promoters have, from time to time been in touch with Indian and western chains. The search for partnership has now ended by the tie up with the Japanese chain and both sides claim that their collaboration will expand through an exclusive agreement for development of additional hotel projects in the country.

The Japanese style and ethos, which will be obvious in these hotels looks from reinforcement in the growing economic cooperation between India and Japan. The volume of trade between the two countries in the last two decades has gone up from Rs. 80 crore to Rs 8,000 crore and turned many Japanese brand names like Hitachi, Honda, Mitsubishi, Soni and Panasonic familiar to the Indian customer.

The hospitality industry, however, was not among them. And, now Nikko fills in the slot bringing with it another famed brand in Japanese restaurant business, Sakura, Metropolitan Nikko Hotel in New Delhi, as the property will be called, will have as its main attraction apart from the

Japanese style of hospitality, a Sakura restaurant. Considering the popularity of Tokyo, the Japanese restaurant at the public sector Ashok Hotel, there is every reason to expect success for Sakura. Metropolitan Nikko will be commissioned in the coming spring.

At the same time as the Sunair-Nikko announcement was made, industry representatives turned out in large numbers to greet the promoters at a pre-lunch function of the Goa Marriott in the Capital. Here too the alliance is marked by a management tie-up between Palm Hotels and Marriott International. Three previous – management partnerships in the hotel industry bind Meridien, Inter-Continental and Hyatt in alliances with Indian partners. In fact, Meridien has announced that its alliances for the future will be only for management. This relationship seems to be mutually advantageous as the compensation is linked to the turnover. The higher the turnover which foreign management and marketing can bring to the property, the better it will bring returns to both.

To return to the Marriott function, it was organised by Mileage Communications with innovative features. The vary entrance to the banquet hall of the Capital's Habitat Centre had been turned into a midship aerobridge promising all the delights of Goa Marriott at the other end. Dattaraj Salgaocar, director of Palm Hotels maintains, "we are indeed proud of our alliance and management tie-up with Marriott International, the leaders in the hospitality business worldwide with whom we share common values and objectives."

While Nikko has already 53 hotels worldwide and targets 100 by 2001, Marriott has 1,800 operating units in more than 50 countries. Goa Marriott, which has 188 rooms, is being commissioned as a deluxe five-star hotel in the middle of December, and is the state's first business hotel. Also, to be commissioned around the same time is Marriott Executive Residences close to Mumbai to be followed by Renaissance, another Marriott brand, with a convention centre six months later. And next year, Chennai will have a top-of-the-line JW Marriott.

Needless to say, the brand names earn a globally loyal clientele. This applies equally to all chains like Sheraton, Radisson and Quality Inns. A significant development in the segment of foreign connections has been the change of ownership of Quality Inns India, the main franchiser for the family of Quality Inn brands, since renamed Choice Hotels. Quality Inn India launched by A K Dave, one-time chairman and managing director of ITDC, has now been acquired by Sushil Gupta of Hyatt Regency.

His son, Sandeep, is the new generation director who promises to continue where Dave left—brining in greater quality to the mid-market hotels.

Customised Service: An Honourable Custom

The hospitality industry, assailed by threats of technological advances manifest as the Internet and other communication tools, will have no option but to insist on customised service. That is the only sure way of survival. It applies as much to the travel trade as to the hotel industry. There is happily a growing recognition of the role of technology but the problem is that by its very nature it cannot be set to a pattern. It has to be attuned to preferences of the individual customer and these are prone to change. What was relevant yesterday may well not be answering the demands of customers today. Essentially, it is the human dimension of the demand that counts. The transformation that the industry itself is going through conditions these changes. The trend is towards mergers, acquisitions and affiliations. Not only hotels, even travel agencies experience these changes. And when one speaks of customised service in such mega institutions, the problem assumes greater magnitude calling for far greater emphasis on training and development. For no reason, should it be taken to mean that the tools of technology can be avoided. The internet can be put to as much use for customised service as the threat it poses to the trade. In any event, internet possibilities are immense, Ravi Saligram, Bangalore-born CEO of the global major Bass Hotels & Resorts, claims that the Net has 250 million users which according to him represent something approaching 90 per cent of the world's purchasing power. He forecast that in a decade spending on the Net, will amount to one per cent of the global economy. The challenge before the industry is not to be overwhelmed by technology but to capture new opportunities provided by the Net. Saligram has a simple prescription: Add value, specialise and provide a unique service which in simple terms is customised service.

One great product reputed for customised service is the Rolls Royce car. Any customer can ask for a modification to suit his need or taste. In hotels, Saligram's slogan is a "Can Do Friendly" response. In operational terms, it means a waiter does not get away by saying the item asked for by the customer is not on the menu. The way the bed is positioned should reflect the preference of the guest and not of the interior designer. The tourism product has to be a pleasurable experience that cannot be repeated elsewhere because it is far too personalised. Since experience is often related by word of mouth, any favourable assessment improves the image of a destination. This is something India particularly needs. Such service fashions the brand.

To return to Saligram, "it will have to be unique; it has to be relevant and it needs to keep in mind that a brand is a promise that generates trust if delivered consistently".

Linked to the unique nature of service are designs for the future which encompass everything from architecture to decor to auto service. Chandu Chhada who claims to have designed more than 100 hotels around the world sums up the need for customised service, "a tourist may visit a destination for various purposes be it for a holiday, leisure, relaxation, business, professional, pilgrimage, health or even just curiosity. He or she needs a place to stay in for a few hours in transit, a few days or even a few months. Obviously, his needs will have to be catered to... No matter which millennium, be it the 21st, 22nd or thereon, the most essential feature or design requirement of a hotel would be to cater to the function and comfort of a guest."

Interestingly, the designs of new hotels according to Chhada will have to meet social needs as well. These have to be eco-friendly, with a drastic reduction in the use of wood and replacement of natural materials such as marble stone which may be extinct in the next twenty to thirty years. Also, with the shortage of space and constraints on plot ratios in preferred sites, he foresees a reduction in the provision of vast public areas such as hotel lobbies and circulation spaces which are not only a waste of space and of energy in keeping them cool or warm, but in most cases, are non-revenue-producing. According to him, there will also be a decline in the number of restaurants and entertainment facilities even in five-star hotels especially in cities where standalone restaurants provide excellent food and service.

All this goes to show that extravagance and glamour do not substitute for customised service, the sheet anchor of the hospitality industry in the coming century.

Resolve Tariff Dispute for Greater Harmony

An avoidable controversy that has placed hoteliers and tour operators on opposite sides of the fence with the award of the arbitrator, Department of Tourism (DoT), prompting a writ petition in the Delhi High Court could not have come at a worse time for Indian tourism.

In their own business interests, hoteliers and tour operators need not take a confrontationist attitude when it is their shared objective that the country should earn more from tourism in foreign exchange. Now that the controversy has been taken to the court one hopes that its final verdict will resolve once and for all the issue pending for the last five years.

The High Court has restrained the DoT from imposing any penal action on hotels for persisting with the dual tariff in convertible currency as far as foreign tourists are concerned, and Indian currency from Indian nationals. There was a tariff differential too. The hotels keeping in view the paying capacity of Indians or perhaps with a view to showing concessions had been charging Indians much less.

Incidentally, the number of hotels practicing dual tariff was around 100 in a total of nearly 1,200. The bulk of the 100 was in metro cities and belonged to the deluxe categories, serving exclusively the upmarket traveller.

The tour operators who bring travel groups have been complaining that this dual tariff goes against the grain of making India a less expensive destination in a competitive neighbourhood. They also argue that the tariff scale discriminated against the foreigner and always used to take Southeast Asia as a role model. But, a review by the World Tourism Organisation (WTO), the international organisation of the global industry, has released figures which dispute the four operators claim.

The per tourist realisation per day in 1996 in India was 46 dollars while the comparable figures for Asean nations and even China, touted as a success story in tourism, are: Thailand 160 dollars, Malaysia 118 dollars, Indonesia 124 dollars, Singapore 492 dollars and China 162 dollars.

Certainly, if one goes by these figures which are most authentic for the international industry, India is not an expensive destination. Besides, hotels account for 50 per cent spending by tourists and if the Indian hotels are really priced high it should be reflected in the earnings per traveller.

Besides, it is common knowledge that India is inadequate in infrastructure in respect of accommodation. In a free market, prices are ruled by demand and supply. It cannot be anybody's case, even that of the tour operator, that in recent months Indian hotel tariffs have not been a bargain.

The reason is obvious: low occupancy and lesser demand. Delhi and Mumbai have 7,000 rooms each and three years ago when the current currency aggravated business travel peaked and the receipts in forex soared because of the pressure on supply and more so the willingness of the customer. The room availability is 58,000 in Bangkok, 33,000 in Hong Kong, 30,000 in Singapore and 52,000 in Beijing.

Interestingly, in the wake of the currency meltdown, most of the Asean countries have opted for a dual tariff for the same reason India did. In fact, India was complimented by Asean travel industry leaders at a Chennai meet for initiating the dual tariff system.

The development that triggered the writ petition was the DoT deadline for enforcing a single tariff as otherwise they would lose their approval classification. The petition was filed after the Hotel Association of India (HAI) had failed to persuade the new Minister for Tourism to get the order stayed.

The HAI in its submission to the minister pointed out that the dual tariff is based on several factors commensurate with international standards of facilities and services provided for foreign tourists and for mobilising exchange resources. Also, to be noted is that foreign direct investment (FDI) has not materialised in the hotel sector while there is a growing shortage of rooms, which if is to be covered would require an investment of as much as Rs 20,000 crore.

In a bid to strengthen their plea for retention of the dual tariff, the hotel industry informed the Department that it has commissioned The National Institute of Public Finance and Policy under Dr Raja Chelliah to undertake a study of the tariff structure and the Department would do well to wait for its findings. It may be mentioned here that hotels were not the first to take to dual tariff. The railways and Indian Airlines have for years enforced dual rates.

In any event, at a time of a depressing slowdown in tourism growth, for the three agencies, the DoT, the hotel industry and the tour operators, to get embroiled in a fruitless dispute is unfortunate. They could pool their resources for better purposes in pursuance of what the minister calls a pragmatic tourism policy.

Lucky

Bharat Hotels which first acquired the Holiday Inn flag under a franchise arrangement gave it up in favour of a more up-market association with Hilton giving the foreign chain complete management rights. In less than two years, Bharat Hotels has gone Inter-Continental under a modified management contract. Owner Lalit Suri said at the launch that he "hoped to be lucky the third time around."

Inter-Continental on the other hand established its presence in India two decades ago first with the Oberoi group and then with the Taj, the arrangement with the latter coming to an end in March this year. Daniel Desbaillet, president Asia Pacific region said the New Delhi hotel will be the chain's 219th property. Spread over nearly 80 countries, Inter-Continental has a strong presence in the Asia Pacific region with hotels in Australia, Thailand, Malaysia, China, Japan, Taiwan, Indonesia, Vietnam and Sri Lanka.

The New Delhi launch also marked Bharat Hotels emergence as a chain. Suri confirmed earlier press reports that he is investing some 60 crore of rupees on the famous Palace hotel in Srinagar overlooking the Dal lake. Describing it as a 'bold venture' he said 58 executive rooms are already operational and the hotel has been re-christened as The Grand Palace. The main palace block of 60 rooms and 10 cottages are under product restoration and will be opened to guests by the end of the year. The next door nine-hole golf course, owned by the J&K government will be available to hotel guests. He said The Grand Palace will play a significant role in reviving tourism in Kashmir.

Suri has also chosen The Grand as his brand name for two more of his hotel projects under construction. The Grand Resort on the Cana Cona beach in Goa, expected to be ready in December 1999, is being built on an 86 acre site straddled between two rivers. It will have 256 rooms and 20 vilas with a private swimming pool. Claiming that it will be the country's finest beach resort with state-of-the-art conference facilities for upto 500 participants, it will also have an international standard shopping mall, a marina with water sports, a nature cure centre, an equestrian centre and a nine-hole international class golf course.

The Grand Mumbai near Sahara airport is Suri's fourth project, slated for completion in just two years. Its 400 rooms will be supplemented by a 1,00,000 sq ft business and commercial complex and service apartments – an innovation. Total investment on the projects including Srinagar is estimated at Rs 300 crore. Apart from a $50 million loan from Merryl Lynch no other borrowings were planned.

Media persons were keen to know if Inter-Continental would extend cover to Bharat Hotel's properties in Srinagar, Goa and Mumbai. Desbaillet said he was talking to Suri on the possibilities but a final decision would take time. He was categorical, however, in one respect: Inter-Continental is not looking for franchises. "We are interested only in management tie-ups," he said. He also made it clear that there was no exclusivity in Inter-Continental's relationship with Bharat Hotels. He did not disclose details but said he was looking at possible arrangements with other hotels in this country.

Suri also confirmed that he broke the agreement with Hilton because it had not lived up to its performance projections but he was confident that the new relationship with Inter-Continental would be 'long lasting'. Describing it as a "closely integrated management agreement" he said Bharat Hotels will be paying out three percent of AGOP and 1.5 per cent of the total turnover.

He explained that while he would have control over financial matters, Inter-Continental will look after day-to-day operations conceding that this was a modified version of the agreement with Hilton which enjoyed financial control also. Apart from day-to-day operations, the foreign partner will also be responsible for "implementation, integration and upgradation of the hotel to Inter-Continental standards and sales and marketing, in close coordination with the owners." The Inter-Continental connection, Suri said, will also give additional benefits to guests like access to Six Continents Club – Inter-Continental's frequent guest recognition programmes and Global Mileage Rewards – Inter-Continental's airline and travel alliance programme. Industry observers will be keenly watching the working of the 'modified' management arrangement at the New Delhi Inter-Continental.

More the Merrier

The travel trade must be counting the budget costs though at the time of writing the finance minister had not presented the first estimate of the BJP-led government. It would not be far wrong to say that the expectations have been great. If the general trade has been looking forward to what Yashwant Sinha has to offer after tourism minister Madan Lal Khurana's much talked about persuasive efforts, there have been other developments that have evoked keen interest in the hotel segment. These related to the government's decision to repeal the Urban Land Ceiling and Regulation Act (ULCRA) and tie-ups, some old, some renewed and some totally new.

The decision on urban land ceilings has not come a day too soon. Promulgated to take away 'excess' land in private hands for public housing, the end results have been dismal. Only an insignificant percentage of land could be acquired and not all of it could be converted into housing while leading at the same time to sky rocketing of land prices for such activities as hotel projects.

With the repeal of this law, scheduled to be completed in the current session of Parliament, the hospitality industry can look forward to some easing of the paucity of land situation, particularly in the metro and other large cities, to bring about a faster growth, of the accommodation sector. As Habib Rehman, president, Hotel Association of India (HAI), had recently pointed out "there is no dearth of money in the country (to invest in hotels) but dearth only of land."

The industry has also been representing to the government to amend Section 37(i) of the Income Tax (IT) Act which requires prior approval before sale of land. This is considered another hindrance in the growth of hotels. This column had reported the reappearance in Delhi of the Inter-

Continental flag, this time over the Bharat Hotels with a modified management tie-up. Earlier in the year, the first Radisson-affiliated hotel had opened its doors. The Apeejay Group-owned Park Hotel in the capital announced it has become a member of the prestigious Small Luxury Hotels of the World (SLH) alongwith its flagship in Kolkata.

The young chief of Park Hotels and a functionary of HAI, Priya Paul, told a largely-attended media conference that it was a matter of prestige to gain membership of SLH as it "brought together some of the finest quality hotels around the globe, including the glamour of city hotels, the charm of resort hotels, historic chateaux and country houses." Paul said membership of SLH confirmed the Park Group's position of boutique hotels which are "stylish, luxurious and intimate."

For company the two Park properties will have such big and famous names as The Ritz in London, The Oberoi in Bali, The Mark in New York, Hotel Balzac in Paris and The Raffles in Singapore. A surprise in store for the media persons was the fact that SLH had made a quiet entry into India some three years ago when it conferred membership on the Neemrana Fort Palace, off the Jaipur highway, promoted by the conservation duo, Aman Nath and Francis Wacziarg.

Both were present at the news conference and told EH&C that they had not felt the need for publicity in India as they were already getting the full benefits of their membership because of SLH's access to potential travellers abroad. A fallout of this was also the promotion of India as a destination, they added.

SLH Asia-Pacific, general manager, Lynne Ireland, said the two Park hotels had met with "all our stringent selection criteria of local recognition, compatible marketing approach, personal service, high quality cuisine, comfortable and stylish surroundings." Without disclosing names, she said two more hotels, one in Mumbai and the other in Jaipur, had been cleared for membership and were awaiting completion of formalities,

SLH considered India as an important and emerging market and it had set a target of twenty members in the next two or three years. In all, SLH has 230 members spread over fifty countries and in the Asia-Pacific region it has a concentration in Australia from where the region's marketing is handled. SLH is not a franchising outfit but it does help members with their international marketing, reservations and promotions.

Ireland said the smallest number of rooms to quality for membership could be as little as four and the maximum permissible is 250 for Asia-Pacific, and 200 for the West. She declined to share information on membership fees saying only that these were size-specific.

Yet another foreign chain which will be making its debut in this country is the Canada-based upmarket Four Seasons group. Its first port of call is Goa where it will manage the Leela Beach, which is awaiting its relaunch later this year after a complete renovation. Promoted by Capt Krishnan Nair's Leela Venture, the resort now has fewer but more spacious rooms and more upmarket, high quality facilities.

Leela Venture has also signed up with Four Seasons for managing four of its projects in the pipeline. Two of these, in Udaipur and Bangalore, are slated for commissioning in 1999 and the other two, in New Delhi and Mumbai, a year later.

Waiting in the wings is Marriott. It has a franchise agreement for an Ansals-promoted hotel in the Saket area of South Delhi, also scheduled for opening in 1999. As they say, the more the merrier.

A Tale of Three Hotels

Three hotels in the Capital have lately been making waves: The Imperial, a Lutyen era landmark which in its new avatar is a spectacular presentation of the Raj nostalgia: The Claridges, the first to come up in the early years of independence (it will be 50 this year); and, Tivoli Gardens, which has gone through an unusual transformation from an open air farmhouse famous for wedding receptions to a sophisticated resort with loads of banqueting and conference facilities.

The Imperial has recently been bestowed the prestigious Five Star Diamond Award by The American Academy of Hospitality Sciences, the only Indian hotel to be so recognised. The Academy president, Joseph Cinque described the Imperial "a most extraordinary establishment in every respect of its operation". Recipients of the award in other parts of the world include Four Seasons Hotel, New York; The Dorchester, London; Island Shangri-La, Hong Kong; the Oriental, Bangkok.

To celebrate the occasion, The Imperial's general manager, Pierre Jochem left it to chef Bruno Cerdan to make the event memorable. Choosing the theme of trees, Cerdan used a variety of ingredients such as gooseberries, star anise, wheat, lentils, cherries, strawberries and peppercorn to create the trees. The cinnamon tree, for instance, was made by fixing cinnamons on a broomstick. The food displayed on the buffet was exotic and consisted of a wide range of colourful and creative cold cuts, lobsters, prawns, salmons, scallops, caviar and a range of desserts – a magnificent culinary experience enjoyed by over 300 guests representing the travel trade, government, diplomats and media.

The Claridges, in the heart of the original New Delhi, is on a three acre plot where a Khanna family lived in bungalows. On advice from friends the family decided to convert it into a hotel. Of its existing 168 rooms in a three-storey structure, it opened in its first phase with just 12 rooms. Last year the family sold the hotel to Suresh Nanda, NRI, ex-Navy, son of a former Navy chief, and a global entrepreneur, for Rs 96 crore. Determined to make the Claridges join the ranks of the world's finest hotels, he is spending Rs 40 crore on its renovation. He told this writer he wants to reposition The Claridges "as a fine boutique hotel with world class facilities and service levels," The hotel now has newly appointed spacious deluxe rooms and designer suites, a new business centre with state of the art facilities, the latest in internet services and the most modern fitness centre.

Asked if he is content with the present size and boutique character of The Claridges, Nanda said ideally he would like to build a new highrise hotel of 220 rooms with an international class spa. But, that he pointed out would depend on whether he could go above the Lutyen rule of three storeys. After all, Meridien, Kanishka and Taj Mansingh were permitted highrises. He would perhaps have to wait until after the elections when it would be possible to get a policy decision.

Rohit Gupta, successful in his father's leather garment exports, pioneered in the early '90s the use of farmhouses as venues for wedding banquets. Christening the family owned seven acre plot in South Delhi as Tivoli Gardens (the name was borrowed from Tivoli restaurant in Connaught Place), he did good business in open air marriage celebrations for six years until 2000 when the government banned such activities. The entrepreneur in him soon found a solution – build a resort with vast indoor and outdoor spaces and continue to cash in on his recognised brand of banqueting. Eighteen months later and with an investment of Rs 15 crore (not counting the cost of land) rose Tivoli Gardens in the Spanish hacienda architecture surrounded by beautiful landscaped and manicured gardens. It boasts of 36 well furnished rooms, many opening into courtyards, an inviting lobby, an English Pub (Trafalgar), a multicuisine restaurant (Marbella) and multi-purpose meeting rooms which can accommodate up to 500 delegates. An innovative idea introduced at Tivoli Gardens is that the conference and banqueting areas have separate entrances and parking lots so that guests staying at the resort are not disturbed. Tivoli Gardens' popularity can be seen from its list of patrons which include such big names as Airtel, Samsung and LG.

Its success has made Gupta more ambitious. He has started work on a 200 room hotel with the most modern convention centre for 1,500 persons theatre style. The location is two kilometre short of Manaser on the Jaipur highway on a ten acre piece of land. Half the rooms will be studio apartments. The hotel-cum-convention centre will be commissioned in two-and-a-half years.

Hoteliers in Disguise

Hospitality services and defence forces have one tiling in common which is the accent on punctuality, discipline and motivation. This shared quality enables resettlement of ex-servicemen in the hospitality services with greater facility than from any other section of employees. This has been recognised lately by a major chain like ITC Hotels and sainik welfare bodies.

The ITC experience according to its managing director, Habib Rehman himself a former army Major, has been rewarding so much so that the company has a special division under a retired Brigadier and has many sided programmes of not only for training but also for encouraging those who want to start new enterprises in this sector.

The potential of ex-servicemen as a resource base is immense considering that as many as 60,000 officers and jawans retire every year while they are still in reasonably good health and spirits. Many of them would be in their forties after two decades or so of service in responsible positions which call for leadership, initiative and innovation, which are equally valued qualities in the hospitality industry.

The possibilities of this resource base were broughtout last week at Ludhiana where four hundred comparatively youthful retired personnel assembled for an interface with the government, industry leaders and representatives of the travel trade.

The Ludhiana meet was the fourth in the series promoted by the Chandigarh-based Training and Research Centre for Tourism, Fashion and Management studies. Its ebullient director, Gulshan Sharma, a retired Major with a doctorate in tourism, has been the brain behind the exercise, the earlier meetings having been held at Hyderabad, Shimla and Chandigarh itself.

Sharma has received support from the defence ministry's resettlement directorate, defence welfare organisations of the state governments and the travel industry. He managed to bring to the Ludhiana meet two Punjab ministers, one of whom is in charge of finance and is also a former army captain, Kanwaljit Singh.

The other, Sardar Janmeja Singh Sekhon, is minister for defence welfare. The meeting occasioned a commitment by the finance minister to fund a research-based data programme for information on both job opportunities as well as self-employment avenues so that servicemen could plan their second career well in time.

The Ludhiana conference, as with earlier meetings, helped the participating officers to be acquainted with the possibilities which the tourism sector could offer. The response at these gatherings indicates a made for each other situation between the travel trade and ex-servicemen and could be profitably repeated in different parts of the country. Skilled manpower shortage has been a problem for the industry, particularly in the northern and western parts of India.

Special courses could be formulated for services people just or about to retire. Even the spouses could be easily trained in not only housekeeping but other tourism-related activities. ITC Hotels has been able to provide employment to the wives of quite a few officers in their establishments.

New entrepreneurship is an area for resettlement, The Punjab promoters have also been holding seminars on investments and sources of funding. ITC Hotels too has a commendable scheme for encouraging establishment of wayside facilities under the brand name of Welcomstop. The facilities include refreshments as well as automobile service stations and telecom centres.

Hopefully, other hotel chains will emulate the ITC example. The distinctive contribution by institutions like ITC Hotels and Gulshan Sharma's directorate is that would be entrepreneurs cannot fall into the hands of con men or fly by night operators. And, if the Punjab scheme gets off the ground for authentic information and guidance there will be a dedicated window on service person's rehabilitation.

Punjab, with the largest contribution to the armed services with the consequential proliferation of retired personnel, needs special consideration which Sharma's initiative has been able to provide. While resettlement should be a matter for national concern, it is to be noted that every eighth retiring person is from the Punjab. The number of retired personnel in the state now adds up to 7,00,000. And the State also has to look after one thousand war widows.

The announcement by the finance minister that he would most handing over Punjab tourism hotels and other services to service officers is a welcome beginning which other non-governmental organisations and other state governments could take up for consideration.

In India, to the Hilton

After several abortive attempts in the past few years, hospitality major Hilton International with a US $2.4 billion turnover and some 400 hotels in its chain, has finally found a firm toehold in India. The latest and apparently more enduring venture is a "strategic alliance" with the country's premier hospitality outfit, EIH, popularly known as the Oberoi group. Under the new tie-up, which became effective. Seven Trident hotels in the EIH stable have been renamed Trident Hilton. In addition, Oberoi Towers, adjacent to The Oberoi in Mumbai, has changed its name to Hilton Towers. The seven Trident Hiltons are located in Gurgaon (commissioned barely two months ago), Agra, Jaipur, Udaipur, Bhubaneswar, Chennai and Kochi. One more will join the Trident Hilton brand in Mumbai which is scheduled to be opened in 2007.

At a joint press conference at the Gurgaon Trident Hilton, EIH chairman, P R S (Biki) Oberoi and Koos Klein, president, Hilton international Middle East and Asia Pacific, said that "the strategic alliance is the basis for a franchise agreement that builds on the combined strength of Trident's domestic brand position and operational expertise together with Hilton's strong global brand and vast sales and marketing network." The EIH chief pointed out that the launch of the alliance is a culmination of six months of intensive brand preparation and training between his group and Hilton International. EIH, he said, will continue to manage all hotels and will undertake domestic marketing, promotion and reservations in India, while Hilton will be responsible for international marketing, promotion and reservations through its global network.

Biki claimed that the tie-up will enhance Oberoi's strong leadership position, both in the Indian and overseas markets. And guests will get additional benefits and services like access to Hilton Honours, one of the largest loyalty programmes in the world. The Hilton president had his own reasons to be upbeat and said, "In one powerful stroke, Hilton customers from around the world can visit India and stay in a network of Hilton-branded hotels in eight great locations."

The Oberoi-Hilton pact is for ten years to begin with. Asked if Hilton would also be interested in acquiring equity, Klein said there was no such proposal right now but he could not rule it out in the future. He also made it clear that there was no exclusivity in the arrangement and both parties were free to enter into arrangement with other chains.

Hilton's country manager in India, Lenny Menezes, told this writer that there would be consultations between the two sides in the event of any proposal for a tie-up with a third party. In any event, he said, Hilton would not consider any affectation which would be in competition with EIH.

Biki was asked why the alliance with Hilton which was primarily for its Trident brand was being extended to the Oberoi Towers. He explained that The Oberoi and Oberoi Towers being side by side had caused some confusion in names. Hilton, he said, will give the erstwhile Oberoi Towers a distinct identity.

When a scribe commented that the Oberois already enjoyed a high reputation for service standards and so what was it that Hilton could teach them, Klein conceded that this indeed was so. But, he pointed out that "nobody knows everything; we can learn from each other. There is certainly room for cross pollination." In any case, he said, the basic objective of a franchise is to provide the global strengths of a brand.

Biki welcomed the recent increase in hotel occupancy and said that with the encouraging growth of GDP a better future seemed to be ahead. But he did not buy the argument that we were already in a mode of severe shortage of rooms. He said that even with what seemed like a boom in the last few months, occupancies averaged only a little over 70 per cent. Metros like Mumbai, Kolkata, Chennai and even Delhi had adequate supply. But if the demand increases significantly, he said, the industry is ready to meet the challenge, as it had done in the past. The Oberois alone, he said, have added ten hotels in seven years. He said in reply to a question that with rebranding there was no plan to raise tariffs yet but pointed out that market forces will determine prices in the future.

Hilton International's first foray into India was some years ago with Bharat Hotels with its property in the capital. The relationship did not last more than two years. The second was with actor Sanjay Khan's spa near Bangalore which had even a shorter life span. The third attempt, towards the end of 2002, was in association with an Indian pharmaceutical company, Morepen Labs. This was to be a joint venture with a one third stake from Hilton for three hotels in Mumbai, Bangalore and Goa to begin with. There was no mention of the status of this joint venture but according to the grapevine the Indian promoters have not been able to get their act together.

Industry observers are impressed that Hilton this time round had made a grand entry with eight operational hotels that have already established their presence, an unmatched feat for any overseas chain.

Partnerships Run a Ground

In the Hilton flag will be lowered from the only hotel where it had been fluttering for less than two years. It signifies the end of a linkage ushered in with great fanfare as it was the international chain's first breakthrough into Indian hospitality services. The forging of the Delhi connection spurred hopes of a spread of presence across the country for the Hilton chain, which unlike many other international groups had tied for management of the property.

At least the arrangement with one of the hotels, which is situated in Chennai will continue. The Delhi episode, however, has prompted tourism analysts to examine the why and how of foreign linkages, especially managements. At the time of writing Hilton's Delhi associate, Bharat Hotels has not formally announced a pact with any other chain but insiders say that it will settle for a franchise agreement with Inter-Continental.

Apart from Hilton, Hyatt is the only hotel in the capital with foreign management. For historic reasons, hotels in India have not tied-up for management although they have used foreign brand names under franchise agreements. For one, the government of India did not permit foreign management for hotels in India until the onset of the economic reforms in the early 1990s.

Secondly, the Indian hotel chains have themselves developed sufficient management expertise to hardly require any assistance from abroad in this regard. Thirdly, no foreign chain, Hilton included, has been willing so far to have an equity stake that will entitle them to management share automatically. And, finally, some of the Indian groups have their own overseas properties which they have been managing with a measure of success. In fact, in some developing countries like Egypt, Sri Lanka and Nepal, Indian hotel companies have invested and also take management.

Still, the need for foreign brand names identifying these properties with international standards has been considered a USP by many hotels, particularly as the overseas partner undertakes marketing, promotion and training. Tie-ups have been snapped when the expectations in revenues and profits have not materialise. This is not unexpected as often within the country arrangement between single property entrepreneurs and big hotels chains are not renewed for the simple reason that the owner does not find the balance sheet as rosy as he expects within a short time.

Nonetheless, foreign chains seeking an Indian presence and their Indian partners requiring an overseas marketing set up will continue, which explains why Sheraton, Holiday Inn, Ramada, SPHC, Meridien, Quality Inn, Days Inn, Trident, Best Western are all here and soon to come are Radisson and Four Seasons. Generally, under these agreement the overseas partners receive anything upto three per cent of the total revenue or of the room rent.

While there is a ceiling of three per cent, the agreement depends on the need for each other. There is even a case of the fee being fixed at one and a half per cent because of the chain's eagerness to come to India, Speaking of foreign partners, in their home base too they do not very often own properties, which are held by not single entrepreneurs or families but by a group of investors.

It is not rare that a chain that boasts of hundreds of hotels in its international network may hardly own a couple of them. But in most of these cases they professionally manage the properties. It is this expertise that some Indian companies would like to avail of.

This was not possible until the reforms were introduced. Now, foreign managements are allowed to operate hotels and the normal fees that are charged vary between seven and ten per cent of gross operating profit (GOP) and three per cent of revenue. The environment in which foreign chains operate elsewhere in the world is not the same in India. In the West, for instance, a management company is free to recruit, layoff, promote or discount and generally take decisions on totally commercial considerations.

In India, apart from the ownership patterns, labour laws do not permit the freedom to layoff at will. In a hypothetical situation a foreign management would like to layoff a percentage of the staff during the lean season. At the same time, hotels in India would do well with expert foreign managements. In that case, the way out suggested by a knowledgeable hoteliers is that Indian owners should not only resist the temptation to back-seat driving and but evolve a system in which the foreign manager has autonomy in operations but the owner will retain financial control. Ideally, there should be 'participative management.'

The Hilton episode might trigger variations in partnerships. But the duration of the Delhi association was too short to produce a miracle, particularly when the business and leisure tourism has been at a low ebb.

Time Share Demands its Share

The world over time share is looked upon as one of the fastest growing segments of the hospitality industry. Although in its infancy in India (it made its debut barely a decade ago), in the west, particularly north America and Europe, the number of time share owners runs into millions and those exchanging their vacation periods into hundreds of thousands. According to statistic available with RCI – Resort Condominium International – which acts as a bank for time share exchange globally and has a presence in India too, over 212 million travellers took time share holidays during 2000. The industry has a turn over of US$ five billion. Big league chains like Hilton, De Vera, Hyatt, Four Seasons, Sheraton and Marriott are active participants in time share.

In India the number of time share resorts is now over 50 and more than 40,000 families are unit owners. Interestingly, a large number of time share owners overseas exchange their holidays in Indian resorts through RCI. And as far as UK is concerned, India is among the top ten preferences for time share exchange while this country is nowhere near that position in terms of general tourists.

It is true that in the initial years, thanks to some unscrupulous developers, time share's image suffered a set back. But concerted efforts by RCI through a stricter regime of affiliation and self-regulation attempted by the Chennai-based All India Resort Development Association (AIRDA) has led to consumer confidence largely being restored. It was at this stage that the time share segment started looking forward to recognition and support from the tourism authorities. It managed to take in its stride the absence of any reference in the national tourism policy to the potential of time share (or even a mention of it). But it was not prepared for the bombshell that dropped when the revised norms for hotel classification were announced. Far from even providing a restricted or stringent procedure for classification, or leaving the door open for later entry, the department of tourism (DoT) has rather harshly provided that any hotel which spares even a few of its rooms for time share will be denied classification.

There has been no official statement from DoT explaining the reasons for excluding time share from the classification loop or for creating a separate category or procedure for it. Unofficially it is learnt the department is wary of associating itself with a segment with an image problem. But, this does not explain why hotels which see merit in tune share, both as a facility for travellers as well as a business opportunity, should be forced to deny themselves this economic activity, especially when it helps the growth of international tourism.

Faced with this road block, AIRDA has approached CII for help. A meeting of CII's national committee on tourism and heritage in the Capital, a member Ravi Santhanam, CEO, Mahindra Holiday Resorts, a major player in time share, presented a draft proposal towards CII accreditation for the segment. B S Rathor, a management expert who is principal advisor to AIRDA, was a special invitee. Santhanam felt that CII accreditation would considerably strengthen the credibility and stature of time share apart from ensuring government recognition. FHRAI secretary general, Shyam Suri said in the discussion that followed that not enough was known in the official circles about time share and its contribution to tourism. He agreed that image too was a factor which may have influenced the DoT's thinking. He suggested that a seminar or workshop on time share be organised to which DoT and other officials functionaries be invited to create greater awareness of what time she could contribute to tourism. Finding a consensus emerging, committee chairman Maharaj Gaj Singh decided that a seminar/workshop will indeed be part of the next meeting of the committee in about three months time. AIRDA now has its work cut out and Rathor told this writer that the association would seek assistance from RCI in putting the seminar/workshop together.

Members were also briefed about the China initiative launched by CII during prime minister Vajpayee's recent visit. The good news for tourism is that China has become a partner country in CII's international conference, which will be attended by the country's tourism ministry as well as the head of the national carrier. China is also opening a tourist office in Delhi. And, as is already known, Air India is starring a bi-weekly service to Shanghai via Bangkok.

In a presentation on Rajasthan the state tourism secretary Arvind Mayaram said Jaipur would soon be an international airport with daily charters from Finland.

At Your Service

Much water has flowed down the Yamuna since the unhappy experience of an NRI who wanted to build a hotel in his homestate of Gujarat. Although the venture had the blessings of the then prime minister, it failed to make it even to the drawing board because the promoter wanted to introduce the concept of service apartments as part of the hotel project. The wise bureaucrats decided that service apartments amounted to 'housing', investment in which was banned even for NRIs. Now, thanks to economic reforms and the industry's response to changing customer preferences, particularly business travellers, foreign direct investment (FDI) is welcome in the hotel sector. It is another matter that investors are not rushing in but the door is open. What is even more welcome is that an Indian company, Ascot Hotels and Resorts Ltd. based in Delhi, has given the Capital its first standalone service apartments under the brand name of Savoy Suites in Noida, the upcoming satellite town.

Service apartments (or serviced apartments as they are known in the Asia Pacific region) became popular in the '80s in the west and also in Asia when long staying corporate travellers (15 days to six months) started complaining about services at hotels geared for the transit visitor. They desired larger rooms with additional facilities, more privacy and a reasonable tariff for long stay. According to Prakash Wadia, CEO, Ascot Hotels who has several decades in hoteliering, service apartments account for 10 per cent of the hotel market, in Hong Kong 11.5 per cent and in Australia 14.5 per cent. They enjoy higher profitability and occupancy and are less prone to occupancy fluctuations. Savoy Suites, he says, caters to the new generation business traveller. The emphasis is on providing a fully furnished, clean, user-friendly, efficient, comfortable and informal apartment in a pleasant, secure environment with recreational facilities, and most importantly at a 'compelling value'.

Savoy Suites consists of 44 apartments with a choice of one or two bedrooms, all enjoying a generous living area with a spacious bathroom. It has an Italian kitchenette equipped with appliances like refrigerator, microwave, electric kettle, toaster crockery, cutlery, and glassware. Other conveniences such as a workplace, telephone and internet facility are also available. Two of the 44 units are larger apartments with two separate bedrooms suitable for families and 12 apartments have inter-connecting doors. The central atrium of the complex is a special feature with an informal lounge around a water body, a bard and a sidewalk cafe. On the roof top is a state-of-the-art health club and a swimming pool. There are two conference rooms too. Also available are multiple dining options within the building. These include two old world hospitality restaurants and McDonald's for fast food. An in-house convenience store meets the daily needs of guests. Savoy Suites has its own assured power supply, round the clock concise and laundry service. Local transport, excursion to Agra and other places can also be organised through Savoy Suites. Tariff, which covers free breakfast, is graded according to length of stay.

Wadia Prakash says he had no difficulty in getting Savoy Suites being treated as part of the hotel industry insofar as approvals of the department of tourism (DoT) are concerned and he has access to entitlements like EPCG. He is confident that big chains will soon be going in for service apartments, for the facility will not only meet the preference of the modern travellers but also help their bottomlines through a mix of short-term and long-term guests.

As for Ascot Hotels' future growth, he says plans are in an advanced stage for a bigger project in Gurgaon which has a wider market because of the presence of a large number of multinational companies in this satellite town. This will be a greenfield project. He adds that the initial client response has been encouraging since the Savoy Suites opened its doors. Apart from senior and middle level corporates who have been attracted to experience the Capital's first brush with service apartments, he has had quite a few queries from NRIs planning holidays in India.

Before embarking on the project Prakash had used the services of a reputed agency for a survey on the desirability of service apartments as well as customer expectations. The facilities that Savoy Suites offers were then tailormade.

The hospitality industry will be watching with interest the debut of the service apartment segment.

A Successful Meeting of Minds

Delegates to the 39th annual convention of the Federation of Hotel and Restaurant Associations of India (FHRAI), especially those coming to the eastern metropolis after a long interval had several welcome surprises awaiting them. It started with a touchdown in Kolkata with a much improved airport, bypasses and flyovers which have added an incredible smoothness to the movement of traffic (could you imagine doing the airport to city hotels in 35 minutes flat?). More importantly, Kolkata has also emerged as a major convention destination. This was aptly demonstrated by the efficient and successful manner in which the FHRAI conference was held at Kolkata's new address – the ITC Sonar Bangla – supported ably by the Hyatt Regency and Taj Bengal which hosted the social events. Across the road from ITC's super deluxe hotel is the Science City which has an auditorium for 1,600 persons. And adjacent to Sonar Bangla is coming up Kolkata's Pragati Maidan (the centre is being completed with assistance from ITPO (India Trade Promotion Organisation) which manages the Pragati Maidan in New Delhi). A new township at Rajerhat is coming up closeby and hoteliers are upbeat about the arrival of large companies and multinationals that will increase flows of corporate travellers. One of the tourist-specific mega projects undertaken by the West Bengal government is a unique floating hotel (25 per cent on land and 75 per cent in water) in the Sunderbans area, a world heritage site.

West Bengal's tourism secretary, R K Tripathy speaking in the interactive session for states made a strong pitch for investments in his state. Among the many incentives, he said, is the one which exempts new projects from sales tax for seven years. Referring to complaints of lack of land for hotels and related ventures he gave the assurance that all an entrepreneur has to do is to choose a vacant piece of land. "If it is owned by the government it would be allotted forthwith and if it's privately owned the government will acquire it for the promoter."

He clarified that West Bengal is free of land use laws prevailing in other parts of the country which bar the construction of hotels in residential or other specified areas. For instance he pointed out that there are hotels plots allotted in Rajerhat.

Sikkim tourism chief, Karma Gyatso had his own bits of good news to share with the delegates. The future of tourism in his state, he told this writer, has significantly brightened up with the proposed revival of the silk route through Nathu La (the 14,400 feet pass into Tibet) following the recent agreement between India and China. The state government has set up a core group to draw up a blueprint for the infrastructure required. Once the pass is opened to trade and travel, Gyatso said visitors would save huge amounts of time going to Lhasa or Mansarovar. The distance to Lhasa would be 500 km shorter than the route through Nepal. The proposal for an airport in Sikkim, he said, has finally been approved by the centre after overcoming environmental concerns. The site chosen is Pakyang, some 30 km from Gangtok and the project to be built by the Airport Authority of India will take two years. ATRs will be able to land there.

The Tourism Finance Corporation of India (TFCI) has been in existence for more than a decade but this was the first time TFCI was invited to make a presentation for FHRAI delegates. M Narayanan, the managing director, talked of the liberalised policies of the corporation and how it had extended its assistance to projects other than, hotels. So far, he said, 460 hotel and other projects had been funded and in the current year as much as Rs 2,500 crore had been sanctioned.

The retiring president SK Khullar in passing the baton to the new president, Vivek Nair got a commitment from his successor that the initiative for the unity in the industry launched in Kolkata will be carried forward for implementation.

Not The Last Resort

The recent visit to India of the chief executive of RCI (Resort Condominium International) Kenneth May, the global outfit that acts as a bank for millions of time-share owners to exchange their vacations, could not have come at a more appropriate time. He came at a moment when the nascent time-share segment of the Indian hospitality industry had reasons to smile. Given a bad name by a few unscrupulous developers, time-share has just begun to float again, thanks to the hard work put in by the All India Resort Developers Association (AIRDA) and RCI's India outfit, now headed by veteran hotelier Raju Shahani. When the department of tourism (DoT) far from encouraging the segment to take its rightful place with the rest of the world not only denied it recognition but also threatened to deny classification to hotels which gave away a part of their room inventory to time-share. Fortuitously, that phase is over and DoT has since persuaded itself to review the new classification norms after intense lobbying by trade associations and even a chamber of commerce like the CII. DoT has in fact put the onus for justification for extending recognition (and support) to time-share on the industry itself. It has asked FHRAI and HAI, the two main hotel associations, to suggest the norms for classifying time-share and the associations in turn have asked their members for assistance in this regard. The exercise will take some time but time-share promoters must be conscious of the need to create confidence both among hoteliers (whose participation is crucial to the growth of the segment) and DoT's concern for consumer protection.

It is in this context that the RCI chiefs visit assumes significance. With the softening of DoT's approach to time-share, Kenneth May must have experienced a receptive audience both in the department of tourism as well as with the hotel industry leaders who are yet to see merit in what is one of the fastest growing segment of the travel and tourism industry. Worldwide the number of time-share members has increased since 1990 from 1.53 million to 6.7 million. The turnover if the segment is estimated at USD 59 billion. Big names like Hilton, Hyatt, Four Seasons, Sheraton and Marriott are active participants in time-share. According to Raju Shahani, even in India some prestigious hotels (the big chains have yet to make up their minds). Hotels like the Le Royal Meridien in Mumbai, Holiday Inn Goa and Ahmedabad, and Radisson in Fort Raichak near Kolkata, have set apart a number of suites, rooms and villas for time-share and are taking part in RCI's exchange programmes.

Kenneth May builds a strong case for time-share's relevance and importance to the hospitality industry by recalling the mantra that "In the best of times or the worst of times, hotel operators must employ the fullest possible range of initiatives to maximise occupancy, revenues and profits as well as to survive the periodic downturn in travel." He then goes on to suggest that time-share strengthens the resilience of the hotel industry; it plays a major role in utilising rooms which would perish when occupancies are low thus enhancing returns. Besides motivating global travel, it also helps destinations seeking inbound visitors, something, he says, India could cash in on especially through its heritage hotels. Affiliation through RCI, May adds, encourages uniform quality centres through regions like franchises, apart from improving standards.

Talking about India, the RCI chief executive says he is upbeat about the country's tourism prospects. It is time he says, time-share is integrated with the hospitality sector and its role is recognised by the government. "I am happy that moves are afoot in this direction," he says. RCI, he adds, works closely with government and he looks forward to that happening in

India also. We would like to see a tenfold increase in time-share members in the next decade so that the country could emerge as a leading time-share destination globally.

In an update on RCIs operations in India, Shahani said it now has 41,000 member families. The typical Indian member takes between 1-2 holidays per year, travelling a group of 4-5 persons. Most members own one week at an Indian resort and have bought time-share because of its exchange value. Quality, he said, is the most important factor governing the member's holiday choice. Technology, he added, is a tool that has enhanced RCI's business and its call centres in Bangalore and Mumbai use the latest systems to respond to customer needs.

Industry observers will be watching with interest time-share's quest for a place in the sun.

The Year of Expectations

It would have been appropriate if the year of expectations had concluded with the millennium sunrise radiating its rays over at least a single national asset for tourism, As if turns out, the day will be only a hang over from celebration bashes. Otherwise, it will be like any other day after the New Year Eve except that the revellers may have on a binge on a more extensive scale and at many more places.

The packages offered by almost all classy hotels across the country are priced at sky high levels. One coming from Goa quotes Rs 1,00,000 for a single day in a suite. Instead of being an occasion to remember for all times, for the coming generation as well, the millennium binge will be forgotten with a hangover.

Still, the year that has passed has engendered new hopes for Indian tourism. Political stability has returned with the new government in which a person committed to tourism has lost little time in taking initiatives. The trade too, though divided, is set to put in collective effort to regain the lost momentum.

Greater coordination between the centre and the states as well as among the ministries related to tourism and travel has been invested with more meaningful content. The coming months should see more global carriers flying into the country at greater frequencies and into newer destinations. These are the impressions one gets observing the tourism scene in this season of goodwill.

Last year opened, in contrast, on a despondent note with stagnation continuing in international arrivals and leading to shrinking bottomlines. Elections came and poll time is no tourist season.

Even the peak season that brought little cheer. The summer super savers could not mitigate the situation either. The redeeming feature was the hotel industry, which in the face of set backs not only remained resilient but also went ahead with investment plans.

Their determination to do so in spite of unfavourable financial results demonstrated the industry's faith in the future.

The authorities on their part did their considerable bit in helping the industry sustain its morale. The long sought after demand for export house status was granted. In some states, tourism-related taxes were revised to the benefit of the sector although rationalisation of tourism taxes still has a long way to go. The silver lining is the states agreement to a common sales tax approach.

Besides, state tourism ministers, called to Delhi for a conference by Uma Bharati soon after she assumed office as minister in charge of tourism, preferred to entrust to her the task of persuading the finance minister to initiate measures on tax reforms. In other words, they were broadly in agreement with the need for streamlining taxes but were helpless as the matter was within the jurisdiction of their colleagues in charge of finance and chief ministers.

A responsive union minister agreed to go to the finance minister, or for that matter, anybody else to take up the cause of tourism. The revival of the inter-ministry coordination committee comprising representatives of all departments which concern tourism, demonstrates her sincerity of purpose.

The Explore India year was another enterprise of 1999 that failed to enthuse the international market. Now that it has been extended to the end of 2000, there is some time for concerted action by the industry and the government. A marketing initiative with major players in the lead is also another positive step that hold promise in the new millennium.

Returning to the millennium preparations, it is surprising that few thought of creating a fitting memorial, which would be a lasting attraction embodying the cultural ethos. It need not have been on the scale of what is being done at Greenwich or in other parts of the world. But we could have created an asset. An opportunity has been missed. Both the trade and the tourism ministry can be faulted on that account.

Midnight revelry is certainly no substitute. Anyway, hopefully the year of expectations will be succeeded by a year of fulfillment – in some measure at least.

Index